4 W The New British Politics

The New British Politics

third edition

Ian Budge Ivor Crewe David McKay Ken Newton

PEARSON
Longman

London • New York • Toronto • Sydney • Tokyo • Singapore
Hong Kong • Cape Town • Madrid • Paris • Amsterdam • Munich • Milan

Pearson Education Limited

Edinburgh Gate
Harlow
Essex CM20 2JE
England

and Associated Companies throughout the world

Visit us on the World Wide Web at:
www.pearsoned.co.uk

First published in Great Britain in 1998
Second edition published in 2001
Third edition published in 2004

ISBN 0582473357

ISBN-10: 0-582-47335-7

ISBN-13: 978-0-582-47335-5

British Library Cataloguing-in-Publication Data
A catalogue record for this book is available from the British Library

10 9 8 7 6 5 4
06

Typeset in 10/12pt Times by 35
Printed and bound by Ashford Colour Press, Gosport, Hants.

Contents

INTRODUCTION

PART 1 STRUCTURE AND DEVELOPMENT IN BRITISH POLITICS

PART 3 BEYOND WESTMINSTER

PART 5 REPRESENTATION BY PARTIES

PART 8   A NEW BRITISH POLITICS?

Preface

The third edition of *The New British Politics* has been updated to focus on the second New Labour Government (from 2001 onwards). To understand contemporary events, of course you have to put them in context (Chapters 1–4). But most of the book deals with what is going on now in central government (Chapters 5–7), in Europe (Chapters 8–9), in the regions and localities (Chapters 10–12). Politics is not just about institutions but also the pressure groups and parties operating within them (Chapters 13–18). Television and press (Chapter 14), elections and voting (Chapter 15), and Parliament (Chapter 18) are particularly relevant here.

The end result of politics are the policies which affect us all – from the war against crime and terrorism (Chapters 19–22) to the environment, health, welfare, race and gender discrimination and equal opportunities (Chapters 23–26). As students of politics we also need to ask how democracy in Britain could be improved (Chapters 27 and 28) – particularly in light of growing apathy and, some would say, alienation from the political process.

We present these analyses comprehensively but directly, through text, tables, graphs, photographs and cartoons. Each chapter has a similar structure with an introduction, frequent 'briefings', historical 'milestones', suggestions for essays and projects, a chapter summary, further reading and internet resources. The book has an associated web site and teachers' manual available on request, which should help to promote an interactive relationship with the arguments and information contained here, rather than a purely passive absorption of the points we make. Active debate and argument should additionally be facilitated by the 'controversies' and 'briefings' inserted at key points in the text and also updated for this edition.

The way to use these for your own purposes and to best effect, is to plan your route through the book in advance. If you want a comprehensive introduction to British politics, before taking a course or without taking one, the best thing is to read the text right through. The overall order of the chapters is planned for this, so you go in a logical progression from the historical background through governmental processes and political actors to policies and how the system works overall.

Often, however, you will have more specific purposes in mind – for example, the core processes of British government. In that case, read Part 2 on central government and Chapter 18 on Parliament. If relationships with the EU are the focus then Chapters 8 and 9 provide a succinct account. Most topics on which A-level or first-year university students might be asked to write essays appear as separate chapters. If you have a choice of topic or can volunteer one yourself you might score by taking a relatively neglected topic such as politics and law (Chapter 19) or security (Chapter 21) which have quite specialised treatments in the book.

The way you organise your reading of an individual chapter may vary with the time you have. With enough time there is nothing like reading the text right through. For those with less time and a tight focus start with the summary and bullet points at the beginning, read the summary at the end and go over the milestones, then read the bits of the text relevant to you. Chapters are divided into sections to make this easy.

Do not, in any case, try to cope with all the material in the chapter at a first reading. Stick to the text, ignoring the briefings for the time being. The briefings are designed to be free standing. Their purpose is to explain details and references in the main text which you might not understand or which you might want to follow up – after reading the chapter text. The same is true of tables and graphs. They are all commented on and summarised in the text, so on a first or quick reading stick to that. The more specialised material inside and around a chapter is useful for writing essays or papers, and pursuing the topic in relevant papers or books and on the internet.

The companion website includes advice on how and how not to write essays. In general, use this book as a starting point but do not just reproduce its arguments and material – engage with them, question them (with reasonable arguments!) and extend them. We ourselves have found our judgements on many topics have changed between the first edition of the book (1998) and this one (2003). That is inevitable as events unfold, so never be afraid to challenge and debate our conclusions – but always with arguments and evidence of your own.

We have to take final responsibility for the opinions expressed here, with our contributing authors for Chapter 19 (David Robertson), Chapter 20 (Nigel South) and Chapter 23 (Albert Weale), also for any factual errors that may have crept in. We thank our specialist authors for their help, Emil Kirchner for advice on Europe, and John Bartle for much useful electoral and legal material. Judith Bara, our Research Officer, has been to all intents another author of the book. Julie Lord has gone beyond processing the manuscript to compiling, collating and formatting. Abigail Woodman at Pearson has been a model book editor. Without all of them the book would have been much inferior and we thank them for their help.

Ian Budge
Ivor Crewe
David McKay
Ken Newton
Colchester, Essex
May 2003

Acknowledgements

We are grateful to the following for permission to reproduce copyright material:

Plate 1.1, 'The Houses of Parliament, Westminster', reproduced by permission of Stockwave, COI; Table 1.1 taken from A. H. Halsey, *Trends in British Society Since 1900*, 1982, p. 146, reproduced by permission of Palgrave Macmillan; Table 1.2 from Office for National Statistics, 2002, Table 3.19, 'Percentage distribution of ethnic minorities by region Great Britain, 2001', URL: www.statistics.gov.uk; Figure 1.1 from Office for National Statistics, 'Current ethnic composition of the British population 2000–01', computed from Labour Force Survey; Figure 1.2 from Office for National Statistics, 'Unemployment rates: by region, Spring 2000'; Plate 1.3 PA Photos Ltd, reproduced by permission; Figure 1.3 Adapted from *OECD Outlook*, various years ©OECD, 'Unemployment in Britain compared with other developed countries 1974–2000' ©OECD; Plate 1.4 (top) PA Photos Ltd; Plate 1.4 (bottom) Gleeson Homes, www.gleeson-homes.co.uk; Figure 1.4 from Office for National Statistics, 'Unemployment rates; by gender 1959–2000', taken from Dept. for Work & Pensions/*Social Trends, No. 32*, chart 4.1, 2002; Table 1.3 from Office for National statistics, 'The distribution of wealth in Britain, 1976–1999' taken from *Social Trends, No. 32*, 2002, Table 5.4; Table 1.4 Adapted from *OECD in Figures: Statistics of Member Countries, 2002*, ©OECD, 'Annual GDP growth for major industrialised countries, 1962–2001' ©OECD; Figure 1.5 from Office for National Statistics, 1999, 'Growth of British gross domestic product over the post-war period'; Plate 2.1 'The House of Commons' reproduced by permission of Stockwave, COI; Table 2.1, 'Major trade unions in Britain, 2002' taken from TUC website http://www.tuc.org.uk ©TUC, by permission; Plate 2.3 'The trading floor of JP Morgan in the City of London', PA Photos Ltd, reproduced by permission; Plate 3.1 'Festival of Britain' from the Hulton Archive, Hulton Getty Picture Collection, reproduced by permission; Figure 3.1 from Office for National Statistics 'Inflation, UK, 1961–2001' taken from *Social Trends, No. 32*, 2002, chart 6.15; Plate 3.2 'Minister of Technology, Anthony Edgewood Benn opens Oceanology International . . .' from the Hulton Archive, Hulton Getty Picture Collection, reproduced by permission; Plate 3.3 Nicholas Garland cartoon in *Daily Telegraph* 23.9.81, reproduced by permission; Figure 3.2 Adapted from *OECD Outlook*, various years, ©OECD, 'Percentage of GDP in the Public Sector, related countries 1977–2000' ©OECD; Plate 4.1 'The Queen at the State opening of Parliament . . .', reproduced by permission of Stockwave COI; Plate 4.2 Steve Bell cartoon in the *Guardian*, 8 October 1996 reproduced by permission of Steve Bell; Table 6.1 from *Annual Abstract of Statistics 2002*, HMSO; Figure 7.1 from 'Number of civil servants 1945–2001' www.civil-service-gov.uk; Figure 7.2 from *Civil Service Statistics, 1999*, Table 5, March 2000, www.civil-service-gov.uk; Table 7.1 from 'Top Ten Executive Agencies by Staff & Expenditure, www.civil-service-gov.uk; Plate 6.1 'Aerial view of Whitehall looking towards the Houses of Parliament' reproduced by permission of Stockwave, COI; Figure 8.1 from *European Union and European Community* (Harverster 1994) Figure 9, Pearson Education Ltd; Plate 8.3 Nicholas Garland cartoon in the *Daily Telegraph*, 1992, reproduced by permission; Table 8.2 from COM 'Public opinion on membership of the European Union in constituent countries' taken from *Eurobarameter*, various issues; Plate 9.1 PA Photos Ltd, reproduced by permission; Figure 9.2 Public finance figures of the European Union from the website http://europa.eu.int/comm/budget/pubfin/index_en.htm; Plate 10.1 PA Photos Ltd, reproduced by permission; Table 10.1 'Regional disparities within Northern Ireland' updated by the Northern Ireland Statistics Research Agency; Plate 10.2 PA Photos Ltd, reproduced by permission; Table 10.2 from Northern Ireland Electoral Office, 'Voting in Northern Ireland Assembly Elections by Region'; Plate 11.1 PA Photos Ltd, reproduced by permission; Table 11.1 from Office for National Statistics: ONS *Regional Trends* NO. 36, 2001 edition & ONS *Social Trends* 2001, HMSO; Table 11.2(b) from *Working Papers in Politics 2002W10 (Iain McLean & Alistair McMillan)*, reprinted by permission of Iain McLean, Nuffield College, Oxford; Plate 11.3 PA Photos Ltd, reproduced by permission; Table 11.3 Support for Scottish independence and devolution, 1. from MORI polls (figures to 1999) and 2. (2000 & 2001) from ESRC, reprinted by permission from both sources; Plate 11.2 Bill McArthur cartoon in the (Glasgow) *Herald, 25 July 1997*. Reproduced by permission of Bill McArthur; Map 12.1 from *Local Government for England*, 1995, Map 2, HMSO, URL: www.statistics.gov.uk; Table 12.1 from Byrne, *Local Government in Britain*, 2000, pp. 84–85, Table 12.1, *Services of local authorities in England, Scotland and Wales*. Reproduced by permission of Penguin Books Ltd; Table 12.2 Council Committees in Colchester, Essex reprinted by permission of Colchester Borough Council; Table 12.3 'Party control of British local councils 1999' reprinted by permission of Prof. Colin S. Rallings, LGC Elections Centre, University of Plymouth; Table 13.1 from COM 'Voluntary Organisation Membership, Western Europe 1998' taken from *Eurobarometer 50.1* (Autumn 1998); Plate 13.1 'Newbury Bypass demonstration', PA Photos Ltd., reproduced by permission; Plate 13.2 'Anti-Nuclear demo at the French Embassy', PA Photos Ltd., reproduced by permission; Plate 13.3 PA Photos Ltd, reproduced by permission; Figure 14.1 from C. Seymour-Ure, *The British Press and Broadcasting since 1945*, Blackwell, 1992, pp. 196–7, reprinted by permission of Blackwell Publishing Ltd.; Table 14.1 'National Newspaper sales', taken from ABC data, reprinted by permission; Table 14.2 from *British Social Attitudes: the 14th Report*, 1996, reprinted by permission of NATCEN; Table 14.3 from R. Negrine, *Politics and the Mass Media in Britain*, Routledge, 1994, p. 42, reprinted by permission of Thomson Publishing Services; Figure 14.2 from D. McKie, 'Fact is free but comment is sacred', in I. Crewe and B. Gosschalk, (eds) *Political Communications: The General Election Campaign of 1992*, 1995, reprinted by permission of Cambridge University Press; Figure 14.3 from R. Negrine, *Politics and the mass media in Britain*, Routledge, 1994, p. 2, reprinted by permission of Thomson Publishing Services; Plate 14.3 A meeting of the moguls, reproduced by permission of Popperfoto; Plate 14.4 front page of the *Guardian* showing Neil Hamilton, ©*Guardian*, reproduced by permission; Plate 15.2 PA Photos; Table 15.3 from MORI polls. Reprinted by permission; Figure 15.3 from Shamit Saggar, 'Racial politics', *Parliamentary Affairs*, 50 (1997), Table 3, p. 699, reproduced by permission of Oxford University Press and The Data Archive, University of Essex; Table 15.5 from Shamit Saggar, 'Racial Politics', *Parliamentary Affairs* 50 (1997), p. 696; Data Archive, University of Essex (data set SN 3887), 2001 figures from BES 2001, reproduced by permission of University of Essex, NATCEN and Professor Paul Whiteley, University of Essex; Plate 16.2 Matthew Pritchett cartoon in *Daily Telegraph*, 21.4.97, reproduced by permission; Plate 16.3 the Conservative Party; Table 16.1 from Butler and Kavanagh: *The British General Election of 1997*, pp. 202–204, reproduced by permission of Palgrave Macmillan; Plate 17.1 PA Photos Ltd, reproduced by permission; Plate 18.1 PA Photos Ltd, reproduced by permission; Table 18.1 'The passage of Welfare Reform and pensions Bill 1999', from HMSO; Plate 19.2 MAC (Stanley McMurty) cartoon from the *Daily Mail* (Atlantic Syndication) 10 September 1996, reproduced by permission; Plate 20.1 Peter Shrank cartoon from *Independent on Sunday*, 23 February 1997, reproduced by permission; Figure 20.2 'Percentage of female police officers, England and Wales' from *Report of Her Majesty's Chief Inspector of Constabulary for 1997–98*, House of Commons, 10 (1998) pp. 74–75, HMSO; Figure 20.3 'Percentage of ethnic minority police officers, England and Wales' from *Report of Her Majesty's Chief Inspector of Constabulary for 1997–98*, House of Commons, 10 (1998) pp. 74–75, HMSO; Plate 21.1 'MI5 headquarters on the River Thames' reproduced by permission of Stockwave, COI; Table 22.1 from *The Government's Expenditure Plans 2000/2001 to 2001–2002*, MOD, Cm 4608, April 2000, Table 6, HMSO; Plate 24.1 'Lloyd's, home of the famous insurance exchange . . .' reproduced by permission; Plate 24.4 'Kick starting the economy' Cartoon by Nicholas Garland, ©Telegraph Group Limited, 1992; Figure 24.1 'Central government expenditure 2002' taken from 'Budget 2002 Summary', HMSO; Table 24.1 from *OECD Economic Outlook*, June No. 71, Vol. 2002, Issue 1. ©OECD, 2000, reproduced by permission. Figure 24.2 'Central government income 2002' taken from 'Budget 2002 Summary', HMSO; Figure 24.3 'Public Sector Net Cash Requirement, 1992–2002', taken from House of Commons Library Research Paper 02142, I July 2002, p. 16. HMSO; Table 25.2 taken from *Social Trends*, 27 Table A. 2, HMSO; Figure 25.1 taken from *Social Trends*, 32, 2002, Chart 8.3, HMSO; Figure 25.2 taken from *Social Trends*, 32, 2002, Chart 10.3, HMSO; Figure 25.3 taken from *Social Trends*, 32, 2002, Chart 10.5, HMSO; Figure 25.5 from Robert Leach & Janie Percy-Smith, *Local Governance in Britain*, Fig. 3.7, 1999, reproduced by permission of Palgrave Macmillan; Table 25.3 taken from *Social Trends* 32, 2002, Table 3.1, HMSO; Table 26.1 taken from *Social Trends* 32, 2002, Table 1.4, HMSO, taken from *Social Trends* 27, 1997, Figure HMSO; Figure 26.1 taken from *Social Trends 29*, 1999, Figure 4.17, HMSO; Figure 26.2 taken from *Social Trends 29*, 1999, Table 5.10, HMSO; Table 26.3 taken from *Labour Force Survey*, 2000–2001, HMSO; Table 26.5 taken from *Social Trends 32*, 2002, Table 4.8, HMSO.

In some instances we have been unable to trace the owners of copyright material, and we would appreciate any information that would enable us to do so.

Companion Website

A Companion Website accompanies *The New British Politics*, Third edition by Budge, Crewe, McKay and Newton

Visit *The New British Politics* Companion Website at www.booksites.net/budge to find valuable teaching and learning material including:

For Students and Lecturers:

- Study material designed to help improve results
- Learning objectives for each chapter
- Self assessment questions to help test learning
- Statistical data for manipulation
- Guidance on effective essay writing
- Extensive links to websites of organisations related to each chapter

TOPICAL ELECTION COVERAGE!

- This website will be updated twice yearly. The website will feature a General Election briefing and overview of results, followed later by a more detailed analysis

Also: This regularly maintained site has a syllabus manager, search functions, and email results functions.

List of abbreviations

ABC	Aubrey, Berry, Campbell (Trial, 1977)
ACAS	Advisory, Conciliation, and Arbitration Service
ACPO	Association of Chief Police Officers
AEEU	Amalgamated Electrical Engineering Union
All ER	All England Reports
ASH	Action on Smoking and Health
BBC	British Broadcasting Corporation
BCC	Broadcasting Complaints Commission
BCS	British Crime Survey
BMA	British Medical Association
BPBNC	Both Parents Born New Commonwealth
BSB	British Satellite Broadcasting
BSC	Broadcasting Standards Commission
BSE	Mad Cow Disease
CAP	Common Agricultural Policy
CAT	Computerised axial or computer-assisted tomography
CBI	Confederation of British Industry
CCT	Compulsory Competitive Tendering
CEO	Chief Executive Officer
CFC	Chlorofluorocarbon
CFER	Campaign for the English Regions
CFoI	Campaign for Freedom of Information
CGT	Capital Gains Tax
CID	Criminal Investigation Department
CLA	Country Landowners' Association
Cm	Command
CND	Campaign for Nuclear Disarmament
CNN	Cable News Network
Con	Conservative
CONVOTE	Conservative voting support in the current month
COPA	Committee of Professional Agricultural Organisations
COREPER	Committee of Permanent Representatives (Ambassadors to the EU)
CPAG	Child Poverty Action Group
CPRS	Central Policy Review Staff
CPS	Crown Prosecution Service
CRE	Commission for Racial Equality
CSA	Child Support Agency
CSC	Civil Service College
CSD	Civil Service Department
CSI	Committee on the Intelligence Services
CSR	Comprehensive Spending Review
CWU	Communications Workers Union

DCMS	Department for Culture, Media and Sport
DEA	Department of Economic Affairs
DES	Department of Education and Science
DETR	Department of the Environment, Transport and the Regions
DEFRA	Department for Environment, Food and Rural Affairs
DfES	Department for Education and Skills
DfID	Department for International Development
DHA	District Health Authority
DIS	Defence Intelligence Staff
DM	Deutschmark
DNA	Deoxyribonucleic Acid
DoE	Department of the Environment
DoH	Department of Health
DoT	Department of Transport
DTI	Department of Trade and Industry
DWP	Department of Work and Pensions
EC	European Community
ECHR	European Convention on Human Rights and Fundamental Freedoms
ECJ	European Court of Justice
ECR	European Court Regulation
ECSC	European Coal and Steel Community
EDP	Economic and Domestic Policy
EEC	European Economic Community
EGO	Extra-government organisation
EMS	European Monetary System
EMU	European Monetary Union
EOC	Equal Opportunities Commission
EP	European Parliament
EP	Ministerial Sub-Committee on European Issues
ERASMUS	European Community Action Scheme for the Mobility of University Students
ERM	Exchange Rate Mechanism
ETUC	European Trade Union Confederation
EU	European Union
EURATOm	European Atomic Energy Authority
EUROPOL	European Police Office
FCO	Foreign and Commonwealth Office
FMI	Financial Management Initiative
FoI	Freedom of Information
G7	Group of Seven
GATT	General Agreement on Trade and Tariffs
GCHQ	Government Communications Headquarters
GCSE	General Certificate of Secondary Education
GDP	Gross domestic product
GEC	General Electric Company
GLA	Greater London Authority
GLC	Greater London Council
GM	Genetically Modified
GMB	General and Municipal
GMG	Glasgow Media Group
GNP	Gross National Product
GP	General Practitioner
GPMU	General Public and Municipal Workers Union

HAT	Housing Action Trust
HMCIC	Her Majesty's Chief Inspector of Constabulary
HMIC	Her Majesty's Inspectorate of Constabulary
HMSO	Her Majesty's Stationery Office
HoC	House of Commons
IBA	Independent Broadcasting Authority
ICPSR	Inter-University Consortium for Political and Social Research
ID card	Identity card
IDEA	Institute for Democracy and Electoral Assistance
IEA	Institute of Economic Affairs
ILEA	Inner London Education Authority
ILO	International Labour Organization
IMF	International Monetary Fund
IRA	Irish Republican Army
IS	Intelligence Services
ITC	Independent Television Commission
ITN	International Television Network
ITV	Independent Television
JCC	Joint Consultative Committee (of the Cabinet)
JIC	Joint Intelligence Committee
JP	Justice of the Peace
JSA	Job Seeker's Allowance
Lab	Labour
LCC	London County Council
LEA	Local Education Authority
Lib Dem	Liberal Democrat
LTE	London Transport Executive
M3	A measure of money supply
MAFF	Ministry of Agriculture and Fisheries
MEP	Member of the European Parliament
MINIS	Management Information Systems for Ministers
MoD	Ministry of Defence
MORI	Market and Opinion Research International
MP	Member of Parliament
MPC	Monetary Policy Committee
MPO	Management Personnel Office
MSFU	Managerial, Scientific and Financial Union
NASUWT	National Association of Schoolmasters and Union of Women Teachers
NATO	North Atlantic Treaty Organisation
NCCL	National Council for Civil Liberties
NCIS	National Criminal Intelligence Service
NCS	National Crime Squad
NDPB	Non-department public body
NEC	National Executive Committee (of the Labour Party)
NEDC	National Economic Development Council
Neddy	National Economic Development Council
NHS	National Health Service
NI	Northern Ireland
NRC	National Reporting Centre
NSM	New Social Movement

NSPCC	National Society for the Prevention of Cruelty to Children
NUM	National Union of Miners
NUS	National Union of Students
NUT	National Union of Teachers
NW	North West
ODM	Ministry of Overseas Development
OFCOM	Office of Communications
Ofgas	Office of Gas Supply
Oftel	Office of Telecommunications
Ofwat	Office of Water Regulation
OMCS	Office of the Minister for the Civil Service
OPEC	Organization of Petroleum Exporting Countries
OPS	Office of Public Service
OPSS	Office of Public Service and Science
OSCE	Organisation for Security and Co-operation in Europe
PA	Press Association
PAC	Public Accounts Committee
PACE	Police and Criminal Evidence Act
PC	Plaid Cymru
PC	Police Constable
PC	Politically correct
PCA	Parliamentary Commissioner for Administration
PCA	Police Complaints Authority
PCB	Police Complaints Board
PCC	Press Complaints Commission
PESC	Public Expenditure Survey Committee
PFI	Private Finance Initiative
PLC	Public Limited Company
PM	Prime Minister
PMQs	Prime Minister's Questions
PPBS	Planning, programming and budgeting systems
PPS	Private parliamentary secretary
PR	Proportional representation
PRT	Petroleum Revenue Tax
PSBR	Public Sector Borrowing Requirement
PSI	Policy Studies Institute
PUSS	Parliamentary under-secretary of state
QBD	Queen's Bench Division
QC	Queen's Counsel
QMV	Qualified majority voting
R&D	Research and development
RAF	Royal Air Force
RFSR	Russian Federal Socialist Republic
RIPA	Regulation of Investigatory Powers Act
RSG	Rate Support Grant
RSPB	Royal Society for the Protection of Birds
SDLP	Social Democratic and Labour Party
SDP	Social Democratic Party
SEA	Single European Act
SEU	Social Exclusion Unit
SERPS	State Earnings Related Pension Scheme

SIS	Secret Intelligence Service
SMSP	Single-member simple plurality system
SNP	Scottish National Party
SOGAT	Society of Graphical and Allied Trades
STV	Scottish Television
STV	Single Transferable Vote
TEC	Training and Education Council
TGWU	Transport and General Workers Union
TIC	Taken into consideration
TUC	Trades Union Congress
TV	Television
UDF	Ulster Defence Force
UHT	Ultra heat treated
UK	United Kingdom
UKREP	United Kingdom Permanent Representation to the EU
UN	United Nations
UNIEU	Union of Industries of the European Union
US	United States (of America)
USA	United States of America
USDAW	Union of Shop, Distributive and Allied Workers
USSR	Union of Soviet Socialist Republics
UVF	Ulster Volunteer Force
VAT	Value Added Tax
WLR	Weekly Law Reports
WTO	World Trade Organisation

Introduction

Statue of Winston Churchill

British politics in context: International, social, and historical settings

This chapter places British politics in context by reviewing the key features of the political system. Some of these are shared with other democracies in Europe and overseas, while some are unique to Britain. They are all affected, however, by globalisation and moves to European integration. Current British politics are not simply an internal affair. Some of the most important influences are international, and these are imposing new strains on institutions, political parties and on territorial relationships between England, Ireland, Scotland and Wales.

British institutions and political practices were 'fixed' in the mid-nineteenth century and continued in many ways to operate as they did then until the last third of the twentieth century. They coexist uneasily with a society in continual and rapid change under the impact of world developments. Are British institutions well adapted to respond to such demands? Or to handle the political and economic problems of the twenty-first century? How far have the Blair governments gone in their attempts to reform Britain's political structure? Answering these questions helps us assess the quality of British democracy, a major aim of this book.

The specific features covered in this chapter are:

- liberal democracy and the Westminster Model of government
- the international context
- social change in post-war Britain
- demands and constraints on British governments
- the class/territorial division in Britain
- the British 'Establishment'
- 'Europe' and Britain
- Britain: decline or adaptation?

Globalisation
The growing linkage of all countries of the world with each other through travel, tourism, trade and electronic communication. As anything done in one area now affects all the others, this means that countries like Britain can act less and less on their own and so creates a need for international political institutions such as the United Nations (UN) and the European Union (EU).

LIBERAL DEMOCRACY

Britain is a liberal–democratic state. Liberal democracy means that institutions such as the Civil Service and the armed forces, which administer and defend the national territory, operate under the supervision of a regularly elected government and Parliament. These arrangements guarantee citizens certain rights and freedoms. Free elections to choose governments define Britain as a democracy, while the liberal element comes in the form of restrictions on state interference with the lives of private individuals and families.

BRIEFINGS

1.1 Liberal democracy

Liberal democracy exists in states that have regular elections for choosing the government, in which all citizens are entitled to vote, and which guarantee rights for individuals and groups that cannot be taken away. There have been liberal states that guaranteed legal rights without being full democracies (for example Britain during most of the nineteenth century); and there have been democracies that infringed rights, such as the United States before the granting of civil rights to African Americans in the 1960s.

Elections are important for maximising the probability that the government will act in accordance with majority wishes – a characteristic that is fundamental to democracy. However, most people would agree that minorities also need to be protected, even against the majority if the majority want to discriminate against them. It is important for minorities to be allowed to persuade others of the correctness of their view and perhaps become the majority later. This possibility has to be left open if democracy is to function properly, so the protection of minorities is as important in its way as majority rule. Liberalism has traditionally stressed individual rights (freedom of speech, assembly, religion, movement). That is why democracies that incorporate guarantees for such rights are called liberal democracies.

MAKING COMPARISONS

Britain is one of about 25 fully liberal democracies in Europe and about 40 elsewhere in the world. British institutions, such as Parliament and political parties, are broadly similar to those that operate in other democracies. This is particularly so where other countries are 'Parliamentary democracies' like Britain and not 'presidential democracies' like the United States of America or Russia. In a Parliamentary democracy the members of the government are drawn from the national legislature or Parliament, and the government itself depends on the support of Parliament. This contrasts with the USA, where the head of government is separately elected and independent of the elected legislature.

Britain was the first Parliamentary democracy in Europe. Many of the other European countries modelled their political institutions and ways of doing things on Britain when they too introduced responsible governments and elected Parliaments. In the 1950s and 1960s the British system (known as the 'Westminster Model') was exported to many of the colonies and territories of Britain's old Empire when these countries became independent. As a result many British procedures and practices exist in other liberal democracies too. Good examples are the ways in which the courts function and some of the ways in which political parties operate.

BRIEFINGS

1.2 The Westminster Model of responsible party government

Britain is a 'representative democracy' because popular votes are usually cast for party candidates who advocate a policy programme, rather than for individual policies themselves (a practice termed 'direct democracy'). The party that gets a majority of candidates elected to the House of Commons then forms the government, until the next election.

The 'Westminster Model', so called after the area of London where the Houses of Parliament stand, is the term used to describe this form of representative democracy. Its most important feature is the fusion of legislative and executive power in the hands of the majority party in the Parliament.

The majority party leader becomes Prime Minister and nominates close party colleagues and supporters to form the Cabinet and government. They make national policy that their majority in the House of Commons can be guaranteed to support, owing to the strict discipline the party leadership in the government enforces on the majority party. All members of the government must support its policy (in public anyway). All members of Parliament (MPs) of the ruling party vote for government policy. The opposition parties can only oppose, as the Westminster Model denies them any direct power.

This system is supported by many commentators on the grounds that it makes for decisive, strong government and fixes responsibility for government actions on the party in power. The fact that one or other of the two main parties will form the next government gives voters a clear-cut choice between their policy programmes.

The Westminster Model has been criticised, however, for making the ruling party too strong. It creates an 'elective dictatorship' of the majority party leadership, which can ignore all opposition and criticism, however justified, of what they propose to do. Moreover, the fact that an election may transfer total power in a matter of days from a party with one set of policies to another that opposes them (as with Conservatives and Labour in the 1997 general election) creates uncertainty and instability for business and for people in general, who have no secure guidelines on what the future will look like after a change of government.

Constitution
The fundamental rules or laws governing the relationship between the public institutions of a state.

However, some features of British politics were not copied elsewhere. A good example is Britain's unwritten constitution: there is no one basic document that specifies the relationships between government, Parliament, the courts and the ordinary citizen.

When other countries made the transition to democracy, often after an internal revolution or defeat in war, they had to make a blueprint of the way their new democratic politics should operate. British institutions and practices evolved more gradually, so there was never a definitive turning point that called for the codification or writing down of the main relationships between institutions and between institutions and the citizenry in one document. (Chapter 4 discusses the constitution in more detail.)

The absence of a codified constitution does not necessarily make Britain less democratic than other democracies. Having regular elections and the opportunity to vote governments in or out is what counts. In many respects, however, it does make British politics different. For example, given the absence of a written document that specifies precisely what governments can and cannot do, it is more

Plate 1.1 *The Houses of Parliament, Westminster: the seat of British government. Built between 1840 and 1852 by Sir Charles Barry with designs by Augustus Pugin*

Source: Stockwave, Central Office of Information

difficult in Britain to claim that a government has acted unconstitutionally. Some groups, such as 'Charter 88', a group of reforming lawyers and academics, claim that Britain needs a written constitution for precisely that reason. Most governments, contrariwise, feel that they exercise their powers in a reasonable way and that a written constitution would be unnecessarily restrictive and cumbersome.

We can make a judgement as to which side is right by looking at those liberal democracies that do have written constitutions and seeing whether these documents are indeed important in safeguarding individuals and minorities, as Charter 88 would claim. Or it could be that they are unnecessarily restrictive, as most British governments have claimed.

Comparisons with the experiences of other democracies help us to answer important questions about British politics on a factual basis, instead of just advancing our own opinions. Would a change in the method of electing MPs lead to parties rarely or never having a majority in the House of Commons, and thus encourage them to combine to form coalition governments? Would coalition governments be more representative than single-party ones or would they instead be weak and helpless? We can look at other countries such as Italy or the Netherlands to see if such consequences necessarily follow when coalition governments emerge.

INTERNATIONAL CONTEXT

Making comparisons is useful because it highlights the ways in which British politics resemble those of other countries, and the ways in which they are unique. They also help us to put British politics in an international context. This is important because we cannot really understand British politics unless we take account of developments outside the country. It is easy to lose sight of this during political debates that focus on things British governments can do on their own, such as regulating or deregulating industry or raising and lowering taxes. However, even these actions can have important international dimensions such as their effect on competitiveness or their compatibility with European Union law.

One need only think of British involvement in the Gulf War (1991) or the invasions of Afghanistan (2001–2) and Iraq (2003) to see that politics in Britain cannot be isolated from what goes on elsewhere in the world. Britain's close involvement in the military alliance that dominates relations between the world's major military powers (NATO – the North Atlantic Treaty Organisation) makes this even truer, as does Britain's growing integration into the European Union (EU), including all Britain's neighbours. Whether or not Britain goes on to form a closer union with the other European countries or, on some issues such as monetary union, continues to stand apart, the EU and its decisions will affect it ever more closely, often more so than decisions taken by British governments alone.

HISTORICAL CONTEXT

Attitudes to Europe, to British institutions and to political processes, all emerge from history. This is probably more true of Britain than of other liberal democracies. Britain was the first major country in the world to base itself on an industrial and commercial economy, to see the bulk of the population shift from the countryside into cities, and to design social and political institutions to deal with that situation. As a result the key British institutions – Parliament, political parties, the Cabinet, Civil Service, local government, trade unions, and financial institutions in the City of London – all took on their modern shape during and after the Industrial Revolution.

Some institutions have adapted to modern developments while others remain essentially unchanged. In the course of the twentieth century other European countries were taken over by dictatorships or defeated in war and occupied.

Among the major powers, only Britain, owing partly to its island position, managed to avoid this. Most Continental European countries thus experienced a sharp break with their political past, which pushed them into changing and updating their political practices. Only Britain had no immediate need to do this.

Consequently, a degree of stability and continuity have characterised British political institutions since the mid-nineteenth century. To take one example, two out of the three big political parties – the Conservatives and Liberal Democrats – in their modern form date back to the 1870s. The third, Labour, is only slightly younger, having been founded in 1900.

Such stability and continuity may be welcomed as evidence of the strength of British democracy. Particularly during and after the Second World War British institutions stood out like an island of stability and a beacon of hope in a chaotic world. When post-war Europe was divided and its democracies were threatened by communist subversion within and Soviet aggression without, Britain seemed admirably free from internal divisions and was perceived as democratic and strong. These characteristics made Britain the chief ally of the USA in the military and political confrontation with the Soviet Union known as the Cold War (1948–90).

The flipside of continuity and stability, however, was a reluctance to keep up with developments, internationally and internally. Eventually, the other European democracies found political stability and re-planned their institutions. They recovered economically from the devastation of the Second World War, and spearheaded a move to European integration from which Britain initially stood apart. Germany gained a large share of world trade and challenged Britain for the position of leading ally of the USA. As the Cold War declined in intensity, world bases were abandoned. British colonies were given independence in the face of nationalist and independence movements. Britain's influence on the international scene diminished. In such a situation, Parliamentary debates over foreign policy, conducted in the grand style of earlier days, seemed more like a charade to bolster pretensions of grandeur than the world-shaking decisions of the old days.

Indeed, British world preoccupations increasingly looked like excuses for not tackling basic problems nearer at hand, such as relative economic decline and relations with Europe. Overseas preoccupations, together with opposition from French governments, prevented Britain from joining the European Community until 1973. At home they diverted attention from the ever-accelerating social changes that started with the creation of the Welfare State in the late 1940s, continued in the midst of economic change and immigration in the 1950s, and created growing difficulties thereafter. The inability or reluctance of political leaders to deal with such developments forms the stage on which recent British politics has been played out.

SOCIAL CHANGE IN POST-WAR BRITAIN

The post-war Labour governments (1945–51) consolidated all the existing schemes for health care and social protection into a unified body of legislation, along with institutions to implement it. Collectively these went under the name of the Welfare State.

BRIEFINGS

1.3 The Welfare State

This is a generic term for the provision by the state of collective goods and services to its citizens: health, education, housing, income support and personal social services for children, the old, the sick, the disabled and the unemployed. The state uses public funds to provide a minimum standard of living, or safety net, for its citizens. There are many different forms of welfare intervention: some work primarily through cash benefits, others by providing services directly; some provide universal benefits, others selective benefits; some try to redistribute incomes and resources, others are more concerned with raising sufficient funds for basic services. Some of these services are highly developed, some are more minimal. The proportion of national wealth spent in Britain on the Welfare State rose particularly rapidly from 1950 to 1980. The term 'welfare state' also refers very often to the array of institutions – hospitals, health trusts, insurance, employment and training agencies – set up to care for those in need.

The basic aim was to ensure that everyone got support in all the major crises of life: poverty, sickness, old age and unemployment. State help was to be provided whether or not recipients could pay. In this sense, the Welfare State was based on the notion of universal rather than selective benefits: all citizens, irrespective of their financial position, were to be provided with Welfare State support. This basic support was supplemented by schemes to provide everyone with decent housing and education.

In themselves, these welfare reforms would have produced major social changes. They allowed poorer groups – generally urban manual workers – to improve their basic standards of living and to get better jobs through improved educational opportunities. This contributed to the breaking down of class barriers and produced more geographical and social mobility (see Table 1.1).[1]

Table 1.1 *Increasing social mobility among males in Britain in the 1970s*

| | Sons or sons-in-law in occupational class | | |
	Non-manual	Manual	Total
Father's occupational class			
Non-manual	16.8	7.8	24.6
Manual	18.8	56.6	75.4
Total	35.6	64.4	100%

Source: A. H. Halsey, *Trends in British Society since 1900*, London: Macmillan, 1982, p. 146

---

[1] The major 'class' division is between manual occupations, often involving hard physical effort, and non-manual occupations, which usually involve desk or computer work. Table 1.1, based on social surveys conducted in the 1970s, shows that 18.8 per cent of the population had fathers in manual work but were themselves in non-manual jobs (or had husbands in non-manual jobs). That is to say that almost one-fifth of the old manual working class had 'risen' to the non-manual middle class. This is balanced by the 7.8 per cent who had fathers in non-manual work but were themselves now in manual work (or had husbands who were). Even taking this into account, however, the general movement between generations in the middle of the post-war period was 'up', both in terms of the relative magnitude of these percentages and the fact that the working class was much larger than the non-manual groups.

Table 1.2 *Percentage distribution of ethnic minorities by region of Great Britain, 2001*

Northern England	1
Yorkshire and Humberside	6
Northwest England	8
East Midlands	7
West Midlands	14
Eastern	4
Greater London	46
Rest of southeast England	7
Southwest England	2
Wales	2
Scotland	3
Total, Great Britain	100

Source: Office for National Statistics, 2002, Table 3.19, http://statistics.gov.uk

Economic expansion and change also encouraged this, however. In the first 20 years of the post-war period (1945–65) the traditional industries expanded and some prospered. New service sectors such as tourism and personal finance developed. Many of the new jobs were non-manual but attracted sons (and increasingly daughters) from the working class.

Unemployment was low, partly because governments made it a major priority to expand employment. The economy also grew every year and provided more jobs. This situation made it easy to absorb refugees from eastern Europe after the end of the war. The prospect of a job attracted growing numbers of immigrants during the 1950s and 1960s, at first from Ireland, then from the colonies and ex-colonies in the West Indies, Africa and the Indian sub-continent.

The arrival of these groups gave Britain for the first time a section of the population who obviously differed from the rest in terms of appearance and, in the case of Asians, in religion and many of their social customs too. Although restrictions on immigration were imposed from 1962 onwards, by 2000 around 4 million of Britain's 59 million people were classified as ethnic minorities mainly of Asian, Caribbean and African origin.

At 7 per cent of the total this is not enormous, but of course, the job seekers naturally concentrated in the more prosperous and populous areas, notably Greater London, the Midlands and (when jobs were available in the 1950s and 1960s) the northern textile towns (see Table 1.2). Their growing presence was sometimes followed by tensions with the white population, which from the 1960s erupted in sporadic rioting and sometimes encouraged racist appeals in elections.

It must be said, however, that Britain is not unique in this respect. Compared with some countries, restraint and goodwill on both sides have usually characterised British race relations. This held true even when economic and social conditions deteriorated in the later 1970s and early 1980s. The presence of immigrants stresses the fact that Britain is a multiethnic society (see Figure 1.1). Awareness of this was heightened by the claims of territorial minorities inside Britain – the Scots, Welsh and (Catholic) Northern Irish – to recognition. The overwhelming majority (just over 83 per cent) of the British population live in England. However, the Scots (9 per cent or 5 million), the Welsh (nearly 5 per

Figure 1.1 *Current ethnic composition of the British population, 2000–01*

Source: Computed from Labour Force Survey, Office for National Statistics

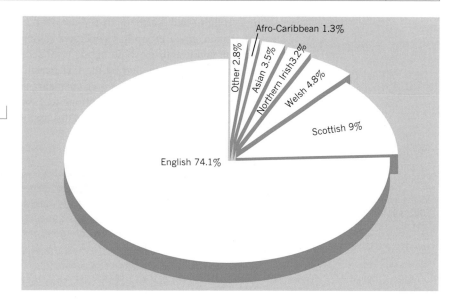

Afro-Caribbean 1.3%

Other 2.8%

Asian 3.5%

Northern Irish 3.2%

Welsh 4.8%

Scottish 9%

English 74.1%

Plate 1.2 *Britain – a multiethnic society*

cent or 2 million) and Northern Irish (just over 3 per cent) dominate their own areas of Britain. Each group has generated nationalist parties that seek greater political autonomy and, in some cases, total secession from the British State. Their claims have been fuelled by the fact that the peripheries have been much less prosperous than the London and southeast area over the post-war period. Hence, some sections of their populations feel they can do better on their own (see Chapters 5, 10 and 11 for a detailed discussion).

Figure 1.2
Unemployment rates by region, spring 2000

Source: Social Trends 32, 2002, Chart 4.25

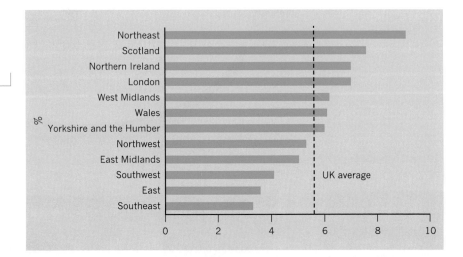

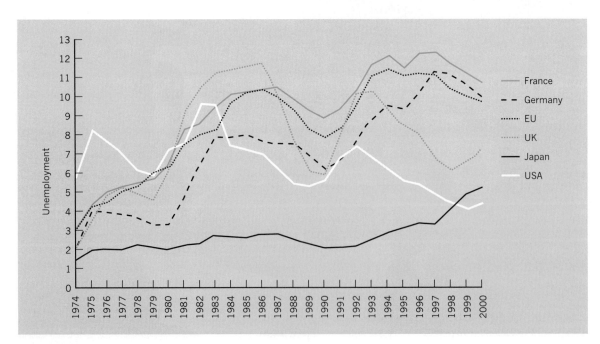

Figure 1.3 *Unemployment in Britain compared with other developed countries 1974–2000*

Source: Economic Outlook, Paris: Organisation for Economic Co-operation and Development, various dates

There was a general economic downturn in Britain after the early 1970s. Just as prosperity had been unevenly shared among the various regions in the earlier post-war period, so the suffering fell unevenly, mostly on the peripheries – including the north and Scotland – in the 1980s. Even by the year 2000 this pattern persisted (see Figure 1.2).

The main reason was that traditional industries such as textiles, coalmining, steel and shipbuilding were heavily concentrated in the north, Scotland and Wales and newer light industries such as car manufacture were concentrated in the English Midlands. By the 1980s these industries were facing huge pressure from competitors around the world, particularly East Asia. Thousands of jobs were lost as firms introduced cost-saving measures to improve their efficiency. Meanwhile the government, committed to 'New Right' economic policies, refused to intervene to try to save factories and mines from closing, believing that it was up to the management of the industries themselves to respond to the pressures of the market by becoming more efficient. As a result, unemployment reached 12 per cent in the mid-1980s and rose again in the mid-1990s. Figure 1.3 shows how the percentage of unemployed peaked in the early 1980s and 1990s. British unemployment rates have sometimes been higher and sometimes lower than the average for European Union countries. They have been lower than this average recently, particularly since 1998. In July 2003 unemployment in the EU 11 countries (those in the European Monetary Union) was 8.9 per cent, in the USA it was 6.2 per cent, in Japan 5.3 per cent while in Britain it was 5.0 per cent.

BRIEFINGS

New Right
The politicians and theorists of the 1980s who believed in the efficacy of market competition as the best means of guaranteeing political freedom and economic growth.

1.4 **Thatcherism and the New Right**

'Thatcherism' is a term used to describe the attitudes and policies of the Conservative governments from 1979 to 1990, when Margaret Thatcher was party leader and Prime Minister. These attitudes have been summed up in the words 'free market, strong state'. On the economic side, the object was to 'get the government out of business' and restore individual initiative. This was achieved by 'privatisation' (selling off) government enterprises such as electricity, water, gas, public housing and railways. Many regulations were abolished and serious attempts made to reduce the number of government employees (from 700,000 to 590,000 in the course of the 1980s).

Strong and authoritative state action was needed, however, to break trade union resistance to these changes or even to initiate them in the first place against internal Conservative Party opposition, parts of the Civil Service, local governments and other groups. Mrs Thatcher and her supporters built up state power by, for example, strengthening police and security forces (see Chapter 21) and taking powers away from local government (see Chapter 12).

The emphasis of Thatcherism on freeing markets tied in with the thinking of 'neo-liberal' or 'New Right' economists, who saw the market as more efficient than the state (including the Welfare State) at providing everyone with goods and services. Mrs Thatcher is therefore often described as a 'neo-liberal' or 'New Right' politician. (For more on these ideas see Chapters 2 and 17.)

Figure 1.4 *Employment rates by gender, United Kingdom 1959–2000*

Source: *Social Trends 32*, 2002, Chart 4.1

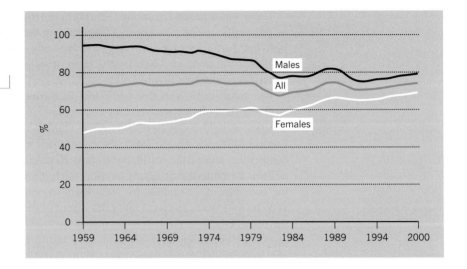

Table 1.3 *Distribution of wealth in Britain, 1976–99*

	1976	1981	1986	1991	1997	1999
Marketable wealth: percentage of wealth owned by:						
Most wealthy 1%	21	18	18	17	22	23
Most wealthy 5%	38	36	36	35	43	43
Most wealthy 10%	50	50	50	47	54	54
Most wealthy 25%	71	73	73	71	75	74
Most wealthy 50%	92	92	90	92	93	94
Total marketable wealth (£ billions)	280	565	955	1711	2248	2752
Marketable wealth less value of dwellings: percentage of wealth owned by:						
Most wealthy 1%	29	26	25	29	30	34
Most wealthy 5%	47	45	46	51	54	58
Most wealthy 10%	57	56	58	64	66	71
Most wealthy 25%	73	74	75	80	83	86
Most wealthy 50%	88	87	89	93	95	97

Note: Data is taken from *Social Trends*, **32**, 2002, Table 5.4. Most people's wealth is the value of their house. When that is taken out of the calculation, in the bottom half of the table, disparities increase markedly

Economic change was not confined to the unemployed. Many men, for example, dropped out of the labour force altogether, taking early retirement on the basis of their savings or pensions. Many more women took jobs outside the home, until the numbers of women working approached those of men (see Figure 1.4). Women tended to be more flexible and to take the service and part-time jobs that now became available.

Unemployment and a changing pattern of family and lifecycle employment created new demands on the Welfare State at the same time as the Conservative government wanted to cut social spending and strengthen citizens' self-reliance. As the eligibility criteria for unemployment and social benefits were tightened in order to reduce expenditure and cut taxation, disparities between rich and poor increased (see Table 1.3). Interestingly these disparities continued to increase throughout the 1990s, so that by 1999 just 1 per cent of the population owned 34 per cent of the wealth (excluding wealth held in housing).

Post-war Britain therefore remains a remarkably unequal society. In contrast to the immediate post-war period, however, the middle classes are much more numerous. A vote of 40 per cent is enough to give a national party a majority in Parliament and to sustain a government. Thus groups that benefit from the current distribution of income and wealth are numerous enough to vote a government in, regardless of the situation of the approximately 20 per cent living in poverty. These social developments partly account for the long tenure of Conservative governments under Mrs Thatcher (1979–90) and John Major (1990–7) who were committed to tax cutting and reducing government spending on the social services. They also help to explain why the New Labour governments have accepted many – although not all – of these policies.

POLITICAL DEMANDS AND INSTITUTIONAL CONSTRAINTS

Some critics have argued that this situation does not seem healthy or stable. If, partly as a result of government policy, groups that are suffering deprivation, see no way of changing this through peaceful persuasion and elections, they are liable to react in ways that are undesirable for a democracy. Either they can back parties with more extreme demands – in the most exaggerated case revolutionary parties that endanger the electoral process itself – or they can threaten to secede from the United Kingdom if they live in a particular area such as Northern Ireland or Scotland.

Of course, the election of an alternative government can bring relief and hopes of reintegrating the marginal groups into society. This is why democracies, which offer such an escape mechanism through elections, are often strong and stable.

Not only electoral considerations but international and institutional constraints limit what a British government can do. The two come together in the financial institutions and markets of the City of London. The major British financial institutions, such as banks, trust funds and insurance companies, conduct their worldwide business here. Much of their business consists in buying and selling shares in British and international companies and in lending governments money. The City is a major influence on what foreign lenders and investors think about British economic prospects. It also has a broader influence on British commerce and industry generally.

The major way in which the City's influence is felt is through the price it and other lenders charge the government for loans, or whether it is even prepared to lend money for the day-to-day operations of government in the first place.

Plate 1.3 *The City of London. Work in progress on the new building, designed by Norman Foster, that will house the London offices of Swiss Re. The 180-metre high structure, nicknamed 'the gherkin', will be topped by a glass dome and will become the second highest building in the City, after Tower 42 – formerly known as the NatWest Tower – which stands at 200 metres. The tallest building in London is a few miles away at Canary Wharf, whose tower reaches 243 metres*

Source:
www.paphotos.com

British governments often spend more than they take in revenue. Any improvement in educational or health standards costs money, which may have to be borrowed. Therefore, it is clear that any government is heavily dependent on the goodwill of the financial markets. A loss of goodwill can result in a reduction in the value of the British currency, through the loss of world financial confidence. This could plunge not only the British government but the whole of the economy into crisis.

In the past, City influence pressed particularly on Labour governments because Labour governments traditionally needed to tax and spend to fulfil electoral promises. Plans to take more money in taxes rather than letting it emerge in higher profits reduces the value of shares. Since the mid-1990s, however, the

BRIEFINGS

1.5 The 'City'

This is a geographical area, referring to the old core of London within the medieval city wall, between the modern centre and the residential East End. Most of the head offices of the financial institutions of Britain, including the Stock Exchange and Bank of England, are physically located there. The term is used metaphorically to refer to British financial institutions in general, many of which are located elsewhere in London and the rest of the country.

These institutions dominate the British economy for two reasons. The first is because, collectively, they own most of the large businesses and firms through their shareholdings. Second, manufacturing industry borrows from them to finance production and expansion. Bank decisions about whether to make loans and how much to charge for them thus affect the activity of the whole economy. In addition, the City is the major global centre for insurance and many exchange markets such as currency, precious metals and other commodities.

The City is one of the three leading financial centres of the world (the others being New York and Tokyo). Thus its collective judgements about how well the British economy is performing, and whether to hold onto British currency, influences foreign investors as well. If the City's judgement is negative money markets across the world will sell pounds for ever-decreasing amounts of foreign currency, thus effectively reducing the value of savings in Britain and of sales overseas. This gives financial interests a crucial influence over government economic policy, often to the extent of obliging governments to favour financially prudent policies such as low government debt and low inflation over expansion of manufacturing industry and of public services.

Social democratic
The ideology of that part of the political Left which holds that political and social change can and should be achieved by means of peaceful reform rather than revolutionary violence.

Labour Party, along with other Social Democratic parties in Europe, has largely abandoned high-tax, high-spending policies in favour of fiscal rectitude (ie low taxation and restraints on public spending and inflation). This sea change in policy has had important consequences for British politics and for the British economy. We will return to this theme in Chapter 3.

CLASS/TERRITORIAL DIVISION

The financial markets' desire for expenditure cuts, limited taxation and hence generally limited government tied in very well with Conservative government policies from 1979 to 1997. Financial services directly or indirectly employ millions of the new middle class in southeast England. So the views of the financial markets and the new middle classes form one side of a political division that traditionally separated the Conservative and Labour parties. Labour's core support has usually come from groups which by and large have been disadvantaged by recent social changes and government policies: the unemployed, the shrinking numbers of manual workers represented by trade unions, immigrants and all those dependent on and working in old industries. Only when Labour adopts a more centrist position, which broadens its appeal beyond its core supporters to the mass of middle class voters, can it win elections. This is precisely what happened in May 1997.

Because of the way industry developed in Britain the social divisions separating the parties are also reflected in a territorial division of political opinion. The availability of water power and coal meant that the manufacturing industries of the Industrial Revolution – textiles, coalmining, steel and shipbuilding – were located in the 'Celtic fringe' – Scotland, Northern Ireland and Wales – and in the Midlands and north of England.

The 'Celtic fringe'
Coined around 1900 to describe the northern and western peripheries of the British Isles (Scotland, Wales and Ireland) that voted Liberal, Labour or Nationalist rather than Conservative. The term is now used to refer to the Celtic periphery of the UK (Scotland, Ireland and Wales) whatever the voting patterns.

The large new nineteenth-century cities – Glasgow, Manchester, Newcastle, Liverpool, Leeds, Cardiff, Belfast – developed in these regions, along with Birmingham and Nottingham in the Midlands. They housed the new industrial class of manual labourers and factory workers, often in appalling conditions. These cities and their inhabitants depended on manufacturing and extractive industries, unlike London, which remained the seat of government, administration, commerce and finance. Although a large working class grew up in central and east London, the capital and its surrounding area (the 'Home Counties') were the centre of an even larger and more prosperous middle class.

Class contrasts between manual and 'white-collar' workers were thus reinforced in Britain by a territorial division between the geographical areas in which each predominated. From this point of view the Labour (and Liberal) parties have often seemed more like coalitions of London and the British peripheries against the south and southeast England than class-based parties. This is particularly true now, following the Labour victories in the 1997 and 2001 elections. In 2001, 124 out of 166 Conservative MPs came from the south and southeast of England. Also significant is the fact that in 2001 not one Conservative MP was elected in Wales and just one was elected in Scotland.

Divisions between these two territorial–class coalitions go beyond party politics. Financial interests trading worldwide from the City of London need above all a stable currency and low inflation to preserve the value of their cash and investments. This need has often conflicted with the requirement of manufacturing industry for devaluation of the currency to help their exports, and for mildly rising inflation to give people more money to buy their products. In turn, this situation stimulates investment and employment.

Of necessity, government policy has usually favoured financial prudence because inflation can provoke an immediate financial crisis with both national and international repercussions. Industrial consequences are long term: once older manufacturing industries decline, it is very difficult to revive them. These industrial changes clearly have negative consequences for older mining and manufacturing communities. Contrariwise, the jobs created in other sectors such as finance and retailing are often better paid and less arduous. The problem has been distributing them geographically in a way that helps the distressed industrial areas rather than the southeast.

By the mid-1990s the Labour Party had reconciled itself to the fact that, to achieve electoral success, it was obliged to follow a policy of fiscal and monetary

Map 1.1 *The regions of the British Isles*

Key

——— Regions as defined by the EU

Scotland

Northern Ireland

North

Yorkshire and Humberside

Northwest

East Midlands

West Midlands

East Anglia

Wales

Southeast

Southwest

restraint. This meant avoiding tax large increases, attempting to balance the national budget and, above all, keeping strict controls on inflation. With the abolition of restrictions on the movement of capital across national borders during the 1980s and 1990s governments in all countries felt pressure to control inflation and thus prevent a decline in the values of currencies. In this sense, the values represented by the City of London throughout the post-war period (lower taxes, balanced budgets and low inflation) became the economic orthodoxy almost everywhere. As we shall see, this development has had the effect of putting strict limits on what governments of all political complexions can do in terms of public expenditure.

Plate 1.4 *Working class housing and a middle class estate*

Sources: (upper picture) www.paphotos.com; (lower picture) Gleeson Homes Ltd

THE BRITISH STATE AND THE BRITISH 'ESTABLISHMENT'

State The set of public bodies and institutions within a given territory that exercise a monopoly of the legitimate use of physical force. In Britain, the State consists mainly of Parliament, the military, the courts, the police, the Civil Service and local government.

The Establishment A vague term referring to the elite of public and private life that, some claim, run Britain irrespective of which party is in government.

The class/territorial division is at the heart of the left–right cleavage between the British parties, which we shall discuss in Chapter 17. Labour wants help for disadvantaged groups and regions, the Liberal Democrats desire their greater empowerment, while Conservatives want a strengthening of the existing order and of the disciplines underpinning it. As we have seen, important institutions such as the City of London as well as many business people and business groups have historically sided with the Conservatives. Many commentators have therefore concluded that all the leading British institutions, including State institutions such as the Civil Service and the security services, are biased against the left and covertly do their best to thwart them when they achieve power. Some variants of these 'conspiracy' theories saw the whole set of central institutions, including the Crown, judges and even the clergy of the Church of England, as lined up to thwart any left-wing threats to their privileges and position.

BRIEFINGS

1.6 The 'Establishment'

This was a term coined in the 1960s to describe the British equivalent of the 'power elite' felt to exist in most countries, that is to say, powerful figures in business, the Civil Service and the armed forces who ran the country regardless of what party was elected to government. The term 'Establishment' was borrowed from ecclesiastical terminology, where it referred to the bishops and higher clergy of the State Church (of England). They were felt to epitomise the fuddy-duddy and inert nature of the traditional British elite, deriving from exclusive private schools and Oxford and Cambridge universities. Radicals in the 1960s depicted these people as powerful enough to thwart necessary change and as contributing to the snobbery and hierarchical nature of British society. They were depicted also as brakes on progress, being influenced by old-fashioned ideas of Empire and of British world dominance.

Ideas of this kind were quickly discredited when Mrs Thatcher came to power in 1979 and started to change British institutions and practices ruthlessly without effective resistance from anyone. Ironically, the Church of England 'Establishment' then emerged among her most socially minded critics.

Speculation about an 'establishment' was always far fetched – there was never a conspiracy. Bishops figured among the major critics of Conservative policies on the grounds that they were hurting the weak. Civil servants and government departments rarely agreed among themselves: if the Treasury favoured City financiers, the Department of Employment often supported trade unions.

Nevertheless, the Treasury and the Home Office are the most powerful and central of the departments dealing with internal affairs. Spending departments, such as Education and Skills, Health, Transport do not deal with core policies. The Treasury shares its values with the City of London and supports their preferences for tight expenditure controls and tax cutting, putting the maintenance of financial confidence at the top of its list of priorities. A certain structural bias is thus built into British central institutions, which favours the private versus the public, tax cutting against services, London and the Home Counties against the peripheries. However, low inflation and fiscal rectitude have become the orthodoxy for all political parties. Put another way, they determine the limits of what even the most radical governments can do in the taxing and spending domain. In areas independent of economic policy, and especially constitutional reform, major changes can still be achieved. But the acceptance of economic orthodoxy by all political parties has significantly changed the nature of British politics.

EUROPEAN INTEGRATION

How British institutions emerged in the form they have today will be examined in the next chapter. They were heavily shaped in the mid-nineteenth century by Britain's then position as the leading industrial country, dominant in world trade.

New international influences are emerging, however, that may redress the balance of the old. These stem in part from Britain's increasing integration into the European Union. By creating additional pressures from outside the existing set of British institutions the European Union may give Labour governments an opportunity to call on countervailing forces that could tip the balance towards their own preferred policies.

This opportunity exists because most other members of the EU have better social protection than Britain. Paying less for social benefits does, of course, enable firms to cut prices, particularly if there is no legislation enforcing a minimum wage (as was true in Britain until 1998) or the minimum wage is set at a low level in comparison with other EU states. Other EU governments are therefore afraid that in the Single European Market, which they are creating, British firms will have a competitive advantage because of lower wage and welfare costs.

Precisely for this reason the Treaty of Maastricht, which envisaged an emerging federal union between Member States, had a 'Social Chapter' binding all governments to give social rights to workers to ensure a 'level playing field' for competition. However, the Conservative government of John Major 'opted out' of the Social Chapter, the only one of the member governments to do so.

The Major government also reserved its position on the question of whether to enter a currency union with the other Member States. Such a union would have the advantage of creating a strong, stable European currency that would command international confidence and avoid financial crises better than a purely British pound. However, it would also remove control of most financial policy from the British government and Treasury and place it in the hands of a European central bank.

Large sections of the Conservative Party see this as an unacceptable surrender of British national sovereignty to the Union. Hence no Conservative government would now agree to European Monetary Union (EMU). Financial and industrial interests are split, as many see British firms being excluded from a lucrative and expanding market if they stand aloof.

This situation provides an unprecedented opportunity for Labour governments to pursue their policies with the consent of both industrial and financial interests. By accepting EMU (as well as the Social Chapter, which the government signed on coming to power in 1997) Labour could advance its social policies without creating a crisis of confidence.

The price would be a diminution of British autonomy over monetary policy. No longer would the Bank of England be able to 'fine-tune' the economy by adjusting interest rates to promote activity, or raise them independently of their European partners as a way of coping with inflation. Now the value of the pound changes roughly in line with the objective performance of the British economy and thus provides an automatic guide to the value of exported and imported goods. With monetary union British goods would be valued in terms of a European-wide currency, which might not be as sensitive to British performance.

But the freedom to encourage economic activity by making money cheap has often been abused in the past. Governments often created an economic boom before an election in order to make people feel good and collect votes, only to provoke a crisis immediately after the election. Indeed, in recognition of this, one of the first actions of the present Labour government was to grant the Bank of England the power to set interest rates without direct government interference, through its nominated Monetary Policy Committee. Transferring financial control to the European Central Bank in Frankfurt might therefore not be a bad thing for many sections of British society.

BRITAIN: ADAPTING TO A NEW INTERNATIONAL ENVIRONMENT

Whether we think European influence is a good or a bad thing, British politics cannot be explained without taking it into account. This would be the case whether Britain were in or out of the EU. So closely are its economy and defence now bound up with Europe that they will be vitally affected by European Union decisions. That is not a choice. The only real question is whether the government chooses to influence European policy from outside or inside. In the case of the Labour government there seems much to be gained from going in and little from staying out.

The inability of Britain to go it alone, evident in the case of Europe and in Britain's relationships with the world superpower, the USA, seems a far cry from its position in the mid-nineteenth century when it was at the centre of a world-wide Empire and an even more extended trading network. The contrast has prompted many critics to see post-war British politics as a series of unsuccessful attempts to cope with national decline.

'Decline' is an emotive word, with all sorts of implications beyond the specific political area to which it applies. It has undertones of moral and spiritual decay, which did indeed inform certain analyses of the British situation in the 1980s. A more neutral characterisation of British politics is that they have been adapting to an unstable and shifting world environment, in which the British position has also changed quite radically.

Clearly, the British State is much less powerful militarily and economically at the beginning of the twenty-first century than it was at the beginning of the twentieth century, when it was the leading naval power in the world. This enabled it to trade everywhere and to build up an Empire that at its height covered a quarter of the land area of the world. At the same time, Britain was, along with the United States and Germany, a leading world industrial power and the leading provider of investment capital in the new markets of Asia, Africa and South America.

All this was due to the fact that the Industrial Revolution was carried through first in Britain, making British firms the undisputed leaders in a variety of manufactures ranging from textiles to steel. This unique situation could not last. Even to sell their goods abroad British entrepreneurs had to invest in overseas infrastructures such as railways, which then provided the basis for other countries to industrialise too. Their doing so was a precondition for Britain to continue its industrial expansion, as purely agricultural societies could take only a limited supply of British exports.

Clearly, Britain no longer enjoys the commercial and military pre-eminence that it did then. However, it has been on the winning side in two world wars and in the Cold War, and it disengaged from its colonies relatively painlessly. The British were able to recognise the formidable power of local nationalism, and avoided becoming embroiled in the sort of long and corrosive wars fought by France and Portugal in the 1950s and 1960s. Britain has kept its options open in Europe up to the present time. All this looks less like drift and decline than successful adaptation to a changing world situation.

Much of the debate on decline and change, however, focused on the economy rather than directly on foreign affairs. The British share of world trade fell consistently over the last 100 years, from one-third in 1899 to one-quarter in 1950, to around one-twentieth today. British economic growth was also sluggish for most of the post-Second World War period. However, since about 1990 the British economy has performed remarkably well, outstripping the growth rates of Germany, France, Italy and Japan by a considerable margin (see Table 1.4 and Figure 1.5).

The relatively poor performance of the British economy in the 1950–90 period was to have profound effects on British politics. The Labour and Conservative parties competed with one another on how best to redress this situation and allow Britain to 'catch up' with such countries as France, Germany and Japan. As we will see in later chapters, radical alternatives were provided by both the left and the right, which led to a particularly abrasive and confrontational style of politics. Poor economic performance also led to a sense that British politics was in a state of almost permanent 'crisis' with parties and governments lurching unsteadily in the face of uncontrollable economic events. This sense of economic crisis

Table 1.4 *Annual GDP growth for major industrialised countries, 1962–2001*

	1962–72	1977–88	1991–2001
France	4.7	1.6	1.9
Germany	3.6	1.3	1.5
Italy	3.9	2.2	1.6
Britain	2.2	1.8	2.7
United States	3.0	2.3	3.4
Japan	9.2	3.9	1.1

Source: OECD, *OECD in Figures: Statistics of Member Countries*, Paris, OECD, 2002, pp. 14–15

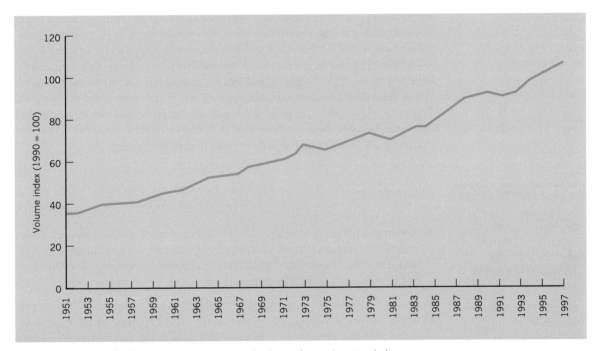

Figure 1.5 *Growth of British gross domestic product over the post-war period*

Source: Office for National Statistics

abated during most of the 1990s and was almost wholly absent after 1997. This fact helps explain the remarkable renaissance of the Labour Party in British politics.

Geographically, Britain is an island group off the northwestern shore of Europe. Its proximity to Europe means that it has always been involved in European affairs. Its strategic location on the Atlantic means, however, that it was also in a position to expand westwards. British emigration and trade, therefore, have been predominantly overseas, away from Europe. They ended up creating new English-speaking countries in North America and Australasia, with which

Britain has closer cultural links than with France and Germany, despite being much closer to those countries geographically.

Since 1960, British governments have therefore been pulled in two directions, often proving unable to make up their minds between them. The European Union, particularly under the influence of France, has wanted to create a strong European bloc of countries with external trade barriers against the rest of the world. Britain, with strong commercial and, particularly, financial links overseas, has wished the EU to pursue relatively liberal, open trading policies. It has also wanted the EU to co-operate with the USA rather than rival it.

These conflicting pulls are behind British membership of the EU on the one hand and its opposition to an exclusive, federal, largely autonomous and self-sufficient EU on the other. Britain would maximise its influence and prosperity by pressing ahead with integration into the EU, which increasingly seems likely to emerge as a world superpower. Yet, this would weaken its overseas links, particularly with the USA, with which it shares a language and – to some extent – a culture. The choice is hard. As an American observer, Dean Acheson, acutely observed in the 1950s, 'Britain has lost an empire but not yet found a role.' It is still hesitating between two roles: that of world free trader and that of good European. New Labour may tip it towards the latter, because of the social and economic benefits from membership. If it does it will resolve the conflicting external pulls that Britain has felt for more than half a century.

ESSAYS

1. What role does the City play in British politics? Has its role been beneficial or detrimental to British interests?

2. What is meant by the British 'Establishment'? Is its influence declining or increasing in British politics?

3. What evidence is there that recent Labour governments have not been obliged to increase taxation and public expenditure?

SUMMARY

■ Britain is a liberal democracy. As such it shares many political characteristics with other countries that are also liberal democracies, both in Europe and overseas. The most obvious are regular, free, competitive elections, and parliaments and governments chosen by popular vote.

■ However, Britain also has unique characteristics deriving from its own particular history and geography. Some of the most important of these are associated with the Industrial Revolution. Britain was the first European country to create institutions such as mass parties, a representative Parliament, popular press, trade unions, international, financial and commodity exchanges and markets.

■ Many of these institutions still exist, largely in their original form. A central question of this book is how well such relatively unchanging institutions serve the needs of a continually changing society, divided between different ethnic groups, classes and regions.

■ A further question is how well they can cope with the international pressures that Britain, like all countries, continually faces. It has become hard to distinguish between purely national politics and foreign relations, particularly with globalisation and the move to European integration. Britain now has to decide between committing itself fully to Europe or remaining in its present uneasy position between Europe and the rest of the world.

PROJECTS

1. How would you go about testing whether the class territorial divide in British politics is increasing or decreasing? Answer with respect to both economic and political variables.

2. What statistics would you use to test the claim that Britain is no longer in 'economic decline?' How reliable are these statistics?

3. Using information available from the annual publication *Social Trends* show that:
   (a) gender inequality in employment in Britain remains high
   (b) women are, however, more important in the workforce.

■ Labour governments, now committed to free market principles, are likely to decide in favour of Europe as a way of securing long-term economic growth while helping to protect citizens and consumers from some of the harsher aspects of the free market economy. In this way it may end the long series of hesitations and fudges that contributed to the sense of economic and social crisis in the 40 years to the mid-1990s.

■ British politics can only be explained by a combination of national and international factors, set within a unique historical and geographical context. Historical influences are channelled through the institutions that the country inherited from the late seventeenth century. The origin and development of these institutions are examined in Chapter 2.

FURTHER READING

A provocative account of some of the general themes discussed in this chapter is Will Hutton, *The State We're In* (London: Vintage, 1996). See also his *The World We're In* (London: Little, Brown, 2002). Andrew Gamble, *The Free Economy and the Strong State* (London: Macmillan, 1988), assessed the 1980s in Britain and also wrote *Britain in Decline* (London: Macmillan, 1989). For the British role in Europe and the world see Ian Budge et al, *The Politics of the New Europe* (London: Addison Wesley Longman, 1997), Chapters 1 and 2. For lively updates on current developments see the quarterly *Monitor* published by the Constitution Unit at University College London, and the associated web site (see section at end of chapter).

USEFUL WEB SITES ON BRITISH POLITICS

Hot links to these sites can be found on the CWS at http://www.booksites.net/budge. As a general introduction to important web sites concerning British politics, try www.ukpolitics.org.uk, which has many links to other political web sites. There are sites for the main institutions of the British State and government. For example, see the monarchy (www.royal.gov.uk), the Anglican Church (www.cofe.anglican.org), the House of Commons and House of Lords (www.parliament.uk and www.explore.parliament.uk), the new Scottish Parliament (www.scottish.parliament.uk), the Welsh Assembly (www.wales.gov.uk/assembly.dbs) and the Northern Ireland government website www.nics.gov.uk. Other useful introductory sites related to British politics: www.historylearningsite.co.uk/gbpolitics.htm offers a comprehensive glossary of terms including liberal and representative democracy; for specific information on the Westminster system refer to www.ukpol.co.uk, as well as data on central and local government in the UK; finally there are accessible complementary resources at www.britpolitics.com.

Political party sites

All the major political parties have web sites, and there are other sites that may be of interest to students of British politics such as www.ucl.ac.uk/constitutionunit/ and www.bubl.ac.uk/uk/parties.htm. See also the following list and subsequent chapters. (For further study aids on this subject, please see the self-assessment test for this chapter on *The New British Politics* website at http://www.booksites.net/budge.)

Labour www.labour.org.uk
Conservative www.conservative-party.org.uk
Liberal Democrats www.libdems.org.uk
Scottish National Party www.snp.org.uk
Plaid Cymru www.plaid-cymru.wales.com

(See Chapters 16 and 17 for more links to party sites.)

Other sites of interest

The government-sponsored www.ukonline.gov.uk is a recommended source of information for central and local institutions. www.open.gov.uk is a good first point of entry for internet information on the public sector in the UK, as is www.number-10.gov.uk

www.hmso.gov.uk for Her Majesty's Stationery Office, contains legislation, statutory instruments and other official government publications
www.britannia.com is a private site on all things British, in particular see www.britannia.com/gov
www.bankofengland.co.uk for the Bank of England

Economic and social statistical data can be found at www.statistics.gov.uk. The Cabinet's site at www.cabinet-office.gov.uk provides valuable information on the ministerial structure, the Civil Service and the public sector standards. General information about British culture and traditions can be obtained from www.english-heritage.org.uk.

PART 1

Structure and Development in British Politics

The London offices of Swiss Re in construction

CHAPTER 2

The first industrial country: Ideas and institutions, 1688–1931

From the seventeenth through to the early twentieth centuries Britain experienced two crucial – and in comparison with other countries – unique developments. First, the country made a long and peaceful transition from autocratic monarchy to modern democracy. No other comparable state made this transition entirely through peaceful means. Instead, such countries as Germany, France, Italy and even the United States experienced revolutions, civil war or wars of independence in their evolution to democracy. Second, and related, Britain was the first country to industrialise and make the transition from a predominantly rural society to an overwhelmingly urban one. At the same time, Britain acquired the world's largest colonial empire, which was at once a source of raw materials and cheap agricultural produce and a market for British manufactured goods and financial services. These developments required new political, economic and social institutions, many of which – Parliament, the Civil Service, local government, courts and police, the City of London, the armed forces – are still with us. Externally, Britain got locked into a pattern of relationships with the rest of the world that also persists, although both Britain and the world have changed greatly in the meantime.

How adaptable these institutions have been in the face of the quite dramatic changes to British society and to Britain's role in the world over the last several decades, was a question raised in Chapter 1, and will be a theme throughout the book. However, we cannot provide a clear answer until we have looked in detail at how British politics and institutions function in practice. To understand them fully we also need to look at the critical formative period in which they emerged and see what influences shaped them. We do this here, before going on to post-1930 developments in Chapter 3.

This chapter looks at the ways in which industrialisation and urbanisation changed both political institutions and the main ideas that shape politics. Discussion will be divided into the following historical periods and episodes:

- the triumph of Parliamentary over royal power, 1688–1830
- urbanisation and the rise of mass democracy, 1830–1928
- the British world system, 1850–90
- institutional change and reform, 1840–1900
- free markets, protection and industry, 1890–1931
- external defences against an unstable international environment, 1890–1931
- the rise of socialism and trade union power, 1890–1931.

THE TRIUMPH OF PARLIAMENTARY OVER ROYAL POWER, 1688–1830

A crucial date in English (and hence British) history is 1688, because it marks one of the very few occasions when English political institutions made a clear break with the past. Until 1688 royal power enshrined in the doctrine of the divine right of kings (that monarchs were chosen by God to rule their subjects) remained influential, even if few political leaders actually believed in it. In England,

James II who had succeeded the Catholic-leaning Charles II to the throne in 1685 was openly Catholic and contemptuous of Parliament. Moreover, he had a Catholic son who was due to succeed him. The most influential grouping in Parliament, the Whigs, were Protestant and determined to assert Parliamentary power over the monarch. James II's insensitivity to Parliament also offended the other main grouping, the Tories and in 1688 seven Whig and Tory leaders invited Protestant William of Orange and his wife Mary, Protestant daughter of James, to take the English throne. Although James at first resisted, he eventually fled to France and William and Mary acceded to the throne.

A new constitutional settlement, known as the Glorious Revolution, established the necessity to consult Parliament, especially on matters of taxation. It also established that all subsequent monarchs would be Protestant. Although a Bill of Rights was published this was not so much a guarantee of citizen rights in the modern sense, as it was a guarantee of the rights of Parliament. These included free elections, free speech in Parliament and the abolition of the monarch's power to dispense and suspend laws. Further refinements were added through the Act of Settlement in 1701 and through the Act of Union with Scotland in 1707 (see Chapter 11).

During the course of the eighteenth century, many of the remaining ambiguities surrounding the limits on royal power were removed as successive Prime Ministers and their Cabinets assumed the role of chief executive in the British system. Even so, important residual powers remained with the monarch, including the formal power of dissolving Parliament and appointing a new government. These residual powers continued through the nineteenth century and indeed remain in a much-attenuated form to this day (see Chapter 4).

In spite of free speech in Parliament and free elections, eighteenth-century Britain was hardly democratic by today's standards. Parliamentary seats could be secured from large landowners or by bribing a few electors. The right to vote was confined to just a few men of property. And, of course, the landed aristocracy retained an important role in government through their membership of the upper House of Parliament, the House of Lords. Even so, the British elites considered their system democratic and free in comparison with the absolutism that characterised most major Continental powers. Towards the end of the eighteenth century two foreign events were to have a profound impact. First, the American War of Independence and the subsequent establishment of democracy in the United States showed up the weaknesses and inadequacies of British politics as practised in the late eighteenth century. Second, the French Revolution showed what could happen to states that denied rights and freedoms to their citizenry. Anarchy and rule by the mob could result. The French Revolution thus provided a salutary lesson on what could happen in states that failed to make a peaceful transition to full democracy.

URBANISATION AND THE RISE OF MASS DEMOCRACY, 1830–1928

The ascendancy of Parliamentary over royal power was accompanied by dramatic economic developments. First agriculture and then manufacturing experienced rapid technological changes greatly increasing productivity and speeding the move of population from the countryside to the towns. The development of factory machinery powered by steam led to the concentration of manufacturing in towns where markets were close by and transport links good. An industrial working class clustered around the new factories and eventually older towns expanded rapidly and new towns were created where previously there had been villages. By 1850, a quarter of the British population lived in cities of over 100,000 and more than a half in conglomerations that could be described as urban. However, most of these areas had no political authority to police, regulate or represent them. The new middle class in the urban areas felt personally threatened by disorder and disease, and wanted in any case to have a healthier and more disciplined workforce in the factories.

BRIEFINGS

2.1 The Industrial Revolution

During the eighteenth century technology was increasingly applied to manufacturing processes, from cloth to iron, which had previously been carried out by hand in scattered artisan workshops. The most notable development was the use of mill machinery, which utilised water and steam power to spin and weave cloth and to shape metal. As a result, a large number of unskilled workers could produce more, better quality goods at a lower price. The use of a single power source and of a large, concentrated labour force prompted the invention of the modern factory. When steam was substituted for water power, factories were grouped near to coalfields and close to each other. These groupings of factories and associated workers' housing produced industrial towns and cities, which developed an infrastructure of canals, roads, transport and services. By 1850 more than half the population of Britain lived in such settlements and Britain had become the first urbanised society. The factory owners, professionals and merchants who dominated the new cities formed a new political grouping that wanted a share in political power, and eventually the organised working class also wanted representation to improve their conditions. Thus the economic changes associated with the Industrial Revolution destabilised the old political order in which landed aristocrats and gentry dominated Parliament.

New Poor Law Passed in 1834 to deal with the poor cheaply and efficiently. 'Workhouses' were set up everywhere into which those who needed relief had to go. Conditions inside were harsher than those of the worst paid employment outside to deter 'welfare dependence'.

Middle class agitation for local and national change produced the 'Great Reform Act' of 1832 and the repeal of the Corn Laws in 1846. The Great Reform Act was in fact a very limited measure. It extended voting rights to all the wealthy and the upper middle class. Parliamentary reform was followed by municipal reform that set up new councils in urban areas which were able, where they wished, to tackle local health and crime. The New Poor Law created uniform, minimal and often harsh facilities for those in desperate need.

BRIEFINGS

2.2 The Reform Acts 1832–1928

The Great (First) Reform Act of 1832 was passed by the unreformed Parliament under pressure from the politically mobilised middle class (industrialists, merchants, and their supporters and dependants). It was a limited measure, abolishing most 'rotten boroughs' (constituencies with very few electors) and 'pocket boroughs' (constituencies controlled by one big landowner), where MPs could buy their seats from electors or obtain it from a landed proprietor. These seats were redistributed to counties or to the large new industrial towns. Inside the redrawn constituencies the vote was given to property holders, resulting in limited numbers of electors in each constituency.

The Great Reform Act was not a very radical measure, but it did show that the electoral system could be changed peacefully in favour of previously excluded groups. Further agitation later in the century brought about:

- the Second Reform Act (1867), which gave the vote to the better off workmen in towns
- the Third Reform Act (1884), which extended the franchise in towns and gave it to agricultural labourers
- the extension of the vote to the third of adult males who were still excluded, along with women over 30, in 1918
- finally, in 1928, the granting of the vote to women on the same terms as men.

These changes were accompanied by reforms of the constituency system which ensured that constituencies were relatively equal in size, thus weighting votes more equally. It was typical of the cautious and incremental nature of political change in Britain, however, that all reforms left intact the 'first past the post system', in which the individual candidates compete in small constituencies and the one with the most votes wins, whether or not he or she gets a majority of the total votes cast.

The new middle classes followed up these successes by abolishing all protective taxes on imports, notably of food (the repeal of the Corn Laws, 1846). Their reason for wanting this was logical and simple. British industry was incomparably bigger and more efficient than that in other countries and therefore had nothing to fear from competition or imports. What manufacturers did want, however, was cheap food for their workforce, so that wages and prices could be kept down. Protective tariffs on imports of food left food prices high, to the benefit of British farmers and country dwellers in general. The abolition of tariffs on wheat signalled the end of all such protective measures, marking the dominance of urban interests over rural and of the new middle class (the 'bourgeoisie') over the landed gentry.

The abolition of protective tariffs produced the 'great transformation' of British society and of Britain's place in the world. For the first time, a country took the gamble of making itself dependent on foreign imports for its basic survival. By the beginning of the twentieth century half of what the British ate was imported, much of it from the Americas and Australasia. This meant in turn that Britain had to export to survive. (It also rendered it particularly vulnerable in the First and Second World Wars to submarine attacks, which sank ships carrying food and munitions.)

Agitators such as John Bright and Richard Cobden who attacked protection did not foresee this military consequence. They were, however, quite prepared to gamble on manufactured exports paying for food imports. Given British industrial supremacy in the world this seemed a safe bet. In support of Corn Law repeal they developed a series of interlocking arguments in favour of free trade, that is, the abolition of all protective tariffs on a worldwide basis.

The free trade advocates believed that without 'artificial' tariffs the pressure of competition would force each area of the world to concentrate on what it produced most efficiently. Efficiency might be linked to natural advantages such as the presence of minerals or a beneficent climate. It was marked in practice by the ability to produce and market the good at a lower price than elsewhere in the world, provided political barriers such as tariffs did not distort market judgements. Hence the importance of eliminating them.

In this way universal free markets would stimulate the production of goods, and distribute them at the lowest possible prices, thereby maximising human well-being. They also reduced the possibility of war, whose prime cause was thought to be poverty or covetousness. Now the populations of all countries would enjoy all the benefits that were humanly attainable, or so the argument went.

Free trade The idea that trade should not be restricted by protection in the form of tariffs, custom duties or import quotas that are designed to protect the domestic economy from foreign competition.

Liberalism With a small 'l', liberalism is the political belief that individual rights should be protected by strictly limiting the powers of government.

Liberalism With a capital 'L' Liberalism refers to the beliefs and policies of the Liberal Party.

Neo-liberalism The ideas associated with the New Right of the 1980s that market competition is the best means of guaranteeing political freedom and economic growth.

GATT General Agreement on Trade and Tariffs – the series of agreements heavily promoted by the USA since the Second World War and designed to promote free trade in all products throughout the world.

WTO World Trade Organisation. The international organisation set up in 1993 to 'police' the GATT agreements, which now replaces it.

BRIEFINGS

2.3 Free trade, free markets, protectionism, and classical (neo)liberalism

Classical economics (the ideas of Adam Smith, David Ricardo and Jeremy Bentham) concluded that trade and well-being would be maximised in a market of independent producers who could trade freely with each other. Victorian politicians such as Richard Cobden and John Bright adopted this argument enthusiastically on behalf of the new middle class. They believed that once free trade was extended, both nationally and internationally, it would eliminate the causes of war, since everybody would receive the maximum benefits possible from the operation of the market, and this would remove the causes of conflict between nations.

Although this summary of the argument may seem a little naive, belief in free markets and free trade gained new force in the second half of the twentieth century from adherents such as Margaret Thatcher. Many countries accordingly tried to sweep away their own barriers to trade and continue to eliminate them internationally through the General Agreement on Trade and Tariffs (GATT) (later renamed the World Trade Organisation (WTO)).

In the nineteenth century the new free trade ideas seemed to provide an answer to everything and were taken up enthusiastically by reformers and liberals everywhere. Hence their label of 'classical' (or neo) liberalism. The antithesis of free trade was protection, where special taxes or tariffs were applied to goods to keep another country's products out. The classic example of this were the Corn Laws in Britain, which excluded cheaper foreign grain in order to raise prices for farmers and were accordingly abolished in 1846.

Free trade ideas fit nicely with the development of parallel ideas relating to the general role of the individual in society. Hence, thinkers such as John Stuart Mill argued that the state should not interfere with the tastes and choices of individual citizens unless their actions adversely affected others. Mill also advanced the notion that the free clash of contrasting political ideas would more likely expose falsehood and lead to the triumph of ideas that were 'true'. Censorship and the restriction of free speech might lead to society being dominated by 'wrong' or 'false' ideas. Moreover, no social group or gender had a monopoly on the truth. By implication, all educated citizens irrespective of background, race, class or gender should participate in the marketplace of ideas. It followed that free speech, universal education and a universal franchise (all should be eligible to vote) were essential to a good society.

Such notions gradually gained currency in Victorian Britain. Clearly they influenced the rise of mass democracy and the idea of 'one man one vote' (later one person, one vote). It follows that if any individual (although only men until the early twentieth century) wanted to stand for Parliament he or she should be free to do so by making direct appeals to the electorate. During the nineteenth and early twentieth centuries the social makeup of MPs did indeed change with much larger numbers being drawn from the middle classes and eventually the skilled working classes. Moreover, as the franchise expanded to include the lower middle and working classes so it was necessary for candidates to appeal to the electorate by differentiating themselves from the opposition in a coherent and intelligible manner.

Liberal individualism
All forms of liberalism implies individualism, but the recent tendency to combine 'liberal' and 'individual' in one phrase, suggests neo-liberal views that reject modern liberal ideology, which is fairly sympathetic to some state intervention, and a return to classical nineteenth-century liberalism, which believes in a minimal state.

By the second third of the nineteenth century the main vehicle for these appeals were the political parties who by then had developed effective means of communicating with voters including party manifestos, political advertising and mass meetings or the 'hustings' where candidates could speak to voters and exchange views.

Generally, Mill and his adherents were *liberal individualists*. They believed that society should be made up not of strictly stratified social classes, but of individuals expressing free will both in the marketplace of political ideas and in the economic marketplace. It is also obvious that such liberal ideas clashed with older notions of class and privilege and with the new socialist ideas based on equality of condition that were rapidly gaining influence in the second half of the nineteenth century. Political party programmes reflected these contrasting views of society with the Tories (later Conservatives) championing aspects of the old order, the Liberals defending liberal individualism, and, from 1901, Labour advancing socialism. We will return to this later in the chapter.

THE BRITISH WORLD SYSTEM, 1850–90

As indicated, a free market in political ideas was accompanied by support for an economic free market. Free trade and free competition constitute a set of ideas that British politicians and most parties have been strongly attached to ever since the 1850s. Concrete examples of their influence today are British entry into the European Union (conceived as an extended 'Common Market'), support for the

Single European Act of 1986 and enthusiasm for opening up world trade in successive GATT (now WTO) negotiations. World trading conditions and British economic competitiveness have changed enormously since the mid-nineteenth century. Regardless of such changes, British policy makers have opened up the country to foreign trade, and done their best to abolish protection internationally, apart from a brief period during the economic recession of the 1930s and the Second World War.

The explanation for this steadfast adherence to free trade and economic liberalism is not simply historical and cultural but is also institutional and structural. In the period of its industrial and commercial supremacy Britain created institutions such as the international financial markets in the 'City', and made enormous overseas investments that depended on world free trade and the unhampered flow of money.

These developments followed naturally from Britain's overwhelming dominance in the world economy from 1850 to 1870. With efficiently produced industrial goods that nobody else could produce as cheaply and all of which could not be absorbed by the domestic market, manufacturers depended on overseas outlets. However, something needed clearly to be traded for manufactured goods. Other countries could go into debt, of course, and many did, contributing to a massive growth of British assets overseas. Ultimately, however, they needed to balance their imports with exports.

The abolition of protection in Britain, under the influence of free trade ideas, helped solve the problem. Increasingly, Britain imported food and raw materials for industry (such as raw cotton, timber and mineral ores). The most plentiful supplies of these were in the less developed world, notably North and especially South America, and Australasia.

Consequently, British trade turned increasingly towards these areas. In line with free trade ideas about each country doing what it did best, Britain manufactured, while overseas trading partners raised animals and crops, or dug and quarried, exploiting the extensive natural resources which they had and Britain did not.

There was a snag, however. Often the natural resources were inaccessible, or under the control of hostile governments or indigenous peoples who had no desire to trade. To deal with the latter Britain rapidly expanded its direct control of likely territories, converting them into 'colonies'. It used its large and highly trained navy to protect trade routes and the army to destroy indigenous opposition (and often the indigenous peoples). Until around 1880, British naval power was close to being hegemonic – that is it dominated to the extent that no other power could challenge it in size and geographic scope.

In other cases, it supported like-minded governments that could subdue internal opposition. In terms of transport, British banks could supply capital for building railways for the transportation of settlers and crops. These were usually built by British-owned companies, which used British iron for the rails, imported locomotives and rolling stock from Britain and employed British personnel, thus creating another British asset overseas.

Britain was able to accept universal free trade in the nineteenth century because its industry and commerce could take on the world. This was an attitude that was natural for the first industrialised country to have but which was obviously much harder for later developing ones to accept. Primary producers of food and raw materials could accept it for a while. They had products to export that Britain wanted, and by accepting their role as British suppliers they could attract investment and build up their economic infrastructure of roads, railways, houses, and supporting facilities.

By the second third of the nineteenth century, however, some European countries (notably Germany) and the United States began to catch up with Britain. Moreover, because they developed their industries later than Britain they could take advantage of the most recent techniques in manufacturing and transport. By 1880, both Germany and the USA were expanding rapidly. Expansion was helped in the Continental countries by state subsidies, by tariffs (taxes on imports) and quotas (physical limits on what could be imported) imposed on British goods. These governments, therefore, embarked on a series of measures collectively known as 'protectionism', which went directly counter to all the doctrines of free trade.

Germany was the major exponent of protectionism in the late nineteenth century, but all the developed countries apart from Britain followed suit. Thus the free trade system – an early form of globalisation with London at its centre – which Britain managed to impose on most of the world, had its exceptions and dissenters. For a time, however, these were not too important in the British scheme of things – especially as the Empire continued to provide an outlet for British goods. Free trade operated without many impediments until the 1890s, and survived, although with increasing difficulty and interruptions during the First World War, until the great world economic depression of the 1930s. Meanwhile free trade ideas and their supporters generated internal developments and opposition.

INSTITUTIONAL CHANGE AND REFORM, 1840–1900

The reform of Parliament and the municipalities, creation of the New Poor Law to deal with poverty and the abolition of protective tariffs clearly demonstrated the dominance of the industrial, commercial and professional classes over the old landed aristocracy. In the middle years of the nineteenth century this dominance was reinforced through the reform or foundation of a whole series of cultural, economic and political institutions that reflected the values of the Victorian middle classes and catered to their interests.

These ranged from the reform of the armed forces and Civil Service, which began to recruit on the basis of open competition and merit rather than the ability to buy a position, to the creation of schools, institutes and later universities in the industrial provinces that trained the children of the new middle classes and 'respectable' skilled working class for positions in trade, business and the professions. The social and geographical extension of the franchise led to the election of many more businessmen and professionals to the House of Commons. The reform of the Stock Exchange and commodity exchanges expanded trade and finance, to the benefit of the commercial middle class. Eventually, a national, mass-circulation press and book publishing industry emerged that disseminated middle class values more widely in a society with rapidly improving literacy rates.

Franchise In its political sense, the right to vote.

2.4 Class and its importance in Britain

Britain is a particularly class-conscious society. This is partly because social, and particularly geographical, mobility has been less than in comparable industrialised societies. Britain has not experienced the sweeping social and political changes brought about by revolution and war as experienced in most other European countries or the mass immigration that opened channels of mobility in the USA. Thus the class divisions fixed by the Industrial Revolution remained almost unchanged until the 1940s, although they have been very much modified by economic and industrial changes since.

The strength of class in Britain lay in the fact that it was reinforced by a whole series of social characteristics and life opportunities. In the industrial cities of the nineteenth century there was a clear demarcation between the areas and type of housing occupied by industrial workers and those of both the lower middle and upper middle class. Each had its own type of school, club, church; each had its own social habits and lifestyle. Manual workers left school at the minimum age, went straight into work, spoke with a particular accent and even looked different from the prosperous middle class. They would travel little, marry and die young, earn minimal wages, spend some of their working lives unemployed and live in or near industrial cities.

Of course, there were many exceptions to this pattern and many variations within the working and middle classes. But large blocks of the population were marked out by these cumulative differences. The working class relied on collective action to improve their situation while the middle class were more disposed to adopt individualistic solutions, which their better resources and education made possible. A corollary of this was that the working class increasingly supported Labour, with its message that state intervention could help them, while the 'solid' middle class became increasingly Conservative from the 1880s onwards. Social differences were thus reinforced by political ones.

Most of these institutions are familiar because they exist in much the same form today. This is clear in the case of Parliament. As earlier noted, the political struggles of the nineteenth century between reformers and the old landed interest led politicians to group themselves in two major parties: Liberals (reformers) and Conservatives (defenders of established interests). By the 1870s both had organised themselves on a countrywide basis and were imposing party discipline on their members.

This meant that the House of Commons, the popularly elected chamber, was regarded as a national forum for the confrontation of two great political parties. All its procedures were arranged so as to focus and enhance this confrontation, from the physical arrangements of the debating chamber that forced MPs of different parties to choose sides, to the procedures for debates and committees that allowed government and opposition to confront each other. The state of the parties from 1868 to 1878, in the first truly reformed parliaments, was thus built into the constitutional arrangements still prevailing in the 2000s. When Labour came to the fore in the 1920s it simply squeezed out the Liberals as a serious competitor for government power.

Plate 2.1 *The House of Commons. The Conservative and Labour Parliamentary parties face each other on confrontational lines in the debating chamber during Prime Minister's Question Time*

Source: Stockwave, Central Office of Information

These consequences of Britain's Parliamentary institutions were reinforced by the single-member constituency system that Britain has inherited for electing MPs (Chapter 15). Any one candidate can be elected if he or she receives more votes than any other candidate does. This gives an advantage to large parties with strong support across the whole country rather than to a small party with a wide national appeal or small parties such as the Scottish Nationalists with strictly regional support, and explains why today governments are formed by either the Labour or Conservative parties rather than the Liberal Democrats.

Another Victorian institution that was to have a strong, if diffuse, influence over national life was the 'public school' (in fact, a particularly exclusive private school open only to the wealthy). Such schools had developed in the eighteenth century to educate aristocrats. From the 1830s onwards they were reformed and opened to the wealthy middle classes. Their aim was redefined as producing Christian gentlemen with a strong moral sense and commitment to public duty. This was to be achieved through the study of Latin and Greek, with literature and history thrown in, and an emphasis on competitive sport.

Plate 2.2 *An Oxbridge college with undergraduates*

A by-product of this was the fusion of aristocracy, gentry and upper middle class in a single upper class marked out by accent, background and lifestyle. The contacts made at public school rendered entry to politics and business easier and helped secure advancement. To an extraordinary degree, therefore, most institutions founded in Victorian times were – and to an extent still are – dominated by graduates of public schools and of the exclusive universities, Oxford and Cambridge.

This made contacts between the people at the top easier, as they shared a common background. Links were reinforced by the fact that many MPs, particularly in the Conservative Party, came from and continued in business after they were elected. The Victorians approved of MPs having personal wealth, because it made them independent, and of MPs engaging in activities outside Parliament, because it kept them in touch with the broader society. Although MPs were paid from 1911 onwards (a reform that opened the way for those without inherited wealth or high incomes to serve in Parliament) the practice remains of taking directorships, consultancies and other jobs to supplement this. The fact that business links increasingly involve the financial corporations of the City of London reinforces the latter's influence over political decisions.

FREE MARKETS, PROTECTION AND INDUSTRY, 1890–1931

The Victorians also modernised the Stock Exchange, where the ownership of companies was bought and sold. By extending the idea of a limited liability company – where the maximum individual investors could lose was the value of their holding in the company – they increased the incentives for individuals with money to buy and sell their 'shares' in its ownership as their price fluctuated. Such individuals were usually not actively concerned with the development of the company they bought into. They were simply concerned with the price they could sell the share for. If it fell, they sold rapidly, causing a general collapse of the price. This could bankrupt a company by preventing it raising money through share sales or bank loans (since banks would not lend to a company in trouble). Share prices might fall for many reasons other than bad management – for example a temporary fall in demand that, given time, a firm might overcome. Or companies might wish to invest more of their profits in better machinery to increase profits in later years.

The divorce between investment and management meant, however, that the predominant concern of investors was the current share price, not the underlying performance and prospects of the company. If it failed to pay out high returns each year it would be in trouble, regardless of whether it could promise higher returns in the future.

'Short-termism'
A criticism often made by politicians of British managers and investors who are unwilling to pay for research and other developments that do not give an immediate profit.

Such 'short-termism' on the part of investors has often been criticised. Manufacturing firms are tied to immediate results and cannot make long-term plans to deal effectively with overseas competition. However, one must also realise that it is a structural feature of the economy. British investors simply follow the logic of a free market, in which shares are necessarily a product to be bought and sold. In such a market investors themselves would be in trouble if they let considerations other than immediate profit and loss enter in. This was particularly true for the British financial markets as the world was opened up from 1850

Plate 2.3 *The trading floor of JP Morgan in the City of London*

Source:
www.paphotos.com

onwards. Banks, insurance companies and individual investors had an increasing choice between various overseas outlets, with high and immediate rates of return. British industrial shares came late into the financial markets in any large quantity. This was because it was easier financing expansion from their high rate of profits than from loans or share sales. The development of more sophisticated and expensive technology ruled this option out. Profits themselves were cut into by a slowdown in the rate of growth during the great depression of 1870–92. Firms amalgamated in order to survive. The new industrial conglomerates turned to banks and the Stock Exchange to finance development by selling their shares.

Britain has thus inherited from the nineteenth century financial markets that are highly efficient, internationally oriented but largely divorced from British industry. A better appreciation of the consequences can be obtained by comparing them with the very different path other countries, particularly Germany, the United States and Japan, took towards industrialisation.

The second, third and fourth industrialising nations could not follow the free trade path marked out by Britain. To open their markets to free competition simply meant that cheaper British products would ruin their home industry. If they wanted to build their own industrial base they had to protect developing industries by imposing taxes on any incoming products that threatened them. This meant that the home consumer had to pay higher prices. By the same token, the industries protected in this way also provided growing opportunities for employment and domestic prosperity.

The economic policies adopted by the Continental countries and the United States were thus very different from Britain's internationally focused free trade, where home industry had to compete with foreign imports and other investment opportunities. The concern abroad was rather to nurture home industry and agriculture, consolidate interlocking of directorates with banks which allowed long-term financing and to allow international competition only when industries were strong enough to sustain themselves.

This contrast in attitudes affects present-day relationships, particularly between Britain and its partners in the European Union. For Britain, the attraction of the EU has always been the prospect of abolishing tariffs and extending free markets across Europe, as a preliminary to extending them to the rest of the world. France and Germany, by way of contrast, have always seen the European Union primarily in terms of building a strong Europe that can protect and develop its industries on a Continental rather than a national scale. The British preference for a looser economic association rather than a federal union stems in part from the structure and functioning of its financial markets inherited from the nineteenth century.

The ways in which political ideas developed in Britain paralleled these economic contrasts. In Germany, France and Russia the state played a major role not only in economic development, but also in most aspects of social and political life. Citizens came to expect the central 'state' to take a lead in education, law enforcement, transport, and the regulation and finance of industry. In addition, a major rationale for the strong state was military defence. Therefore, these countries – and later Japan – maintained large standing armies and eventually developed navies, some of which came to rival British dominance. Except in France, democracy and democratic institutions remained undeveloped. *Collectivist* rather than *individualist* notions prevailed whereby citizens believed that the interests of central state institutions could take precedence over those of individuals. Increasingly, the idea that the *nation* and nationality were inherently superior to markets or liberal notions of freedom held sway – an idea carried to an extreme in European Fascist and Nazi regimes of the 1930s.

Although such ideas were not entirely absent from Britain, they had little influence compared with liberal individualism and older notions of class division and inherited privilege. Liberal individualism was even more influential in the United States where, by mid-century, democracy (for white males at least) was fully developed.

EXTERNAL DEFENCES AGAINST AN UNSTABLE INTERNATIONAL ENVIRONMENT, 1890–1931

Eventually, these contrasting ideas of the role of the state were to be tragically played out in two world wars and in the subsequent Cold War. From the late nineteenth century through to 1914, the British were drawn into increasing military competition with the other great powers and in particular Germany. At the same time there was a 'rush for empire' as Britain, France, Germany and other powers established control over almost all of Asia and Africa. Eventually military and economic competition resulted in the First World War, which transformed the role of the UK in international affairs. Although Britain and its allies (the USA and France) triumphed, the economic, human and military costs were very high. One million British, Empire and Commonwealth soldiers died, Britain incurred massive external debts to finance the war and British industry was obliged to keep producing basic industrial goods (iron and steel, ships, coal, textiles) rather than develop new industries and technologies.

These costs were graphically illustrated in the fortunes of the pound sterling after the war. Historically, the pound was freely convertible into gold and the British currency was effectively the reserve currency for international trade (that is, governments and firms used pounds to finance international transactions). This was known as the Gold Standard. After the war, however, international confidence in sterling collapsed and the Bank of England increasingly had to intervene in the foreign exchange markets to maintain full convertibility. Eventually the pressure was too great and in 1919, Britain suspended the Gold Standard. Many in the City and the Conservative Party considered this an economic mistake and the Gold Standard was re-established (by Chancellor of the Exchequer Winston Churchill) in 1925. The pressures returned however and Britain finally abandoned the Gold Standard in the context of deep economic crisis in 1931.

The consequences of maintaining the Gold Standard for so long were little short of disastrous for British industry. Already inefficient by international standards, the strong pound reduced industrial competitiveness further by making imports cheap. Unemployment rose rapidly especially in the older industrial areas. While many other countries such as the United States prospered during the 1920s, Britain remained mired in economic recession – a development that helped precipitate a damaging general strike in 1926. As a result, opinion began to shift towards the idea of protecting British industry from foreign competition through the imposition of tariffs and quotas. We will return to this theme in the next chapter.

On the broader international stage, the war shattered the old world order. Imperial Germany was replaced by a geographically much smaller democratic republic. The communist Soviet Union replaced imperial Russia and Japan emerged as a strong regional economic and military power. By refusing to sign up to the League of Nations, a new international organisation designed to enforce international order, the United States withdrew into isolationism, although its industrial base went from strength to strength. Above all, the war reduced British international status. The UK was no longer able to dictate to other countries; its naval hegemony was over and it became just another, albeit important, European power.

RISE OF SOCIALISM AND TRADE UNION POWER, 1890–1931

As British industry suffered increasingly from foreign competition from the 1880s onwards, so insecurity grew. Foreign firms operating from a protected home base took full advantage of free trade to penetrate both the British and colonial markets. Ideological and structural constraints meant that British governments resisted internal pressures to impose protective tariffs until the 1930s, when it became obvious that the First World War had completely disrupted the old world trading arrangements.

For the unskilled working class, these developments aggravated the general precariousness of their position in an unregulated free market. They had no savings to fall back on and no particular skills to make them especially valued. They were employed on a weekly or even a daily basis, and when there was no work they had no money to pay the rent or even to buy the next meal. Prolonged unemployment would force them into a New Poor Law workhouse where their family would be split up and where they would live under conditions deliberately made harder than those of the poorest paid worker outside, to discourage 'dependency' and reduce the tax burden on the working population.

In this situation, workers sought security through organised action. Their first successful attempt was through consumer co-operatives, which reduced prices and shared out profits to their members. Other collective organisations such as funeral and sickness clubs followed. These all operated on the basis that large numbers of tiny contributions could finance a strong collective organisation, which then protected individuals in times of need. Such organisations were often associated with churches, particularly Nonconformist churches and the Catholic Church, the majority of whose adherents were working class.

In spite of this, the middle class resented co-operatives. Small shopkeepers and professionals saw them as offering unfair inducements that undermined the free market in goods and services.

This was even truer when workers banded themselves together to bargain about the price of their labour. Employers saw this as an unfair attempt to raise costs, which in a competitive market would drive them out of business. They much preferred to deal with individuals where they could offer what they felt they could afford on a take it or leave it basis. Workers on their side saw this as an inherently unequal bargain, in which their sole source of support – their wage – could be reduced or cut off according to the vagaries of employers and markets.

The remedy was to join collective organisations – trade unions – that could bargain on a more powerful basis than any individual. If a trade union could persuade the whole workforce of a particular factory or firm to withhold their labour, profits would be severely hit and so it would be worthwhile for an employer to make a better offer, even though this cut into profits to a certain extent. For established interests, trade unions represented a direct attack on the free market, and in the first half of the nineteenth century, trade unions were outlawed. In the second half they were severely regulated and restricted by, for example, being made liable for damages caused by anyone who could be regarded as acting as their agent (eg a worker on strike).

Employers often brought in non-union labour to break a strike by the existing workforce. 'Pickets' of striking workers confronted these and violence sometimes ensued. Thus the collective responsibility of unions for damage caused by their members was a serious liability for them, rendering them ultra-cautious in their actions and weakening their finances. The police normally took the side of

Plate 2.4 *A picket line – a group of strikers*

the employers, protecting their property and maintaining free access for strike breakers to the factory premises.

Trade unions and their supporters wanted to change the balance of power in the workplace by getting Parliament to absolve them from collective responsibility for individual actions. They also wanted governments to act more neutrally in industrial disputes.

BRIEFINGS

2.5 Business cartels versus labour cartels

A cartel is an organisation, usually of firms or manufacturers, that aims to establish monopoly control of a particular product so as to regulate its price. In this way market demand by consumers and competition among producers will not drive down the price, which will be decided by what producers think is a reasonable profit over and above their costs of production. The temptation for producers, especially if they face no competition and their product is a necessity of life, is to set the price and their profits very high.

Cartel
An arrangement between economic interests to limit competition by controlling their market in some way.

A cartel is a direct attack on the free market, since it undermines or dominates competition. With the growth of big firms and multinational companies many semi-cartels exist today. As they tend to drive prices up and stifle innovation, governments try to regulate them, for example through the Monopolies Commission and regulators such as Ofwat (the Office of Water Regulation) in Britain.

Trade unions can also be seen as cartels, trying to ensure that no worker undercuts another in terms of wages, and thus operating to drive the price of labour up. Late nineteenth-century liberals and business people regarded them as such and opposed them or regulated them closely. Margaret Thatcher and her Conservative governments (1979–90) also looked on unions this way.

Trade unions argue, however, that workers' wages are not just a commodity price to be set by the market. Individual workers competing against each other, and helpless against wealthy companies that can afford to pick and choose, would drive their own wages down. The saving in 'labour costs' would be counterbalanced by increasing human misery in terms of poverty, health, family stability and crime, problems that would affect the rest of society and eventually incur general costs in social security, health care and policing.

BRIEFINGS

2.6 The rise and fall of union power: trade union legislation 1868–2000

In 1868 the various small trade unions (mainly of craftsmen) that had been locally organised in Britain held a joint meeting resulting in a federation with a governing council, the Trades Union Congress (TUC). The Liberal government's Trades Union Act (1871) gave them legal recognition and protection of funds against embezzlement. The Conservative government's Conspiracy Act (1875) declared that no trade union could be prosecuted for anything that would not be illegal if done by an individual. On this foundation trade unions grew, most importantly by organising unskilled labourers as well as (relatively well-off) craftsmen (the 'new trade unionism' of the 1890s). Trade unions also began to use their funds to send 'Labour' candidates to Parliament. This helped the foundation of the fully fledged Labour Party in 1900.

One stimulus to taking direct political action was the Taff Vale decision by the courts (1901) which decided that a trade union could be held responsible and sued for the actions of members during strikes. The Liberal government's Trades Disputes Act (1906) effectively reversed this decision. Only an individual could be sued for illegal actions. The Trade Union Act (1913) stated that unions could use funds for political purposes if they were separated from general funds, and if members who objected would not be forced to pay into them.

On this legal basis, trade unions grew rapidly from 1906 to 1926, mounting direct actions and strikes with considerable success. Adverse economic conditions after the First World War produced more industrial action, culminating in the general strike of 1926. All trade unionists were called on to strike, basically in support of miners' attempts to avoid wage cuts and dismissals. The Conservative government defeated the strike after a week but took relatively restrained action against the trade unions, stipulating that members had to 'opt in' to paying the political fund rather than 'opt out'.

With the election of the Labour government in 1945 trade unions secured a reversal of this measure. More importantly, they were consulted on all issues relating to labour and industrial relations by the government. The 'closed shop' and factory negotiating committees were recognised as normal practice. Neither Conservative nor Labour governments from 1951 to 1970 challenged the legal powers of trade unions. The Conservative government of Edward Heath (1970–4) tried to regulate trade unions through a special code of industrial law and a special court, the Industrial Relations Tribunal. The miners' strike in 1973–4 precipitated a general strike that brought down the government. The Labour governments of Harold Wilson and James Callaghan (1974–9) tried to conciliate trade unions by reaching formal agreements with them on prices and wages. A failure to agree on wage restraint in 1978 led to a near general strike in 1979 (the 'winter of discontent'). This rendered Labour so unpopular that it lost the general election of 1979.

The 'New Right' Conservative government of Margaret Thatcher regarded trade unions as a major impediment to the free market, echoing the views of free market economists of the late nineteenth century. In a series of legislative measures the 1979–83 and 1983–7 governments:

- required regular trade union ballots on whether they should keep a political fund
- required regular re-election of trade union leaders
- required ballots of members before strike action could be taken
- perhaps most importantly, outlawed secondary picketing, that is, industrial action against any firm not directly involved in an industrial dispute.

Thus strikers could picket a newspaper, for example, if they were in dispute with it. But they could not stop another firm delivering newspapers, even if this was vital to keep the newspaper going. Enterprising employers could thus split their companies into two to avoid union reprisals, since the law would hold that the one not in direct dispute should not be picketed in any way.

Concurrent developments also weakened trade unions. A growth in unemployment reduced their membership from 12 million to 7.5 million in the course of the 1980s. In a set-piece confrontation the government defeated a year-long miners' strike in 1984–5, brought about by closures of mines. The media proprietor, Rupert Murdoch, also broke the print and journalists' unions' power in the Wapping dispute (1986–7), with the help of the secondary picketing legislation.

In a curious way, however, the reforms imposed on the unions also helped them, making them internally more democratic, leaner and fitter. In their glory days from 1950 to 1979 they had become very bureaucratised, with policy and leadership chosen by agreement among leaders and little contact with the rank and file. Having to submit themselves to democratic election actually strengthened leaders' claims to represent their members. This was reflected in a cautious return to industrial action in the ▶

1990s, especially as economic conditions gradually became more favourable. Even though the 'New Labour' Party of Tony Blair distanced itself from too close a connection with the trade unions, the unions worked hard for its return to office in 1997 and in 2001. They have been rewarded by British adoption of the European Social Chapter (1997) and the upholding of a minimum statutory wage for all workers. Even so, by 2002 the Labour government faced a series of public sector strikes that in character were similar to those of the 1960s and 1970s.

To achieve both objectives they had to gain political power. The Second Reform Act (1867) and the Third Reform Act (1884) gave the vote to substantial numbers of working class men. In order to attract their votes both the Conservatives and Liberals passed legislation favouring trade unions. Various attempts were also made to organise a specifically 'Labour Party', which eventually emerged in 1900 as an alliance of trade unions, co-operatives and some of the small socialist parties that had already elected a few MPs.

At the same time employers and landowners had been steadily leaving the Liberal Party and joining the Conservatives, whom they saw as more likely to protect their interests at home and abroad. The Liberals became more dependent on working class votes and Labour Party support in Parliament. This produced a radical shift in the political views of many of their leaders. Retaining individual freedom as a central value, they began to feel that political and social freedom was impossible unless individuals had a reasonable economic basis from which to pursue it. If they did not know where the next meal would come from they would hardly pay any attention to politics.

In line with these ideas, a Liberal government with Labour support passed the National Insurance Act of 1911. This provided for contributions by employees, employers and the state towards the provision of health and unemployment insurance. What this meant was that everyone who had worked and paid contributions would get free health care when they were sick, from payments guaranteed by the state. The same applied to unemployment: all who lost their job would be entitled to weekly payments until they found another. When there was a Labour government supported by Liberals (1923–4), a Housing Act was passed to help local councils build subsidised houses to rent to those with little money.

As technological developments encouraged the concentration of production in ever-larger plants, so trade unions became larger as well. It was no longer enough to stop work at one factory in order to get better offers from employers. Firms could always shift work from one factory to another, or even close down factories affected by a strike. What was necessary was to disrupt all the factories controlled by a firm in order to induce it to negotiate.

However, in seeking more members, unions did not grow in accordance with any very rational plan. Although they initially based themselves on one particular group of craftsmen or workers, the desire to reinforce themselves in one factory or inside one company often led to recruitment of very different types.

Moreover two, three, four, or even more unions might operate inside one factory. They might put different demands to management and one might go on strike when others did not, because workers were, and are, a sharply differentiated group. Trade unions representing skilled workers were anxious to maintain

Table 2.1 *Major trade unions in Britain, 2002*

Union name	Number of members	Industrial or service sector covered
UNISON	1,272,470	Public employees including health workers
AMICUS (merger between AEEU and MSF)	1,132,211	All sectors of industry
T & G (Transport and General Workers)	858,804	All sectors of industry including communications
GMB (General and Municipal)	712,010	Distributive sector and local government
USDAW (Shop, Distributive and Allied Trades Workers)	310,222	Shops and stores, transport
CWU (Communications Workers)	284,422	Electronics, particularly communications
PCS (Public and Commercial Services union)	267,644	Government, public sector and private sector IT and service workers
NUT (National Union of Teachers)	206,100	Teachers in state schools, particularly primary schools
GPMU (Graphical, Paper & Media)	201,296	Mainly local government
NASUWT (National Association of Schoolmasters and Union of Women Teachers)	183,681	Teachers in state schools, particularly secondary schools
UCATT (Union of Construction, Allied Trades and Technicians)	123,000	Building and construction workers
ATL (Association of Teachers and Lecturers)	113,059	Teachers in secondary schools and colleges
PROSPECT	103,942	Engineering, scientific, managerial and professional staff

Source: TUC web site: http://www.tuc.org.uk

'differentials' between their members' wages and those of unskilled workers. Therefore, when one union obtained its demands another might well strike to obtain more for its members in order to maintain their 'differential'.

The messy nature of British trade unionism, with large unions often overlapping each other, and with multiple unions present in the same factory is now largely a thing of the past. As Table 2.1 shows, recent mergers and rationalisations have greatly simplified the structure of unions in Britain. The size of the largest unions is quite striking: the ten largest account for three-quarters of the 6.5 million members in the country as a whole. Note also that by the beginning of the twenty-first century many unions represented service and public sector workers. Just 20 years previously most of the main unions represented workers in manufacturing, mining and transport. Union activity is co-ordinated by the Trades Union Congress (TUC), a committee and annual delegate conference supported by a permanent bureaucracy. But its powers are very limited compared with those of individual unions.

The rise of trade union power and the Labour Party was partly fuelled by the spread of socialist ideas. On the Continent, socialist and Marxist ideas had taken strong hold in such countries as Germany and France. They came in three varieties. Marxists believed that a transition to a communist society where the workers own the means of production, control and exchange could only be achieved by the violent overthrow of the existing capitalist order. Social democrats believed that it was possible to make a peaceful transition to socialism through winning representation in national legislatures such as the British Parliament. Perhaps unsurprisingly, social democratic ideas were more influential in countries with democratic institutions such as Britain and Australia, than in autocracies such as Germany and Russia where Marxist ideas were dominant. Finally, some on the left believed that it was possible to achieve a good society that combined some common ownership of natural monopolies such as transport and utilities, welfare state protection for workers with elements of the capitalist system in naturally competitive sectors of the economy such as retailing and agriculture. Eventually, most social democrats shifted to this last, moderate position, including most members of the Labour Party.

That a moderate form of socialism would develop in Britain is not surprising given the influence of liberal individualist ideas and the absence of revolutionary change. Although many in the Conservative Party feared that a Labour government would bring revolution and the end of capitalism, no Labour government has ever attempted such a project. As later chapters will show, Labour governments instead called for the nationalisation of basic industries, the strengthening of the Welfare State and greater income equality. In addition, the vast majority of Labour MPs and party members were and remain strong supporters of traditional liberal values, including freedom of speech and religion and race and gender equality. In its historical development, British socialism fits well with broader traditions in British society – gradual change through existing institutions and a belief in the intrinsic worth of the individual in society.

ESSAYS

1. What were the main electoral reforms of the nineteenth century? Why were they passed and what were their effects on party politics?

2. What were the costs and benefits of the free trade policies pursued by Britain for much of the nineteenth and early twentieth centuries?

3. What are 'liberal individualist ideas'? What influence have they had on British politics?

4. Account for the rise and decline of trade union power in Britain.

SUMMARY

This chapter has concentrated on the most important institutional and ideological features of British politics deriving from Britain's experience as the first urbanised and industrialised nation in the world. To put these developments in their historical setting the milestones section charts the key events, both nationally and internationally, up to 1945.

The political and economic developments of the eighteenth and nineteenth centuries that led to the spread of democracy and Britain's industrial and commercial pre-eminence are:

■ a deep attachment to free trade and the ideal of a free competitive market

■ the associated rise of liberal individualism or a belief in free speech and the value of the free marketplace of ideas

- the persistence of political and other institutions that continue in an essentially nineteenth-century form (eg Parliament, the political parties, the Civil Service, local government)

- a working class defence against the uncertainties of the free market that relies on collective action and is fuelled by socialist ideas, focused particularly on trade unions and the Labour Party.

MILESTONES

Milestones in British history, 1688–1945

BRITAIN	WORLD
The Glorious Revolution, 1688, established the primacy of Parliamentary over royal power	
Late eighteenth century, adversarial party politics in Parliament, but voting limited to the wealthy	American Declaration of Independence, 1776; French Revolution, 1789
1832 Great Reform Act widens the franchise and removes most electoral corrupt practices followed by Municipal Reform and New Poor Law	1830 revolutions against absolutist rule break out across Europe
1846 Britain abolishes the Corn Laws and establishes free trade	1848 further often violent revolutions across Europe
Conservative–Liberal Alternation in Government 1867–86	
Home rule for Canada, 1867	
Second Reform Bill extends franchise, 1867	
Great Economic Depression, 1870–92	Franco-Prussian War, 1870–1 makes newly united Germany dominant on the Continent of Europe
Liberal reforms in health, Civil Service, army, universal education, 1868–74	
Trades Union Act, 1871	
Unions protected from liability for individual members' acts, 1875	
Control of Suez Canal and Egypt secures sea route to India; Indian Empire consolidated, 1878	
Expansion in South Africa, 1879–80	
80 Irish Nationalist MPs elected to House of Commons and disrupt Parliamentary proceedings, 1874–80	
Irish 'Land War', 1879–83	
Third Reform Act extends franchise further, to almost all adult males, 1884	1884–5: the 'grab for Africa': European powers set out to conquer as much territory as possible; most falls to France and Britain
First Home Rule Bill for Ireland splits Liberal government, which is defeated, 1886	

▶

BRITAIN	WORLD

BRITAIN

Conservative Predominance in Government 1886–1905 (Liberals, 1892–5)

Local Government Act extends elected councils to counties, 1888

Second Irish Home Rule Bill defeated, 1893

Scottish Office centralises Scottish administration in Edinburgh

Home Rule movements grow in Scotland and Wales during 1890s

Labour Party founded 1900 with support of trade unions

Home Rule for Australia and New Zealand, 1901

Liberal Predominance in Government 1905–16

Trade Union Acts, 1906 and 1913, strengthen unions

Home Rule for South Africa, 1909

Parliament Act, 1911, strengthens power of House of Commons (elected) against House of Lords (unelected)

National Health Insurance Act – extensive government intervention to protect and pay sick, unemployed and old, 1911

Third Irish Home Rule Bill initiated 1912 – Lords' now limited veto can only block it until 1914

Rising violence by Irish Protestants, paramilitary organisations founded, 1912–14; 'Curragh Mutiny' of army officers in Dublin against having to enforce Home Rule, 1914; Home Rule postponed

1915 – submarine attacks almost cut off British food supplies

1916–22 Coalition Governments Between Liberals and Conservatives

Representation of the People Act (1918) extends franchise to almost all adult males and women over 30

1919 Britain suspends Gold Standard

Civil war in Ireland, 1918–22

Ireland partitioned between Irish Free State and Northern Ireland, 1922

WORLD

Boer War, 1899–1902; Britain conquers independent white republics of South Africa with difficulty

Anglo-French military co-operation initiated 1904; extended to Russia 1907, creating an informal alliance against Germany

Naval arms race between Britain and Germany for dominance of North Sea, 1906–14

First World War begins 1914 – Britain, France and Russia against Germany, Austria–Hungary and Turkey

US enters war against Germany, 1917 German defeat, 1918

1919–23 Treaties of Versailles and Trianon reduce and disarm Germany, break up Austria–Hungary, create Poland and other new central and eastern European countries and extend French and British control of Arab Middle East

League of Nations set up without USA

Russian Revolution, 1917–22, Communist government takes over (reduced) Russian empire

BRITAIN	WORLD
Conservative Predominance in Government 1922–9 (First Labour minority government 1923–4)	
Housing Act provides for subsidised housing, 1924	
General economic depression from 1920 – many strikes by individual unions. Britain re-establishes Gold Standard, 1925	
General strike fails, 1926	
Equal Franchise Act (1928) extends vote to all adult women	
Labour Government 1929–31	
Labour splits over cutting social payments, 1931. Britain leaves Gold Standard	Wall Street Crash (collapse of US share values) ushers in Great Depression of 1930s: world trade slumps, millions unemployed in all countries
National Coalition Governments of Rump Labour and Liberals Dominated by Conservatives 1931–40	
Cuts in social benefits, abandonment of free trade, protectionist measures create cartels and monopolies to regulate market	1933–9 rise and consolidation of Nazi regime in Germany, rearmament and takeover of adjoining territories; leads to Second World War, 1939
Government of India Act 1936 gives India limited Home Rule as a response to growing nationalist agitation	
Coalition Governments of Conservatives, Labour and Liberals 1940–5	
Full wartime planning and control of society and economy	Germans conquer most of European mainland except Russia, 1940
	Germany attacks Russia, 1941
	Japan goes to war against USA and UK, 1941
	USA enters war on British side, 1941
	Defeat of Germany and Japan, 1945

FURTHER READING

Karl Polanyi, *The Great Transformation* (Boston: Beacon Press, 1957) is the classic account of the triumph of free trade in Britain. Eric Hobsbawm's three-volume history traces out the social and economic consequences of the Industrial Revolution. The one most relevant to this chapter is Eric Hobsbawm, *Industry and Empire* (Harmondsworth: Penguin, 1968). Andrew Gamble, *Britain in Decline* (London: Macmillan, 1989) reviews many of the developments discussed in this chapter from a rather pessimistic point of view. P. J. Cain and A. G. Hopkins, *British Imperialism* (Harlow: Longman, 1993) is an influential two-volume account of Britain's imperial and commercial history. Cain, 'British capitalism and the State', *Political Quarterly*, **68** (2), 1997, pp. 95–8, is also relevant.

PROJECTS

1. Analyse the role of class in the House of Commons over time by researching the educational backgrounds of MPs between 1900 and 2003.

2. Obtain statistical evidence on the patterns of British overseas trade in the twentieth century.

3. Research the changing pattern of trade union membership since 1945. Answer with regard to the level of trade union membership and the type of trade union.

USEFUL WEB SITES ON INSTITUTIONS AND RELATIONSHIPS

Hot links to these sites can be found on the CWS at http://www.booksites.net/budge. There are a variety of excellent sites dealing with the historical evolution of British political, social and economic institutions. A comprehensive introduction to the major developments in different periods can be found at www.spartacus.schoolnet.co.uk/Britain.html. Useful material regarding political and social reforms is also available at www.britishhistory.about.com and this site also contains valuable information on foreign policy relevant to the British Empire.

Additional data can be obtained from www.academicinfo.net/histuk.html. For students willing to dig deeper into British history we suggest you visit the Historical Manuscripts Commission at www.hmc.gov.uk/index.html and the Institute of Contemporary British History at www.history.ac.uk/icbh.

British trade union sites

The Department of Trade and Industry offers constructive information on trade unions and collective rights at www.dti.gov.uk/er/union.htm. History and news about trade unions can be found at the Trade Union Congress site www.tuc.org.uk, the General Federation of Trade Unions www.gftu.org.uk and the public service workers' union www.unison.org.uk. See also the *Guardian*'s special report on trade unions www.guardian.co.uk/unions/archive.

There are a variety of web sites from other trade unions in the UK, for example, the Amalgamated Engineering and Electrical Union www.aeeu.org.uk; the Communications Workers Union www.cwu.org; the Transport and General Workers Union www.tgwu.org.uk; the Public and Commercial Services Union www.pcs.org.uk; the Broadcasting, Entertainment, Cinematograph and Theatre Union www.bectu.org.uk; the Association of University Teachers www.aut.org.uk; the National Union of Students www.nus.org.uk.

International union sites

For students interested in the international union arena, you can visit the International Labour Organisation www.ilo.org and also the International Confederation of Free Trade Unions web site at www.icftu.org. Valuable information on this topic is also obtainable from www.global-unions.org as well as www.etuc.org (European Trade Unions Confederation).

CHAPTER 3

International crisis and economic change: Ideas and institutions, 1931–2004

By the early 1930s, the whole system of world free trade had broken down. This was one of the effects of the First World War, where the leading trading nations had fought each other to a standstill. The destructive impact on Germany in particular destabilised international trade and finance – illustrating that relationships between national economies are not so much competitive as interdependent.

The final breakdown was signalled by the world depression, which began with a general collapse of financial confidence from 1929 to 1931 and continued for most of the 1930s. This chapter discusses how this led to major ideological and policy shifts in Britain involving the abandonment of free trade and to massive government intervention in economy and society. This was designed both to protect British industry and to guarantee minimum living standards for the population. The reforms initiated by the 'national governments' of the 1930s were carried further by the Labour governments of 1945–51, and supported by both Conservatives and Labour from 1950 to 1979 (the 'social democratic consensus'). Intellectually this was underpinned by 'Keynesian' economics, which gave a central place to government action to smooth out the economic cycle.

The end of the long post-war boom in the early 1970s demonstrated the limits of government intervention. Free trade and free markets reasserted themselves vigorously under the Conservative governments led by Margaret Thatcher (1979–90), replacing the earlier 'social democratic consensus' with a 'neo-liberal' one. Many of the policies and issues of the 1980s and 1990s in Britain, linked to growing world 'globalisation', thus hark back to the mid-nineteenth century rather than to the 1930s and 1940s. The new element was 'Europe', which has increasingly become the central issue dividing the Conservative Party from Labour today. Finally, the chapter reviews the main ideas underpinning the New Labour project that has attempted a 'Third Way' between socialism and unbridled free market capitalism. Both 'Thatcherite' and New Labour ideas have had important effects on the ways in which political and social institutions operate in Britain today.

The chapter describes:

- the rise of government intervention from 1931 to 1945
- Labour's particular brand of socialism: the creation of the Welfare State and nationalisation of basic industries, 1945–51
- the 'social democratic consensus', 1951–79
- the return to free market principles in the 1980s and the emergence of a 'neo-liberal' economic consensus
- New Labour's Third Way, 1997–present

Keynesianism
Economic theories and policies propounded by J. M. Keynes (1883–1946) which advocate government intervention to achieve economic stability, growth and full employment.

INTERVENTION, PROTECTION AND PLANNING, 1931–79

The rise of intervention, 1931–45

The collapse of world trade and of much of British industry by 1931 prompted even the Conservative-dominated national governments of the 1930s to previously unheard of interventions in society and economy. Externally they finally imposed protective tariffs to safeguard what was left of British manufacturing against foreign competition. Internally they forced surviving businesses to merge into cartels and conglomerates to keep prices up and costs down. Their protectionist policies however helped the growth of new industries close to the large consumer markets of the Midlands, London and southeast England – cars, washing machines, wireless sets, domestic furnishings and so on. There were almost two manufacturing economies – one based on the old industries in the industrial north and one based on new industries in the Midlands and south.

The problem from the government's point of view was the location of the new industry in places that were already reasonably prosperous. Many difficulties could be overcome if some of the new industries could be persuaded to move out of the congested areas into the depressed ones. A number of commissions and their reports set out planning proposals for this involving government inducements and controls. The most significant was the Beveridge Report, which reported on income maintenance (unemployment benefit, pensions, national assistance, welfare services and health) – thus laying the foundations for the post-war Welfare State. This was not created completely from new – elements of a social support and welfare system had been in place since the early twentieth century – but it was the first time that it was proposed to create a comprehensive system of social support.

Beveridge Report
Produced in 1942 by a government commission chaired by Lord Beveridge (1879–1963), an academic economist, which recommended welfare services and income support for citizens 'from the cradle to the grave'. Its recommendations provided the intellectual basis for both the 'Welfare State' and the 'social democratic consensus' (1945–79).

BRIEFINGS

3.1 Wartime rationing

Very soon after the outbreak of war in September 1939 the government introduced petrol rationing, followed in January 1940 by food rationing. Few British citizens expected rationing to last for long, partly because few expected the war to last for long. In the event almost every commodity, including clothes, fuel and food, was subject to rationing by the end of the war. On most items rationing lasted until the late 1940s and was not completely removed until 1952. Every household was issued with a ration book, containing stamps that had to accompany money purchases.

Ration allowances were meagre – for example, as late as 1951 the meat ration was four ounces per person per week – and designed to provide the very minimum necessary to feed, clothe and heat a family. Rationing was necessary because Britain depended on imports of fuel, food, textiles and other commodities. Shortages in all these developed as production was disrupted by war and enemy action, and as resources were diverted to the armed forces. After the war shortages actually worsened as the demand for food and fuel in war-ravaged Europe soared. In 1947 the fuel quota was reduced during a severe winter and, in 1949, some of the most restrictive rationing was introduced because Britain was running out of the dollars needed to buy goods on the international markets. Most commentators agree that the continuing austerity of the 1940s and early 1950s contributed to the defeat of the Labour government in 1951.

Between 1936 and 1945 public and elite attitudes towards state intervention were transformed by two events: the acceptance of Keynesian economics and the total modification of the economy during the Second World War. The monetarist orthodoxy accepted by the national governments of the 1930s held that industrial development could only take place if there was general confidence in the currency, maintained by government budgets in which revenues equalled or surpassed expenditures. Keynes showed that the economy could function under these conditions well below the level it might attain with full use of available resources. Since the main underused resource was labour, this implied long-term unemployment for large sections of the workforce. Governments could, however, raise the economy to nearly full capacity by increasing government expenditure and therefore stimulating demand.

BRIEFINGS

3.2 Orthodox economics and Keynesian economics

Orthodox economics
The dominant economic approach before Keynesian theory, which argued for minimal state intervention in the economy.

Orthodox economics assumes that the most efficient system of economic organisation is based on minimal government intervention and free markets. National accounts – the relationship between income (taxes) and expenditure (government spending) – should always be in balance. For a government to spend more than it receives in taxation leads to inflation. During the 1930s, however, tax revenues fell as a result of the Depression, leading governments to cut expenditure – including unemployment and other benefits. The Cambridge economist John Maynard Keynes (later Lord Keynes) noted that the effect of this was to reduce the level of total demand in the economy and therefore to depress it even further. He demonstrated that it was possible for the economy to reach equilibrium (that is, when supply matches demand) at a level far below full capacity with resulting high levels of unemployment. The government therefore needed to stimulate demand by increasing expenditure, the precise opposite of what governments actually did for most of the 1930s. Budget deficits were acceptable, therefore, when the economy was operating below full capacity. Once full capacity had been reached, government accounts should once again be brought into balance. If they were not, inflation would return. The experience of the Second World War seemed to confirm this thesis: massive government spending led to full employment and eventually to labour shortages and inflation. After the war all British governments accepted Keynesian thinking: governments had a duty to intervene to maintain full employment via government spending. Not until the 1970s, when rising inflation and rising unemployment occurred at the same time, were the basic principles of Keynesian economics challenged. As a result, orthodox economics became again a feasible alternative for policy makers.

The war seemed to confirm the validity of this assumption. Spending on armaments was massively increased in the late 1930s. By June 1943, only 60,000 people were registered as unemployed, and by 1945, few political leaders opposed

Keynesian demand management. The war also gave planning an enormous boost, both in theory and practice. Central committees strictly controlled prices, incomes, industrial relations and production. Never before or since has the British economy been so rigidly disciplined.

A notable feature of this policy transformation is that it was accompanied by remarkably little in the way of institutional reform. For although a number of new bureaucracies were created before and during the war, the machinery of central government continued to operate much as it always did. Local government, the Civil Service, Parliament and the 'Establishment' functioned as before. *Policies* changed but political and bureaucratic values and practices did not.

FOUNDING AND ADMINISTERING THE WELFARE STATE, 1945–62

Privatisation
The opposite of nationalisation, privatisation is the returning of nationalised industries wholly or partly to the private sector.

Nationalisation
Taking businesses or whole industries into public ownership.

Under the government elected in 1945 basic industries were nationalised, the Welfare State created, regional policy strengthened dramatically and landuse planning by local authorities established as mandatory. All these policies remained in place until the 1980s. Only then did Conservative governments challenge them through privatisation, the dramatic scaling down of regional policy, and the creation of 'internal markets' in education and health.

Post-war policy was dominated by a driving desire to maintain full employment. Keynesian demand management, nationalisation and regional policy were either primarily or partly designed to achieve this and, combined with a generally favourable international trading position, did so until 1951. Industry readapted to peacetime conditions quite efficiently and Britain's share of world trade actually increased during these years. Nationalisation and Keynesianism carried with them a marked increase in government intervention. However, there was no support for overall national planning or for new administrative organisations to carry it through. All Labour's political and economic initiatives were channelled through the traditional institutions and ministries. Government structures, although larger, remained much what they had been in the 1930s or for that matter the 1870s. When the Conservatives came to power in 1951 the basic relationships between government, unions, finance and industry were thus almost unchanged. The trade unions played no integrated role in economic or industrial policy. Big business was quite happy to accept a regulative government role, especially in foreign trade, but they too were excluded from central economic policy making. Administrative changes were largely confined to the creation of new bureaucracies to implement the programmes of a burgeoning Welfare State. The public sector had expanded enormously, but the basic tools available to governments to guide and control the public sector changed very little. The divorce between industrial and financial sectors, and between both of these and government, continued to be almost as wide as in the earlier free trade era.

This made it easier for the Conservative governments from 1951 to 1964 to accept most of what Labour had done. They continued to administer the Welfare State, simply relaxing some of the more rigorous measures such as rationing

Plate 3.1 *Festival of Britain. General view of the River Walk showing The Islanders and part of the Skylon. The Festival came to symbolise national post-war hopes for modernisation*

Source: Hulton Getty

of food and clothes that had been adopted during wartime. Such 'decontrol' was possible because of the recovery of world trade and growing prosperity of the 1950s.

In one sense, the Conservatives had little choice in the matter, for the Welfare State – and especially free universal health care – was immensely popular with the electorate. Thus, a sea change had taken place in British politics and society. Following the experience of the 1930s and the Second World War, the British had become convinced that universal welfare provision was essential to the good of society. Recognising this, all political parties became enthusiastic supporters of the Welfare State.

3.3 Decolonisation and disengagement from Empire, 1946–83

The Second World War created not only domestic but also overseas preoccupations for British policy makers. The most important of these was the confrontation between the American-led, and British-supported, North Atlantic Treaty Organization (NATO) and the Soviet Union, from 1948–88 (the Cold War). Britain was subsidiary to the United States in this. Successive post-war governments had, however, to deal directly with the vast colonial Empire inherited from the nineteenth century, and no longer possible to dominate with military power. The Second World War, fought in the name of freedom and democracy, exacerbated the problem of dealing with the Empire since it had stimulated native nationalist movements that demanded independence.

It was clear to the post-war Labour movement that India, with its vast population, would be impossible to control. Independence was accordingly granted in 1948, and internal divisions between Hindus and Muslims met with a deadline for withdrawal, after which they were left to fight it out and separate into India and Pakistan. The same solution was applied to Jews and Arabs in Palestine. In Malaya, the British, allied with Malays, defeated a Chinese communist insurrection (1948–58).

Withdrawal as a solution quickened pace after a last attempt to assert control in the Middle East failed with an abortive takeover of the Suez Canal in 1956. In the years between 1959 and 1963 Britain granted independence to most of its African colonies. The final stage of the retreat from Empire was the strategic defence review of 1967–8, which concluded that Britain could not afford a naval presence east of Suez – a decision which soon extended to the Mediterranean too. These withdrawals left Britain with only vestigial colonial dependencies – one of which, the sparsely inhabited Falkland Islands, involved Britain in war with Argentina in 1982.

On the whole, the disengagement from Empire was managed peacefully and skilfully. Friendly governments were left in charge, British interests safeguarded and ties with the West firmly cemented. Contrariwise, disengagement accentuated Britain's transition from being a world to a regional power, and contributed to the crisis of morale in the 1970s and 1980s.

Government intervention, 1959–79

Until about 1960, government intervention in industry was minimal but Keynesian demand management of expenditure and interest rates continued. Aware that Britain's growth rate was falling behind those of France, Italy and Germany, after 1960 governments used Keynesian methods in combination with incomes policy and some embryonic planning devices both to control inflation and to achieve a higher rate of economic growth. Using fiscal and monetary policy to stimulate or depress economic activity in the Keynesian fashion, the government soon found itself in a vicious 'stop–go' cycle characterised by successive rounds of economic stimulation followed by the reigning in of demand with expenditure cuts and interest rate hikes (see Briefing 3.4).

3.4 'Stop–go' and the British economic cycle

During much of the post-war period British economic management was characterised by periodic rounds of economic growth followed by government-induced deflation to stem the inflationary effects of growth. Typically, the cycle went something like this: in year one, the government would reduce taxation and interest rates in order to stimulate employment and growth. This in turn led, in year two, to an upsurge in imports on which the expansion of the British economy depended. With a growing balance of payments deficit the pound would come under pressure on the foreign exchanges, forcing the government, in year three, to dampen demand by raising interest rates and taxation. This resulted in increased unemployment, and pressure by the trade unions for government action. Given the commitment of all governments to full employment, chancellors of the exchequer would then be obliged, in year four, to stimulate the economy in order to reduce unemployment. The cycle would then begin again. This pattern led to a vicious cycle of under-investment in British industry: it was because British industry was uncompetitive that growth in the economy led to import-led inflation, but, without a period of steady increase in demand with sustained investment, industry could not catch up with its foreign competitors. In other words, as soon as the conditions for sustained investment appeared they were undermined by the government's need to protect the pound.

Not until the 1980s, when the pound was bolstered by North Sea oil revenues, did conditions change in ways which allowed the cycle to be broken, and it was not until the post-1992 period that surviving British industry had become sufficiently competitive to support a period of sustained growth.

Figure 3.1 *UK inflation, 1961–2001*

Source: *Social Trends 32*, 2002, Chart 6.15

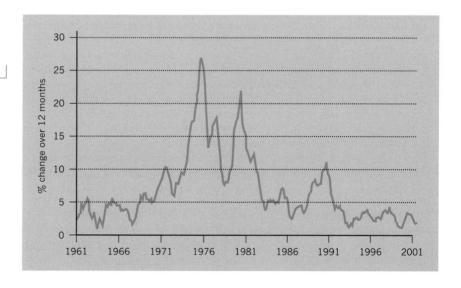

Such 'stop–go' tactics became common between 1953 and 1970. A related problem was inflation, which accelerated during 'go' periods and declined during 'stop' periods. Compared with the 1970s and the 1980s inflation was low (Figure 3.1) but, crucially, it was higher than those of comparable countries.

Indeed, as the decade wore on, the fundamental problem with the economy was increasingly defined as failure to achieve a rate of economic growth comparable to other major industrial countries.

The Tories flirted with economic planning during the early 1960s and when elected in 1964 Labour created the Department of Economic Affairs (DEA) in which a full-blown government department was assigned the job of long-term economic planning, while the Treasury was confined to its traditional role as short-term controller of expenditure. The DEA's brief was extensive: to devise a longer term national plan; to revitalise industry and improve efficiency, working partly through planning by industrial sector; to work out a prices and incomes policy; and to reorganise regional policy.

However, the DEA really operated for less than two years, owing to the accelerating rate of economic crisis from 1965 to 1967. Britain's competitive position had been deteriorating for some years and balance of payments deficits were slowly increasing. Sterling was clearly overvalued, mainly because of the need to maintain the stability of the pound as an international reserve currency. The

International reserve currency A currency that many smaller and third world countries not directly linked with the sponsor country choose to make payments in, because it has a stable value.

BRIEFINGS

3.5 The changing fortunes of the pound sterling

When the leading industrial countries established a fixed exchange rate regime for post-war trade at Bretton Woods in 1944, it was agreed that the US dollar would be the main currency of international trade. In addition, however, the pound sterling would also perform this role. In other words, when countries traded with each other they would use either dollars or pounds as a medium of exchange. The pound was accorded this status because a large number of countries used pounds as their main reserve. These included British colonies and dominions but also some Latin American, Middle Eastern and Scandinavian states. Bretton Woods allowed for devaluations but only under emergency circumstances. Britain was, therefore, expected to maintain the value of the pound in relation to the dollar. Any forced devaluation would undermine confidence in the whole sterling area. Under the worst circumstances, a flight from the pound would lead to a collapse in its value. From 1945 until the end of the Bretton Woods system in 1971 successive British governments were under pressure to maintain the value of sterling. The two forced devaluations in 1949 and 1967 were regarded as major government failures, and these pressures intensified the problems of the stop–go cycle (see Briefing 3.4). Most countries gradually moved out of the sterling area during the 1950s and the 1960s. Even after 1971, when currencies floated freely in relation to one another, the problem of currency weakness remained, but this was mainly because the lack of competitiveness of British industry led speculators to believe that the pound was a poor long-term prospect. In 1976 such sentiments led to a run on the currency, and only large loans to the government and intervention from the International Monetary Fund (IMF) prevented economic collapse.

Since then the value of sterling has not been so central to government economic policy, partly because governments have acted more responsibly in fiscal matters and partly because of the existence of a floating exchange rate regime. One major exception was the British involvement with the Exchange Rate Mechanism (ERM) of the European Monetary System (EMS) between 1990 and 1992. (This subject is covered extensively in Chapter 4.)

Labour government was committed to economic growth and the expansion of public services and found it impossible to reconcile its policy objectives with economic reality. An already bad situation was aggravated by the government's deference to the official Treasury and City line of giving priority to the value of sterling. In 1966 a serious balance of payments crisis and a crippling seamen's strike coincided, inducing investors to sell pounds, and the government opted to abandon national planning and industrial expansion, and instead to safeguard the currency by restricting credit. Under the new Chancellor of the Exchequer, Roy Jenkins, economic policy reverted almost to a pre-Keynesian strategy: some government expenditure was cut (mainly in defence), foreign loans were repaid and taxes increased. Interestingly, the Jenkins deflation was not so damaging to employment as might have been expected (Figure 3.1), largely because a 1967 devaluation did produce something of an investment boom.

In comparison with the 1945–50 period, Labour had hardly been a radical reforming government. Rather than institute institutional reforms the government simply increased spending on existing programmes, and especially on the Welfare State. Taxation increased dramatically from 32 per cent of gross domestic product (GDP) in 1964 to 43 per cent in 1970. The government's failure to carry through a radical programme alienated many supporters within the Labour movement. By 1970 increasingly militant trade unions were demanding more fundamental reforms and were prepared to use their bargaining muscle to extract higher wages from employers.

Gross domestic product The total value of all the goods and services bought and sold in the domestic economy.

Therefore, the new Conservative government of Edward Heath, which unexpectedly won the 1970 election, was intent on reforming industrial relations, by imposing a more rigid framework of law on trade union activity. What transpired was the 1971 Industrial Relations Act, which sought to make unions accept certain legal restrictions on their activities, notably on their right to strike, and to submit themselves to a special court. From its inception, this inspired their fiercest hostility.

Along with other countries, the new government abandoned a fixed exchange rate for its currency, letting international financial markets determine its value. In conjunction with this it negotiated British entry to the European Community (now called the European Union) in 1972. Entry was expected to stimulate British industry by exposing it to new competitive pressures while at the same time opening up new markets.

Strangely, the Conservative government failed to exercise real control either over incomes or over public expenditure and inflation took off, soaring from 6.4 per cent in 1970 to 9.4 per cent in 1971, by far the highest figure since 1950 (Figure 3.1). This situation could not last long. The rapid increases were bound to undermine the balance of payments and Britain's trading position, especially with a floating exchange rate. In a famous 'U-turn' of November 1972, Edward Heath announced a prices and incomes policy. Although at first accepted by the unions the miners and other unions later resisted controls on wages. Faced with crippling strikes, the government called a general election early in 1974.

The government's U-turn on incomes policy in 1972 was accompanied by another change of heart on industrial policy that was now adapted to aid, succour and guide industrial recovery. Bankrupt companies such as Rolls-Royce and Upper Clyde Shipbuilders were bailed out, regional incentives and development

Plate 3.2 *Minister of Technology, Anthony Wedgwood Benn, opens Oceanology International, the world's first fully international conference on underwater technology, at Brighton. The Labour government had come to power on a modernising platform, with Harold Wilson famously speaking of the 'white heat' of technology*

Source: Hulton Getty

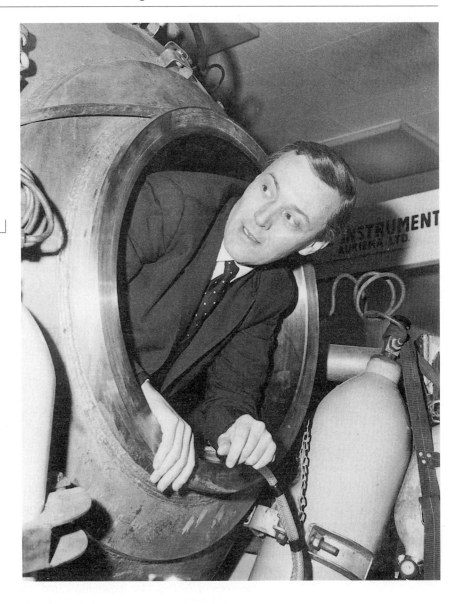

grants were strengthened, a Minister for Industrial Development was attached to the new Department of Trade and Industry, and workforce retraining was organised and greatly strengthened. All this did not amount to planning in the sense of economic targets being set over a fixed time period, but it did represent a new institutionalised liaison between government and industry.

When they left office the Conservatives thus presided over a larger public sector than in 1970, in terms of the government share of GDP and the number of enterprises it owned. This demonstrates how much the Heath government was relying on incomes policy to harness inflation. Talk of controlling the money supply, which dominated the policy agenda in the late 1970s, was almost completely absent.

On returning to power in February 1974, the new Labour government continued the Conservatives' interventionist policies while trying to conciliate the trade unions. However, they did so with much greater ideological commitment. Indeed, the Party was split between social democratic gradualists and more fundamentalist socialists who were determined to avoid the mistakes of the last Labour government. For about 18 months, the fundamentalists were in the ascendant. The Industrial Relations Act was repealed, a state holding company to encourage investment and improve productivity was created, and a system of planning agreements between industries and state established. A new 'Social Contract' bound both government and trade unions to moderate wage demands. In fact, the Social Contract resulted in anything but moderation. Weekly wage increases jumped from 12.2 per cent in 1973 to 29.4 per cent in 1974. Inflation too bounded ahead, reaching 16.1 per cent in 1974 and a staggering 24.2 per cent in 1975 (Figure 3.1). Finally, the Conservatives' quite generous public expenditure targets for 1974 and 1975 were met in full.

The year 1974 was a bad one for all the developed countries. The quadrupling of oil prices by the Organization of Petroleum Exporting Countries (OPEC) in late 1973 precipitated a sharp downturn in world trade and an acceleration of inflation everywhere. A good part of the 1974–5 inflation can be attributed to these international forces.

BRIEFINGS

3.6 OPEC and the oil crises of the 1970s

Partly as a result of the increased economic activity associated with US intervention in the Vietnam War (1964–72), oil and other commodity prices increased rapidly during the late 1960s and early 1970s. As a result the bargaining power of commodity producers also increased. Most of the world's oil came from Arab states and poorer third world countries that formed a cartel called the Organization of Petroleum Exporting Countries (OPEC) to increase the price of oil by bargaining. When war broke out in the Middle East in 1973 OPEC decided to increase the price of oil in order to punish Israel and its western backers. Within a year oil prices increased fivefold on the world markets, bringing severe inflation to the industrialised countries. Those such as Britain were particularly hard hit, having no indigenous oil supplies. In addition, powerful trade unions were able to insist that wages kept up with or exceeded price increases, thus fuelling further inflation. The disruptive effects of this inflation were considerable and led indirectly to the bailing out of the British economy in 1976 by the International Monetary Fund. Later in the decade a second oil crisis with accompanying price increases was caused by the Iranian revolution. The new regime in Iran was deeply hostile to the West and persuaded OPEC to precipitate another price rise. By 1979–80, however, Britain's North Sea oil began to be extracted. As a result, Britain benefited from the increased oil price and the pound sterling appreciated rapidly on the foreign exchange markets. Since the early 1980s OPEC has often been in disarray as a result of conservation measures in the West, increases in oil production in such areas as Alaska and the North Sea, and internal divisions within the original OPEC countries.

However, Britain suffered from additional problems. Its industrial competitiveness continued to decline. British trade unions were more successful than those in many other countries in keeping wage rates up to or beyond the rate of inflation. Like the Conservatives before them, Labour announced an incomes policy that, although not statutory, was in effect compulsory. After early compliance by the unions, the government faced growing resentment and industrial unrest, which culminated in a 'winter of discontent' during 1978/79. Most commentators agree that this almost certainly cost Labour the election in May 1979.

Just as important as incomes policy was the government's conversion to a limited form of monetarism. During 1976 the selling of sterling reached panic proportions. Fixed exchange rates (the Bank of England commitment to buy sterling for fixed sums in other currencies) had been abandoned in 1971 and left free to fall. And fall the pound did, to a low of $1.57 at one point (until 1971 the pound was fixed at $2.40 to the dollar). Britain was approaching the point where the government could not meet immediate payments on outstanding debts. In exchange for massive loans from the International Monetary Fund (IMF), Denis Healey, the

Monetarism A revised version of neo-classical economics that, contrary to Keynesianism, argues that government should minimise its involvement in economic matters, except for controlling the money supply as a way of holding down inflation.

BRIEFINGS

3.7 The Public Sector Net Cash Requirement (PSNCR)

Public Sector Net Cash Requirement (PSNCR) The amount borrowed by government to help finance its annual expenditure.

Put simply, the PSNCR (previously known as the Public Sector Borrowing Requirement (PSBR)) is the difference between government revenue and expenditure. As was noted in Briefing 3.2, after the Second World War British governments were committed to full employment, and running up the national debt was deemed necessary for this end. With the intervention of the IMF to bail out the economy in 1976, holding down public spending became a priority (see Briefing 3.4), and the Conservative government elected in 1979 was determined to make a reduction in the PSBR (as it was then called) a top priority. In 1980 the government launched its medium-term financial strategy, which aimed to reduce the PSBR in stages from 4.8 per cent of GDP in 1979–80 to under 3 per cent by 1983–4. In the event the PSBR increased to 5.7 per cent of GDP in 1980–1 and induced the government to produce a very deflationary budget in 1981. This, together with a period of sustained economic growth from 1983, reduced the PSBR to 0.9 per cent of GDP in 1986–7 and gave a surplus in the following two years, which was helped by proceeds from selling off nationalised enterprises. By the early 1990s, however, recession took its toll on government revenues and the PSBR once again moved into deficit, reaching over 5 per cent of GDP by 1996. The Labour government elected in 1997 pledged to reduce this figure to well below 3 per cent over a five-year period. Helped by the general recovery of the economy they achieved this by the second part of their first term of office. Note that the Maastricht convergence criteria require governments to keep their annual debt liability to below 3 per cent of GDP.

Chancellor, agreed to new controls on the money supply. Interest rates rose to a record 15.5 per cent and public expenditure was cut. After complex negotiations the IMF and the Treasury agreed that the Public Sector Borrowing Requirement (PSBR) (now known as the Public Sector Net Cash Requirement), the amount needed by the government to cover the gap between resources and expenditure, should be trimmed by £3 billion over two years. In fact, public spending did not fall quite as rapidly as planned. But the very idea of using public sector spending as the major instrument of economic policy was new, notwithstanding Roy Jenkins' more limited efforts in this direction between 1968 and 1970. These radical adaptations to political and economic reality represented a defeat for 'old Labour' ideas, and although a form of traditional socialism was to return under the leadership of Michael Foot (1979–83), thereafter, the Labour Party moved steadily to the right.

The combination of incomes policy and public expenditure cuts reduced inflation quite quickly to a low of around 8 per cent between 1978 and 1979 (Figure 3.1). However, unemployment remained stubbornly high. Labour's plans both for industrial reorganisation and social reforms were rendered ineffective by the spending cuts. As with its predecessor, crisis management rather than social reform became the government's overriding preoccupation, and more and more problems focused on the reaction of the trade unions to government intervention.

One further characteristic of this turbulent period was the relative absence of institutional reform. Parliament, the Civil Service, the health service and local government operated in the traditional manner. It is true that controls on public expenditure instilled a sense of crisis in the public sector, but in terms of operating procedures and the relationship between central authority and other public sector actors, very little changed.

BRIEFINGS

3.8 The 'social democratic consensus', 1945–79

This is the name given to the implicit agreement between all political parties, up to 1979, that the fundamental reforms and policies of the post-war Labour government should remain unchanged. The most obvious of these was the Welfare State. Both Conservatives and Labour governments of this period increased social benefits and health provisions. Another feature was the acceptance of state ownership of coal, gas, electricity, rail, air transport and telephones. Steel and road transport were partially denationalised and then renationalised throughout the period. The third 'leg' of the consensus was economic management: Keynesian policies of avoiding unemployment by government overspending and relaxation of monetary controls were followed by both Conservatives and Labour. From 1960 both also tried to control prices and incomes directly through various monitoring bodies.

This consensus between the parties broke down under the successive economic crises of the 1960s and 1970s and the confrontations with increasingly aggressive trade unions that income controls provoked. In retrospect we can see it depended on the early post-war prosperity in which Britain shared. When this became more difficult to sustain both state intervention and Keynesian economic policy were discredited and became targets for attack by the Thatcherite Conservative governments of the 1980s and 1990s.

RETURN OF FREE MARKET PRINCIPLES IN THE 1980S AND EMERGENCE OF A NEO-LIBERAL ECONOMIC CONSENSUS

Government intervention, whether of the Labour or the old Conservative variety, seemed increasingly to create more problems than it solved. Perhaps the solution lay in a return to the free trading and free market ideas associated with the golden age of the mid-nineteenth century? These were particularly attractive as they had encouraged hard work, thrift, saving and respect for authority, virtues which many thought the country had lost in the preceding 20 years and that were traditional sources of support for the Conservative Party.

Indeed, the Conservatives under Margaret Thatcher won the general election of May 1979 amid a wave of popular revulsion against the strikes and trade union excesses of the 'winter of discontent'. The new Prime Minister and her closest associates had been converted to the belief that Britain was suffering from political and moral breakdown, traceable to the excessive government intervention fostered by socialism. They believed that the 'nanny state', as they called it, gave everybody an assurance that they would be bailed out if things went wrong for them. Consequently, the public engaged in all sorts of irresponsible behaviour, since they did not have to suffer the consequences of their actions.

According to Thatcherite ideology, those who suffered were the solid moral majority who did behave responsibly, saved for their old age and worked hard. These were denied the fruits of their labour by a swollen state apparatus that took away their savings in taxation and depressed their initiative by over-regulation, while rewarding 'scroungers' and the irresponsible.

A major imperative, therefore, was to cut government down to size and limit its interventions in society. By doing so it could distance itself from those who had usurped its authority, particularly trade unions, and act with force where it had to intervene, notably in support of law and order and free market reform. A strong government could also assert British interests abroad, in collaboration with like-minded US administrations. Bolstered by the enhanced economic growth that these policies would bring it could also push the European Union in a free trade direction.

These leading ideas inspired government action both under Margaret Thatcher (1979–90) and her successor as Conservative Prime Minister, John Major (1990–7).

Thatcherism, 1979–90

Until 1983, the Thatcher government favoured monetarism: a belief that control of the amount of money circulating in the economy would alone improve general economic efficiency, in spite of the exceptional unemployment it caused (over 11 per cent in 1982). From 1983, however, monetary targets were rarely met and ministers became less and less dependent on the theory. They stuck to their free market philosophy, denationalisation (or 'privatisation'), reducing trade union power, and increasing penalties and incentives in the public sector all being central to government policy. The British National Oil Corporation, Jaguar Cars,

Deregulation
The opposite of regulation, it involves the weakening or removal of state regulations in the interests of market competition.

British Leyland, British Telecom, the Trustee Savings Bank, British Gas, British Airways, Rolls-Royce and many council-owned homes were sold. In the late 1980s water companies, electricity supply and other 'natural monopolies' traditionally within the public sector were also privatised.

Major legislation in 1980, 1982 and 1984 transformed industrial relations law. 'Closed shops' (ie factories where all the workforce have to join a union) had to be approved in a secret ballot by four-fifths of the workers; secondary picketing (ie the picketing of firms not themselves party to an industrial dispute) was outlawed; secret ballots were introduced to endorse industrial action, to elect top union officials, and to approve the collection of union political funds. These laws, together with continuing high unemployment, substantially weakened the trade unions. From 1979 to 1995 their membership halved. They were further debilitated by the costly and often violent miners' strike of 1984–5, which ended with a split in the National Union of Mineworkers and an effective victory for the government. Many mines were closed and the remnants of the coal industry were sold off in the mid-1990s. By the end of the century, little was left of the industry. In 2002 it was noted that the country had more Elvis Presley impersonators than coal miners!

Unemployment remained the Thatcher government's Achilles heel. By 1987, the number and scope of youth employment schemes, retraining programmes and other employment creation schemes had increased considerably. However, in 1985, the economy began to expand very rapidly by British standards, culminating in the frenetic 'boom' of 1987–8.

Plate 3.3 *Nicholas Garland cartoon in the* Daily Telegraph, *23 September 1981, showing unemployment about to go through the 3 million mark under Thatcher*

The Thatcher project involved a renewed effort to reduce the size of government and attempts at major institutional reform. High levels of unemployment had become what looked like a long-term feature of many inner city areas, especially in the north, Scotland, Northern Ireland and Wales. Intervention in these areas had traditionally involved high levels of public expenditure on housing, transport and social services, with central government relying on locally elected councils to effect its policies. The Conservatives, in line with their free market philosophy, sought instead to remove what they saw as the dead hand of Labour-dominated local government. The centrally controlled Youth Training Scheme, channelling the energies of the young unemployed, was extended and made semi-compulsory; enterprise zones with suspension of normal planning regulations were set up under nominated boards; council house sales continued and private renting and buying of houses was encouraged. State schools were given the right to opt entirely out of local authority control and thus gain much greater autonomy. Subsidies for public transport were effectively removed and competition was encouraged. Meanwhile moral and administrative pressure was applied to those receiving Unemployment Benefit to take any form of work available, however low paid and unattractive. Vigorous attempts were made to break away from national pay settlements, so that firms operating in areas of high unemployment could pay less.

In addition, the government embarked on major reforms of the Civil Service, education and the health service. Most of these involved introducing market or market-like principles into operating procedures. Until the 1970s there was an implicit assumption that publicly provided services were a good thing. From the 1980s, many politicians, academics and commentators seriously questioned this assumption and argued that the private sector (or in some cases private sector practices applied in the public sector) were often superior in terms of quality and value for money.

The attempt to get government out of the economy appeared by the end of the 1980s to have had real but limited success. In areas of traditional strength – finance and services centred on southeast England – free enterprise policies had strengthened Britain's competitive position in an era of growing interdependence and internationalisation of markets. They had accelerated the industrial decline of the outlying areas, however and events were to show that the recovery was fragile. A further downturn in the global economy from 1990 arrested the move to the market. Spending as a percentage of GDP increased once more after having declined in the early 1980s (Figure 3.2).

The stock market 'crash' of October 1987 convinced the government that in order to avert a recession it was necessary to stimulate the economy by lowering interest rates. At the same time, the third Thatcher government was less intent on holding down public expenditure. It had a surplus of revenue over expenditure and had eliminated the annual PSBR by 1987. However, the expected downturn in economic activity following the collapse of world stock market prices in October 1987 never transpired. As a result the economy became seriously over-heated in 1988, culminating in an inflation rate of close to 10 per cent (Figure 3.1). Remedial action in the form of punitively high interest rates followed rapidly, which in turn depressed the housing and property markets and helped precipitate the 1990–2 recession.

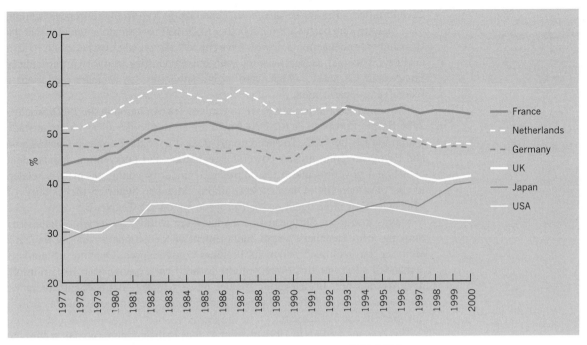

Figure 3.2 *Percentage of GDP in the public sector, related countries, 1977–2000*

A number of other countries went through a similar boom/slump cycle during the late 1980s and early 1990s. In few others was the initial stimulus to growth and inflation so great or the subsequent deflationary reaction so draconian. Britain experienced a longer, deeper recession than any comparable country except Japan.

Modified Thatcherism, 1992–7

The Conservatives' surprise election victory in 1992, giving them a record fourth term, was not just a confirmation of the Thatcher policies of the 1980s. Some of the Thatcherite agenda was dropped: most importantly, the Major government no longer pursued orthodoxy in the national accounts. Public expenditure was allowed to rise to a point where by 1995 the PSBR was above 6 per cent of GDP. Money was initially pumped into health, education, transport and a range of other areas before further cuts were imposed from 1994 onwards to finance reductions in income tax. But equally much of the Thatcher agenda remained or was even strengthened including lower taxes on incomes and profits, further privatisations such as British Rail and increasing competition and self-management within the public sector.

From 1993 the British economy recovered ahead of its European partners and a great deal of the government's energy went into managing the boom to sustain steady growth and avoid a subsequent recession. Much of the Major government's attention had also to be given to relationships with the European Union. Mrs Thatcher had been a strong upholder of British sovereignty – the idea that the British government should always have the last say on what was done on British territory. This had caused tensions with other countries in the EU, particularly France and Germany, which were strong supporters of a closer (and even a federal) European Union.

The single most important move towards European union in the 1980s was the 1986 Single European Act (SEA) which aimed to abolish all restraints to trade within the EU by 1992. To speed up progress it gave the European Commission and European Court greater powers of regulation and intervention, independent of national governments. It also introduced majority voting, on matters related to the development of the market, among Member States in the Council of Ministers. (For more detail on the European Union see Chapter 8.)

Moves towards a European free market were wholly in line with Thatcherite thinking. Mrs Thatcher's warm endorsement of the economic aims of the SEA seems to have blinded her to its political consequences. Opening up markets demanded strong political intervention, as her own experience in Britain might have warned her. In delegating greater powers to the 'Brussels bureaucracy', even to enforce free trade, she was undermining the autonomy of the British government and Parliament.

This was masked up to 1991 by the fact that British commissioners within the EU, British advisers and many neo-liberal economists were at the forefront in striking down protectionist measures in countries such as France and Germany. Under John Major, however, it became clear that the free market was simply a stage on the road to closer political union. The Treaty of European Union (also known as the Maastricht Treaty) (1992–3) committed countries of the European Union to closer integration of social and economic policies, and to collective decision making in many areas. Britain reserved the right to opt out of the creation of a single currency, which it exercised when it abstained from joining the euro in 1999 and refused to accept the Social Chapter on minimal working conditions for European employees (now adopted by the Labour government).

Even so, the treaty seemed to a substantial body of 'Eurosceptics' in the Conservative Party to go too far. Their scepticism was reinforced by the improvement in the British economy after the country was forced out of the European Monetary System (EMS), which had obliged members to keep their currencies within narrow limits in relation to each other.

As France and Germany powered ahead with their project of 'ever-closer union', and as the European institutions became more active in Britain, the persistent opposition of the Conservative Eurosceptics spread to other aspects of government activity. They objected to the slackening pace of Thatcherite reform and threatened to vote against a whole series of government measures unrelated to Europe.

With a minuscule majority in Parliament the Major government (itself split internally) took an increasingly negative stance in Europe to retain Eurosceptic support. This in turn alienated the pro-European Conservatives. Supported by much of industry and the City, they wanted to go along with European Monetary Union (EMU), either because they feared the consequences if Britain were left out or because they saw positive benefits for London as the financial centre of a more integrated Union. Divisions both in Cabinet and in Parliament contributed to the impression of an indecisive, do-nothing government, which helped lose them the election of 1997.

There is no doubt that the Conservative governments of the 1979–97 period transformed the political landscape of Britain. Above all, they changed the nature of political discourse by creating a completely new policy agenda. With the collapse of the social democratic consensus in the 1970s Britain had become something of an ideological battleground between old Labour ideas such as nationalisation and high rates of income tax designed to redistribute wealth, and free market ideas based on individual initiative and self reliance. To be sure, there were many shades of opinion within the main political parties and between them, but almost all political discourse took on a left versus right character. The Conservative years changed all this. By the mid-1990s almost all politicians accepted that the market was the best mechanism for producing and delivering a wide range of goods and services. This applied not just to traditional industries but also to 'natural' monopolies such as utilities and transport. It even might apply to the ways in which public services like health, education and law enforcement could be delivered. At the same time, few argued for higher taxation. The assumption was that lower rates of (especially) income tax provided an incentive to work and to save. Old Labour policies were effectively discredited.

A THIRD WAY? NEW LABOUR, 1997–2004

It comes as no surprise then that when after nearly 18 years in opposition the Labour Party returned to office in May 1997, it accepted most of the Thatcherite agenda, including the need for strict financial discipline and income tax reductions. Indeed one of the first things the self-styled 'New Labour' government did was to adhere strictly to the Conservatives' spending plans. Combined with the increased tax revenues that resulted from continuing economic prosperity this resulted in a large budget surplus that allowed some relaxation of spending controls before the next election. Increasingly, Labour steered political debate away from the questions of how industry should be structured and levels of spending and taxation determined, towards an emphasis on the quality of public services, notably health, education and law and order. The hard-line, Eurosceptical Conservative Party under William Hague failed to note this change of emphasis and argued that the future lay in low taxes and reduced public expenditure – a position that helped account for the Conservatives' second resounding defeat in 2001. His successor, Iain Duncan Smith, played down both the European issue and lower taxes and argued instead that the Conservatives too were interested in improving public services.

In spite of this emphasis on public services, there is no question that by 1997 the nature of the policy agenda had changed. Old Labour appealed to voters not only on the question of nationalisation but also on issues of wealth and equality. Traditionally, Labour governments had advocated higher taxes for the rich and

Plate 3.4 *Prime Minister Blair with his wife, Cherie, at No. 10 Downing Street*

lower taxes for the poor. At the same time, they generally opposed the private provision of such services as education, transport and housing. By 1997 references to redistributive taxation (taxing the better off and redistributing tax revenue to the poor) had almost passed from political discourse. Instead, New Labour supported the idea of increasing the size of the national economic cake, so that everybody would benefit. At the same time, they no longer opposed private education and the private provision of transport, and they had become positively enthusiastic about owner-occupied housing.

They also distanced themselves from the trade unions, whose advice was much less important to the government than that of financial interests and in particular proponents of fiscal orthodoxy – a combination of low inflation and a balanced budget. Financial interests dominate the Monetary Policy Committee of the Bank of England, which sets interest rates. Beating inflation and maintaining a stable currency are seen as the prerequisites for a generally healthy economy in the long term, even if there are casualties, especially in manufacturing, in the short term. Central controls on local government spending were maintained and indeed tightened. Tough law and order policies were supported by the first two Labour Home Secretaries, Jack Straw and David Blunkett, while the Prime Minister never tired of extolling 'family values'. In general too New Labour shared Mrs Thatcher's suspicions of public employees and the government devised ever tighter means of control of schools and teachers, for example. In many ways therefore Mrs Thatcher's goals of 'free economy, strong state' have been accepted by New Labour.

These policies have been projected to the public as a 'Third Way' between unfettered capitalism and state socialism. However, it is not easy to pinpoint what exactly the Third Way is. In an influential book published in 1998, the sociologist Anthony Giddens attempted to spell it out. Most of the emphasis is on the

Third Way
The theory that governments should follow policies that are based neither on free market capitalism nor state socialism. In British politics it is closely associated with Blair and New Labour, and represents a rejection both of Thatcher's free market policies and of old Labour's socialist policies.

BRIEFINGS

3.9 A neo-liberal consensus?

Just as Conservatives and Labour agreed from 1950 onwards on the acceptance of Labour reforms such as the Welfare State, so we can see an implicit agreement between the major parties today on acceptance of the Conservative privatisations of the 1980s, together with their supporting 'free market' philosophy. New Labour and Conservatives agree that the economy is best left to run itself with a minimum of government regulation. What regulation there is will be undertaken on financial grounds, favouring the City of London, and aimed at reducing inflation. Public services are to be run on a 'market model' as far as possible with bigger incentives for efficient providers and penalties for the inefficient. This applies even to the Welfare State, the big holdover from the previous period. Conservatives and Labour still divide over the extent to which social benefits should be raised and taxes cut. Even though they share many of the same policy ideas, therefore, Conservatives and Labour still divide on the extent to which government should intervene in society, by targeting benefits, or reduce its role by taking less in taxes.

'restructuring of government and civil society', which usually means making government more responsive to what should be a better informed and more politically active public. In policy terms, this translates into making government programmes more *efficient* but not necessarily bigger or more egalitarian. The Third Way also involves copying the best practice of other countries in such areas as welfare and health care. Almost by definition, the Third Way can mean institutional and constitutional reform. While its advocates believe strongly in protecting the weak and vulnerable in society (the disabled, the poor, the sick), they also believe that welfare benefits should go only to the deserving poor or the genuinely needy. As far as income security is concerned, most individuals should be self-reliant rather then depend on the state. Only those who cannot help themselves should be supported by the government. To be fair, in health and education, New Labour supports free provision for all who need it – although it also respects the wishes of those who prefer private provision. However, it no longer believes that income and wealth inequality should be addressed directly through redistributive taxation.

None of this adds up to socialism or even to social democracy as practised in most European countries in the post-Second World War period. But it does mean renewal and reform. New Labour was quite prepared to accept most of the reforms of the Thatcher period because many of them did make government more efficient. Labour has also embarked on major constitutional reform, which the Conservatives opposed. This has involved signing the European Convention on Human Rights, and giving devolution to Scotland, Wales and Northern Ireland. In addition the House of Lords has been reformed and some devolution to a London Assembly and Mayor has been implemented.

BRIEFINGS

3.10 Inequality in Britain

Among the OECD states (Organisation for Economic Co-operation and Development which represents the richer industrial countries), it is widely recognised that Britain has a relatively high degree of income and wealth inequality. Along with the United States (and in contrast to such countries as Japan and France) a small number of rich people control a large proportion of wealth. In 1999, for example, the richest 1 per cent of the population owned 23 per cent of the wealth, up from 18 per cent in 1981 (see Table 1.3). More disturbingly, there is evidence that this inequality spreads to other areas of social life, including health and education. People living in Scotland, Wales and the north of England have a considerably lower life expectancy than those living in the south. This difference is largely explicable in terms of income and wealth distribution. More poor people live in Wales and northern Britain than in the south. In education, although standards have been increasing in recent years, so has educational inequality. A recent OECD report found that a high level of socio-economic segregation in Britain encouraged by private and elite public sector schools has led to a growing gap in the educational attainment between rich and poor (*Knowledge and Skills for Life*, OECD, 2000).

Although New Labour is committed to reducing these inequalities, some of its policies, such as maintaining grammar and special subject schools, may actually have the opposite effect.

One final characteristic of Labour's 'Third Way', which also distinguishes it from earlier Thatcherite ideas, is what has been called *liberal internationalism*. Tony Blair and other Third Way adherents believe that with the proper safeguards, globalisation can produce benefits. These safeguards include international treaties on environmental protection, aid for poorer countries and, most controversially, multilateral military efforts to contain terrorism and the aggression of 'rogue' states such as Iraq. Liberal internationalists also support free trade and such bodies as the EU, the World Trade Organisation and the International Monetary Fund. We will return to this theme in later chapters.

By the first years of the twenty-first century, therefore, the ideas that inform British politics had changed. Market values dominated in most areas of economic life, and market-like mechanisms had been introduced to most parts of the public sector. Labour has not dropped its hope of a more egalitarian society, but it assumes that this will come through economic growth and public services that are more efficiently run. In fact, rather than Britain becoming a more equal society it has become more unequal over recent decades (Briefing 3.10). This was not, of course, the intention of Labour governments, but it has happened nonetheless. Labour has gone further than its predecessors in the area of constitutional change. However, reforms of the 'core' institutions of British political life – Parliament, Civil Service, local government – have lagged behind. Later chapters will review these developments in detail.

ESSAYS

1. Why did government intervene so extensively in society from 1931 to 1951? What remains of this legacy in the early twenty-first century?

2. What was the nature of the post-war 'social democratic consensus'? To what extent has Labour's 'Third Way' broken with this consensus?

3. Why has the question of the value of the pound sterling declined in importance in British politics since 1992?

SUMMARY

This chapter has shown how British governments broke away from free trade doctrines in the 1930s and 1940s to protect industry and society from the consequences of global recession. In particular, governments intervened to:

- nationalise basic industries (coal, steel, transport and public utilities) so as to guarantee price and production levels and a minimum level of service

- use monetary policy to achieve a high level of activity in the economy with top priority being given to full employment

- use planning to direct investment and employment towards reviving older industrial regions and alleviate crowding in the inner cities

- create a comprehensive Welfare State to provide all citizens with basic health care, education and adequate housing.

From the 1950s to the late 1970s few governments challenged these policies. However, it became increasingly difficult to fund them because:

- Britain suffered from chronic balance of payments problems that led to repeated bouts of 'stop–go', ie overheating of the economy followed by the need for deflation.

- The international economic environment became more difficult during the 1970s, with the abandonment of fixed exchange rates and the rapid increase in commodity prices.

■ Britain's economic performance was poor compared with other countries as strikes and low productivity led to an ever-present sense of economic crisis. The preferred solutions to these problems – incomes policy and economic planning – gradually became discredited.

■ By the mid-1970s intellectual and political opinion moved in favour of market solutions to economic problems, although sections of the Labour Party continued to support strong state intervention.

■ Since the 1980s a combination of market solutions together with fiscal and monetary discipline have dominated the political agenda. Full employment has been given a lower priority, although the Labour Party remains more concerned about it than the Conservative Party. Similarly, both parties now accept that Welfare State benefits have to be selective rather than universal. The major difference between the parties is on the degree of selectivity, with Labour favouring higher benefit levels.

■ By the mid-1990s the performance of the British economy recovered to reach the average (or, by some measures, above the average) of the developed countries.

■ New Labour's 'Third Way' involved renewing the relationship between government and citizen, constitutional reform and social justice. Under Prime Minister Tony Blair it also involved an interventionist foreign stance and support for multilateral treaties as well as military intervention to oust dictators.

MILESTONES

Milestones: events, policies and governments, 1931–2004

BRITAIN	WORLD
'National' governments, 1931–40 (MacDonald, Baldwin, Chamberlain), Conservative dominated	
Abandonment of Gold Standard, 1931	World depression, 1928–39
Mass unemployment, 1930–8	Rise of Hitler in Germany
Tariffs on foreign imports, 1931–5	
Formation of industrial cartels, 1931–8	
Marketing boards for Agriculture	
Special Areas Acts, 1935, 1936, 1937	
Rearmament, 1936–40	
Series of reports on landuse, town planning, population distribution, 1938–40	Nazi annexations: Austria, 1938, Czechoslovakia, 1939, attack on Poland, 1939, precipitates war
Wartime coalition, 1940–5 (Churchill)	
Unprecedented control of labour, supplies, food, production, 1940–5	Second World War, 1939–45
Beveridge Report on Social Insurance, 1942	

BRITAIN

Labour government, 1945–51 (Attlee)
National Health Service Act, 1946
National Insurance Act, 1946
State ownership of coal industry, gas, electricity,
    transport and steel
Town and Country Planning Act, 1947

Full employment policy, wage and dividends
    freeze, control of production in many areas,
    rationing

Conservative governments, 1951–9
(Churchill, Eden, Macmillan)
Deregulation of trade and financial controls
Limited denationalisation of iron and steel
    industry and road transport

Conservative governments, 1959–64
(Macmillan, Home)

Wage and price freeze, 1962–3
Unsuccessful application to join EC, 1962

Labour governments, 1964–70 (Wilson)
Balance of payments crisis, 1964–66

National economic plan effectively abandoned,
    1966–7
Increasing credit, wage and dividend restrictions,
    1966–9
Devaluation of pound sterling, 1967
Unsuccessful application to join EC, 1968
Plan to regulate trade union and industrial
    relations, 1969–70 (revealed in green paper In
    Place of Strife, 1969) defeated by trade union
    and internal Labour opposition
Intervention of British troops in Northern
    Ireland, 1969

Conservative governments, 1970–4 (Heath)
Floating exchange rate for pound sterling,
    1971
Industrial Relations Act, 1971 (legal regulation of
    trade unions); 'U-turn' from not interfering in
    industry or wage negotiations to restrictions on
    wage and salary increases
Suspension of Northern Ireland Parliament and
    Direct Rule, 1972

WORLD

German surrender, 1945
Japanese surrender, 1945
Dislocation of international trade after Second
    World War
Berlin crisis, 1948–9, marks start of Cold War
    with Soviet Union and intensification of
    western alliance (NATO)
Independence of India, Pakistan, Burma and
    Ceylon, 1948

Korean War, 1950–3
World economic growth, Invasion of Suez, 1956
Formation of European Community, 1956

Independence of most African colonies
Détente with Soviet Union, 1960–79
Relaxation of Cold War and arms race

Britain keeps out of US involvement in Vietnam
    War, 1964–73
Increasing liberalisation of world trade under
    GATT

Arab/Israeli War, 1967

Abandonment of Bretton Woods system of fixed
    exchange rates, 1971–3

▶

BRITAIN	WORLD
Reorganisation of local government units into larger ones, 1972–5	
Entry to EEC, 1973	
Easy credit and high inflation, 1973–4	Arab/Israeli War 1973
Successful strikes by National Union of Mineworkers, 1972 and 1974, which disrupt entire country	
Discovery of oil in British North Sea	Rise in world oil prices, 1973–4

Labour governments, 1974–9 (mostly in minority) (Wilson, Callaghan)

BRITAIN	WORLD
Major election gains by Scottish and Welsh Nationalists, 1974	
High inflation, 1974 onwards	
Social Contract with trade unions, involving limits on prices and incomes and legal concessions, 1975–8	
Referendum for continuing membership of EC, 1975	
Balance of payments crisis, 1976	
Severe credit restrictions and increasing cuts in projected government expenditure, 1976–9	
High and increasing unemployment, 1975 onwards	
'Winter of discontent', 1979 (strikes by numerous groups of workers including transport strike)	British oil revenues from North Sea equal payments for foreign oil
Defeat of government proposals for Scottish and Welsh devolution, 1979	

Conservative governments, 1979–97 (Thatcher, Major)

BRITAIN	WORLD
Policy of restricting stock of money to bring down inflation involves further cuts in government and central restrictions on local government expenditure	Increasing friction between Soviet Union and the West from 1979
	Iranian Revolution and world oil crisis, 1978–81
Legal restrictions on union's rights to picket during strikes and to extend scope of stoppage	World economic depression intensifying up to 1981
Falling inflation and greatly increasing unemployment, 1980–2	
Extensive urban riots, 1981	
Foundation of Social Democratic Party and leadership defections from Labour, 1981	Falklands War, 1982
	World economic recovery, 1982–6
Re-election of Conservatives with large majority, Liberal–Social Democratic Alliance comes close to Labour in terms of votes but not seats, 1983	
Miners' strikes, 1984–5: most bitter industrial dispute since war	
Renewed urban riots, 1985	

BRITAIN

Unemployment reaches 13 per cent, then begins
to fall

Renewed balance of payments problems with
drop in oil revenues, 1988–97

'Privatisation' of many nationalised industries
including gas

Re-election of Conservatives with large majority,
1987, Labour fails to recover significantly and
Alliance fails to break through

Economic boom, 1987–9, followed by severe
recession, 1990–4

Britain joins Exchange Rate Mechanism (ERM), 1990

Replacement of local rates by Community Charge
(poll tax) provokes massive non-payments and
riots, 1989–90

Replacement of Mrs Thatcher as Prime Minister
by John Major, 1990

Conservatives returned with a majority of 21 with
John Major as Prime Minister, 1992

Britain forced out of ERM by currency crisis, 1992

Increasing internal conflict in Conservative Party
between 'Eurosceptics' and pro-Europeans

Government forced into increasing opposition
to 'Europe'

Slow economic recovery, 1994–6

'New Labour' wins election, 1997

Labour governments, 1997– (Blair)

Bank of England given autonomy to act on interest
rates through Monetary Policy Committee

Labour endorses strict financial orthodoxy

British economic performance improves:
accelerating boom 1997–2001

Referendums approve a Scottish Parliament and
devolution for Wales, September 1997

Devolved assemblies start work, September 1999

'Peace Process' in Northern Ireland succeeds in
reaching agreement on a power-sharing Assembly
in 1998. Uneasy peace continues through 2003

Labour second landslide victory, 2001

Slowdown of British economy 2002–3

WORLD

Approval of Single European Act (SEA) 1986 by
members of EU including UK

Oil and other commodity prices fall, 1986

Relaxation of Soviet–western relations, 1986–7,
serious disarmament negotiations between the
USSR and USA

Single European market planned for mid-1990s

Break-up of Soviet Union follows peaceful
liberation of East European states, 1989–91

Maastricht Treaty on further European union,
Britain opts out of Social Charter and reserves
decision on monetary union

Gulf War, 1991

Bosnia crisis 1992–5: British intervention along
with other EU members and USA

Intergovernmental conference on closer European
Union, 1997

Russia accepts eastward expansion of NATO

European Monetary Union, 1999, all members
join except UK, Sweden and Denmark
(Greece joins later)

Kosovo intervention and bombing of Serbia by
USA and UK, 1999

Terrorist attacks on USA, September 2001

Allied intervention in Afghanistan 2002 and
Iraq 2003

World economic difficulties

PROJECTS

1. Write a review of the differences in economic management between the Conservative governments, 1979–1997 and the Labour governments of the subsequent period. Answer with specific reference to the role of taxation in funding public expenditure.

2. Catalogue the main differences between the Conservatives and Labour on the funding and organisation of the Welfare State since 1979.

3. Outline the main privatisations carried out since 1980. Produce a report card on the success and failure of privatisation.

FURTHER READING

A very large literature on British economic policy exists. A balanced assessment of the question of economic decline is David Coates, *The Question of UK Decline* (London: Harvester Wheatsheaf, 1994).

On the politics of economic change see, for the early period, Samuel H. Beer, *Modern British Politics* (London: Faber, 1965) and, for the 1970s, Keith Middlemas, *Politics in Industrial Society* (London: Deutsch, 1979).

On the Thatcher era see David Marsh (ed.), *Implementing Thatcherite Policies* (Milton Keynes: Open University Press, 1992). On the 1990s see C. Crouch, 'The terms of the neo-liberal consensus', *Political Quarterly*, **68** (4), 1997, pp. 352–60. On New Labour's economic and social policies see Gerald R. Taylor (ed.), *The Impact of New Labour* (London: Macmillan, 1999). On the Third Way, see Anthony Giddens, *The Third Way* (Oxford: Polity, 1998). Giddens replies to his critics in *The Third Way and its Critics* (Oxford: Polity, 2000).

USEFUL WEB SITES ON THE BRITISH ECONOMY

Hot links to these sites can be found on the CWS at http://www.booksites.net/budge. For students interested in the historical development of economic theories and practices that shaped modern Britain, there is an excellent set of entries in the Economic History Network at www.eh.net/HE, especially in their 'resources on specific topics' page (www.eh.net/HE/he_resources/topics.php). A comprehensive historical approach to the period surrounding Keynesian economic theory can be found at www.libertyhaven.com/theoreticalorphilosophicalissues/economics/keynesianism/index.html. Contemporary economic models of relevance to today's world are regularly discussed in the web site of the World Economic Forum www.weforum.org.

The main policy goals and achievements of economic and fiscal policy can be found at www.number-10.gov.uk; there are other relevant sites related to economic and fiscal policies. These include the Treasury site www.hm-treasury.gov.uk; the Bank of England www.bankofengland.co.uk; and the Department of Trade and Industry www.dti.gov.uk. It might also be worth looking at the British Chambers of Commerce web site at www.chamberonline.co.uk/index.jsp.

A number of societies and research groups provide critical assessment of economic theories such as the Institute of Fiscal Studies www.ifs.org.uk; the National Institute for Economic and Social Research www.niesr.ac.uk; the Centre for Economic Policy Research www.cepr.org; the Adam Smith Society www.adamsmith.org.uk; the Institute for Economic Affairs www.iea.org.uk; and DEMOS www.demos.co.uk. The *Financial Times* www.ft.com and the *Economist* www.economist.com offer regular market, financial and economic analysis.

PART 2
Government

Portcullis House

A British constitution?

The history and developments reviewed in the last two chapters have strongly shaped present-day institutions and practices. The slowly evolving nature of the British State, perpetually introducing new processes under old forms has left its mark, particularly on the constitution. A constitution enshrines in law the rights and duties of citizens and the functions and powers of the state and its major branches, such as the Crown, Parliament, regional and local government, and the courts. The British 'constitution' is almost unique among the world's democracies for its pre-modern origins, gradual evolution and unwritten status. Until recently most commentators celebrated it for producing strong but flexible and responsive government that has worked well over the centuries. Its major features – Parliamentary sovereignty, the rule of law, the unitary state, and responsible and accountable government – were seen as evidence of British pragmatism and political genius. We shall examine these claims in the next set of chapters as we see how government operates in practice under the constitution. In fact many of its original principles were eroded in the 1980s and 1990s by government actions themselves and by membership of the European Union. The constitution also came under criticism for not working as it was supposed to, and for being less democratic than it should be. Some sceptics even questioned whether Britain has a constitution at all, hence the question mark in the chapter title. Demands for reform grew louder in the 1990s, and at the turn of the century New Labour embarked on a major programme of constitutional reform.

This chapter discusses the traditional British constitution, criticisms of it, and the ways in which it has changed in the recent past. It covers:

- the status and sources of constitutional authority
- Parliament, government, and the constitution
- the principal doctrines of the traditional 'British constitution'
- the myth and reality of the traditional constitution
- the movement for constitutional reform
- New Labour's 'constitutional project'.

BRITAIN'S 'UNWRITTEN' CONSTITUTION: STATUS AND SOURCES

Constitution A set of fundamental laws that determine what the central institutions and offices of the state are to be, their powers and duties, and how they relate to one another, and to their citizens.

People talk of a country's constitution in two different ways. Sometimes they refer broadly to the general body of laws and rules that define the functions and powers of the state, and its relations with ordinary citizens. In this sense every country, including Britain, has a constitution.

At other times they refer to a single document, typically written on vellum and solemnly ratified with a grand seal, which incorporates the most fundamental laws and rules. Examples are the US Constitution of 1787, and Germany's 'Basic Law' of the constitution of 1949. In this second sense, Britain, along with Israel, is almost unique among democracies: there is no single constitutional document.

Table 4.1 *Sources of the British 'constitution'*

1 Statutes	Acts of Parliament, which override all other British constitutional sources and account for a growing proportion of the 'constitution'
Examples	■ Representation of the People Acts, 1832–1969 (extended the right to vote) ■ the Peerage Act, 1963 (created life peers) ■ European Communities Act 1972 (UK joined the European Community)
2 Royal prerogative	Functions performed by ministers acting on behalf of the monarch; their authority derives from the Crown, not Parliament. Executed by Orders in Council or through proclamations and writs under the Great Seal. A gradually diminishing sphere of the constitution, but still important for foreign affairs and security matters
Examples	The power to: ■ dissolve Parliament ■ declare war and make treaties ■ dispense honours ■ appoint ministers
3 Common law	This means customary rules, especially 'precedents' established by judicial decisions in particular cases. Important for civil liberties
Examples	■ Freedom of speech and assembly ■ Individual rights in relation to the police and the courts
4 Authoritative commentaries	Books and writings widely recognised as interpretations of constitutional rules
Example	■ T. Erskine May, *Treatise on the Law, Privileges, Proceedings, and Usage of Parliament*, the classic guide to Parliamentary procedure
5 Conventions	Established customs and practice which are considered binding but lack the force of law. Applies particularly to the practices of the Crown and the Cabinet
Examples	■ the impartiality of the Speaker of the House ■ Cabinet and ministerial responsibility ■ the Prime Minister should be a member of the Commons
6 European Union law	EU law has precedence over UK law, where the two conflict. British courts are required to strike down UK laws which contravene EU law. Important for social and economic legislation, including the rights of workers
Example	■ *Factortame* case: House of Lords judge 1988 Merchant Shipping Act to be unlawful in light of EU agreements

One has to visit the British Library (or the cathedrals at Lincoln or Salisbury) to look at Magna Carta of 1215 for the anything resembling a written constitution in Britain.

Statute law The sum total of laws passed by Parliament.

Common law Law that is overtly made by judges and that has become part of custom and precedent.

To say that the British constitution is totally 'unwritten' is misleading. Many laws and rules that regulate Britain's political system are in fact written down. They appear in acts of Parliament (statute law), treaties with foreign states, orders in council (government directives made in the name of the Crown), judgments handed down through the ages by the courts (common law), European law, and the commentaries of experts (Bagehot and Dicey in the nineteenth century, Jennings and Bogdanor in the twentieth). Table 4.1 defines these sources and gives examples.

However, these writings have never been assembled, codified and ratified into a single document. Moreover, important aspects of Britain's constitutional arrangements are not written down at all, but take the form of widely accepted understandings: constitutional 'conventions'. Britain's constitution is, therefore, more accurately described as partly written and wholly uncodified. It is the unplanned and unsystematic product of slow evolution.

The lack of a single constitutional document in Britain reflects the exceptional continuity of the British State. It has been spared the dictatorships, civil wars, colonisation and foreign invasions that, after liberation, herald a fresh start, a new and written constitution. There has been no historical moment since the 'glorious revolution' of 1688 when a strong need for a new constitution has occurred.

The British 'constitution' also differs from most other countries in another significant respect: it has no special legal status. Written constitutions are normally 'entrenched': they can only be changed by special procedures that do not apply to ordinary legislation. For example, an amendment to the US Constitution requires the assent of two-thirds of both Houses of Congress and ratification by the legislatures of three-quarters of the states. In some countries major constitutional changes must be approved by referendum. In Britain, Parliament can repeal or amend a constitutional law exactly as it would any other law. Referendums have increasingly been held, but there is no legal requirement for them.

And last the British constitution differs from many others where the courts (sometimes a special Constitutional Court) have powers to interpret the constitution and to rule that government legislation or action is unconstitutional. In Britain, the courts have ruled that government and ministerial action are inconsistent with the law, but they cannot rule that the law itself is unconstitutional. (Although since the Human Rights Act (1998) laws can be declared inconsistent with it.)

PARLIAMENT, GOVERNMENT, AND THE CONSTITUTION

The British constitution allows for a pronounced concentration of power in the hands of central government to such an extent that the party in government can reshape the constitution to its own advantage. This is because the most important single influence on the constitution is statute law, and so long as the government enjoys a secure majority in the Commons it can pass laws that shape the constitution, however controversial and partisan. Although blatantly partisan constitutional legislation has been rare in Britain since 1918, there are a few recent examples:

Bill of Rights A formal statement of the rights and privileges that may be actually or theoretically claimed by citizens. Unlike a modern Bill of Rights, however, the one passed by Parliament in 1689 was more concerned to restrict the royal prerogative and assert the powers of Parliament.

- A 1984 Act required trade unions to ballot their members about political donations, which go mainly to the Labour Party. No matching legislation was introduced requiring companies to ballot their shareholders about political donations, which go mainly to the Conservative Party.

- A 1986 Act abolished the Greater London Council, and the six other metropolitan councils, which were normally under Labour control.

- The government's willingness in 1994 to change the ancient Bill of Rights (1689) at short notice in order to help one of its MPs sue the *Guardian* in 1994 shows how easily – and, at times, recklessly – statute law can be used to change the constitution. (See Briefings 4.1)

BRIEFINGS

4.1 **The Hamilton affair and the amendment of the Bill of Rights of 1689**

In 1994 the *Guardian* newspaper published allegations that the MP and Trade Minister, Neil Hamilton, had accepted payments from the millionaire businessman and owner of Harrods, Mohamed Al Fayed, without recording the payment in the Register of Interests, as required by Parliamentary rules. Hamilton started libel proceedings against the *Guardian*, which successfully applied to the court to have the action struck out on the ground that in order to defend it properly they would need to rely on evidence of Hamilton's conduct in the House of Commons, which was precluded by the terms of Article Nine of the Bill of Rights of 1689, and by the rules of Parliamentary privilege. Many Conservative MPs and peers considered this unfair because it prevented Hamilton from using the courts to clear his name. The government hurriedly passed a new law permitting an MP to waive Article Nine of the Bill of Rights in order to bring a libel action. In the event Hamilton abandoned his libel action, was defeated in the May 1997 general election and soon after was found by the Parliamentary Commissioner for Standards to have acted improperly.

This is a recent example of how government can use its majority in the House of Commons to overturn, at short notice and without careful consultation, a long-established provision of the constitution. This may illustrate either the flexibility of the constitution, or the government's ability to alter the constitution for short-term partisan advantage.

(For more detail see Dawn Oliver, 'Regulating the conduct of MPs: the British experience of combating corruption', *Political Studies*, **45**, 1997, pp. 539–58.)

Royal prerogative
Functions performed by ministers on behalf of the monarch. Before a constitutional monarchy was established the Crown had powers that were subject to no check or veto by Parliament, but now the royal prerogative is generally exercised by ministers.

Some of the other sources of constitutional authority listed in Table 4.1 are effectively controlled by the government:

- The royal prerogative is exercised by ministers who derive their authority, not from Parliament, but from a wholly compliant Crown.

- Common law and judicial decisions sometimes prove a temporary embarrassment for the government, but can be overturned by an act of Parliament.

- Constitutional conventions only bind the executive to the extent that they are recognised and implemented by the government.

As a result, the British 'constitution' is little different from 'what the government decides to do'.

PRINCIPAL DOCTRINES OF THE TRADITIONAL CONSTITUTION, 1911–72

Despite its untidiness and vagueness, there is some structure to the traditional British constitution which was in operation between 1911, when the Parliament Act reduced the power of the House of Lords, to 1972, when the European Communities Act enabled Britain to join the EU. Its central principles are: a unitary state; Parliamentary sovereignty; constitutional monarchy; centralised power; government accountability; and a representative form of democracy. All are important features of the British system of government, and we will discuss them in greater detail in chapters that follow, but a quick review of them here is necessary before looking at the way in which the constitution has started to change in recent times.

The unitary state

Unitary state A state in which there is a single sovereign body, the central government. Unlike a federal state, the central government of a unitary state does not share power with smaller territorial areas within the state (states, regions or provinces) although it may devolve some powers to them.

The British State is unitary rather than federal or confederal. This means that there is only one constitutional centre of power – Parliament – which can create any sort of sub-central system of government it wishes. In federal systems, such as Germany, Australia, Switzerland, and the USA, sub-central levels of government (states, regions, and provinces) have their own independent and constitutionally guaranteed status and powers. The federal (ie central) government cannot change these, unless it alters the constitution, because power is shared by the different levels of government. There are, of course, regional and local units of government in Britain with powers and duties, but the important point is that they only have these because the Westminster Parliament permits them, not because any constitutional document says so. In fact, central government can create or abolish regional Parliaments and councils as it wishes, just as it can change their powers and responsibilities. The Heath government, for example, suspended the 50-year-old Stormont Parliament in Northern Ireland in 1972, replacing it eventually with direct rule from London. The Thatcher government abolished the Greater London Council and the six Metropolitan Counties in 1986. The Blair government then re-established both the Stormont Parliament and a form of London government.

It is, of course, true that central government has reformed regional and local government in major ways in other unitary states such as France, Italy, and Denmark, yet in these unitary states, regional and local government is *relatively* powerful and autonomous compared with Britain. Even among democratic unitary states, political power in Britain is concentrated in central government. Britain is not just a unitary state but a comparatively highly centralised one. (For more on the UK's unusual form of unitary state see Chapters 10 and 11.)

Parliamentary sovereignty

A. V. Dicey, the foremost authority on the British constitution in the late nineteenth century, described Parliamentary sovereignty as 'the one fundamental law of the British constitution' and 'the ultimate political fact upon which the whole system of legislation hangs'.

Parliamentary sovereignty means that no institution other than Parliament (strictly speaking 'the Queen, Lords and Commons assembled') can make law. An act of Parliament is not subject to, or constrained by, a higher law, such as a written constitution, or another body, such as a regional parliament or a court of law. In this sense, Parliamentary sovereignty means that Parliament can do whatever it wants – pass any new law and abolish any old one without *formal* restraint. Parliamentary sovereignty means that Parliament can make or unmake any law. It cannot be bound by its predecessors, neither can it bind its successors.

Legal power, of course, is not the same as practical power or political power. For example, Parliament has the *legal right* to do all sorts of things that would be unconstitutional in other democracies – to prohibit football, dancing, television and alcohol, even to abolish all elections – but it does not have the *political capacity* to do these things. The constraints on it, however, are practical and political, not formal or constitutional.

Constitutional monarchy

Britain has a 'constitutional monarchy', which means that the Crown plays a largely ceremonial role as head of State and symbol of the national community, having gradually ceded its political powers in the eighteenth and nineteenth centuries, as the price of survival. In the nineteenth and early twentieth century the monarch's rights were 'to be informed, to encourage and to warn' in the famous words of Walter Bagehot, the nineteenth-century constitutional expert. In practice, it is not clear that the present-day monarch has even these rights.

Plate 4.1 *The Queen at the State opening of Parliament. The Crown plays a largely ceremonial role as head of State and symbol of the national community, having gradually ceded its powers in the eighteenth and nineteenth centuries. The Crown retains the right to dissolve Parliament, on the Prime Minister's advice, and to choose the Prime Minister*

Source: Stockwave, Central Office of Information

Concentrated and centralised power – elective dictatorship?

Just as the political power of the monarchy has dwindled to virtually nothing, so the power of aristocracy in the House of Lords has dwindled to very little. The 1911 Parliament Act prohibited the House of Lords from blocking financial measures and limited its delaying powers on a non-financial bill. Neither will the Lords block measures included in the government's election manifesto (the 'Salisbury doctrine'). Occasionally, the Lords defeats a bill sent to it from the Commons, but usually the Commons simply approve the bill again, possibly after minor amendments, and the House of Lords is then required to accept it. If the

Lords is particularly resistant the government can invoke the Parliament Acts of 1911 and 1949 to bypass the Lords altogether.

The combination of a constitutional monarchy and of the diminished powers of the House of Lords means that the House of Commons is supreme. Some constitutional systems provide for two powerful representative assemblies (bicameralism). In Britain's 'asymmetric bicameral' system, the Upper Chamber, the House of Lords, is clearly secondary to the Lower, the House of Commons.

More than that, power is concentrated in the party that controls the majority of seats in the House of Commons. This is because Britain's first past the post electoral system (see Chapter 15) normally provides the winning party with an overall majority in the Commons. So long as the government can impose party discipline (see Chapter 18), the party leadership will get Parliamentary approval of its policies.

In most other democratic states, the power of the state is restrained by written constitutions and by the courts that interpret them, and it is generally shared between different levels of government (federal, state and local), between different representative assemblies (the upper and lower houses of central government), between different branches of government (the executive and legislative), and between different parties that form coalition governments. In Britain, more than almost any other democracy, power is centralised at the national level, and largely concentrated in the hands of the majority party in the House of Commons – in other words 'elective dictatorship'.

Governmental accountability

One consequence of the concentration of power, and one of the great merits claimed for the British system, is the accountability of government. Central government cannot easily blame others for its failings – it cannot blame opposition parties, the House of Lords, local government, the courts, the Civil Service, or anybody else for action taken in its name. Moreover, the electoral system and the party system create a direct and unbroken chain of accountability that stretches for the individual electors right up to the Cabinet and Prime Minister: electors send a single-party representative for their constituency to Parliament; the majority party forms a government; the government creates a Cabinet led by a Prime Minister; and so the government, Cabinet, and Prime Minister are held directly accountable by the voters for what gets done. There are no multiple-member constituencies, and no coalition governments to complicate matters.

Representative government

British government is representative government. For much of the nineteenth and twentieth centuries, the public elected MPs, who were left to get on with the job of running the country. The principle was enunciated in 1774 by Edmund Burke, who did not mince his words when he told the people who had just elected him as their MP that he was always prepared to work hard for them, and to listen to

Plate 4.2 *Steve Bell cartoon in the* Guardian, *8 October 1996. Sir Geoffrey Johnson Smith, Chairman of the Select Committee on Privileges, fiercely denies being influenced by the whip, David Willetts, over the Ian Greer cash for questions affair. This was another example of so-called Tory sleaze in the run-up to the 1997 general election that was seized on by advocates of constitutional reform*

Source: Steve Bell

what they said, but that his actions in the House of Commons would always be determined by his own judgement.

Representative government of this type contrasts with participatory or direct democracy, where citizens exercise closer control over their elected representatives by participating more directly in government. Referendums – a direct form of participation – were rarely used in Britain until quite recently and are not part of the traditional constitutional order.

STRENGTHS OF THE TRADITIONAL CONSTITUTION

The traditional British constitution was widely thought to have great strengths: it provided a durable and adaptable foundation for democracy; it helped to create stable government; and it produced moderate and effective government. Above all, it was said, it worked.

Durable democracy

The UK is one of the world's oldest democracies. It has gradually evolved from Magna Carta in 1215 to its present form, and during this time it has avoided authoritarian and totalitarian governments, military coups, and extremist political threats. It has adapted to huge social and economic changes, and survived wars and the rise and decline of the Empire. Throughout all this it has protected most of the basic social and political rights of most of its citizens.

Stable government

Most British governments are in office for four or five years, providing a stability and continuity not often found in coalition systems. In post-war Italy and France, for example, there has been much more government instability. There have been unsettled periods in Britain since 1945 (1964–6, 1974, 1976–9) but they have been brief and exceptional.

Moderate government

For the most part, British government has been moderate government. Radical reforming governments have been relatively rare (the 1945–51 Labour government, and Thatcher governments of 1979–90) and, moreover, a broad consensus has usually spanned the two main parties. This has been called 'Butskellism', after R. A. B. Butler, on the left-wing of the Conservative Party, who had much in common with Hugh Gaitskell, on the Labour right.

Effective government

More controversial, and less easily demonstrated, the British constitutional system is said to produce effective government. Because power is centralised in the hands of the majority party in the House of Commons, government is better able to take effective action, so far as any government is able to do this. This does not mean that government policies are good or successful, but that governments can take decisions and implement them. There are not many veto points in the system and governments can take action if they have the will to do so.

The pragmatic virtue – it works

In the last resort, defenders of the traditional British constitution have argued that it works. It provides for stable, moderate, effective, and accountable government in normal times, and is flexible enough to respond to crisis. For example, although it is a prime example of strong, single-party government, it has moved smoothly into coalition government when the need arose. It did this when the country was threatened by the great depression (1931–36) and again during the Second World War (1940–45). The Labour government of 1974–9 was kept in power by an informal Parliamentary agreement with the Liberals and Scottish Nationalists.

Similarly, although the UK is a prime example of a centralised unitary state, there was a degree of devolution to Scotland, Ireland, and Wales, even before the creation of the Scottish Parliament and Welsh Assembly in 1999, and the restoration of Home Rule to Stormont. The electoral system is one of the least proportional in the democratic world, but it often produces a government that is close to the opinions of the average elector (see Chapter 28). The British constitution is a strange and unusual animal, it is true, but its defenders argue with some truth, that it works as well as most, and better than many.

THE TRADITIONAL CONSTITUTION: MYTHS AND REALITY

Conventions

At the same time, critical voices have grown more insistent in recent times. At the heart of the criticism is the fact that the British constitution is only partly written and wholly uncodified. It depends not on formal, written rules, but on conventions, that is on unwritten understandings based on custom and practice, which are supposed to be observed, but which lack the force of law. 'The British Constitution presumes more boldly than any other the good sense and the good faith of those who work it,' said W. E. Gladstone, the nineteenth-century statesman.

Defenders of the traditional constitution emphasise the flexibility of conventions and their ability to fill gaps in the written parts of the constitution. They are what the constitutional expert Lord Norton calls 'the oil in the machinery of the constitution'. Sceptics point out that governments lubricate their own machinery nicely, leaving the opposition's to rust.

Some conventions are so firmly fixed that it is almost impossible to imagine their changing: the Crown assents to bills passed by both Houses of Parliament; the monarch calls on the leader of the largest party in the Commons to form a government; the Prime Minister always sits in the Commons; the Speaker is impartial; Parliament must meet every year. Other conventions are more fluid. For example, the nineteenth-century convention that the Cabinet as a whole advises the monarch when to dissolve Parliament has yielded to the convention that it is the Prime Minister alone who does so. This recognises the power of present-day Prime Ministers. Often, however, the flexibility of a convention depends not on constitutional principles, but on political expediency – and here we are back again to the power of the government.

Governments will bend the accepted rules for short-term advantage if they think they can get away with it, and the combination of party discipline, a majority in the Commons and the legal supremacy of Parliament means they often can get away with it. In 1977 the Labour Prime Minister, James Callaghan, decided to allow a free vote on the rules for regulating European elections. Challenged in Parliament to say whether this breached the convention of collective Cabinet responsibility, he nonchalantly replied: 'The convention still applies except in cases I announce that it does not.'

The convention that a government resigns if it loses a vote of confidence is a case in point. The principle may be firm but the definition of a 'vote of confidence' is not. In the nineteenth and much of the twentieth century any financial or legislative measure that was central to a government's programme was regarded as a matter of confidence. This understanding was simply ignored by the Labour government, which was elected with a tiny Parliamentary majority of three in October 1974, and became a minority government in March 1977. It was defeated on a number of major measures but insisted that only a defeat on a censure motion required it to resign.

The 1994 Conservative government, beset by a dwindling majority and growing backbench rebellion, took the same line when an important part of its

Constitutional convention Unwritten understandings based on custom and practice that are held to be binding and are commonly observed even though they are not enforced by law or sanctions. An example in the British constitution is that of the Crown assenting to bills passed by Parliament.

budget was defeated (increased VAT on fuel). Ironically in the same month the Prime Minister, John Major, defined the proposal to increase Britain's contribution to the EU as an issue of confidence in order to pressure reluctant Conservative MPs into supporting it. When is an issue an issue of confidence? When the Prime Minister says it is.

Ministerial responsibility

'Ministerial responsibility' offers a telling example of how changing political circumstances and government self-interest have together eroded the once firm constitutional convention that ministers are responsible for what they and their officials do (or omit to do). In theory they are answerable to Parliament for the conduct of their department and are held accountable – expected to resign – for major personal lapses or departmental errors.

A good example is the resignation of Lord Carrington and two junior ministers in 1982 for ignoring warnings of an Argentine invasion of the Falklands. In 1986 the Minister for Trade and Industry, Leon Brittan, resigned for leaking a letter designed to damage his government colleague, Michael Heseltine, during the Westland affair. Peter Mandelson, the only minister ever to resign twice, was forced out in 1998 (over an undeclared home loan) and again in 2001 (over the British passport application of an Indian businessman, Hinduja, who had donated 1 million pounds to the Millennium Dome). Stephen Byers eventually resigned in 2002, although it is not clear whether this was over the important issue of railways, or less important departmental matters. In quite a few cases ministers have resigned not because they complied with the convention of ministerial responsibility, but because they were forced out of office by backbench opinion.

However, in the 1980s and 1990s many other ministers presided over serious policy failures and refused to resign. They include:

- James Prior, the Northern Ireland Minister, over the breakout of prisoners at the Maze prison in Belfast in 1983

- Norman Lamont, the Chancellor of the Exchequer, over Britain's forced exit from the Exchange Rate Mechanism (ERM) in 1992

- Michael Howard, the Home Secretary, over a series of prison escapes in 1994 and 1995

- William Waldegrave, for misleading the Commons, and Sir Nicholas Lyell, the Solicitor-General, for wrongly instructing ministers on the arms to Iraq scandal in 1996

- Douglas Hogg, the Agriculture Minister, over the concealment of 'mad cow' disease in the early 1990s

- Jack Straw, the Home Secretary, for the accidental publication of the addresses of witnesses to the Macpherson inquiry on the police handling of the murder of Steven Lawrence, in 1999

- Jack Straw, the Home Secretary, for the protracted delays in the processing of passport applications in 1999

- Keith Vaz for misconduct in 2001.

It might be argued that it is no longer reasonable to hold ministers personally accountable for the actions of thousands of civil servants in their ministry. The huge growth of government, the rapid turnover of ministers, and the delegation of much of the administration to executive agencies at arm's length from the department (see Chapter 7) may well be reasons for weakening the convention in some instances.

This argument might exonerate Prior, who could not be personally blamed for prison breakouts, but hardly excuses Lamont, Waldegrave, Lyell, Hogg, and Vaz, who had direct personal responsibility for their errors. They clung to office to avoid damaging not only their own careers but, more important, their government's reputation. The convention, in reality, is to cling on to office for as long as possible, and only resign if forced to. If it is true that the convention of ministerial responsibility often does not work, then one of the mechanisms of government accountability is severely weakened.

Secrecy

The British political system is one of the most secretive among modern democracies (see Chapter 21). Not only are state institutions and officials protected by the sweeping and powerful Official Secrets Act 1989, but freedom of information provisions are by most standards, weak and ineffective. If a virtue of the British constitution is that it concentrates power in a way that makes government effective, a weakness is that it protects government from close and constant inspection. If we cannot find out what public officials have done, how can we hold them accountable for their actions?

Unaccountable government?

In the 1960s and 1970s Britain was widely admired for its accountable single-party government. In the 1990s it was increasingly criticised for an executive that was too powerful and insufficiently accountable to Parliament and public opinion. The poll tax was probably the most conspicuous example (see Chapter 12). Hailed as 'one of the worst ideas in the world', it was approved by almost no one, except a few senior government members who pushed it through Parliament and against the will of the great majority of ordinary people. There is much truth in Gladstone's claim that the British constitution relies heavily on the good sense and faith of those who work it. What if they lack sense and good faith?

Inflexibility

While it is true that the British constitution has been flexible and adaptable, it is also true that it has difficulty in responding to some demands for reform – the reform of the House of Lords has been an unresolved issue for 100 years now. Government secrecy and the electoral system are other examples. The British constitution puts great power in the hands of the government, and they often have no wish to change rules that give them this power.

A democratic deficit?

Critics have pointed to many democratic weaknesses and failings of the British constitution – the unelected nature of the House of Lords, the unfairness of the electoral system, the absence of any Bill of Rights, the weakness of freedom of information provisions, secrecy, the over-centralisation of power in the hands of central government and the weakness of regional and local government, the weakness of the House of Commons, the strength of the executive, and an over-reliance on representative rather than participatory forms of government. As the cracks in the traditional constitution began to show more clearly towards the end of the twentieth century, the movement for constitutional reform grew stronger.

THE MOVEMENT FOR CONSTITUTIONAL REFORM

In the Victorian and Edwardian eras (1837–1914) issues of constitutional reform dominated the political agenda, pitched the parties into battle and inflamed the passions of politicians and people alike. The Chartist movement (a popular movement of the 1830s and 1840s that pressed for universal suffrage, a secret ballot, the abolition of the property qualification, equal constituencies, payment of MPs and annual elections), the Home Rule movement in Ireland and the Suffragette movement were associated with mass demonstrations, riots and even violence.

After 1918, constitutional issues played a smaller role. Combined Labour–Liberal attempts to introduce electoral reform in 1918 and 1929 were blocked by the House of Lords and killed by the landslide election victory of the National (effectively Conservative) government in 1931. After 1945 the Labour Party no longer favoured electoral reform, having been elected with a landslide victory in that year. In the 1960s and 1970s disgruntled backbench MPs occasionally complained about the growing dominance of the executive over Parliament. Sporadic electoral successes for the Welsh and Scottish nationalist parties in the 1960s and 1970s led to calls for greater autonomy or independence, but proposals failed in the referendums of 1979. The issue subsided under the newly elected Conservative government of 1979, which was strongly opposed to any form of devolution.

Since the mid-1980s, however, constitutional reform has returned to the political agenda. It remains an issue of no great interest to most voters in England. Even in Wales and Scotland, where it is more important, the 'bread and butter' issues of jobs, taxes, pensions and housing take priority. However, in political circles and the 'chattering classes' there has been a significant resurgence of interest in constitutional reform, focused particularly on the programme of the Charter 88 movement.

Charter 88

The core of the Charter 88 programme consists of:

- Scottish and Welsh Parliaments directly elected by some form of proportional representation, and with powers to tax

- devolution of power to the English regions, although not necessarily in the Welsh/Scottish form

- a proportional electoral system for national, local and European elections

- the reform of the House of Lords, to create a (mainly) directly elected second chamber and the abolition of hereditary members

- a freedom of information act to reduce secrecy in government

- a bill of rights, achieved by the incorporation of the European Convention on Human Rights into British law

- a written constitution and the establishment of a 'constitutionalist' culture.

RECENT CONSTITUTIONAL CHANGES

We have referred, so far in this chapter, to the 'traditional' constitution of 1911–1972 for the simple reason that the system has changed in the past 25 years. Much of the traditional constitution remains, of course, but starting with Britain's membership of the European Union in 1973, a serious of events and reforms have created a shift in constitutional arrangements.

Impact of Europe

It is not too much to say that Britain's joining (what was then called) the European Communities caused a constitutional earthquake. Earlier in this chapter (p. 92) we quoted Dicey's comment that Parliamentary sovereignty is the one fundamental law of the British constitution. Membership of the EC ended that (see Briefing 4.2) for it was completely unlike any previous international agreement. Signing a foreign treaty or joining an international organisation does not necessarily contravene Parliamentary sovereignty. Long before it joined the European Community Britain was a member of the United Nations, the North Atlantic Treaty Organisation (NATO) and GATT (the General Agreement on Tariffs and Trade). They imposed obligations on the British government but did not affect the right of Parliament to make or unmake any law.

BRIEFINGS

4.2 European law and Parliamentary sovereignty

The sovereignty of Parliament is the dominant characteristic of our political institutions... the principle of parliamentary sovereignty means neither more or less than this, namely, that Parliament thus defined has, under the English Constitution, the right to make or unmake any law whatever; and further, that no person or body is recognised by the law of England as having the right to override or set aside the legislation of Parliament.

A. V. Dicey, *Introduction to the Study of the Law of the Constitution*, London: Macmillan, 1952, p. 29

On the basis of the powers thus conferred on them, the Community institutions can enact legal instruments as a Community legislature legally independent of the Member States. Some of these instruments take effect directly as a Community law in the Member States, and thus do not require any transformation into national law in order to be binding, not only on Member States and their organs, but also on the citizen.

European Commission, *ABC of Community Law*, Luxembourg: European Documentation Series, 1991

Joining Europe was altogether different. The act of Parliament that legalised Britain's membership (the 1972 European Communities Act) incorporated the Treaty of Rome, and all the secondary legislation of the EC into British law, as well as the decisions of the European Court of Justice. For all practical purposes the 1972 Act commits Britain to obeying all present and future European laws, and therefore, binds successor Parliaments to accepting European law. Some constitutional commentators argue that Parliamentary sovereignty remains intact because Parliament can always repeal the 1972 Act, and rescind any other agreement with the EU. Technically this is so, but it remains a pure technicality so long as the chances of leaving the EU are negligible. Meanwhile, British courts must give precedence to European law.

The most striking example of a British court using European law to judge Parliamentary legislation is the *Factortame* case, which involved a claim by the owners of a Spanish fishing boat that the Merchant Shipping Act 1988 was contrary to EU law and should not be applied. The House of Lords unanimously held (subject to a European Court of Justice ruling in support of the EC rights claimed by the fishermen) that EU law should prevail over the 1988 Act. The *Factortame* case is significant because it showed, beyond all doubt, that British courts could now do more than declare government actions illegal – they could declare acts of Parliament illegal, which ended the principle of Parliamentary sovereignty. There are many similar, although less fundamental, cases of British law being overturned by European law. Briefing 4.3 gives a small but telling example.

In sum, membership of the EU has:

1. brought an end to Parliamentary sovereignty
2. strengthened the constitutional power of the courts.

BRIEFINGS

4.3 Case 121/85 *Conegate v Commissioners of Customs and Excise* [1986] ECR 1007

Inflatable sex dolls imported into the UK were seized by Customs and Excise. The importers claimed that seizure was contrary to Article 30 of the EC Treaty, which prohibits obstructions to free trade between member states. The ECJ held that the fact that the goods cause offence was not enough to justify a ban on their import. Imports could not be banned when there was no corresponding prohibition on their internal domestic distribution.

Referendums

The UK has increasingly used national referendums to ratify major constitutional changes, even though referendums do not fit easily with the principles of Parliamentary sovereignty and representative democracy, and even though the constitution itself does not require referendums for constitutional change. The first, a national referendum on the European Union in 1975, was followed by referendums on Scottish and Welsh devolution in 1979 and 1997. Referendums have been used by local authorities to decide which political structure to adopt (Local Government Act 2000), and a national referendum is promised on whether the UK should join the euro.

Judicial review

The growth of judicial review started before membership of the EU gave the courts additional power. Some of the most important cases are discussed in Chapter 19, but here it is important to note that:

- The courts of Britain have been increasingly willing since the 1960s to take a more proactive role in reviewing the decisions and actions of politicians in both central and local government.

- A small proportion of cases have introduced radically different constitutional principles. For example, in 1993 the House of Lords ruled that the Home Secretary was in contempt of court in his action on an asylum case. The case was important because it deprived ministers of their age-old right to claim Crown immunity for their actions.

- The number of applications for judicial review has multiplied many times since the early 1980s. Many of them fail, but the growth shows that judicial review, like referendums, are an integral part of the constitutional system.

NEW LABOUR'S 'CONSTITUTIONAL PROJECT'

The constitutional implications of membership of the EU, referendums, and judicial review are profound in themselves, but the election of New Labour in 1997 resulted in even more far-reaching change.

From the mid-1930s to the mid-1980s the Labour Party was traditionalist about constitutional issues, although a few MPs (eg the left-wing MP Tony Benn) supported it. Labour supporters of Charter 88 were an exception. Most Labour leaders saw little need for reform, given that the system enabled them to win power periodically. Left-wingers such as Michael Foot (Labour leader 1980–3) were as likely to take this view as right-wingers.

Labour's change of heart had several causes:

1. The Party had been an impotent opposition for 18 years (1979–97) and the fear that it might not win another election made constitutional reform more attractive, as well driving it closer to the nationalists and Liberal Democrats, who favoured reform. This might have been especially important in a 'hung Parliament' (where no one party has a working majority) requiring coalition government.

2. Many were dismayed by what they regarded as the Conservative governments' (1979–97) excessive secrecy, disregard for individual and group rights, and increasing concentration of political power in their own hands.

3. The lack of power of backbench MPs in the two main parties.

4. In theory, the House of Lords acts as a constitutional backstop, but its large Conservative majority on most issues meant that it rarely opposed Conservative government measures.

5. Scottish Labour was converted to the merits of a Scottish Parliament because from 1979 to 1997 Scotland was ruled by a Conservative government, even though an overwhelming proportion of Scots voted against it. Scottish Nationalists effectively exploited this situation to campaign for an independent Scotland, steadily increased their vote, and replaced the Conservatives as the main challengers in Labour areas. For the Labour Party acceptance of a Scottish Parliament – which Labour would anyway expect to dominate – was seen as a small but necessary price to pay for heading off the SNP and dishing the Tories in Scotland.

6. Once the case for a Scottish Parliament was conceded, it followed that the Welsh should have an Assembly of their own (see Chapter 11 on Scotland and Wales), and perhaps also the English regions and the large metropolitan areas as well.

In office the Labour government moved with remarkable speed on some matters, but slowly on others.

Independence for the Bank of England

Within four days of being elected, Gordon Brown, the Labour Chancellor of the Exchequer, announced to almost everyone's surprise, that the Bank of England would follow the pattern of many central banks in Europe, and have the power to set interest rates independently of the government. Although not a major constitutional change in itself, this signalled the willingness of the central government to devolve power.

Human rights

After many calls for a British Bill of Rights, and quite a few failed attempts in Parliament, the Human Rights Act was passed in 1998. This incorporates into British law the European Convention on Human Rights which is implemented by the European Court of Human Rights (ECHR) in Strasbourg (see Chapter 9). It empowers the courts to strike down British secondary legislation that is inconsistent with it. For its part, the government is now required to ensure that its legislation is consistent with the Convention. One important little corner of the Act, however, tries to protect the old constitutional order. To preserve 'Parliamentary sovereignty' (or the myth that it still exists) the courts cannot strike down Parliamentary legislation, but can only issue a 'declaration of incompatibility'. It is not clear what would happen if the government or Parliament chose to ignore such a declaration.

It is much too early to tell what the effect of the Human Rights Act will be. Many cases with important constitutional implications are before the courts, and critics claim that they will grow to the point where they choke the system, and give the judges too much political power. Defenders claim that the Act is long overdue as a protector of individual rights, that the courts will act cautiously, and that the current backlog of cases before the House of Lords will decline as the new system begins to work. Some go further and argue that a special court, a Constitutional Court, should be created to deal with important constitutional cases.

Scottish and Welsh devolution

After the two referendums on Scottish and Welsh devolution in 1997, the Scotland Act 1998 turned over large areas of Scottish government to the Scottish Parliament, including most social, educational and health services, police, transport, agriculture, housing, local government, and economic development. However, the Parliament has only limited taxation powers and most of its money comes in central government grants. The Government of Wales Act 1998 gives fewer service responsibilities and no taxing powers to the Welsh Assembly. Some feel that the arrangements in Scotland and Wales are inherently unstable: they will result in attempts by both regions to wrest more power from central government, and in demands for equal powers to be devolved to English regions. They also create an anomaly (the 'West Lothian question') whereby Scottish

MPs in the House of Commons can speak and vote on questions of relevance to the English regions, but English MPs in the Commons cannot speak or vote on matters of relevance to Scotland before the Scottish Parliament. The same is true of Welsh members of Parliament.

Home Rule in Northern Ireland

Between 1972 and 1997 Northern Ireland was ruled from London, but as a result of the Good Friday Agreement of 1998 (confirmed by a referendum in the same year) the Northern Ireland Assembly at Stormont was re-elected in June 1998. Its powers are similar, but not identical, to those of the Scottish Parliament. The long-term fate of the NI Assembly remains in the balance, however, after devolved government was suspended in October 2002 (see Chapter 10).

London government

The Greater London Authority Act 1999 provides for a directly elected executive Mayor of London and a separately elected London Assembly with 25 members. They took office in July 2000, and have responsibility, in consultation with the 32 London boroughs, for metropolitan-wide policies, including London transport, police, fire, emergency planning, economic development, the environment, and culture. Most of the Authority's £36 million budget is met by a central government grant. Although the London Mayor has little formal political power, the current holder Ken Livingstone, has high political visibility and, along with the First Minister in Scotland and the First Secretary in Wales is a political influence outside central government. Livingstone's battles with central government over the funding of the London underground have hit the newspaper headlines many times, and the introduction of a £5 charge on vehicles driving into central London was also well publicised.

The House of Lords

As a first stage of reform the House of Lords Act 1999 removed most hereditary peers from the Lords (they have now gone), leaving Life Peers in control. The second stage of reform is not yet decided, although the opposition parties and many Labour MPs want an almost wholly elected Chamber with greater powers than the present House of Lords.

The Labour government therefore has to decide between a largely appointed or elected Upper House. An appointed House, composed of elder statesmen and eminent figures from various fields of life, might lack democratic legitimacy, being regarded as the creature of party patronage, particularly the Prime Minister's. Contrariwise, a directly elected Upper House would have democratic credentials, but might, therefore challenge the House of Commons. This dilemma slowed the second stage of Lords reform after 1999, and stalled it in February 2003 when all the government's proposals for reform were rejected by the House of Commons.

Electoral reform

From the beginning Britain has used the first past the post electoral system in general elections. This simple voting method often produces single-party government in Parliament. Hence the voting system is associated with the constitutional merits of stable and accountable single-party government in the House of Commons. By the same token, it is also associated with electoral unfairness (disproportionality) in which major parties are favoured and minor ones discriminated against. In the general election of 1983, for example, the Conservatives took 42 per cent of the general poll but 62 per cent of Parliamentary seats, compared with the Liberal Democrats who took 25 per cent of the poll and 4 per cent of seats. In the 2001 election Labour took 41 per cent of the vote and 63 per cent of the seats.

Labour has contemplated electoral reform for some time, and when it came to power in 1997 it introduced the additional member system for Welsh, Scottish, and London Assembly elections (for details of voting systems see Chapter 15). For the London mayoral elections, however, Labour introduced the supplementary vote, while in elections for the European Parliament it introduced, in accordance with a European directive, a version of the regional list system (the European Parliamentary Elections Act 1999). In Northern Ireland the single transferable vote system is used for the Assembly and the European Parliament. So far, however, general and local elections still use the first past the post or simple majority systems. The result is that five different election systems are currently used in the UK. But the main target of criticism – the use of the first past the post voting in general and local elections – remains unreformed.

Labour is deeply ambivalent about reforming the voting system for general elections. A Labour Party commission on electoral reform (the Plant Commission) was divided on the issue. On the one hand, Labour is acutely aware that the Conservatives won four successive elections with a minority of votes between 1979 and 1993, and had sufficiently large Parliamentary majorities to push through unpopular policies such as the water and railway privatisation, the poll tax, and VAT on fuel. On the other hand, changing to a proportional representation (PR) system would have two major drawbacks for Labour. First, some Labour MPs would lose their seats under PR. Second, no party has won more than 50 per cent of the Parliamentary vote since 1935, and a proportional system would almost certainly mean coalition government in the House of Commons. Electoral reform might well mean the end of single-party Conservative government, it is true, but by the same token, it would mean that Labour would always have to share power with the Liberal Democrats or nationalists, or perhaps both.

Disproportionality (the opposite of proportionality)
Occurs when the seats in a representative body are not distributed in relationship to votes. Proportionality (proportional representation) occurs, therefore, when there is a closer relationship between the distribution of seats and votes.

Referendums

New Labour built on the practice of calling referendums on major national issues by holding four within the first two years of its office (Welsh and Scottish devolution in 1997, and London government and the Good Friday Agreement in Northern Ireland a year later). It has promised two more on a new electoral system and Britain joining the euro, when the time comes.

Freedom of information

After delay, backbench revolts and much criticism, the Freedom of Information Act was passed in 2000. The Act is supposed to provide a general right of access to all types of recorded information held by public authorities. It places obligations on public authorities to observe these rights, and creates an Information Commissioner to enforce them. However, there are a great many exemptions to the Act (on commercial and public interest grounds) and, in any case, ministers and local government can simply veto requirements by the Information Commissioner to divulge information. As a result many believe that the Act is no real improvement on the voluntary code of practice it replaced.

It is also argued that even if the Freedom of Information Act is claimed to be a small step forward, two other Acts are a step back. The Regulation of Investigatory Powers Act 2000 gives government access to electronic information previously not available to it, and the Terrorist Act 2000 broadens and strengthens government powers.

Department for Constitutional Affairs

In 2003 the office of the Lord Chancellor (1,400 years old) was replaced by a Secretary of State for Constitutional Affairs. This means the end of the Lord Chancellor as Speaker of the House of Lords, cabinet member, and head of the judiciary. A new Supreme Court, to replace the Law Lords, and an independent judicial appointments commission are promised.

The incomplete programme

Experts on constitutional matters differ widely on the significance of New Labour's constitutional project. Some claim that British government is pretty much as secretive, powerful, and unaccountable as it ever was. Others argue that it has modified but not transformed the cohesive, unitary, and flexible nature of the traditional system. A third school of thought claims that the innovations after 1972, and even after 1997, amount to nothing less than a constitutional revolution.

What is probably beyond argument, however, is the claim that New Labour's project is unfinished and may yet turn out to be unstable. The Welsh, Scottish and London authorities are likely to push for greater devolved powers, and English regions may want the same powers. With the Northern Ireland Assembly suspended, the fate of the Province is uncertain. After failing to get agreement in 2003, reform of the House of Lords is incomplete. Some important reforms of the Lord Chancellor's functions are to be decided. Election reform is hanging. Other fundamental matters have barely been tackled: the weakness of the House of Commons, government secrecy, the financing of political parties. Freedom of information is still unresolved.

We will return to the issue of democracy and the British constitution at the end of the book (Chapter 28), after looking at greater depth at particular parts of it in the chapters that follow. Meanwhile we can note that the issue remains a hotly contested and very topical one that is still far from resolved.

SUMMARY

This chapter has summarised the main sources and features of Britain's 'unwritten constitution', starting from the question of whether it really is a constitution at all. Certainly its informal and diffuse nature leaves it open to manipulation by the powerful central governments it has helped to create, and this has been a source of growing concern. The particular constitutional features highlighted by this chapter are:

- the partially written and wholly uncodified nature of the British constitution

- the extent to which these have to be supplemented by 'conventions', practices or customs that can, however, be radically reinterpreted, or even ignored, if it suits the party in power

- the principal doctrines of the traditional constitution: a unitary state; Parliamentary sovereignty; constitutional monarchy; power concentrated within central government; government accountability; and representative (rather than direct) democracy.

However:

- Defenders of the traditional constitution argue that it has produced a durable basis for democracy with stable, effective, and moderate government that works pragmatically.

- Critics argue that the conventions of ministerial and Cabinet accountability do not always work, and that secrecy, inflexibility, and too much power in central government's hands, create an 'elective dictatorship'.

- Changes in the traditional constitution were brought about by membership of the EU, and by the willingness of British courts to play a larger role in constitutional matters (judicial review).

- New Labour's constitutional project resulted in an unprecedented series of reforms in the short span between 1997 and 2000. Some argue these have had profound effects on the traditional constitution, some that the effects are modest, but all agree that the reform programme is still incomplete.

ESSAYS

1. Do you agree that Labour reforms, 1997–2000, have changed the British constitution profoundly?

2. Is it fair to say that the traditional British constitution of 1911–72 was marked by the characteristics of government secrecy, conventions of ministerial and Cabinet responsibility that often did not work, lack of government accountability, and elective dictatorship?

3. Do you agree that Britain needs a written constitution? Why or why not?

MILESTONES

Milestones in British constitutional development

1215 Magna Carta (The Great Charter). English Barons force King John to recognise their personal rights (which later extend to all freemen) and their right to collective consultation about important matters

1296–1306 Edward I begins to summon representatives of towns and counties, regularly, along with the Lords, to agree to taxation for the Scottish wars. In return, the King makes concessions to meet their requests, a process that continues for the next 200 years

1532–59 Parliament is used by the Tudor monarchs to ratify the most important royal actions (settling succession, setting up Protestant Church, etc)

1640–51 Parliament fights Civil War against Crown and wins. Establishes its supremacy over the Law Courts

1688–9 Bill of Rights. Parliament deposes James II and installs William III as king (the Glorious Revolution). It reaffirms that taxes can only be raised with its consent and affirms specific citizens' rights

1701 Act of Settlement. Parliament establishes (Protestant) succession

1707 Act of Union with Scotland. The English Parliament absorbs the Scottish one, but accepts the separate Scottish legal system and Church

1715–1832 The 'Eighteenth-Century Constitution'. The government has to be acceptable to the King but must also maintain a majority in the House of Commons. Party organisations ('Whigs' and 'Tories') develop from time to time to secure and organise this majority

1832 Great Reform Act substitutes election for ownership of seats as the basis for representation in the House of Commons. Election is within small constituencies by plurality vote on first past the post system

1838 Accession of the 18-year-old Victoria marks end of active involvement of monarch with the government, which is now effectively nominated by the largest party in the House of Commons

1867 Second Reform Act (Representation of the People Act) extends franchise to most male town dwellers

1868–89 Conservative and Liberal parties create mass organisations throughout Britain and alternate in government with support of a Commons majority

1884 Third Reform Act (Representation of the People Act) extends franchise to most male country dwellers

1911 Parliament Act. Reforming Liberal government with support of Commons majority restricts powers of (hereditary) House of Lords: (a) over financial bills, (b) to delaying any legislation for only three years

1918 Representation of the People Act enfranchises all remaining males over 21 and women over 30

1922 Government of Ireland Act sets up regional Parliament and government in Northern Ireland

1928 Representation of the People Act gives women the vote on the same terms as men

1949 Parliament Act. Reforming Labour government restricts delaying powers of House of Lords to one year

1963 Peerage Act. Creation of 'life peers' to serve in House of Lords but not to pass on title to children

1969 Representation of the People Act reduces voting age to 18

1972 European Communities Act. Britain accedes to the EU Parliament and accepts that all previous European legislation and judicial decisions are binding and European legislation superior to British legislation

1973–4 UK Parliament abolishes Northern Irish government and Parliament

1986 Single European Act extends competence of EU. Qualified majority voting in the Council of Ministers means that UK government cannot veto European provisions it disagrees with, in the areas where they apply

1993 Treaty of Maastricht further extends European Union's area of jurisdiction and use of qualified majority voting

1997 New Labour government accepts the Social Chapter of the Treaty of Maastricht. Bank of England given powers to set the interest rate. Referendums on Welsh and Scottish devolution

1998 Human Rights Act. Scotland Act. Government of Wales Act. Referendum on the Good Friday Agreement followed by Northern Ireland Act and reintroduction of Home Rule for Northern Ireland. London referendum

1999 First election to Scottish Parliament and Welsh Assembly, under system of proportional representation. Greater London Authority Act. House of Lords Act. European Parliamentary Elections Act to introduce the regional list voting system

2000 Freedom of Information Act. Representation of the People Act (introduces various measures to encourage turnout)

2002 Official proposals for regional government in England

2003 Department for Constitutional Affairs replaces Lord Chancellor's Department

PROJECTS

1. Imagine that you are Home Secretary. How would you complete reform of the House of Lords and how would you change, if at all, the electoral system for general and local elections?

2. (For groups) Each member of the group to take one of the following and discuss the respects in which it does and does not change the traditional British constitution of 1911–72: the Human Rights Act 1998; the Scotland Act and the Government of Wales Act 1998; the Greater London Authority Act 1999; Freedom of Information Act 2000; and the Regulation of Investigatory Powers Act 2000.

FURTHER READING

The best and most recent introduction to the traditional constitution and recent changes is Anthony King, *Does the United Kingdom Still Have a Constitution?* (London: Sweet & Maxwell, 2001). Assessments of Labour's constitutional project can be found in David Beetham, Pauline Ngan, and Stuart Weir, 'Democratic audit: Labour's record so far', *Parliamentary Affairs*, **54**, 2001, pp. 376–90, and R. Hazell, et al, 'The constitution: coming in from the cold', *Parliamentary Affairs*, **55**, 2002, pp. 219–34.

For a recent and brief summary of constitutional reform see A. Granath, 'Constitutional reform: a work in progress', *Talking Politics*, **14** (3), 2002, pp. 103–6; and N. Smith, 'New Labour and constitutional reforms', *Talking Politics*, **14** (1), 2002, pp. 24–7.

The publications of the Charter 88 group provide the standard arguments for constitutional reform. The Constitution Unit of University College London publishes a series of papers and up-to-date articles on various aspects of constitutional reform. For the details of Charter 88 see R. Holme and M. Eliot (eds), *1688–1888, Time for a New Constitution* (London: Macmillan, 1988).

USEFUL WEB SITES ON THE BRITISH CONSTITUTION

Hot links to these sites can be found on the CWS at http://www.booksites.net/budge. As a first step you can visit www.historylearningsite.co.uk/british_constitution.htm, which provides a comprehensive introduction to the core doctrines informing the British Constitution. There are also some sites containing information on the sources of constitutional authority, for example, the British Library offers an electronic version of the Magna Carta at www.bl.uk/collections/treasures/magna.html. An interesting description of the 1689 Bill of Rights can be found at www.royal.gov.uk/output/page100.asp. For the Reform Act of 1832 see www.spartacus.schoolnet.co.uk/PR1832.htm, which contains historical information as well as comments from contemporary actors. The main governmental site containing constitutional information is the Parliament site www.parliament.uk.

The evolution of constitutional reform can be traced in various sources. The constitution secretariat page offers important insights into devolution and the reform of the House of Lords www.cabinet-office.gov.uk/constitution/. The main advocate of constitutional reform in the UK is Charter 88, whose web site is available at www.charter88.org.uk. Academic commentary and analysis on constitutional issues are available from The Constitution Unit at University College London www.ucl.ac.uk/constitution-unit. Finally, it is worth consulting the *Guardian*'s special report on constitutional reform www.politics.guardian.co.uk/constitution.

For the implications of British membership of the EU on the constitution, see www.europa.eu.int; the Home Office at www.homeoffice.gov.uk. Specific information on the European Court of Justice is available from www.curia.eu.int/en/index.htm.

CHAPTER 5

The Prime Minister, the Cabinet, and the Core Executive

As we have seen, the British constitution gives exceptional power to governments supported by a majority in the House of Commons. The Prime Minister is the most powerful member of the Cabinet and the Cabinet effectively *is* the Government. This makes them the most powerful people in Britain. The way they work together and with a small core of other political influentials raises a set of important and controversial questions about the British system of government. Has the office of Prime Minister (PM) been transformed from the traditional 'first among equals' into a powerful political executive akin, in many ways, to a president? Or is the Cabinet still the effective centre of all important decision making? How do the Prime Ministerial styles of Thatcher, Major and Blair compare, and what effect does this have on the fate of their governments?

The chapter is divided into seven main sections. They describe how the machinery of government works at this, the highest level, of government, and how different officials and agencies interact in the decision-making process. The chapter focuses on:

- the Prime Minister
- the Cabinet
- the Cabinet, departments, and joined-up government
- the eternal political triangle: departments, Cabinet, and Prime Minister
- Prime Ministerial styles: Thatcher, Major and Blair
- Prime Ministerial versus Cabinet government
- the Core Executive.

THE PRIME MINISTER

Prime Minister
The head of the executive branch of government and chair of the Cabinet.

Since Britain has no written constitution, the powers and duties of the Prime Minister are neither clearly defined nor legally limited. They have evolved according to historical circumstances since the first Prime Minister, Robert Walpole, took office in 1721. Since then there have been 51 Prime Ministers (post-war premiers are listed in Table 5.1), each exercising different authority in different ways. Consequently, it is difficult to state exactly what the job of the PM is. As one incumbent (Herbert Asquith, Prime Minister 1908–16) remarked, it is 'what the office holder chooses and is able to make of it'. It is clear that the Prime Minister is the head of government at home (the monarch is the Head of State), and the political representative of the country abroad, but this job description tion hides a multitude of responsibilities and powers. Among other things, the Prime Minister:

Table 5.1 *Post-war Prime Ministers*

Prime Minister	Dates	Party
Clement Attlee	1945–51	Labour
Sir Winston Churchill	1951–5	Conservative
Sir Anthony Eden	1955–7	Conservative
Harold Macmillan	1957–63	Conservative
Sir Alec Douglas-Home	1963–4	Conservative
Harold Wilson	1964–70	Labour
Edward Heath	1970–4	Conservative
Harold Wilson	1974–6	Labour
James Callaghan	1976–9	Labour
Margaret Thatcher	1979–90	Conservative
John Major	1990–7	Conservative
Tony Blair	1997–	Labour

- Decides the number and nature of Cabinet and government posts and who is to fill them. This requires restructuring the Cabinet and its membership from time to time.

- Chairs Cabinet meetings, manages their agendas and discussion, calls on speakers, sums up discussion, and directs the writing of minutes.

- Decides the number and nature of Cabinet committees, subcommittees, and ministerial groups, and appoints their chairs and members. Chairs some of the most important committees.

- Oversees the armed forces and security services.

- Manages relations between the Cabinet and the wider world of Parliament, the media, other countries, and international organisations – far and away the most important being the EU.

- Manages the flow of government information to the outside world.

- Answers formal questions in the House of Commons (Prime Minister's Questions – PMQs).

- Approves senior positions in the Civil Service and the diplomatic service. Recommends senior appointments in the Church of England, the judiciary, the Privy Council, quangos, and other civil positions.

- Recommends names for the honours list.

- Dissolves Parliament before calling an election.

- Takes the lead in any unexpected crisis of government and the governing party.

- Manages the majority party and maintains contact with its MPs and party headquarters.

- Maintains contact with heads of other states as necessary.

- Keeps watch on the broad political agenda and the course of government.

Even this list, long though it is, does not capture the staggering range and responsibilities of the Prime Minister. Being head of government involves many tasks ranging from formal representation of the nation and crisis management at home and abroad, to guiding the daily work of the government and maintaining contact with senior figures in the government, Parliament and Civil Service at home, and senior statesmen abroad. This means constant travel, a ceaseless round of meetings, an endless chain of decision making, and incessant public appearances.

BRIEFINGS

5.1 A day in the life of the Prime Minister

07.00	Wake
07.30	Family breakfast
08.00	Go over the day's diary with PM Office staff
08.30	Briefing meeting on political issue of the day
09.00	Meeting with No. 10 staff on education
10.00	Meeting on election reform
10.30	Briefing on PM question time
10.45	Visit the secretariat in the PM's Office
11.45	Briefing on freedom of information seminar
12.00	Seminar on freedom of information
	(Salad/sandwich lunch)
13.15	Interview with journalist
14.15	Seminar with policy advisers
15.15	Meeting with foreign head of state
16.00	Meeting with national politician
16.30	Meeting with top civil servant
17.00	Meeting with Cabinet colleague
17.30	Meeting with Cabinet colleague
18.00	Meeting about Cabinet committee business
19.30	Private dinner/family time
22.00	House of Commons vote/read official documents
23.00	Sleep

Note: Based on different sources

Margaret Thatcher, stormbird of British politics

It is clear, even from recent history, that Prime Ministers bring very different qualities, aptitudes, and interests to the job. Margaret Thatcher was possibly the most memorable Prime Minister of the post-war period, and she was unique in many respects. Although no feminist, she is the only woman to have held the post. She was also a woman with a mission – to regenerate Britain – and the force and energy she applied to the task stirred strong feelings of love or loathing.

From lower middle class origins (her father was a shopkeeper, but mayor of his town of Grantham) she went from the local grammar school to a chemistry degree at Oxford. She was elected President of the University Conservative Association. After a taking a law qualification, she pursued a conventional political career, entering Parliament as Conservative MP for Finchley in 1959. Within 11 years she was Minister of Education in the Heath government of 1970. After that her political career was not typical, however.

Two events precipitated her break with the 'social democratic consensus' that had prevailed since the war. One was the election defeat of the Conservative government in 1974, following strike action by trade unions. The other was her conversion to free market policies on the grounds that government failure was due to 'overloading' the state with too much taxation and too many responsibilities.

Winning the 1979 general election as the result of a general reaction to trade union action in the 'winter of discontent', she set out on a radical campaign to 'get government off the backs of the people' by cutting taxation and public services, reducing government regulation, and privatising state enterprises. Her three successive general election victories (1979, 1983, 1987) had a lot to do with her forceful and dynamic politics, which seemed to make her political position impregnable, in spite of an increasingly autocratic style. When this led to the hugely unpopular poll tax (substituting a personal for a property tax in local government), and open hostility with the Europhiles in her own party, her Cabinet dumped her for fear of losing the 1992 general election. She was the longest serving Prime Minister for 150 years and was replaced in No. 10 by John Major in 1990.

John Major: over-reaction to Thatcher?

John Major came from a poor London family. His father was a circus performer and a manufacturer of garden gnomes, and he left grammar school at 16 with almost no qualifications. He rose through banking and, after serving as a Conservative councillor in London, entered Parliament in 1979, four years earlier than Blair and in the same election that took Thatcher to power in Downing St. He was favoured by her during the 1980s precisely because he had no connections with the traditional Conservative grandees.

Ten years after his election to the Commons Thatcher made Major the Foreign Secretary, and in short order he became Leader of the House, Deputy Prime Minister, and Chancellor of the Exchequer. He replaced Thatcher as Prime Minister in 1990. Although a Thatcher supporter in the 1980s, he rapidly distanced his government from hers by abolishing the poll tax, taking up a more pro-European political stance, and adopting a radically different political style. He replaced the autocracy of the Thatcher era with something more collegial and unassuming. He succeeded in winning the 1992 election as a result but immediately ran into serious trouble when a mismanaged currency crisis forced the pound out of the European Monetary System. Subsequent government in-fighting over Europe, and a growing national concern over government 'sleaze' added to his reputation for being a weak and ineffective leader, and he was defeated spectacularly in the general election of 1997 by Blair and New Labour.

Tony Blair and New Labour

Blair and Major are a striking contrast in style and background. The paradox is that the Conservative Major comes from the kind of underprivileged background usually associated with Labour, while Blair shares an exclusive background with many Conservative MPs.

Born in Edinburgh in 1953, the son of a barrister and lecturer, Blair attended Fettes public school and went to Oxford to study law, then practised as a barrister in London. He was attracted to Labour by his Christian Socialist beliefs developed at university. He won his first Parliamentary election in 1983 and, with his excellent debating and political skills, rose quickly to a shadow Cabinet post in 1988. When the Labour leader, John Smith, died suddenly in 1994 Blair stepped into his shoes, and immediately set about changing the Labour Party along lines already initiated by his predecessors Kinnock and Smith.

Under the slogan 'New Labour New Britain', Blair led Labour away from its old policies of nationalisation, high taxation, universal welfare benefits, and alignment with the trade unions. In their place he put centrist ('Third Way') policies, cautious economics, low taxation, a leaning towards free markets, and support for the EU. He loosened Labour's close ties to the unions, and introduced the most modern of public relations systems into the party. He abolished Labour's Clause 4, which committed the party to public ownership, but emphasised the importance of high-quality education ('education, education, education'), and changed its image on law and order. As opposition spokesman on Home Affairs he caught the headlines and outflanked a startled Conservative government by claiming to be 'tough on crime, tough on the causes of crime'.

By taking the centre ground, he was able to maximise Labour's advantage over an unpopular and factious Conservative government in the mid-1990s, and was elected as Prime Minister by a landslide in 1997. Labour had been in opposition for 18 years. At 43 he was the youngest Prime Minister in almost 200 years, and the only post-war Prime Minister to take office without any previous government experience. He was also the first to have a child born at No. 10 Downing St for 150 years. Blair's goal, however, was not one term in office (five years) but two or three – to have the time to complete New Labour's agenda. The first term (1997–2001) was cautious in policy terms. Labour initially adopted the outgoing Conservative government's budget, but engaged in an ambitious programme of constitutional reform (see the previous chapter). The result was another landslide election victory in 2001.

Hiring and firing

As we have seen, Prime Ministers have an amazing array of powers and can do all sorts of things, in theory; in practice, their options are limited by the force of circumstances. To illustrate this we will focus on the power to hire and fire members of the Cabinet and the government, partly because it is so important, and partly because it illustrates the powers and limitations of the office very well.

In theory Prime Ministers have a free hand to decide how large or small their Cabinets are. In practice there are natural limits to Cabinet size. It is presently 23 strong, but it has been as small as 16, and during the war Churchill's Cabinet had ten members. For the most part, however, much less than 15 is too small to cover all the important aspects of modern government, and much more than 25 is too large for an effective committee. Most recent Prime Ministers have settled for a Cabinet of 20–23.

In theory, Prime Ministers can combine or divide Cabinet posts in any way they want. Major created the National Heritage Department with a Cabinet seat in 1992, but this was later changed to the Department for Culture, Media, and Sport. Harold Wilson created the Cabinet post of Deputy Prime Minister in 1964, and the position lives on today. Education can be a ministerial post on its own, or it can be combined with training and/or employment, and/or skills. Environmental matters could be grouped with agriculture, or local government, or with food and rural affairs (as at present). In practice, however, many Cabinet posts are more or less fixed – Chancellor of the Exchequer, Home Secretary, Foreign Secretary, and posts identified primarily with education, health, social services, transport, the environment, Scotland, Wales, and Northern Ireland (with devolution, these could conceivably be combined into a regional ministry).

In theory, Prime Ministers can fill Cabinet posts as they wish. In practice, they may be severely restricted in their choice:

- The convention is that most Cabinet members, and especially the most important ones, must be answerable to, and therefore members of, the House of Commons. This has 659 members.

- In single-party government Cabinet members must be drawn from the majority party – usually between 300–400 individuals.

- Some powerful figures virtually select themselves for high office – Blair must find Cabinet places for Prescott, Brown, Straw, and Blunkett.

- Other posts must be filled from a small pool of possibilities – the Welsh or Scottish offices are normally filled by Welsh and Scottish MPs.

- Some MPs are ruled out of holding government positions. Blair is unlikely to be able to reappoint his confidant Peter Mandelson to a Cabinet post.

- The Cabinet should be a balance of men and women, maturity and promise, different political factions (left and right, Europhiles and Europhobes). The PM must take care to keep the government together and not leave out a potentially disruptive faction.

- Having filled Cabinet posts, the PM must fill another 100 government posts from a total pool of as few as 300 people.

Once the political has-beens, the never-will-bes, and those with difficult political and personal histories have been ruled out, the Prime Minister may be left with rather little choice.

This is not to say that the PM has no room for manoeuvre. Some powerful political figures have been kept out of the Cabinet by their Prime Minister, or out of the Cabinet post they really wanted. Thatcher increasingly filled her Cabinet with political 'dries' (free market supporters), giving leading 'wets' (moderates) the minor jobs. Moreover, Prime Ministers reshuffle their Cabinet from time to time to bring in new talent, damage the careers of enemies, or to signal a shift in policy direction. The most famous recent example is the 'night of the long knives' in 1962, when Harold Macmillan sacked six Cabinet members. Between 1979 and 1990 Thatcher sacked 12 senior Cabinet members, and in a reshuffle in 1989 she changed 62 government positions.

Although some Cabinet reshuffling is normal and expected, it is notable that the changes of 1962 and 1989 were soon followed by Macmillan and Thatcher themselves falling from power. Drastic action seems to have signalled loss of Prime Ministerial control, rather than the exercise of it.

In sum, the PM's powers to hire and fire government members are, like many other functions of the office, a mixture of surprising freedom and tight constraint. There is often little choice, and some ministers choose themselves by virtue of their political position and stature. At the same time, some PMs have juggled with the careers of powerful people and have shaped governments to their own taste.

The Prime Minister's Office

We have emphasised the enormous number of Prime Ministerial tasks, and the extreme pressures of the job. Naturally, the PM does not carry this burden alone. He is supported by a staff of about 45 senior officials, and a total of over 200 people who constitute the Prime Minister's Office. Some are Civil Service appointments and others are purely political. The number in the Office is steadily rising and its organisation constantly changing, but the Office presently revolves around three basic units:

1. The **Policy Directorate** is the main point of contact between the PM and the government machine. It has two main sections:

   - The Private Office sifts the documents that flood into Downing Street, manages the PM's diary, briefs him, takes notes at his meetings, and liaises between him and the outside world. It has about 20 senior staff and works round the clock.

   - The Policy Unit has about a dozen senior advisers who draft policy documents.

2. The **Communications and Strategy Unit** has two main jobs:

   - Deals with government political communications of all kinds, both Prime Ministerial and departmental. *All* government press releases and briefing documents flow through this office. The Prime Minister's Press

Secretary is very influential, to the extent that Thatcher's (Bernard Ingham) was known as the 'real Deputy Prime Minister'.

- Strategic planning.

3. The **Government Relations Unit** handles relations with ministers, departments, the Labour Party, and other outside bodies.

The Prime Minister's Office works closely with the Cabinet Office (see later), and with the Whip's Office in Parliament (see Chapter 18), and has close and constant contact with all the main executive agencies and government departments in Whitehall, including the Deputy Prime Minister's Office, which was created in 2002. Under Blair, the PMs Office and the Cabinet Office have become, in effect, a single, centralised executive office.

The kitchen Cabinet

Kitchen Cabinet
The loose and informal policy advice group that Prime Ministers may collect around them, and that may include politicians, public officials, and private citizens.

This is not the end of the story. Prime Ministers often gather around them a collection of personal friends and advisers they can trust. They are often private individuals, not government officials, but they have direct access ('face time') to the PM. They are often resented by 'regular' politicians and civil servants, although one can appreciate the PM's need for advice he can trust from outside official circles. Thatcher and Blair seem to have made extensive use of their kitchen Cabinets, but Major relied more on the Cabinet.

We can only speculate about the Blair kitchen Cabinet, for it is, by definition, a changing and closed circle of people, but the same names tend to reoccur: the Chief of Staff, Jonathan Powell; policy advisers, David Miliband (now an MP), Geoff Norris, and Fiona Millar are all members of the Prime Minister's Office; Professor Anthony Giddens, former Director of the London School of Economics and theoretician of the 'Third Way'; Lord Levy, party fundraiser and envoy to the Middle East; Philip Gould, a strategy and polling adviser. Peter Mandelson is no longer such a central figure.

THE CABINET

The Cabinet must not be confused with the government. There are usually 20–25 Cabinet members but over 100 people in the government, which includes Cabinet ministers, junior ministers, and Parliamentary private secretaries. Most Cabinet members are drawn from the House of Commons because of the convention that they should be accountable to the elected chamber of government, but some come from the Lords. The Lord Chancellor, the highest legal officer in the country, is the main member of the Lords to hold a Cabinet position. Most Cabinet members are ministers who run Whitehall departments, but some do not have such duties and can range over policy issues without the burden of departmental responsibilities (Table 5.2).

Cabinet
The committee of the leading members of the government who are empowered to make decisions on behalf of the government.

The Cabinet, like the office of Prime Minister, has changed over time. Churchill had only five to eight members in his wartime Cabinet, and experimented with

Name	Office	Age 2003
Tony Blair	Prime Minister, First Lord of the Treasury, Minister for the Civil Service	50
John Prescott	Deputy Prime Minister	66
Gordon Brown	Chancellor of the Exchequer	53
Lord Falconer of Thoroton	Secretary of State for Constitutional Affairs and Lord Chancellor for the transitional period	51
Jack Straw	Secretary of State for Foreign and Commonwealth Affairs	58
David Blunkett	Secretary of State for the Home Department	57
Margaret Beckett	Secretary of State for Environment, Food and Rural Affairs	61
Baroness Amos	Secretary of State for International Development	58
Alistair Darling	Secretary of State for Transport, Secretary of State for Scotland	51
John Reid	Secretary of State for Health	46
Paul Murphy	Secretary of State for Northern Ireland	56
Peter Hain	Leader of the House of Commons, Lord Privy Seal, and Secretary of State for Wales	53
Geoff Hoon	Secretary of State for Defence	51
Andrew Smith	Secretary of State for Work and Pensions	50
Lord Williams of Mostyn	Leader of the House of Lords	62
Patricia Hewitt	Secretary of State for Trade and Industry, Minister for Women	63
Charles Clarke	Secretary of State for Education and Skills	53
Tessa Jowell	Secretary of State for Culture, Media, and Sport	57
Hilary Armstrong	Parliamentary Secretary, Treasury and Chief Whip	59
Ian McCartney	Minister without Portfolio and Party Chair	57
Paul Boateng	Chief Secretary to the Treasury	53
Also attending the Cabinet		
Lord Grocott	Lords Chief Whip and Captain of the Gentlemen at Arms	64

Table 5.2 *The Labour Cabinet, 2003*

Note: Salaries: the Prime Minister's salary is £171,554. Other Cabinet ministers are paid £124,979, with a few exceptions.

Source: The government web site

16 'overlords' in 1951. The experiment did not last long and soon the Cabinet returned to its normal size. Whatever its size and composition, the Cabinet is the central committee of government. Its main purposes are:

- to take major government decisions and approve government policy
- to reconcile the responsibilities of ministers to their individual departments with their responsibilities to the government as a whole
- to resolve any differences between ministers acting in their departmental capacities.

The Cabinet co-ordinates the policies of Whitehall departments and directs the work of government as a whole. As such it is the 'central committee' of the government executive, and it either discusses and makes important decisions, or ratifies the decisions of Cabinet committees. The main concepts of Cabinet government are listed in Briefing 5.2.

BRIEFINGS

5.2 Key concepts of Cabinet government

Adversarial decision making The clash between differing department views, which extends to the departmental ministers in the Cabinet, and which conflicts with Cabinet collegiality and collective responsibility.

Cabinet government The theory that the Cabinet forms a collective political executive in British government and thus constrains the power of the Prime Minister. In Cabinet government the principle of collective responsibility means the Cabinet discusses and makes important political decisions, or is consulted about them.

Collective responsibility The principle that decisions of the Cabinet are binding on all members of the government, who must support them in public in order to maintain a united government front, or resign their government post.

Core Executive The web of institutions, networks, people and practices that operate around the Prime Minister and Cabinet, and the people and agencies that serve them. The Core Executive is made up of the most influential officials, individuals, committees, bodies, and agencies with an influence on important government decisions.

Departmental government The theory that British government is made up of a set of distinct and autonomous Whitehall departments, each with its own long-term plans and commitments, and relatively unco-ordinated by the Cabinet and Prime Minister.

Joined-up government The attempt, particularly associated with New Labour, to overcome departmental government and produce integrated and co-ordinated policies stretching across all relevent Whitehall departments.

Prime Ministerial government The theory that the office of the Prime Minister is now so powerful that it forms the political executive, the 'efficient secret of government', that effectively makes the decisions, with the Cabinet little more than a 'dignified' part that rubberstamps Prime Ministerial decisions.

Collective responsibility
The principle whereby decisions and policies of the Cabinet are binding on all members of the government who must support them in public, to maintain a united front, or resign their government post.

Collective responsibility

As a collective decision-making body the Cabinet is bound by the principle of 'collective responsibility'. It may be the centre of acute conflict in the privacy of the Cabinet room, but it must present a united front in public. As the nineteenth-century Prime Minister, Lord Melbourne, said: 'It doesn't matter what we say as long as we all say the same thing.' Cabinet discussions are secret (members sign the Official Secrets Act) and, to preserve the appearance of unanimity, the Prime Minister sums up the mood of the meeting, which adds to the PM's power. Votes in Cabinet are rare.

As we saw in the previous chapter, the nature of collective responsibility is changing. Originally applied only to the Cabinet, it now covers all government members. Between 1994 and 1997 the Labour Party also extended it to members of its shadow Cabinet. Contrariwise, the government suspended collective responsibility in 1975 and 1977 over the issue of the European Union. In 1994 a Cabinet minister, Michael Portillo, made thinly veiled criticisms of the Cabinet's European policy, but was not disciplined in public. Some ministers have also circumvented collective responsibility by leaking documents. The principle of collective responsibility, it seems, is now applied more broadly but also more weakly.

Cabinet committees

Established during the crisis years of the Second World War as a way of doing Cabinet work quickly and efficiently in small groups, Cabinet committees now play an important part in government. According to Cabinet Office information: 'Both Committees and Subcommittees act by implied devolution of authority from the Cabinet and their decisions therefore have the same formal status as decisions of the full Cabinet.' This means, presumably, that committee decisions do not need Cabinet agreement or ratification.

The Prime Minister decides the number, terms of reference, membership and chairs of committees (Table 5.3). Most are composed of Cabinet members, but some include junior ministers and senior civil servants. There are two main types of Cabinet committee:

- **Ministerial committees and subcommittees** These deal with the permanent policy areas of government, such as domestic affairs and economic affairs. Subcommittees cover special topics within committee areas. Normally committees are chaired by the Cabinet minister responsible for the area.

- **Ministerial groups** These deal with short-term matters, such as the Millennium Dome, Wembley Stadium, and the Manchester Commonwealth Games.

Ad hoc committees were a device much used by Mrs Thatcher to bypass formal discussion in her Cabinet and committees. She could fill them with her own nominees and so get her own way. John Major's more consensual style resulted in more discussion in full Cabinet. Blair comes between Major and Thatcher: on some matters he seems to push his own initiatives through ad hoc committees; on others he uses the full Cabinet. One of the most interesting Blair initiatives is a Joint Consultative Committee with the Liberal Democratic Party (JCC). Although the work of the Committee was suspended in 2001, it was important because it broke the constitutional convention that government committees were composed only of government members and total confrontation with opposition parties. It provided a political device to put pressure on traditionalists within the Cabinet who opposed change, as well as being a way of isolating the Conservative opposition.

The Cabinet Office

Just as Prime Ministers have their Office, so the Cabinet has its Cabinet Office or secretariat. It consists of about 50 senior civil servants and more than 2,000 staff, whose job is to timetable meetings, prepare agendas and documents, and draft and circulate minutes. The secretariat is so important that its head, the Secretary

The Cabinet | 123

Table 5.3 *Cabinet Committee structure*

Cabinet committees change over time, and ad hoc groups dealing with specific matters often have a short life. In 2002 there were 20 committees, 23 subcommittees, and six ministerial groups. The following are examples.

Ministerial Sub-Committee on European Issues (EP)

Chair	Secretary of State for Foreign and Commonwealth Affairs
Membership	This a large committee with 21 Cabinet ministers, plus the Attorney-General, the Minister for the Cabinet Office, the Minister of State, Foreign and Commonwealth Office, the UK Permanent Representative to the EU, and others as business requires
Terms of reference	'To determine the United Kingdom's policies on European Union issues; and to oversee the United Kingdom's relationships with other member states and principal partners of the European Union'

Ministerial Subcommittee on International Terrorism (DOP (IT))

Chair	Prime Minister
Membership	PM plus seven senior Cabinet members representing Home, Foreign, and Defence affairs, International Development, Defence, and the Treasury, plus the Chief of Defence Staff and Attorney-General and other ministers and heads of intelligence agencies, as necessary
Terms of reference	'To keep under review the government's policy on international terrorism, in particular the political, military and humanitarian response to the attacks in the United States on 11 September and preventative security measures in the United Kingdom and overseas'

Ministerial Group on Wembley Stadium (MISC 12)

Chair	Secretary of State for Foreign and Commonwealth Affairs, and for Culture, Media and Sport (alternate chair)
Composition	Two Cabinet ministers representing Transport and the Treasury, plus the Junior Minister for Culture, Media and Sport
Terms of reference	'To consider options and policies for the government's approach towards the redevelopment of Wembley Stadium'

Source: The government web site

of the Cabinet, is the country's senior civil servant. The Cabinet Secretary is in daily contact with the Prime Minister and Cabinet members, attends Cabinet meetings (although not for party political items) and some Cabinet committees. Cabinet committees, made up mainly of politicians, are shadowed by a set of 'official committees' of civil servants who prepare the work for committees, and follow up their decisions.

The Cabinet Office is a nerve centre of government. It liaises closely with the Prime Minister's Office. Through its Office of Public Service (OPS) it oversees the management of the Civil Service, through its European secretariat it co-ordinates government business with the EU, and through its six main secretariats it helps to co-ordinate the work of the government and Whitehall departments.

THE CABINET, DEPARTMENTS, AND JOINED-UP GOVERNMENT

The Cabinet has many responsibilities and roles. Politically, it must decide government policy and what legislation to put before Parliament. Administratively, it must ensure the efficient and effective functioning of government departments. Collectively, it must resolve disputes between departments, political factions, and individual ministers. These functions overlap, of course, with those of the Prime Minister, which is why the Cabinet Office and Prime Minister's Offices collaborate so closely.

As the highest committee of government, the Cabinet is especially important as the place where final decisions are made if they cannot be taken elsewhere, either because they are so important, or because they arouse inter-departmental conflict. Naturally, each ministry is deeply concerned with its own business and interests, and since these often conflict, they have to be resolved somehow. Cabinet is the place to do it.

Even if there is no conflict, policies still have to be co-ordinated, for few policy decisions can be made by one department acting alone. Building a motorway affects the environment, has an impact on agriculture and consequences for other forms of transport, and costs money that could be spent on other services. One of the most difficult problems of government is that ministries often take a narrow view of their own policy interests and neglect their effects on other departments. It is actually very easy for one department to pursue a policy that is simply incompatible with another's, and even for units within the same ministry to do the same. The larger and more complex modern society and the larger and more complex its administration, the more difficult it is to achieve 'joined-up' government, and the more crucial the role of co-ordinating institutions. The Cabinet is supposed to be the centre of joined-up government, and a hallmark of the Blair government is the drive to integrate and co-ordinate government policies.

To this end a set of bodies and procedures have been created within the Prime Ministerial and Cabinet Offices:

- the Social Exclusion Unit to implement a single policy against poverty and deprivation

- the Policy and Innovation Unit, later merged with the Strategy Unit, to deal with policy not covered by the Social Exclusion Unit (similar in some respects to the Central Policy Review Staff)

- the Strategic Communications Unit to co-ordinate all government communications (later merged with the Policy Unit to form the Communications and Strategy Unit)

- the Comprehensive Women's Unit

- the Anti-Drugs Unit

- the Treasury's Comprehensive Spending Reviews

- and the virtual merger of the PM's and Cabinet Offices in an attempt to integrate and co-ordinate government policies.

We will return to the subject of joined-up government in Chapter 7.

THE ETERNAL POLITICAL TRIANGLE

Decision making within the Cabinet rests on three important principles, which often conflict with each other:

1. **Departmental autonomy** Whitehall departments are among the largest organisations in the country, and most ministers spend most of their time running them. This requires departmental autonomy, partly because different departments have separate types of work – education, defence, transport, health – and partly because they have their own practices and cultures. The job of ministers is to defend their departments; the more effective they are, the higher their political reputation. The Cabinet may, therefore, be the centre of intense departmental conflict.

2. **Cabinet collegiality** At the same time the Cabinet must be a collegial body capable of resolving conflict and making collective decisions. Whatever their rivalries, Cabinet members must form a united front, and to do this they must have the chance of discussing issues.

3. **Prime Ministerial authority** Prime Ministers are leaders. Even the most powerful and ambitious ministers want the Prime Minister to lead the Cabinet, the party and the country. Besides, ministers are often so overburdened by their departmental duties that they have little time for general policy issues. It is the Prime Minister who must try to hold all the many reins of government. It is also the PM's job to rise above conflict in Cabinet and settle disputes authoritatively. In this sense the PM is not a colleague of Cabinet members, but their boss.

Cabinet collegiality
The feeling among Cabinet members that they must act closely and co-operatively together, even when they conflict over policy issues and departmental interests.

The three principles do not always fit well together. Departmental autonomy clashes with collegiality when ministers fight for money or over policies. Too little discussion and consultation undermines Cabinet collegiality. A dominant Prime Minister can easily undermine collegiality, and one who interferes with departmental affairs too much will erode autonomy. Conversely, a weak Prime Minister will not control departmental and personal rivalries. A good PM must know when to talk or listen, when to lead or follow, when to control or delegate. In short, a good PM balances the demands of autonomy, collegiality and leadership. It is an exceedingly difficult and delicate task, and there are recent examples of it going badly wrong, as we will now see.

Thatcher as Prime Minister

When Thatcher came to power in 1979 she seemed the kind of strong and dynamic leader who could take charge of government and reverse national decline. The Falklands War strengthened popular belief in her leadership qualities. Yet when she lost power in 1990, as the longest serving Prime Minister of the century, she was widely seen as dogmatic and autocratic. For much of her time in Downing Street she dominated government and stretched Prime Ministerial leadership to its limits. She was an ambitious and driving force, but she also intervened too much in the departmental affairs of her ministers, and undermined Cabinet collegiality with her critical style.

The poll tax is a case in point. This policy to shift local taxation from a graduated property tax to a flat-rate tax on individuals was described as the worst idea in the world, and there was little government or even Cabinet support for it, but Thatcher pushed it through Parliament, forcing her colleagues to support it publicly against their own judgement. Its unpopularity was one of the more important factors leading to her Cabinet colleagues forcing her from office. Other examples of her leadership style are listed in Briefing 5.3. In general, Thatcher placed the principle of Prime Ministerial authority way above departmental autonomy and Cabinet collegiality – the eternal triangle was balanced on one corner, so it fell over.

BRIEFINGS

5.3 Prime Ministerial style: Thatcher

- Ensured that 'dries' (right-wing free marketeers) dominated the Cabinet and its committees.
- Sacked 12 Cabinet ministers, 1979–90.
- Reduced the frequency of Cabinet and Cabinet committee meetings. Wilson's annual average of Cabinet meetings was 59, Thatcher's was 35.
- Greater use of ad hoc committees and the kitchen Cabinet. It is said that some of her ministers knew nothing about some ad hoc committees, although they made important decisions.
- Intervened a great deal in departmental affairs.
- Publicly criticised some of her ministers, or used leaks against them, but strictly enforced collective responsibility.
- Started Cabinet discussions by stating her own views, rather than listening and summing up.
- Did not consult her Cabinet about some major policy decisions (eg the banning of trade unions from Government Communications Headquarters (GCHQ) in 1984).
- Appointed weak ministers who could be controlled.
- Kept some major issues off the Cabinet agenda. Michael Heseltine claimed this as the reason for his Cabinet resignation in 1986.
- Attended Parliamentary debates less frequently than any other modern Prime Minister.

Major as Prime Minister

When Major replaced Thatcher in 1990 he adopted a more collegial and consensual style (see Briefing 5.4). Initially this succeeded in healing political wounds and unifying the government. He also came out of the Gulf War (1991) with much respect as a political leader. Yet after a while his quiet and unassuming style was described as 'grey', dithering, and ineffective. The Cabinet was described as a collection of 'political chums', and was accused of being 'in office but not in power'. Intense conflicts about economic policy, social policy and the

EU surfaced. The government appeared weak, divided and directionless. In the end, the eternal triangle of Major's Cabinet was balanced on departmental autonomy, so it toppled over.

BRIEFINGS

5.4 Prime Ministerial style: Major

- Made more use of the Cabinet, less of committees.

- More emphasis on Cabinet collegiality and consensus, less on leadership.

- A greater mix of opinion in the Cabinet, especially wets and dries, Europhiles and Eurosceptics.

- Greater openness in government.

- Less intervention in departmental affairs.

- Lapses of collective responsibility: Portillo's veiled criticism of the government in 1994 went publicly unchecked.

Blair as Prime Minister

In the first years of his administration Tony Blair combined some of the best characteristics of Thatcher's dynamism and leadership, with Major's informal and unassuming style. He managed to combine two contradictory tendencies:

- He has further centralised the Labour Party and imposed unprecedented discipline on it, reversing some traditional policies (Clause 4, public spending) with little debate and a great show of unanimity. He has gradually appointed more of his supporters to Cabinet and government positions. He has reduced the number and length of Cabinet meetings, working (as did Thatcher) through Cabinet committees. He has placed great emphasis on managing the media, and acquired the reputation for being a 'control freak'. He has greatly increased the size and power of the Prime Minister's Office. His unprecedented popularity in the country, until the Iraq issue at least, has enhanced his leadership. In short, he is strong on Prime Ministerial authority.

- He also has the full support, so far, of the Cabinet on many of the most controversial policies, such as taxing and spending, and Scottish and Welsh devolution. He has kept his Cabinet together by approaching some controversial issues (the EU, the euro, electoral reform) slowly and cautiously. His project on constitutional reform is the equivalent of Thatcher's project for economic change, but is far less unpopular. Although said to be a control freak, he allows his senior Cabinet colleagues much autonomy – especially Gordon Brown on economic matters. In short, he is strong on departmental autonomy and Cabinet collegiality.

Up until the early years of his second term in government, at least, Blair's Cabinet was a balance of the three principles of Prime Ministerial authority, departmental autonomy, and Cabinet collegiality.

BRIEFINGS

5.5 Prime Ministerial style: Blair

- Took on major agenda and policy-setting powers of the government and made it clear that he would not tolerate dissent either from his Cabinet or from the Parliamentary Labour Party.

- Has reduced the number and length of Cabinet meetings (it meets for about an hour a week) using committees and private discussions more.

- Spends even less time than Thatcher in the Commons, more and more on public speeches, press conferences, and high-level meetings.

- Allows considerable discretion to strong Cabinet ministers (Gordon Brown, Jack Straw, and David Blunkett), provided their policies are broadly in line with government policy.

- Is careful to keep the Cabinet united on potentially divisive issues – Europe, the euro, electoral reform, Lords reform – but Iraq may have been an exception.

- Carefully cultivates his leadership image and places great importance on media management and 'message discipline' (repeating the same theme many times).

- At the same time, he has an open and informal Prime Ministerial style – 'Call me Tony'; refusing to wear a morning coat at the Queen Mother's funeral.

WHO GOVERNS: CABINET OR PRIME MINISTER?

Prime Ministerial government
The theory that the office of the Prime Minister has become so powerful that he or she now forms a political executive similar to that of a president.

A classic and long-running debate about British government revolves around the question of whether the power of the Prime Minister has increased relative to the Cabinet. It is said that the PM is no longer 'first among equals', but a dominant political executive, and the result is not Cabinet, but Prime Ministerial government. The Cabinet, once said to be the 'efficient secret of government' because it, and not the Commons, made decisions, is now a 'dignified' part of government, which hides the real power of a presidential Prime Minister. This assertion dates back at least to Churchill's war government, but it surfaces again whenever forceful Prime Ministers emerge – Macmillan, Wilson, Thatcher, and Blair. The 'Controversy' that follows summarises some views on the matter.

Prime Ministerial government

Arguments for Prime Ministerial government are found in John Mackintosh's *The British Cabinet* and Richard Crossman's introduction to the 1960 edition of Bagehot's *The English Constitution*. Both claim that the British Prime Minister is

BRIEFINGS

5.6 Cabinet, Cabinet Committees, and other executive meetings, 1950–2000

Cabinet   Since the 1950s the number and duration of Cabinet meetings has steadily declined from about 100 a year to about 40. Under Blair they rarely last for more than 60 minutes.

Cabinet Committees   Between 1970 and 2000 the number of Cabinet Committee meetings fell more than 50 per cent.

Other meetings   Since 1979, and especially under Blair since 1997, business has increasingly been handled by:

- ad hoc meetings of senior ministers
- kitchen Cabinet meetings
- bilateral meetings between the PM and senior colleagues, especially Brown, Prescott, and Irvine.

now so powerful that the office is more like that of a president. Key decisions are made by the PM, plus a few powerful members of the Cabinet and kitchen Cabinet. Key Cabinet committees are under Prime Ministerial control, and the full Cabinet is often only a rubber stamp, and may not even be consulted on important matters. The Prime Minister directs the flow of government information and dominates relations between the Cabinet and the wider world.

> **Cabinet government**
> The theory that the Cabinet, not the Prime Minister, forms a collective political executive that constrains the power of the Prime Minister to the role of 'first among equals'.

Cabinet government

This school of thought argues that the political system limits the PM's power and ensures that the Cabinet forms a collective political executive. In the short run, PMs may be formidable, but in the long run they depend on Cabinet and party support, and most important matters will have to be agreed by Cabinet. Since the power of the Cabinet rests on the support of the majority party in the House of Commons it must, to some extent, reflect its political complexion. This, in turn, places constraints on the power of both the PM and the Cabinet, and ensures a degree of accountability of the political executive to the majority party in the Commons.

Cabinet or Prime Ministerial government?

There is no question that the British Prime Minister holds one of the most powerful political offices in the western world. What is not clear, however, is whether there is a trend towards greater Prime Ministerial power:

1. There is nothing new about powerful Prime Ministers – British history is full of them from the very first, Sir Robert Walpole, to Thatcher and Blair.

2. Strong Prime Ministers, such as Churchill, Macmillan and Thatcher, have often been followed by weaker ones, such as Eden, Douglas-Home and Major.

CONTROVERSY

Prime Ministerial or Cabinet government?

Prime Ministerial government

- The powers of the Prime Minister are very considerable.

- There are no constitutional limits to the power of the Prime Minister.

- The fusion of the executive and the legislative branches of government gives the Prime Minister direct influence over both.

- One-party government and strict party discipline ensure the power of the Prime Minister over the governing party in Parliament.

- The apparatus of Whitehall government is hierarchically organised with the Prime Minister at the peak and in control.

- The office of the PM accumulates power over time, ratcheting up with each new incumbent. Wartime conditions gave Churchill special powers that were expanded by strong successors: Attlee, Macmillan, Wilson, Thatcher, Blair.

- The Prime Minister is at the centre of mass media attention. This gives the PM power over government colleagues.

- The Prime Minister represents the country in international meetings (often widely covered in the mass media).

- The Prime Minister's Office and the Cabinet Office are increasingly linked under the direction of the Prime Minister.

- All government communication with the media is increasingly controlled by the PM's office.

Cabinet government

- Modern government is now so complicated and demanding that one person cannot possibly control all key decisions.

- Important political factions in the party need to be represented in the Cabinet if confidence in the Prime Minister is to be maintained.

- The Prime Minister has powerful and ambitious rivals for office. Some, but not all, may be ignored. Blair cannot keep Brown out of a senior Cabinet position.

- Ministers can use the weapon of resignation against the Prime Minister (Nigel Lawson in 1989, Sir Geoffrey Howe in 1990), although it may do the minister more harm than it does the Prime Minister in the short term.

- Politics is a hard and ruthless game. PMs need to be constantly watchful and careful, listening carefully to advice from all quarters – party whips, the Prime Minister's Office and advisers, commissions and committees of enquiry, Whitehall staff, the media, and especially friends and advisers who speak their minds.

- The media can be a powerful critic of the Prime Minister. Douglas-Home, Wilson, Heath and Major were weakened by a hostile press.

- Powerful PMs have been driven from office – notably Macmillan and Thatcher.

3. Relations between the Prime Minister and Cabinet members are largely secret, although surrounded by rumour and hearsay. It is difficult to know what really goes on, and easy to overestimate the power of the PM.

4. It is often assumed that there must be rivalry and competition between the PM and leading Cabinet members, where there may actually be agreement and

unity. Blair and Brown are often assumed (by the media looking for trouble) to be locked in battle. In fact, they often seem to be close colleagues.

5. The memoirs of leading political figures, as well as commentators outside the system, are entirely contradictory.

In short, the controversy about whether we have Prime Ministerial or Cabinet government seems to be unresolvable. Consequently, political scientists have turned to a different way of analysing the political executive, using the concept of the 'Core Executive'.

CONTROVERSY

Prime Ministerial or Cabinet government? What commentators say

It is no exaggeration to declare that the British Premiership has turned not into a British version of the American presidency, but into an authentically British presidency.

M. Foley, 'Presidential politics in Britain', *Talking Politics*, **6** (3), 1994, p. 141

Cabinet does not make all the decisions but it does make all the major ones, and it sets the broad framework within which more detailed policies are initiated and developed.

M. Burch, 'Prime Minister and Cabinet: an executive in transition', in R. Pyper and L. Robins (eds), *Governing the UK in the 1990s*, London: Macmillan, 1995, p. 103

The Prime Minister is the leading figure in the Cabinet whose voice carries most weight. But he is not the all-powerful individual which many have recently claimed him to be. His office has great potentialities, but the use made of them depends on many variables – the personality, the temperament, and the ability of the Prime Minister, what he wants to achieve and the methods he uses. It depends also on his colleagues, their personalities, temperaments and abilities, what they want to do and their methods.

G. W. Jones, 'The Prime Minister's power', in A. King (ed.), *The British Prime Minister*, London: Macmillan, 1985, p. 216

Centralisation of power in the hands of one person has gone too far and amounts to a system of personal rule in the very heart of our parliamentary democracy.

Tony Benn, 'The case for a constitutional premiership', in A. King (ed.), *The British Prime Minister*, London: Macmillan, 1985, p. 22

The Prime Minister leads, guides and supports his team, but relies upon their energies and expertise, just as they in turn rely upon his leadership . . . The relationship is subtle and variable, but essentially it is one of mutual reliance. A strong Prime Minister needs strong ministers.

S. James, *British Cabinet Government*, London: Routledge, 1992, pp. 133–4

The more I've been here, the clearer it's become to me that Cabinet government is a reality; let's say that the power of departments and departmental ministers is strong . . . I should perhaps add that this is the way this Prime Minister, in particular, likes to work . . . He's a conciliator and therefore goes with the grain of the system of Cabinet government, rather than against it.

1993 interview with senior civil servant, quoted in C. Campbell and G. K. Wilson, *The End of Whitehall*, Oxford: Blackwell, 1995

THE CORE EXECUTIVE

Frustrated by endless controversy about whether we have Prime Ministerial or Cabinet government, some political scientists have pointed out that both are embedded in a wider network of power relations that spread well beyond Downing Street and the Cabinet room. Increasingly during the twentieth century, and especially under Thatcher and Blair, the power of the political executive has been strengthened and centralised, and far from including only the Prime Minister and the Cabinet, its tentacles use and control many other influential bodies, agencies, committees, and individuals in Whitehall and Westminster. This network of power and influence at the apex of government has been termed 'the Core Executive' (see Figure 5.1). It consists of:

- The Prime Minister, leading members of the Prime Minister's office, and the more influential members of the Prime Minister's kitchen Cabinet.

- The Cabinet and its main committees, leading members of the Cabinet Office, and the more influential ministerial advisers.

Figure 5.1

The concentric circles of power: the Core Executive

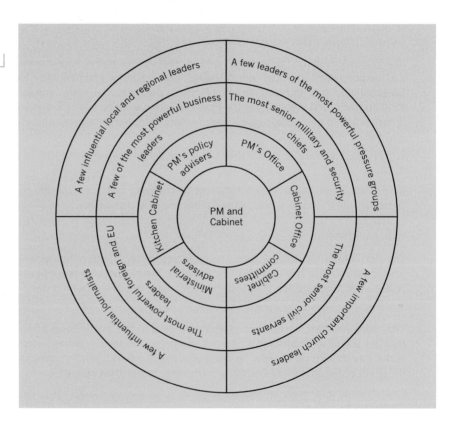

- The most senior officials in Whitehall departments, agencies, and other bodies (eg the Bank of England and the main security and intelligence organisations).

- The individuals and organisations that circle around the Prime Minister, the Cabinet, and those who serve them.

- Some members of the House of Commons and the Lords – government whips and a few chairs of Commons committees.

The advantage of focusing on the Core Executive is that it avoids the old and (some claim) sterile argument about Prime Ministerial versus Cabinet government to focus on the broader picture of decision-making power and influence. However, the concept also has three main problems as an analytical tool in political science.

Numbers

How many people are included in the Core Executive – 100, 500, 1,000, 5,000, or more? Almost certainly the Core Executive includes the whole Cabinet, but should we also include, perhaps, another ten, 20 or 30 of the most influential junior ministers in, perhaps, the Treasury, Home Office, and Foreign Office? Almost certainly the Core Executive includes the most important Cabinet committees, but should we also include some important subcommittees as well? How many? Almost certainly the Core Executive includes the most influential members of the Prime Minister's Office, but is this ten, 20, 30, or 40 people? Discussions of the Core Executive are often rather vague about even approximate numbers.

Changing circles of power

The answer to the numbers problem is that a lot depends on the particular issue under discussion, for the Core Executive is not fixed but changes according to circumstances. A small circle made strategic decisions about the Falklands and Gulf Wars, including senior military chiefs; a larger circle will influence the key decision to join the euro or not, excluding military chiefs but including senior staff of the Bank of England and Treasury. Some involved in one decision are not involved in others. But this answer simply raises a more difficult question: if different individuals and bodies are influential on different key issues, then the composition of the Core Executive will change from one issue to the next. In this case, is there any such thing as the Core Executive at all? Are we back to identifying the Prime Minister and Cabinet as the 'inner core', with many, constantly changing 'outer cores' circling around it, moving in and out of influence according to issues and circumstances? In which case the composition of the Core Executive is not at all clear.

What does the concept of the Core Executive explain?

The concept of the Core Executive is useful in directing attention to the wide network of power and influence at the highest level of government, but it does not help much to answer the important questions of who wields power, why, in whose interests, and to what effect? Why are some groups and individuals more powerful than others? How and why do they come to be powerful? How do they exercise their power, and in whose interests? To answer these questions we have to turn to substantive theories of power and influence, such as class, pluralist, elite, and bureaucratic theory, which is what we will do in following chapters.

ESSAYS

1. What do you understand by the term 'joined-up government'? Why is it necessary but difficult to achieve?

2. Discuss the claim that Thatcher's period in office provides clear evidence of Prime Ministerial government, Major's clear evidence of Cabinet government, and Blair's clear evidence of both.

3. How useful do you find the concept of the 'Core Executive' in the analysis of British government?

SUMMARY

- There is no question that the British Prime Minister has considerable power. A series of strong Prime Ministers since 1940 testifies to the fact.

- Neither is there much doubt that the Cabinet can be a powerful body. It reasserted its power over Thatcher in 1990, and it is not a body that even an authoritative leader such as Blair can easily ignore.

- An effective political executive rests on the three principles of Cabinet collegiality, departmental autonomy, and Prime Ministerial authority. If these are unbalanced, the system will not work effectively.

- The power of the Prime Minister relative to the Cabinet has swung substantially from one Prime Minister to the next, and within the term of office of the same PM. Thatcher started in a more collegial mode than she ended. Major's Cabinet started collegially but ended divided. So far Blair has managed successfully to blend Prime Ministerial authority, departmental autonomy, and Cabinet collegiality.

- Consequently there is much evidence to support both the theory of Prime Ministerial government and that of Cabinet government.

- Some political scientists have stopped arguing about Prime Ministerial versus Cabinet government to focus on the much wider network of power and authority relations found in the Core Executive. There are many indications that the power of the Core Executive has been increased and centralised, especially under Thatcher and Blair.

MILESTONES

1721 Robert Walpole acknowledged as the first Prime Minister

1735 Walpole makes No. 10 Downing St his official residence

1782 Resignation of the Lord North government on the principle that collective Cabinet responsibility links the Prime Minister with his Cabinet

1914–18 Lloyd George's wartime Cabinet has fewer than ten members

1916 Lloyd George creates the Cabinet Office

1922 Prime Minister Bonar Law creates a peacetime Cabinet with only 16 people

1931 Appointment of the first Prime Minister's press officer

1937 First statutory reference to the office of Prime Minister in the Ministers of the Crown Act

1940–5 Wartime emergency gives Churchill great powers as Prime Minister. The modern Cabinet committee system created. The wartime Cabinet had ten or fewer members

1945–51 Attlee (Deputy Prime Minister under Churchill) continues as a strong leader

1951 Churchill's short-lived experiment with 16 'overlords'

1962 Macmillan's 'night of the long knives'

1964 Wilson creates a Political Office in 10 Downing St. Ministers allowed their own special advisers

1970 Central Policy Review Staff (CPRS) created by Heath to help Cabinet work. Superministries created: the Department of Trade and Industry, and the Department of the Environment

1974 Wilson sets up first PM's Policy Unit

1975 Collective responsibility suspended during the EC referendum. Collective responsibility again suspended over the issue of the voting system to be used in EC elections

1989 Thatcher starts process of expanding and strengthening the Prime Minister's Office. Gives special role to the PM's press secretary

1983 Thatcher abolishes the CPRS. Cabinet secretary becomes head of the Civil Service

1989 Thatcher shuffles 62 government positions. Lawson (the Chancellor of the Exchequer) resigns from government, criticising Thatcher's leadership and her economic advisers

1990 Sir Geoffrey Howe resigns from the Cabinet, criticising Thatcher's leadership. Thatcher's domination of government contributes to her downfall. Major introduces a more collegial style of Cabinet government

1992 Information about Cabinet committees made public for the first time

1994 Michael Portillo ignores the principle of collective Cabinet responsibility with criticisms of the government's EU policy

1994–7 Principle of collective responsibility applied to the Labour shadow Cabinet

1997 Blair's new Cabinet includes a predominance of strong party notables but marked by consensus on central policies. PM's office expanded and strengthened

2002 Office of Deputy Prime Minister created

FURTHER READING

S. James, *British Cabinet Government* (London: Routledge, 1998) and G. Thomas, *The Prime Minister and Cabinet Today* (Manchester: Manchester University Press, 1998) are both short general books, while A. King (ed.), *The British Prime Minister* (London: Macmillan, 2nd edn, 1985) is the classic collection of readings. A useful collection of articles on the Core Executive is contained in R. A. W. Rhodes and P. Dunleavy (eds), *Prime Minister, Cabinet and Core Executive* (London: Macmillan, 1995).

Short and up-to-date articles are M. J. Smith, 'The core executive', *Politics Review*, **10** (1), 2000, pp. 2–4; G. Thomas, 'The Prime Minister and Cabinet', *Politics Review*,

PROJECTS

1. Read this chapter carefully and pick out the bodies, agencies, and offices that contribute most to the centralisation of executive power in British government. Explain how they do so, and say whether such centralisation is inevitable.

2. Read carefully through this chapter and make a note of the different bodies, agencies, and committees that can help to produce joined-up government, and those that are more likely to produce fragmented government.

4, 2002, pp. 22–5; and P. Barberis and F. Carr, 'Executive control and governance under Tony Blair', *Talking Politics*, **12** (3), 2000, pp. 395–9. On Prime Ministers between 1970–98, see D. Kavanagh, 'The powers behind the prime minister', *Talking Politics*, **12** (3), 2000, pp. 400–3, and on Blair, see D. Kavanagh, 'Tony Blair as prime minister', *Politics Review*, **11** (1), 2002, pp. 14–17; M. Garnett, 'The Blair essentials', *Politics Review*, **10** (4), 2001, pp. 8–11; and P. Hennessy, 'The Blair style and the requirements of twenty-first century premiership', *Political Quarterly*, **71** (4), 2000, pp. 386–95. On Cabinet committees, see C. Brady and P. Catterall, 'Inside the engine room: assessing cabinet committees', *Talking Politics*, **12** (3), 2000, pp. 404–7; and on Prime Ministerial advisers, see J. Burnham and G. Jones, 'Advising the prime minister, 1868–1997'; *Talking Politics*, **12** (2), 2000, pp. 333–6.

The classic works on Cabinet and Prime Ministerial government are J. Mackintosh, *The British Cabinet* (London: Stevens, 1962) and R. Crossman, 'Introduction' to W. Bagehot, *The English Constitution* (London: Fontana, 1963).

USEFUL WEB SITES ON THE CORE EXECUTIVE

Hot links to these sites can be found on the CWS at http://www.booksites.net/budge. Given the centralised, unitary nature of British government, the key sites for the Core Executive are those of Number 10 Downing Street (www.number-10.gov.uk) and the Cabinet Office (www.cabinet-office.gov.uk) which provide relevant links to all matters of concern for the Prime Minister and Cabinet. Some useful data on the structure of central government and its development can be obtained from www.nuff.ox.ac.uk/politics/whitehall. You might also want to visit the recently created Office of the Deputy Prime Minister's web site at www.odpm.gov.uk.

The web sites for the key Whitehall departments within the Core Executive are the Treasury (www.hm-treasury.gov.uk), the Foreign Office (www.fco.gov.uk), the Home Office (www.homeoffice.gov.uk) and the Department for Constitutional Affairs (www.lcd.gov.uk). Others may be accessed through links within the Cabinet Office web site (www.cabinet-office.gov.uk).

In addition, a variety of sites deal with individual Prime Ministers in recent British history, the most informative being: www.margaret-thatcher.com, www.guardian.co.uk/Thatcher and www.johnmajor.co.uk. Information on Tony Blair is available at www.controversy.net/blair.html and www.politics.guardian.co.uk/person/0,9290,-463,00.html.

CHAPTER 6

Ministries, ministers and mandarins: Central government in Britain

The ministers who direct government departments must work very closely with the civil servants who administer the departments. Ministers, of course, are elected politicians, but civil servants are non-political, permanent, and appointed officials – bureaucrats, in other words. There are hundreds of thousands of civil servants, ranging from filing clerks to a small number of very senior administrators who are often referred to as 'mandarins', after the top civil servants of ancient China. The implication is that British mandarins are also highly trained, exceptionally able, totally dedicated, and no less inscrutable than their Chinese counterparts. This chapter is concerned with the relationship between government ministers and their mandarins, most of whom work in government departments that are headquartered in Whitehall.

The relationship is crucial to the modern state. It is the government departments that actually produce public services – health, education, public transport, national defence – and it is the mandarins, not ministers, who have specialist knowledge and experience of how to run the huge organisations that deliver these services. In theory, ministers have the political function of making public policy, and mandarins the administrative task of advising on policy matters and implementing whatever ministers decide. In practice, it is impossible to draw such a simple distinction between the role of the minister and the top civil servants.

For this reason, the relationships between ministers and mandarins are both important and complex, and raise all sorts of important issues. What is the proper relationship between ministers and mandarins? Should civil servants be responsible to the public, to Parliament, or only to their ministers? Should ministers be responsible for everything their civil servants do? Do civil servants really run the country? How has the relationship between ministers and mandarins changed since the Whitehall reforms of the 1980s and 1990s? What special features has New Labour brought to Whitehall operations?

This chapter examines:

- departments and ministries of Whitehall
- ministerial roles and responsibilities
- ministers and civil servants
- mandarin power?
- politicisation of the Civil Service?
- New Labour and the mandarins.

DEPARTMENTS AND MINISTRIES OF WHITEHALL

The central administration of Britain, like that of almost all other countries, is organised into separate departments or ministries (there is no real distinction between the two). There are about 70 of these. Seventeen of the major ministries are headed by Cabinet ministers (Table 6.1).

Department/ministry	Main function	Civil Service staff (thousands)	Budget (millions) (b)	Web site address
Cabinet Office	To support the Prime Minister	6.9	£0.2	www.cabinet-office.gov.uk
The Treasury	Management of the economy. Central government budgets	94.2	Not available	www.hm-treasury.gov.uk
Foreign and Commonwealth Office (FCO)	Foreign policy, relations with the Commonwealth	5.5	£1.4	www.fco.gov.uk
Home Office	Justice, police, prisons, law and order, public safety, immigration, race	60.1	£10.5	www.homeoffice.gov.uk
Ministry of Defence (MoD)	Defence	98.3	£24.5	www.mod.uk
Office of the Deputy Prime Minister	Regional and local government, urban renewal, social inclusion	25.4	Not available	www.odpm.gov.uk
Department of Work and Pensions (DWP)	Employment, unemployment, related benefits, pensions (administration)	Not available	Not available	www.dwp.gov.uk
Department of Health (DoH)	Health and well-being	7.2	£50.7	www.doh.gov.uk
Department of Trade and Industry (DTI)	Trade, industry, productivity	11.4	£4.5	www.dti.gov.uk
Department for Environment, Food and Rural Affairs (DEFRA)	Environment, sustainable development, fishing, food and food safety, water, countryside, animal health	Not available	£2.9	www.defra.gov.uk
Department for Education and Skills (DfES)	Education and training	38.3	£19.5	www.dfes.gov.uk

Department	Responsibilities			Website
Department for International Development (DfID)	International aid and development	1.3	£0.3	www.dfid.gov.uk
Department for Transport (new ministry)	Transport	Not available	Not available	www.dft.gov.uk
Department of Culture, Media and Sport (DCMS)	Museums, galleries, libraries, arts, sport, heritage, media, tourism, National Lottery	0.6	£0.9	www.dcms.gov.uk
Lord Chancellor's Department	Administration of justice in England and Wales (all legal departments)	25.0	£3.0	www.lcd.gov.uk
Privy Council Office	Royal charters and proclamations, orders-in-council, scrutiny of bylaws	Not available	Not available	www.privycouncil.gov.uk
Northern Ireland Office	Northern Ireland	0.2	£1.2 (plus £6.0 for Northern Ireland Executive)	www.nio.gov.uk
Scotland Office	Representation of Scottish interests in the UK, especially in respect of non-devolved government responsibilities	13.7	£16.5	www.scottishsecretary.gov.uk
Wales Office	Representation of Welsh interests in the UK, especially in respect of non-devolved government responsibilities	3.2	£8.6	www.walesoffice.gov.uk

Table 6.1 *Major departments and ministries of central government*

Note: Because of departmental reorganisation not all figures are available

Source: www.cabinet-office.gov.uk and *Annual Abstract of Statistics 2002*, London: The Stationery Office, 2002, p. 92

6.1 British central administration

Civil servant A servant of the Crown (in effect of the government) who is employed in a civilian capacity (ie not a member of the armed forces), and who is paid for wholly and directly from central government funds (not by local government, agencies, nationalised industries, or quangos).

Mandarin A term given to the thousand or so top civil servants who have regular, personal contact with ministers and act as policy advisers. They are collectively known as the Senior Civil Service, and consist mainly of permanent secretaries (the senior civil servant in each department) under-secretaries and deputy secretaries. They constitute not much more than about 0.2 per cent of all civil servants.

Mandarin power The theory that top civil servants exert a powerful influence over government policy making because of their ability, experience, expertise, training and special knowledge. One version of the theory claims that civil servants, not ministers, run the country.

Minister There are more than 90 government ministers ranging from 23 full Cabinet ministers (plus two who attend the Cabinet), through ministers of state, to Parliamentary undersecretaries of state (PUSS – or 'pussies' for short), and down to the lowest rank of (unpaid) Parliamentary secretaries. Collectively the last three are known as junior ministers. They usually look after the work of a particular part of their department, under the general direction of their senior minister. As government has grown so has the number of junior ministers from 23 in 1945 to 68 in 2003.

Ministerial responsibility The principle that ministers are responsible to Parliament for their own and their department's actions. In theory ministers take responsibility for administrative failure in their department, and for any individual injustice it may cause, whether they are personally involved or not.

Special adviser Special advisers are not civil servants but political appointees who are either policy experts or general political advisers to ministers.

Both the number and nature of ministries may change – just as Cabinet posts change – when the government reorganises departments. National Heritage, for example, was created in 1992, and in 1988 the functions of the Department of Employment were split between the then Department of Education and Science (DES), the Department of Trade and Industry (DTI) and the Department of the Environment (DoE). The Blair government has not restructured Whitehall departments in a major way, except for creating the Deputy Prime Minister's (John Prescott) huge ministry, in 1997 which used to cover regional and local government, housing and planning, social exclusion, and regeneration and neighbourhood development. It was probably too large for effective co-ordination and was split up after the election of 2001.

The most important department is the Treasury, because it manages the national economy and controls the spending of other government departments. Its Comprehensive Spending Review (CSR – introduced by Gordon Brown) requires departments to justify their spending plans for a rolling three-year period. Whereas the Treasury used to have a limited co-ordination role, the CSR gives it greater powers to control spending and direct future spending plans for Whitehall as a whole – another example of the centralisation of executive power and of the attempt to create joined-up government.

Ministries are sometimes conglomerates of responsibility that have grown up rather haphazardly. The most obvious example of this is the Home Office, which has retained all the activities of government that have not been hived off into specialist ministries. Even the Home Office is primarily concerned with public order, however, and many ministries focus fairly clearly on one policy issue, such as foreign affairs, transport, health, trade and education, as well as the regional departments for Scotland, Wales, and Northern Ireland.

This focus contributes to the development of the 'departmental view', already noted (Chapter 5) as adding to the clash of views and adversarial nature of decision making in British administration. Clearly, having a department charged with one service – transport, health, or education – means that it will press its special interest. Moreover, the evidence shows that over the years departments have developed their own cultures and views of how best to do things.

Pressing one concern means that there will be fewer resources for others. Thus there are often clashes between the 'spending' ministries over which should have priority. These are compounded when one ministry's priorities directly conflict with another's: where new roads have a negative effect on the environment, for example. As no ministry has total control of everything it does, they sometimes have to negotiate or fight with others through a inter-departmental committees, right up to the Cabinet if necessary. The result can be 'turf warfare' between departments and cabinet ministers who compete rather than co-operate with each other.

Potential conflicts are not confined to relations between ministries, but may also involve groups within a ministry. An obvious cleavage is between the ministry itself and the executive agencies to which its work has been increasingly hived off under the 'Next Steps' initiative of the Thatcher governments. (We consider these in detail in the next chapter.) There may also be conflict between minister(s), representing the government in power, and the civil servants running the ministry. Civil servants should be non-partisan and impartial, but what if government priorities run counter to long-standing and deeply held 'departmental views' about policy? It should not be assumed that conflict of this kind inevitably arises on a daily basis, for often differences of opinion are resolved by amicable agreement. But conflict can and does crop up, and to understand its subtle but important nature we must first consider: (a) the general structure of ministries and departments; and (b) the enormous dependence of politicians on civil servants that this structure creates, a dependence which, if not unique to Britain, is certainly notable here.

Ministry structure

Each major department is run by a senior minister or Secretary of State, who usually holds a Cabinet seat. To try to keep pace with the huge increase in government

Figure 6.1 *Structure of a typical Westminster department/ministry*

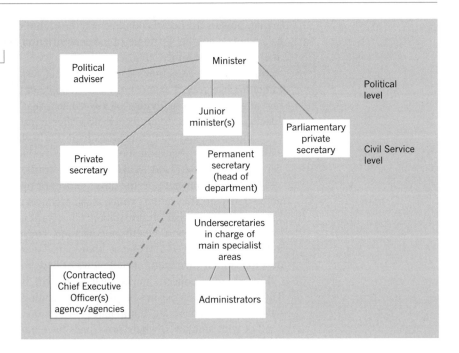

work post-war governments have appointed increasing numbers of junior ministers. In 2002 the Blair government consisted of:

- 21 Cabinet ministers (plus one more who attended Cabinet meetings), most of whom were department heads

- 34 ministers of state who are usually responsible for specific aspects of their department's work

- 34 Parliamentary undersecretaries of state, and Parliamentary private secretaries (PPSs) who assist ministers

The more important the department, the more senior and junior ministers it has. The Treasury has two full Cabinet seats (the Chancellor and the Chief Secretary to the Treasury) and three ministers of state, but the Welsh Office has a Cabinet minister and a Parliamentary undersecretary. See Figure 6.1 for the structure of a typical department. Many Cabinet ministers have served an apprenticeship by rising through the ranks of the government from Parliamentary secretaries (unpaid ministerial bag carriers), often in a range of different departments.

Ministers are, legally speaking, powerful agents of government in the sense that most acts of Parliament empower them – not the Prime Minister, the Cabinet, or senior civil servants – to do certain things. For this reason ministers are also formally responsible for what goes on in their department, and are answerable to Parliament for all that the department does in their name. Since government departments are among the largest organisations in the country, this is a huge responsibility.

Plate 6.1 *Aerial view of Whitehall looking towards the Houses of Parliament*

Source: Stockwave, Central Office of Information

MINISTERIAL ROLES AND RESPONSIBILITIES

Ministers have an incredibly busy and crowded schedule. In an average day a minister may meet with mandarins to talk about departmental matters, attend a press meeting, travel to a public function, be briefed about Parliamentary business, receive a deputation from the public or a foreign government, attend a political meeting, a dinner, or a late-night sitting of the House of Commons, and then work late into the night on a dispatch box full of papers to be read in time for an early start the next day. Ministers also attend Cabinet and Cabinet committee meetings, travel to Brussels and to their Parliamentary constituencies, and attend party meetings and conference. During the year they are likely to have to handle time-consuming department and political crises, as well.

The daily workload of a minister is varied and crushingly heavy because it involves many different activities:

- **Administration** The departments ministers run are among the largest organisations in the country.

- **Policy making** Ministers set the policy of their department and are involved in general government policy making in the Cabinet and its committees. They are involved in many meetings with other ministers whose business overlaps with their own, and they have to fight for their department and its resources in the Cabinet.

- **Politics** Ministers are accountable to Parliament, and attend its sessions to answer questions, speak in debates, vote, and pilot legislation through Parliament. They also have party meetings and constituencies to nurse.

- **Public relations** Ministers meet the media regularly to explain departmental policy and further their own careers. They keep up a demanding schedule of travel around the country to dinners, conferences, meetings and openings of various kinds. They meet deputations from interest groups, and receive a huge volume of mail.

- **The EU** Many ministers read mountains of documents, attend innumerable meetings, and travel thousands of miles on EU business.

In spite of these huge demands, ministers are amateurs with no special background or training for their jobs. They are largely drawn from the approximately 300–400 people who get elected to Parliament for the majority party. If their party has been in opposition for some time they may have no experience of government or Whitehall when they take power. Not one of the members of the Labour government elected in 1997 had any previous governmental experience.

Moreover, ministers usually spend little time in any one department before being moved in a government reshuffle. On average they spend two years in one job before switching to another. Between 1945 and 2003 there were 28 ministers of education, each lasting, on average, barely more than two years in office. One, Kenneth Clarke, was Chancellor of the Duchy of Lancaster, and Secretary for Health and then Education, and Home Secretary, all within a six-year period, before becoming Chancellor of the Exchequer in 1993, a post he held until 1997. It is said to take over a year to master the work of a department, and at least another year to make any sort of impact on it, by which time ministers have often moved to another job.

Ministerial responsibility
The principle whereby ministers are responsible to Parliament for their own and all their department's actions. In theory, ministers are responsible for administrative failure in their department, and for any injustice it may cause, whether they are personally responsible or not.

Ministerial responsibility

Untrained and inexperienced though they may be, ministers are responsible to Parliament, and can be forced to resign if they or their departments perform badly. According to convention they bear responsibility for administrative failure in their departments, for any injustices it may cause, and for general policy failures, whether or not they are personally responsible. In theory, ministers are responsible for everything that goes on in their departments. The classic example is the famous Crichel Down affair of 1954 when the Minister of Agriculture, Sir Thomas Dugdale, resigned because of departmental maladministration about which he knew nothing.

6.2 Ministerial responsibility: what they say

The individual responsibility of ministers for the work of their departments means that they are answerable to Parliament for all their department's activities. They bear the consequences for any failure in administration, any injustice to an individual or any aspect of a policy that may be criticised in Parliament, whether personally involved or not.

Central Office of Information, *The British System of Government*, HMSO: London, 1994, p. 42

The evidence of this study destroys the Crichel Down Affair as the key example of ministerial responsibility. The true convention regarding ministerial resignations is hang on for as long as you can. How long a minister can hang on depends upon his or her stock of political capital.

Keith Dowding, *The Civil Service*, London: Routledge, 1995, p. 169

In theory, the convention of ministerial responsibility is a cornerstone of the British constitution because it is the basis of government accountability to Parliament, and hence the main mechanism for holding ministers responsible for their actions. In practice, however, ministerial responsibility does not work this way. Since the Second World War no minister has resigned because of Civil Service mistakes. Table 6.2 shows that most ministers resign for personal reasons (sex scandals or drunken driving) or because of an error in their ministerial role (the Falklands in 1982, or salmonella in 1988). Even the much-quoted precedent of Crichel Down can be explained in terms of the minister losing backbench support, rather than taking responsibility for Civil Service errors.

There are many more recent examples of ministers hanging on to their posts, in spite of departmental failures. To take just one small policy area as an example – that of prison escapes – we find four recent cases of ministers refusing to take responsibility for departmental failures: in 1983 (Secretary of State for Northern Ireland, James Prior), 1991 (Home Secretary, Kenneth Baker) and 1994 and 1995 (Home Secretary, Michael Howard).

There are five main reasons why the convention of ministerial responsibility is not always followed in practice:

1. Conventions are by definition not legally binding, but depend on the willingness of politicians to abide by them.

2. Ministers cannot possibly know everything about their huge departments or be held responsible for every one of its actions. It is estimated that they usually know little more than 1 per cent of departmental matters.

3. While ministers are supposed to resign because of 'failure' or 'injustice', or 'criticism' in Parliament, these are difficult terms to define. Besides, ministers are continuously criticised in Parliament.

4. A minister who should resign may be protected by his or her Cabinet colleagues for political reasons, although in different circumstances the same minister might be sacrificed to public opinion for the same failing. Sometimes governments make a political gesture and find a scapegoat, and sometimes they close ranks to protect themselves.

Year	Minister	Cause of resignation
1982	Nicholas Fairbairn (Solicitor-General for Scotland)	Private life and handling of a departmental matter
1982	Lord Carrington (Foreign Secretary), Humphrey Atkins (Lord Privy Seal), Richard Luce (Minister of State, Foreign Office)	Failure to take due note of warnings that Argentina was planning a Falklands invasion
1985	Cecil Parkinson (Transport Secretary)	Private life, the Sara Keays affair
1986	Leon Brittan (Secretary of Trade and Industry)	Leaking official documents about the sale of Westland helicopters
1986	Michael Heseltine (Defence Secretary)	Disagreement with Cabinet over sale of Westland helicopters
1988	Edwina Currie (Undersecretary of State, Health)	Claimed (correctly) that British eggs are infected with salmonella and forced to resign
1990	Patrick Nicholls (Undersecretary of State, Environment)	Drunken driving
1992	David Mellor (National Heritage Minister)	Private life and acceptance of hospitality from businessmen lobbying government
1993	Michael Mates (Minister of State, Northern Ireland)	Relations with Asil Nadir, businessman who jumped bail in a fraud trial
1994	Tim Yeo (Minister of State, Environment)	Private life and illegitimate child
1994	Lord Caithness (Minister of State, Transport)	Private life
1994	Tim Smith (Undersecretary of State, Northern Ireland)	Accepted cash for asking Parliamentary questions
1994	Neil Hamilton (Undersecretary, Corporate Affairs)	Cash for questions
1995	Allan Stewart (Undersecretary, Scotland)	Waving pickaxe at anti-road demonstrators
1995	Charles Wardle (Undersecretary, Industry and Energy)	Opposition to government's immigration policy
1995	Robert Hughes (Parliamentary Secretary)	Private life
1996	David Willetts (Parliamentary Secretary)	Secretly directing Conservative members of Privileges Committee when he was a whip
1998	Ron Davies (Secretary of State for Wales)	Private life
1998	Peter Mandelson (Minister without Portfolio)	Conduct in office – undeclared personal loan from Paymaster-General, and Hinduja passport affair
1998	Geoffrey Robinson (Paymaster-General)	Conduct in office – personal loan to Peter Mandelson
2000	Peter Kilfoyle (Undersecretary of State, Defence)	Disagreement with government policy
2001	Keith Vaz (Minister of State for Europe, Foreign Office)	Misconduct (technically did not resign as a minister but was reshuffled out of office after suspension from the Commons for misconduct)
2002	Stephen Byers (Transport Secretary)	Various transport problems, especially Railtrack, plus behaviour of special advisers
2002	Estelle Morris (Education Secretary)	Various problems concerning schools' policy, especially controversy over 'A' Level results – exacerbated by negative media coverage
2003	Robin Cook (Leader of the House of Commons) John Denham (Minister of State, Home Office)	Disagreement with government Policy (Iraq)

Table 6.2 *Some ministerial resignations and their causes*

5. The creation of Whitehall agencies with a degree of independence from ministers (Chapter 7) makes it more difficult to distinguish between the policy failures of ministers and the bureaucratic failures of agencies. Each side can blame the other.

As a result the convention of ministerial responsibility is vague, and mainly results in resignation where ministers have lost the support of their government colleagues and/or their party backbenchers.

MINISTERS AND CIVIL SERVANTS

Civil servant
A servant of the Crown (ie the government) who is employed in a civilian capacity (ie not a member of the armed forces) and who is paid wholly and directly from central government funds (not local government, nationalised industries or quangos).

Mandarins
The comparatively small number (about 1,000) of very senior civil servants who have close and regular contact with ministers in their capacity as policy advisers.

Senior and junior ministers constitute the top, political layer of Whitehall departments, which is superimposed on an elaborate hierarchy of appointed, politically neutral, and professional civil servants. At the head of these armies of officials is a permanent secretary who, as the equivalent of the chief executive officer of the department, oversees its administration, acts as a policy adviser to the minister, and is supposed to act as the channel for all communications from lower levels of the Civil Service to the minister. In the post-war years permanent secretaries were powerful figures, and they still constitute an important part of the Core Executive. However, the Civil Service is now less hierarchical and more flexible than it was, and ministers have a much wider range of contacts and methods of working within their departments than before, so permanent secretaries may not be such powerful gatekeepers nowadays.

Nevertheless, British ministers are dependent on their career civil servants to a degree that is unusual in western democracies. In many countries, incoming ministers bring with them a whole layer of political appointees – both administrators and policy advisers – who also leave their posts when the minister goes. In Britain, where the Civil Service is supposed to be strictly politically impartial, serving whichever political master happens to be in government, a new minister works with the Civil Service team he inherited from his or her predecessor. Ministers have rather little control over the selection of the most senior civil servants (mandarins) they have to work so closely with. Only if 'things don't work out' between a minister and his senior officials can the minister demand changes of staff, but there are limits to how many changes can be demanded. Ministerial dependence on permanent officials will be heightened if he or she is new to the department – as they often are when they are members of a new government, or when they have just been moved as part of a government reshuffle.

The special circumstances of British civil servants requires them to play a special role in the administration of the state.

The Civil Service role

While most ministers are elected politicians who hold their posts for a short time, civil servants are permanent, appointed servants of the Crown. Their role has four main features: impartiality, anonymity, permanence and confidentiality.

BRIEFINGS

6.3 Civil Service impartiality and anonymity

In the determination of policy the civil servant has no constitutional responsibility or role distinct from that of the minister. It is the civil servant's duty . . . to give the minister honest and impartial advice, without fear or favour, and whether the advice accords with the minister's views or not . . . When, having been given all the relevant information and advice, the minister has taken a decision, it is the duty of civil servants loyally to carry out the decision with precisely the same energy and goodwill, whether they agree with it or not.

Civil Servants and Ministers: Duties and Responsibilities, London: HMSO, 1986, pp. 7–8

The Civil Service as such has no constitutional personality or responsibility separate from the duly constituted Government of the day . . . The duty of the individual civil servant is first and foremost to the Minister of the Crown who is in charge of the department in which he or she is serving.

The Armstrong Memorandum, *Civil Service Management Code*, Issue 1, London: HMSO, 1993, paras 3–4
(Sir Robert Armstrong, Cabinet Secretary, 1979–88, and Head of the Civil Service, 1981–8)

Although my generation of civil servants has been brought up to regard every act taken by an official as an act in the name of the Minister, our successors may . . . have to be prepared to defend in public and possibly without the shield of ministerial protection, the acts they take.

Sir D. Wass, 'The public sector in modern society', *Public Administration*, **61** (1), 1983, p. 12
(Sir Douglas Wass, Permanent Secretary at the Treasury, 1974–83, and Joint Head of
the Civil Service, 1981–3)

■ **Osmotherly Rules**   A set of rules for the guidance of officials appearing before House of Commons select committees and designed to protect the principle of civil service impartiality, anonymity and confidentiality.

■ **The Armstrong Memorandum**   The official statement on the duties and responsibilities of civil servants, including their role in relationship to ministers.

Civil Service impartiality The principle whereby civil servants should be politically neutral and serve their Cabinet ministers regardless of which party is in power and of what they may personally feel about their minister's policies.

1. **Impartiality**   Civil servants must serve their political masters – their ministers – and be strictly impartial about party politics and ministerial policies. Ministers must not, therefore, ask civil servants to perform political tasks, and civil servants must not enter the political fray. Appointments and promotion in the Civil Service should not involve political considerations, or be affected by a change of government. According to the Osmotherly Rules (after Edward Osmotherly, the civil servant who wrote them) Commons committees must not ask civil servants 'questions in the field of political controversy'.

2. **Anonymity**   Civil servants are anonymous. The Osmotherly Rules state that Parliamentary committees must not ask questions about the conduct of particular civil servants or about the advice they give to ministers.

Osmotherly Rules
A set of rules, named after their author, Edward Osmotherly of the Civil Service Department, for the guidance of civil servants appearing before Commons select committees and designed to protect civil service impartiality, anonymity and secrecy.

Civil Service anonymity
Civil servants are the confidential advisers of ministers and must not be asked questions about politically controversial matters or the policy advice they give.

3. **Permanence**   Unlike the system in many other countries, top British civil servants do not change with a change of government. Impartiality and anonymity should mean they can serve whichever party is in power.

4. **Confidentiality**   The advice civil servants give their ministers is confidential, and the Osmotherly Rules and Armstrong Memorandum state that they cannot be asked to reveal their advice. Civil servants sign the Official Secrets Act.

Events in the 1980s and 1990s, however, suggest that these four principles have been changed under the pressure of political events:

- **Impartiality and the Tisdall affair**   In 1983 the civil servant Sarah Tisdall was sentenced at the Old Bailey to six months in prison for leaking information about the arrival of Cruise missiles at Greenham Common. She believed the defence secretary was avoiding ministerial accountability. Her case raises the question as to whether the Civil Service should carry out all ministerial directives, even those they feel are morally or legally dubious. Is their first duty to the public interest, or to their minister?

- **The Ponting affair**   Clive Ponting was a civil servant who was prosecuted in 1985 for releasing secret information suggesting that the battleship *Belgrano* was sunk during the Falklands War for political reasons and not for military ones, as the government claimed. He argued that civil servants have a duty to the public interest that might, under certain circumstances, require them to 'go public'. The judge instructed the jury to find him guilty, on the grounds that ministers should judge what is in the public interest, but the jury acquitted him.

- **The arms to Iraq affair**   The Scott inquiry into the 'arms to Iraq' affair (where the Conservative government had secretly relaxed the rules on exporting arms to Iraq) found that ministers had asked civil servants to help them misinform Parliament and the public, and that civil servants seemed to have colluded with them.

- **Anonymity**   An inquiry into the collapse of Vehicle and General Insurance in 1971 placed the blame on named officials. An inquiry following the Westland affair in 1986 criticised five named officials for their role in leaking a letter, and another, Sir Robert Armstrong, the Cabinet Secretary, for failing to take disciplinary action against them. In recent times the anonymity of civil servants has been increasingly difficult to maintain, as the media, political memoirs and official inquiries have publicised Civil Service and ministerial conduct.

- **Permanence**   Civil servants are also now less permanent than they used to be. The chief executive officers in charge of executive agencies are on fixed-term contracts.

In sum, the theory and practice of the Civil Service role are not the same thing, and the practice has changed in recent decades under the pressures of modern government.

MANDARIN POWER?

In theory, ministers are the elected politicians who make public policy; civil servants provide policy advice and carry out ministerial decisions. Civil servants 'are on tap, but not on top', as the saying goes. In practice, it is impossible to draw a clear distinction between policy and administration. First, policy inevitably involves administrative questions. For example, the poll tax, whether or not it was a good idea in principle, was inevitably difficult and expensive to implement and might have been rejected on administrative grounds alone. Second, administration often involves important policy issues. A series of administrative decisions about how to run a programme can easily affect the goals it is supposed to achieve. Toughening up security in prisons, for example, can easily subvert their educational and reformative role.

Consequently, the roles of ministers and their Whitehall staff are blurred. Where the minister's job ends and the permanent secretary's begins is not at all clear. As Sir Humphrey, the caricature of the archetypal mandarin, says in the TV programme *Yes Minister*, with deliberate lack of clarity:

> I do feel that there is a real dilemma here, in that while it has been government policy to regard policy as the responsibility of ministers, and administration as the responsibility of officials, questions of administrative policy can cause confusion between the administration of policy and the policy of administration, especially where the responsibility for the administration of the policy of administration conflicts or overlaps with the responsibility for the policy of the administration of policy.

J. Lynn and A. Jay, Yes Minister, *London: BBC, 1982, p. 176*

The overlap of policy and administration is not just of theoretical interest. It has important implications for the power potential of Whitehall mandarins.

According to the German sociologist Max Weber permanent officials, especially civil servants, hold the reins of power in the modern bureaucratic state. 'For the time being', he wrote, 'the dictatorship of the official, not that of the worker, is on the march.' His argument for making this claim was that permanent officials have the training, the ability, and the experience that enables them to control or manipulate their nominal political masters. Officials are full-time professionals; politicians are part-time amateurs.

There are many arguments for and against this startling claim when we apply it to the British Civil Service, and for every argument in favour of mandarin power there seems to be another contradicting it. While the arguments do not necessarily cancel each other out, we have to turn to other ways of trying to resolve the controversy. One obvious way is to call on the evidence of insiders, and the obvious place to search is the growing body of political memoirs of ministers and mandarins who have written about their personal experience within the Whitehall machine. Unfortunately, these are also inconclusive. Not only is the evidence anecdotal and patchy, but for every minister – Benn, Castle, Crossman – claiming that civil servants were unhelpful or obstructive, there is another – Wilson, Carrington, Heath, Healey, and Crossman – saying that they are professionals who can be controlled. Crossman appears to disagree with himself, so he appears in both lists.

Mandarin power/ dictatorship of the official The theory that, no matter which party forms the government, civil servants will exert a powerful influence over government, or even control it, because of their ability, experience and expertise.

Mandarin or ministerial power? The theory

Mandarin power

Numbers
About 1,000 civil servants have a direct input into the policy-making process compared with about 60 ministers and junior ministers

Time
Civil servants are full time; ministers divide their time between many activities

Permanence and experience
Civil servants are permanent; ministers are temporary; civil servants often have many years' experience; ministers have few (if any)

Ability and training
Top civil servants are exceptionally able, usually have excellent educational qualifications. Ministers are untrained and not elected for their educational qualifications

Monopoly of advice and information
Ministers are heavily dependent on their civil servants for policy advice. This is a uniquely British situation, as elsewhere they take independent policy advisers in with them, as a matter of course

Tricks of the trade
Civil servants may use tricks of the trade: putting important documents at the bottom of the dispatch box; concealing major policy issues in long, complex reports; giving ministers little time for decisions; selective use of facts; getting other departments to intervene in matters of mutual interest

The departmental view versus vague party platforms
Departments have a comprehensive policy view; ministers have sketchy guidance from their party manifesto

Civil Service ambition
Those at the top of the Civil Service hierarchy are able and ambitious. Some ministers are weak, appointed because they can be controlled by Cabinet colleagues

Civil Service empire building
Civil servants are ambitious for their departments: they want to build empires

Evidence
It is not difficult to draw up a long list of ministers who were run by their departments

Ministerial power

The boss
Numbers may not count for much when ministers can use their legitimate power to overrule civil servants

Time is not the essence
It does not take a good minister long to come to grips with the essentials of policy decisions

Permanence and experience
Some ministers take charge of their department quickly: a few have a lot of government experience if their party has been in power for some time

All amateurs
Civil servants are generalists, not specialists, and have no more professional training for their job than ministers. Some ministers are exceptionally able

Outside advice
Ministers are not totally dependent on civil servants or advice; they have their own (non-Civil Service) advisers, professionals, the party, pressure groups, academics and the media

Ministerial experience
It does not take ministers long to learn these tricks and ways of countering them. They have tricks of their own, and may be able to make life difficult for non-compliant civil servants

Cabinet and party backing
Ministers can use the party election manifesto and the weight of Cabinet opinion to force (if necessary) civil servants to accept a policy

Personality
Ministers are not famous for being shy and uncertain; many have great ambition, confidence and force of character to drive their will

Professional ethos
The Civil Service has a strong and well-developed ethos or ethic of serving ministers to their best ability

Evidence
It is not difficult to draw up a long list of ministers who ran their departments

Mandarin or ministerial power? Some insider evidence

The trouble with the Civil Service is that it wants a quiet life. The civil servants want to move slowly along the escalator towards their knighthood and retirement and they have no interest whatsoever in trying to develop new lines of activity.

Tony Benn, *Out of the Wilderness, Diaries 1963–1967*, London: Arrow Books, 1987, p. 195

I believe that civil servants like to be under ministerial control. There is nothing they dislike more than to have a minister whom they feel is weak, who does not know his mind and who wants to leave it all to them . . . What they like is to have a minister who knows a policy he wants to pursue.

Edward Heath, quoted in Peter Barberis (ed.), *The Whitehall Reader*, Buckingham: Open University Press, 1996, p. 83

Even at the ODM [Ministry of Overseas Development] I remember Andy Cohen, the Permanent Secretary, trying to wear me down . . . He would be in my office about seven times a day saying, 'Minister, I know the ultimate decision is yours but I would be failing in my duty if I didn't tell you how unhappy your decision makes me.' Seven times a day. One person [the Minister] against the vast department.

Barbara Castle, *Mandarin Power*, quoted in Barberis, op cit, p. 66

Ministers set the policy agenda, often with help from officials, and make decisions within it. They seek, and officials offer, advice within the framework of the policy agenda.

Lord Burns, Permanent Secretary of the Treasury, 1991–8, quoted in Theakston, 2000, p. 40

I think the minister who complains that his civil servants are too powerful is either a weak minister or an incompetent one.

Denis Healey, quoted in Barberis, op cit, p. 81

Already I realise the tremendous effort it requires not to be taken over by the Civil Service. My Minister's room is like a padded cell . . . there is a constant preoccupation to ensure that the Minister does what is correct.

Richard Crossman, *The Diaries of a Cabinet Minister*, vol. 1, London: Hamilton and Cape, 1975, pp. 21–2

Broadly speaking, I would say that it is quite untrue to believe that Whitehall, if you are firmly committed to anything, would try to stop you doing it.

Richard Crossman, *Socialism and Affluence: Four Fabian Papers*, London: Fabian Society, 1967, p. 80

We concentrate on what *can* happen, not what *ought* to happen.

Sir Brian Cubbon, Permanent Secretary of the Northern Ireland Office, 1978–88, 'The duty of the professional', in R. Chapman (ed.), *Ethics in Public Service*, Edinburgh: Edinburgh University Press, 1993, p. 10

Only bad ministers blame the Civil Service, because only bad ministers let themselves be dominated by the Civil Service.

Gerald Kaufman, 'How to be a minister', *Politics Review*, **7** (1), 1997, p. 13

If neither abstract argument nor insider evidence offers a conclusive answer to the controversy about mandarin power, perhaps the most significant evidence is provided by developments under Thatcher and Major. Their governments reformed the Civil Service structure and mode of operation in fundamental ways and, moreover, won big battles against determined opposition from almost all sections of Whitehall. This constitutes clear evidence that British civil servants can be brought under government control, if the government is determined to push its reforms through. Perhaps this is a lesson to learn from the insider evidence just quoted – strong and determined ministers can get their own way, even against Civil Service opposition, if this is forthcoming. At any rate, whatever may have been the case before 1979, Whitehall mandarins were not 'on top' in the 1980s and early 1990s. On the contrary, civil servants were severely criticised at the time for being too compliant, and giving in to ill-thought out and hastily implemented government plans. Indeed, it was even argued that the Civil Service had abandoned its traditional political neutrality to become a political tool of the government.

POLITICISING THE CIVIL SERVICE?

Since the 1980s the problem has not been that civil servants use their powers for their own purposes but, on the contrary, that the government has used civil servants for its own party political purposes. Critics argue that under Thatcher the Civil Service became politically partial. There is some evidence for this view:

- The Cabinet Secretary, Sir Robert Armstrong, was used to defend the government policy of banning the publication of the book, *Spycatcher* (which contained relevations about the security services) in an Australian court.

- Civil servants were used to leak a confidential document in the Westland affair.

- The Scott Inquiry into the arms to Iraq affair found that some civil servants complied with the government's attempts to use them politically to implement its secret policy, and then used them again to try to cover up the affair.

- It has been claimed that civil servants have been promoted and others blocked on political or ideological rather than professional grounds. Mrs Thatcher was credited with asking the question, 'Are they one of us?' in relation to appointments. The danger is that civil servants may be reluctant to give advice they think might put their own career at risk.

- Most intangibly of all, it has been suggested that after years of one-party rule, civil servants came to accept the government's view of things without question.

Although there is some clear evidence of the politicisation of the Civil Service in the 1980s, much of the evidence is circumstantial and inconclusive. How can one tell if civil servants have withheld good advice? How can we know whether some civil servants were promoted on political and ideological grounds? Secrecy and confidentiality make it difficult to draw any firm conclusions, although circumstantial evidence suggests that there may have been a problem.

Concern about the politicisation of the Civil Service built up from the mid-1980s onwards. In 1994, after much pressure, the government accepted a formal Code of Ethics drafted by the Treasury and Civil Service Select Committee of the House of Commons. An appeals procedure was set up for civil servants who felt under pressure to compromise their political neutrality. It is not yet clear how effective these reforms will be. Nevertheless, the Blair government has been accused of trying to use civil servants in department press officer jobs to defend the government's party political record.

NEW LABOUR AND THE MANDARINS

The Thatcher/Major Conservative governments were in power for 18 years. In that time they reshaped almost every aspect of government policy, appointed almost every senior civil servant, tried to remodel large parts of the Whitehall machinery, and did their best to instil a Thatcherite culture in Whitehall. As a result, some observers in 1997 suggested that the Blair government would need to sweep clean the top levels of the Civil Service and replace it with its own people. No such thing happened, and the transfer of power from Conservative to Labour government was relatively uneventful. There were a few 'hiccups' in the form of policy problems, some early retirements of permanent secretaries, and some departmental transfers, but these were relatively minor. Many top information officers (spin doctors) in Whitehall were replaced, but they held politically sensitive posts. By and large, the Civil Service seems to have adapted to its new political masters, and New Labour has no significant plans at present to reform the Civil Service.

However, the Blair government has done two things to change working patterns in Whitehall. It has significantly enlarged and strengthened the role of special advisers, and it has created a large number of task forces.

Task force
Task forces are usually comparatively small, official groups set up to do a particular and fairly limited job (write a report, investigate an issue or event), and dissolved when they have completed the task.

Special advisers

In the past the British Civil Service used to enjoyed something close to a monopoly of advice to ministers. This was partly because British parties did little to turn their vague campaign promises into specific policies. For example, Richard Crossman, a new minister in 1964, noted with dismay in his diary that the file at Labour's headquarters on one of its longest standing commitments was almost empty. 'Think tanks' (outside centres which provide policy advice) were relatively new to Britain, and limited in number and resources, policy working groups in the main parties were relatively weak, and Parliamentary select committees (Chapter 18) were ignored as often as they were used as sources of advice. Thus, when British ministers needed advice their first port of call was, until recently, the Civil Service. In recent decades, however, this has changed as governments become aware of their dependence on the mandarins, even though they did not appoint them in the first place.

A response to this has been the appointment of special advisers from outside the Civil Service. These are not new to British government: Harold Wilson brought in Thomas (Lord) Balogh as an economic adviser in 1964, and Mrs Thatcher used Professor Sir Alan Walters, also as an economic adviser. The Labour government of 1974 allowed each Cabinet minister one special adviser. Since the 1980s, however, and especially under New Labour, special advisers have increased in number and influence. Compared with the eight special advisers in Major's Downing Street organisation, and a total of 38 in Whitehall, 53 were appointed by Labour in 1997, and there are now more than 81 of them, 27 in Downing Street. Many Whitehall advisers are senior businessmen brought in to give the benefit of their experience, and, in addition, private firms such as the business consultants PricewaterhouseCooper have been used.

There are two kinds of special advisers. The first are policy experts with specialist knowledge, and the second are political advisers (not a Civil Service function) who think generally about political tactics and strategy for their minister and the government. Many are part-time or on short-term contracts. As outsiders who are answerable only to the minister who employs them, they are independent of the civil servants. On the one hand, special consultants give the government a greater range of advice and greater freedom of action; on the other, they may undermine the traditional advisory role of senior civil servants. Moreover, there has been a crossing of lines between the Civil Service, the government, and the Labour Party. Two essentially party political appointments, Alastair Campbell (now resigned), and the Prime Minister's Chief of Staff, Jonathon Powell, are authorised to give orders to civil servants.

Task forces

The most notable change in Whitehall since 1997 is the growth of task forces. Such groups can ignore the traditional Whitehall approach to problems, and search for new and pragmatic solutions to government problems. For example, in 2002 there were 12 National Health Service task forces, composed of medical professionals and patients, charged with finding ways to improve the service. Officials records show that in the financial year 2000/1 there were 48 task forces, 240 ad hoc advisory groups, and 71 reviews at work. About 300 task forces were created between 1997 and 2001.

Their advantage is the ability to use outside expertise and experience, and their ability to take a fresh look at policy problems. They are also good at cutting across departmental boundaries, and hence they can help joined-up government. Their effect, however, is to further undermine the policy adviser role of mandarins, and to bypass the traditional Whitehall structures of departmental and interdepartmental committees.

ESSAYS

1. Argue the case for and against a permanent layer of civil servants at the top of Whitehall departments.

2. In what ways, and for what reasons, has the role of Whitehall mandarins changed in the last 30 years?

3. Are ministers really responsible to Parliament in their departmental capacities?

SUMMARY

- In theory, ministers are responsible for policy and civil servants for administration, but in practice, no clear line can be drawn between policy and administration.

- In theory, ministers are responsible to Parliament for their own actions and those of their departments and civil servants. In practice, the principle of ministerial responsibility is often breached.

- In theory, civil servants are impartial, anonymous, permanent, and protected by secrecy. In practice, all four features of the civil servant's role have been undermined in recent years.

- The old controversy about mandarin power is unlikely to be resolved, because arguments for and against the theory are inclusive, and insider evidence is contradictory. However, it is clear that politicians wielded decisive power over their mandarins in the 1980s and 1990s when the Thatcher and Major governments implemented sweeping reforms of Whitehall.

- New Labour has no current plans for further Whitehall reforms, but its increasing use of special advisers and task forces has tended to undermine the traditional policy adviser roles of senior civil servants, and bypass normal departmental methods for policy making.

- Critics of the Whitehall system claim that the doctrines that are supposed to regulate ministerial and Civil Service relations are more mythical than real. They argue for clearer and firmer rules, especially on the role of the Civil Service, and for better procedures, especially to protect civil servants from ministers who try to use them for political purposes.

MILESTONES

Milestones in relations between ministers and mandarins in the post-war period

Nineteenth century The modern principles of Civil Service permanence, neutrality, and anonymity become established along with ministerial responsibility

1954 Crichel Down affair. Secretary of State for Agriculture, Sir Thomas Dugdale, resigns because of maladministration in his department. Later research suggests that he was forced from office because he lost backbench support

1955 Creation of junior minister posts (to fill in for ministers away from London)

1964 Junior ministers given specific departmental responsibilities. Named Ministry of Aviation officials blamed for excessive profits paid in defence contracts to Ferranti Ltd for Bloodhound missiles

1968 Foreign Office officials named by Commons select committee for failure to compensate British victims of the Nazis (the Sachsenhausen case)

1971 Collapse of Vehicle and General Insurance Co. A named civil servant is blamed, but the minister, John Davies, does not resign

1973 Cabinet Office sets up its European Secretariat to co-ordinate departmental policy on the EEC

1976 Publication of Osmotherly Rules for guidance of officials appearing before Commons select committees

1983 Departments of Trade and Industry amalgamated

1983 Sarah Tisdall jailed for leaking documents about the siting of Cruise missiles on Greenham Common

1984–5 Ponting trial. Clive Ponting had leaked documents that showed the political motives for sinking the Argentine cruiser, *Belgrano*, in the Falklands War with the loss of 700 lives. Acquitted by jury against judge's instructions

1985 Publication of the memorandum of Sir Robert Armstrong (the Cabinet Secretary) on the duties and responsibilities of civil servants

1986–7 Westland helicopter affair. Colette Bowes, a civil servant, publicly identified for leaking a secret letter on the instruction of her minister, Sir Leon Brittan, who then resigned

1987 A revised version of the Armstrong Memorandum

1988 Department of Health split from Department of Health and Social Security. Department of Employment split between Departments of Education, Trade and Industry, and Environment

1992 Creation of National Heritage Department

1995–6 Controversy about Scott Report into the 'arms for Iraq' affair (also known as the Matrix Churchill affair). The government had used civil servants to try to suppress embarrassing information at a trial on grounds of 'national security'

1997 Smooth transfer of power from Conservatives to Labour after May general election

1997–2002 Growing numbers of special advisers and task forces used in Whitehall

PROJECTS

1. Playing the roles of a minister and a permanent secretary, argue the case for and against special advisers and task forces in central government.

2. Find out what you can from newspaper reports about any cases involving ministerial responsibility (eg Sir Thomas Dugdale and the Crichel Down affair, 1954; Norman Lamont and the withdrawal of the pound sterling from the EMS in 1992; James Prior, Kenneth Baker, and Michael Howard and prison escapes in 1983, 1991, 1994, and 1995; Stephen Byers, Transport and the Millennium Dome, 2002; and Keith Vaz and misconduct, 2002.) What, if anything do these case histories tell us about ministerial responsibility?

FURTHER READING

A general account of the Civil Service can be found in R. Pyper, *The British Civil Service* (London: Prentice-Hall/Harvester Wheatsheaf, 1995), and K. Theakston, *The Civil Service Since 1945* (Oxford: Blackwell, 1995). Longer, but very readable, is P. Hennessy, *Whitehall* (Secker and Warburg, 1989), and a more advanced text is K. Dowding, *The Civil Service* (London: Routledge, 1995). For an excellent set of insider views on the relationships between ministers and mandarins see P. Barberis (ed.), *The Whitehall Reader* (Buckingham: Open University Press, 1996). The same book has a section on Civil Service loyalties, responsibilities and ethics. An excellent account of the decline of the Whitehall Model based on extensive interviews is Colin Campbell and Graham K. Wilson, *The End of Whitehall: Death of a Paradigm* (Oxford: Blackwell, 1995).

Recent articles include K. Theakston, 'Ministers and civil servants', in R. Pyper and L. Robins (eds), *United Kingdom Governance* (Basingstoke: Macmillan, 2000, pp. 39–60); T. Butcher, 'The Civil Service under New Labour', *Politics Review*, **11** (3), 2002, pp. 29–31; R. Pyper, 'The Civil Service under Blair', *Politics Review*, **9** (3), 2000, pp. 2–6; R. A. W. Rhodes, 'New Labour's Civil Service: summing-up joining-up', *Political Quarterly*, **71** (2), 2000, pp. 151–66 and D. Kavanagh and D. Richards, 'Departmentalism and joined-up government: back to the future?, *Parliamentary Affairs*, **54**, 2001, pp. 1–18.

USEFUL WEB SITES ON MINISTRIES, MINISTERS, AND MANDARINS

Hot links to these sites can be found on the CWS at http://www.booksites.net/budge. A good way to start your research on the structure of ministries and departments is to visit the Cabinet Office web site www.cabinet-office.gov.uk, where you will find a comprehensive description of the ministerial network and the organisation of the Civil Service. The site also provides links to all major departments' web sites, including the Foreign Office www.fco.gov.uk, the Home Office www.homeoffice.gov.uk, the Treasury www.hm-treasury.gov.uk, the Lord Chancellor's department www.lcd.gov.uk, and the Ministry of Defence www.mod.gov.uk, among many others. Information on Northern Ireland, Scotland and Wales can be obtained from www.nio.gov.uk, www.scotland.gov.uk, and www.wales.gov.uk respectively.

The British Council offers an interesting analysis of the evolution of the civil service which you can find at www.britishcouncil.org/governance/manag/civil. The official reference point for the Civil Service is their home page www.civil-service.gov.uk. In addition there are various sites where the functioning of the Civil Service is scrutinised. The FDA is the trade union and professional body for Britain's senior public servants (www.fda.org.uk). Using their search engine enables access to a variety of reports and articles on the Civil Service. Valuable information on the Osmotherly Rules and the Armstrong Memorandum can be obtained from www.epolitix.com (here again we recommend you use their search engine). It is also worth visiting the BSE Enquiry home page www.bse.org.uk as well as the Study of Parliament Group at www.spg.org.uk, both of which contain helpful data on the institutional relations between ministries, departments and civil servants.

CHAPTER 7

The changing state: Administrative reforms

This chapter continues the discussion of the Civil Service in Britain, but broadens out to cover the major reforms to the administration of the central state and its public service over the past 30 years. While the previous chapter concentrated on relationships between politicians and bureaucrats at the very highest levels of the Whitehall machine, this one turns to basic reforms of the structure and operations of public services as a whole. The traditional model of the Civil Service is examined first, then the ways the Conservative governments of Thatcher and Major changed the system between 1979 and 1997. The chapter finishes with an account of how New Labour has adopted, adapted, or dropped Conservative reforms.

This chapter discusses:

■ the traditional model of British public administration and its radical critique
■ reforming the public services in the 1980s and 1990s
■ the spread of quasi-government
■ an assessment of public sector reforms in the 1980s and 1990s
■ New Labour and the public sector: joined up or gummed up?

THE BRITISH CIVIL SERVICE: THE TRADITIONAL MODEL AND RADICAL CRITIQUE

The traditional model

The traditional model of the Civil Service operated between 1854, when the Northcote-Trevelyan Report created a blueprint for it, and the early 1980s, when the Thatcher governments started their programme of changes. The main features of the traditional model are:

Administration
Either (1) the process of co-ordinating and implementing public policy through the machinery of public administration; or (2) another word for government – as in 'the Blair administration'.

- a Civil Service staffed by qualified and experienced bureaucrats

- public service

- accountability of the Civil Service through ministers who are answerable to Parliament for all the actions of their departments

- a centralised system for recruiting, training, promoting, and paying civil servants

- promotion according to experience and ability (a meritocratic public service)

- a permanent, politically neutral, anonymous, and confidential Civil Service, with no constitutional role or responsibility distinct from ministers (see Chapter 6).

The Fulton Report

In many ways the Fulton Report of 1968 represents the culmination of the traditional model. The most fundamental review of the system since Northcote-Trevelyan, it attacked what it saw as an exclusive and aloof administrative class of mandarins, drawn predominantly from a narrow social background. Most of these were Oxbridge-educated generalists whose first concern was serving and advising ministers, rather than the efficient management of their departments. Put another way, the British Civil Service was run by a largely untrained and amateur upper class elite, mobility between grades was low, technical knowledge limited, management techniques and practices antiquated, and outside advice largely excluded or ignored. The report produced 158 recommendations for change, but the most important were:

- less dependence on gifted all-rounders and more on highly trained specialists and graduates from a variety of backgrounds

- the creation of a single Civil Service career stream to encourage the advancement of the most talented from all grades

- the creation of a Civil Service Department responsible for all recruitment and a Civil Service College responsible for post-entry training

- the hiving off of some responsibilities to semi-autonomous agencies and departments.

Fulton's main concern was to create a service that was more efficient and professional, but in spite of widespread publicity, only some of its recommendations were implemented. The Civil Service Department and the Civil Service College were created to centralise recruitment and training, and the administrative class was nominally merged with the executive and clerical grades. However, a de facto administrative class remained. With intensifying economic crisis in the late 1960s and the 1970s, governments' attention was diverted elsewhere, and in the end it was left to the Civil Service to reform itself, which meant minor changes rather than major reform.

Nevertheless, it became increasingly evident that the traditional model of the Civil Service did not always apply. We have already seen, in the previous chapter, how the principles of neutrality, anonymity, permanence, and confidentiality were undermined. In any case, the Civil Service of the Northcote-Trevelyan Report was no longer adequate for the demands of late twentieth-century society. In addition, criticism of the traditional Civil Service was beginning to grow: right-wing politicians increasingly criticised it for promoting its own interests by favouring a larger state machine; left-wingers criticised it for being part of the Conservative Establishment. More important, perhaps, the growth of the state combined with increasing financial pressures in the 1970s and 1980s meant that the Civil Service came under increasing scrutiny. As a result attention switched from questions about the political power of civil servants – mandarin power – to concern about their capacity and efficiency in running the vast bureaucracies of the modern state.

The radical critique

Rational choice
An approach to political science that treats politics as the outcome of the interaction between rational individuals pursuing their own interests.

By the late 1970s right-wing intellectuals in the USA and Britain developed a radical critique of public services, centring on the efficiency of their administrative operations. Drawing on the increasingly influential rational choice theory, they assumed that what drove politics was the rational self-interest of politicians and officials. From this assumption they argued that the very organisation of public services provides officials with an incentive to maximise their own interests, not those of the general public. The structure of public bureaucracies favour ever-expanding government programmes and spending, not to benefit the public, but for the aggrandisement of bureaucrats themselves who would gain power, prestige, and pay in this way. At the same time the public service ethos of the British Civil Service, it was said, insulates it from modern and efficient management practices.

Many of the problems relating to government 'overload' in the 1970s – ever-increasing public expenditure, a growing army of officials, and inefficient public services – were linked to this view of the selfish incentives of civil servants. In effect, the public sector lacked the discipline that market competition forced on the private sector.

BRIEFINGS

7.1 Rational choice theory and politics

Rational choice theory (sometimes known as public choice theory) assumes that all actors in the political process (politicians, voters, officials, interest groups) are self-interested and seek to maximise their own benefits, whether it be votes, income or power. Left to their own devices public offficials will seek to maximise their budgets to accumulate personal benefits (promotion, salary, prestige). As a result, there will be an overprovision of public service, and, shielded from market competition, costs will be high.

Privatisation will, according to the theory, eliminate this problem. Where full privatisation is not possible, governments should change the institutional rules and procedures in ways that alter officials' incentives to maximise spending. Creating quasi-independent agencies run by managers on commercial contracts, with predetermined cost and performance targets, results in changed incentives and reduces costs because officials' careers and pay will depend on efficiency.

These ideas were pioneered by a number of American economists, including William Niskanen and Gordon Tullock. They also provide the basis for the influential book by David Osborne and Ted Gaebler, *Reinventing Government: How the Entrepreneurial Spirit is Transforming the Public Sector* (Reading, MA: Addison Wesley, 1992), which influenced reforming politicians in both the USA and Britain.

With this general approach to public management in mind, the Thatcher governments of the 1980s, and the Major government of the 1990s set about changing and reforming the British Civil Service in order to:

- reduce its size
- reduce its costs
- improve value for money

- increase competition and efficiency, partly by privatisation, and partly by introducing business culture and incentives into the Civil Service
- increase freedom to manage – giving organisations the resources and freedom to maximise efficiency, unrestricted by centralised Civil Service rules and regulations
- de-privilege Civil Service salaries, pensions, and job security
- pay greater attention to the consumers and customers of public service.

REFORMING PUBLIC SERVICES: A MANAGERIAL REVOLUTION?

New Right ideas became increasingly influential during the 1970s and, on coming to power in 1979, Margaret Thatcher was determined to apply them to the Civil Service. As part of her campaign against big government she immediately set about reducing the size of the Civil Service and curtailing many of its privileges (pay rises, job security, special pension schemes). Performance-related pay was introduced and secondments to and from the private sector were encouraged. As Figure 7.1 shows, civil servant numbers dropped sharply after 1979, although the largest decreases were among industrial rather than regular civil servants.

This provoked a reaction from the Civil Service unions which took strike action, but after 21 weeks they capitulated to the government. Also in 1981 the government abolished the Civil Service Department, which was regarded as too powerful and partisan a supporter of Civil Service interests, and created a new Management Personnel Office under the control of the Cabinet Office. In 1984 the government signalled its power over public service trade unions by banning them from the General Communications Headquarters (GCHQ) in Cheltenham following a shutdown of this security information-gathering service during the strike.

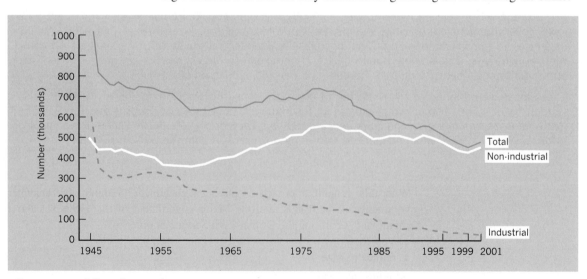

Source: www.civil-service.gov.uk

Figure 7.1 *Number of civil servants (full-time equivalents), 1945–2001*

BRIEFINGS

7.2 **Management of the Civil Service, 1965–2000**

Until 1968 most of the personnel and training functions of the Civil Service were the responsibility of the Treasury. Indeed the head of the Home Civil Service was also the head of the Treasury. In 1968 the Civil Service Department (CSD), responsible for all personnel matters, was created, along with a Civil Service College (CSC), responsible for training. However, the CSD was viewed with increasing hostility by the Thatcher government, which abolished it in 1981, transferring most of its functions to the Management Personnel Office (MPO) in the Cabinet Office – ie under the PM's control.

In the late 1980s the MPO was transformed into the Office of the Minister for the Civil Service (OMCS), then into the Office of Public Service and Science (OPSS) in 1992, and finally into the Office of Public Service (OPS) in 1995, which was incorporated into the Cabinet Office in 1998, making the office the corporate headquarters of the Civil Service. These new units remained under the wing of the Cabinet Office, and in 1988 the Cabinet Secretary was also made the head of the Home Civil Service. Significantly, the OPS is now responsible for the overall implementation of the Efficiency Unit, Next Steps and the Citizen's Charter, as well as recruitment and training. Compared with the old Civil Service Department, the OPS facilitates a greater degree of central control. In July 1998 the OPS was no longer identified as a separate part of the Cabinet Office.

These changes signal the government's strong interest in Civil Service management reform, but pale into insignificance compared with a number of further initiatives taken later in the 1980s. The impetus was a conviction that market or market-like arrangements were the only way of making government services more cost effective and responsive to the needs of citizens. Gone was the public service ethos of the 1960s; what mattered was cost and efficiency – any change that furthered these objectives was desirable.

One of Thatcher's first acts was to create an Efficiency Unit under the leadership of Sir Derek Rayner, who had been Chairman of Marks & Spencer. The Unit's objective was to identify areas where major savings could be achieved including, if appropriate, the abolition of unnecessary tasks. The Efficiency Unit continued its work for the remainder of the 1980s with Sir Robin Ibbs replacing Sir Derek (later Lord) Rayner in 1983 (see Briefing 7.3). It was the Efficiency Unit under Ibbs that produced the most important single set of Civil Service reforms in its *Improving Management in Government: The Next Steps. Report to the Prime Minister* in February 1988. The Ibbs Report identified a serious management deficit in the Civil Service and recommended radical change. Its tone was very different from Fulton. As one advocate of the reforms puts it:

Next Steps
The short title of the Ibbs Report (1988), which identified serious management failure in the Civil Service and recommended far-reaching reforms in the shape of executive agencies.

Next Steps is more like a report from a management consultancy firm than a traditional Civil Service review. It is glossy, bold and evangelical. The traditional mandarin style of drafting to avoid commitment has been replaced by a fresh passion for revitalisation and change ... It is predicated on the belief that there is an important discipline of 'management' which has been traditionally and mistakenly overlooked by the Civil Service in favour of traditional 'policy skills'.

Patricia Greer, Transforming Central Government: The Next Steps Initiative, *Buckingham: Open University Press, 1994, p. 6*

BRIEFINGS

7.3 Drive for efficiency, 1979–97

1979 Rayner's Raiders Thatcher appoints Sir Derek (later Lord) Rayner as head of a new Efficiency Unit. Based in the Cabinet Office, the Unit's brief was to improve efficiency by reducing costs and eliminating waste. Derek Rayner was replaced by Sir Robin Ibbs in 1983. By the early 1990s the Unit was claiming savings of £1.5 billion.

1982 MINIS As Environment Secretary, Michael Heseltine introduces Management Information Systems for Ministers (MINIS) to provide him with a continuous and systematic information about the running of his department. Designed to improve management accountability, this had not been been attempted before, many in Whitehall believing it was inappropriate for ministers to become involved in the detailed running of their departments. No other department adopted MINIS in full, though some used watered-down versions.

1982 FMI The Financial Management Initiative (FMI) required departments to identify clear policy objectives and to test performance in relation to these objectives. Managers within departments were given more control over their budgets or 'cost centres' and required to operate within cash limits. FMI was not fully implemented, mainly because it is difficult to identify clear objectives with some public services.

1988 Next Steps The Efficiency Unit's *Improving Management in Government: the Next Steps. Report to the Prime Minister* proposes the separation of policy from management: the government to set policy; executive agencies with considerable operational and budgetary autonomy to be responsible for management.

1991 Market testing The white paper *Competing for Quality* heralds the adoption of market testing throughout government.

1991 Citizen's Charter Designed to make public services increasingly responsive to the needs of consumers (regarded as market customers rather than public service clients).

1992 PFI The government launches the Private Finance Initiative (PFI) to encourage the private financing of public facilities. Private consortia raise capital and then, with contracts from the government, create facilities that generate income for them for a fixed period.

1994 *The Civil Service: Continuity and Change* This white paper gave executive agencies greater discretion on recruitment and pay.

1995 Annual efficiency plans Departments required to plan for increased efficiency and to state how they would keep to their budgets.

1996 Benchmarking Introduced to establish best practices for Next Steps agencies and to encourage them to learn from private management practice.

Executive agencies
Also known as 'Next Step agencies' – the semi-autonomous agencies set up to carry out some of the administrative functions of government that were previously the responsibility of Civil Service departments.

White paper
White papers are government documents outlining proposed legislation in order to permit discussion and consultation of the policy. White papers may be preceded by green papers, which are also consultative documents, but which outline various policy alternatives, rather than the firmer policy proposals that government set out in their white papers.

Market testing
The process of deciding whether a public service should be produced at all, and, if so, whether it should be produced by the public sector, contracted out, or privatised.

Benchmarking
The practice of measuring public sector cost efficiency against the standards of the private sector.

Next Steps: the theory

The main recommendations of Next Steps were:

- To separate 'steering from rowing' or policy from management. Once the government has made policy and set the targets, the management and delivery of services can best be done by separate administrative units working to agreed costs and targets.

- This decentralised system to be based on two main devices: semi-independent and specialised executive agencies to carry out particular functions; and business contracts between agencies and government.

- The heads of the agencies (chief executives) should have limited contracts according to the agreed business plan, and staff should be rewarded according to performance.

- The centralised Civil Service should be decentralised into a series of executive agencies, each with its own powers (within the terms of the contract) to set the pay, recruitment, and conditions of work.

BRIEFINGS

7.4 Patricia Greer on contract government

One of the basic principles of Next Steps is that executive agencies are provided with the freedom and the tools to get on with their 'businesses' and that in return agencies must deliver certain outputs or standards of service within the available resources. This basic principle is enforced through a series of 'contracts' which essentially specify what freedoms an agency has, how much money it has and what ends the agency must achieve.

At a more detailed level agencies contract other agencies through 'service level agreements' to perform particular functions such as computer services, providing contribution record data or accommodation services. In other words, the 'contractor' becomes a 'client' organisation which must manage its dealings with other contract agencies.

Patricia Greer, *Transforming Central Government: The Next Steps Initiative*, Buckingham: Open University Press, 1994, p. 60

Next Steps: the practice

The government accepted these recommendations with enthusiasm and immediately set about the business of setting up executive agencies. Within five years (1993) 97 executive agencies had been created, employing nearly two-thirds of all civil servants. Most of these are quite small – the Debt Management Office has 25 employees, the national Weights and Measures Laboratory has 55 – but some are very large and involve important government functions. There are no exact figures, but between 1979 and 1997 the number employed under Civil Service

Figure 7.2 *Staff working in executive agencies, or on Next Steps lines by department, 2001*

Source: www.civil-service.gov.uk/statistics

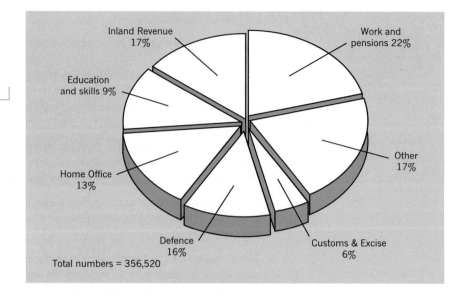

regulations fell from around 730,000 to fewer than 500,000, and by 1999 more than 75 per cent of all civil servants were working in 133 executive agencies in the UK (see Figure 7.2 and Table 7.1). Most agency chief executives were appointed through open competition, rather than internally (for details see the Cabinet Office web site).

In 1991 the white paper, Competing for Quality (Cm 1730, London: HMSO, 1991) extended much of the thinking inherent in Next Steps to other areas of government by means of 'market testing'. Designed to explore whether value for money can best be achieved by contracting out to private producers – known, more simply, as shopping around for the best service at the best price – market testing resulted in contracting out such things as the Inland Revenue's information technology service. By 1996 some £3.6 billion worth of services had been tested, with total savings claimed in excess of £700 million. However, depending on the agency or service concerned, in-house bids from those already providing it could be included, and these won most of the contracts.

Various other experiments to introduce market or quasi-market forces into public services were also tried, namely:

- Some services (notably the NHS) tried to create quasi- or 'internal' markets by separating the provider of a service from the purchaser.

- In other cases, services were not contracted out, but agencies were actually sold to the private sector. In 1996: the Chessington Computer Centre (providing payroll, financial and accounting services) was sold for £15.5 million pounds; the Recruitment and Assessment Services (providing recruitment and personnel services) for £7.25 million; and Her Majesty's Stationery Office (HMSO) for £54 million.

Table 7.1 *Top ten executive agencies by staff and expenditure, 2001*

By staff (full-time equivalent civil servants)		By expenditure (pounds million)	
Agency	Staff		
Social Security Benefits Agency	66,295		2,420
Inland Revenue	49,385		1,804
HM Prison Service	39,365		2,089
Employment Service	28,610		1,371
HM Customs & Excise	23,400		770
Defence Evaluation and Research Agency	11,065		983
Court Service	8,670		400
Social Security Child Support Agency	7,910		212
HM Land Registry	7,810		223
Social Security Contributions Agency	7,382		250
		Social Security Information and Technology Services Agency	316
		HM Land Registry	223
Total: Largest 10	249,892	Total: Largest 10	9,045
Total: All agencies	332,830	Total: Largest 50 Agencies	14,101

Note: Based on 105 agencies, plus two departments (Customs & Excise, and Inland Revenue) that operate along agency lines. A total of 131 agencies operate in the UK

Source: www.civil-service.gov.uk/statistics

- Voucher schemes were experimented with in nursery education.

- The Private Finance Initiative (1992) got off to a slow start but by 1997 the Dartford and Skye road crossings, and a few hospital and prison buildings had been financed this way. Labour endorsed the idea in 1997 by approving the private financing of the Birmingham Northern Relief Road, and, controversially, planning for private investment in the London Underground and hospitals.

SPREAD OF QUASI-GOVERNMENT

Another aspect of the reforms that swept the public sector in the 1980s and 1990s was the spread of quasi-government. The government itself refers to the strange creatures that inhabit this world as non-departmental public bodies. Academics and journalists usually call them quangos (quasi-autonomous non-governmental organisations), or extra-government organisations (EGOs). They are large in number and varied in function, but are all run by people appointed by the government, not by elected politicians or career civil servants.

Along with other democracies, Britain has long had public or semi-public bodies that are distinct from government. For example, the BBC is a quango run at arms' length from the government to avoid political interference in news broadcasting. There was a rapid spread of quangos in the 1980s for two main reasons:

1. The central government tried to bypass politically independent local authorities (often Labour controlled) and deliver particular services in line with its own policy through quangos. The government argued that they were less bureaucratic than other public sector organisations.

2. Privatisation of utilities and public services led to the setting up of regulatory agencies – eg Oftel, Ofgas and Ofwat to monitor the pricing and quality of telephone, gas, and water services.

BRIEFINGS

7.5 Classifying quasi-government

The government identifies four types of quango:

1. Executive non-departmental public bodies (NDPBs). These include such bodies as the utility regulators, the Arts Council, and the Commission for Racial Equality.

2. Advisory NDPBs such as the Electoral Commission.

3. Tribunals with judicial functions such as the Supplementary Benefits Appeals Tribunals and Rent Tribunals.

4. NHS bodies.

To this list must be added a number of other agencies, including opted-out schools and colleges, training and education councils (TECs), and housing action trusts (HATs). It could be argued that executive agencies (because they have operational autonomy) resemble quangos more than traditional local or central government departments. According to the Democratic Audit, in 1994 no fewer than 6,708 quangos existed, of which 5,521 had executive powers. In 1979 the Conservative government pledged itself to reduce the number of quangos, but actually increased them rapidly. New Labour has promised to open up public appointments to quangos by broadening the social and educational base of appointees.

Public sector reform: an assessment

The 1979–97 reforms were not the product of a master plan, but a piecemeal, step-by-step process which found its way more by accident and experience. Nonetheless, reform in the UK was part of a much wider set of changes that occurred across many western states in the 1980s and 1990s, often referred to as 'the new public management'. Thatcher was a leading exponent of the new public management, but by no means alone in the world.

The Thatcher–Major public service reforms

For	Against
Efficiency With fewer employed and lower costs public services are better value for money	*Efficiency? Who can tell?* There are no market tests for many public services (which is why they are public in the first place) so we cannot tell whether efficiency and quality have improved. Besides, central government did not monitor its own service performance (before and after measures)
Quality Service standards are higher	*Quality? Who can tell?* There is no clear evidence about public service quality. Besides, it would be expected to rise over time without the reforms
Decentralisation The old, hierarchical, centralised, rigid, bureaucratic Civil Service has been replaced by flexible and decentralised agencies with modern management practices	*Fragmentation* Government bureaucracies are even more fragmented than they were, and joined-up government is more difficult
Responsiveness Helped by the Citizens' Charters, executive agencies are more responsive to consumer demands	*Unresponsiveness* Executive agencies are more responsive to market forces than client needs. If they respond it is to the most vocal and articulate groups – ie the educated middle class, who know how to work the system
Specialised skills Executive agencies develop specialised skills to perform their particular jobs	*Specialised monopolies* Skills lost to the public sector are not likely to be regained, and then costs of agencies with a monopoly of skills will tend to rise
Sweeping away bureaucracy Reforms replaced bureaucracy with more efficient market or quasi-market mechanisms	*Extra bureaucracy* Reforms in hospitals, schools, and universities have created a huge extra burden on bureaucracy in these institutions and society as a whole
Deregulation Removing red tape has set service providers free to do their jobs effectively	*Reregulation* Deregulation is inevitably followed by reregulation to prevent crises such as mad cow disease, foot and mouth, and railway disasters
Separating steering from rowing Creating executive agencies leaves ministers and senior civil servants free to get on with policy making	*Policy making and administration* Policy making and administration are inseparable. Predictably, ministers interfere endlessly with agency administration
Customers not clients Public service consumers should be treated as markets treat customers	*Clients not customers* Many public service core users (pupils and students, prisoners, hospital patients, children, the mentally ill) are not customers, and public service professionals (teachers, doctors, and social workers) are not business or salespeople
Accountability Ministers and agencies have clear lines of responsibility and accountability. Ministers 'steer', agencies 'row'	*Lack of accountability* Lines of ministerial accountability are more confused and weaker with semi-autonomous executive agencies. There is no clear distinction between steering and rowing
Markets Market reforms have greatly improved public services	*Public service* The public service ethos, essential between the state and its services, has been severely damaged

There were, perhaps inevitably, some teething problems with the British reforms. For example, Group 4's contract with the prison service to transport prisoners brought public derision following a number of escapes. The Child Support Agency (CSA), responsible for ensuring maintenance payments by absent fathers, came under attack for what was claimed to be insensitive and aggressive action. The long-term effects of the reforms, however, are not at all clear and have aroused great controversy. The outlines of the argument are contained in 'Controversy' (see p. 169), but it is worth looking at three especially important aspects in greater detail – fragmentation, accountability, and efficiency.

Fragmentation

One of the major problems of British government in the post-war period – perhaps of almost any government in the modern world – is the fragmentation caused by the inevitable division of the state bureaucracy into separate departments and units. This tends to create overlapping, confusing, competing, and incompatible policies and services. The reforms of the 1980s and early 1990s make the problem worse.

The fragmentation of the public and quasi-public sector is now so great and confusing that it is difficult to obtain reliable statistics even on something as straightforward as the simple number of organisations, bodies, and agencies. One estimate is that there are now over 5,500 special purpose bodies spending more than £40 billion a year of public money, involving more than 70,000 ministerial appointments to governing bodies. This may well help to create more policy incoherence than ever before. New Labour's concern with joined-up government can be seen as a response to the problem of fragmentation created by the reforms of the 1980s and early 1990s.

Accountability

Fragmentation undermines accountability partly because it can be difficult to find out who is responsible to whom for doing what, partly because quasi-public bodies often work and take decisions in secret, and partly because many of them are not accountable to anybody in particular. This is all the worse if, as often charged, the Thatcher and Major governments stacked quangos with their own party supporters, otherwise known as local notables, 'reliable chaps', and 'safe hands'. The first report of the Standing Committee on Standards in Public Life (the Nolan Committee) reacted to this state of affairs by recommending:

- appointment to quangos by merit
- a commissioner to vet appointments
- the declaration of party interests
- a code of conduct for members similar to that of the Civil Service.

The Blair government has pledged to implement the Nolan recommendations, and has managed to increase the proportion of working class and minority group appointments. Inevitably the press has responded with comments about 'Tony's Cronies'.

The accountability problem of executive agencies is different but just as serious. It occurs when ministers, who remain responsible for the overall operation of their departments, pass the buck to chief executive officers when a problem arises. If 'operations' are separated from 'policy' the strong implication is that the agency chiefs are responsible for errors or maladministration, although constitutionally ministers are responsible. This problem was graphically illustrated in the case of the Prison Service Agency when, in 1995, the chief executive, Derek Lewis, was obliged to resign following a series of successful prison breakouts. The Home Secretary, Michael Howard, said it was an operational and not a policy problem, though he was accused by Lewis of interfering repeatedly in operational matters.

Efficiency

There are serious questions about the efficiency of some of the new bodies. Many quangos are not run by professionals or experienced managers, and devolving services to small, independent agencies can involve considerable additional administrative costs and inefficiencies. The Democratic Audit found that clerical and accounting costs had risen rapidly in opted-out school and hospital trusts, and that cost management in some bodies was defective. In 1994 the House of Commons' Public Accounts Committee found that the management standards of quangos, rather than rising had actually fallen during the early 1990s. In some instances, corruption, serious maladministration, and waste of public money was uncovered, and the Committee was 'seriously concerned', 'surprised', and even 'appalled' by the record of one Regional Hospital Authority.

One response to the problems of fragmentation, lack of accountability, and inefficiency is to add a new layer of regulation and inspection to government. A whole new industry of 'auditing' and monitoring has been created including the National Audit Office, the Prisons Inspectorate, the Office of Public Service, the Better Regulation Unit in the Cabinet Office, the Benefit Fraud Inspectorate, the Commission for Health Improvement, and so on. The list runs to about 150 organisations, spending close to £900 million, and probably incurring a roughly equivalent amount from the inspected and regulated bodies.

NEW LABOUR AND THE PUBLIC SECTOR

On coming to power, New Labour accepted many of the broad reforms of the Thatcher–Major governments. It:

- declared the Next Steps agencies 'an integral part of the government machine'
- accepted Citizens' Charters and revived them in 1998 as *Service First*

- agreed to benchmarking and contracting out in both central and local government (see Chapter 12)

- accepted the principle of selling central government assets (a majority stake in the Commonwealth Development Corporation was sold)

- relaunched the Private Finance Initiative as Public–Private Partnerships

- developed the practice of setting public policy targets, penalties and rewards, and using league tables.

At the same time, New Labour has given two new twists to reform. It has:

1. made service quality and value for money its first priority, using the People's Panel of 5,000 randomly selected citizens as a sounding board for opinion about public services (the Panel was discontinued in 2002)

2. adopted a pragmatic approach to reforms, accepting those which work and rejecting others. The internal market in the NHS and the nursery school voucher scheme were quietly abolished.

New Labour has produced two major documents on public sector and civil service reform. The first, the white paper on Modernising Government (1999), promised better services, more use of outsiders, and greater efforts to produce joined-up government. The second, later in the same year, was the Wilson Report (after the Cabinet Secretary and Head of the Home Civil Service, Sir Richard Wilson) on the Civil Service, which argued for stronger leadership, better performance, and more outsider and minority recruitment into the Civil Service. There is evidence that outside recruitment has increased substantially.

Joined-up government

New Labour's main contribution to public sector reform, however, is its drive for joined-up government, sometimes called holistic governance (see also Chapter 6). This is by no means new to British government: Churchill experimented (1951–3), with 16 'overlords' to co-ordinate the activities of Whitehall departments; Wilson (1964–70) tried merging departments to create 'superdepartments', like Health and Social Security; and Heath created the Central Policy Review Staff (CPRS) in 1971 to give collective advice to ministers and overall direction to government policy. Now New Labour has created its 'action zones', particularly in education, health, social exclusion, electronic commerce, and government, to do the same thing.

All modern governments wrestle with the intractable problem of departmentalism and fragmentation because joined-up policy making and implementation are difficult, perhaps impossible, to achieve in the sprawling, departmentalised, specialised and competing public (and private) bureaucracies of the modern world.

At worst, creating new units and agencies of government to foster co-ordination and integration simply adds a new layer of co-ordinating bodies to the bodies to be co-ordinated.

There is also an inherent tension between Labour's drive to produce joined-up government and higher performance standards, on the one hand, and its efforts to decentralise, on the other. Joined-up government and the monitoring of performance standards both rest on centralisation, which is why many of the new units created to achieve them are located in the PM's or the Cabinet Office. Yet the constantly changing machinery of central intervention and co-ordination may actually add to fragmentation and uncertainty about who does what and how. One very senior ex-civil servant described the Blair government as 'more gummed up than joined up'.

One can easily imagine Sir Humphrey, of *Yes Minister*, describing, to his befuddled minister: 'The new Cabinet unit set up to co-ordinate the central agencies that manage the decentralised agencies earlier established to monitor the co-ordination of decentralisation.'

ESSAYS

1. Which of the Thatcher–Major reforms of Whitehall has New Labour adopted, and which has it rejected? Why has it done so?

2. Do special advisers in Whitehall politicise the Civil Service?

3. Why is joined-up government essential but difficult to achieve? What effect did the Thatcher–Major reforms have, and how successful are New Labour's attempts to create joined-up government likely to be?

SUMMARY

- The traditional Whitehall model of the Civil Service presents it as a hierarchical, centralised, public service bureaucracy, with clear lines of responsibility from impartial civil servants to elected ministers, to Parliament. This has never been a precise portrayal of British public administration, although it has approximated the ideal in some respects.

- The public sector reforms of the Thatcher–Major governments, 1979–97, were intended to radically transform the traditional model by introducing market competition and business management in order to improve public service quality and reduce costs.

- The most important single innovation was the separation of policy making (steering) from management (rowing) by turning over most Civil Service administration to more than 100 semi-autonomous executive agencies, run on commercial lines, and with chief executive officers on short-term contracts.

- Another change was the creation of a large quasi-government sector.

- There is much controversy about the effects of the 1979–97 reforms, and no clear-cut conclusions, although some evidence that government by quango lacks in efficiency and accountability.

- New Labour has accepted many Thatcher–Major reforms and added a few of its own.

- Most notably, New Labour has tried to create joined-up government, although success has been hard to achieve.

MILESTONES

Milestones in administrative reform

1968 The Fulton Report aimed at a more professional Civil Service that recruited more widely

1968 Civil Service Department (CSD) set up

1968 Civil Service College founded

1979 Efficiency Unit set up by Margaret Thatcher to review departmental performance

1981 CSD abolished. Management Personnel Office more closely linked to Cabinet Office

1983 Financial Management Initiative requires policy objectives to be specified and more managerial autonomy

1983 Cabinet secretary emerges as head of the Civil Service

1983 Privatisation of state-owned property and industry begins in earnest

1988 Efficiency Unit publishes Next Steps, which proposes the separation of management from policy and creation of autonomous executive agencies in central government. Many such agencies created in the following years

1991 Citizen's Charter launched, specifying consumer rights in various areas

1992 Private Finance Initiative (PFI) encourages private finance of government projects

1995 Office of Public Service succeeds CSD but remains under control of Cabinet Office

1997 New Labour government accepts the major administrative changes of 1979–97. Appoints more political advisers to Whitehall, and is criticised for continuing Thatcher's policy of politicising the Civil Service. The Social Exclusion Unit, the first of the attempts to create joined-up government, is set up

1998 White paper, *Modernising Government*, and Wilson Report on Civil Service reform

1999 Neill Committee on Standards in Public Life recommends a limit to the number of special advisers in Whitehall, and a code of conduct for them

FURTHER READING

A vast literature exists on public service organisation in general and recent Civil Service reforms in particular, but see especially C. Pilkington, *The Civil Service in Britain Today* (Manchester: Manchester University Press, 1999); K. Theakston, *The Civil Service Since 1945* (Oxford: Blackwell, 1995); R. Pyper, *The British Civil Service* (London: Prentice-Hall/Harvester Wheatsheaf, 1995), and D. Richards, *The Civil Service under the Conservatives 1979–1997* (Brighton: Sussex Academic Press, 1997). For a careful empirical study of the demise of the Whitehall model, see Colin Campbell and Graham K. Wilson, *The End of Whitehall: Death of a Paradigm* (Oxford: Blackwell, 1995). Two useful collections of the readings are P. Barberis (ed.), *The Whitehall Reader: The UK's Administrative Machine in Action* (Milton Keynes: Open University Press, 1996) and P. Barberis (ed.), *The Civil Service in an Era of Change* (Aldershot: Dartmouth, 1997).

Useful and up-to-date reviews of the Thatcher–Major reforms and the New Labour record so far are R. A. W. Rhodes, 'New Labour's Civil Service: summing-up joining-up', *Political Quarterly*, **71** (2), 2000, pp. 151–66, and D. Kavanagh and D. Richards, 'Departmentalism and joined-up government: back to the future?' *Parliamentary Affairs*, **54**, 2001, pp. 1–18. Shorter articles are T. Butcher, 'The civil service under New Labour', *Politics Review*, **11** (3), 2002, pp. 29–31 and R. Pyper, 'The Civil Service under Blair', *Politics Review*, **9** (3), 2000, pp. 2–6; T. Butcher, 'The Civil Service: structure and

1. (For class debate) What are the reasons for claiming and denying the idea that hospital patients, old people, young children, prisoners, the mentally ill and handicapped, and single parents are customers of public services? What are the implications of your answer for replacing the public service ethos with a market approach?

2. (For class debate) What are the reasons for believing that public service efficiency and quality have improved since 1979 as a result of reforms? Why is it so difficult to know?

management', in R. Pyper and L. Robins, *United Kingdom Governance* (Basingstoke: Palgrave, 2000); and M. Moran, 'The new regulatory state in Britain', *Talking Politics*, **13** (3), 2001, pp. 109–13.

USEFUL WEB SITES ON THE CHANGING STATE AND ADMINISTRATIVE REFORM

Hot links to these sites can be found on the CWS at http://www.booksites.net/budge. The web has much information concerning the British Civil Service and its transformation. A detailed account of changes between 1967 and 1997 can be obtained from the report of the Select Committee on Public Services at www.parliament.the-stationery-office.co.uk/pa/ld199798/ldselect/ldpubsrv/055/psrep03.htm.
The British Council also offers interesting insights in the reform of the civil service (www.britcoun.org/governance). Since 1997, there have been major transformations in this area, for which the best source of information is the Cabinet Office web site www.cabinet-office.gov.uk and the Civil Service official site www.civilservice.gov.uk. A general overview of the reforms introduced by the Labour government in this area and others in the last five years can be found at www.politics.guardian.co.uk/fiveyears. A good deal of documentation on the renewal process can be obtained by using the search engine of the Archive of Official Documents web site at www.archive.official-documents.co.uk.

If you are interested in a comparative perspective on the reform of the Civil Service, visit the World Bank web site at www.worldbank.org/publicsector/civilservice.

There are also many sites offering information on myriad quasi-non-governmental organisations (quangos). The first step is to visit the public bodies web site at www.quango.gov.uk. You can also check the Office of the Commissioner for Public Appointments (www.ocpa.gov.uk). We suggest that you also visit the Committee on Standards in Public Life (www.public-standards.gov.uk) and the Local Government Association (www.lga.gov.uk). Academic analysis of the public administration can be obtained from www.sourceuk.net/indexf.html.

The Parliamentary Commissioner for Administration (PCA) maintains a web site to address citizen grievances concerning the activities of government departments or agencies (www.parliament.ombudsman.org.uk). Her Majesty's Stationery Office (www.hmso.gov.uk) has full documentation on the Local Government Act 1992 and the Citizen's Charter. Visit the Council of Europe site (www.coe.fr/index.asp) for the full text of the European Convention for the Protection of Human Rights. Reports on the quality of British Democracy in general can be found at www.democratic.org.uk. For comments and feedback on the public sector and its management visit www.publicnet.co.uk.

PART 3

Beyond Westminster

European Parliament, Strasbourg

Britain in Europe

As our discussion of central government, and even of the constitution shows, British politics have increasingly taken on a European dimension. The former European (Economic) Community (EC, EEC) changed its name to the European Union (EU) by the Treaty of Maastricht (1992). This symbolised the intention of the member countries, particularly France and Germany, to transform it into a federal state. An important stage was marked by the adoption of a common currency, the euro, by 11 of these members in 1999. Britain stood aloof but clearly will have to decide whether to join the European Monetary Union (EMU). The Conservative Party is increasingly united in opposition to this move while Labour remains equivocal.

'Europe' has thus become the major issue dividing British parties. However, it also affects British politics in two other ways. One is the role Britain plays as one of the major Member States of the EU, which is the subject of this chapter. The other is the impact of the EU in Britain itself (Chapter 9), where the increasing integration of the country into European administrative structures means that British politics cannot be adequately described without the European dimension. The inseparability of European from domestic politics was shown in such an everyday but far-reaching matter as the specification of a minimum wage following EU practice (despite Conservative opposition).

The fact that European bodies can now legislate for Britain independently of the government shows that national sovereignty is being eroded. By the same token a new federal entity, in which Britain constitutes just one unit, is clearly emerging. The decision whether to go ahead and accept the single currency is the most crucial waiting to be taken by any British government at this time.

This chapter describes the institutional development of the European Union and the British role within it. It covers:

- the nature and development of the European Union
- the British role within it
- the Single European Act, the Treaties of Maastricht, Amsterdam and Nice; towards a European federal state?
- Europe as a crisis issue in British politics
- enlargement of the Union: how this affects Britain.

THE EUROPEAN UNION: ORIGINS AND DEVELOPMENT

Britain is currently one of 15 Member States of the European Union (which should expand to 25 in the near future). It is not one of the Founding Members, however, since the Union originated in 1951 as the 'European Coal and Steel Community' (ECSC) grouping France, Germany, the Netherlands, Belgium,

Luxembourg and Italy. Although severely functional in form and designed ostensibly to rationalise the Continental iron and coal industry, the project actually masked political ambitions to integrate France and Germany so thoroughly that they would never be able to go to war again as they had in 1914 and 1939, provoking colossal destruction and 20,000,000 deaths.

While supporting this initiative Britain did not join it. In the 1950s British governments saw their interests in terms of three overlapping spheres of influence: the Empire, the USA and Europe. The financial transactions of the City and its world trading relationships gave Britain stronger overseas links than with the Continent.

Although British and Continental attitudes to European co-operation have varied over the half century since, the generally enthusiastic approach of the Continentals to integration and the scepticism of the British have been constants throughout. Underlying this contrast has been the British commitment to free trade and thus to a purely economic Common Market, as distinct from Continental support for full-blooded political union.

> **Functional integration**
> Integration based on pragmatic co-operation between states in specific areas of (usually) economic activity. In the European context, functional integration is often contrasted with deeper and wider political integration of a federal kind.

BRIEFINGS

8.1 The Council of Europe

The Council of Europe was an early attempt to integrate the European countries, set up in 1949 as an intergovernmental consultative organisation designed to advance co-operation between members and help encourage democracy and human rights throughout Europe. The Council meets in Strasbourg, France, and is made up of a Committee of Ministers, a Parliamentary Assembly and a Congress of Local and Regional Authorities. Meeting four times a year, the Assembly adopts resolutions and the Council then makes recommendations to members. In spite of this statelike structure, the Council of Europe has no legislative powers. Decisions are taken by consensus of all members. Until recently the most important function of the Council was the operation of the European Convention on Human Rights, which was created in 1954 and whose rules are enforced by the Court of Human Rights. Note that this Court, whose decisions are binding on members, is not an EU institution.

> **Intergovernmental organisations**
> International organisations that allow national states to co-operate on specific matters while maintaining their national sovereignty.

By 1996 the Council of Europe had 44 members, and one with 'guest status'. Since the fall of communism the Council's role as a forum for advancing democracy has increased substantially. A newly created European Commission for Democracy through Law advises emerging democratic countries on constitutional and other matters. In addition, membership of the Council is seen as a first step towards membership of the EU.

Plate 8.1 *Vicky cartoon in the* Daily Express, *1961, showing Harold Macmillan's reluctance to join the European Union:* 'If they want us they will have to make it easy for us.' *Charles de Gaulle and Konrad Adenauer, Prime Ministers of France and Germany, lead on their bicycles*

Source: *Daily Express*

"IF THEY WANT US THEY WILL HAVE TO MAKE IT EASY FOR US" —MR. MACMILLAN

Plate 8.2 *Vicky cartoon in the* Evening Standard, *1962, showing Britain (personified by Harold Macmillan) caught in a dilemma between its Commonwealth commitments and a new European future*

Source: *Daily Express*

"BUT MY DEAR, YOU KNOW — ALL THESE RUMOURS OF OUR BREAK-UP ARE RIDICULOUS!"

Map 8.1
The enlargement of the European Union, 1957–2004

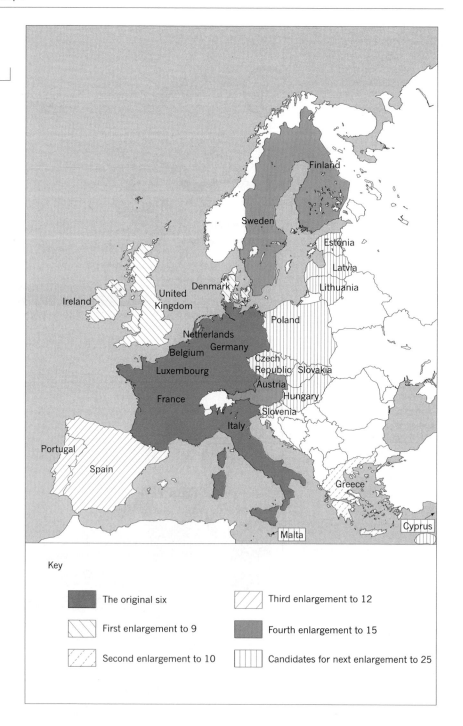

Key

The original six

First enlargement to 9

Second enlargement to 10

Third enlargement to 12

Fourth enlargement to 15

Candidates for next enlargement to 25

8.2 Functional integration and the Common Agricultural Policy (CAP)

Following failures to create a European state directly after the war, Continental leaders decided that functional integration would make the members of the EC interdependent economically and that this would encourage political integration. The reasoning was that, if the countries of the six shared common production and pricing policies in such essential goods as coal, steel, atomic power and agriculture, they would be locked into economic interdependence and would therefore have every incentive to co-operate on other matters (a phenomenon that social scientists have called spillover). This would then eliminate the sort of competition and conflict that led to the Second World War.

As an economic project functional integration proved less than successful. By the late 1950s national rather than EC priorities dominated policy in coal, steel and in the generation of atomic energy. Only in agriculture did co-operation flourish, mainly because of the political benefits of pleasing large numbers of small farmers in France, Germany and Italy. The Common Agricultural Policy set artificial prices for all the major agricultural products. Whenever the world market price of a product fell below this price, the EC imposed tariffs on imports to make up the difference between the market price and the CAP price. Inefficient farmers were, therefore, given an incentive to remain inefficient. Consumers were paying above-market prices for food and in addition a surplus was built up that had to be stored. These surpluses – the 'butter mountains' and 'wine lakes' – resulted in a widespread ridiculing of the CAP.

A further difficulty with the projected enlargement to Eastern Europe is that payments to the large numbers of farmers there would bankrupt the scheme.

During the 1980s and 1990s a number of reforms were initiated, all of which were designed to reduce the level of price support and eventually to replace the intervention price mechanism with direct income supports. While the proportion of the EU budget devoted to the CAP has declined in recent years – as indeed has the agricultural population, which at around 5 per cent is just one-third of the 1958 figure – inefficiencies remain and constitute an obvious area for reform. Whether there is the political will to do this, particularly in the major recipients of subsidies (the Mediterranean countries and Ireland) remains to be seen.

The ECSC was important because it established the principle of functional integration – integrating specific industrial or economic sectors under a supranational institutional authority responsible for policing a European policy. It became the precursor of the European Economic Community created by the Treaty of Rome in 1957. In turn this was to develop into the European Union in the 1990s. From its very beginning the EEC opened up the possibility of evolving from a loose confederation of countries concerned only with integration in certain functional economic sectors into a much tighter organisation resembling a federal state. Aware of this ultimate objective, the founding fathers of the EEC created a comprehensive institutional structure which resembled that of a national government. The European Commission seemed very like a European government. Originally it was confined to implementing directives agreed by national governments, but powers of autonomous decision making were much expanded by the Single European Act (SEA, 1986) and the Treaties of Maastricht (1993) and Amsterdam (1997). Figure 8.1 shows the institutional structure of the

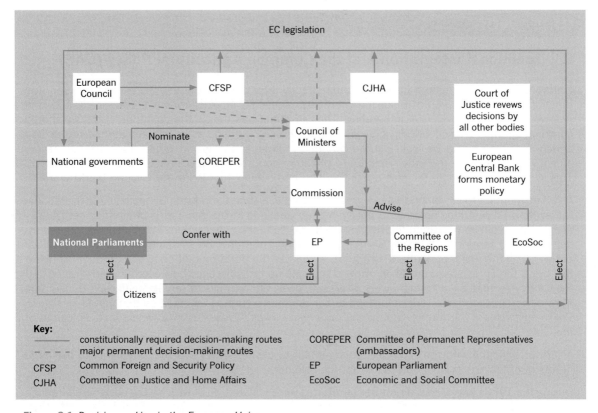

Figure 8.1 *Decision making in the European Union*

Federal A political structure that combines a central authority with a degree of constitutionally defined autonomy for sub-central units of government – usually states, regions or provinces.

EU in the 1990s, which is broadly similar to that laid down in the Treaty of Rome of 1957.[1]

The Treaty of Rome set up a grouping of the original six members of the ECSC with a much greater range of functions and tasks than the original body. To symbolise this it changed its name to the European Economic Community. In particular the new body was to harmonise trade by removing internal barriers and enforcing common rules on all the Member States; and to reform agriculture through the Common Agricultural Policy (CAP). This was a system of guaranteed price supports for the numerous and often inefficient farmers of France, Italy and other Member States. CAP payments dominated the budget, which gave the EEC

---

[1] Decision-making procedures in the EU are complex and can only be provided schematically in Figure 8.1. The most important relationship is between the citizens of the individual member states, national governments, the Council of Ministers and the Commission. For major policy and political initiatives the Council representing national governments remains the key body. For the details of implementation the Commission is centrally placed. These relationships are shown in the figure. A secondary, but increasingly important, body is the European Parliament which, via the co-decision-making procedures introduced by the Maastricht Treaty (1992), now plays a role in a range of policy areas. Finally, the meetings of government leaders (the European Council, not to be confused with the Council of Ministers) can launch major initiatives that are later endorsed by the Council of Ministers (see also Figure 9.1 and related text).

the reputation of a protectionist agricultural grouping rather than a promoter of free trade and open markets.

Despite this, economic activity among the six expanded enormously and they increasingly attracted British exports. By the early 1960s British trade was shifting from overseas towards Europe. The British were keen to share in community prosperity. Changes in both the Conservative and Labour parties encouraged a more pro-European position. Under the leadership of Harold Macmillan the Conservatives had become a modernising, centrist party committed to rapid economic growth and technological change. Similarly, the Labour Party under Harold Wilson was intent on modernisation. For both leaders participation in an economically dynamic Europe looked attractive. However, both the Conservative government's application for EC membership in 1963 and the Labour application in 1967 were vetoed by the French. Finally in 1973 Britain was admitted along with Ireland and Denmark.

BRITAIN AS A MEMBER STATE

In joining the EC Britain now acquired a voice in its affairs equal to that of each of the original 'Big Three' countries, France, Germany and Italy. However, the UK was only one among a number of members, and could always be outvoted by a coalition of the others. Given that Britain continued to view the EC primarily in economic terms while most other countries saw it as a political project, this opened up a line of potential conflict. This was not very apparent until the late 1980s, for two reasons.

First, within the EC, a period of inertia and stagnation followed the rapid expansion of the 1960s. A crisis of identity developed as attempts at further integration faltered. In the face of the economic dislocations of the 1970s national governments tended to rely on national rather than collective solutions to their problems. At the same time, the CAP was increasingly perceived as expensive, wasteful and inefficient. By the late 1970s agricultural surpluses in the form of food 'mountains' had built up, through the inability of European farmers to sell their produce at the market-determined world price. Instead, the EC bought the produce at a higher price and stored it for future use. These 'mountains' emphasised the protectionist and interventionist side of EC policies and deprived it of support for other initiatives. Each Member State had a veto over new developments. As British hostility to any deepening of political integration was known, this in itself acted as a deterrent to any non-economic initiatives during the 1970s and early 1980s.

Britain was itself partly responsible for ending this state of affairs through excessive use of its national veto in the early 1980s. Threatened vetoes over a whole series of unrelated EC policies secured reluctant support for Britain in the Falklands War (1982) and a large budget 'rebate', ie return to Britain of some of the money paid in tax to the EC (1982–4).

This all established an image of Britain as a 'bad European' among the officials and politicians of the other Member States. Events since then have reinforced, rather than challenged, this reputation. This was unfortunate as a new EC initiative now undermined the power of veto and accelerated the processes of integration within the EC, thereby posing new dilemmas for the British.

THE SINGLE EUROPEAN ACT AND MAASTRICHT: QUANTUM LEAPS FORWARD FOR THE EC

Until the mid-1980s the EC was an intergovernmental organisation with responsibilities mainly in agriculture, environmental protection, regional and competition policy. For important decisions such as enlargement, or major budget and policy changes, a unanimous vote in the Council of Ministers was required. Although the European Parliament (EP) had been directly elected by voters since 1979, its powers were confined to approving or rejecting the EU budget as a whole. From 1985 to 1992 all this was to change as the EC evolved into an embryonic federal state.

BRIEFINGS

8.3 Intergovernmental and federal organisations

When discussing forms of international organisation it is common to characterise them in terms of a continuum ranging from loose organisations that have no power to impose rules or sanctions on members, to full-blown federal governments that can oblige a member (or constituent state) to adhere to legislation and punish it for non-compliance. One of the loosest intergovernmental organisations is the United Nations: members can leave at will and there are effectively no sanctions that the Security Council can impose on them.

Since the late 1980s the EU has developed into what might be called a 'strong' intergovernmental organisation. The Council of Ministers can, by majority vote, oblige members to follow certain policies (although on major matters, such as enlargement of the Union, unanimity is still required). Moreover, the EU has all the trappings of a state including a legislature, courts and a bureaucracy. Most scholars agree that, for a true federation to exist, the central government should have control over defence and macro economic policy. With its single currency, therefore, the EU has taken a significant step towards federalism – reinforced by the discussions on a common defence set in motion by the Treaty of Amsterdam (1997). Note, however, that compared with other federations the EU has a weak central government. In countries such as the USA, Australia and Canada the federal government controls defence, the economy and a vast range of social policies. No one expects the EU to take on equivalent roles for many years, although proponents of a united Europe clearly want such a transformation. Note also that in the strongest federations the central government is often prepared to go to war to keep the federation together, as is the case with Russia's intervention in Chechnya. Membership of the EU is effectively voluntary: if a country wanted to leave, serious economic consequences might follow, but the other members would respect its decision. In this sense the EU resembles a confederation, where membership of the collection of states is voluntary, more than a federation, where membership is considered irreversible.

The impetus came from a growing perception that the Member States could not compete successfully at world level unless they were truly integrated. In addition, the experience of the 1970s and the early 1980s had convinced many that national governments on their own would find it increasingly difficult to control inflation. The solution to these problems lay in a single economy with a single currency. Such arrangements would also require a degree of political integration so as to enforce them properly and to make European-wide institutions accountable to electors. Political integration was also seen, not least by Chancellor Kohl, the German leader, and François Mitterrand, the French President, as a way of binding an enlarged Germany into Europe, and preventing it from threatening its neighbours.

BRIEFINGS

8.4 The changed international situation during the 1980s and the impetus towards monetary co-operation

Competing theories exist to explain the acceleration of moves towards European union during the 1980s, but most agree that monetary co-operation is a key factor. From the 1970s most countries agreed to abolish exchange and other controls on the movement of capital across national borders. As a result, investors from around the globe could move their money to those countries that were likely to produce the best return. The key factors determining where to invest are the stability of exchange rates, level of interest rates and political and social order. With the internationalisation of capital movements, governments in all the EU countries had an incentive to keep their investment environments as attractive as possible. Previously they could literally stop money from leaving the country, but with the abolition of controls they had no power to do so. Moreover, during the 1970s and 1980s a number of governments (including Britain, Belgium, France, and Italy) had been unable to stop the export of capital by raising interest rates and had been forced into humiliating devaluations. Thus opinion started to harden around the idea of pooling currencies in a European Monetary System (EMS) that, through the operation of an Exchange Rate Mechanism (ERM), would oblige governments to keep their currencies within specified bands around a central rate. During the early 1980s the ERM did not work well, as many countries failed to keep within the specified bands. However, from 1983 to 1989 things improved so much that the ERM was increasingly viewed as a precursor to full monetary union. During 1992 and 1993, however, the system unravelled as the international markets decided that the currencies of the vulnerable economies (in particular Britain and Italy) were overvalued and ripe for mass selling. German unification had forced the Germans to raise interest rates to hold down inflation, so capital moved rapidly to Germany and out of other Member States' currencies. Governments proved incapable of stemming the outward flow of capital and were forced to leave the ERM, effectively devaluing their currencies. This crisis destroyed public confidence in the Conservatives' capacity to handle economic affairs and thus led to their election defeat in 1997.

Since the events of the early 1990s, two schools of thought have emerged about monetary co-operation. The right wing of the Conservative Party sees these events as evidence of the folly of trying to link currencies together. It argues that a single currency is even more dangerous, because it removes an individual country's ability to devalue and leads to high unemployment and economic recession. Others argue that the problems with the ERM in 1992 and 1993 demonstrate the need for a single currency that stabilises all the European currencies at one level, with the euro (the new currency unit) forming a strong and highly sought-after international currency.

Table 8.1 *Arrangements for qualified majority voting in the EU*

Country	Weighting	Country	Weighting
France	10	Austria	4
Germany	10	Sweden	4
UK	10	Denmark	3
Italy	10	Finland	3
Spain	8	Ireland	3
Belgium	5	Luxembourg	2
Greece	5	Total	87
Netherlands	5		
Portugal	5		

Source: Commission of the European Communities, *Adapting the Institutions to Make a Success of Enlargement*, COM (2000) 34, Brussels, 2000, p. 61

The first step in this transformation was the Single European Act. Signed in 1986 it was designed to achieve the original aim of the 1957 Treaty of Rome: the creation of a single market in goods, capital and labour. In addition, the Act strengthened the federal as opposed to intergovernmental nature of EC decision making. Unanimity in the Council of Ministers remained for major issues such as enlargement. But the details of implementation could be expedited through 'qualified' majority voting (QMV).[2] The powers of the European Parliament were also strengthened, although not dramatically, and the Treaty made bold declarations on the need for greater political (ie defence) co-operation (Table 8.1).

The British government enthusiastically supported the free market provisions of the SEA, but were critical of the political changes. Achieving a genuine common market in goods and services had long been an objective of Conservative governments. It was the marriage of this objective to political integration that was unacceptable to many members of the party.

Their objections paled into insignificance beside Conservative reactions to the Treaty on European Union (the Maastricht Treaty), signed on 7 February 1992. Maastricht represented a radical departure from preceding initiatives because of its ambitious economic and political objectives. The most important of these were:

- creation of a European Union with a common citizenship

- creation of a single currency by 1999 under the control of a European central bank

---

2 Each country represented in the Council of Ministers is given a weighting as shown in Table 8.1; for a measure to be adopted a total of 62 votes is necessary. The Single European Act and the Treaties of Maastricht, Amsterdam and Nice greatly extended the number of areas covered by QMV (they had previously required unanimity). Great controversy has surrounded the size of the blocking minority required under QMV. The British, in particular, are concerned that with enlargement the position of the bigger states would be weakened. From the very beginning the EC gave to smaller states a weighted vote greater than they would have been given in proportion to their populations. The present arrangement is a compromise. Following the 1995 enlargement the British wanted the blocking minority to be set at 23, whereas the final agreement was 25. In anticipation of further enlargement slightly more weight has been given to larger countries, in provisions due to enter into force in 2004–05.

- strict 'convergence criteria' for joining the currency

- acceptance of a Social Protocol (sometimes also known as the 'Social Chapter') on minimum working and social conditions for all citizens of the European Union

- creation of a Cohesion Fund to help the poorer states and regions adjust to economic change

- co-decision making between the Council and the Parliament in further areas so as to strengthen the role of the European Parliament. Decisions resulting from this procedure were subject to QMV in the Council of Ministers. The treaty also extended the number of policy areas subject to QMV.

BRIEFINGS

8.5 Convergence criteria for European Monetary Union (EMU)

To join the European Monetary Union (EMU), a country has to demonstrate that it has achieved a 'sustainable convergence with the economies of the other Member States'. This is because currencies cannot be united unless countries experience reasonably similar economic conditions and pursue similar economic policies. To qualify, therefore, countries have to meet the following criteria:

- price stability or a rate of inflation close to that of the three best performing states

- the achievement of a public sector deficit of not more than 3 per cent of gross domestic product (GDP) in any year and not more than 60 per cent accumulated debt as a percentage of GDP

- stability of a Member's currency in the ERM for two years with no devaluations within two years

- the achievement of a level of long-term interest rates as low as the average of the three best performing states in the EU.

These criteria proved very difficult to achieve in the 1992 to 1998 period, when many Member States experienced economic recession. In both 1996 and 1997 the interpretation, if not the wording, of the criteria was loosened so as to accommodate the particular problems of Germany and Italy, neither of whom looked likely to meet the strict interpretation of the criteria by 1999, when EMU was scheduled to take effect. This demonstrates that EMU was really a political step towards full federation as much as an economic measure. Similarly the economic 'tests' proposed by the Labour government to determine whether joining EMU would be good for Britain will be interpreted in terms of political considerations and popular reactions to such a move.

The Conservative Prime Minister, John Major, eventually signed the Treaty in 1993. But he did so only after extensive negotiations that secured an opt-out for Britain from the final stage of the Single Currency, which is still in force. British objections were partly political and partly ideological. Major was vulnerable to the vociferous and significant minority of 'Eurosceptics' within the Parliamentary Conservative Party, convinced that a single currency would end British sovereignty.

Plate 8.3 *Garland cartoon in the* Daily Telegraph, *1992: Margaret Thatcher warns that the EU is headed for severe problems unless plans for a centralised economy and political union are drastically changed. Her bow is aimed at Jacques Delors, Commission President, who is flanked by Douglas Hurd, John Major, François Mitterrand and Helmut Kohl*

Source: *Daily Telegraph*

The then Conservative leadership assumed a more pragmatic line: that membership would be in Britain's interests 'when the time was right', particularly in terms of keeping inflation down. If there has been a constant in British economic policy since 1979 it has been a commitment to keeping inflation low. The debate created deep divisions within the Conservative Party. Labour and the Liberal Democrats supported the Treaty, particularly its Social Protocol, which guaranteed limited working hours and a minimum wage.

EUROPE AS A CRISIS ISSUE IN BRITISH POLITICS

As the controversies over recent treaties show, EU policies now affect many aspects of British economic and social life. However, for most of the population the Union remains remote. In their everyday lives people feel more directly affected by the activities of local councils, regional executives and the Westminster government. This is confirmed by the large number (one-quarter in 2002) who continue to hold 'no opinion' about membership of the EU. British antipathy to Europe is among the highest in the EU (Table 8.2). Moreover, at 23 per cent in 1999, British turnout in the European Parliamentary election was much less than half of that at the 2001 general election, and was the lowest in the EU.

There are, therefore, deep divisions over Europe among many sections of the public and in particular among British political leaders, the deepest of which now exists between the Conservative and Labour parties. This derives from a broader cleavage between internationalists and nationalists. The former see Britain's future as an active but by no means dominant partner in a multicultural Europe. The nationalists see Britain essentially as an independent economic and political

Table 8.2 *Public opinion on membership of the EU in constituent countries*

Country	1973			1980			1990			1994			1998			2002		
	Good	Bad	No opinion/ no reply	Good	Bad	No opinion/ no reply	Good	Bad	No opinion/ no reply	Good	Bad	No opinion/ no reply	Good	Bad	No opinion/ no reply	Good	Bad	No opinion/ no reply
Belgium	57	5	38	57	2	41	69	5	26	56	10	36	47	9	43	56	25	19
Denmark	42	30	28	33	29	38	49	25	26	53	26	21	56	20	25	72	19	10
Germany	63	4	33	65	6	29	62	7	31	50	12	38	48	11	40	44	34	22
Greece				42	22	36	75	5	20	64	9	27	67	9	25	78	14	9
Spain				58	5	37	65	8	27	50	14	36	63	7	30	60	20	21
France	61	5	34	51	9	40	63	7	30	50	13	37	52	12	36	53	25	22
Ireland	56	15	29	52	19	29	74	8	18	72	7	21	79	4	17	90	5	6
Italy	69	2	29	74	3	23	75	3	22	68	5	27	68	5	26	57	19	24
Luxembourg	67	3	30	84	3	13	72	8	20	71	9	20	77	6	18	71	19	10
Netherlands	63	4	33	75	3	22	82	3	15	77	5	18	75	6	19	67	18	15
Portugal				24	6	70	62	4	34	54	13	33	58	9	33	73	13	15
United Kingdom	31	34	33	21	55	24	52	19	29	43	22	35	37	22	41	36	39	26
Austria													38	19	43	46	37	17
Finland													45	21	29	39	49	12
Sweden													35	36	29	31	54	15
Averages	56.5	11.3	32.2	53	13.5	33.5	66.6	8.5	24.9	59	12.1	28.9	54.1	12.0	34.2	52	27	21

Source: Commission of the European Communities, *Eurobarometer*, Brussels, various issues

Sovereignty
The exclusive right to wield legitimate power within a territory. A sovereign state has complete control over its own affairs.

force in an increasingly complex global economy. While this division is discernible within both main parties, it is increasingly associated with differences between them. It is a division that underlies attitudes towards EU institutions and in particular the European Parliament. The internationalists accept the interdependence of Britain with Europe and the rest of the world, and adopt an essentially pragmatic stance towards the increasing power of supranational institutions: they agree with them if they bring concrete benefits. For the Eurosceptics, any attempt to strengthen EU institutions is a direct affront to Parliamentary sovereignty and must be resisted at every turn. The depth of these feelings is clear in speeches by the Conservatives Enoch Powell and Margaret Thatcher in the 1980s.

BRIEFINGS

8.6 Enoch Powell and Margaret Thatcher on Europe

Our Parliament is a homogeneous body. It wills a single nation which elects the disparate members who sit together in the House. It is the Parliament of the United Kingdom. The parliament which assembles at Strasbourg is an assembly of those who have been elected in different nations... They do not come together as the representatives of a single self-recognising community... We are performing a type of solecism in attributing the term parliament to that Assembly... [it] is not a 'Parliament' and it is not the wish of the people of this country that it should ever be a parliament in the sense of being the ultimate repository of the legislative and executive powers under which the people of the United Kingdom are to live.

Enoch Powell, speech to the House of Commons, 26 June 1986

To try and suppress nationhood and concentrate power at the centre of a European conglomerate would be highly damaging and would jeopardise the objectives we seek to achieve. Europe will be stronger precisely because it has France as France, Spain as Spain, Britain as Britain, each with its own customs, traditions and identity... We have not successfully rolled back the frontiers of the state in Britain only to see them reimposed at a European level with a European superstate exercising a new dominance from Brussels.

Margaret Thatcher, speech at Bruges, 20 September 1988

The following 'controversy' puts the arguments for and against further integration of Britain with the European Union. The depth of these divisions and the continuing impetus within the EU to ever closer union mean that the European question now threatens to dominate British politics, with the two major parties moving towards direct opposition on it. This was amply demonstrated in the aftermath of the Labour victory in the 2001 general election. In the ensuing Conservative leadership election the pro-European candidate, Kenneth Clarke, was decisively defeated by Iain Duncan Smith. Deeply hostile to the EU his first act as leader was to appoint only Eurosceptics to the shadow Cabinet.

The Labour Party in the meantime has found itself increasingly comfortable in the EU. It agreed to tightening integration in the Treaties of Amsterdam (1997) and Nice (2001). Formally it accepts the position negotiated by the Conservatives at Maastricht in 1992, that it will join EMU 'if and when the time is right'. However, Labour decided in 2003 not to join the monetary union until after the next general election.

The need to cope with a united and determined opposition, always prepared to capitalise on popular hostility and indifference, aways acts as a strong constraint on Labour efforts to take a lead in the EU. The case for any EU action has almost always to be argued in terms of narrow British interests, which does not go down well with the other European partners. This, together with his close co-operation with the US (Chapter 22) prevents Tony Blair asserting a lead in Europe or emerging as a truly European statesman. Continued abstention from monetary union further marginalises Britain within the EU and leaves the initiative to France and Germany.

EFFECTS OF ENLARGEMENT

The enlargement of the EU to central and eastern Europe is likely to give the organisation even more of a Continental bias and further marginalise the British position on its far western flank. The likely ten candidates to join the Union – the Czech Republic, Slovakia, Hungary, Poland, Estonia, Slovenia, Latvia, Lithuania, Malta and (Greek) Cyprus – have strong links with Germany and France and are generally federalist in orientation. In order to cope with a 25-nation member-ship and prepare for even more expansion later, most countries agree on EU procedures being streamlined. For the British this seems an opportunity to hive off some policy areas from a 'remote Brussels bureaucracy' back to the Member States and thus reclaim some British sovereignty. Britain also argues against any bold new political initiatives being taken, leaving time to accommodate the new partners.

Most politicians and officials in other countries see this position as yet more evidence of British foot-dragging and limited commitment to Europe. To operate with more members they would argue that EU powers need to be strengthened and decision-making procedures rendered less dependent on national vetoes.

Although most other states are agreed in principle on this, little has been done in advance of the first enlargement in 2004. Indeed the larger states have slightly increased their blocking powers in the Council of Ministers, while the large pay-ments made under the Common Agricultural Policy to existing producers will have to be continued one way or another.

At some point however there are likely to be moves to challenge this 'institu-tional sclerosis' by moving on to stronger federal arrangements. Britain, owing to its internal divisions and ties to the USA, is likely to appear once again as a 'reluctant European' confronting a committed Franco–German axis. Only if the Labour government manages to win a referendum on joining the eurozone will Britain succeed in strengthening its European credentials. Such a campaign is likely however to have major repercussions within Britain itself, as we shall see in the next chapter.

CONTROVERSY

Should Britain agree to closer European union?

The case for Britain strengthening and deepening the EU

The danger from Germany

The EEC transformed Franco-German relations but Germany – especially a united Germany – is still the dominant economic power in Europe. Any possible threat from this is best thwarted or pre-empted by locking Germany into closer political union with the rest of Europe.

The danger from outside

The collapse of the Soviet Union and the increased uncertainties of the post-Cold War era mean that Europe needs to meet any new threats or challenges that might emerge from Asia, the Middle East or from an unstable eastern Europe. Europe needs to move towards a common foreign and defence policy, which can only be achieved by strengthening the central institutions of the European Union. At the same time, the EU should be enlarged to include most of the former communist states of eastern Europe.

The democratic deficit

EU policy makers are subject to very limited popular control. The Council of Ministers is not answerable to the European Parliament and the unelected and largely unaccountable Commission has far greater decision-making autonomy than any national Civil Service. The way forward therefore must involve the strengthening of democracy in the EU, which means making central institutions stronger and more accountable directly to the people of Europe.

The bicycle analogy

Unless the EU keeps moving forward – towards ever closer integration – it will atrophy.

The case for Britain resisting EU federalism

Dangers of a common currency

It is too risky to have a common currency when real economic convergence has not occurred among the economies of the EU's Member States. The Maastricht convergence criteria (inflation, interest rates, debt/GDP ratios) are inappropriate. The real criteria are employment rates, economic activity and growth rates. Without convergence on these, poor areas will remain depressed, because they will be unable to devalue themselves into activity and the EU will not possess sufficient central funds to stimulate economic activity there.

The democratic deficit

EU integration needs to proceed at a rate that has the overwhelming majority support of electorates in the Member States. 'Real democracy' may be impossible in such a large and diverse community.

The dangers of judicial legislation

Judicial legislation (judges in effect creating new law by interpreting established legal principles or commitments in the light of new situations) is dangerous because the judiciary are not accountable to electors. This applies particularly to the European Court of Justice, which has been very assertive in the EU.

Injustices in EU rule operation

Uneven rule implementation in different Member States means Britain loses out by having an efficient administration. Such losses will increase with enlargement and stoke up massive popular resentment.

World economic competition

Changes in technology are creating an increasingly competitive global economic system. Deepening the EU in economic and financial terms will enable European producers to compete more effectively in the internal EU market and strengthen the European Union's bargaining position in world markets more generally.

Foreign and defence policy

A common EU foreign and defence policy really means lack of agreement, inaction, and impotence – witness European ineffectiveness in the continuing Middle East crisis.

Fortress Europe versus global market

The real market of the future is the global market. An insulated EU market – economic fortress Europe – will atrophy.

Flexibility

British interests, as in the past, are best served by retaining maximum strategic flexibility in terms of trade patterns and political–military alliances. Circumstances constantly change. The EU will be too unwieldy to respond effectively to new economic, political, ecological and military challenges.

ESSAYS

1. Account for the sceptical attitude of British governments towards European union.

2. Has British hesitation about European union damaged British interests?

3. Will enlargements result in a European federal state?

4. What is the Common Agricultural Policy? Why has it been so controversial?

SUMMARY

■ Britain has traditionally been sceptical about European integration, because of its stake in world markets and its links with English-speaking countries overseas. It suffers from a structural and cultural dilemma which other countries do not have and that have caused it to be seen as a 'bad European'.

■ However, it did support the Single European Act (1986) creating a single market in goods, labour and capital, but was suspicious about moves towards full political integration.

■ 'Eurosceptics' have now taken over the Conservative Party.

■ New Labour is reasonably united around a pragmatic attitude to Europe: they support it if there are clear benefits. This is far removed from the political commitment of the Continental states to union, and weakens the British bargaining position within the EU.

Milestones in the development of the EU

1951 Treaty of Paris. Belgium, the Netherlands, Luxembourg, France, Italy and West Germany (the Six) set up the European Coal and Steel Community (ECSC)

1957 Treaty of Rome. The Six set up the European Economic Community (EEC) and the European Atomic Energy Authority (Euratom)

1962 Common Agricultural Policy (CAP) created. The EEC regulates farm prices and decides on agricultural priorities right across the community

1966 President de Gaulle establishes the right of national veto (the 'Luxembourg Compromise')

1967 Creation of the European Communities (EC) by the merger of EEC, ECSC and Euratom under a Commission and Council of Ministers

1968 Creation of European Customs Union

1973 Denmark, Ireland and the UK join the EC

1974 Heads of government meet as European Council. The Regional Fund created to help poor or declining regions inside Member States

1979 First direct elections to the European Parliament. The European Monetary System (EMS) with its Exchange Rate Mechanism (ERM) and European Currency Unit (ECU) created

1981 Greece joins EC

1985–6 The Milan Summit and the Single European Act (SEA) amend the Treaty of Rome to introduce the principle of qualified majority voting in areas related to the single market, and take the first steps towards a common foreign policy

1986 Spain and Portugal join the EC

1992 Treaty on European Union (Maastricht Treaty) amends the Single European Act and presents a plan for economic and political union. The Treaty covers co-operation on political, economic, defence, social, environmental, cultural and legal matters. Britain and Denmark opt out of the Social Chapter on welfare and regulation of working conditions, and reserve decision on European Monetary Union

1992/3 Maastricht Treaty narrowly approved in a French referendum and, at the second go, in Denmark

1992 UK is forced by a currency crisis to withdraw from ERM and EMS, to be followed in the next few months by many other EU currencies

1993 Single internal market inaugurated

1995 Austria, Finland and Sweden join EU

1997 Treaty of Amsterdam strengthens defence and foreign policy co-operation, extends qualified majority voting in the Council and establishes common rules on immigration and citizenship

1999 Single currency zone set up inside 11 (later 12) countries of EU. Britain announces it will decide on membership later. Series of scandals produce resignation of the Santer Commission in face of censure by European Parliament. This greatly increases the power of the European Parliament. The new (Prodi) Commission takes more power over the nomination and resignation of its members, limiting the power of Member States in this regard. It thus enhances its position as an autonomous EU government responsible to the European Parliament

2001–2 Treaty of Nice effectively codifies failure to agree on extensive institutional reform in advance of enlargement. It was rejected in Irish and Danish referendums, although Ireland held a second referendum in which it was accepted

2004 Enlargement in central and eastern Europe will take EU membership to 25

1. Document the likely terms on which current candidate members will be admitted to the EU in the next enlargements.

2. Critically examine the economic criteria the British government has laid down for joining the EMU.

3. Analyse the likely way the central institutions of the EU would evolve if it became truly federal. What would be the UK position within these?

FURTHER READING

Anthony Forster and Alasdair Blair, *Britain's European Foreign Policy* (London: Macmillan, 2001) and Stefano Falla, *New Labour and the European Union* (London: Ashgate, 2002) are up-to-date analyses of British inability to choose decisively between the US and the EU. The latter is described in Ian Budge et al, *The Politics of the New Europe* (London: Addison-Wesley Longman, 1997), Chapter 2. Lively, up-to-date accounts of British–European relationships are: J. Baker, 'Britain and Europe: more blood on the Eurocarpet', *Parliamentary Affairs*, **55** (2), 2002, pp. 317–30: T. Buller, 'Understanding contemporary Conservative Euroscepticism', *Political Quarterly*, **71** (3), 2000, pp. 319–27: D. Stephens, 'The Blair government and Europe', *Political Quarterly*, **71** (3), 2000, pp. 67–75: 'In focus: *is* the UK the most Eurosceptic member of the EU?', *Politics Review*, **10** (3), 2001, p. 34. David McKay, *Federalism and European Union* (Oxford: Oxford University Press, 1999) is an informed analysis of European aspirations to federalism.

USEFUL WEB SITES ON BRITAIN IN EUROPE

Hot links to these sites can be found on the CWS at http://www.booksites.net/budge. The amount of information on the European Union in general, and the role Britain plays in it, increases almost on a daily basis. There are certain web sites that can be regarded as thresholds for entering into this debate.

The Labour Party (www.labour.org.uk) sets out what is essentially the government's view and the pro-integration lobby is exemplified by the views of organisations such as the European Movement at www.euromove.org.uk/ and the coalition known as Britain in Europe (www.britainineurope.org.uk); you can also visit the Young European Movement at www.yem.org.uk.

The Conservative Party (www.conservative-party.org.uk) reflects the views of the 'Eurosceptic' position. Other groups on this side of the debate provide material at www.eusceptic.org, Youth for a Free Europe (www.free-europe.org.uk), Bruges Group (www.brugesgroup.com), the Democracy Movement (www.democracy-movement.com), the Libertarian Alliance, (www.libertarian.co.uk) and www.no-euro.com. Material on Eurosceptics across Europe can be accessed at www.keele.ac.uk/socs/ks40/eurocrit.htm.

For excellent media coverage of the debate see the *Guardian*'s special reports on Britain and the EU (www.politics.guardian.co.uk/eu/), Britain and the euro (www.politics.guardian.co.uk/euro) and the more general report on European integration (www.guardian.co.uk/eu). Daily news reports and comments on European affairs are available from www.euobserver.com. You might also want to visit www.europolls.co.uk for information on opinion polls. The official EU website is www.europa.eu.int.

Europe in Britain

Chapter 8 looked at the part Britain plays within the European Union. This chapter will examine the other side of the coin: the impact of the EU on government and politics within Britain. It will discuss the decisions British governments have to take about Europe, the constitutional effects of membership up to the present, how the EU itself makes decisions and what effects this has in Britain. In addition we shall see how membership of the European Union has affected the machinery of government and the ways in which public policy is made inside Britain. The chapter will also address the problem of the 'democratic deficit' of the EU and tackle the question of 'subsidiarity', that is, which level of government is best equipped to deal with particular responsibilities.

This chapter discusses:

- the centrality of the EU to contemporary British politics
- the EU and the British constitution
- how the EU is governed and Britain's part in this
- how British civil servants interact with their EU counterparts
- how British interest groups deal with EU policies
- how the EU affects public policy
- the nature of the 'democratic deficit'
- subsidiarity: which level of government should be responsible for which policy area inside Britain.

UNION OR SECESSION: THE BRITISH DILEMMA

Federation A political organisation in which power is divided between a central authority and other units, usually geographical, that retain some independent authority in the system. The term is a controversial one in Britain because it can either mean a fairly centralised form of government (eg a United States of Europe) or a loosely organised one, in which the member states retain much autonomy.

The most important decisions the British government has to take in the next decade are about its relationship with Europe. This is not just a matter of foreign policy, for such decisions will crucially affect Britain's own power and standing inside the national territory, what is commonly termed its 'sovereignty'. What the government has to decide is how far it is prepared to become a constituent part of a European federation. In such a federation a European government in Brussels, only partly elected from Britain, would decide British social policy, for example, and largely regulate the economy. Perhaps it might even direct foreign policy and deal with matters of peace and war involving British lives.

Put this way, it seems as though Conservative 'Eurosceptics' are right in claiming that British national sovereignty will disappear. They argue that industry and finance will be constrained by European regulations, bureaucracy will dominate, British competitiveness will diminish and overseas investments will go elsewhere. Much else will go, including most of the traditions and practices which make Britain distinctive.

Eurosceptics see no benefits from this, since their ideal is an autonomous British state regulating all its own internal and external affairs. Pro-Europeans, by the same token, see the loss of autonomy as a price worth paying for the influence

British governments and individuals can exert in a much larger political unit. Better to be part of a new superpower, they argue, than an independent third-class state on the fringe of world developments. They cite the new opportunities available for finance and industry within the European Union, and claim that economic and social development will be faster and smoother within a more dynamic economy, in which British financial expertise is joined with German industrial strength.

The pro-Europeans believe that loss of political autonomy would be balanced by the British share in electing a European Parliament and government. European institutions would not be 'foreign' but representative of European citizens in Britain as much as they would be of European citizens in Spain, France, Italy and Scandinavia. Only if one thinks of the British Parliament and government as the sole bodies authorised to represent the British people, can one regard a wider European democracy as threatening.

This is, of course, exactly what Conservative Eurosceptics do think. Many groups in Britain, however, are positively attracted by Europeanisation. Scottish, Welsh and Irish nationalists see it as a way of easing the stranglehold of the British State on their own countries (see Chapter 10). The Labour Party is reassured by the social protection the European Union offers to vulnerable groups such as low-paid workers. From the trade unions' point of view, undermining Conservative reforms might be no bad thing. Employers' competitiveness is their employees' poverty. Constitutional reformers see in the guarantees offered by the European treaties a protection for the civil liberties threatened by British governments. Even Conservatives such as Kenneth Clarke, the unsuccessful contender in the leadership election of 2001, see Europeanisation as a necessary step to consolidating Britain's world trading position, rather than as a threat to it.

CONTROVERSY

European federalism

Federalism has a clear meaning in political science, but in public discussion it takes on different meaning according to who is using it and for what political purpose. In political science, a federal state combines a central authority (the federal government) with a degree of constitutionally defined autonomy for sub-central units of government – usually territorial units of government such as states, regions or provinces. In other words federal government is a form of decentralised government that guarantees some autonomy for units of government below the central state. It contrasts with unitary and centralised states such as Britain has been traditionally.

In Britain, however, the term 'federal' is sometimes used by politicians as a codeword for a highly centralised 'European superstate' – for rule by a centralised bureaucracy in Brussels, with all the red tape, rigidity, and loss of sovereignty this implies for Britain. Europhobes often use the word 'federal' to imply centralisation, which they hate. British objections to the use of the word 'federal' to describe the European Union in the Maastricht Treaty led to the term being removed. Nonetheless, the federal nature of some EU institutions remained, and were actually supported by the British government.

For others in Britain, 'federal' means decentralised government that preserves substantial rights of Member States to administer their own territory in their own way. These rights are protected by the principle of subsidiarity (see later). Hence, Europhiles often use the term 'federal' to describe a degree of decentralisation, which they like.

These issues are not theoretical ones likely to affect us only later. The European Union already operates in Britain, parallel to but independently of the British government and Parliament. On a range of questions British courts take their precedents from the European Court in Luxembourg, just as British civil servants and local councils follow directives from Brussels. The EU does not have (and is not likely to have) its own administration in Britain to enforce decisions directly. It relies on British institutions to do that. But, as the example of the courts shows, they can be quite effective in enforcing European interventions.

BRIEFINGS

9.1 Subsidiarity and its possible consequences in Britain

Subsidiarity
The principle whereby decisions should be taken at the lowest possible level of the political system.

The principle of subsidiarity states that public policy should be made and implemented at the lowest appropriate level of government compatible with efficiency and accountability, that is, at the point closest to ordinary citizens. Only decisions that have to be taken at the European level should be made there; all others should be made by national, regional or local government.

One reason for doing so is to make decision making more open and accessible to those whom it affects. In the (clumsy and vague) words of Article 3B of the Maastricht Treaty:

> In areas which do not fall within its exclusive competence, the Community shall take action, in accordance with the principle of subsidiarity, only if and insofar as the objectives of the proposed action cannot be sufficiently achieved by the Member States, and can, therefore, by reason of the scale or effects of the proposed action, be better achieved by the Community.

The subsidiarity principle therefore protects the interests and powers of nation states where there is no good reason to take decisions at the European level. However, it can easily be extended within Member States to relations between the centre and the regions or localities. It is therefore something of a two-edged sword so far as protecting existing state power is concerned and may serve to empower Scotland or Wales, for example, in relation to the UK as a whole.

This chapter looks at the way in which EU institutions operate in Britain and the way in which their interventions have already changed British political practices and structures. We can expect more changes as the Labour government supports closer integration and federal union. Having said that, the EU will always rely more on indirect rather than direct means of intervention. Thus, what we can expect is continuing adaptation by the British Civil Service and local government to the European dimension, rather than any immediate restructuring to meet EU needs. Adaptation has already gone a long way, as we shall see when we examine the European presence in Britain more closely.

EUROPE AND THE BRITISH CONSTITUTION

Practical and Parliamentary sovereignty

Parliamentary sovereignty
The power of Parliament to make or repeal any law it wishes.

The main constitutional issue raised by membership of the European Union concerns Parliamentary sovereignty. In Britain, legal sovereignty is vested in Parliament. The concept of Parliamentary sovereignty means that Parliament can pass any law it wants. In effect, as we saw in Chapter 4, this gives extensive and undefined powers to the majority Government.

From the mid-nineteenth century until 1973 Parliamentary sovereignty was one of the cornerstones of the British constitution. Joining the European Community – and therefore accepting the 43 volumes of legislation and more than 3,000 regulations and directives already passed – changed all that. British law must now be consistent with European law, and British courts must both accept and enforce European law. In cases of disagreement the European Court of Justice in Luxembourg has the final word, and British citizens may directly approach the European Court if they believe the British government is acting unlawfully. The British government may even have to compensate citizens for actions judged by the European Court to exceed its powers. It was clear that European law would take precedence over British law when Britain joined the EC, but the principle was underlined strongly by the Factortame case of 1991. This required British law to fall into line with European law on the registration of shipping, a matter that had been jealously controlled by the sovereign British State for centuries. More recently, in 1996, the Conservative majority in Parliament was forced by decisions of the European Commission and the Court to accept the right of employees to opt for a 48-hour week, even though the government resisted this strongly and had in fact declared it would not accept it. Loss of sovereignty could hardly go further than that.

In a practical sense, Britain has long since ceased to have exclusive and total control over its own affairs (if, indeed, any country ever does have total control). Joining the North Atlantic Treaty Organisation (NATO) or signing the General Agreement on Tariffs and Trade (GATT) on free trade, for example, requires agreement with other nations and the loss of some national autonomy. To this extent practical sovereignty is limited in even the most powerful modern state.

But the question of constitutional sovereignty and the EU is more complicated than this. Membership of the EU hugely limits practical sovereignty, but it also legally limits Parliamentary sovereignty. This makes the issue supremely important in the minds of some politicians.

Others contend that this legal loss of sovereignty is neither final nor absolute. They argue that Parliament could, if it wished, revoke membership of the EU tomorrow, so regaining its old sovereign status. The process of leaving the EU would, of course, be long, messy, disruptive and expensive. Thus for all practical purposes it may be impossible. To the extent that British secession remains theoretically possible, however, Parliament has not lost its legal sovereignty. To the extent that it is in practice unlikely, absolute Parliamentary sovereignty no longer exists in Britain.

JUDICIAL REVIEW UNDER THE EU

Judicial review is the power of courts to invalidate Parliamentary legislation or government actions on the grounds that they infringe some higher body of law, such as a constitution (see Chapter 19 for a more extensive discussion). English judges have traditionally not asserted such a right (Scots ones occasionally have) – partly because there is no clearly defined body of constitutional law in the UK (Chapter 4), and partly because their licence to interpret common law and the 'real' meaning of legislation gives them extensive powers anyway.

However, the overriding nature of the EU Treaty obligations and the authority of the European Court of Justice to lay down binding interpretations of them, do mean that British courts now have written standards against which to evaluate Parliamentary legislation and government decisions. This has substantially reinforced their willingness to intervene in the administrative process even at detailed levels of decision, most notably in defence of immigrants' rights to a fair process and hearing.

This tendency has been strengthened by the European Court of Justice's adoption of the European Convention for the Protection of Human Rights as the practical standard for evaluating human rights in the EU, and its direct incorporation into English and Scots law by the New Labour government in 1998–9. This provides a body of written 'higher' legislation defining individual rights in relation to government, just as the EU treaties delimit areas in which the British government cannot act, or act only in certain ways. Both set clear limits on unlimited Parliamentary sovereignty, which has been the legal basis for effective government autonomy.

Nowhere is this clearer than in immigration appeals. Partly because of the EU's abolition of internal barriers to mobility the number of foreigners from outside its area seeking permission to reside in Britain has increased enormously (over 20,000 new applications were made in the second quarter of 2002). The government has sought to reject most of these to avoid stirring up racist and religious tensions at home. Such 'administrative' decisions may have enormous implications for individual and family safety, so the courts have shown themselves quite prepared to consider appeals against government decisions. The number of appeals in all areas increased eight times between the start of the 1980s and the end of the 1990s, and continues to rise rapidly. The European Court itself now considers cases initiated by individual citizens. The title of a booklet issued to civil servants – *The Judge Over Your Shoulder* – clearly underlines the extent to which the courts are involved in decision making at all levels, from the most general to the most detailed. It is clear that membership of the EU has accelerated this process, which was however already underway (for more detail, see Chapter 19).

European Parliamentary elections and voting reform

From 1979 the European Parliament in Brussels has been directly elected by the citizens of the EU. Elections have been held simultaneously across Europe within the Member States. Currently the UK elects 87 out of 626 Euro MPs.

9.2 **Britain and the European Convention on Human Rights**

The European Union is not the only body in Europe with an influence over British government and politics. The Human Rights Bill passed by the Blair government in 1998 originates in the European Convention on Human Rights signed by 15 West European countries in 1950. The Convention is implemented by the European Court of Human Rights (ECHR) in Strasbourg. This is not to be confused with the EU's European Court of Justice (ECJ) in Luxembourg, which, however, uses the convention as its reference point. The EU's Charter of Fundamental Human Rights, approved at its 2000 Nice Meeting, also draws heavily on the Convention.

Main provisions of the Convention

- the right to life (Article 2)
- freedom from torture and inhuman or degrading punishment (Article 3)
- freedom from slavery or enforced labour (Article 4)
- the right to liberty and security of the person (Article 5)
- the right to a fair trial (Article 6)
- freedom from retroactive criminal accusations and punishment (Article 7)
- the right to respect for private and family life (Article 8)
- freedom of thought, conscience and religion (Article 9)
- freedom of expression (Article 10)
- freedom of assembly and association (Article 11).

Britain and the ECHR

Britain was the first country to sign the Convention in 1950 but did not make it part of its own law, claiming this was unnecessary because the rights were already part of common law. Consequently it was not possible for individual British citizens to bring a case against the British government to the ECHR until 1966, when the law was changed.

ECHR cases against Britain

The decisions of the ECHR have had a considerable impact on British government. Between 1966 and 1998 some 100 cases were brought against the British government and in 50 of these the ECHR found the government guilty of breaching the Convention. The cases include:

- **GCHQ (1984)**   The government's ban on trade unions at GCHQ was upheld by the Court.
- **Prevention of terrorism (1993)**   The power of the Secretary of State for Northern Ireland to detain terrorist suspects for up to seven days without charges was upheld.
- **Death on the Rock (1994)**   The British government was ordered to pay £38,000 towards the legal costs of those who brought a case about the killing of terrorist suspects in Gibraltar.
- **Age of homosexual consent (1996)**   British law about different ages of consent for heterosexuals and homosexuals was upheld by the Court.
- **Juvenile murders (1996)**   The Home Secretary (Michael Howard) was found in breach of the Convention when he decided on special terms of imprisonment for juvenile murderers.

Incorporation into British law

In 1998 the Labour government incorporated the Convention into Scots and English law through the Human Rights Act (HRA). Britain has thus acquired a written body of fundamental law – a major innovation in the Constitution – which provides a strong basis for judicial review of administrative acts.

Depending on their political affiliations the elected members join different party groups within the EP: Conservatives, the European People's Party; Labour, the Socialists; Liberal Democrats, the Liberal Group; Greens and Welsh and Scottish Nationalists, the one entitled Group of Greens/European Free Alliance. MEPs tend to be more pro-European than their home parties, and of course integrated into their pan-European groups, so there is often some tension between the Brussels and Westminster party line. This is exacerbated by the Euroscepticism of the British Conservative Party.

BRIEFINGS

9.3 Relations between British Euro MPs (MEPs) and members of Parliament (MPs)

The British Conservative Party is now almost wholly Eurosceptic. They hate the loss of national sovereignty involved in membership and if not advocates of total withdrawal at least want to wrest back many powers from Brussels to London. They dislike the social dimension of EU policy (the Social Chapter, for example); and claim that Brussels stands for the remote and stifling bureaucracy of a European superstate. On the Labour side, some feel that the EU is a club for wealthy countries, while others also resent the loss of sovereignty. The fact that both main parties have their pro- and anti-Europe wings makes the issue difficult for them to handle, and the issue being so highly charged increases the problem. Only the Liberal Democrats are united, having always been strongly pro-European. In short, Europe has been a source of rancorous conflict both within and between the two main parties for three decades, and the conflict shows no sign of going away.

Relations between the party groups in the European Parliament and in Westminster are thus not particularly good, especially on the Conservative side. Conservative members of the European Parliament (MEPs) are allowed to attend the Backbenchers' Committee in Westminster (the 1922 Committee) but there are few other direct connections. There are stronger ties on the Labour side: MPs and MEPs frequently meet, and the latter have rights and powers within the national organisation. For example, the leader of the Labour group in the European Parliament sits on the Party's National Executive Committee, and Labour MEPs may vote in the national leadership elections.

A weakness of the trans-European parties however is that they have no grass-roots organisation in any country and depend on the local party apparatus to select candidates, campaign and organise the vote. British Euro-elections are run by the British parties (Table 9.1). The latter regard the elections primarily as a national popularity contest, in which the British government record and domestic issues play the major part. Europe is an issue in Britain of course. But instead of competing on what the EU should be doing about the current problems facing it, the debate continually looks back to whether the EU should be tackling them at all and whether Britain should be in it.

All this weakens the claims of Euro MPs and of the EP itself to have a popular mandate comparable to that of the Westminster Parliament. Elections

PARTY	1979 %vote	1979 MEPs	1984 %vote	1984 MEPs	1989 %vote	1989 MEPs	1994 %vote	1994 MEPs	1999 %vote	1999 MEPs
Conservative	48.4	60	38.8	45	33.0	32	27.0	18	35.8	36
Labour	31.6	17	34.7	32	39.0	45	42.6	62	28.0	29
Liberal Democrat	12.6	0	18.5	0	6.2	0	16.1	2	12.7	10
Green					14.5	0	3.1	0	6.2	2
UKIP									7.0	3
SNP	1.9	1	1.7	1	2.6	1	3.0	2	*	2
Plaid Cymru	0.6	0	0.7	1	0.7	0	1.0	0	*	2
Dem Unionist	1.3	1	1.6	1	1.0	1	1.0	1	*	1
Ulster Unionist	0.9	1	1.1	1	0.8	1	0.8	1	*	1
SDLP	1.1	1	1.1	1	0.9	1	1.0	1	*	1
Pro-Euro Conservatives									1.4	0
BNP									1.0	0
Socialist Labour									0.9	0
Liberal									0.9	0
% turnout	31.6		32.6		36.2		36.4		24.0	

Table 9.1 *Results of UK elections to the European Parliament, 1979–99*

* Due to changes in the electoral system, voting figures for UK are not given. Figures for Scotland, Wales and Northern Ireland are as follows: Scotland: SNP polled 27%; Wales: Plaid Cymru polled 29.6%; Northern Ireland: Democratic Unionists polled 28.4%; Ulster Unionists polled 17.6%; SDLP polled 28.1%; Sein Fein polled 17.3% but failed to win any seats

Source: European Parliament UK Office, *Election Facts*, August 2002. Accessed via http://www.europarl.org.uk/guide/Gelectionsmain.htm

usually go against the British party currently in national office, as Euro-voting is a cheap way to express dissatisfaction with it, carrying none of the consequences for a change of government that general elections would. This also explains why turnout in European elections is so low in Britain – 24 per cent in 1999.

One consequence is that small or new parties have a better chance to make an impact in the European elections and even to gain seats, as the Greens did with 6 per cent of the vote and two seats in 1999. As the EP still has very limited powers this is marginal to the mainstream of British politics however.

Where Euro-elections may have an important impact is in the constitutional sphere – on the conduct of general elections to the Westminster Parliament itself. These are the central mechanism of power distribution in the UK, deciding which party will form the government for the next five years. As we shall see in Chapter 15, the method of translating party votes into seats in Parliament, which then determines who forms the government, is biased in several ways at the moment, favouring Labour over the Conservatives and both over all the other parties. This is because individual MPs are elected in small constituencies with a plurality of the vote, ie if they receive more votes than any single rival (often only one-third of the total) they win. The system favours parties with concentrated regional support over those like the Liberal Democrats who receive fairly equal support from all parts of the UK.

The European elections were originally held on this basis in the UK. But from 1999, under pressure from the EU, they have been held in large regional constituencies under a proportional system, which makes the seats received by a party list of 10–15 candidates proportional to the votes they get. This is the reason why the Greens in 1999, with 6 per cent of the vote, got two seats – whereas in 1989 with over 14 per cent of votes they got no seats under the small constituency plurality system.

The Euro-elections thus offer an outstanding example of how British elections could be made fairer to small parties. The change to PR was in fact one of the constitutional reforms carried through by the Labour government when it came to power in 1997, along with semi-proportional elections in Scotland, Wales and London. Indeed all national and regional elections in Britain are now more proportional than general elections. This creates an increasing pressure for the latter to be reformed, although any real change will be resisted by the two large parties which would lose by it.

Any move towards proportional general elections would change the current 'elective dictatorship' into a coalition government in which the Liberal Democrats would decide to govern either with a Labour or Conservative partner. Whether this is regarded as a good or bad thing there is no doubt it would introduce enormous changes into the way Britain is run. Thus the role of the Euro-elections in demonstrating the feasibility of PR in Britain and setting up pressures for changing to it have important constitutional implications.

Executive power

Executive One of the three branches of government (with the legislative and judiciary). The executive is concerned with making government decisions and policies rather than the legislative function of law making. In Britain the executive is, in effect, the Cabinet or the Prime Minister.

Just how important this could be is illustrated by another, contrary, tendency of EU membership – an increase in the political power of the government and Cabinet. This is because the main centres of power in the EU are no more accountable to the British Parliament than to the European, or to other national parliaments for that matter. The Council of Ministers, the main executive body in Brussels, is composed of representatives of national governments. It cannot become embroiled in the domestic politics of its Member States. Thus any influence the British Parliament brings to bear on the Council must pass through the British government. And this, of course, gives the government a crucial role.

Parliamentary approval is not required for EU legislation. On the contrary, the British Parliament may only scrutinise legislation on a 'take note' basis, and even then may only deal with proposed, future legislation. 'Taking note' means recording legislation and the action it requires, but doing nothing to change it in any way. Officers of the EU do not attend Parliamentary meetings, and neither explain nor justify their actions to Parliament. Parliament can only advise ministers about the policy they should adopt and await the outcome. Ministers may take note of Parliamentary opinion, but they may also ignore it if they please.

9.4 Scrutiny of European legislation by the House of Commons

The best that Parliament can do to control EU legislation is to exert control over the British government's negotiating position within the European bodies. In practice this has been difficult. The various committees of the House of Commons charged with examining European legislation have had extremely limited powers once they received the documents, usually sending them on rather than discussing their substance. With 30–40 documents arriving every day there have been few that could be given further consideration.

Once an issue is earmarked for debate there remains the problem of how Parliament is to influence the government's Council negotiating position. No specific amendments are allowed to be made to Commission proposals, and the House or standing committee may only debate on a 'take note' motion. During Parliamentary vacations even less can be done. A statement by the supposedly radical Michael Foot, then Labour Leader of the House, sums up procedures nicely:

> Ministers will not give agreement to any legislative proposal recommended by the Scrutiny Committee for further consideration by the House before the House has given it that consideration, unless the Committee has indicated that agreement need not be withheld, or *the minister concerned is satisfied that agreement should not be withheld for reasons which he will at the first opportunity explain to the House.*

The italic section emphasises the almost unlimited freedom of action that the British government has been able to reserve for itself. The House of Commons reorganised its procedures in 2000. The European Scrutiny Committee now considers all proposed legislation and refers matters needing further scrutiny to one of two standing committees. They report to the House of Commons but Parliamentary approval is still not required for European legislation. The government may note Parliamentary opinion but may also ignore it if it wants.

Legislative
The law-making branch of government. In Britain it is the Queen in Parliament – the Queen, the House of Lords and the House of Commons.

Other aspects of the constitution

Membership of the EU has so far had little effect on other aspects of the British constitution. The three-tier structure of government (central, regional, and local) has been retained, as has the same set of central ministries. The highest court in the land remains the House of Lords and there is still no fully written-up constitution. The same rules of Parliamentary procedure apply and much the same Parliamentary timetable is followed. In these respects EU membership has changed British practice very little.

HOW THE EU IS GOVERNED

Before seeing how the EU has affected government in Britain we need to see how it manages itself. The most important EU institutions are located at Brussels in Belgium (see Map 8.1), about an hour's flight from London. The European Court sits further away in Luxembourg, and the European Parliament is located even further away at Strasbourg on the French–German border (but its committees operate in Brussels close to the other centres of EU power).

Figure 9.1 identifies the central institutions of the EU and British participation in them. Decision making in the EU is complicated by the fact that it has two executives and governments rather than just one.

The body that might become the European government if the EU becomes a truly federal state is the European Commission. This is a body of 20 politicians nominated by each member country (two each by the bigger members, Britain, France, Spain, Italy and Germany; one each by Sweden, Finland, Denmark, Ireland, the Netherlands, Belgium, Luxembourg, Portugal, Austria and Greece). The Commission as a whole is scrutinised and approved by the European Parliament at the beginning of its term of office.

This procedure emphasises that Commissioners' loyalties are not to their home country but to the EU. The Commission has increasing powers to act auto- nomously in implementing the Single European Market and the general industrial and trade policies of the EU. We have already seen how action under its work, health and safety powers, in allowing workers to opt for a 48-hour minimum week,

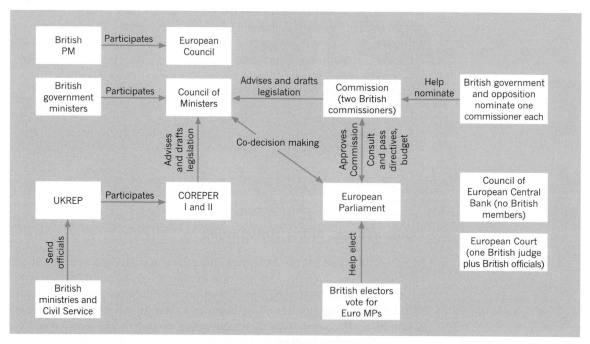

Figure 9.1 *British participation in the central European Union institutions*

Plate 9.1 *European Parliament building, Brussels*

Source: www.paphotos.com

cut across Conservative government policy in 1996. The Commission runs the EU's central bureaucracy, divided into 36 directorates-general. These resemble the functional ministries of Member States which act in each separate policy area.

However, the Commission and its Civil Service are not autonomous. In many areas their function is to prepare policy proposals for decision by the Council of

Ministers. The latter is the parallel, second and in most respects more powerful organ of the EU. Because it consists of representatives of national governments it is easy to think of the Council as an executive. In fact, however, as the ultimate source and approver of policy initiatives, the Council performs many of the functions carried out by legislatures in other political systems.

The Council consists of a General Affairs Council and various technical councils. The foreign ministers of Member States meet in the General Affairs Council, while ministers for particular policy areas such as agriculture meet in the technical councils. Associated with the ministerial councils is the Committee of Permanent Representatives (COREPER in EU jargon). COREPER I 'shadows' the foreign ministers and consists of the national ambassadors to the EU, while COREPER II consists of the deputy ambassadors. There are numerous committees and working parties of appropriately qualified national civil servants associated with it. All these bodies carry out detailed preparatory work for the meetings of corresponding ministers.

Thus the Council of Ministers also has a Civil Service working for it, which in many respects overshadows the permanent 'Eurocrats', just as the Council overshadows the Commission. Most new initiatives come from it or from the European Council (not to be confused with the Council of Europe), which is the meeting of prime ministers and heads of governments of the Member States that often has to take decisions over matters on which the Council of Ministers cannot agree. Any major new initiatives or proposals for the extension of EU powers have to be agreed here. It is only the ministers who can commit national governments to courses of action not already agreed in the founding treaties, particularly in foreign and defence policy.

Because of the powers of the Council of Ministers and of the European Council it has often been said that the EU is more of an intergovernmental than a truly federal structure. Decisions have to be negotiated and agreed between the governments of the Member States rather than autonomously by the supranational bodies. It is here that the British government can hold out for what it considers to be British interests.

This was reinforced by the original practice of taking decisions in the Council unanimously. Every country had a veto, so by withholding its consent any national government could block any proposal. This is how British governments would have liked the situation to continue, so that they could veto any action affecting Britain with which they did not agree.

Since the Single European Act of 1986, however, and even more under the Treaty of Maastricht (1992), qualified majority voting (QMV) has been introduced into the Council of Ministers for all but very major policy decisions such as the enlargement of the EU. Under this procedure not even two of the larger countries, acting together, can block proceedings. This has put the initiative – even in the intergovernmental Council of Ministers – into the hands of France, Germany and the smaller countries, which want to speed up integration. Increasingly in the 1990s, therefore, an anti-federalist British government found itself isolated even on the body that might have been expected to protect its interests. Its position has also been undermined by the decisions of the European Court, which tends to support the Commission. Meanwhile the European Parliament has also proved itself pro-integrationist. It has often carried with it not only British Labour and Liberals but also British Conservative 'Euro MPs', who have thus found themselves at loggerheads with their own party at Westminster.

Of course, as Figure 9.1 also shows, standoffs between British and European institutions are not a simple matter of 'us' versus 'them'. This is because British MPs and civil servants participate in EU institutions and shape EU policy just as much as any other national group. In fact, as one of the leading Member States in the EU, the British play a disproportionate part compared with most others. This was particularly true of the framing and implementation of the Single European Act (1986) with its free market principles, which the former Conservative Commissioner Leon Brittan pushed through with the help of British economic advisers.

THE EU AND THE BRITISH CIVIL SERVICE

In spite of spreading integration, membership of the EU has had little impact on the way government actually works in Britain. The EU has no direct administration of its own within Member States. Instead it relies on the existing national machinery to carry through its directives and legislation.

Thus no special ministry has had to be created in Britain to look after EU affairs. Instead, the European Secretariat of the Cabinet Office and the Foreign and Commonwealth Office (FCO) co-ordinate the work of Whitehall ministries, and of the British staff in Brussels through a constant round of interdepartmental meetings. Whitehall departments that are most deeply embedded in European affairs – the Treasury, DTI, DEFRA – have special European divisions within them. The rest deal with matters on an ad hoc basis as required. Where they are affected, regional governments and ministries are brought in.

The implementation of EU policy is thus handled by central ministries and departments, very much as is the implementation of national policy. This is because it is now national policy, even if decided by European bodies. What has called for more of an administrative effort is the fact that Britain, through its membership of the Council of Ministers, and its associated committees (COREPER I and II) is now heavily involved in the process of preparing and passing European legislation in the first place.

Such legislation is not wholly, or even largely, 'political' in nature. However, the fact that policy is decided through negotiations between national governments, and that there is, on occasion, considerable controversy, pervades the entire policy formulation process. The British government has to define and defend its interests in relation to the EU as a whole and to the other Member States. The result is that the FCO, which traditionally represents British interests abroad, has become the central co-ordinating ministry for EU policy. It organises the UK Permanent Representation in Brussels and acts as the link between the home civil servants based in Brussels and their counterparts in the Whitehall ministries. The European Communities Section in the FCO is responsible for most of the co-ordinating work. It consists of several sub-departments covering different EU policy areas.

Although the FCO plays a co-ordinating role in formulating Britain's EU policy it does not have the technical expertise to determine that policy by itself. The specification for an industrial product, for example, is hardly within its competence. So there is considerable reliance on the functional ministries that do possess such expertise. Departments closely involved in formulating British EU policy in their areas of competence are the Treasury, DEFRA, DETR and DTI, most of which have EU sections co-ordinating their involvement with the EU. Departmental representatives liaise with the FCO, but also participate directly in meetings of specialists held under the aegis of the Commission, in the working parties and associated committees of COREPER, and also in ad hoc British Civil Service committees shadowing European Council meetings. The functional departments also play a major role in the preparation of briefs for Council meetings.

Co-ordination of British policy is achieved for the most part through a series of informal contacts among officials from interested government departments. But there is also a committee system through which EU policy can be discussed. At a basic level, there are a series of interdepartmental committees in the major policy areas. There are also temporary committees, bringing together the people most immediately concerned with a particular policy issue, and usually organised at the instigation of one of the functional departments. Their composition varies widely. A committee meeting on shipbuilding subsidies, for instance, would be chaired by a representative from the DTI and include officials from the Treasury, the DTI, the FCO, and possibly the Welsh, Scottish or Northern Irish administrations. Only the FCO would be represented on every committee. Above the specialist policy committees is a European Union Committee that oversees the preparation of briefs for the Permanent Representation and the Council meetings, and is generally responsible for the co-ordination of Britain's EU policy.

In its capacity as a central co-ordinating body the Cabinet Office also plays a significant role in the formulation of British policy. Officials from the Cabinet Office attend the regular committee meetings of the EU and are very closely involved in the more controversial issues. They also play a mediating role in ironing out differences between British government departments. Such a mediating role is especially important in the European context, where the government tries to present its views in terms of a national consensus.

Besides all the interdepartmental Civil Service committees concerned with formulating Britain's EU policies there are also political inter-ministerial committees. These include a Cabinet committee, composed of the ministers most affected by EU activities, which regularly discusses EU issues and is chaired by the Foreign Secretary.

Many of these arrangements for co-ordinating policy form an extension of interdepartmental committees and negotiating sessions inside Britain itself. What is new is the central co-ordinating role of the FCO, and the opportunities for civil servants from different ministries to work closely within the same organisation in Brussels, at the UK's Permanent Representation to the EU (UKRep).

Indeed, the major effect of the EU on the British Civil Service is the addition of a major European dimension to every civil servant's work. Most departments are involved one way or another with European policy matters, and most home civil servants have to keep a careful eye on developments in Brussels. Many have to attend the London meetings or travel regularly to EU meetings, apart from being seconded to UKRep. This means that many civil servants have to incorporate the European dimension into their daily working lives, and attend frequent training or refresher courses to keep them abreast of developments.

This creates a huge workload for politicians and civil servants. Every week tons of documents arrive from Brussels, Strasbourg and Luxembourg. Almost every week there is a high-level EU meeting involving the Prime Minister and/or other ministers. Apart from the Council of Ministers there are many other political meetings, and civil servants may spend as much time in Brussels as in London. There is also a meeting every week or so of the Cabinet EU Committee. Even without the EU, pressure on senior politicians and civil servants is enormous. With it, demands on their time and energy are even greater.

THE EU AND BRITISH PRESSURE GROUPS

Pressure groups
Private, voluntary organisations that wish to influence or control particular public policies without actually becoming the government or controlling all public policy.

Pressure or interest groups are organisations representing bands of people with some condition or activity in common that might be affected by politics. The most obvious of these are trade unions, grouping manual workers, craftspeople, or white-collar workers. But there are thousands of others: churches, sports and professional organisations, animal and environmental protection groups and many more. Almost any activity or interest one can think of has an organisation to protect or advance it.

Politics inevitably affects these aspects of life. Any proposal for regulation or intervention affects somebody who either wants intervention to take an advantageous form or to be left alone. In either case groups exist or are formed to influence the political outcome.

Traditionally, interest groups in Britain have enjoyed close relationships with particular ministries. The extent to which they have enlarged their 'lobbying' in Brussels is a good indication of how far British policy is now being decided there rather than in London.

Among the pressure groups whose interests are affected by the EU, the larger ones are now organised at both national and international levels. They operate in Brussels, as in London, maintaining offices in both places in order to keep a close watch on policy developments and to lobby for their interests. At the European level groups act mainly on the Commission and Parliament, both of which are fairly open to outside interests. However, both also try to simplify life by dealing with only one or two large organisations in the same policy field. Therefore British pressure groups look for close working relations with their European partners. They are more likely to get a hearing if they act together, and more likely to be successful if they pool resources and speak with one voice. For example, the National Farmers Union is part of the Committee of Professional Agricultural Organisations (COPA), which maintains a strong presence in Brussels; so also do other umbrella groups such as the European Trade Union Confederation (ETUC) and the Union of Industries of the European Union (UNIEU).

PUBLIC POLICY

Policy development in pursuit of European integration has often been patchy, and implementation of policy erratic, as the budget and the bureaucracy of the EU are relatively small. The budget is fixed at under 2.007 per cent of the combined gross national product (GNP) of Member States. The EU employs approximately 25,000 people in Brussels and Luxembourg, which is smaller than a medium sized department of central government in Britain or the administration of a large city such as Amsterdam or Barcelona. Nevertheless the EU already has an enormously powerful and wide-ranging policy impact, covering almost everything from the routines of daily life all the way up to the grand issues of monetary union and foreign policy. Every year the EU issues more than 12,000 legal instruments in the form of regulations, directives, decisions, recommendations and opinions.

BRIEFINGS

9.5 How policy is implemented by the EU

Decisions in the EU are implemented by means of five types of 'legal instruments', as follows:

1. Regulations are general and, since they have the force of EU law, they are directly binding on all Member States.

2. Directives are more frequently used than regulations and, similarly, are binding on all Member States. Unlike regulations, however, directives leave it open for Member States to decide how best to achieve the desired goal.

3. Decisions are binding on all those to whom they are addressed.

4. Recommendations have no binding force, and are sometimes not defined as 'legal instruments'.

5. Opinions have the same characteristics as recommendations.

Economic affairs – the euro

This is probably the most important single area so far as national policies are concerned. The Single European Act, passed in 1986 and implemented patchily in the 1990s encourages free movement of goods, services, capital and people throughout the EU. Among other things this means the free movement of university students (promoted by programmes which pay the extra expenses). Many technical specifications in manufacturing and services have been standardised (the EU term is 'harmonisation'). And since the EU itself is funded by each nation paying a proportion of its receipts from value added tax, VAT rates have also been partly standardised. The EU would like the whole tax structure in member countries to be standardised across Europe, a logical complement to the idea of a unified market.

The most ambitious, difficult and controversial part of the whole agenda, certainly in Britain, has been the introduction of a common currency, the euro, now functioning in 12 states of the Union. Britain is the major Member State holding aloof from this, with a corresponding marginalisation of its influence in the EU which we have already discussed. Decisions about financial (and hence implicitly economic) policy for the EU are taken by the Council of the European Central Bank on which Britain is not represented, though decisions to increase or slow down European economic activity inevitably affect her.

The problem for the Labour government, generally disposed to go in, is that any decision to do so involves calling and winning a referendum campaign against impassioned Conservative opposition. They will not initiate this if it gets in the way of their internal political agenda, particularly winning the next general election. They have thus taken refuge in a formula. They will recommend joining the eurozone if their economic 'tests' are met. Unlike the EU's own conditions for joining the European Monetary Union (EMU), the British criteria stress economic convergence rather than financial considerations. However they are both vague and highly technical and can probably be interpreted to favour whatever conclusion the government wants, once it decides what the political circumstances dictate. Under the mask of economic debate most decisions about the EU are political ones. The real question for Britain in the monetary debate is not what effects the euro would have on its economy (nobody knows) but whether it wants to go ahead with the EU or the US.

BRIEFINGS

9.6 British economic 'tests' for joining European Monetary Union (EMU)

Gordon Brown, New Labour Chancellor of the Exchequer (ie Minister of Finance) postponed controversy in October 1997 over a decision to adopt the euro by laying down five economic tests which had to be met for a decision to be made. These were:

- sustainable convergence between the UK and the economies already using the euro
- sufficient flexibility to cope with economic change
- positive effect on investment
- impact on British financial services
- impact on employment.

Compared with the EU's criteria for whether a country is capable of adopting the euro (see Briefing 8.5) the British tests stress economic rather than purely financial considerations – would the British economy integrate well with the Continental ones or not? However, they are more vague.

Of course, in a world boom (or recession) the economies would show convergence but at other times might be out of kilter. So all depends on when the campaign is initiated. What is flexibility? If the test were seriously applied to the northern industrial and southern financial service economies within Britain itself they would probably show non-convergence and lack of flexibility in the north. But should the United Kingdom be split up politically as a result? Few politicians outside the Scottish National Party would argue so.

All this implies that the British tests, like the EU's own convergence criteria, are a front for decisions that have to be taken on political grounds – does Britain wish to integrate with the EU or not? It may remain as it is and occupy a half-way house, but this will in the long run deprive it of influence within the wider Europe.

Other aspects of EU harmonisation

These have been less controversial. National governments are no longer permitted directly to subsidise industries. But the EU provides money for industrial restructuring and technological development, offering loans at special interest rates through the European Investment Bank. The basic principle is that public subsidies should be distributed on an EU basis to strengthen the EU economy, and not by national governments in a way that interferes with a free market. There are also rules about public procurement. Public bodies, such as governments, are obliged to seek tenders for large contracts on the open market across the EU. Finally, attempts have been made to regulate conditions of work, including minimum pay, employment laws, and such things as the enforced use of tachographs (monitoring machines) in the cabs of long-distance trucks, a measure the European Court forced on an unwilling British government in 1979.

By and large the EU has been successful in creating a single, integrated market, although its difficulties and failures have often attracted more attention than its successes. Examples of problems involving British interests are: the banned export of British meat to France (blocked on health grounds after the mad cow and foot and mouth scares): ending the practice in some countries of favouring home-produced spirits, a decision that helped the Scottish whisky industry. Once again these examples show how deeply EU policy reaches into national economic affairs. EU authority is supreme in competition policy (the EU policy of encouraging free competition between firms in the same sector and discouraging monopoly practices), although few mergers or acquisitions of note have been blocked by the Commission. Similarly, although the Maastricht Treaty speaks optimistically about a free labour market, linguistic, cultural and other barriers have resulted in low levels of mobility between Member States.

Regional aid

Britain receives substantial grants from the European Regional Development Fund, created in 1975 to help poor or industrially run-down areas. Of the 50 million people in the EU living in such regions, 20 million are in Britain (Wales, Scotland, Northern Ireland and the north of England). The standard of living in Britain as a whole is almost exactly the EU average, but only in the southeast of England is it higher (by about 20 per cent), while in Northern Ireland it is 25 per cent lower. The special regions of Britain benefit from funds and policy initiatives aimed at building up small businesses and the tourist trade, retraining workers in declining agricultural areas, restructuring industry and retraining workers, rebuilding urban infrastructure and revitalising the economy in areas of industrial decline. Merseyside alone now receives about £1.3 billion from London and Brussels.

Consumer affairs

Common standards for the labelling and selling of foods have been adopted. Well-publicised examples in Britain involve the production of ice cream, sausages and beer, but EU regulations cover a large proportion of the goods sold in shops. The EU has ruled that tobacco products must not be advertised on television, and it carefully regulates the amount and the timing of television advertising. Recently it cleared British meat after the foot and mouth epidemic of 2001, and took judicial action against the French government for continuing to ban it.

Agriculture and fishing

The Common Agricultural Policy (CAP) is the largest single item on the EU's annual budget, accounting for almost half the total, although it used to be three-quarters. It is intended to give some economic security to the large number of poor farmers and agricultural communities in western Europe. Although British farmers benefit very substantially from the CAP the country as a whole pays more than it gets because British farms are relatively large and efficient. Currently the EU's fishing policy is even more controversial because, in trying to preserve fish stocks, it has affected the livelihoods of fishing communities in Britain.

Environmental policy

The EU has developed a wide range of policies to protect the environment involving, among other things, forests, birds, plants, animals, drinking water, waste disposal, bathing beaches and recreational areas. Many of these have caused difficulties for the British government: substandard water supplies and bathing beaches, inadequate industrial pollution controls, new roads that fail environmental impact norms (the M3 at Twyford Down, for example), and new conifer forests inconsistent with EU standards. In 1993 Lancashire County Council successfully prosecuted the British government in the European Court for its failure to clean up three bathing beaches. EU policy in these matters may be embarrassing for the government but serves to protect British consumers.

Social policy

The EU has enacted a broad range of social measures. For example, industrial training has been financed by the European Social Fund since 1972. Some policies have attracted much publicity, such as the case of *Smith* v *Macarthy*, in which the European Court forced a British employer to observe equal pay rules. The controversial Social Chapter of the Maastricht agreement laid down a broad range of regulations on, among other things, social conditions, working hours, minimum wages and health and safety standards. The Chapter was not signed by the Conservative government of the time, but has been accepted by the Labour government.

Justice and home affairs

This is an area where the Member States jealously guard their own autonomy, so common European policies on policing and internal security have to be arrived at by intergovernmental negotiations and unanimity or not at all. In some cases such as the Schengen agreement to abolish frontier controls inside the EU, some States have agreed to go in together leaving others including the UK outside. Free internal mobility within the EU poses problems for frontier controls as it is more difficult to exclude aliens who have already been admitted to another EU country. This particularly affects the British concern to exclude purely 'economic' immigrants to the UK. Under the terms of the Treaty of Amsterdam (1997) the EU is now able to act more directly in the area of justice and home affairs.

Foreign affairs and security

On foreign economic policy the EU has been relatively successful in framing a common European policy. It now acts for its members in the vitally important GATT negotiations, and appears alongside the most powerful nations in world economic meetings. But on diplomatic and defence matters its success is limited. Some Member States, including Britain, jealously guard the power to decide their own foreign and defence policies, or else prefer to work through NATO. Consequently, Europe failed to provide international leadership during the various crises of the 1990s and has been unable to formulate a common response to the US 'war on terrorism' or the continuing Middle East crisis.

Two points should be noted about the impact of the EU on public policy. First, some of the rules and regulations which exist on paper are only partially enforced, if at all in some Member States. There are many ways of breaking, bending or ignoring them. This means that many areas of public policy remain largely unaffected by EU directives and law (law and order, for example). Also unaffected are all those very important areas – agriculture apart – where the nation state provides direct cash payments for individuals: pensions, social and unemployment benefits. In other words EU competence is mainly confined to regulation rather than the direct distribution of benefits. This may, of course, change with further integration and monetary union and consequent pressures to redistribute across countries and regions to help adjustment. Figure 9.2 shows the budget of the EU in 2002. Note the continuing importance of agricultural subsidies and of structural funds used to help poorer regions 'catch up' with the more affluent regions.

The rules on public procurement are complex, and can easily be twisted and evaded. Britain has a good record of compliance with EU directives. In 1991 only Denmark, Luxembourg and the Netherlands were found to be more compliant, and some countries were much worse. Figure 9.3 shows the degree of compliance with Single Market laws in the mid-1990s and the number of complaints against countries for flouting the trade rules. Again, Britain's performance is relatively good compared with many Member States, in particular Germany. However, Britain continues to have the worst ice cream and the best beer in Europe, despite EU attempts to change both!

Whatever the actual impact of EU policy, the fact remains that many of the policy areas previously controlled by national governments are now partially or even wholly in the hands of European decision makers. To this extent it is certainly true that EU policy has an important and expanding effect on daily life in Britain.

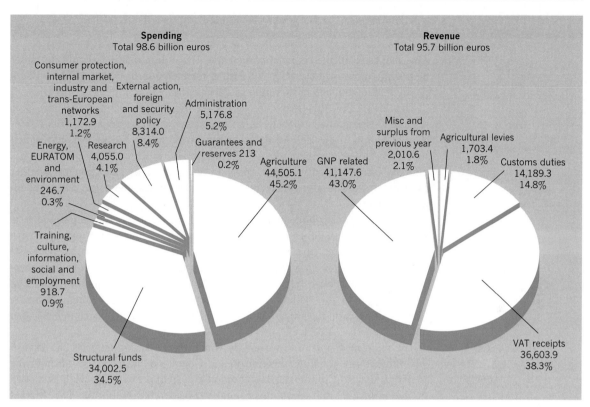

Spending
Total 98.6 billion euros

Revenue
Total 95.7 billion euros

Consumer protection,
internal market,
industry and
trans-European
networks
1,172.9
1.2%

External action,
foreign
and security
policy
8,314.0
8.4%

Administration
5,176.8
5.2%

Energy,
EURATOM
and
environment
246.7
0.3%

Research
4,055.0
4.1%

Guarantees and
reserves 213
0.2%

Agriculture
44,505.1
45.2%

GNP related
41,147.6
43.0%

Misc and
surplus from
previous year
2,010.6
2.1%

Agricultural levies
1,703.4
1.8%

Customs duties
14,189.3
14.8%

Training,
culture,
information,
social and
employment
918.7
0.9%

Structural funds
34,002.5
34.5%

VAT receipts
36,603.9
38.3%

Figure 9.2 *European Union budget, 2002*

Source: Public finance figures of the European Union from the website http://europa.eu.int/comm/budget/pubfin/index_en.htm

Figure 9.3 *Single
Market laws enacted by
national governments,
31 December 1995,
and complaints against
countries for rule violation,
1995*

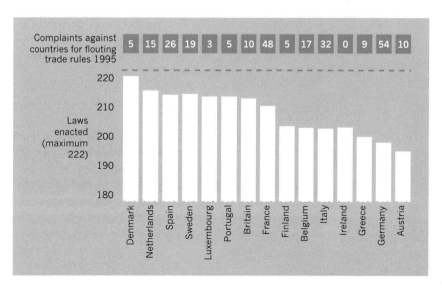

Complaints against
countries for flouting
trade rules 1995

| 5 | 15 | 26 | 19 | 3 | 5 | 10 | 48 | 5 | 17 | 32 | 0 | 9 | 54 | 10 |

Laws
enacted
(maximum
222)

220
210
200
190
180

Denmark Netherlands Spain Sweden Luxembourg Portugal Britain France Finland Belgium Italy Ireland Greece Germany Austria

THE 'DEMOCRATIC DEFICIT' OF THE EU

Democratic deficit
A phrase usually applied to the EU to describe a lack of democratic accountability in its decision making.

This makes it all the more important that EU policy making should be under democratic control. One effect of British membership has been to place much policy making outside the scrutiny of Parliament.

The blame for this rests on successive British governments. They have regarded Parliamentary debate as an unnecessary interference with their freedom of action in the EU. So they have given no lead that might have resulted in a substantial restructuring of Parliamentary procedures to give the EU effective scrutiny. This failure raises in acute form the question of whether Parliament's essentially nineteenth-century procedures can cope with modern developments.

That national Parliaments can exert real power over EU negotiations is shown by the case of Denmark, which provides an interesting example of a national Parliament (the Folketing) exerting considerable authority over EU legislation. The Folketing secured its position during the debate on EU membership. Under the Danish Act of Accession the government is required to make an annual report to the Folketing and to keep it informed of Council business. General debates on the EU are held at regular intervals, and special debates also take place.

The main mechanism, however, by which the Folketing controls the Danish government's negotiating position in the Council of Ministers is through the Market Relations Committee. The committee system is extremely well developed in the Folketing and committees enjoy considerable authority. The Market Relations Committee is the most authoritative of all and also the most prestigious: its 17 members, elected proportionately from the various political parties, include many former Cabinet ministers. Under the rules of procedure the government is committed to consult with the Market Relations Committee on all Council business. The Committee meets weekly and may question ministers and civil servants involved in EU policy. The government is obliged to seek mandates from the Committee before important Council decisions. In many Council sessions Danish ministers have had extremely narrow mandates and on some occasions they have had to seek new mandates from the Committee before reaching agreement on a particular issue.

In the light of Danish experience, the inability of the British Parliament to control its government's negotiating position may be part of a general decline in its power, attributable to the dominance of a single party in government at any one time, government control of the Parliamentary agenda, and the poor access of MPs and peers to information. In Chapter 18 we shall consider the general question of Parliamentary power.

In the European area, however, there is another body that might be able to hold governments to account: the directly elected European Parliament itself. It holds its legislative meetings in the French city of Strasbourg, far away from the real centres of power in Brussels, and meets in full session for only one week a month.

BRIEFINGS

9.7 The European Parliament

Since 1979 the EP has been directly elected every four years. Seats in the EP are allocated among Member States in rough proportion to their population.

Although the EP is charged with the duty of supervising the Commission and the Council of Ministers it lacks power and has mainly a secondary and advisory role. Although its jurisdiction has expanded, the Parliament is still primarily a delaying or amending body with limited powers of veto, especially on budgetary matters. It is logistically and bureaucratically hampered by having to meet in Brussels for committees and in Luxembourg and Strasbourg for plenary sessions. Moreover, the main secretariat is located in Luxembourg. Business is conducted in all the official languages of the EU, which imposes a huge burden of translation.

The European Parliament is increasingly flexing its muscles, however. In 1998 it forced the resignation of the European Commission en bloc, after the publication of a damning report on corruption on the part of some Commissioners.

This indicates that its influence is limited. The Parliament is the least weighty of the four major European bodies (Council of Ministers, Commission, Court, Parliament). However, it is not quite so limited as its peripheral position and short legislative sessions might suggest.

For one thing, it does most of its work in specialised committees, and these meet in Brussels where they cross-question Commissioners and European civil servants on all aspects of European policy. Increasingly these meetings receive press coverage, especially when they uncover frauds or anomalies in EU policy.

The EP has also been given increased powers in every revision of the original treaty (Treaty of Rome, 1957), so it can reject the budget or national nominees to the Commission (but only as a whole). Parliament has to be consulted on a whole range of social and economic policy (Single European Act 1986) and it has positively to approve policy, or at least not reject it, in other areas, under the Treaties of Maastricht (1992), Amsterdam (1997) and Nice (2000).

The weakness of the European Parliament is that it mainly controls the Commission. The body it really wants to control is the Council of Ministers, since that is where initiatives on most EU matters originate. Until it can affect the Council's decisions, or until the latter's governmental powers are mostly transferred to the Commission, much of what the EP does seems like shadow boxing. Parliament really has no desire to punish or hamper the Commission when it is its ally in campaigning for a transfer of power from national to EU level.

This fact also mutes party conflict within the European Parliament. MEPs are organised into six main party groups: Communists, Socialists (with British Labour included), Greens, Liberals (including British Liberal Democrats), European People's Party (Conservatives and Christian Democrats) and Democracies and Diversities. The major groupings are Socialists and Populars, who compete for Parliamentary control with each other. However, most politicians who get themselves elected to the Parliament are naturally Europhile and federalist. Hence party conflict is muted, rendering Parliamentary proceedings rather dull as well as irrelevant to core decision making.

The European Parliament's significant asset is that it is the only elected European body. Direct elections are held every four years, more or less simultaneously across all the countries of the EU. Hence it can claim to have more of a democratic, popular mandate for what it says than can the Commission or the Court.

However, the Council of Ministers can also claim that its members, chosen to represent their country by their respective national governments, owe their position ultimately to popular election. In Britain, general elections are clearly regarded as more important than Euro-elections, as evidenced by the fact that they attract about double the number of voters.

Indeed, as campaigning in Euro-elections is in the hands of the British parties rather than an all-European Socialist or Conservative organisation, they often appear as a pale reflection of the general election. European issues only enter in a negative way (eg 'resisting Brussels bureaucracy') and elections are fought mostly on issues of domestic politics. It is difficult, therefore, for British members of the European Parliament (MEPs) to claim a very convincing mandate for wresting power from the Council of Ministers, when they have been elected on the basis of (or as a protest against) the British government's domestic record.

The powerlessness of the British Parliament in European affairs is not counterbalanced, therefore, by any greater authority or effectiveness of the European Parliament. The latter has only marginally greater power of scrutiny over European legislation and no greater control over the Council of Ministers. This detracts even from its direct election, by lowering its visibility to electors and ultimately their turnout. The EP has the potential for democratic control should the EU become a real federation. Until that day, however, it remains the weakest of the European institutions and the most limited in its functions.

SUBSIDIARITY AND LOCAL GOVERNMENT

This 'democratic deficit' might be made up within the structure of the EU – at least to some extent – by implementing the idea of 'subsidiarity', which is frequently talked about and is even written into the Treaty of Maastricht as a vague commitment. 'Subsidiarity' has been seen by 'Eurosceptical' countries such as Britain as a way of limiting future transfers of power from London to Brussels, or even of getting some powers back. This hardly guarantees democratic control, given the weakness of Parliamentary scrutiny.

A better idea might be to go all the way and transfer some European and central powers to local and regional governments, the third set of directly elected bodies in Britain. They have the advantage of being much closer to their electors than either the European or British governments and Parliaments.

Traditionally, many 'personal' services that were centralised in other European countries – education, police, public health – have been controlled by local authorities in Britain. The tendency under governments from 1976 onwards however has been quite the opposite. Such services have either been taken over by central government or given to unelected 'quangos' nominated by the government – the only exception being the 'hiving off' of these services in Wales and Scotland to elected regional executives. Centralisation has been justified in terms of controlling public expenditure, benefiting from the 'economies of scale' of larger, if non-elected, units, and of introducing competition. An unstated reason, arising from the election cycle in Britain (which ensures that most local councillors are elected at the government's mid-term, when its popularity is low), is that councils are often controlled by opposition parties. Governments have often found it easier to work with nominated bodies whose members were more likely to be 'one of us' (in Margaret Thatcher's phrase).

This erosion of local democracy has been one factor stimulating demands for local autonomy in Scotland, Wales and Northern Ireland. We shall discuss these regions and their local nationalist parties in the next chapter. Here we need only note that regional elected assemblies are also boosted by the doctrine of subsidiarity. There are few tasks outside foreign affairs and defence that government at this level would not be fitted to do. Even if Scottish and Welsh independence became an option it would be easier to contemplate within the Single Market and the structure of the EU. Hence, the Scottish National Party uses the slogan: 'Scotland in Europe' to indicate that an independent Scotland is viable. Paradoxically, the centralisation of western Europe under the EU helps its decentralisation, a point noted in the next chapter.

Quite apart from the possibility of carrying 'subsidiarity' to its logical conclusion, the EU has already had an effect on the British regions and local government. The EU has substantial regional funds and many of its policies have a direct impact on local services. As a result a large and increasing number of local and regional bodies have built their own special links with Brussels. Some maintain an office and staff there to keep a close watch on events, to try to influence European bodies, and to raise money. Others employ consultants in Brussels to act on their behalf. Some authorities group together to form consortia, but the larger ones act separately.

It often suits both local interests and Brussels to work directly with one another, thereby short-circuiting the government in London. This is consistent with subsidiarity, but it is also a convenient political device that allows the localities and Brussels to build political alliances independently of national governments. This is notably true for Britain, where the government has the reputation of being the 'awkward partner'. Thus, the EU strengthens the position of local and regional government as against the central government in London. This is a concrete example of centralisation in Brussels developing hand in hand with the decentralisation of power to the local and regional levels, something that is taken up within the context of regionalism in the next chapter.

ESSAYS

1. Why is the issue of European Union so divisive in British party politics? Is it likely to become less divisive in the next ten years or so?

2. What organisational impact has membership of the EU had on Whitehall and Westminster? Have they restructured around Europe or adapted existing organisations? Why?

3. The EU's main areas of policy interest are economics, the environment, consumer affairs, regional policy, agriculture and fisheries, and security and foreign policy. Pick any three and trace the impact of EU policy on British affairs.

SUMMARY

This chapter has examined the impact of the European Union on government and politics in Britain. The effects have been deep and profound but they also vary considerably, as follows:

■ Constitutional effects have been limited, with the single and major exception of Parliamentary sovereignty. Parliament must accept EU law, and cannot change, repeal or even debate it. Legal sovereignty in relevant policy areas has therefore shifted from Westminster to the EU. With this important exception, the British constitution has changed little as a result of membership.

■ Much policy, particularly in economic, social and environmental matters, is now made in Brussels rather than London. The common currency poses a dilemma for British policy makers which they will have to confront decisively at some time.

■ In terms of the machinery of central government the UK has adapted existing structures rather than changed them. There is no special Ministry for European Affairs, as there is in many countries. Instead, European affairs are handled by a series of interdepartmental committees, co-ordinated by the Cabinet Office, and by the Foreign and Commonwealth Office. Nonetheless, the sheer volume of EU work has added enormously to the pressures on leading politicians and civil servants. They have also had to develop a European awareness in almost everything they do.

■ Pressure groups whose interests are affected by the EU have responded by moving into Brussels, where they have replicated their London lobbying activities and organisations. They often join forces with other European partners to form 'umbrella' organisations that represent many national organisations with similar interests. It is estimated that about 500 'Eurogroups' are recognised by policy makers in Brussels, and that over 3,000 full-time lobbyists operate in the city. British groups are fully involved with both.

■ Local governments and regional organisations have followed suit and made direct contact with European decision makers in Brussels. The advisory 'Committee of the Regions' gives them an institutional basis inside the structures of the EU.

■ The impact of the EU varies considerably in different policy areas. In some its effects are pervasive, in others less so. But EU policies now affect many aspects of daily life in Britain, and their influence is likely to grow.

FURTHER READING

For the fullest account of the impact of the European Union on the government, politics and policy of the UK, C. Pilkington, *Britain in the European Union Today* (Manchester: Manchester University Press, 2001), Janet Mather, *The European Union and British Democracy* (London: Palgrave-Macmillan, 2000) and J. A. Cygan, *The UK Parliament and EU*

PROJECTS

1. Identify the main effects of membership of the EU on the executive, legislative and judicial branches of British government. Where does most power and influence lie?

2. Imagine you are the leader of a major European pressure group. How would you try to influence EU policy on a matter of interest to your group? Answer with reference to:
   (a) agricultural policy
   (b) environmental policy
   (c) competition policy.

3. Locate the interests of Scotland and Wales in relation to the EU. Does British membership of the EU make the devolution of legislative powers to Wales and Scotland more or less likely?

Legislation (Dordrecht: Kluwer, 1998) are very useful. Recent articles are: H. Macmillen, 'Political responsibility for the administration of Europe', *Parliamentary Affairs*, **52** (4), 1999, pp. 703–18; N. Kinnock, 'Accountability and reform of internal control in the European Commission', *Political Quarterly*, **73** (1), 2002, pp. 21–8. A stimulating 'political' read is Robert Worcester, *How to Win the Euro Referendum: Lessons from 1975* (London: Foreign Policy Centre, 2000).

USEFUL WEB SITES ON EUROPE IN BRITAIN

Hotlinks to these sites can be found on the CWS website at http://www.booksites.net/budge.

The impact of the European Union in the design and implementation of governmental policies in Britain cannot be underestimated. In our previous chapter we focused on the conflicts responses to such influence within Britain may engender. Now in turn we can suggest some useful web sites on the structure and functioning of the European Union and its impact on Britain.

The inevitable first step is to visit the EU official web site at www.europa.eu.int/index_en.htm, where you can find links to the European Parliament, the Council of Ministers, the European Commission and other relevant institutions. A comprehensive analysis of the historical evolution of the European Union after the Maastricht treaty is available at www.europarl.eu.int/code/maastric/default_en.htm. Detailed information on the political outcomes of the Amsterdam Treaty can be found at www.europa.eu.int/abc/obj/amst/en/. We suggest you consult the European Committee of the Regions (www.cor.eu.int/home.htm) and the European Economic and Social Committee (www.esc.eu.int/pages/en/home.htm). Reliable statistical data on the EU is available at www.europa.eu.int/comm/eurostat. The official publications of the EU can be accessed from www.euros.ch. There are critical voices within the European Union structure itself: you can find them at www.europarl.eu.int/edd.

For official British policy towards Europe visit the Foreign and Commonwealth Office site (www.fco.gov.uk). For UKRep (the UK's Permanent Representation to the EU) see www.ukrep.fco.gov.uk. You might also want to visit the European Foundation at www.europeanfoundation.org.

An excellent source for academic approaches to the EU is the European Research Papers Archive (www.eiop.or.at/erpa/). Visit also the Centre for European Reform (www.cer.org.uk) and the working papers of the Jean Monnet Programme (www.jeanmonnetprogram.org).

Disuniting the Kingdom: Ireland

Besides Europe Britain is embroiled in another set of territorial relationships affecting its sovereignty – in Ireland. The whole of Ireland was once part of the 'United Kingdom of Great Britain and Ireland' – up to 1922. Then the south and west of the island broke away from Britain after a violent armed struggle to form the independent Republic of Ireland. Britain is the only member of the EU to have lost part of its territory through twentieth-century violence. Its current territorial sovereignty as the 'United Kingdom of Great Britain and Northern Ireland' is threatened by developments there, which may also set precedents for Scotland and Wales.

This chapter covers:

- nationalism and state building in western Europe – are current states really the unified nations they claim to be?
- how relationships with the British State worked out in Ireland
- Northern Ireland – origins of the 'Troubles'
- the 'Troubles', 1969–97: rival claims of nationhood
- the 'peace process', 1997–2003
- the Northern Irish Assembly, keystone of the political settlement
- prospects for a lasting peace.

MINORITY NATIONALISM AND STATE BUILDING IN BRITAIN AND EUROPE

Britain is unique among the countries of the EU in having had part of its national territory secede in a violent struggle for independence. The present-day Republic of Ireland broke away from the United Kingdom in 1922 by force of arms. Irish nationalists have continued the guerrilla war in Northern Ireland and on the British mainland up until recently. Only Spain among the Member States of the EU has experienced anything similar to this, in the form of Basque terrorism.

Minority nationalism, by way of contrast – peaceful demands for political autonomy on the part of cultural or religious minorities – is common throughout western Europe. Belgium has effectively split itself between Dutch-speaking Flemings and French-speaking Walloons; Italy and Spain have granted extensive powers to regional minorities; and Bavaria has its own political party inside Germany.

BRIEFINGS

10.1 England, Britain, Great Britain, the United Kingdom, and the British Isles

There is often confusion between the terms England, Britain, Great Britain, the United Kingdom, and the British Isles. This is partly because geographical entities get mixed up with political ones. The largest geographical entity, the British Isles, consists of the two main islands and many smaller ones. The larger island, Great Britain, contains England, Wales and Scotland, and the smaller one, Ireland, comprises Northern Ireland and the Republic of Ireland. The largest political entity is the United Kingdom of Great Britain and Northern Ireland, which consists of England, Scotland, Wales and Northern Ireland. This is often shortened to the UK. The largest part of the UK is England, often confused with Great Britain or even the UK by the English. The Republic of Ireland was part of the UK until 1922 when it broke away after the War of Independence.

BRIEFINGS

10.2 State nationalism and minority nationalism: are nation states really nations?

'State' is another word used to describe a 'country' or 'polity'. It refers first to a territorial unit governed by a single supreme (or 'sovereign') authority and secondly to the military and administrative institutions that defend and organise that unit. In the context of international relations the idea of an autonomous territorial unit is usually uppermost. References to the activities of the 'state' inside Britain usually mean the executive and its administrative apparatus.

The British State was consolidated by English kings and rulers, based around London, who conquered the outlying regions of England from 800–1200, then Wales and Ireland. They tried but failed to conquer Scotland, which was, however, incorporated by negotiation through the dynastic Union of the Crowns in 1603, and the Union of Parliaments in 1707. Southern and western Ireland broke away violently from the British State at the end of the First World War (1919–22) and set up a separate State, the Republic of Ireland. The 'six counties' of Northern Ireland are still disputed between the British and Irish states and violence continues. The Scottish Nationalist Party (SNP), which gained 21 per cent of the Scottish vote in the 2003 Scottish Parliament election, advocates Scottish independence through peaceful means. Welsh Nationalists organised in Plaid Cymru want more autonomy inside Britain.

The growth of independence movements stems from the influence of nationalism. This is the idea, which originated in the nineteenth century, that each 'people' defined by a particular language and culture should have its own state. In practice, this was often reversed by the dominant group as each existing state imposed its own language and culture on the minorities claiming that as there was one state it ought to have a unified people. 'Unionists' often claim that Britain is a nation state, as most 'Britons' speak English and have a common culture. Welsh, Scottish and Irish nationalists oppose this, arguing that the existence of a separate culture in their country justifies an independent state for them. Nationalism is thus a two-edged sword. Depending on what groups are identified as important, it can be used either to argue for the legitimacy of the existing 'nation states' such as the United Kingdom, or for the right of secession of the Irish, Scots and Welsh.

Nationalism
The belief that the people identified as belonging to a national community should form their own sovereign state.

Irish (and Scottish and Welsh) nationalism are thus not anomalies on the European scene; on the contrary, they are a familiar phenomenon. That is in part why the EU has created its advisory 'Committee of the Regions' to represent minority groups, bypassing the claims of the existing Member States to be homogeneous nations.

Indeed, there are some European federalists who advocate a 'Europe of the Homelands' (*Europe des Patries*), which would cut out existing states altogether and base a European federation on the traditional regions. One does not have to go this far to see that regional aspirations might be a useful ally in attempts to take power away from the Member States.

The reason why so many regional minorities exist goes back to the very formation of the European states. Most were created by powerful rulers expanding from their fortified capital to seize surrounding territories. Sometimes these were inhabited by people speaking the same language and sharing a similar way of life to the original subjects, but sometimes they were very different. Whatever the case, they could be taxed and used to support an even more powerful army for further territorial expansion.

The traditional state tried to impose the same religion on all its subjects but did not concern itself with their culture or language. After the French Revolution, however, the idea that the state should be 'one and indivisible' – all citizens should be equal to each other but also similar – gained ground. This was the origin of nationalism, according to which every people or nation should have its own state. Universal education gave those in control of existing states an opportunity to create a corresponding nation by imposing the state language on all schools and educating all children in it. The growth of a mass press, and later radio and television – all using the majority language – aided this process.

State attempts to impose a single language provoked resistance from minorities who saw their own culture and language disappearing under state pressure. Their remedy was to create their own political institutions in order to sustain, rather than depress, their culture. Thus they too found support in the ideas of nationalism. One only had to recognise the minority as a separate nation to argue that it should have its own state. However, minority secession or even autonomy was resisted by the majority, who saw this as splitting 'their' nation, and redoubled their attempts at assimilation of the minorities. What these conflicts call into question is what constitutes the nation: the region, or the state in which it has become embedded?

These conflicts have worked their way through British politics. The core of the British State is formed by southeast England, which conquered or assimilated the other parts of the islands in a process lasting 1,000 years (up to the Parliamentary union with Ireland in 1801).

In some respects state formation in Britain was more permissive than in other European countries: because of its island position it had less need to exert an iron control over its borders – it could afford to leave local leaders in charge (in mainland Britain at least); provided they paid taxes and kept order they could do more or less what they wanted within their own region or county. Nineteenth-century political reforms were aimed at freeing local initiatives rather than promoting centralisation. It was, for example, native Scottish educationalists, and not a

Plate 10.1 *The aftermath of the Easter Rising, 1916, which initiated the violent secession of southern Ireland from the UK*

Source: www.paphotos.com

London government, who tried to replace both Gaelic and Scots with standard English.

In Ireland, however, the British government – because the island was a potential area of military weakness – acted much more like an imperial power towards a colony, planting settlers and ruling through an alien bureaucracy. Differences were exacerbated by the fact that four-fifths of the population were Roman Catholic in a largely Protestant British state. Doctrines of nationalism thus found fertile ground among the Catholic Irish of the south and west in the nineteenth century. Like many such European nationalist movements the struggle for independence fused with movements for political emancipation, social advancement and cultural autonomy. These sparked off a century-long series of revolts against British rule (1798, 1848, 1867–8, 1879–83, 1919–22). The last of these succeeded in establishing an independent state, the Republic of Ireland, in the south and west of Ireland.

Plate 10.2 *Ulster volunteers take on the Republicans in the Northern Irish Civil War, 1920–22*

Source: www.paphotos.com

The Irish example illustrates the ambiguity and interchangeability of the concepts of nation and minority, region and state. It all depends on whether a territorially concentrated group has state institutions of its own or whether its area is run by a state in which a larger group dominates. Ireland was a region of Britain and is (mostly) now a separate state. The same could conceivably happen in Scotland and Wales and may well happen in Northern Ireland over the next 20 years.

Northern Ireland illustrates another phenomenon, however, which is equally characteristic of nationalist movements. The nationalist struggles set off reactions not only from the state majority but also from other minorities or from representatives of the state majority within their own region. In the case of Ireland the Protestants, a local majority in the north, strongly opposed Irish nationalism and upheld the union with Britain. The Irish War of Independence was also a civil war between largely Catholic nationalists and largely Protestant unionists. When Irish independence was granted the latter retained their own territory in the north as part of the British state.

Like Russian dolls, however, such territorial solutions always reveal another minority lurking underneath. Northern Ireland contained a substantial nationalist, Catholic minority who supported a takeover by the Republic. This led to continuing guerrilla warfare and terrorism (1919–23, 1936–41, 1956–63, 1969–96) in mainland Britain as well as in Northern Ireland.

BRIEFINGS

10.3 Guerrilla warfare, terrorism, and freedom fighters

Nationalist groups frustrated with constitutional procedures for expressing their demands may turn to violence, often calling themselves 'freedom fighters' or a 'liberation front'. The main example in Britain is the Irish Republican Army (IRA). The mainstream Welsh and Scottish nationalists are dedicated to non-violent ways of expressing their claims for self-determination, but fringe groups in both cases have used violence. (The most notable example is the burning of English-owned holiday homes in Wales.) Nationalists may be tempted to follow such tactics because they are minorities within the British State, where the inbuilt English majority can always vote them down. The danger in resistance to all claims for autonomy is that the frustrated nationalists may turn to violence.

One group's terrorism is another group's liberation struggle. The very definition of the situation is one element in the conflict between the IRA and the British State. The latter has infinitely more soldiers, weapons and resources than the IRA. The 'freedom fighters' or 'terrorists' thus have to adopt hit and run tactics, killing individual members of the armed forces or leaving bombs that will injure or kill civilians indiscriminately. Through these actions they hope to provoke the authorities into indiscriminate action against Catholics as a whole, thus provoking general resentment and providing recruits to their own movement. Once 'guerrilla warfare' of this kind starts it can generate its own grievances and become self-perpetuating, as the example of Ireland shows.

DEVOLUTION

Devolution
The delegation of specific powers by a higher level of government to a lower one.

A way in which compromises might be achieved between a minority and the central state is also suggested by Northern Ireland. From 1922 to 1972 it had a provincial Parliament and government largely responsible for internal affairs. Its record was marred by discrimination against Catholics, but in other respects the Northern Irish administration modernised the province and vastly improved social conditions.

The Northern Irish case provides a precedent for the way Welsh and Scottish demands for more autonomy have been met, without breaking up the British State. A more sweeping form of 'devolution' to Northern Ireland, with equal power sharing between Protestants and Catholics, has formed the basis of Labour's 'Peace Process' in the troubled province.

Devolution is not a curious British anomaly. Most member countries of the EU have self-governing arrangements within culturally distinctive regions. The argument that any grant of political devolution will break up the United Kingdom is mistaken. Indeed, by compromising with local nationalists before they become totally frustrated, devolution may prevent an Irish situation developing. However, devolution clearly does have constitutional implications, which we shall explore in this chapter and the next.

NORTHERN IRELAND: ORIGINS OF THE 'TROUBLES'

Historical and social background

Northern Ireland had no history as a separate political entity before 1922. It was created at that time out of the six counties of Ireland that had a Protestant majority. These were set up with a separate Parliament and government as part of the Government of Ireland Act (1922), which effectively recognised the remaining 26 counties as a separate state.

BRIEFINGS

10.4 Northern Ireland, Ulster, and the 'six counties'

The largest concentration of Protestants in Ireland was in the northeast around the industrial town of Belfast. They thinned out towards the northwest of the island, although there was a concentration in the town of Derry (or Londonderry). In the 'Troubles' of 1919–22 the Protestant paramilitary groups, supported by the British Army, gained the upper hand in this part of Ireland. When the British government decided on partition between a Catholic-dominated free state (the future Republic of Ireland) and the Unionist-Protestant north as the only stable solution to the Irish conflict, they carved out the largest area Protestants could dominate within the historic province of Ulster, following county boundaries. They left out the three western and southern counties of the historic Ulster because these had Catholic–Nationalist majorities. The remaining 'six counties' had no previous tradition as a political unit and Derry, in particular, was cut off from its natural hinterland. Because it comprised the bulk of the historic province of Ulster the region was often referred to, loosely, by that name. However, the official term was 'Northern Ireland' (even though the tip of Donegal, in the Republic, lies further north!). This is the entity that had full internal home rule from 1922 to 1972, with its own Parliament and government based at Stormont, near Belfast.

The British government believed that the new unionist entity of 'Northern Ireland' would not be viable without a respectable territory. Hence it included many areas where Protestants were in only a tenuous majority, or were actually a minority. Substantial numbers of Catholic nationalists were thus incorporated against their will in this 'Protestant state for a Protestant people' as Viscount Craigavon, its first Prime Minister, described it. Thus there is a major division inside Northern Ireland between the Protestant heartland of North Down and Antrim – on the east – and Armagh and the counties of Fermanagh, Tyrone and Londonderry – in the west. This division is not only a religious one, but a social and economic one too, as Table 10.1 shows.

The western part of the province is more rural and less developed. Such east–west differences exist in the Republic of Ireland too. They were exacerbated in Northern Ireland, however, by the tendency of the Protestant-dominated 'Stormont' government (1922–72) (so called from the suburb of Belfast where it was located) to concentrate investment in Antrim and Down.

Table 10.1 *Regional disparities within Northern Ireland*

	Belfast and district	Rest of east	West and south
Percentage of unemployed, 2002	4.2	4.5	5.7
Average weekly earnings of full-time workers (£)	401	335	341
Religious groups, 2001 Percentage Roman Catholic	37.4	31.6	59.6
Percentage Protestant	58.3	65.0	38.4
Percentage other	0.7	0.3	0.2
Percentage no religion	3.7	3.6	1.8

Source: Northern Ireland Office Statistics Research Agency

Map 10.1 *Northern Ireland, showing local government districts shaded according to religious affiliation*

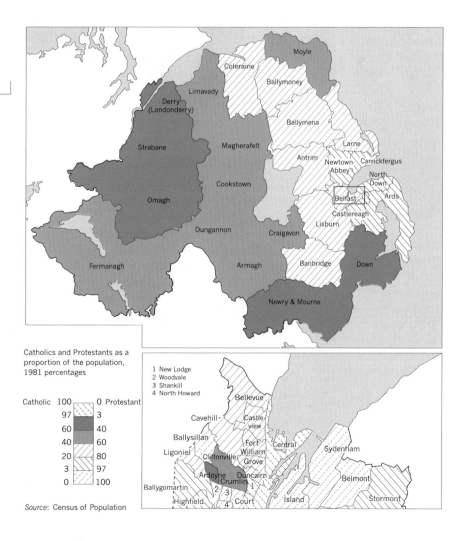

Catholics and Protestants as a proportion of the population, 1981 percentages

1 New Lodge
2 Woodvale
3 Shankill
4 North Howard

Source: Census of Population

Religious divisions

Practically the whole of the politics of the province can thus be traced back to the Protestant–Catholic religious division. This extends to voting too. Nowhere else in the United Kingdom, not even in Scotland, does a person's religious affiliation so emphatically determine their vote. The parties themselves are founded on the basis of such divisions. Sinn Fein is the Irish nationalist party associated with the underground Irish Republican Army, while the Social Democratic and Labour Party (SDLP) is the representative of moderate Catholics. The Alliance Party attempts to bridge the sectarian divide and attract both Protestant and Catholic votes from the working class. The various Unionist groupings represent Protestants of varying degrees of extremism. As their name suggests, they advocate 'no surrender' to Catholic nationalist demands and support continuing union with Britain.

This pervasiveness of religion in politics is not surprising. Northern Ireland was created on the basis of the politico-religious division in Ireland. Its continuing existence perpetuates this unless a way can be found to accommodate the demands of both sides within it. However, such a settlement would have implications for both the territorial integrity and sovereignty of the existing British State, as we shall see.

Outsiders, including the English, cannot understand why religion should be such an explosive force in the province. In the rest of Britain it is regarded as an individual matter, having nothing to do with politics and certainly not party politics. To understand why religion goes to the root of personal and political identity in Northern Ireland one must go back into Irish history and Irish relations with the rest of the British Isles.

In the course of the seventeenth century the Gaelic-speaking Catholic tribes of Ireland were colonised by Protestants from Great Britain, just as happened to the Algonquian-speaking tribes of North America. Settlements were planted, the natives converted, massacred or driven out in Ireland just as they were in New England or Virginia. The native Irish managed to survive better than the native Americans, but only as an exploited peasantry with no political rights.

It was in northeastern Ireland that colonisation succeeded best in driving the natives out because of the continual flow of poor Protestant settlers from south-west Scotland (only 30 miles away). The growth of Catholic Irish nationalism in the nineteenth century was seen in the northeast as threatening the very existence of the 'Protestant people'. It provoked a popular resistance to nationalism unparalleled in other parts of Ireland where Protestants were thin on the ground. Semi-underground movements, above all the Orange Order, were created to oppose it, with violence if necessary.

BRIEFINGS

10.5 The Orange Order

In the eighteenth century Catholic resistance to the 'Protestant ascendancy' in Ireland often took the form of secret societies (Whiteboys, Defenders) which took reprisals against obnoxious landlords. These continued in the south during the nineteenth century (the Fenian Brotherhood). As Protestants began to feel threatened they formed their own secret societies, most notably the Orange Order, which took its name from William of Orange (William III) who established the Protestant ascendancy with his victory at the Battle of the Boyne (1690).

Widespread at one time on the British mainland and among army officers, the Orange Order came to have its main strength in Ireland, particularly the north. Modelling itself on the Freemasons, with which it had many links, it has a strong local organisation of 'lodges', and an overall hierarchy of Grand Masters, lodgemasters, and so forth. What gave it a unique force was its ability to unite the Protestant governing elite with a strong grassroots, working class organisation.

The Orange Order does not get directly involved in conflict itself. But it forms a valuable recruiting base and communications network for paramilitary groups. Its elaborate symbolism and annual marches to commemorate Protestant victories are a constant provocation to violence and confrontation with Catholics during the 'marching season' (most of the summer). There are also Orange lodges and marches in central Scotland and Liverpool. However, their activities are very muted compared with the assertions of Protestant dominance in Northern Ireland.

Northern Ireland, 1922–72

The local Unionist politicians joined the Conservative Party in Great Britain to defeat any concession to Irish nationalism, such as Home Rule, up to the First World War. The settlement of 1922 was a defeat for the Northern Unionists, because their object was the preservation of British rule (and support for Protestants) everywhere in Ireland. Instead they found themselves partitioned off in the north, while a Catholic nationalist republic was built up in the rest of the island.

However, the Protestants did have a secure majority in Northern Ireland. The region had been created expressly to ensure this: Protestants constituted 60 per cent of the population. The Unionist leaders organised their built-in majority to control the Northern Irish Parliament and government for 50 years (1922–72). The British Parliament and government were content to turn over the internal running of the province to them, incidentally making nonsense of the claim that such a delegation of powers subverts the constitutional sovereignty of the British Parliament. No constitutional difficulties arose during the existence of the 'Stormont' Parliament and government.

Unionist policy was aimed primarily at ensuring the viability and stability of Northern Ireland as a territorial unit separate from the Republic of Ireland. They could count on British armed support, but they also built up their own paramilitary Protestant militia. This was sufficient to deter open opposition from the minority for most of the time.

No lasting settlement, however, could be built on armed force alone. Politically the Unionist government had to balance three groups. These were the Protestant working class, anxious to protect their jobs and differentials against Catholic competition; the Protestant middle class with something of the same anxieties, but also a concern with modernisation and development, who would be alienated by too open a display of sectarianism; and the Catholic population, who had to have some concessions if they were not to pose a constant threat of disorder.

A major Unionist achievement was to get the British government to agree in 1936 to parity of social provision between Northern Ireland and the British mainland. Thus the post-war Welfare State operated fully in Northern Ireland, providing the unemployed and sick with infinitely better payments and facilities than in the Republic. This appealed to all segments of the population, and it was a powerful argument for Catholics to put up with political discrimination in return for better living conditions. The other major concession to the Catholic Church was state support for Catholic schools, again carrying over practices on the British mainland.

Both these measures enabled the Protestant middle classes to convince themselves that Northern Ireland was as tolerable a solution to bigotry and violence as could be found in Irish conditions, and preferable to living under the domination of a reactionary Catholic Church in the Republic. Throughout its existence the Stormont government pursued an active policy of modernisation of the traditional agricultural and industrial economy, thus creating more middle class jobs in management and administration.

These activities also demonstrated to the Protestant working class that the government was trying to conserve their jobs and improve their living conditions. Where Protestants faced the most severe job competition, in the depressed west of the province, local councils and government agencies actively discriminated in their favour. The Orange Order, a semi-secret society dedicated to maintaining Protestant supremacy, enrolled the working class as its rank and file while keeping control firmly in the Unionist leadership's hands. Anti-Catholic rhetoric and rituals contented the membership while keeping it out of real policy making.

Until 1965 Northern Ireland functioned in this way without major difficulties. Successive British governments, Conservative and Labour, saw no need to intervene in its internal affairs. The Unionist MPs affiliated to the Conservative Party (at that time called the 'Conservative and Unionist Party'). When the British Conservative government of 1951–5 depended on their votes for its majority the Labour opposition did not object. Nobody saw any anomaly in Northern Ireland MPs voting on domestic English and Scottish legislation when MPs from these regions could not vote on Northern Irish affairs.

THE 'TROUBLES', 1969–97

The old system collapsed because of the rise of a new, educated Catholic middle class which organised a non-violent civil rights movement inside Northern Ireland to protest against discrimination and sectarianism (1967–9). Their peaceful protests provoked violent Protestant reactions, culminating in armed attacks on the Catholic areas of Belfast and Londonderry in 1969. A new factor was the television reporting of these conflicts, rendering it impossible for the old tactics of repression to be quietly employed.

The riots and publicity forced a British military intervention to separate the two sides. They finally led to the abolition of the devolved Parliament and government, in an attempt to create a new power-sharing settlement. The disorder provided an opening for both extreme Irish nationalism and extreme Protestant loyalism. The first is represented by the Provisional Irish Republican Army (the 'Provos' or IRA), the second by the Ulster Defence Force (UDF) and smaller groups. Over 28 years both sides carried out regular attacks on each other, on the British Army and on the Northern Irish police, as well as indiscriminately against anyone of 'the wrong sort'. The IRA also engaged in terrorism on the British mainland, mainly with explosives and bombs.

The 'milestones' section at the end of the chapter summarises events from the creation of Northern Ireland in 1922. Since 1970 its history has been dominated by political violence, on the one hand, and attempts at political settlement, on the other. The most important of these were the arrangements for intergovernmental negotiations between Britain and the Irish Republic from the mid-1980s on, which recognised that the heirs of the Irish independence struggle had a legitimate interest in the territory.

THE 'PEACE PROCESS', 1997–2003

The last Conservative government made a determined effort to resolve the political situation by negotiations with all sides to the conflict in 1995–6, which produced a cessation of violence for over a year. Its insistence on the IRA surrendering its weapons before they could join a constitutional conference proved a demand that the political leadership could not get their rank and file to accept.

Hardly had New Labour got into power than they initiated further meetings with all sides to the conflict. The government tried to break through previous deadlocks by involving not just the parties and paramilitaries of the province itself but also the Irish and even the US governments (Irish-Americans are the main financial backers of the IRA).

These negotiations produced the 'Good Friday' agreement in April 1998 on:

1. keeping Northern Ireland as a separate political entity

2. which would however have an autonomous power-sharing Parliament and government where action could be taken only with the agreement of representatives of the two communities

3. the province would remain part of the UK

4. but the Irish government would have a right to be consulted on everything the UK government did in the province and in effect exercise a veto over policy.

Both communities made considerable concessions in the agreement – Nationalists stopping short of incorporation into the Republic but Unionists tolerating its formal right of intervention in the province. Not surprisingly the agreement split both sides but the Protestants most seriously, almost down the middle. In a referendum on whether to accept the agreement slightly over 70 per cent of the total population voted to accept it (May 1998). In an election for the new Assembly in June the Ulster Unionists and smaller Protestant parties supporting the agreement got enough votes to form a power-sharing executive with the Social Democratic and Labour Party, representative of moderate Catholics, and Sinn Fein representing militant Catholic Nationalists.

The Assembly and the projected executive managed to survive the summer 'marching season' when extreme Protestant groups sought to provoke violent confrontations and riots. They foundered, however, on the IRA refusal to make even a token surrender of its arms in the following year. The negotiated compromise had included the understanding that no group linked to paramilitaries could take its place in the Assembly or executive without its allies surrendering their arms. Sinn Fein protested it was independent of the IRA. But nobody believed it, least of all Protestant Unionists. They refused to participate in the Assembly until arms began to be surrendered.

This stalemate lasted for the best part of a year, constantly threatened by riots and confrontations between the communities, atrocious murders and reprisals by extremist groups outside the settlement, by paramilitaries asserting claims to control their own areas, by punishment beatings and shootings of alleged social deviants and drug dealers. A major effort by the British and Irish governments in November 1999 produced a fudged compromise. The IRA declared an intention to review arms and the Unionists agreed provisionally to go into the executive subject to reviewing progress.

The 12-member executive that emerged comprised representatives of all parties in the Assembly including the Democratic Unionists hostile to the agreement.

It was thus hardly in a position to agree any policy initiatives, far less controversial ones. This is beside the point, however. The executive's major achievement is to exist at all, as a concrete symbol of peace and compromise between the warring factions.

This achievement was threatened in February 2000 as a result of reiterated IRA refusals to make even symbolic surrenders of arms. In turn this led to a threatened Unionist withdrawal from the executive. To avert this the British government suspended it again, after less than three months of life (February 2000). Concerted pressure by the Irish and US governments on Sinn Fein and the IRA and British reform of the Protestant-dominated Royal Ulster Constabulary produced promises of IRA arms inspection by international representatives that the Unionists could live with. The executive was therefore reconstituted in May 2000. Further suspensions (to date four) followed over the next two years, leading the IRA to make token surrenders of arms to conciliate the Unionists.

One may expect similar cliff-hangers during the next few years – one indeed is in progress now. What the history of the peace process indicates however is that a large-scale return to guerrilla action and bombings by any of the main groups is unlikely. Disputes will be conducted through words and symbolic gestures using the Assembly as the arena. In a sense both sides have got what they want – Catholic Nationalists now feel they are under the (admittedly very) extended jurisdiction of an Irish government, while Unionists have preserved the separateness of the political order in the north.

THE NORTHERN IRELAND ASSEMBLY: KEY TO POWER SHARING – AND BRITISH CONSTITUTIONAL CHANGE?

The Assembly and Executive which sporadically occupy the old seat of government at Stormont, near Belfast, are of prime importance as the symbol and guarantee of power sharing, the basis of the peace settlement. On this they work with intergovernmental bodies, such as the North–South Council, with the Irish government, and the British–Irish Council consisting of the Westminster government and all the devolved administrations in Britain. The Executive also participates in the Joint Ministerial Council with the British, Welsh and Scottish administrations on immediate practical matters such as EU negotiating stances on agriculture, fisheries, environment and social affairs.

Frequent suspensions of the Assembly mean that policy making often falls into the hands of the British Secretary of State for Northern Ireland, a member of the British Cabinet at Westminster. (S)He may enforce controversial reforms like those of the police, which local politicians are reluctant to take responsibility for. But these would never be pushed through without their tacit consent, and support from the Irish government in Dublin.

Just to describe the diffuse nature of policy making in Northern Ireland illustrates how tenuous the idea of national sovereignty has become, especially as existence of the EU renders the strict demarcation of national boundaries increasingly irrelevant. In Ireland there has long been free movement of people and goods across the unpoliceable border. Natives of Northern Ireland are simultaneously British and Irish citizens owing to the claim of both States to the territory. Carrying anomalies even further, Irish citizens resident in the UK may vote in local and national elections – a relic of the old union between the countries.

The all-incorporating political structures of Northern Ireland may have been driven by the need to get a settlement by sharing power. But they clearly have constitutional implications for the general relationship between regional administrations and the centre within the UK. If the still very centralised British government can cede its powers in Northern Ireland, why not also in Scotland, Wales and even the English regions? The Northern Irish situation with its mutual vetoes clearly cuts across the doctrine of absolute Parliamentary sovereignty which lies at the base of the unwritten British constitution (Chapter 4).

Workings of the Assembly

The Assembly consists of 108 members, six from each of the 18 constituencies. These are grouped into parties. The second Assembly elections of May 2003 were not held owing to the suspension of the assembly. Had they been, it is likely that the Democratic Unionists, opposed to the peace process, would have emerged as the largest party on the Protestant side, and Sinn Fein as the largest Catholic party. This would have put the whole peace process in jeopardy. This remains a very likely outcome in any future election.

The power-sharing institutions are designed among other things to prevent any one party having sole power over anything. Thus the Unionist, Protestant, First Minister – David Trimble from 1998–2003 (occupying that position because the Ulster Unionist support was essential to buttress the agreement) – had to do everything with his SDLP Deputy First Minister, representing the largest (Catholic) party. In practice, the few decisions that have been made through the Assembly mechanisms were taken by the 12-person Executive as a whole and endorsed in the Assembly.

Executive posts have been shared out among all the parties in the Assembly in proportion to their seats. The Opposition – notably the Democratic Unionists, who are against the power-sharing agreement as a whole – have also been represented on the Executive, and have been in nominal control of ministries like its other members. Even so they have often boycotted its meetings.

Each Executive 'minister' is in addition responsible to a specialist Assembly Committee, chaired by party members from the opposing side of the religious-political divide. Thus the Sinn Fein Minister of Education, Martin McGuiness (1998–2003), faced a Committee chaired by a Democratic Unionist, assisted by an Ulster Unionist. Table 10.3 gives the policy areas in which the ministers and committees operate. These spell out the broad social and economic matters over which the Assembly and Executive have autonomous powers. The Westminster government retains responsibility for constitutional and security issues, including courts, law and prisons. If the Assembly could agree on requesting the transfer of such 'reserved' powers it would get them. In that sense 'rolling

Table 10.2 *Voting in Northern Ireland Assembly elections, percentage by region, 1998*

1998	Belfast	Rest of east	West and south	Northern Ireland
UUP	14.9	29.1	18.7	21.1
SDLP	17.6	11.6	30.7	21.9
DUP	17.1	22.1	15.9	18.7
SF	22.3	3.88	24.2	17.7
APNI	7.9	12.4	2.6	6.5
UKUP	2.6	9.8	2.0	4.5
NIWC	3.0	1.57	1.1	1.6
PUP	8.3	1.56	0.3	2.6
UDP	2.6	1.99	0.1	1.2
Ind U	2.1	3.75	3.1	3.0

Note: Party abbreviations: UUP Ulster Unionist Party; SDLP Social Democratic and Labour Party; DUP Democratic Unionist Party, some candidates also stood as United Unionists or similar labels; SF Sinn Fein; APNI Alliance Party of Northern Ireland; UKUP United Kingdom Unionist Party; NIWC Northern Ireland Women's Coalition; PUP Progressive Unionist Party; UDP Ulster Democratic Party; Ind U Independent Unionist

Source: Information for 1998 based on the official result forms (AE115 and AE116) and supplementary data published in *The New Northern Ireland Assembly Election*, 25 June 1998, Belfast: Chief Electoral Officer for Northern Ireland, 1998.

Table 10.3 *Policy areas covered by executive ministries and Assembly committees in Northern Ireland*

Agriculture and rural development
Culture, arts and leisure
Education
Employment and learning
Enterprise, trade and investment
Environment
Finance and personnel
Health, social services and public safety
Regional development
Social development

devolution' still exists in Northern Ireland, but the real problem is getting agreement between two sides who trust external governments more than they trust each other.

TOWARDS A LASTING PEACE?

The likely results of a regional election have again thrown politics into the melting pot in Northern Ireland. Relentless appeals to sectarian fears coupled with intimidation and social pressures will probably make the extreme parties on both sides of the political divide dominant both in terms of votes and Assembly seats. As the precedent is for the First Minister and his Deputy to be chosen from the two largest parties this creates immediate problems for devolved government in the next few years. A Sinn Fein presence at the top would be unacceptable to most Protestants while the Democratic Unionists have the same effect on Catholics. The immediate result is likely to be stalemate and further suspensions of the Assembly.

The ingenuity already shown in cobbling together institutional compromises plus international pressures on the participants may bridge the gap. The peace settlement has survived year-long suspensions before and neither the Executive nor the Assembly are really essential for governing the province. The important thing is to edge back to having them in being as a concrete guarantee of power sharing.

In the long run, with Catholics and Protestants now almost equal in numbers within the province, this is the only tolerable solution that can be reached. The alternative is the previous violent stalemate which neither side can win. The Nationalists have shown there can be no peace without including them. But it is equally clear that the Unionists cannot be bombed into a united Ireland – which is also the last outcome that the government of the Republic would want anyway.

The overwhelming majority of English opinion would accept any solution agreed in Ireland. The latter has never been regarded as part of the Union in the same way as the countries of Great Britain. It is the Northern Irish Protestants who want to continue the Union not the British public as a whole. It is therefore the internal constraints that hinder a lasting settlement and of these the main one is the mutual suspicion of the two communities. This may in the end bring the peace process down. But it remains the best way of enabling Catholics and Protestants to live tolerably together.

That said, the solution will not be a comfortable one. High-level political conflict may diminish but in parts of the province the rule of law has broken down. Normal policing continues in town centres, middle class suburbs and in much of the countryside. The working class areas and housing estates are however dominated by paramilitary groups. The Protestant ones have lost much of their original impetus and degenerated into criminal gangs concerned to enforce their drug monopoly. The IRA seeks to substitute its own administration for that of the State in the areas it dominates through impromptu courts, punishment beatings, and shootings. It has turned the social control it exerts to political ends, pressuring voters to support Sinn Fein in its drive to replace the SDLP as the main representative of the Catholic community. So far its tactic of 'guns and ballots' seems to have succeeded.

Both Protestant and Catholic paramilitaries have an interest in wearing down the new Northern Ireland Police Service to an extent where it will not even contemplate intervening in their areas. Their tactic for doing so has been the street rioting endemic in Belfast from 2001 onwards. With police officers constantly deployed and a high proportion injured in containing the rioters, their objective has to be short-term crisis management rather than long-term resumption of control.

All this makes Northern Ireland a difficult place to live in, although it has to be said that the presence of the army and the high proportion of the population employed on security have given a boost to the economy it would not otherwise have enjoyed. It is a chastening thought that the British State, usually regarded as a model of stability and peaceful resolution of conflicts, has accommodated a near civil war for 30 years and now finds parts of its territory beyond control. The peace process may survive this situation but it will not properly resolve it for a very long time.

ESSAYS

1. Distinguish between the British Isles, Great Britain, the United Kingdom and England. To what extent is the UK a unitary state?

2. What are the main political groupings in Northern Ireland? What accounts for the differences between them?

3. In what politically related ways are the Irish, as an ethnic group, different from Afro-Caribbeans?

4. To what extent does the working of devolution in Northern Ireland offer lessons for the rest of the UK?

SUMMARY

This chapter has shown that:

- The United Kingdom, like most European states, was formed out of different territories with divergent histories and cultures.

- From the seventeenth century Ireland was treated more like an overseas colony than an integrated part of British territory.

- This provoked a Catholic nationalist movement which used violence to create a separate state – a Republic of Ireland – in the south and west of the island (1919–22).

- The Protestant Unionists who dominated the northeast formed a separate statelet, Northern Ireland, which had a devolved government inside the United Kingdom.

- Protestant domination in the north was challenged first by a Catholic Civil Rights movement (1967–9) and then by the shootings and bombings of the Provisional IRA (1970–97), which extended to the British mainland.

- The 'Peace Process' (1997–2004) produced a compromise in which the Nationalist parties accepted the status of Northern Ireland as part of the United Kingdom, and Protestant Unionists accepted power sharing within it.

- Endemic disorders and grassroots violence threaten the peace settlement, already weakened by the IRA–Sinn Fein drive towards total dominance in the Catholic community. Power sharing is, however, likely to continue in some form as there is no viable political alternative to it.

Milestones in Irish history, 1922–2003

Northern Ireland ('six counties', 'Ulster')

Republic of Ireland ('Irish Free State', 'Eire')

1922 Government of Ireland Act effectively divides Ireland between Northern Ireland in the northeast and the Irish Free State (Eire), covering the south and west

1922 Special Powers Act gives Northern Irish government exceptional powers to maintain order

1923–7 Civil war followed by extensive disorder over whether to accept partition and dominion status within British Empire. Pro-treaty side (later Fine Gael Party) wins

1926 Fianna Fáil founded to contest treaty by non-violent means. This splits it off from Sinn Fein and IRA, which remain committed to violence

1929 Abolition of proportional representation in Northern Ireland Parliamentary elections

1932 Unemployed in Belfast hold non-sectarian demonstrations and riot

1932 Fianna Fáil wins general election and forms government

1933–8 'Economic war' with Britain

1935 Serious sectarian riots in Belfast renew old religious hostilities

1936 British government agrees to equality of social support between Northern Ireland and (mainland) Great Britain

1937 New constitution whittles away British Treaty rights and entrenches position of Catholic Church

1938 British return treaty ports (where they had had naval bases) to Irish Free State

1939–40 IRA bombing campaign in England

1939–45 Irish Free State stays neutral in Second World War

1940–43 German bombing of Belfast and (London) Derry

1940–5 Northern Ireland forms base for allied air forces protecting Atlantic convoys

1943–64 Sir Basil Brooke (Lord Brookeborough), NI Prime Minister, maintains system of strict Unionist monopoly of power based on inbuilt Protestant majority

1948–51, 1954–7 Fine Gael forms coalition governments with smaller parties

1949 Bitter Northern Irish election reaffirms Unionist domination

1948 Eire becomes Republic of Ireland and leaves Commonwealth

1956–63 IRA border attacks mostly fail

1959–72 Modernising Fianna Fáil Prime Ministers, Lemass and Lynch

1963–9 O'Neill succeeds Brookeborough as Unionist Prime Minister. Rhetoric favours Catholics but does nothing practical on discrimination

Northern Ireland ('six counties', 'Ulster')

1967–9 As a result civil rights movement formed to press for reform. TV shows non-violent protests broken up by Protestant militants and police

1969 Special police and Protestant militants attack Catholic areas of Belfast and Derry. British troops intervene to protect them

1970–2 IRA provokes army into indiscriminate internment and shooting of nationalists ('Bloody Sunday' 1972)

1972–4 British attempts to introduce power sharing between Protestants and Catholics thwarted by Protestant general strike. Unionist Party splits into small groupings

1972 Joins EU as part of UK

1974–98 Direct rule: province run by Northern Ireland Office as part of British government

1974–95 IRA, UDF, UVF mount terror campaign (extended by IRA to mainland Britain): killings and bombings, often indiscriminate

1982 Elections to a new Northern Ireland Assembly. 'Rolling devolution': Assembly can take over whatever powers it agrees on, but no agreement between Unionists and Nationalists

1985 Margaret Thatcher and Fine Gael Prime Minister, Garrett Fitzgerald, sign Anglo-Irish Agreement providing for joint consultation of two governments on Northern Ireland. These continue and intensify up to present

1994 Downing Street Declaration sets out plans for talks between British and Irish governments and all parties in Northern Ireland. In response IRA and Protestant ceasefires declared

1995–6 Talks stalled and blocked by Unionists on whom British Conservatives increasingly depend in British Parliament

1996 Renewed IRA bombings in mainland Britain. Violent Protestant marches in Northern Ireland

1997 New Labour government in Britain announces accelerated talks: start of 'Peace Process'

1997 New IRA and Protestant ceasefire

1998 Agreement for a political settlement between Irish and British governments approved by referendums on both sides of the border

Republic of Ireland ('Irish Free State', 'Eire')

1972 Joins EU along with UK

1973–7 Coalition government of Fine Gael and Labour

1977–81 Fianna Fáil government

1981–92 Various short-lived minority governments or coalitions alternate

1986 Referendum rejects divorce

1992–8 Stable coalitions of both major parties with Labour

1995 Referendum legalises divorce by narrow majority

1995–2003 Sustained economic boom, active partnership of Irish government with British in Peace Process

1998–2003 Fianna Fail–Progressive Democrat – right-wing coalition government

▶

Northern Ireland ('six counties', 'Ulster')

1998   Power-sharing Assembly elected
1998–9   Assembly only elects executive at end of
   1999 because of IRA refusal to give up any arms
2000   Power-sharing executive suspended, then
   reinstated as IRA makes symbolic concessions
   on arms
2001–2002   Further political confrontations and
   suspensions force IRA to put some arms caches
   'beyond use' under independent verification

2002   Reform of Royal Ulster Constabulary (RUC)
   changed to NI Police Service
2002   Suspension of NI Assembly over
   allegations of Sinn Fein–IRA spy ring within it
2003   The May Assembly elections were not held

Republic of Ireland ('Irish Free State', 'Eire')

2001   Referendum rejects EU Treaty of Nice
   because it might liberalise social
   relationships
2002   Referendum closes last loophole for
   abortion in the constitution
Catholic Church indemnified by government
   against lawsuits over child abuse
Sinn Fein increases electoral support in the Republic

PROJECTS

1. Describe the various institutions now involved in governing Northern Ireland and how they relate to each other.

2. Compare and contrast the ideologies of Irish Nationalism and of Northern Irish Unionism.

3. Assess how far the Peace Process in Northern Ireland has been successful.

FURTHER READING

The Irish background is reported in T. P. Coogan, *The Troubles: Ireland's Ordeal 1966–1995* (London: Hutchinson, 1995). The Northern Irish dilemma is discussed in J. Loughlin, *The Ulster Question since 1945* (London: St Martin's Press, 1998), Paul Dixon, *Northern Ireland* (London: Palgrave, 2001) and D. Norris, 'Northern Ireland: the long road to peace', *Talking Politics*, **11** (1), 1999, pp. 34–6. See also Jonathon Tonge, *Northern Ireland: Conflict and Change* (London: Pearson, 2nd edn, 2002). Short discussions on aspects of the Northern Ireland situation can be found in Barbara Lomas, 'The Good Friday Agreement', *Talking Politics*, **14** (1), 2000, pp. 28–31 and Stephen Hopkins, 'General Election 2001: Northern Ireland, a place apart', *Politics Review*, **11** (2), 2001, pp. 22–5.

Lively and informed comment on the workings of devolution and constitutional reform is provided by *Monitor*, published quarterly by the Constitution Unit, University College London, which also maintains a web site (see end of chapter).

USEFUL WEB SITES ON DISUNITING THE KINGDOM: IRELAND

Hotlinks to these sites can be found on the CWS website at http://www.booksites.net/budge.

Specific sites on Northern Ireland are Northern Ireland Government (www.nio.gov.uk); Official Documents www.hmso.gov.uk/acts/acts1998/19980047.htm); CAIN web site (http://cain.ulst.ac.uk/) and the Mitchell Report (www.irishnews.com/mitchell.html). See also the Constitution Unit web site (www.ucl.ac.uk/constitution-unit).

Devolution: Scotland, Wales, and the English regions

Devolution is the delegation of powers by a state to units within its territory. It differs from a federal set-up in two ways. The state can (at least in constitutional theory) take powers back when it wants. And the powers delegated to different units may differ quite considerably. Devolution is a common arrangement in western and southern Europe and has always existed in Britain (in the Isle of Man, Channel Islands and Northern Ireland 1922–72). From 1998 it has again operated in Northern Ireland, as we have seen and also in Scotland, Wales and Greater London, and is being proposed for other English regions.

This chapter asks:

- why is devolution now being implemented in Britain?
- to what extent is it due to regional differences which make it more efficient to run diverse areas differently?
- how far is it a political response to Welsh and Scottish nationalism, as it certainly is to Irish nationalism?
- how does the devolution of powers actually work in Scotland and Wales?
- is London a model for what may happen in other English regions?
- what are the prospects in general for regional government in England?
- what are the constitutional implications for Parliamentary sovereignty and the centralised state?

NATIONALISM AND DEVOLUTION

Chapter 10 showed the British government had little choice about devolving power to a Northern Ireland Assembly if it wanted to get even an uneasy peace in the province. The driving force in events there has always been violent Irish nationalism (confronted by an equally violent Protestant sectarianism). Even the Unionists, however, were used to the idea of devolution which they had had themselves for 50 years (1922–72).

At its nearest point the Scottish mainland is only 18 miles from Ireland, with which it shares much of its traditional culture and history. It is not surprising therefore that from the late nineteenth century Scottish nationalist sentiment was stimulated by events there and advocated 'Home Rule all round' – that is, devolution not only for Ireland but also for Scotland and Wales. Scottish nationalism differed from Irish, however, in basing itself on the Protestant rather than the Catholic traditions of Scotland and having an obvious focus on the institutions surviving from its period as an independent state – primarily the Scots language and law, Gaelic, and the (Presbyterian) Church of Scotland. It was also different in deploring violence and working through peaceful and constitutional routes to change. These paid off when the Scottish Nationalist Party (SNP) consolidated its support at 20–30 per cent of the Scottish electorate, threatening Labour's strong base in Scotland and pushing it into supporting devolution. (The SNP, however, wants independence.)

Welsh nationalism has developed along the same lines as Scottish – peaceful, constitutional and moderate to the point where it has accepted devolution as an acceptable substitute for independence – provided the Welsh Assembly gets legislative powers. Much more than Scottish, Welsh nationalism is focused on the need to protect and extend the native language and consolidate its social base.

The reason why Welsh and Scottish (and Irish) nationalism are such powerful forces within their own countries goes back to the state-building process discussed in the last chapter. In conquering and consolidating their territories the European states incorporated areas with different languages and cultures to those of the majority population. The natural attachment of such groups to their own culture caused them to resent the state imposition of schooling in the majority language and discrimination in its favour (eg by making access to top jobs dependent on speaking it). Such minorities have felt more and more threatened by developments such as a mass English-language press, radio and television; widespread emigration of their native population because of economic decline; and English immigration to take over businesses, top jobs, land and housing.

These processes are going on throughout Europe. The solution as nationalist parties see it is to have sovereign political institutions to protect their culture and society against takeover. A compromise, by states which want to resist breakup, is often to give the territory devolved political institutions to handle most domestic matters, keeping security, and economic and foreign affairs, in central hands.

Scottish and Welsh (not to mention Northern Irish) devolution can be seen as this kind of compromise, borrowed from other west European countries such as Belgium and Spain. It is politically difficult for any British government to admit it is compromising with Welsh and Scottish nationalism, however, since its official stance is that what unites the British is much stronger than what divides them. Hence devolution rhetoric has stressed themes such as subsidiarity (having problems dealt with at the level most appropriate for them), local democracy, efficiencies from producing solutions tailored to regional characteristics, 'bringing government closer to the people' and so on. There are arguments in favour of all of these, which as a result of regional devolution have now come to the forefront of political discussion. Clearly these apply just as well to the often very distinctive English regions as to Scotland and Wales. As a result English regionalism is now being discussed to an unprecedented extent and serious consideration is, almost for the first time, being given to the prospect of a (more limited) devolution of power within England.

REGIONAL DISPARITIES IN BRITAIN

One paradox of the previous discussion is indeed that we have concentrated on Scotland, Wales and Ireland without mentioning the English regions such as Merseyside or the northeast. In terms of their social and economic profile these are almost as distinctive as Scotland and Wales. However, they do not possess the cultural and institutional differences that act as a focus for separatism or nationalism. All these regions have as good a claim to be 'English' as the London area. Social and regional deprivation has fuelled political reactions, but these have taken the form of overwhelming support for the Labour Party in its struggle for central power. Discontent was therefore expressed in support for Labour at the centre rather than for autonomy and Home Rule for the region itself.

Regionalism Regions are geographical areas within a state, and regionalism involves granting special powers and duties to regional representatives.

Labour and, to a lesser extent, the Liberal Democrats have also attracted disproportionate support in Scotland and Wales for the same reasons. The support of the peripheries makes Labour a territorially rather than a class-based party. The difference is that in Scotland and Wales it has to compete internally with the local nationalist movements, which explains its definite commitment to devolution in these areas compared with its vague rhetoric about greater political freedom for English regions.

The major force behind movements for regional autonomy are feelings of distinctiveness. But they are also fuelled by perceptions of relative deprivation in relation to London and southeast England. Table 11.1 shows a whole series of figures, covering wealth, living conditions and health, that illustrate this point.

Plate 11.1 *The Assembly Hall (of the Church of Scotland), Edinburgh, temporary but dramatic home of the Scottish Parliament. The expensive new Parliament building at Holyrood is a subject of great controversy*

Source: www.paphotos.com

Table 11.1 Disparities between different areas of the UK

	% of workforce with a degree	Average weekly earnings (£)		GDP per head (UK = 100)
		Male	Female	
Scotland	14.1	423	316.1	77
Northern Ireland	12.8	393.3	307.3	96
Wales	12.3	400.5	313.7	81
England	15.6	459.2	341.5	102
North East	10.4	398.9	306	77
North West	12.9	428.6	312.8	87
Yorkshire	12.2	409.9	308.8	88
East Midlands	12.6	407	301.1	94
West Midlands	11.9	425.3	311.2	92
East	14.4	455.5	333.8	116
London	25	593	434.3	130
Southeast	17.8	482.1	353.1	116
Southwest	15.5	418.2	309.8	91

	Mortality rate per thousand births	% of households with no car
Scotland	5	34
Northern Ireland	6.4	n/a
Wales	6.4	27
England	5.7	28
North East	5.5	38
North West	6.6	30
Yorkshire	6.2	31
East Midlands	6.1	26
West Midlands	6.9	28
East	4.9	21
London	6	36
Southeast	4.8	23
Southwest	4.6	23

Source: ONC Regional Trends, **36**, 2001, and ONC Social Trends, 2001

The varying levels of regional unemployment, a central factor underlying other disparities, were shown in Figure 1.2. As Chapter 1 noted, the underlying reason for regional disparities is that nineteenth-century industrialisation took place in the north and Midlands. Its attendant problems of rapid and unplanned urban development, slums, badly paid repetitive work, crime and poverty were most keenly experienced there and linger on to the present day – exacerbated by the collapse of manufacturing at the end of the twentieth century. Attempted solutions (such as rehousing and relocation in vast featureless housing estates on the outskirts of cities) in turn created fresh social problems.

The area around London, in contrast, always benefited from greater government and consumer spending. When industrialisation came in the 1930s, with light engineering and service industries, it was cleaner and paid better wages. The planning and welfare measures discussed in Chapter 3 ensured that living conditions were better.

Map 11.1 *Counties and regions of England and Wales*

Apart from modern industrialisation, southeast England has always benefited economically from the overspill of wealth from London. Government employment has created a disproportionately large middle class that has sustained the largest and most concentrated consumer market in Britain. The end beneficiaries of foreign wars and conquests were the financial interests and markets of the City of London, which reinforced middle class political and economic dominance of the region.

Foreign wars and Empire did provide markets for industry in the peripheries, particularly for coal, steel and shipbuilding. They also provided jobs, but not at home. Emigration to the colonies provided an outlet for the restless and ambitious, supplemented by posts in the colonial administration. The army and navy recruited disproportionately in the more deprived areas: between a quarter and two-fifths of the nineteenth-century army originated in Scotland and Ireland, far in excess of their share of the British population.

Such outlets for the surplus populations can be seen in two ways. They can be viewed positively, as providing economic and social opportunities that would never have been available otherwise; or they could be judged negatively, as a haemorrhage of the brightest and best who, had they been able to stay at home, would have provided an indigenous regional leadership otherwise lacking.

Whatever one's judgement on this, 'economic' emigration certainly helped maintain social stability in the peripheries. During the single decade of the 1950s, for example, a third of a million – out of a total population of $5\frac{1}{4}$ million – emigrated from Scotland, about 6 per cent of the population, mostly young and disproportionately better educated. Half went to (southeast) England, and half abroad. As a result of emigration the Scottish population remained static while southeast England grew. Increased emigration in the 1990s meant the Scottish population actually declined.

The loss of Empire and reduction of military commitments in the 1960s may have contributed to regional discontent by reducing job opportunities. Certainly they helped concentrate attention on domestic rather than foreign problems. Among the more obvious domestic problems were the decline of traditional industries – coalmining, steel making, heavy engineering, shipbuilding and textiles – and the centralisation of the firms that remained in London. Branches in the peripheries, remote from the main consumer markets, tended to be closed first. This applied even to the new industries that found their way there. Meanwhile, British economic management was focused on the southeast. The price of credit and loans was raised when financial markets reacted to 'overheating' in the south at times when the north had barely warmed up. 'Stop–go' economic policies have thus hit particularly hard in the peripheries: from the point of view of peripheral industry it was all stop and no go. The Monetary Policy Committee of the Bank of England has continued to raise and lower interest rates under New Labour in response to London and financial needs, ignoring the decline of manufacturing in the rest of the country as a result of expensive credit and the strong pound, which depresses exports and encourages imports.

Social conditions are poorer and health is worse among the larger numbers of the working class in the outlying regions (Table 11.1). This means that direct government expenditure on social benefits and the health service is greater in these areas than in the more prosperous southeast. Maintenance of roads and infrastructure in large, thinly populated areas, such as the Highlands of Scotland, also costs more. Hence the figures for direct government expenditure show more state money being spent per head in Scotland, Wales and Northern Ireland than in England (Table 11.2). British 'unionists' (ie those who favour retaining the existing United Kingdom) use this to underline the benefits these regions get from being in the British State. Local nationalists say it simply shows that conditions are worse, owing to disparities that can only be eliminated by regional autonomy or independence. They also argue that figures for directly attributed expenditure conceal what happens with indirect expenditures (research and

Table 11.2 *Direct government expenditure per head in the UK*

(a) Identifiable public expenditure per capita as a percentage of UK identifiable expenditure per capita (UK = 100)

	1989/1990	1990/1991	1991/1992
England	95.8	96.1	96.8
Scotland	119.1	118.2	114.6
Wales	107.8	109	106.8
Northern Ireland	151.1	141.5	137.0

(b) Public spending and GDP per head, regions of the UK, 1999–2000 (£)

Region	Public exp/head on 'devolved' services	GDP per head
Southeast	2,281	15,100
East Anglia	2,386	15,100
Greater London	3,367	16,900
Southwest	2,395	11,800
West Midlands	2,504	11,900
East Midlands	2,403	12,100
Yorkshire and Humberside	2,481	11,400
Northwest	2,701	11,300
North	2,783	10,000
Wales	3,069	10,400
Scotland	3,406	12,500
Northern Ireland	3,870	10,100

Source: (a) D. Heald, 'Territorial public expenditure in the UK', *Public Administration*, **72**, 1994, pp. 147–75; (b) Iain Maclean and Alistair McMillan, 'The fiscal crisis of the United Kingdom', Nuffield College Working Papers in Politics, 2002, W10, http://www.nuff.ox.ac.uk/Politics/papers/

development, military, administration), which go almost exclusively to southeast England.

Overall comparisons between the constituent countries of the United Kingdom can also be misleading. Within England, some of the most deprived British regions exist in the north and the west. Similarly, inside Wales, there is a great difference between south, east, and northwest. And in Scotland, Edinburgh, Aberdeen and their regions are in many ways as prosperous as the London area and contrast greatly with the deprived Glasgow conurbation and the declining industrial city of Dundee.

We shall explore these internal differences further when we consider Scotland and Wales separately. What should be noted here, however, is that minority nationalism is not solely social or economic in character. Its basis, whatever the issues it raises, is cultural and derives from feelings of national or regional distinctiveness. Moreover, even if some peripheral areas are prosperous, most are not, and it is their situation that fuels the grievance. This emerges more clearly from the individual cases considered in this chapter.

TERRITORY AND ETHNICITY

Ethnicity
A combination of different social characteristics (which may include race, culture, religion, or some other basis of common origin and social identity), which give different social groups a common consciousness, and which are thought to divide or separate them in some way from other social groups.

There are of course many ethnically and culturally distinctive groups in Britain, as noted in Chapter 1. The most distinctive are recent immigrants from the Caribbean and particularly the Indian sub-continent, who are distinguished racially and, in the case of Sikhs, Hindus and Muslims, by language and religion as well. Accommodating them may raise political problems from time to time, especially when the group suffers from high unemployment, poverty, poor living conditions and social breakup. Riots, crime and delinquency tend to spread under these circumstances.

However, one thing immigrant groups do not do is threaten the sovereignty of the British State. This is because they do not constitute a local majority in any city or region where they have settled. Demands for better treatment or recognition therefore are channelled through all-British institutions, through national parties such as Labour and the Liberal Democrats, or through London-based pressure groups.

The Welsh, Scots and Irish are less culturally distinctive than immigrant groups. Over the last two to three centuries they have evolved within the British context and many of their cultural patterns and institutions mark them out as British. Paradoxically, however, they still pose more of a threat to the integrity of the British State than more obviously 'different' groups, because they occupy a distinct territory within which they constitute a local majority. Their demands, mainly for greater regional autonomy, thus become bound up with their territorial distinctiveness. The British State is nothing if not a territorial unit subject to a central political authority. Thus the territorial demands voiced by the Scots, Welsh and Irish constitute more of a threat to it than the demands of more distinctive groups that can be met without territorial concessions. We start by looking at post-devolution Scotland and Wales, with a particular focus on how the new political arrangements work there, before going on to their constitutional implications for the British State as a whole, and the English regions.

SCOTLAND: SOME CULTURAL BUT MORE INSTITUTIONAL DISTINCTIVENESS

Historical and social background

Scotland covers the northern third of Britain but has a population of just over 5 million. Most Scots live in the central lowland area between the two major cities of Glasgow and Edinburgh, and on the eastern coastal plain stretching through Dundee and Aberdeen. Most of the country consists of mountains and islands that are very thinly populated. Unlike Wales, however, the various regions of Scotland are more accessible from each other than from England.

Map 11.2 *The regions of Scotland*

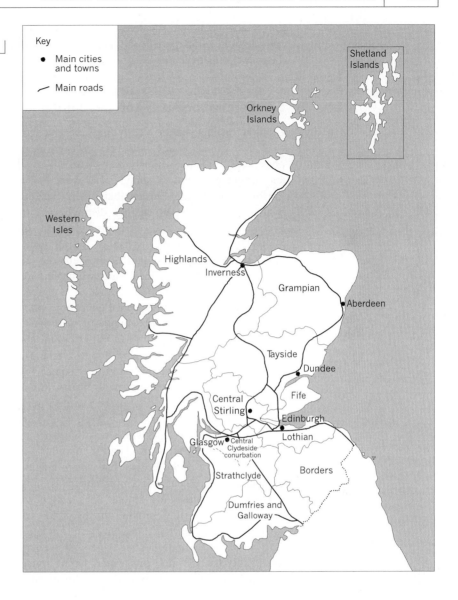

Historically, the differences between the Highlands and Lowlands of Scotland were just as great as those between Scotland and England. The Highlands (the Grampian Massif, west coast and western islands) hosted a tribal, pastoral society speaking a Celtic language (Gaelic). The Lowlands were a feudal, arable society speaking Scots, a form of northern English. The assimilation of the Highlands through internal (often forced) emigration, improved communications and compulsory schooling in English has eliminated the cultural gap. Gaelic remains an important symbol of national distinctiveness but is spoken only by 50,000 people, mostly in the remote Western Isles. Scots has also been eroded by universal education in standard English. Like Gaelic, however, it has an important literature and experienced a cultural revival (the 'Scottish Renaissance') in the mid-twentieth century.

Scottish nationalism and devolution

Cultural distinctiveness clearly provides local nationalism with a focus, as in Wales. Unlike Wales, however, the negotiated union with England in 1707 preserved the distinctive institutions that Scotland had developed as a sixteenth- and seventeenth-century state. These were first a State Church, organised on Presbyterian and not Episcopalian lines (that is, governed by elders and not bishops), and therefore sharply distinguished from the Church of England. Second, the separate body of Scots law, with supporting courts, was retained. Scots law differs from English in basing itself on Roman civil law rather than precedent. The retention of the supreme courts in Edinburgh meant that Scotland had a separate legal elite, which provided a high-level career outside London.

The Church's responsibility for education and social welfare, and the judiciary's for internal order and policing, passed over to other governmental bodies in the nineteenth century. Their initial organisation on a Scottish basis meant that Scottish bodies based in Edinburgh emerged to handle them (eventually grouped together as the contemporary Scottish Office). The separate legal code made this a logical development. It also fostered the emergence of a Scottish banking system more closely meshed with local commerce and industry than its English counterpart.

In contrast with Wales, which was integrated administratively with England, all regions of Scotland focused on Edinburgh. The Scottish institutions, however, were emanations of the British State, more intent on enforcing London's wishes in Scotland than in pushing Scottish interests in the corridors of power.

However, Scottish institutions *do* function separately and they *are* based in Scotland. They thus provide the basis for another Scottish difference: the existence of a distinctive mass media. Press and radio in Britain are generally very centralised. London-edited papers have a national circulation and there are remarkably few morning newspapers based in the 'provinces' (see Chapter 13). Scotland is the major exception, with local mass-circulation newspapers dominating readership in the big cities. Regional programming of radio was strong even under the BBC (British Broadcasting Corporation) monopoly and is stronger now. Television in Britain has been regional since the emergence of independent television. Scotland has its own independent television companies, some of which, such as Scottish Television (STV), have developed into media conglomerates.

11.1 The Scottish media

In an age of mass communication, control of the media – particularly of newspapers and television – is often the major factor influencing cultural identities and the political agenda. Generally, the centralisation of the British media on London serves to depress regional self-consciousness and focus attention on the 'glittering scene' in the capital.

Scotland and Northern Ireland, in part because of their distance from London, are the major exceptions here. Moreover, Scotland has enough autonomous institutions, both political and cultural, to provide something of an alternative focus to London. This has resulted in Glasgow and Edinburgh each having a quality local paper (the *Herald* and the *Scotsman*), which contain all local as well as national and international news, and hence are almost a necessity for middle class reading. The mass circulation *Record* and *Scottish Sun* are based in Glasgow, with 50 per cent Scottish content. Dundee and Aberdeen have local papers that transcend the quality/mass divide (the *Courier*, and *Press and Journal*).

The BBC has always had a strong Scottish regional unit with an autonomous council. The independent television companies (Borders, Scottish, Grampian) have developed Scottish and local programming over the last 20 years. The Glasgow-based Scottish Media Group owns Scottish Television (STV). Scottish programmes provide employment for Scottish actors, musicians and artists as well as writers, who in turn contribute to a distinctive cultural voice.

Thus developments towards deregulation and competition have in this case strengthened the bases of Scottish identity rather than eroding them. The new Scottish Parliament provides even more of a focus for a distinctively Scottish media.

The Scottish media face two ways, as do other Scottish institutions. On the one hand, much of their comment and reporting is of British affairs, and differs little from the London-based media. On the other, their location and the nature of their public mean that they have a particular interest in Scottish news. The coverage may have little to do directly with politics but certainly supports the idea that Scotland is different. From this it is a short step to thinking of it as a cultural and social entity that ought to have its own political institutions.

This sounding board from which to address the whole of the (potential) nation perhaps accounts for the most salient feature of the Scottish National Party (SNP), its tendency to argue the case for independence in economic and material, rather than cultural, terms. The main plank of the SNP platform is that Scotland would do much better economically outside the United Kingdom than by staying inside – for example by setting its own interest rates to favour manufacturing rather than finance; taking over the oil revenues in its sector of the North Sea; or securing direct subsidies from the European Union. This position was summarised in the slogans 'It's Scotland's oil' and 'Scotland in Europe'.

Clearly Scottish cultural distinctiveness offers a focus and a basis for the SNP. Anyone with a strong sense of Scottish identity is likely to be susceptible to its appeals. To gain power in Scotland, however, the party needs to win over a

Table 11.3 *Support for Scottish independence and devolution*

	1. Independence %	2. Devolution %	3. Neither %
1990	34	44	17
1991	33	43	19
1992	34	42	21
1993	34	45	18
1994	35	45	16
1995	32	44	21
1996	30	43	23
1997	28	44	25
1998	47	40	4
1999	36	43	14
2000	30	55	12
2001	29	57	11

Note: Figures to 1999 from MORI opinion polls. The question wording for earlier years is 'Do you favour . . . 1. An independent Scotland that is separate from England and Wales but part of the European Community? 2. Scotland remaining part of the UK but with its own devolved Assembly with some taxation and spending power? 3. No change from the present system?' After 1997 the wording was somewhat changed. Respondents were asked: 'In the long term would you prefer a devolved Scotland within the United Kingdom, or a fully independent Scotland, or neither?' Figures for 2000 and 2001 are taken from political surveys funded by the Economic and Social Science Research Council. Figures do not total 100 per cent because 'don't knows' have been excluded

substantial block of Labour supporters (see Table 11.3). These identify themselves as Scottish but have massive material problems – which they share with the other British peripheries – such as unemployment, poor housing and bad health. To gain their votes the SNP has to convince them that they are not just 'Tartan Tories' but committed to social redistribution and welfare. The SNP has therefore become one of the most left-wing minority nationalist parties in Europe, lauding political radicalism as an essential element in the Scots character.

Opinion polls and election results suggest that about one-third of Scots support total independence. Opposing them are about one-tenth who oppose even devolution. In between there are 50–60 per cent who support devolution. Other survey evidence shows that this group also favours giving more power to the Scottish Parliament within the UK – the referendum of September 1997 showed that it was favoured by a convincing majority of Scottish voters. Devolution got a majority in all areas of the country, unlike Wales.

Regional divisions inside Scotland

The main political division inside Scotland is between the Glasgow conurbation, which contains about half the population and is overwhelmingly Labour, and the rest of the country where Labour is challenged by Scottish Nationalists, Liberals and Conservatives, in more or less that order. The 'service' cities of Edinburgh and Aberdeen give less support to Labour and more to other parties. In the Highlands the Liberal Democrats run equally with Labour and the Nationalists. These political differences are based on considerable social and

Table 11.4 *Social and economic differences between Scottish regions, 2001*

	% with degree-level qualification	% unemployed	GDP per head	Average wage £
Northeast	30	2.2	121	391.6
Eastern	23.8	3.7	99	383.2
West	22.4	4.7	90	389.9
Highlands and Islands	28	3	74	374.5

Note: Percentage with degree and average wages for Orkney, Shetland and Western Isles n/a

The regions include: Northeast – Aberdeen City, Aberdeenshire, Moray; Eastern – Angus, Dundee, Borders, City of Edinburgh, Falkirk, Perth, Kinross, Stirling, West Lothian, Fife, East Lothian, Midlothian, Clackmannan; West – East and West Dumbartonshire, Dumfries & Galloway, Ayrshire, City of Glasgow, Renfrewshire, Lanarkshire, Inverclyde; Highlands and Islands – Western Isles, Orkney, Shetland, Argyll & Bute, Highland

Source: GDP, Office for National Statistics regional accounts; Scottish Executive Economic Advice and Statistics Division

economic differences, which are not without some cultural reinforcement, as Table 11.4 shows.

Scotland as a whole does not appear to differ significantly from southeast England in terms of most social indicators (Table 11.4). The regional figures show that this is due to the relative wealth of Edinburgh and Aberdeen. This prosperity contrasts with severe deprivation in Glasgow and Dundee, both of which have had to cope with the social legacy of early industrialisation followed by later industrial collapse. It is this heritage, shared with other deprived peripheries such as northern England and south Wales, that pushed them into fervent support for trade unions and the Labour Party.

An additional factor fostering such support in Scotland is religion. The core of Labour Party support is the Roman Catholic vote. Catholics in Scotland are descendants of immigrant groups, mostly Irish, who came in the nineteenth and early twentieth century to take the jobs nobody else wanted. Their poverty was compounded by the large families that the Church encouraged. Once the Church accepted that the Labour Party was not hostile to it the social circumstances of Catholics pushed them overwhelmingly into voting Labour. At the same time their religious ties made them less susceptible either to Conservative appeals to support the (Protestant) British State or to nationalists harking back to the traditions of a largely Presbyterian Scotland. The concentration of Catholics in the populous west of Scotland makes the habit of Labour voting hard to break there and Labour is, as a result, the dominant party in Scotland.

However, Labour in its turn has had to safeguard itself against nationalist appeals by going part way to meet them, with its proposals for devolution. We have noted at various points that Labour is as much a coalition of British peripheries against the centre as a class party. Nowhere is this aspect of Labour's character more marked than in Scotland, where it tries to maintain its claim to be the major exponent of Scottish interests against rival claims of the Scottish Nationalists.

ON THE RECORD

Alex Salmond MP, former National Convener, Scottish National Party: why I believe in Scottish independence

Scotland is one of the longest established countries in Europe; her culture, law and institutions preserve her identity as a modern, outward-looking European nation. Yet Scotland has no effective democratic voice. Westminster has misrepresented us with its isolationist attitude to Europe.

The House of Commons doesn't have time or enough interest to meet the real political needs of Scotland. This will change now we have our own Parliament devoted to getting the best deal for Scotland and giving us a real say in the running of our country.

One of the positive actions the Parliament can take is to introduce fair voting at local government level. With fair voting, no one political party will have absolute control. All politicians will have to co-operate in the best interests of the whole country. This will also sweep away the scandals which have resulted from one party's domination of Scotland's councils.

While it is not as powerful as I would like, Scotland's Parliament is still able to abolish Skye Bridge tolls, end the feudal system of land ownership, fight the creeping privatisation of the health service and the galloping privatisation of all our universities and colleges.

The independent Parliament that I seek would put even more power in Scotland's hands. It would be able to remove Trident from the Clyde, demand Scotland's share of the oil revenues and speak up for Scotland in Europe.

Personal statement

Plate 11.2 *Bill McArthur cartoon in the (Glasgow)* Herald, *25 July 1994. Caption: 'Freedom Son? ... It's the right to vary tax by 3p in the pound.' The biggest change in Scotland's links with the rest of Britain for nearly 300 years was heralded as the Blair government proposed an Edinburgh Parliament to raise taxes and make many of its own laws*

ON THE RECORD

Sir Teddy Taylor MP: devolution

As regards devolution, I believe it could lead to the breakup of the United Kingdom because the Scottish Parliament will have very limited powers and the funding available to it will only be of the level of finance they have at present less the substantial costs of the new Assembly, which is estimated at £5 per head. My fear is that the new Assembly will simply become a complaints department about alleged inadequate financing and provision of power from London and this will lead to continuing disputes.

The same problems could arise with devolution in Northern Ireland, without the additional problem of the policies of a devolved Parliament being interpreted as being biased in a particular direction.

I do believe European integration to be a greater danger to democracy and international integrity than devolution of Scotland and Wales. The devolved Parliamentary proposals can, of course, be changed by a future national Parliament if it is found to be utterly unacceptable. However, as far as Europe is concerned, all the power we hand over is wholly and permanently without the control of democracy.

(Sir Teddy Taylor was first elected in 1964 to a seat in Glasgow, was appointed as a junior minister in the Scottish Office and resigned this position because of opposition to the membership of the European Community. He voted against the Treaty of Rome and against all subsequent European treaties. He lost his Glasgow seat in 1979 and was re-elected for a seat in Southend, Essex, where he is still the sitting MP.)

Personal statement

SCOTTISH DEVOLUTION IN PRACTICE

The first Scottish Parliament in almost 300 years was elected on 6 May 1999. It differentiated itself in two ways from the British Parliament:

1. **Electoral arrangements** The new voting system gave top-up seats to party lists of candidates within regions in addition to the seats parties had been able to win individually within the 73 constituencies. This system was deliberately designed to produce a more proportional representation in the Parliament than would have been secured by 'first past the post' constituency voting on its own. This would have resulted in a permanent Labour majority, unacceptable to the other parties. The current balance of seats in the single Chamber after the May 2003 elections is Labour 50, SNP 2, Liberals 17 and Conservatives 18. With an overall membership of 129 this means that no party has a majority. To form the Executive two parties have to go into coalition. A Labour–Liberal one has existed since 1998.

2. Related to the absence of a single-party majority are arrangements for more consensual and informal policy making within the chamber, and closer involvement of all members (MSPs) in Executive decision making. The Executive of 11 ministers including a First Minister is shadowed by Parliamentary committees with broadly comparable coverage of ministerial assignments. These give a good idea of the policy areas in which Scotland can

Table 11.5
Policy areas covered by executive ministries and Parliamentary committees in Scotland

Executive ministries	Parliamentary committees
Justice	Justice 1, Justice 2
Education and young people	Education, culture and sport
Enterprise and lifelong learning	Enterprise and lifelong learning
Environment and rural development	Rural development: transport and environment
Finance and public services	Finance: audit; local government
Health and community care	Health and community care
Parliamentary business	Procedures: standards; public petitions; subordinate legislation
Social justice	Equal opportunities, social justice
Tourism, culture and sport	Education, culture and sport
	European

act on its own. Broadly speaking these are detailed domestic matters. Parliament's remit does not include general decisions about the nature of economic or social policy, still less foreign or constitutional affairs (see Table 11.5).

The emphasis on consensual decision making reflects the precedent set by Northern Ireland on power sharing. But there are not the same compelling reasons to share power in Scotland (or Wales). As a result Scottish Labour, the dominant partner in the Executive, has imposed important decisions on the Parliament despite strong opposition. Thus it decided to build an expensive new building to house it, which has proved a permanent provocation for the Scottish press. Massive cost overruns contribute to the impression that Parliament is more concerned with its own accommodation, working conditions and pay than with the general well-being of the country.

Labour's high-handed behaviour has been prompted partly by British government attempts to use party mechanisms to keep control of the devolved arrangements. There is still a Secretary of State for Scotland with a seat in the British Cabinet whose remit is to 'manage' Scottish affairs. Symptomatic of this is British Labour's concern to get an acceptable nominee as First Minister. A financial scandal however got their preferred candidate (Henry McLeish) out of office, to be succeeded by the more independent-minded Jack McConnell, the current First Minister.

The episode reflected resentment even among Labour MSPs at London's interference. If the party link between Edinburgh and London ever breaks down (eg through a British Conservative election victory) we could expect to see more open confrontations over policy.

One symptom of covert London influence up to date is the thin legislative programme which has been concerned with useful but uncontroversial measures. Controversial proposals in line with general Labour policy have been the abolition of restrictions on what school teachers may say about homosexuality, and of fox hunting within Scotland. The two areas where the Lib–Lab coalition has managed to break away from the straight Labour line has been when they exempted Scottish students from having to pay top-up fees to universities, and demanded free personal care, financed by general taxation, for the elderly.

In 2002–3 by far the most potent, symbolic and potentially explosive Scottish issue was confronted – the land question. More than half of Scotland, and two-thirds of the Highlands, is composed of vast (largely sporting) estates owned by wealthy outsiders. These are run to foster grouse or deer for autumn shooting, often to the detriment of the environment and local economic development. The legacy of the 'crofting wars' of the late nineteenth century, and of the 'clearances' of natives off the land, make the question of its control and ownership a highly symbolic issue. The Land Reform Bill passed in February 2003 took a first step to dealing with it by consolidating open access to all land (except for very special reasons) and giving crofters the right to buy their own land if they want to. These measures do not tackle the complex question of overall ownership but they give the promise of doing so in the future.

Land reform possibly reflects Liberal Democrat influence within the executive coalition. It is important to their credibility at British level to be seen in government. Their major reform – of the constituency-based plurality voting which gives Labour permanent control of almost all local governments in the west of Scotland, and many elsewhere – has however continued to stall. Such a reform would benefit Liberals as much as Nationalists and provide a general boost to public life by freeing it from the dead hand of local Labour oligarchies. An agreement to do this forms part of the present coalition arrangement.

The results of the Scottish elections of May 2003 show that the SNP has been unable as yet to capitalise on the malaise of Executive and Parliament. They are still far from replacing Labour as the dominant party in Scottish politics. Until they do so they will be unable to advance very effectively their agenda for Scottish independence. In the meantime, however, there is strong public support (66 per cent) for increasing the powers of the Parliament, which is a useful intermediate step from a Nationalist point of view and one on which they could make common cause with Liberals and some Labour. Nobody wants to co-operate closely with the Conservatives. This, together with their limited number of Parliamentary seats, renders them ineffective within the Scottish four-party system (Table 11.6).

Table 11.6 *List voting in Scottish Parliamentary elections, by region*

1999	Labour %	SNP %	Lib Dem %	Conservative %	Other %
Highlands & Islands	25.5	27.7	21.4	14.9	6.3
Northeast	25.5	32.3	17.5	18.3	3.9
Mid-Scotland and Fife	33.4	28.7	12.7	18.6	4.9
Lothians	30.2	25.7	14.4	15.8	11.8
South	39.2	27.8	6.2	9.2	12.0
Central	38.5	26.0	11.0	15.7	4.5
Glasgow	43.9	25.5	7.2	7.9	11.2
West	38.5	26.0	11.0	15.7	4.5
Scotland	38.8	28.8	14.2	15.6	2.3
2003					
Highlands & Islands	22.3	23.4	18.8	16.0	19.1
Northeast	20.2	27.3	18.8	17.4	16.3
Mid-Scotland and Fife	25.3	23.0	12.0	17.6	21.3
Lothians	24.5	16.2	11.0	15.1	22.8
South	30.0	18.4	10.3	24.2	16.9
Central	40.4	22.5	5.9	9.2	22.0
Glasgow	34.7	19.1	7.3	7.5	31.3
West	32.6	19.6	12.3	15.4	19.6
Scotland	29.1	20.9	12.1	15.3	21.2

Notes: Votes are the ones cast for party lists in regions, which give a better idea of the parties' overall standing. Percentages add across rows, although not in all cases to exactly 100% because of rounding. 'Other parties' are the Scottish Socialist Party, Socialist Independents, Socialist Labour and Greens – all on the left of the political spectrum

WALES: CULTURAL DISTINCTIVENESS AND TERRITORIAL FRAGMENTATION

Historical and social background

Wales is arguably the part of Britain with the most distinctive popular culture. Like the other non-English areas it emerged from Celtic kingdoms that held out against the invading Germanic tribes after the collapse of the Roman Empire. However its rugged geography, with high mountains protecting it against invasion but hindering internal communications, meant that it was not united under a single political authority before its incorporation into the English administrative structure in 1536.

This mattered less than its cultural and religious distinctiveness. Almost all the Welsh population spoke a separate Celtic language until the last quarter of the nineteenth century. In common with other 'submerged' European languages Welsh experienced a cultural renaissance in the nineteenth and twentieth centuries. However, its popular base was concurrently eroded through universal education in English, exposure to English language mass media, and massive immigration of English speakers into eastern and industrial south Wales. Although there is a special Welsh-language TV channel and schools that encourage bilingualism, Welsh is now spoken by only half a million people (20 per cent of the population), mainly located in north and west Wales (Table 11.7).

Another nineteenth-century development, however, reinforced Welsh distinctiveness. This was religious revivalism, spearheaded by Methodists and Congregationalists, radical Protestant denominations opposed to the torpor and worldliness (as they saw it) of the Anglican State Church. The Nonconformist Churches used Welsh as their medium and penetrated every village and town of the country.

Table 11.7 *Differences between regions inside Wales*

	West	Northwest (Gwynedd and Dyfed)	Northeast (Clwyd and Powys)	South (Gwent and Glamorgan)
Percentage of households with no car	23.7	25.5	24.3	31.8
Average weekly earnings	354	353	368	387
GDP per head (UK = 100)	70.0	71.5	82.0	92.0
Percentage with higher educational qualifications (A level or equivalent)	22.0	17.0	18.3	21.8
Percentage Welsh speaking	44.9	68.4	23.5	9.7

Note: 'Welsh Wales', the northwest, has the highest percentage of Welsh-speaking people and is therefore culturally the most distinctive. It is also the poorest region, with the west

Source: Computed by authors

They demanded the 'disestablishment' of the Anglican Church and loss of its special privileges, especially in education within Wales.

This was a uniquely Welsh demand, met in 1920. By that time, however, religious passions had started to ebb. While the Nonconformist tradition still gives Welsh life a particular flavour it is not particularly influential in contemporary Wales, where only 12 per cent of the population attend church at all regularly.

Nonconformity and the call for disestablishment did, however, give Welsh voters a push towards radical politics as they were enfranchised in the late nineteenth and early twentieth century. This expressed itself in support for progressive Liberalism and subsequently for Labour and nationalist parties in the North and West.

The English-speaking south suffered all the evils of early industrialism: slums, overcrowding, bad health, precarious employment. This too generated votes for reforming Liberals in the nineteenth and early twentieth centuries. The political party that really gained, however, was Labour, the defender of working class interests against the free market. South Wales became one of the earliest trade union and Labour strongholds, and from there Labour spread out to the rest of Wales. In the 2001 general election Labour held 34 out of 40 Welsh seats, the Liberal Democrats 2, Plaid Cymru (PC, the Welsh Nationalist Party) 4, and the Conservatives none.

The Welsh regions

The overall figures mask a marked regional variation inside Wales. Labour predominates everywhere but particularly in the industrialised south, traditionally home to a militant working class. 'English Wales' – the border area of the east – provides the highest level of support for the Conservatives. The strongest support for nationalism comes from the northwest – centred on Gwynedd, the Welsh kingdom that held out longest against English domination. This is the predominantly Welsh-speaking area where the influence of nonconformity lingers. Its economic base is mainly farming and tourism, a fragile means of livelihood. The extractive industries, slate and stone, which supported the population from the mid-nineteenth to the mid-twentieth century, have now substantially disappeared. This may explain why the nationalists have not opted for a separate Welsh-speaking entity in this area, leaving the English-speaking regions to themselves. Another reason is that west Wales with the exception of South Pembroke is culturally like the north.

Attracting support in the rest of Wales is difficult for the nationalists. Unlike the Scottish Nationalist Party, Plaid Cymru is predominantly a cultural defence organisation. The party wants separate political institutions to protect and extend the Welsh language, together with a better economic and social base to support the Welsh-speaking population. This gives it a strong appeal in the north and west. Its problem, however, is how to appeal to the English-speaking borders and south Wales, whose voters are opposed to the extension of the Welsh language, which they themselves do not speak.

Map 11.3 *The three Wales: voting in the referendum on devolution, 1997*

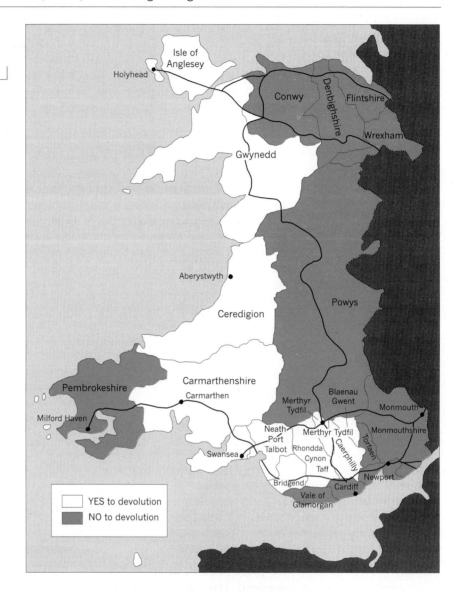

Regional political differences are heightened by geography. Most of the regions of Wales are difficult to reach (the reason the Welsh were able to survive in the first place); but each of them is more accessible from the neighbouring part of England than it is from the rest of Wales. This fact of geography has been underpinned by the building of railways and roads from east to west, rather than from north to south. It is easier for all-Welsh bodies to meet in Shrewsbury, an English town – or even in London – than in far southern Cardiff, the official capital.

Rural west Wales (the coastal strip and its hinterland down to Carmarthen on the Bristol Channel) is linked to the north historically and politically. Here support for the nationalists is strong. The regions over the mountains to the east, bordering on England, are the most anglicised, and here nationalism attracts little support. These differences are almost perfectly illustrated in the referendum votes for a separate Welsh Assembly, shown in Map 11.3. The north and west supported devolution and the east was totally opposed. The south was split between the old mining valleys (for) and the coast (against).

South Wales (the triangle of Cardiff, Swansea and Merthyr Tydfil) is the most populous area of the country and the classic heartland of industrial working class Wales, the country of trade unions and Labour. Labour has controlled all of local government and most of the constituencies of south Wales for generations.

Welsh devolution

In many ways this consistent support for Labour has defined Welsh politics better than sporadic upsurges of nationalism. Support for Labour, the national 'opposition party', can be seen as the main political expression of Welsh distinctiveness. Labour, in its turn, can be seen as a representative of peripheral protest against the centre in Britain, as much as a class-based party. In south Wales both fuse because the region itself is defined by its working class nature.

Welsh Labour MPs may express political demands for their region but some have been bitter opponents of nationalism inside Wales, denouncing it as a distraction from the real task of improving living standards and getting jobs. The Cardiff area's relative proximity to London (200 miles) makes it a favoured location for new industrial development, provided it remains well integrated into Britain.

The opposition of many Welsh Labour MPs to a Welsh Assembly ensured the high vote against it in the Welsh referendum of September 1997. The furthest Labour had gone in the past in terms of devolution was the creation of the Welsh Office in Cardiff in 1965, on the model of the well-established Scottish Office. The Welsh Office is a regional ministry that administers culture, environment, local government, housing, social affairs, agriculture, infrastructure and economic development in Wales. It thus groups administrative areas that in England (and in Wales until 1970) were handled by separate functional ministries from London.

Having a separate administration in these areas means that the Welsh Assembly charged with overseeing it has been set up with relatively little difficulty. The creation of the Assembly was urged on democratic as well as nationalistic grounds, given that the British Parliament has little time for specifically Welsh business. Its specialist committee on Welsh affairs has little power, and is dominated by the party that won most British votes, not necessarily by the parties preferred by Welsh voters.

This is the reason given by New Labour for having put the proposal for a Welsh Assembly to a referendum in Wales, this time with Labour more united in support. From the viewpoint of stimulating local democracy the argument is clearly correct. Labour-dominated councils, particularly in the south where they face little challenge, have often been accused of corruption and nepotism. The Welsh Assembly is open to wider influences and more party competition, so it could bring a breath of fresh air into the closed Labour politics of south Wales.

The new Assembly

This promise was borne out by the results of the first Assembly election on 6 May 1999. Plaid Cymru obtained an unprecedented 28 per cent of the Welsh vote compared with its 10 per cent in the British general election. This could not have been achieved without massive support in south Wales. Large switches from Labour to PC were also recorded in the concurrent local council elections in the southern valleys. With the Conservatives rejected and the Liberals unconvincing, Plaid Cymru emerged as the natural political opposition to Labour throughout Wales.

This status was also reflected in the new Assembly, where the party controlled 17 out of 60 seats, the Conservatives 9 and the Liberals 6. Labour, although the largest party, was short of an absolute majority with 28 seats. These results were achieved, as in Scotland, through an election system where top-up seats distributed through proportional representation in large areas supplemented the traditional first past the post constituency-based results. The result is a much more proportional system of representation where parties have to win a majority or near majority of votes to get a majority of Assembly seats, unlike the British Parliament.

After the election Labour decided to form the Welsh Executive on its own, with the tolerance of the other Assembly parties. This tolerance did not extend

Plate 11.3 *The Welsh Assembly in session. Note the informality in contrast to the House of Commons*

Source: www.paphotos.com

Table 11.8 *Policy areas covered by ministries and Assembly committees in Wales*

Ministries	Assembly Committees
Rural development and Wales abroad	Agriculture and rural development: European and external affairs
Culture and sports	Culture
Economic development	Economic development
Education and lifelong learning	Education and lifelong learning
Environment	Environment, planning and transport: planning decisions
Health and social services	Health and social services
Finance, local government and communities	Local government and housing: audit
Assembly business	Business: standards
	Equality of opportunity
	Subordinate legislation
	Regional committees (mid, north, southeast, southwest Wales)

to a Labour proposal to give wide discretionary powers to the executive outside the supervision of the Assembly. A majority administration would have been able to force this through in the tradition of the elective dictatorships at Westminster, or of the Welsh local councils. In face of the reality of divided power at Cardiff Labour had to drop the proposal, which indeed consorted badly with its own calls during the election campaign for a more inclusive and consensual politics.

The power of the other parties in the Assembly has been reinforced by splits within Welsh Labour's own ranks, notably between New and Old Labour. This, together with the fact that the Assembly's main powers relate to supervising Welsh administration and not to legislation, means that much of its work is done through all-party committees rather than through ministries and departments, unlike the Westminster government. In turn this focuses decision making within the Assembly itself rather than within the Executive.

The party standoff has given considerable potential for influence to the central policy committees of the Assembly. These cover economic development, health and social services, agriculture, environment and higher education. Only two of these are chaired by Labour. Plaid Cymru has two and Liberals and Conservatives one each (Table 11.8).

The legislation setting up the Assembly subordinates it much more to the British government and Parliament than is the case with the corresponding Scottish body. The British Secretary of State for Wales may sit in the Assembly (but not vote). This well underlines his directing and guiding role. In particular, the Welsh Assembly lacks legislative powers, even in areas of prime concern. They allocate funds provided by the British Treasury, and develop and implement policies initiated by the London Parliament and government.

It remains to be seen if the Assembly can in practice extend its role. Almost all the important issues facing it are ones where the central government is heavily involved – the crisis of Welsh upland farming, the 'match funding' needed to

1999	Labour %	Plaid Cymru %	Lib Dem %	Conservative %	Other %
North	34.2	32.3	10.3	19.4	1.7
Mid and west	24.6	38.6	16.7	14.4	5.8
Southwest	42.3	30.4	11.1	12.6	4.7
South Central	36.9	27.0	14.4	16.2	5.6
Southeast	4.5	24.3	12.2	16.8	3.5
Wales	37.6	28.4	13.5	15.9	4.3
2003					
North	31.6	23.8	10.0	22.0	10.8
Mid and west	25.2	28.3	16.4	19.3	10.9
Southwest	41.6	17.2	12.7	15.0	13.0
South Central	41.1	15.4	13.8	18.5	11.3
Southeast	45.1	12.6	10.4	20.2	11.4
Wales	36.9	19.6	12.7	19.0	11.5

Notes: Votes are the ones cast for party lists in regions, which give a better idea of the parties' overall standing. Percentages add across rows, although not in all cases to exactly 100% because of rounding. 'Other parties' are the Socialists and Greens – both on the left of the political spectrum

attract EU aid programmes to Wales and the pressures on a health budget that threatens to spiral out of control.

The failure of the Executive to secure aid from London to 'match' European aid, and the consequent risk of losing it altogether later, sparked a political crisis in early 2000. This failure was seen as part of a supine, do-nothing attitude on the part of Labour ministers headed by Tony Blair's nominee for Labour leader and First Secretary, Alun Michael. On the one hand, he adopted an autocratic attitude to the Assembly, while, on the other, doing nothing that might offend the British Labour government. A vote of no confidence proposed by Plaid Cymru was carried in February 2000, resulting in Michael's resignation and the succession of the 'Old Labour' Rhodri Morgan to his post. Morgan promised a more consensual and consultative approach in politics, working in partnership with the Assembly. His election was certainly an assertion of independence from London, as Blair had strongly opposed him in the earlier leadership campaign. It was followed by a formal coalition with the Liberals and more vigorous Welsh initiatives at Brussels. In May 2002 the Assembly went completely against British government policy by voting for free personal care for the elderly. It also took up Plaid concerns about excessive English immigration driving up house prices and eroding Welsh-speaking communities.

Shared powers and interdependent decision making between Wales and London are clearly a recipe for continuing tensions and quarrels. Plaid Cymru has denied that it ever sought full independence for Wales. But it is committed to seeking full legislative powers in the areas covered by the Assembly. This may well be a winning electoral tactic if too many standoffs develop (Table 11.9). It is likely to push the other Welsh parties in the same direction. However, PC lost ground in south Wales as well as in other areas in the election of 2003.

BRIEFINGS

11.2 Clientelism, corruption, and patronage

Whatever happens in general or regional elections Labour always dominates the local governments of south Wales, often as the only party. Freed from effective accountability, the ruling group of councillors can in these circumstances favour their own supporters and friends in matters over which they have local control – jobs, minor building contracts, priority on public housing lists etc. Patronage of this kind can be used to favour party supporters ('clientelism') and can slide over into corruption if money is given in exchange for favours.

Remarkably little overt corruption has been uncovered in British local government, either in Wales or out of it. Rumours of a 'Taffia' in local politics are widely believed, however. Probably the best solution is more transparency in government (which may be produced by the Welsh Assembly) and challenges to Labour predominance by other parties.

It is noteworthy that Plaid Cymru has made most headway in south Wales as a challenger to Labour predominance on local councils, culminating in its 28.4 per cent share of the Welsh vote in the 1999 Assembly election. If a more proportional voting system were introduced in Welsh local governments that would very much consolidate its political position. Welsh Labour has recently reaffirmed its opposition to such a reform so the stage is set for a party battle on this in the Assembly which may undermine the Lib–Lab coalition.

EXTENDING DEVOLUTION TO THE ENGLISH REGIONS?

The islands of Man, in the Irish Sea, and Guernsey and Jersey in the English Channel, have always had independent Parliaments and governments with full control over their domestic affairs – more so than Scotland, in fact, since they control their own budgets and taxes. Even with devolved government in these areas and in the other countries of the British Isles, the 5/6 of the UK population living in England are directly under the control of central government. It would thus be quite feasible to 'hive off' the more troublesome peripheries while consolidating central control over England. This has indeed seemed to be the strategy of New Labour in regard to English local government.

Contrariwise, the official justification for Scottish and Welsh devolution has always been its greater efficiency, transparency, democracy and ability to 'bring government closer to the people'. What is sauce for the goose is sauce for the gander, and such arguments apply equally well to the regions inside England as to the other countries of the UK. So it is not surprising that there has been increasing discussion and even concrete moves towards setting up regional assemblies and administrations in England.

BRIEFINGS

11.3 Traditional autonomy in the Isle of Man, Jersey and Guernsey (the Channel Islands)

The Isle of Man, Jersey and Guernsey (the last two part of the Channel Islands off the coast of France) have always had their own Parliaments and government. This is because they owed feudal allegiance to the English Crown but were not juridically part of England or under the control of the English (later British) Parliament. In practice, British governments handle their foreign and defence policy, leaving domestic matters to the locals. Autonomy extends to taxation (with income tax set very low to attract wealthy residents). Jersey and Guernsey even issue their own coinage, which is, however, related to the British. This is typical of the political compromise on which the islands are run. Most British domestic legislation is automaticially accepted by the local Parliament and applied. Only occasionally are modifications made to accommodate local preferences. The best known was Man's retention of flogging and birching as criminal punishments until it was struck down by the European Court of Human Rights in the 1970s – even though the island's exact status within the EU is a little uncertain.

These little autonomous areas were regarded as an irrelevant anomaly until recently. With the growth of interest in English regionalism they may come to be regarded as working models of how some relationships with the centre might be organised, particularly in Cornwall and areas like it.

Of these initiatives the most important has been the reconstitution of Greater London as a political entity. Because of their political differences with the Labour-controlled Greater London Council (GLC) in the mid-1980s, the then Conservative government had abolished it outright, leaving only a lower tier of urban government, the London boroughs, in place. The lack of even a planning authority for Greater London as a whole made it difficult to make integrated decisions for the whole region, and it became increasingly obvious that this was necessary particularly for transport and planning.

New Labour set out to remedy this but in a novel way – by having an executive mayor elected directly by the whole area, overseen by a small council. This 'presidential' arrangement is completely different to the assembly-dominated systems that operate in Wales and Scotland and in local government. Labour has been urging this change to directly elected executive mayors on other local governments. But referendums on the subject have mostly defeated the proposals.

Further difficulties were illustrated by events in Greater London. The new arrangements, which took effect in May 2000, create the most powerful directly elected politician in Britain, the choice of 7 million London voters. The actual events of the Greater London campaign in which 'Red Ken' Livingstone, defeated as Labour nominee by Tony Blair's hostility, then ran as an independent and won, show that the post could become a potent centre of opposition to government policies. Livingstone has already fought partial privatisation of London transport all the way to the courts and has begun to charge all private cars entering London a flat daily fee, to relieve congestion.

BRIEFINGS

11.4 **Turn again, Livingstone, twice Mayor of London**

'Red Ken' Livingstone came to political prominence in the early 1980s when he used his position as Chairman of the Labour-dominated Greater London Council (GLC) to institute a number of innovative policies and thumb his nose at Mrs Thatcher at a time when the Labour Party as such was at a low ebb. The GLC operated in County Hall, a massive stone building directly across the Thames from the Houses of Parliament. Typically, Livingstone put up a vast notice recording increases in the unprecedented level of unemployment under the Conservative government, so it could be seen every day by MPs from their own terrace on the river bank opposite.

His impish gestures enlivened what were, at bottom, serious alternatives to Conservative individualism and free market policies. He distributed money to minority groups, particularly Afro-Caribbean ones, at a time of serious racial tensions. This provided them with non-violent political outlets for their activism such as the London carnivals, local liaison groups and neighbourhood councils. He masterminded London Labour's 'Fare's Fair' transport policy whereby cheap flat rates were introduced by the Transport Board with revenues being made up by the London rates if they fell short. Actually the policy was a great success and very popular. Passengers and revenues boomed until the policy was struck down by the Law Lords on appeal by a Conservative Borough Council.

Livingstone's attitudes caused difficulty both with a Labour leadership anxious to shed its 'loony left' image and with the Conservative government. Mrs Thatcher abolished the GLC in 1986 primarily to deprive him of a platform. County Hall was sold to the Japanese as a private hotel (another piece of highly symbolic politics!).

Livingstone declined to being an ordinary backbench MP until Labour's decision to reconstitute Greater London as a political entity with an Executive Mayor. Running for the Labour candidacy he was so violently opposed by Tony Blair that he had a good justification for standing as an Independent when the party rejected him. In an unprecedented result he beat the official party nominees on a low turnout, and used this as a basis to fight New Labour's partial privatisation of London transport all the way through the courts (where he lost). The prospects for Labour's transport policy are not good and Livingstone should benefit politically – which may counterbalance some of the hostility stemming from his proposal to charge each car entering London a flat rate for the privilege. The initial introduction of the 'congestion charge' in February 2003 proved quite successful, once again confirming Livingstone's potential for creative policy innovation.

None of this creates good precedents, from Labour's point of view, for regional bodies elsewhere. This was however one of the few policy areas left to John Prescott, the Deputy Prime Minister, reduced to Blair's shadow after the 2001 election. He was able to make his own mark on the structure of government in Britain with a white paper published in May 2002, containing official proposals for elected English regional assemblies with some important powers – economic development, European funding, local housing and strategic planning, as well as oversight over other regional bodies. The model for this is presumably the Welsh Assembly – a high-level elected body with administrative rather than legislative functions. Financially, the assemblies would have a block grant from the government, rights to tax local authorities in the region and a power to borrow – putting them in as favourable a situation as Wales and Scotland in this respect.

Assemblies would have 25–35 members with an executive of six and would be elected by the additional member system as in Wales and Scotland. The whole region would be used to elect the members additional to the constituency-based ones, presumably choosing proportionally between party lists. Again this would have the effect of breaking up entrenched party majorities and making regional executives mostly coalitions.

A prerequisite for setting up regions according to government proposals is to have only unitary local authorities (Chapter 12). Unitary local authorities are ones which carry out all local functions in their area as opposed to a 'two-tier' system of counties and boroughs. Quarrels over local restructuring will probably delay or preclude the formation of regions except for those that already have unitary authorities. As it happens these are largely in northern England – the northeast, around Newcastle, northwest and Yorkshire and Humberside. With one exception, these are also the regions furthest from London and with the most distinct local identity (Map 11.1). One example of this is the Campaign for the English Regions (CFER) which was formally launched at Newcastle on 20 July 1999. It groups advocates of regional devolution from the northeast, Yorkshire and Humberside and the West Midlands. Its primary aim is to lobby for elected regional government. Significantly it is based at the offices of the Northeast Constitutional Convention in Newcastle – the English city furthest from London and with one of the highest levels of social deprivation.

Plate 11.4 *The Liverpool town hall. In terms of their social and economic profile, regions such as Merseyside and the northeast are almost as distinctive as Scotland and Wales. Regional civic pride, epitomised in the architecture of grand Victorian town halls, diminished under the centralising Conservative governments of 1979–97. The Labour government has promised to restore regional autonomy*

With grassroots pressure and official support it is quite likely that the northern regions may get devolution while the others do not – with the exception of Cornwall, not officially a region at all but only a county. Its remoteness in the extreme southwest, and separate cultural traditions, linked to a Celtic language which died out in the eighteenth century, have generated a Cornish Constitutional Convention proposing an assembly similar to Wales. Clearly, if Man and Jersey are autonomous, Cornwall could be too if the movement generates enough local feeling.

Whatever the details of the final arrangement it is likely that devolution in England will follow the same pattern as in the United Kingdom as a whole, with different regions having different powers and different relationships with the British centre. Areas without a distinct regional identity and at least some grassroots support for autonomy are likely to have to wait longer for devolution. The prospects for devolved government in England do, however, look brighter than before, and may compensate in terms of local autonomies for the central controls increasingly imposed on local government. More space to voice local opinions and reactions will inevitably make decision making more complex and less of an 'elective dictatorship' in Britain. But if it also becomes more consensual and inclusive of regional interests that may be no bad thing.

CONSTITUTIONAL IMPLICATIONS

Traditional constitutional theory has stressed Parliamentary sovereignty as the basis of the British constitution – whatever the majority of the nationally elected House of Commons decides is conclusive. In practice, this meant that the government, with its Commons majority, could not be challenged in policy terms until the next election.

Devolution, like membership of the EU, substitutes a more pluralist conception of politics and policy making. Many more groups will have formal powers which enable them to veto or at least substantially modify central decisions. This will make it essential for the British government to have genuine consultations with regional bodies rather than simply issuing directives for them to carry through. A foretaste of this is given by the Joint Ministerial Committee, which brings together ministers from the Northern Irish, Welsh and Scottish Executives and the UK government to discuss matters of common concern.

Northern Ireland is an extreme example where the UK government is involved in a mesh of institutions and processes which require it to consult at all times not just with the NI Executive itself, but with the Irish government and – through the British–Irish Council – with all the devolved administrations down to the Isle of Man and the Channel Islands! With the creation of English regional governments there is hardly going to be any domestic decision which does not involve consultation with another governmental body and often with many – at a variety of levels, from the European to the local.

The need for consultation is going to be greater because the electoral calendar affecting regional bodies, local governments and central government will be different. Local governments even now are chosen on the basis of annual elections. These only occasionally coincide with general elections. There is thus a tendency for electors to register their dissatisfaction with the party in power at the centre by voting for opposing parties locally – and now also regionally. The same obviously happens at the European elections. The result is that Parliaments and assemblies at the different levels are almost bound to be dominated by opposing parties. In the future the government will not be able to rely, as New Labour has, on manipulating party ties to secure consent. Instead it will have to compromise with opponents to ensure that action does not get blocked. The prospects are for a much more 'consensual democracy' in Britain in place of confrontation between an all-powerful government and an effectively powerless opposition.

All this could be seen as subsidiarity – the doctrine that decisions should be made at the lowest level of government appropriate for them – in action. However, in an increasingly interdependent world it is unlikely that many decisions can actually be isolated from their broader context and made on their own by only one government. For example, roads and other transport projects in any one region are going to affect the contiguous ones and either facilitate or hinder British and European planning. All interests need to be consulted and aggregated. Perhaps subsidiarity should be reinterpreted as a prohibition on higher levels of government being able to steamroller their decisions through regardless of their impact on lower levels.

This is just what has happened in the past under traditional interpretations of Parliamentary sovereignty. As we have seen, Parliament itself needs more real sovereignty, as its fictive legislative omnipotence has in practice been used to justify the 'elective dictatorship' imposed by single-party majority government. Paradoxically, devolution may end by giving the Westminster Parliament more time and opportunity to scrutinise and challenge central government.

As Chapter 4 indicated, this is still a long way in the future, however. The British Labour government has given devolution to Scotland, Wales and London with one hand, while, with the other, seeking to maintain control through internal Labour party manipulation. One suspects that it regards the Joint Ministerial Committee as a way of letting devolved governments know what it has decided or for persuasion and arm-twisting, rather than as a venue for genuine consultation. This parallels its attitudes to English local government, increasingly subjected to central control under both Conservative and Labour administrations, as we shall see in the next chapter.

BRIEFINGS

11.5 New systems of voting – will they create pressures to reform general elections (and local ones)?

Devolved legislatures on the British mainland are all elected on the additional member system or supplementary vote system. Constituency based first past the post or plurality voting, where the candidate with most votes wins, still takes place for the majority of members. But party preferences are separately aggregated within larger areas and used to elect MPs for parties which did badly in the constituencies compared to their overall vote. This produces a more proportional representation as we have seen. The Northern Irish system of voting where all the Assembly members are elected on the basis of the single transferable vote (STV) is even more proportional. In addition, elections to the European Parliament are now purely proportional: electors vote for party lists of 10–15 candidates in large regions and the seats are distributed on the basis of the party vote.

In contrast, general and local elections still take place in one-candidate constituencies with plurality voting. This notoriously favours parties with concentrated local support, primarily Labour but in the southeast the Conservatives. The result is to distort representation in favour of big parties, leading to 50 years of Labour dominance in many local governments. In both Wales and Scotland the other parties are pressing for change in local election procedures towards a more proportional system. The same argument applies to the House of Commons, however. Why should Labour and Conservatives have a inbuilt bias in their favour while Liberals are artificially under-represented? Tony Blair's counterargument is that a proportional reform of voting would deprive all parties of an overall majority and put power in the hands of the minority Liberals, who would decide between a coalition with Conservatives or a coalition with Labour. Opponents of the 'elective dictatorship' of a single-party majority government might not object to this, however. If proportional representation is good for Europe and the regions, why should it not be good for the UK too? That is a hard position to oppose, so moves towards greater proportionality are likely to come both at local and British level in the next ten years, probably in the shape of an additional member system.

ESSAYS

1. To what extent is the United Kingdom still a unitary state?

2. In what ways is the government of Scotland distinct from that of England?

3. What are the main differences between federal and devolutionary arrangements? Which is better for the UK?

SUMMARY

This chapter has discussed:

- the forces promoting devolution in Britain, primarily Welsh and Scottish nationalism

- regional differences, which play some part in supporting the idea that local problems require local solutions, even in England

- the workings of devolution in Scotland and Wales, together with the internal politics of these countries

- prospects for devolution in the English regions

- constitutional implications of devolution, primarily the undermining of the 'elective dictatorship' of the UK government based on its control of a Parliamentary majority, and the need for more extended consultations over its decisions.

MILESTONES

Milestones in Scottish and Welsh devolution

	Scotland	Wales
1886–1924	Home Rule all round, devolution for Ireland, Scotland and Wales advocated by Liberal and Labour parties but abandoned by Labour after 1924	
1888	Scottish Office created as a separate administration for Scotland	
1886–94	Crofters' land agitation in West Highlands met by land tenure arrangements	
1896–1900		'Young Wales' movement. Lloyd George agitates for Home Rule within the Liberal Party
1920		Disestablishment of the Anglican Church in Wales
1928	Scottish National Party founded	Plaid Cymru (the Welsh Party) founded
1930–1955		Protests and demonstrations against flooding of Welsh valleys to provide water for England
1938–39		Sanders Lewis (major Welsh poet) imprisoned for burning RAF buildings
1945	SNP wins first Parliamentary seat in by-election	
1945–50	Tom Johnston, charismatic Secretary of State for Scotland, institutes massive social and economic reform programmes	
1948–51	Scottish Covenant Association gathers one million signatures in favour of Home Rule	
1960–1974	Some bank raids used to finance 'Scottish Liberation Army'	'Wales Liberation Army' burns English holiday homes and posts letter bombs
1965		Welsh Office created to take over administration for Wales
1974	SNP gains unprecedented one-fifth of the vote in Scotland	Plaid Cymru gains three Welsh seats
1978–79	Devolution for Scotland gains slim majority of Scottish vote in referendum but fails to meet Parliamentary requirement of a majority of all electors	Devolution gains only a minority of Welsh votes in a referendum
1980–82		Gwynfor Evans (ex PC leader) fasts to secure Welsh-language TV channel
1992, 1997	SNP regains one-fifth of the Scottish vote in general elections	PC consolidates vote in north and west Wales
1997	New Labour government holds Scottish and Welsh referendums which approve devolution	
1999	First election to Scottish Parliament results in Lib–Lab coalition. SNP vote increases to nearly one-third	First election to Welsh Assembly results ultimately in Lib–Lab coalition. PC vote increases to nearly one-third
2003	Second Scottish Parliamentary election consolidates Lib–Lab coalition	Second Assembly election consolidates Lib–Lab coalition

1. Write a historical account of the incorporation of Wales and Scotland into the United Kingdom. To what extent do the problems of these territories today have their roots in history?

2. Write a new constitution for the United Kingdom providing for the full representation of all the peoples of the UK.

3. Choose some area of devolved policy making in Wales or Scotland and trace in detail how a particular policy decision is made.

FURTHER READING

Comprehensive analyses of Scottish politics are Peter Lynch, *Scottish Government and Politics* (Edinburgh: EUP, 2001) and Gerry Hassan and Chris Wadhurst, *Anatomy of the New Scotland* (Edinburgh: Mainstream, 2002). Jo Murkens et al, *Scottish Independence: A Practical Guide* (Edinburgh: Edinburgh University Press, 2002) explores the viability of an independent Scotland. Welsh politics is analysed in John Osmond, *Welsh Politics in the New Millennium* (Institute of Welsh Affairs: Cardiff, 1999). On English regionalism see H. Armstrong, 'What future for regional policy in the UK?', *Political Quarterly*, **69**, 1998, pp. 200–14. On 'constitutional implications', *Political Quarterly*, **70**, 1997–9 contains much discussion, including Vernon Bogdanor, 'Devolution: decentralisation or disintegration?', *Political Quarterly*, 1999, pp. 185–94. See also Ben Plimlott and Nirmala Rao, *Governing London* (Oxford: OUP, 2002) Lively and informed comment on the workings of devolution and constitutional reform generally is contained in *Monitor*, published quarterly by the Constitution Unit, University College London. Almost every issue of the journal *Scottish Affairs*, published by the Unit for the Study of Government in Scotland, Edinburgh University, contains discussions of Scottish politics and the devolution arrangements for Wales and the English regions as well as Scotland.

USEFUL WEB SITES ON DEVOLUTION

Hotlinks to these sites can be found on the CWS website at http://www.booksites.net/budge.

The question of devolution and regional politics in the UK has become a central component of the political agenda. There are many sites covering aspects of this process. At a general level, official information on the devolution process can be obtained from www.cabinet-office.gov.uk/constitution/devolution/devolution.htm. Insights on governmental policies on the regions are accessible from the office of the Deputy Prime Minister (www.regions.odpm.gov.uk/index.htm), official documentation is available at www.regions.odpm.gov.uk/governance/whitepaper/index.htm. The Campaign for the English Regions (CFER) is a national organisation campaigning for devolution to the regions of England: you can find them at www.cfer.org.uk. You can also visit the Regional Policy Forum at www.rpf.org.uk. Highly valuable information and feedback on devolution can be found at www.devolution.info, www.devolve.org. For an excellent source of academic research on devolution and constitutional change, see www.devolution.ac.uk. You might also be interested in media coverage, if so visit www.guardian.co.uk/Devolution.

Specific sites on Scotland

Government www.scotland.gov.uk
The National Archives of Scotland www.nas.gov.uk
Institute of Governance – University of Edinburgh www.institute-of-governance.org
Scottish affairs www.scottishaffairs.org
The Campaign for Scottish Independence www.standupforscotland.com
The Scottish Independence web server www.forscotland.com

Specific sites on Wales

Government www.wales.gov.uk
General www.gjwwales.co.uk
Wales official legislation www.wales-legislation.hmso.gov.uk
Political parties and movements www.cymru1400.com and
www.independentwales.com

Specific sites on England

Campaign for an English Parliament www.englishpm.demon.co.uk
English petition online www.petitiononline.com/engfree/petition.html

Specific sites on Northern Ireland

Government www.nio.gov.uk
Official documents www.hmso.gov.uk/acts/acts1998/19980047.htm
CAIN web site http://cain.ulst.ac.uk/
Mitchell Report www.irishnews.com/mitchell.html

Specific sites on the Greater London Authority

Information about the mayor and other aspects of the work of the Greater
London Authority can be accessed via the comprehensive web site at
www.london.gov.uk. For example, material concerning City Hall, the purpose-built
centre for the Authority, can be found at www.london.gov.uk/gla/city_hall/
and data on the Authority and its members can be accessed directly via
www.london.gov.uk/assembly/.

For at least the last 100 years British local government has had a dual function: on the one hand, local authorities are democratically elected and accountable to their local citizens; on the other, local government is the creature of central government and must comply with its decisions. Until very recently, local government was the only elected layer of government other than central government itself, and yet central government has relied on it and controlled it closely because it is local not central government that actually produces and delivers many public services. To complicate matters, local government is often in the hands of different parties from central government, and the local parties naturally have their own ideas about what to do and how to do it.

This dual function has created an ambiguity at the heart of the local government system, and a good deal of political conflict between central and local government. Matters rose to a new level of intensity in the 1980s, when the Thatcher governments reduced local powers and financial capacities, and introduced the poll tax. As a result, a good many health warnings were issued at the time about local government being 'in turmoil', subject to 'massive upheaval' and enmeshed in 'endless futile reform'.

To understand how and why local politics have become such an intense subject of national controversy we will, first, set it in the overall context of the British system of government, then look at its structure and mode of operation, and finally, consider its role in democracy.

This chapter accordingly covers:

- local politics in context
- territorial and functional reorganisations
- how local councils function
- parties, political control, and local politics
- money and power in local government
- councillors and officers
- local government and democracy
- New Labour: local democracy revived?

LOCAL POLITICS IN CONTEXT

To understand local government in Britain we also have to understand the nature of the British State. Effective power is concentrated in central government by the constitutional doctrines of the unitary state, which enables national government to change local government boundaries, powers and functions, and finances at will. Yet, in spite of these draconian powers, central government does not have its own local agents to execute its orders. There is nothing in Britain that remotely resembles the French prefect, a civil servant posted in a locality to implement national legislation directly. Central departments in Britain mostly lack this kind of 'field administration', as it is called, and therefore rely on local governments or quangos to execute their policies. These responsibilities are laid on local authorities either by legislation (requiring them to carry out its provisions) or by central 'circulars' or 'directives' from government departments.

In other European countries the responsibility for service provision is more usually shared between different levels of government, and local discretion over both services and local taxation is greater. This helps to explain why, in the UK, the overwhelming part of local government income comes from central government in the form of grants, and yet more than half of all public employment is at the local level. In effect, central government pays for public services and uses local government as its administrative arm to deliver them.

Central control over local authorities is ensured by two important legal principles, *ultra vires* and *mandamus*. This effectively places them in a straitjacket designed by central government; they must do what the law requires of them, and they must not do anything else. This situation means that most administrative activities are not initiated locally; neither are they accounted for locally. Yet central government cannot simply bypass local government. It has no means of producing or delivering services itself. It has to (1) somehow force the locality to comply, directly or by controlling its supply of money, (2) abolish it, or (3) transfer its powers to other bodies. All these strategies have been pursued by governments in the last 25 years, often creating intense controversy and conflict in the process.

Controversy and tension in local politics are thus paradoxically caused by:

Ultra vires The legal doctrine stating that local authorities may only do that which the law expressly allows them to do.

Mandamus The legal doctrine stating that local authorities must carry out the duties imposed on them by law.

- the close mutual dependency of local and central government. Local government depends on the centre for revenues, central government depends on the localities for many public services

- their shared democratic status, the fact that both are elected and have a 'mandate' from their respective electorates to pursue their own policies, which have often conflicted

- the constitutional latitude that central government has to bludgeon local governments into submission – by abolition, legal action, 'capping', regulation, and inspection – combined with the limited 'blocking' ability of local politicians if they do not wish to comply.

None of this makes for a happy relationship, and the potential for conflict is likely to continue, because it is built into the structure of central–local relationships. This is especially because, unlike many countries, local (and regional) governments in Britain do not have a constitutionally protected position. Instead their fate depends on the unwritten constitution and ultimately on the majority party in Parliament.

TERRITORIAL AND FUNCTIONAL REORGANISATIONS

Nowhere is the centre's legal power shown more clearly than in its ability to abolish or create local authorities, something it has done many times in the past 150 years, and several times in the last 30 years alone. Parliamentary sovereignty and the constitutional traditions of a unitary state (Chapter 4) make it possible for central government to change local areas and functions, more or less at will. Boundaries have been freely revised and functions added or taken away since the modern system was established in the early industrial era.

The most pressing needs in the nineteenth century (drainage and sewers, public health, housing, street lighting, law enforcement, education) were experienced in the rapidly expanding industrial cities. So these were the areas that first enjoyed local democracy and self-government, by virtue of the 1835 Municipal Corporations Act, which instituted town councils elected by property holders. The 1888 Local Government Act extended the franchise for local elections and established county councils for the rural areas. It created a two-tier system in local government, whereby county councils ran the services affecting broad areas (planning, education and police) while lower units within them ran local and more personal services (housing, health and local amenities). The lower units (urban or district councils) also had elected councils and their own administration. London was organised as a county, with a second tier of boroughs beneath it, but other large cities were 'unitary', that is, they had a single-tier city council responsible for all services. Outside England and Wales, Scotland and Ireland were organised on broadly similar lines but with differences in some of the structural detail.

From the end of the nineteenth century until the 1980s Westminster politicians accepted the recommendations of royal commissions that a two-tier system is best. But as economic and population patterns changed in the second half of the twentieth century it became necessary to reform and modernise the system again. However, the recommendations of the Redcliffe-Maud Report on Local Government in England (1969), were largely ignored in the 1972 Local Government Act, which basically rationalised the existing two-tier system. Even its seemingly straightforward allocation of responsibilities was qualified. Arrangements for London were different, as they were for Scotland and Northern Ireland. In addition a number of other local services remained in the hands of ad hoc bodies, and several health services were transferred to the National Health Service (see Figure 12.1).

Two-tier local government
Where the functions of local government are divided between an upper level (counties, for example) and a lower level (boroughs or districts, for example).

Unitary system
Where local functions are controlled by only one layer of local government.

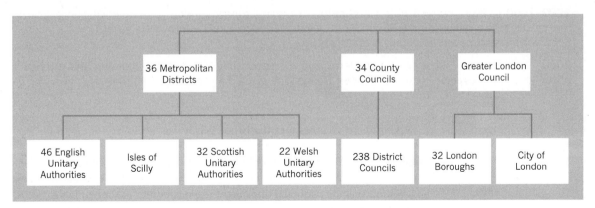

Figure 12.1 *Local government structure in England, Scotland, and Wales*

12.1 Local government reorganisations in England and Wales, 1800–2000

1800 and before   Unelected borough councils (or corporations) were gradually established by Royal Charter for some cities. Benches of magistrates and parish 'vestries' appointed by local notables provided rudimentary government in other areas.

1835 Municipal Corporations Act   Established elections (with limited suffrage) for town (borough) councils. The City of London retained its medieval corporate privileges.

1888 Local Government Act   Established the principle of a two-tier local government system with the creation of counties, with urban and district councils beneath them, all directly elected. The London County Council (LCC) was responsible for education and transport. By 1899 28 metropolitan boroughs became the lower tier of government within the London area.

1894 Local Government Act   Two-tier principle extended with the creation of urban and district councils for cities and small towns. Parish councils retained residual responsibilities in small villages.

1963   The Greater London Council (GLC) was created to accommodate the continuing growth of London. The two-tier principle remained, with Greater London embracing 32 London boroughs. The GLC was responsible for transport and planning, while the Inner London Education Authority (ILEA) was retained with jurisdiction over the old LCC area.

1972 Local Government Act   The major change was the creation of six metropolitan counties and 36 metropolitan districts for major urban areas. In addition, the number of counties was reduced to 39 and urban and district councils replaced with 296 district councils. The two-tier principle was retained and strengthened.

1984–7   The Conservative government abolished the GLC and the metropolitan counties. Responsibilities were devolved to London boroughs, district councils (outside London) and to a variety of quangos. The two-tier principle was abandoned for large urban areas.

1995–6   Local government reforms. A number of unitary authorities were created, but the old two-tier structure remained in many areas. In Wales the two-tier structure was abolished and replaced with 22 county and county borough councils.

1996 Local Government (Scotland) Act   Further wholesale changes involved the abolition of the regional councils and the creation of 29 unitary councils.

1999–2000   1999 Greater London Authority Act creates a new London Assembly with an elected mayor following a referendum in which 72 per cent of London voters approve the government's plans. Plans for elected mayors in other cities drawn up.

2000   New London Assembly with elected mayor is responsible for strategic planning and a range of services in the Greater London area. Ken Livingstone elected as London's first mayor.

Driving these changes was the belief that it was necessary to strike the best trade-off between small-scale democracy and large-scale efficiency: some functions are best provided, or can only be provided by large authorities; but wherever possible local functions should be performed by small-scale authorities. Few now believe that the particular division of responsibilities enshrined in the 1970s' legislation was entirely rational; much was a result of political expediency. The

Plate 12.1 *County Hall, London. The Greater London Council was seen as a high-spending Labour power base and was abolished by the Conservative government in 1984*

Source: Stockwave, Central Office of Information

reforms simply tinkered with the haphazard pattern of local government that had evolved over many centuries.

Two further changes tinkered with the arrangements, also for reasons of political expediency. Between 1984 and 1987 the Conservatives abolished the Greater London Council and the six metropolitan counties in the largest urban areas of England. This was designed to cut local government expenditure by what were regarded as high-spending leftist councils, and it was an attack on Labour power bases in the big urban areas. The powers of the abolished counties were devolved to existing district and borough councils and to a number of non-elected quangos.

The second change was the reforms of 1995/6, which reorganised local government in Wales and Scotland into 22 and 28 unitary authorities respectively. As the Conservatives had little to lose politically the new structure was imposed without much consultation and largely ignored local objections. It was different in England where the Conservatives had their own electoral base and options and objections had to be entertained seriously. New unitary authorities emerged only where local feelings ran predominantly in favour of them, and so far as they had a consistent logic, other than a political and electoral one, it was to give more autonomy to certain areas on the fringes of existing counties that were in themselves strong local communities needing all-purpose local governments (see Map 12.1).

Over most of the country, however, the old two-tier system created in 1972 was retained, and to the extent that this was based largely on the 1888 system, the present-day structure looks, in outline, much like that in England at the turn of the century (see Figure 12.1). The intrusion of unitary authorities here and there, and the horizontal division of local powers with ad hoc bodies and quangos, still support the comment made by an MP in 1871: 'The truth, sir, is that we have a chaos as regards authorities, a chaos as regards rates, and a worse chaos than all

Map 12.1 *The new territorial organisation of local government in England, 1995*

Source: HMSO

as regards areas.' Criticisms of the 1995/6 reforms were particularly bitter, however, they were variously described as inept, an unequivocal failure, shameless and shameful, a costly farce, and a messy compromise. None of this helps democratic accountability and representation in the localities, dramatically shown by the confusing distribution of functions between tiers and types of local government unit shown in Table 12.1.

	England metropolitan		England non-metropolitan		London		Scotland, Wales, and England	
	Joint authorities	Boroughs /districts	Counties	Districts	Boroughs	GLA	Joint/special authorities	Unitaries
Social services		*	*		*			*
Education		*	*		*			*
Libraries		*	*		*			*
Museums and art galleries		*	*	*	*			*
Housing		*	*	*	*			*
Planning – strategic			*			*		*
Planning – local		*	*	*	*			*
Highways		*	*	*	*	*		*
Traffic management		*	*		*	*		*
Passenger transport	*		*			*	*	*
Sport		*	*	*	*			*
Parks		*	*	*	*			*
Refuse collection		*			*		*	*
Refuse disposal	*	*	*	*	*		*	*
Consumer protection		*	*	*	*			*
Environmental health		*	*		*		*	*
Police	*		*			*	*	*
Fire	*		*			*	*	*

Table 12.1 Local authority services in England, Scotland, and Wales

Source: T. Byrne, *Local Government in Britain*, London: Penguin Books, 2000, pp. 84–5

Plate 12.2 *Peter Brooke's cartoon in* The Times, *30 July 1997. Simon Jenkins commented in the same issue of* The Times: *'The government is set to deliver the British constitution its biggest shock since the war. Direct election of a London mayor will overturn the whole cabalist tradition of party politics.'*

Source: *The Times*

In retrospect, the territorial reforms of the 1970s through to the late 1990s were more important for what they did not change than for what they did change. In particular, the legislation really failed to address three vital areas that dominate most of the debate on the shortcomings of local government in Britain today: first, the nature of local democracy; second, the arrangements for local government finance; and third, provisions for regional government. Having looked at the last in Chapters 10 and 11, we now turn to the other two in more detail.

LOCAL COUNCILS AND HOW THEY FUNCTION

Before we can assess the quality of local democracy, however, we need to examine how it functions and organises itself. Local councils are executive bodies as well as legislative ones, unlike Parliament which is a legislative body. Of necessity, local councils have to delegate executive functions and detailed supervision of them to some extent. But they do so by delegating to committees rather than individual ministers, as in central government. Council committees, in contrast to Parliamentary ones, are therefore executive decision-making bodies, rather than simply supervisory ones.

The role of local committees has changed in the last two decades. From 1945 until the 1980s they focused on managing various departments of the authority, such as housing, parks, and social services, and they were intimately involved with policy making and administration. In this they worked closely with their permanent staff, known as 'officers' to distinguish them from elected members.

Table 12.2 *Council and committees in Colchester, Essex*

Committees	Membership
Council	The Mayor of Colchester and all Council members
Cabinet	Chair and six members, responsible for communications; employment, economic development, leisure and tourism; environment and waste; housing; community safety and health; planning and transport; resources
Overall and Scrutiny Panel	Chair and ten members
Best Value Review Panel	Chair and nine members
Economic Prosperity and Tackling Deprivation Panel	Chair and nine members
Environment and Well-Being Panel	Chair and nine members
Quality of Life Committee	Chair and nine members
Planning Committee	Chair and 12 members
Licensing and Regulatory Committee	Chair and 12 members
Standards Committee	Chair and three members

The Cabinet is a Conservative–Liberal Democrat Coalition. Other committees and panels have a mixed party and independent membership drawn from the elected council

But as the powers and functions of local government were reduced in the 1980s, and as much of their property and service provision was privatised, so local committees increasingly turned to the role of facilitators of local services, rather than direct producers of them. In many ways these changes have cleared the way for a more political role to be taken by the council. Under New Labour, the system changed yet again, this time to replace the old council committees organised around particular services (education, housing, health, transport, planning, etc) with new forms of executive power based on mayors or council leaders, and cabinets (see Briefing 18.7). Table 12.2 shows a typical set of committees and panels for Colchester, an urban council within the administrative county of Essex.

Local democracy, like Parliamentary democracy, is also party democracy. If there is a majority of one party on the council, policy will be decided at the party meeting. Party discipline will generally ensure that party decisions are voted in as council policy, even if individuals disagree with them. The convenors of all-important committees will be members of the majority party and will implement its policy in their committee. Thus what seems to be a somewhat rambling and disarticulated structure of separate committees will actually be co-ordinated through parties and the party executive committee.

This is, of course, what happens in central government too. The difference at the local level is that three (or more) party competition often results in coalitions, or in no overall party control. Table 12.3 shows the distribution of party control across England and illustrates the extent to which coalition or minority government has become a usual state of affairs locally, again contrasting with Westminster.

| | Council control | | | | | | |
	Con	Lab	LD	Ind/other	Nat	NOC*	Total
Scotland	0	14	0	6	2	10	32
Wales	0	8	0	3	3	8	22
London	8	15	3	0	0	6	32
Mets	1	25	2	0	0	8	36
Counties	17	7	0	0	0	0	34
Districts	76	47	19	12	0	84	238
Unitaries	7	20	3	0	0	16	46
Total	109	136	27	21	5	142	

*No overall control

Source: Local Government Chronicle Elections Centre, University of Plymouth, 2002

Where there is a coalition, committee chairs are distributed between the parties. In some cases they are also given to minority parties to get their support, and in such cases the party meetings are necessarily less effective in determining policy. It then tends to be decided by interparty negotiations on central co-ordinating committees. The absence of a majority party, therefore, makes the council as a whole more important, as it would Parliament (Chapter 18).

Corresponding to each council committee there is an administrative department with a chief officer, who attends council and committee meetings and takes instructions from them. Depending on their area of responsibility, local officials are often professionally trained with specialised qualifications. Public health requires a medical doctor and public works architects and engineers, for example. Because of the way that councils have been compelled by central governments to contract out services and simply buy them from competing suppliers, this is, however, less true today.

Traditionally, administrative co-ordination was handled by a town clerk, a solicitor, but most councils today have replaced the clerk with a chief executive officer or manager with business experience and a qualification in administration, who leads the permanent staff of the council. This reflects general tendencies in the society towards greater professionalism and the need for a more sophisticated approach to modern administration. We should not assume, however, that local government is only about administration. Its history over the past 100 years and more is, in large part, the history of the growth of local politics.

PARTIES AND POLITICAL CONTROL

Much discussion of local government concentrates on the administration of local services rather than its political dimension. This is because it was less politicised in many places before the reorganisations of the 1970s, and the highly partisan actions of central government in the 1980s. Two things changed the situation:

1. The Conservative governments from 1979 to 1997 cut support for services, forcing local councils to make highly political decisions about if and what to cut.

2. The parties excluded from power at the centre became more radical in the localities, and, where they took power, sometimes chose to oppose central government cuts outright, thereby sparking off unprecedented confrontation and crisis.

It was the Liberals who first built themselves up locally by espousing 'community politics', a concentration on highly local issues and grievances that sometimes provoked confrontation with bureaucratic and unresponsive Labour councils. This tactic gained the Liberals widespread local support, which stimulated Labour to base their national recovery on local politics. Labour and Liberal successes were also helped by the fact that local elections were held annually and their results reflected popular discontent with the party in power in central government. Thus councils became increasingly Labour and Liberal dominated from 1979 to the extent that only 6 per cent were left in Conservative hands in 1997. The result was that national political divisions between the parties within Parliament came more than ever to be reflected in the confrontation between central and local government.

Local government is, therefore, more of a party democracy than ever. It is worthwhile noting that this has had two effects, in particular, on the national parties themselves, thus making the point that local and national politics are closely tied together:

- The decline of party membership has been counterbalanced by the emergence of a body of 20,296 locally elected and active politicians who control large local organisations and their resources.

- Party activists have often been thought of as idealists and ideologues who, without first-hand political experience themselves, press the national leadership into more extreme and impractical policies. In reality, local activists are well versed in pragmatic local politics, and they constitute an important group both among New Labour and Liberal Democrats: two-thirds of new Labour MPs and 70 per cent of Liberal Democrats in the 1997 Parliament had been local councillors.

MONEY AND POWER IN LOCAL GOVERNMENT

Money was at the centre of the battle between central and local government in the 1980s. Up to the 1980s local revenues were traditionally based on the 'rates', a tax based on the notional rental value of residential and commercial property. For many years the rating system worked moderately well. Property owners paid the tax directly, and tenants paid indirectly through their rent. The tax raised less than half of local income, and the shortfall was made up by central government grants, known as the rate support grant (RSG). This was also designed to equalise the financial resources of rich and poor authorities, and did so to a fair degree according to a complicated formula that took account of the wealth and needs of authorities.

During the 1970s pressure grew in some circles to abolish the rates because:

Regressive taxation
Where lower income groups pay proportionately more in taxation than higher income groups.

- There was a widespread myth that they were unfair because only the property-owning middle classes paid them. In fact, tenants paid them indirectly, and the rates were actually a mildly regressive form of taxation, because lower income groups pay proportionately more.

- The size of the RSG grew as local government costs increased. In the late 1930s the RSG stood at around 30 per cent of total local spending, but by 1977 it was closer to 60 per cent. The Conservative government of the 1980s did not like this, claiming that it encouraged councils to overspend.

- Adjusting the rates to pay for a larger proportion of local services was politically difficult. With inflation and house prices rising rapidly, adjustments resulted in *apparently* sharp increases in the rates – although, in fact, the real costs barely rose at all as a percentage of disposable household income.

In their 1974 election manifesto the Conservatives pledged that they would reform the system, and once in office they replaced the RSG in 1980 with a new system called grant-related expenditure, which enabled the central government to set detailed spending targets and to cut the grant if local authorities exceeded them. Central government also gave itself the power to punish 'overspending' authorities by 'clawing back' more in grants than councils overspent.

In response, many authorities simply increased their rates, especially Labour-controlled authorities in the larger cities that were increasingly hostile to the Conservative government. This provoked a new round of reforms in which central government tried to enforce its spending policies by 'rate capping'. Properly implemented, rate capping would affect overspending Conservative and Labour-controlled councils (for example, Portsmouth Council in 1983), but the government fixed the system so that only Labour authorities were punished.

Rate capping
The practice introduced in the 1980s whereby central government set a maximum rate level for local government in an attempt to control their expenditure.

By 1985 this issue had become a source of major conflict between the two parties. Sixteen Labour councils declared that they would not meet the government's rate target and would either not set a rate or would indulge in deficit spending. This was illegal as in a unitary system such as Britain, national government has complete authority over local government matters. In the event, and following a change of heart by the Labour leadership, who urged compliance with government policy, all but one of the rebel councils set a rate. The exception was Liverpool City Council where a group of left activists, led by Deputy Leader Derek Hatton, decided that they would close local services down rather than comply. They eventually kept services running by borrowing from Swiss banks. But their actions were illegal, and led to several council members being charged for the losses. Hatton and several of his colleagues were made personally bankrupt and were subsequently expelled from the Labour Party.

12.2 What is the best system of local government finance?

Type of tax system	For	Against
Rates (up to 1989 in Scotland, 1990 in England and Wales)	Well established (until abolition) and easy and cheap to collect	Subject to *apparently* large increases during periods of inflation. Falls only on residential and commercial property owners. Difficult for central government to control
Community charge (poll tax) 1989–93	A flat rate tax everybody has to pay. Simple and highly visible so should provide an electoral check on high spending local authorities	Proved very difficult and expensive to collect. Very regressive. Highly unpopular
Council tax (1993 onwards)	Relatively simple and easy to collect. Levied on households, but the amount paid is determined by the value of the properties, which are placed in value bands. It assumes a two-person household, but rebates are available for single people, the poor and disadvantaged	Banding can be arbitrary. May prove as unpopular as the rates during periods of inflation. Progressive element is linked to property values rather than income or ability to pay
Uniform business rate (effective since 1990–1)	Easy to collect and to understand. Linked to property values as with the old rating system	Not really a local tax at all as the revenue goes to the central government, which then redistributes to localities. Unpopular with small business. Can be regressive as it is unrelated to the profit or turnover of business
Local income tax	Easy to collect and to adjust. Strongly progressive and linked to the ability to pay. Highly visible and accountable	Could be inflationary and encourage spending. Not amenable to control by central governments and therefore unlikely to be adopted in Britain outside Scotland where the Scottish Parliament will be given limited power to raise income tax for the whole of the Scottish jurisdiction
Local sales tax	Could be hidden in prices (such as VAT). Its 'invisibility' makes it less unpopular than more visible taxes. Easy to collect	Highly regressive and unrelated to ability to pay. Its invisibility reduces accountability. As with income tax, highly unlikely to be adopted because central government cannot control spending levels

Community charge or **poll tax** The local tax that replaced the rates (or property tax), in which every adult resident of a local authority paid the same amount. It came into operation in 1990 and was replaced by the council tax in 1993.

These events strengthened the government's conviction that reform was needed of the local government finance system. From a number of alternatives, however, the government chose the one that was the least effective, and most likely to arouse opposition: the community charge or poll tax. The idea behind the poll tax was simple: every individual adult living in a particular area would pay a flat charge to the local council. The charge would be reduced for the poor and disadvantaged, but the vast majority of people would pay the same amount. Occupants of stately homes who previously had paid large rates bills would pay the same as occupants of tiny council flats.

Defenders of the tax argued that the poll tax would:

- be highly visible, so making a clear connection between the cost of local services and paying taxes for them

- apply to all residents, and therefore force everyone to weigh up the cost of local services against taxes

- make councils more accountable for their policies and therefore force spending down

- be initially unpopular, although people would get used to it and come to see its merits.

Critics of the tax – most of the country – argued that the poll tax was 'the worst idea in the world', because:

- it was unworkably difficult and expensive to collect

- it was highly regressive, since the rich and poor paid the same amount

- it had been abolished in all civilised countries centuries before

- it would discourage people from voting because the poll tax list was widely believed to be the local electoral registration list.

The critics proved right. Without exaggeration, the introduction of the community charge represents one of the most important policy mistakes in British government in the twentieth century. It proved excessively expensive to collect (in some poorer areas collection costs exceeded revenues) and was deeply unpopular, causing some of the most widespread protests and serious civil disturbances seen in the country for many decades. It was also a major cause of Thatcher's downfall. When John Major became leader, a new local tax was the first priority of the government.

Council tax The local tax, which replaced the community charge in 1993, in which, like the rates, payment is related to property values and levied on all occupants of property.

What emerged was the council tax and the uniform business rate. The former is similar to the old rating system. Every property is rated in one of seven (later eight) bands of property value (A to H), and the tax falls on the current occupant of the property. Rebates are available for the poor and the disadvantaged. The tax has worked without too much public attention or adverse publicity, it has proved easy to collect and an element of fairness was incorporated into the banding system by weighting the tax towards the occupants of more expensive properties.

Part of its success is also due to the simple fact that it accounts for a smaller and smaller proportion of local expenditure.

In retrospect it is difficult to understand the whole poll tax business. It was based on political myths about the old rating system that were easily destroyed; it chose the worst from the list of available options; it was forced on the country by a tiny minority against the better judgement of a huge majority of politicians and civil servants, and virtually all experts; it proved, as predicted, to be a hugely expensive and wasteful disaster; and it was replaced by something close to the old rating system.

COUNCILLORS AND OFFICERS

Elected councillors

There is no job specification for local councillors, but as elected representatives they are involved in local policy making, the administration of services, the representation of interests, and in community and political leadership. They are not paid for this, although they receive expenses and attendance allowances for approved duties. A complicated electoral system exists whereby county councillors are elected every four years, but the timing of district council elections can be varied. Districts can hold elections concurrently with county council elections, or at the mid-term of county elections, or by thirds, that is, one-third of district councillors elected every year that there is no county council election. All elections are held on the first Thursday in May. Eligibility is different from national elections: Commonwealth citizens may vote, as may citizens of the EU.

Council members are not typical of the population. They are:

- generally older than the general population, the 55–69 group being heavily over-represented

- mostly male, although there were more female local councillors (29 per cent in 2001) than women MPs until 1997

- more middle class, and more likely to be professionals, employers, or managers (65 per cent)

- better educated, with about 53 per cent having a degree or professional qualification

- often school board members (56 per cent) or on other public boards and joint committees (44 per cent).

The unrepresentative nature of councils probably has a lot to do with the fact that councillors are not paid and, therefore, the job attracts either those who are not employed (38 per cent retired, 10 per cent not in the labour market) or the self-employed (16 per cent) who can organise their working day around council meetings. As a result there have been calls for the proper payment of councillors, even for full-time paid elected officials, along the lines of the new Mayor of London. The job has, as we have seen, become more professional and politicised than before, with the average councillor spending more than 30 hours a week on the job, and council leaders and chairs putting in many more. The average councillor has served for nine years.

In 1986 the Widdecombe Report into the conduct of local authority business recommended pay for councillors and a formal recognition of the role of political parties. In the event the government rejected most of the report. Instead it legislated to prohibit council publicity of a party political nature.

Officers

Elected council members are supported by the local government equivalent of the national civil service, consisting of full-time paid officers (bureaucrats) who are professional managers and experts. There are about 750,000 of them in local government, and in many ways they are organised along the same lines as the national Civil Service (see Chapter 7).

CHIEF OFFICERS

Like permanent secretaries in their Whitehall departments, local government has chief officers such as the chief fire officer, director of social services, education officer, chief financial officer, a registration officer (for elections), and (most usually) a chief executive officer (CEO), who also acts as the 'head of paid service' and often acts as a 'monitoring officer' who is responsible for reporting any illegal or improper council activity.

POLITICAL IMPARTIALITY

Like the Civil Service, local government officers are required to be politically neutral, and serve which ever party or coalition is in power. By convention they refrain from open support of parties, and under the Local Government and Housing Act 1989, senior officers are not allowed to stand for political office or engage in party political activity.

PROFESSIONAL MANAGEMENT

Many local services are of a highly technical nature – education, health, refuse collection and disposal, traffic management, etc – so local government officers have long been more specialised and professional than the generalists of the Civil Service. But in recent years they have become caught up by the new public management practices. Mission statements, value for money, management gurus, loose–tight structures, corporate planning, planning programming and budgeting systems (PPBS), enhancement, visions, customer charters, cost-benefit analysis, and multi-project scheduling are the order of the day. Chief officers are paid market salaries for senior executives – more than five figures in some cases.

DICTATORSHIP OF
THE OFFICIAL?

Like civil servants (see Chapter 6), the chief officers of local government are often accused of running the show, using their professional drive and ambition to dominate their nominal political masters – the part-time, amateur, and untrained elected councillors. Just as often officers are accused of being lazy, time serving, incompetent, and old fashioned. Both are stereotypes, and some analysts suggest that council leaders and their officers form a dual or joint elite.

LOCAL GOVERNMENT AND DEMOCRACY

Most democratic theorists agree that local democracy is an essential part of the system of government for several good reasons:

- **Size and subsidiarity**   Other things being equal, small-scale democracy is better than large-scale democracy. Participation is easier, knowledge of local issues is greater, and the gap between voters and leaders is smaller. This is similar to what the EU calls the principle of subsidiarity (Chapter 9).

- **Efficiency**   Local people with a knowledge of special local conditions are likely to make more sensible and efficient decisions than central bureaucrats. In any case, there is no reason for a Whitehall office to make decisions about the opening time of public parks in Cornwall.

- **Training ground for democracy**   Local government is a democratic training ground that gives citizens first-hand experience of how to organise public affairs.

- **Experimentation**   It is easier to experiment with services on a small local scale: failures are not large scale and expensive, and successes can easily be transferred to other authorities.

- **Pool of talent**   Local government provides a pool of experienced political talent that can be recruited into national politics.

- **Pluralism**   Many different political arenas, and a fragmentation of political power between different levels of the political system is a democratic virtue.

One of the most enduring debates in democratic theory concerns the proper division of powers between different levels of government. It is generally agreed that central government should be responsible for national defence and security and macro economic planning, while local government can handle parks, street lighting and refuse. In between, however, there are a large number of services that can be assigned to either national, or local, or regional/provincial government, or any combination of them – education, health, housing, social welfare, public transport, police, regional and local development, planning. In most democratic countries, responsibility is shared between two or three levels of governments.

12.3 Division of functions among different levels of government

With the growth of powers of the European Union, and the devolution of power by central governments to regional and local governments, the debate about which level of government should do what has received fresh impetus in recent discussions about subsidiarity. Unfortunately, which level is best at doing what is usually a matter of tradition or political expediency rather than efficiency or fairness. As long ago as 1861 the political philosopher John Stuart Mill argued that there are three levels of responsibility:

- the purely local where such tasks as street cleaning, lighting and refuse collection should be performed

- those where because of 'spillovers' to other areas, such as education or policing, the central government should administer policy

- those areas such as sanitation and welfare where the central government should set minimum standards, but localities should administer and pay for the services.

Writing in the US context, the political scientist Paul Peterson has argued that:

- central government should play a major role in redistributive policies such as income support (welfare), pensions, health and housing

- lower levels of government should provide what he calls developmental policies – such things as sanitation, transport, education and utilities.

In fact this division is not so very different from that which prevails in Britain today, except that successive Conservative governments have privatised or centralised a number of developmental policies.

One thing is for sure: debate over the proper division of responsibility, including which level of government should pay for what, will continue for many years, because there is no simple, uniform or rational solution. The debate will probably intensify following Scottish and Welsh devolution and the possible creation of regional governments in England.

In Britain, services have been increasingly centralised, on the argument that they are better provided and paid for by central government, and on the grounds that there should be a uniform, standardised level of provision. Services that can respond to local conditions have often been left at the local level. For example, until the 1980s, the amount and quality of local council (public) housing was left to local authorities, even if the housing programme was largely funded by central government. This meant that large urban authorities, often with poorer populations and under Labour control, provided more council housing than the counties, which tended to be richer and under Conservative control. Similarly, education, law enforcement and many other services were provided locally, although they also depended heavily on central government grants.

In this way, local people and their elected councillors had a direct say in the provision of local services – to some extent, at least. Beginning with the election of a Conservative government in 1979, this system was slowly but surely undermined, and by the late 1990s relatively few direct links exist between the local provision of services and the local democratic process.

LOCAL GOVERNMENT REVOLUTION, 1979–97

Local government changed in the first part of the twentieth century in response to changing social, economic, and political circumstances. Generally speaking the system became more highly centralised, and the localities lost services to other bodies. But from 1979 to the early 1990s it was cut and centralised faster than ever before:

1. **Financial centralisation** Local taxing powers were cut, and central grants increased, so giving central government more power of the purse over local government. This was intended to cut local spending significantly, and local current expenditure fell from its all time high of 8.6 per cent of total national domestic expenditure in 1975/6 to 7.6 per cent in 1993/4. Capital spending fell much faster. Total local government employment (including teachers, police officers, firefighters, and social service workers) fell from 2,360,000 in 1979 to 1,971,000 in 1998.

2. **Privatisation and deregulation** Many services previously provided by local governments were privatised or opened up to private competition. Bus and rapid transit systems that used to be local public monopolies were privatised and deregulated. Street cleaning and refuse collection were turned over to private companies. Compulsory competitive tendering (CCT) became obligatory for a range of services in 1988 and extended to almost all services in 1992.

3. **Council house sales** Between 1980 and 1996 2.2 million dwellings previously owned by local authorities were sold to sitting tenants or housing associations. This massive transfer of housing units has greatly reduced the role of local authorities.

4. **Educational reform** Local authority responsibility for education, easily the most expensive local service, was reduced or eliminated. The former polytechnics (now universities) were removed from local control, the management of schools (including decisions over hiring and firing and resource allocation) were devolved to school governors, and schools given the opportunity to 'opt out' of local government funding altogether and instead receive finance direct from central government. The opt-out rate has been low, but has tended to involve higher status secondary schools. The introduction of the National Curriculum, the testing for standards of both teachers and pupils, and the publication of performance tables, has increased central control.

Implications for local democracy

These changes were enormously controversial at the time, some arguing that local democracy had been emasculated by making an already highly centralised political system even more centralised. Others claimed that local government became modern, efficient, and responsive to citizens. The changes were not necessarily bad in themselves, and some, such as the sale of council houses, have been popular in some circles, although they have some highly adverse consequences for the poor and homeless. There is no doubt, however, that they have changed the nature of local government. Instead of administering national programmes and tempering them to the needs of the locality, they have become purchasers of local services and thus constrained by the guidelines laid down by central government (cheapest bids) and the alternatives offered by the market.

There are two opposing views about the effect this transformation has had on the nature of local democracy.

ENABLING OR FACILITATING ROLE OF LOCAL DEMOCRACY

The first view is that it has changed the role of local governments from providers of public services according to local needs and demands, to enablers or facilitators of a range of policies decided on by central government or by the market. By enabling is meant the assessment of needs, and the organisation and purchase of services to meet them, rather than the direct provision of services by local authorities. At best, the 'enabling authority' is the central player that co-ordinates formal and informal networks of organisations (government bodies, quangos, businesses, and voluntary organisations) that think imaginatively about local problems and the public services to solve them. At worst, enabling means reducing the political power of local authorities and degrading the quality of local services. It may also cause the further erosion of the link between citizens and local services.

BRIEFINGS

12.4 Politicisation of local government in Britain

Party politics were introduced into local government by the Conservatives who organised themselves locally after the 1867 and 1884 Reform Acts in order to try to capture the vote of the newly enfranchised population. For the first half of the twentieth century however, local government in Britain was relatively free of party politics. Elections in the large urban areas were organised along party lines and councillors organised into party groups, but many councillors in the smaller and rural authorities were labelled 'independents', 'ratepayers', or 'homeowners', although they were often Conservatives in all but name. Many seats in local elections were uncontested, and many councillors were willing to serve the community provided they were spared the embarrassment of an election. From the 1960s onwards, more seats were contested, and candidates increasingly stood as representatives for the main national parties. Majority parties (sometimes coalitions) took control of committees and the leadership of the council.

The politicisation of local government reached new heights in the 1980s, which saw fierce battles between opposing party groups over such contentious issues as council house sales, secondary education and the poll tax. Some left-wing inner city councils also became associated with a variety of issues (gay rights and nuclear policy), which infuriated the Conservative government. It reacted with the abolition of the Greater London Council and the six metropolitan authorities, and the progressive reduction of local government responsibilities and taxing capacity.

At the 1984 Conservative Conference the government announced that the Widdecombe Committee would look into the conduct of local councils. It recommended a number of reforms to strengthen local democracy, but the major legislation stemming from the committee involved a ban on the use of local authority resources for politically motivated publicity and advertising.

Some commentators argue that the link is weak in Britain because local government is little more than an agent of central government and the provider of its national services. The link is also weak because local elections are fought by national political parties, and local elections are simply mini-versions of general elections – they are not won or lost on local issues or according to local party performance, but according to how central government is doing. Local democracy has, according to this argument, simply merged into national democracy.

Some on the political right go further and claim that market provision of services is the best guarantee of quality and value for money, so there is little need for elected local government. Such a perspective is difficult to reconcile with the fact that the vast majority of the public do regard a range of services as best provided by government, and that local provision is the best guarantee of public accountability. Whether it is market forces or political accountability that matters, it is worth noting the striking fact that emerges from most surveys on the matter – most citizens are well satisfied with their local government services.

BRIEFINGS

12.5 **Satisfaction with local services?**

It is certainly true that local services have been subjected to strong criticism in certain instances, and service quality may have suffered during the poll tax years, but generally speaking most people seem to be satisfied with their services most of the time:

1. The **Audit Commission**: 'The best of local government is better than the private sector and much better than the NHS or Whitehall at delivering services.'

2. The **Consumers' Association**: two-thirds thought local services good value for money and 80 per cent were satisfied overall.

3. The **Widdecombe Committee**: more than 70 per cent of respondents were very or fairly satisfied with the performance of their councils.

In many political systems accountability is maintained by a close link between locally raised taxes and payment for local services. In Britain this link has been eroded by ever increasing central control over local government finance. As a white paper on local government finance concluded in 1986: 'Local accountability depends crucially on the relationship between paying for local services and voting in local elections. As this link has been evaded so local democracy has been weakened.'

AN EXPANDING ROLE FOR LOCAL DEMOCRACY?

The second view argues not in terms of local public services, but in terms of democracy. The role of enabler and facilitator is not at all trivial, for it gives councils some power to decide from whom to purchase services, and how best to deliver them. It also releases them from the detailed supervision of administration to concentrate on relations with local citizens, who, of course, are customers for services. Besides, the political and representative role of local councils may also become more important, now that the European dimension is opening up and there is a precedent for standing up to national government on local concerns. Both democracy and the cost and quality of local services are concerns of New Labour, which has put local government through yet another set of reforms.

NEW LABOUR: LOCAL DEMOCRACY REVIVED?

As with central administration (Chapter 7) New Labour has left some Thatcher–Major reforms in place, but changed others. It is revealing to list the things it has accepted:

1. **Boundaries and structure**   The old local government boundaries have been left intact, and the old structures largely so (see Figure 12.1).

2. **Powers**   Local government has, so far, been left with pretty much the same set of service responsibilities as before.

3. **Finance**   Although it is not setting global limits, central government keeps the power to control local authority spending, with reserve powers to cap council tax where it is thought to be too high.

In other words, the overall shape of local government as handed down by Thatcher and Major has been accepted (there is much to be said for leaving things to settle down after the turmoil of the 1980s) and local government remains under the close control and supervision of central government. Nonetheless, some highly important changes have been introduced as well, mainly by the Local Government Acts of 1999 and 2000:

New organisation   The Local Government Act 2000 gives local authorities four options for new political structures. In effect the new system creates a local executive (leader/mayor and cabinet), and a legislative council and committees with monitoring and scrutinising powers – along Westminster lines. Supporters of the reforms argue that this encourages modern political management, opponents that is simply creates a new local political elite.

Best values options   Local authorities now have the choice of contracting out services under the old CCT system, or of delivering the service itself. Either way it must produce a performance plan, showing that it has chosen the 'best value' option, and have this plan approved by the Best Value Inspectorate, which is part of the Audit Commission. Councils that do not meet national standards may lose their service powers. Hackney and Leeds have had some education transferred to private direction for this reason.

Services   The Local Government Act 2000 gives local authorities the power to promote the economic, social, and environmental well-being of their communities. Authorities which are judged to perform well in these and other services areas can be awarded 'beacon' status, which gives them some extra autonomy from central government and some extra taxing capacity.

BRIEFINGS

12.6 New Labour's council constitutions

1. **Leader and cabinet** The leader is elected by the council, and the Cabinet is either appointed by the leader or elected by the council from a single party or a coalition of parties. The great majority of councils (82 per cent) have chosen this option.

2. **Directly elected mayor and Cabinet** The mayor is directly elected by the population for a four-year term of office, and selects a Cabinet from among the members of the council who belong to a majority party or a coalition. Ten councils (4 per cent) have chosen this option.

3. **Mayor and council manager** Imported from the USA, this system has a directly elected mayor who is similar to a non-executive chairperson in a business, and a manager who is a powerful chief executive with responsibility for both policy and management. Only the city of Stoke on Trent has chosen this option.

4. **Alternative arrangements** Available to councils with a population of less than 85,000, or those that have rejected a referendum for an elected mayor, this system creates a council with greater policy-making powers, and a more streamlined committee system. Fifty-nine councils (15 per cent) have chosen this option.

Local strategic partnerships with the shift from service provision to facilitating, and from local government to local governance, local authorities are now supposed to enter into partnerships to produce public services with public agencies and quangos, businesses, and voluntary organisations. In Tony Blair's words their 'distinctive leadership role will be to weave and knit together the contribution of various stakeholders', rather than directly to deliver all these services themselves. Public/private partnerships (PPPs) and Private Finance Initiatives (PFIs) are to be the main instruments of local governance.

London government Reform of London government has had a lot of media attention, partly because a directly elected mayor and 25-member assembly are genuinely radical innovations, and partly because the unofficial Labour candidate, Ken Livingstone, easily saw off his Conservative and Labour opponents, to the embarrassment of the Labour government.

Electoral systems The Greater London Authority, the Scottish and Welsh Assembly, and directly elected mayors are elected by the supplementary vote system, not the first past the post system (see Chapter 15).

Devolution The creation of the Scottish Assembly with powers to restructure local government is likely to result in reforms, particularly in the electoral system, although none has been implemented yet. The Welsh Assembly has more limited powers to amend but not make primary legislation about local government.

The question is whether these accumulated changes will do much for local democracy, when the basic structure inherited from the 1980s and early 1990s is left in place. Reviving local democracy would seem to call for a fairly radical reform which gives local government real control over local taxes and services. Anything else may help to improve service quality, which may well be New Labour's main concern, but is unlikely to do much for a vibrant local democracy.

Improving local democracy

The problem Local election turnout is lower in the UK than almost any other western democracy, and falling; local government units are larger than in almost any other western democracy; local government has fewer financial powers than most other western democracies; and local government is subject to closer control by national government than in most other western democracies. New Labour is much concerned by low and falling election turnout and community participation.

Some solutions?

1. Create smaller authorities to encourage local democracy. The problem is that local election turnout is not closely related to local authority size.

2. Change the voting system to one that is more proportional. This may increase local election turnout, but not a lot. However, it would break one-party (largely Labour) dominance of councils.

3. Allow local authorities to create small area committees (as the Local Government Act 2000 does) to encourage community participation. The problem is that community and parish councils do not arouse great participatory enthusiasm.

4. Create directly elected mayors and cabinets. Executive mayors may attract local interest (eg Ken Livingstone). The danger is that they may make local decision making less democratic by creating a strong executive and a weak council that does not attract active or high-calibre members. Concentrating attention on mayors may also erode interest in the lower tier of city government.

5. Create unitary authorities because the two-tier system is confusing and lacks direct accountability. The problem is that election turnout in unitary authorities is not much different from two-tier authorities.

6. Give local authorities more power, so that electors know that serious decisions are taken at the local level. Most know that local government does not count as much as central government and so few take much interest or know much about local affairs. Surveys show that if something went wrong with council decisions, citizens are as likely to turn to their MP as their local councillor. There are various ways of giving local authorities more power:

> Give more discretion over local taxation. Central grants would still be necessary, to ensure equalisation of financial capacity between rich and poor areas, but they could be reduced considerably.

> Give local government more service responsibilities, so reversing the trend of the last 70 or 80 years.

> Remove the dead hand of *ultra vires*, giving local authorities more discretion. The Scottish Parliament may take up this option.

> Reduce the amount of local government regulation, monitoring, and control of local services. New Labour is currently making the central regime tighter, not looser.

It seems that the most effective way of improving local democracy, participation, and election turnout is to give local government more power over its tax options and services. The problem is that while most post-war governments have paid lip service to more local autonomy, they have actually tightened central control. There is however, a last option, which should not be forgotten.

7. Forget about local democracy, and concentrate on improving local service quality and efficiency. Repeated surveys show that citizens are generally quite satisfied with local services. Perhaps one way ahead is simply to recognise that local democracy is not particularly important in the British system of government, and concentrate instead on raising service performance to a still higher level?

SUMMARY

Perhaps more than any other sphere of British life, local politics have reflected the heightened ideological confrontations and clashes of the 1980s, but we may now be moving into quieter waters. This chapter has highlighted:

- the mutual dependency of central and local government in Britain, which produces conflict when political control is divided

- repeated reorganisations, both territorial and functional

- politicisation, privatisation and deregulation, which transformed local government into a 'facilitator' rather than a direct provider of local services

- finance, especially the poll tax, a local issue that for the first time brought down a Prime Minister

- the precarious constitutional and political position of sub-national government in Britain (in many democracies state, provincial or local governments have constitutionally protected status or their position is secured by long-established traditions)

- the limited renewal of local democracy with the election of a Labour government in 1997, not least in Scotland, Wales and London. However, New Labour seems more concerned with trying to improve local services by means of central controls, inspectors, and audits, and by means of strengthened local political executives, than reviving local democracy. It is highly unlikely that Labour will give new taxing powers to local governments. In this sense, the close accountability linkage between local voters, local taxation and local policies, which is the essence of local democracy in many countries, is unlikely to develop in Britain.

MILESTONES

Milestones in local government in Britain

1888 and 1894 Local Government Acts create the local government structure that prevails until the 1970s

1966 Creation of the Greater London Council

1967 Redcliffe-Maud Commission on Local Government

1972 Local Government Act rationalises the system of local government and creates metropolitan counties and districts

1975 Local government reorganised in Scotland

1976 Local Government and Planning Act: overspending curbed, sale of council houses compulsory

1984–6 GLC and metropolitan counties abolished. Local transport subsidies curbed

1986 Widdecombe Report recommends major changes in role of political parties in local government. Only minor changes made in the ensuing legislation

1987 Central government grants are fixed to expenditure

1988 Government announces abolition of rates, creation of community charge and uniform business rate, plus other measures including the opting out of schools

1989 Poll tax (community charge) introduced in Scotland

1990 Poll tax introduced in England and Wales

1991 Government announces phasing out of poll tax and introduction of a replacement council tax

1994–6 Two-tier local government systems abolished in Scotland and Wales. Some unitary authorities created in England

1997 Referendum in Scotland produces a four to one majority for the creation of a Scottish Parliament and three to one majority for the Parliament to have tax-raising powers. Referendum in Wales produces a very small majority for a Welsh Assembly. Plans for devolution to English regions in doubt

1998 Referendum on directly elected executive mayor for London. Local Government Act introduces best value system

2000 Local Government Act introduces directly elected mayors and Cabinet. Representation of the People Act – directly elected mayors elected by the supplementary vote system. Independent candidate Ken Livingstone elected as first Mayor of London

FURTHER READING

A comprehensive and up-to-date textbook is T. Byrne, *Local Government in Britain* (London: Penguin Books, 7th edn, 2000). Another textbook treatment is provided by J. A. Chandler, *Local Government Today* (Manchester: Manchester University Press, 1996). A stimulating collection of essays on local democracy is found in Gerry Stoker (ed.), *The New Politics of British Local Government* (Basingstoke: Macmillan, 2000). The definitive study of central–local relations is R. A. W. Rhodes, *Control and Power in Central Local Relations* (Aldershot: Ashgate, 1999). Recent organisational changes are covered by Steve Leach and Janie Percy Smith, *Local Governance in Britain* (Basingstoke: Macmillan, 2000).

For shorter and more recent work see J. A. Chandler, 'The Blair administration and local government', *Talking Politics*, **13** (3), 2001, pp. 176–82; S. Leach, 'Democratic renewal: Cabinet and elected mayors in local government', *Politics Review*, **10** (2), 2000, pp. 6–8; M. Cole, 'The changing governance of London', *Talking Politics*, **13** (1), 2000, pp. 22–5; and L. Pratchett, 'Local government: from modernisation to consolidation', *Parliamentary Affairs*, **55**, 2002, pp. 331–46.

PROJECTS

1. Playing the role of an expert consultant who has been called in to advise the Minister of State for Local Government and the Regions, lay out the arguments for the different systems of local taxation outlined in Briefing 12.2.

2. (For class discussion) Divide the class into small working teams, each to formulate its own plan for dividing different public services between central and local government. Make sure that you consider national defence, macro economic planning, education, health, housing, transport, EU affairs, parks, police, fire, and libraries. Come back together in the class to compare your plans.

3. Imagine your local authority is to have a referendum on the three forms of local mayor/leader and Cabinet government outlined by the Local Government Act 2000. Which would you vote for and why?

USEFUL WEB SITES ON LOCAL DEMOCRACY

Hotlinks to these sites can be found on the CWS website at http://www.booksites.net/budge.

Although Britain has a highly centralised form of government, local councils offer a fundamental channel of representation for citizens. The first step is to visit the Local Government Association (www.lga.gov.uk) and the New Local Government Network (www.nlgn.org.uk). The Central and Local Government Information Partnership (CLIP) was set up to enable central and local government to work together to develop an efficient and effective infrastructure for policy development, implementation, monitoring and reporting, visit their web site at www.clip.gov.uk. The Improvement and Development Agency (IDeA) was established by and for local government in April 1999, their mission is to support self-sustaining improvement from within local government, visit them at www.idea.gov.uk.

The Local Government Association Parliamentary Monitoring and Intelligence Service (PAMIS), provides specialist coverage of the activities of Parliament as they affect local government, you can find them at www.pamis.gov.uk. The Local Government Ombudsman (www.lgo.org.uk) investigates complaints of injustice arising from misadministration by local authorities and certain other bodies. The Institute of Local Government Studies (University of Birmingham) provides valuable academic insights into the problems arising in relation to local government and administration. Visit also the National Association of Local Councils at www.nalc.gov.uk.

There are also a number of independent associations engaged in the expansion of local democracy; a good example is Localis (www.localis.org.uk). For direct access to data about local government elections visit the Local Government Chronicle's specialist web site maintained by the University of Plymouth at www.politics.plymouth.ac.uk/lgecentre.

PART 4
Popular Participation

Anti-war demonstration in Downing St

Pressure groups

The political institutions we have examined in previous chapters all operate in the context of an open society, where various interests and groups compete to have their concerns recognised and enforced by governments. Although we often read about 'public opinion' on political issues there is no such thing. There are many public opinions because society consists of a complex and variegated patchwork of social groupings divided according to age, gender, ethnicity, class, education, religion, region, occupation, history, culture, and social and political values. Each of these has a characteristic set of interests and opinions, and each forms itself into voluntary associations that express their common interests and organises collective action to promote them. There is a great number and variety of voluntary organisations and associations, including charities, community associations, social clubs, youth clubs, churches, educational, scientific and cultural associations, sports clubs, and occupational groups for businesspeople, trade unionists, and professionals.

Voluntary associations play a vital role in society and politics. They constitute what is often termed 'civil' or 'pluralist' society – an organised sector of society that is outside government and not controlled by it. They are important because, on the one hand, they help to give people a sense of belonging and social involvement, and allow them to co-operate to achieve collective goals. On the other hand, they are also one of the most important ways that citizens can express their democratic rights to be heard and influence government. Most ordinary citizens do not wield any political influence as individuals; if they do so at all, it is through the collective action of their voluntary associations.

This chapter looks at the role and influence of pressure groups in government – both Britain and the EU. It is divided into seven main sections:

- voluntary associations and civil society
- voluntary organisations and politics
- pressure groups, parties, and social movements
- how groups operate: tactics and targets
- the impact of groups
- Thatcher, Blair, and pressure groups
- pressure groups and democracy.

VOLUNTARY ASSOCIATIONS AND CIVIL SOCIETY

Voluntary associations have roots deep in British society. Statistics about them tend to vary a little from one research report to another, because they depend on the particular definitions and questionnaire wording, but most studies (see Tables 13.1–13.3) show that:

- about half of adult citizens are members of at least one voluntary organisation, and a minority are members of a good many of them

	(percentages of population aged 15 and over)					
	France	Germany	Italy	UK	Sweden	Portugal
Sports	19	29	11	20	36	10
Environment	4	7	2	8	15	1
Trade unions and political parties	4	8	4	11	51	3
Social and charity	4	8	8	10	13	4
Religious	3	6	7	11	5	4
Hobbies	2	11	1	11	19	1
Cultural, art	10	4	5	5	10	5
Consumer	1	1	1	1	19	1
Human rights	2	1	2	2	7	0
Youth	2	2	1	5	4	1
Other	8	7	4	7	11	3
Not a member of any group	60	47	66	47	15	74
Member of one group	31	33	25	30	26	21
Member of two or more groups	12	20	8	23	58	6

Table 13.1 *Voluntary organisation membership, western Europe, 1998*

Note: The table shows figures for the four largest countries of western Europe, plus Sweden and Portugal, which tend to be at the high and low ends of organisational membership

Source: *Eurobarometer*, 50.1, Autumn 1998

Table 13.2 *Percentage who are not members of any voluntary organisation in the UK, 1959–98*

1959	1977	1983	1987	1990	1998
52	46	42	47	39	47

Source: K. Aarts, 'Intermediate organisations and interest representation', in H.-D. Klingemann and D. Fuchs (eds), *Citizens and the State*, Oxford: Oxford University Press, 1995, p. 232, and Table 13.1

Table 13.3 *Voluntary associations in Birmingham, 1970 and 1998*

	1970	1998
Sports	2,144	1,192
Social welfare	666	1,319
Cultural	388	507
Trade associations	176	71
Professional	165	112
Social	142	398
Churches	138	848
Forces	122	114
Youth	76	268
Technical and scientific	76	41
Educational	66	475
Trade unions	55	42
Health	50	309
Other	–	75
Total	4,264	5,781

Source: William A. Malone, Graham Smith, and Gerry Stoker, 'Social capital and associational life', in Stephen Baron et al (eds), *Social Capital*, Oxford: Oxford University Press, 2000, p. 220

- Britain has quite a high density of voluntary organisations by western European standards, though by no means the highest

- the number and variety of organisations is astonishingly broad, covering almost every conceivable kind of human activity

- although membership is fairly widely spread in society, 'joiners' tend to be concentrated among the educated, middle and upper class, middle aged, and male sections of the population

- contrary to some claims that voluntary associations are in decline, the general trend for the number of organisations and the number of memberships is stable or upwards. Decline is found in trade unions, many traditional women's organisations and charities, and (recently) in political parties but the trend is upwards for environmental groups, youth clubs, outdoor recreational organisations, educational, and community groups.

Civil society

Civil society
The aspects of social and economic life (primarily voluntary associations and private organisations) that are outside the immediate control of the state. A strong civil society based on a large number and wide variety of private associations and organisations is thought to be the basis for democracy.

The idea of civil society was important in the classical political theory of the seventeen and eighteenth centuries, when absolute monarchy was still strong and democracy in its infant stages. The basic idea was that some aspects of social life should be independent of the state and its rulers, and that people should be free to organise their own lives in their own way, particularly the medieval guilds that regulated employers, tradesmen, and workers. Such groups could provide the foundations for organised political opposition to political tyranny.

Civil society is no less important in modern democracies. A strong civil society has a great diversity of active voluntary associations, many of which have little to do with politics most of the time. However, they provide the organisational basis for civic involvement and collective action that is not regulated by the state. They give people experience of managing their own affairs and teach the civic virtues of co-operation and compromise in the pursuit of common goals. They also provide the social foundations of political discussion and action, if and when this is thought necessary. In this respect it is noticeable that one of the first things dictators do when they come to power is try to get control of voluntary organisations, knowing they are dangerous bases of the struggle for freedom and democracy. The term civil society has come back into fashion recently, particularly to describe the social foundations necessary to sustain democracy in central and eastern Europe, where, under communism, citizen organisations and associations were closely controlled by the state.

Mass society
A society composed of isolated individuals who, because they have no deep roots in community and social life (civil society is weak), are liable to manipulation by political elites.

One variant of civil society theory argues that mass societies with weak civic groups and voluntary associations are especially prone to anti-democratic movements and the seizure of power by autocratic politicians. Mass societies are composed of isolated individuals who have weak links with other citizens, and few voluntary associations and community organisations. Anti-democratic elites find it easier to control and manipulate citizens without social roots and ties, compared with citizens who have vibrant and independent associations of their own.

VOLUNTARY ORGANISATIONS AND POLITICS

Some voluntary associations are set up for political purposes – trade unions and environmental action groups, for example – but a large majority are not political at all. They are interested in football, growing roses, or amateur dramatics. Indeed, the main attraction and strength of these groups is that they are not primarily political, but can be mobilised to take political action if the circumstances require it. No matter how remote from politics a group may seem, it can easily be affected by events that oblige it to take political action. Football clubs, for example, do not attract their fans by talking politics, but safety at stadiums, football hooliganism, and the closure of the Wembley Stadium have been recent issues that have drawn the Football Association into politics.

A surprisingly large proportion of ostensibly non-political groups do get involved in politics from time to time, and research shows that apart from voting, most citizen political activity is prompted by associations. This finding serves to underline the conclusion that groups are relevant to government and politics in two important but different ways:

1. Voluntary associations have an indirect effect on politics in that they help to create stable social foundations, social integration, and civic engagement, all of which are important for democracy.

2. Voluntary associations have a direct effect on politics when they become politically involved and prompt their members to take political action of some kind. Some voluntary associations are created for political reasons, but most are only intermittently engaged in politics.

The rest of this chapter will be concerned with the directly political role of voluntary associations.

BRIEFINGS

13.1 Political participation in Britain

The most authoritative study of the extent to which people undertake political action shows that, apart from voting, most action is stimulated by social groups. About 14 per cent of adults take part in informal group activity and 11 per cent in organised group activity to do with politics (such as writing letters or distributing leaflets to express concerns). Twenty-one per cent had contacted a local councillor and almost 15 per cent had attended meetings to protest against some policy. Sixty-three per cent had signed a petition.

Most people do not do these things very often: three or four of them are undertaken in a five-year period. When they do, however, it is generally at the prompting of some group that organises the action. (The percentages are from Geraint Parry, George Moser and Neil Day, *Political Participation and Democracy in Britain*, Cambridge: Cambridge University Press, 1992.)

PRESSURE GROUPS, POLITICAL PARTIES, AND SOCIAL MOVEMENTS

'Pressure groups' is the term generally applied to social groups when they get involved in politics. Political parties, of course, are voluntary associations that are political, but they differ from pressure groups in four ways:

1. Parties want to become the government, pressure groups only want to influence government. Action on Smoking and Health (ASH), for example, wants to influence a part of government policy, but does not want to fill the elected offices of state.

2. Parties have broad policy interests, pressure groups generally have narrow ones. The Countryside Alliance is concerned only with issues related to the countryside and its way of life.

3. Parties are primarily political, pressure groups are not. Many try to avoid politics as much as possible. The Ramblers' Association becomes involved in politics only when issues arise that are dear to its heart.

4. Parties fight elections, most pressure groups do not. The British Medical Association (BMA) is a powerful pressure group, but it does not run for political office, although one medical pressure group, The Kidderminster Hospital group, fought and won a seat in the 2001 general election.

Plate 13.1 *Single-issue politics: 'tree people' protesting at the site of the Newbury Bypass demonstration*

Source: PA News

At the same time there is no clear distinction between parties and pressure groups in any of these four ways. Some groups have broad policy interests, for example the Trades Union Congress (TUC) and the Confederation of British Industries (CBI). Some (eg Friends of the Earth, Gingerbread) are inextricably bound up with politics because they were set up as pressure groups with a political agenda. Some groups fight elections, although often they seem more interested in publicity than in winning. Others do not fight elections themselves, although some (the TUC, the NFU) sponsor candidates for Parliament. One thing is clear, however: while there are few political parties, the range, diversity and number of pressure groups is enormous.

Pressure groups and new social movements

New social movements (NSMs) differ from both political parties and pressure groups while sharing some characteristics of both. They are marked by four main features:

New social movements
Organisations that emerged in the 1970s in order to influence public policy about such issues as the environment, nuclear energy and weapons, peace, women and minorities. They have wider policy interests than most pressure groups, but are more loosely knit than political parties.

1. **Organisationally**, they are less bureaucratic and hierarchical than traditional parties and pressure groups, consisting of loose-knit networks of networks – rainbow alliances.

2. **Ideologically**, they have broader objectives than most pressure groups, but narrower ones than the parties.

3. Their **methods** are often innovative, direct and eye catching – such as the opponents of the Newbury Bypass who lived in trees and underground tunnels to obstruct building work; or Greenpeace, which sailed its boat, the *Rainbow Warrior*, into nuclear test zones. They often emphasise direct political action and community involvement.

4. Their **membership**, as befits rainbow alliances, often cuts across normal social divisions of class and left–right politics, bringing together different social groups. The 'crusties' of the anti-road movement combined with the 'Land Rover and green welly' country set to defend the countryside.

In some respects there is nothing particularly new about new social movements. The most famous in British history is probably the Chartist movement of the mid-nineteenth century, which brought together a broad alliance of liberal, working class, and left-wing interests to press for political reform. However, it is the movements that emerged in the 1970s and 1980s that attract attention now – the movements for women, the environment, peace, minorities, the anti-nuclear movement, and for animal rights. They are known not just for their reformist goals but also for their unconventional methods of direct political action. For this reason it was claimed that the new movements would undermine the centralised, hierarchical and bureaucratic nature of conventional politics, as practised by the old parties and pressure groups. New social movements were said to be better adapted to the fluid and fragmented social groupings of postmodern and post-industrial society. They were described as 'anti-political', that is anti-traditional, or anti-system. The idea that new social movements would replace the politics of the old parties and pressure groups was strengthened when the membership of parties and trade unions began to decline in the 1980s and 1990s.

Plate 13.2 *Nuclear demonstrators gather outside the French Embassy in London, 6 September 1995, to protest against nuclear tests at the Muroroa Atoll in the South Pacific*

Source: PA News

However, the old parties and many of the old pressure groups proved more resilient than this and responded to the NSM threat. Some had been advocating new social movement goals for a long time (political power for women, animal rights, peace, minority rights), and they simply responded by making them more prominent in their political agenda. Most parties and groups had grassroots organisations and a mass membership already, and they tried to strengthen them. In fact, community organisation in Britain was not pioneered by new social movements, but by the Liberal Party in Birmingham, whose leader in the 1960s, Wallace Lawler, placed a high priority on party organisation in the localities. In the 1990s New Labour has tried with some success to forge a new and broad alliance of interests on which to build its revival. There is no doubt that the new social movements have had an impact on British politics, but they have been added to the old system, and changed it rather than transformed it. They operate alongside the parties and pressure groups, but they have not replaced them.

A last comment on the term 'pressure group' should be made here. Some dislike the term 'pressure group' because they think it implies the use of sanctions, coercion, or illegitimate pressure. They prefer the term 'lobby' or 'interest groups'. Nonetheless, the collective term 'pressure groups' is used for good reasons:

1. Pressure does not necessarily entail illegitimate pressures or sanctions. It may involve nothing more sinister than information or advice.

2. Strictly speaking the term 'interest group' applies to a special kind of pressure group.

3. The term lobby derives from the idea that pressure groups congregate in the lobby of the House of Commons where they can whisper in the ears of MPs. In fact few pressure groups get near the lobby of the Commons. They use quite different methods – as we will shortly see.

13.2 **Types of pressure group**

Pressure groups come in so many shapes and sizes that any attempt to classify them inevitably runs into trouble. For example, interest groups are primarily concerned with the occupational interests of their members, and cause groups promote a wider range of concerns and values. By the same token, the National Union of Farmers (an interest group) argues that it wants to preserve the rural way of life (a cause). Similarly the National Union of Teachers (also an interest group) is concerned with teachers' salaries, and with the quality of education (just like educational cause groups). Similarly, trade unions are less closely aligned with the Labour Party than they used to be, while environmental groups have moved from being outsider to semi-insider groups. Consequently, none of the following categories is watertight but, nevertheless, they are generally helpful in the analysis of the pressure group world.

Interest groups Interest (or sectional) groups represent the interests of occupational groups, mainly business organisations, professional associations and trade unions. Major examples include the Institute of Directors, the British Medical Association, and the Transport and General Workers Union. The National Union of Students (NUS) is also an interest group. Such organisations are mainly (not exclusively) concerned with material (mainly economic) interests.

Cause groups Cause groups (promotional or attitude groups) promote a general cause or idea. Membership is not limited to particular occupations, and the range of interests covered is very wide – religion, education, culture and art, leisure, sport, charity and welfare, community, social, youth, and science. Major examples include the Royal Society for the Protection of Birds (RSPB), Shelter (a housing action group), the Consumers' Association, and Amnesty International.

New social movements These political organisations have broader concerns than many interest and cause groups, but are more loosely knit than political parties.

Episodic groups These groups are not normally political, but may become so when circumstances require (eg the Rum Importers Association).

Fire brigade groups Such groups are formed to fight a specific issue, and dissolve when it is over (eg the Anti-Poll Tax Federation).

Peak associations Peak associations are 'umbrella' organisations that co-ordinate the activities of different pressure groups in the same area of interest. Examples include the Confederation of British Industry (CBI) and the Trades Union Congress (TUC), but equivalents exist for many other areas of activity. There are also international peak associations (Save the Children, Amnesty International, the Red Cross, the International Labour Organisation) that operate across the globe.

Insider groups Groups with easy access to government officials and decision-making bodies. Insider groups (sometimes called established groups) usually speak for legitimate and mainstream interests in society. Most professional associations have an official status within policy-making bodies and some groups are legally entitled to be consulted, for example the National Farmers' Union in the annual farm prices review. Insider groups pay for their privileged status by playing the rules of the Whitehall and Westminster game, which means not being too critical of ministers, and behaving 'responsibly'.

Outsider groups Outsider groups do not have easy access to officials or decision makers. They are kept at arm's length because of who or what they represent. Examples include the Campaign for Nuclear Disarmament (CND) and the Animal Liberation Front. Not all groups want greater insider status, because they fear that they might become 'domesticated' by being too closely involved with government. Sometimes groups move from an outsider to more of an insider status, as the environmental groups did in the late 1980s.

Crossbench groups Some groups are inevitably aligned with a particular party, but others try to maintain party neutrality, knowing that they must deal with whichever party is in power. They are called crossbench groups after crossbench (non-party) members of the House of Lords.

The pressure group world

The group world has three main features, already hinted at: its huge numbers, its great diversity, and the density of its networks.

NUMBERS

There are hundreds of thousands of organised groups in the country, so many that it is virtually impossible to count them. A few are continuously active in politics, but others are only sporadically involved. Government now affects so many people and interests that tens – if not hundreds – of thousands of groups are likely to be politically active in national and local politics at any given time.

DIVERSITY

There is a huge variety of pressure groups, covering almost every conceivable interest, and coming in many forms – large and small, loose knit and highly organised, strong and weak, rich and poor. The size and diversity of the group world means that the political arena is crowded with groups, and there are often rival groups fighting each other on their own issues – for example, fox hunting, abortion, gun control, road building, joining the euro, Scottish and Welsh independence.

NETWORKS

Most groups are organised like a pyramid, with many local branches at the bottom, area and regional organisations in the middle, and national and international bodies at the top. At the same time, many local groups are integrated into a parallel structure of umbrella organisations, also with a pyramid that reaches from local associations to national and international headquarters. This sort of complex web of horizontal and vertical links is found among trade unions, professional associations, business associations, charities, churches, sports, women's organisations, and environmental groups.

HOW GROUPS OPERATE: TACTICS AND TARGETS

There are two general rules for pressure group operations. First, get into the policy making cycle as early as possible, when options are being considered, before government takes a position, and the political parties draw public battle lines. Second, work at the highest possible level of the political system to which you have access, because that is where the least effort has the greatest influence. These two general rules means that there is usually a preferred hierarchy of pressure points.

Civil servants

Efficient and effective groups usually start with civil servants. First, much pressure group activity does not concern great policy issues, as many assume, but detailed and technical matters that are usually handled by middle-ranking Whitehall officials. Second, the policy cycle often starts and ends with the civil servants who draft the early documents and implement final policy decisions, so it is sensible to concentrate early efforts on them. Third, groups try to get their views established before the issue is politicised by government and opposition parties. 'Insider' groups have the advantage of close working relations with Whitehall because both need and use the other: groups provide civil servants with technical information and practical advice; civil servants provide groups with inside political information, and are channels of communication to ministers. Early consultation may avoid much trouble later on.

Ministers and the Cabinet

Civil servants cannot 'deliver' their ministers, any more than ministers can guarantee their proposals being accepted by the Cabinet. If an issue is already politicised, then groups may have to go to Westminster to press their case. They will start with ministers and members of the government, if they can, because this is where the power lies. Insider groups may have access to this high level, where much may be accomplished by small, private meetings – perhaps in Whitehall committee rooms or in London clubs. Outsider groups do not have such access, so use other methods which tend to be more expensive, time consuming and uncertain.

Westminster

Groups that fail to convince the government, or have no access to it, may turn to the House of Commons, although it is a larger and more uncertain arena than the Cabinet or Whitehall offices. Nevertheless, many pressure groups approach Parliament, and most MPs could fill their days just reading mountains of pressure group mail, and receiving delegations. Wealthier groups may employ professional lobbyists with contacts and experience. Groups with a sympathetic MP have been able to take advantage of private members' bills in the Commons (with pressure group assistance the laws on abortion and homosexuality have been changed this way), and some well-connected groups can influence legislative details. Some groups can present their views to Parliamentary committees, others can influence party backbench committees.

Political parties

Groups with strong links to a political party will use them to try to influence party policy. The League Against Cruel Sports and the Howard League for Penal Reform have sympathisers in the Labour Party, and the Electoral Reform Society with the Liberal Democrats. Business and trade organisations have natural links with the Conservatives. However, most groups try to maintain a crossbench status so they can work with whichever party is in power.

BRIEFINGS

13.3 Affecting the detail of legislation

In 1996 a very detailed measure requiring water to be supplied to caravan sites was being considered in a Parliamentary standing committee.

It was uncontroversial and the need was not disputed by the parties. The Country Landowners' Association (CLA), however, was concerned about who would bear the expenses of installing the water-points, the proprietor or the water company. CLA members would gain financially if responsibility were put on water companies by the legislation, and so it was extremely active in the committee, using both professional lobbyists and interested MPs (some of them members of the Association).

The water companies had, of course, spotted this possibility, and they employed consultants and lobbyists too. However, more MPs were landowners than shareholders in water companies, so the CLA had the advantage.

This case illustrates several points:

- even very technical legislation or administration will have consequences for groups' interests
- groups benefiting will often be opposed by groups that might lose, resulting in pluralist debate and politics
- however, the group with more resources will usually win
- given the network of connections between MPs and social groups, there is a very thin line between legitimate 'lobbying' and corruption, especially when MPs are able to avoid declaring an interest. There were a series of scandals under the Major government involving MPs and professional lobbyists.

Local councils

Many pressure groups have purely local objectives: opposition to a new road, support for parking restrictions or traffic controls, better schools. In such cases the natural target is the local council. Even where the issue is a national one, it pays to get the local council on your side. As a popularly elected body it has a legitimate claim to represent local opinion, and resources and expertise to influence central policy. Councils took an increasing number of cases to the courts in the 1980s, even as far as the European Court.

Public campaigns and the mass media

Public campaigns are often the last resort of pressure groups, but less so than they were, given the ability of some groups (Greenpeace, Animal Rights Groups, opponents of GM crops, Stop the War in Iraq) to mobilise supporters or attract attention. But in spite of modern mailshot and advertising techniques, public campaigns tend to be expensive, time consuming and unpredictable. Some groups use advertising firms – also costly – and most also use personal contacts with journalists. Some groups try to get media coverage by the headline hitting methods of demonstrations, protests, petitions, sit-ins, civil disobedience, or violence against people or property. Email and web site campaigns are increasingly used.

Courts

Some groups have taken their cases to court (equal pay, the abolition of corporal punishment in Scottish schools), including the EU's Court of Justice in Luxembourg, and the Council of Europe's Court of Human Rights in Strasbourg. Most groups avoid legal action because it is costly and uncertain.

The European Union

The EU is so important that many groups have turned of lot of attention to it, especially to the Commission, as the main executive body. Consequently, there are now thousands of groups at work in Brussels, as there are in London. Most of them operate at the European level in one of four ways. The simplest is to set up an office to lobby in Brussels, but this is expensive and often groups look around for partners to share the cost. Second, they can combine with similar interests in other EU states to form a Eurogroup. The EU encourages and officially recognises over 1,000 such groups at present, but they tend to be rather weak and fragmented. Third, groups can form a European pressure group drawing support from EU countries. Fourth, groups can try to work through the British government, or regional governments, which takes us back into the kinds of action outlined earlier.

Policy networks and policy communities

Groups often use a combination of targets, but the most prestigious insider groups normally work smoothly and quietly by using their high-level contacts. Outsider groups have to use the noisier methods of public campaigns. Paradoxically, the quieter the group, the greater its influence; the more noisy and obstructive its tactics, the less influential it is likely to be. In some cases contacts between pressure groups and government are so tight that they form what is known as a policy community. The members of such communities are in close and constant contact with each other, and generally agree on the main issues in their policy arena. Policy communities have been formed around food and drink policy, farming, technical education, and water privatisation.

The biggest and most powerful policy community in Britain probably centres on the financial interests of the City of London, which reach into the heart of government through the Treasury and the Bank of England. The need to protect the currency and London's position as the leading financial centre is so obvious to government that the City needs to do little to ensure that its case is heeded. Thus financial interests in favour of high interest rates, to bring down inflation, have normally won out over manufacturing interests which favour low interest rates for expansion and investment.

Sometimes the relationship between Whitehall departments and pressure groups in a policy community is so close that there is a fear that department officials have, in effect, been taken over by the group – they 'go native'. This is a danger, of course, because governments and the Civil Service are supposed to protect the interests of the public at large, not those of a sectional group. Although it is

Policy communities
Small, stable, integrated and consensual groupings of government officials and pressure group leaders that form around particular issue areas.

Plate 13.3 *Fire Brigades Union demonstration: outside groups have to use noisier methods of public compaigns. The firefighters were a very vocal group, with considerable public backing; but they were unsuccessful under the Labour Government*

Source: www.paphotos.com

Policy networks
Compared with policy communities, policy (or issue) networks are larger, looser, less integrated and more conflictual networks of political actors in a given policy area.

difficult to say when this happens, if only because policy communities are by their very nature fairly closed circles of influence, the accusation has sometimes been made about decision making in farming, business, the defence industry, the legal system, and some areas of health policy.

More normally, however, circles of influence take the form of policy networks, policy communities are a special kind of policy network, but many networks are more open and conflictual than policy communities. Policy networks include not just government and core insider groups, but also a range of groups that hover between insider and outsider status, and perhaps even some outsider groups as well. Because a wider variety of opinions are included in networks, there is more disagreement, and decision making is more pluralist – it tends to spill over from Whitehall and Westminster into public arenas.

IMPACT OF PRESSURE GROUPS

So many factors affect the issues provoking pressure group campaigns that it is difficult to unravel the part played by any particular group or set of groups. For example, the death penalty was abolished in 1965 after a long campaign by many groups, but the changes in the law were also accompanied by a new government and the arrival of many new MPs, by a series of widely publicised miscarriages of justice, and by a shift in public opinion. This makes it difficult to know what is due to group pressures, or to other factors. Similarly, various environmental groups claim recent successes for their cause, but these have also been helped by media coverage of environmental incidents (nuclear accidents, petrol tanker disasters, burning rainforests), a shift in public opinion, and by pressure from the EU and other international bodies.

While it is impossible to pin down the exact influence of any particular group, their political power seems to depend partly on their own group characteristics, and partly on the characteristics of the environment they operate in.

Group features

Some of the internal features of groups that affect groups' influence are:

- **Membership size and type**   Groups with a large membership can raise money through subscriptions and contributions. With about one million members the Royal Society for the Protection of Birds (RSPB) has an annual income of over £51 million and runs a network of offices and shops around Britain. In 2000 it organised a petition with half a million signatures to maintain EU bird protection laws.

- **Money**   Some groups are wealthy because of the people and interests they represent. The National Farmers Union (NFU) has 150,000 members, and an income of £23 million, compared with Friends of the Earth whose membership and income are closer to 200,000 and £2 million. This is typical of the difference between interest groups of producers and cause groups of enthusiasts.

- **Organisational advantages**   Some groups are easier to organise than others. Interest group members are easily organised at work, but cause group sympathisers are often scattered, and potential members can be difficult to identify and contact. For this reason producer and occupational groups are far easier to organise than consumer and cause groups. Hospital doctors are easier to organise than hospital patients, producers easier than consumers, and teachers easier than pupils.

- **Membership density**   A group representing practically all its possible members (eg the British Medical Association with 100 per cent density) is in a stronger position than a trade union with 50 per cent density.

- **Divided membership**   The BMA speaks for almost all doctors; miners are divided between competing unions.

- **Internal structure**   Interest groups are often centralised, making political action easier. Cause groups are often more decentralised and participatory, making it difficult to respond quickly and effectively to events.

- **Sanctions**   Some groups have powerful sanctions: businesses may move capital easily; professional bodies may withdraw co-operation; some organisations can call on public sympathy. Other groups have few sanctions: the homeless cannot strike, withdraw co-operation, or move their investments.

- **Leadership**   A charismatic leader is an asset – eg William Wilberforce and the Abolition Society (for the abolition of slavery, one of the first pressure groups) in the late eighteenth century, and Frank Field (Child Poverty Action Group), Des Wilson (Shelter), and Jonathan Porritt (Friends of the Earth) in recent times.

The political environment

Features of the political environment that might affect the impact of pressure groups include:

- **Public opinion**   A group with public support is more likely to get a sympathetic hearing. The poor image of students hinders the negotiating power of the National Union of Students (NUS). Public opinion may also change (on environmental issues, for example), and it is not always important. Nurses seem to get a more sympathetic hearing in public than around negotiating tables.

- **Legitimacy**   A group that is thought to speak for legitimate interests – doctors, lawyers, teachers, business – is likely to get a better reception than one which does not – drug addicts, the unemployed, ex-criminals.

- **Insider status**   Insider groups are more likely to be successful than outsider groups – but not always.

- **Politicisation**   Much group activity concerns policy detail and technicality. On hot political issues groups usually have less room for manoeuvre, since they often compete with parties or other groups.

- **Opposing groups**   Some groups operate alone in their field of interest, especially on technical matters. Others face organised opposition, especially on moral matters such as blood sports, smoking, Sunday shopping and abortion. Groups involved in the same issue are not necessarily equally matched, however. The BMA is powerful, the Patients' Association much weaker.

- **Institutionalised power**   'Institutionalised power' occurs where the interests of a group are implicitly built into the very structures and cultures of decision making, so that the group often has to do very little to protect its interests. Feminists argue that such an institutional bias results in male supremacy, ethnic minorities talk of institutional racism, and workers and trade unionists refer to the 'capitalist system'.

THATCHER, BLAIR, AND PRESSURE GROUPS

Corporatism
A system of policy making in which major economic interests work closely together within formal structures of government to formulate and implement public policies. Corporatism requires a formal government apparatus capable of concerting the main economic groups so that they can jointly formulate and implement binding policies.

Tripartism Compared with corporatism, tripartism is a looser, less centralised and co-ordinated system that brings together three main interests (government, business, unions) in economic policy making. It is a consultative rather than a corporatist method of reaching and implementing decisions.

In the earlier post-war era of consensus politics both Conservative and Labour governments co-operated with business and labour organisations to solve economic problems. The most visible expression of this consensus style of policy formulation was the National Economic Development Council (NEDC), created in 1961 to take joint action on economic policy. A good number of similar bodies were subsequently created in the 1960s and 1970s, and the practice of officially incorporating insider groups into the consultative and decision-making processes was widely spread in central and local government. Some writers describe this period as 'corporatist', though others argue that Britain was never a corporatist state in the way that Austria and Switzerland were. They prefer the term 'tripartite' to refer to the British system of three-cornered consultation between government, business organisations, and trade unions (often described pejoratively as 'beer and sandwiches at No. 10').

Thatcher and the pressure groups

The 'winter of discontent' of 1979 effectively brought the tripartite era to an end. When Margaret Thatcher came to power she dismantled or weakened many tripartite practices and institutions. According to her, close co-operation between government and pressure groups was neither democratic nor functional, giving too much political power to private, narrow interests, and interfering with the efficient operation of the market. Besides, she stated that her party had been democratically elected to run the government, not pressure groups.

It should not be assumed that Thatcher only reduced the power of the trade unions. She confronted many other groups, including business interests, teachers, lawyers, civil servants, doctors, local government associations, universities, and even the Church of England. Official advisory bodies were cut by one-third, and the rest were weakened. Groups were excluded from the early stages of policy formulation, though less often from the final implementation stages, where co-operation is important. In short, the close association between groups and government was broken, and pressure groups often found themselves out in the cold.

Blair and the pressure groups

New Labour has tried to establish warmer working relations with leading groups, but without returning to the old tripartite system:

- It tried to work with the CBI.

- It started quarterly meetings with the TUC in 2000.

- It co-opted group members onto task forces and quangos, although in an ad hoc manner, and as individuals rather than group representatives.

- When a crisis occurred over increases in fuel taxes, it created the Fuel Forum with representatives of the Road Haulage Association, the NFU, and the Federation of Small Businesses. This showed a willingness to consult and co-operate with organised groups in order to solve an urgent political problem.

In large part the Thatcher–Blair contrast is based on their different views of the role of pressure groups in a democracy – a topic we will take a closer look at now.

PRESSURE GROUPS AND DEMOCRACY

As a leading member of the New Right, Thatcher viewed pressure groups as a potential danger to Parliamentary democracy. Are they?

In theory, groups play an important part in democracy:

- They are an important means of political participation and influence, especially for minorities.

- They collect and sort out group opinions to produce an agreed position (interest aggregation), and argue their case in the political arena (interest articulation).

- Groups inform and educate their members about political issues, and act as channels of communication between citizens, and between citizens and political elites.

- They mobilise citizens politically.

- They serve as pools of talent for recruitment to political office.

- They provide governments with aggregated opinion, technical expertise, and practical advice.

Pluralism According to pluralist theory, political decisions are the outcome of competition between many different groups representing many different interests.

For their part, governments obviously have a democratic duty to consult, and may depend on organised groups for policy information and implementation.

In practice, the role of pressure groups has been hotly disputed by competing pluralist, elitist, and New Right theorists. The argument takes many twists and turns, but an important part of it involves not so much the question of whether pressure groups are good or bad for democracy, but how much or how little power they should have.

CONTROVERSY

Are pressure groups good for democracy?

The pluralist case

- The greater number and diversity of groups ensures political struggle and competition. As a result (nearly) all issues are contested by competing groups.

- Groups look for allies in the political struggle, which forces them to compromise.

- All groups have some resources to fight battles: money, members, leadership skills, public sympathy, or access. Group resources are not distributed equally, but the inequalities are not cumulative. No group is powerless, none all powerful.

- Power is distributed between many different groups. There is no fixed 'power structure'; it depends on circumstances.

- Groups that fail in one arena (Parliament) may succeed in another (the courts, local government, the EU).

- Groups cannot get everything they want. They compromise to get something.

- Many groups have veto power – they can rule out proposals they don't like.

- Pluralist democracy is not perfect, but it works reasonably well, 'warts and all'.

The elitist case

- Group resources are often distributed with cumulative inequality. Just as power in society is unequally distributed, so some groups have few resources, others many.

- Some interests are unorganised, some rely on others to protect them, and some are poorly organised – minority groups, children, the mentally ill, the homeless, the poor.

- The group world is dominated by educated, wealthy, middle and upper class 'joiners'.

- Groups fight their battles within a political structure and according to rules of the game which are systematically loaded in favour of middle and upper class interests or even a particular sector, such as the City of London.

- Organisations are internally oligarchic. Group leaders are often unelected and unaccountable to members.

- A small national elite controls all important decisions, but leaves smaller issues to pluralist competition.

- The group world reflects and reinforces the political power structure in which the wealthy dominate.

The New Right case

- Groups represent narrow sectional interests; governments are elected by citizens to represent the public good.

- Groups, especially trade unions, distort market operations but so also do professional bodies and some business groups. Their power should be reduced to ensure market competition.

- Groups fragment policy making and prevent government developing a coherent programme.

- In protecting their sectional interests groups slow economic growth, and cause unemployment, inflation and high public expenditure.

- Groups create 'hyper-pluralism' – too many economic and political demands on government. This undermines good economic policy and democracy and creates 'ungovernability' and 'democratic overload'.

- Group leaders are often unelected and unaccountable to their members.

- Government may consult and groups may advise, but government should hold the reins of power.

Most certainly, groups have a democratic right to try to make their voice heard and to try to influence public policy, but as sectional and often narrowly self-interested actors, they do not have the right to make public policy. Too much group power results either in domination by factional interests, or in fragmented, confused and unaccountable decision making, what is sometimes called 'hyper-pluralism'. Nonetheless, too little group power means that government is too auto-cratic. The difficulty, of course, is knowing what is 'too much' and 'too little' power.

Growth of direct and radical action

The controversy about pressure groups and democracy has been sharpened by claims that radical and direct group action has grown in recent years. Action of this kind has a long history, going back to Wat Tyler's Peasants' Revolt of 1381 and includes the mass demonstrations of the Chartists (1848), suffragette action later in the nineteenth century, the Jarrow march against unemployment in 1936, and pitched battles between Fascists and Anti-Fascists in the streets of East London in the same year. The Campaign for Nuclear Disarmament organised its first Aldermaston March in 1958, and peaceful civil disobedience for the same cause was organised by the Committee of 100. Mass direct action by students, workers, and intellec-tuals spread across practically the whole western world in 1968, and in the 1970s the Anti-Apartheid Movements disrupted sports events against South Africa.

Since the huge publicity given to the demonstrations of 1968, groups seem to have turned increasingly to direct political action in the form of marches, sit-ins, petitions, occupations, civil disobedience, and occasional violence. Such methods often get a lot of publicity. Recent examples include:

- Greenpeace's use of the *Rainbow Warrior* to obstruct nuclear tests, and the blocking of an outlet pipe from the Sellafield nuclear power station

- road protestors on Twyford Down and elsewhere

- protests against cruise missiles on Greenham Common

- hunt saboteurs

- poll tax demonstrations and riots

- protests against live animal exports

- direct action against using animals for laboratory experiments

- sabotage of field tests of genetically modified crops

- anti-capitalist rallies against the World Trade Organisation

- the People's Fuel Lobby defeated government plans to increase fuel tax by organising blockades of petrol refineries and fuel centres in 2000

- many incidents of direct action by farmers – especially the Farmers For Action group;

- mass demonstrations in London of an estimated 400,000 people organised by the Countryside Alliance in 2002

- university student protests against top-up fees

- and, most spectacularly of all, the Stop the (Iraq) War campaign brought tens of millions of people onto the streets of cities around the world in February 2003, including the largest ever popular demonstration in Britain of 1–2 million people in London.

Although not new, direct action by radical groups challenges the traditional structures and organisation of government decision making and consultation. At the same time, it may strengthen conventional groups and procedures, because, faced with radical action from outsider groups, the government may open negotiations with insider groups to resolve the issue. This is exactly what happened when the Blair government set up the Fuel Forum with insider groups to solve the fuel tax issue. Paradoxically, therefore, direct and radical political action by groups may undermine conventional politics in some ways, but strengthen it in others.

SUMMARY

- The dense network of voluntary associations in the UK creates a pluralist or 'civil' society, with indirect and direct consequences for democracy.

- The distinction between pressure groups, new social movements and parties is not clear cut, but groups usually have a narrower range of policy interests than parties, and want to influence the government, not replace it. New social movements usually have broader interests than groups, but narrower ones than parties, are often more loosely organised, and often favour direct action and community organisation.

- The main targets (pressure points) for groups are: top civil servants, ministers and the Cabinet, Westminster, political parties, the mass media and the public, local councils, the courts and the European Union.

- Insider groups are able to work through government officials; outsider groups have to use less certain, more time-consuming methods aimed at the public and the mass media.

- Group influence is impossible to measure but depends on group characteristics (membership size, type and density; income; ability to recruit members; ability to respond quickly to political change; ability to use sanctions; group unity) and outside factors (public opinion; legitimacy; insider status; whether their issue is politicised; and the power of opposing pressure groups).

- The period of tripartite co-operation in the 1960s and 1970s was ended by Thatcher, who was more inclined to confront and exclude groups from government consultation. The Blair government has tried to work more closely with groups, but has not re-created a tripartite system.

- Pluralist theory places great emphasis on the role of groups in democracy, but elite theory claims that group politics reinforce elite or class power. The New Right argues that groups produce hyper-pluralism, ungovernability and overload.

ESSAYS

1. 'Elite theory claims that pressure groups merely reflect and sustain the power structure of modern society.' Discuss.

2. Why do some analysts attach so much importance to civil society, and is Britain such a society?

3. 'Once powerful in Britain, pressure groups have been weakened to the point of powerlessness since 1979.' Is this true?

MILESTONES

Milestones in the development of British pressure groups

1950s British pressure groups 'discovered' by British and American political scientists

1961 National Economic Development Council (NEDC) set up

1965 Confederation of British Industry (CBI) formed

1966 Devaluation of the pound postponed for a year by the Labour government because of financial pressures from the 'City'

1968 Demonstrations and direct action by students, workers and intellectuals spread across the western world

1969 Trade union pressure forces the Labour government to abandon plans for trade union reform ('In place of strife')

1970s Rise of the 'new social movements'

1971 The Conservative Industrial Relations Act reduces trade union powers

1974 The Prime Minister (Heath) calls an election, as a result of the miners' strike, and loses

The Labour government's 'Social Contract' with the trade unions agrees to social legislation and repeal of the Industrial Relations Act in return for a 'prices and incomes policy' but no agreement is struck with business or professional organisations about prices, salaries, or profits

Manpower Services Commission (a tripartite agency for jobs and training) created, followed by **1975** Health and Safety Commission, and **1976** Advisory, Conciliation, and Arbitration Service (ACAS) to deal with industrial relations disputes

1979 Thatcher begins to dismantle the machinery of 'tripartism' and begins a long series of confrontations with a wide range of organised interests and groups

1982 CBI Director-General, Sir Terence Beckett, threatens to 'get the gloves off' with the Thatcher government over its financially orthodox economic policy

1984–5 Miners' strike, the most bitter and prolonged industrial dispute since 1926, lost by miners

1980, 1982, 1984, 1988, 1989, 1990 Employment and Trade Union Acts reducing powers and rights of trade unions

1988 Edwina Currie, Junior Health Minister, is forced out after her statement that eggs are widely infected by salmonella angers egg producers and the NFU

1988–90 Anti-poll tax protests, culminating in demonstrations and riots across the country in 1990

1992 NEDC abolished

1994–6 Payments to MPs and other incidents of sleaze involving pressure groups and lobbyists prompt Nolan Committee to investigate MPs' interests

1997–8 Stronger regulation of MPs' interests by House of Commons

1997 Blair tries to establish working relations with major interest groups, but not under the old tripartite system

1997 The start of a long series of protests by farmers. Countryside Alliance organises demonstration attracting 300,000 people

1998–2000 Destruction of GM crops by Greenpeace

1999 Anti-capitalist and World Trade Organisations rallies in London and Seattle become an annual event

2000 Fuel tax protest

2002 Countryside Alliance attracts 400,000 participants in London demonstration. Student protests against top-up fees

2003 Anti-(Iraq) war coalition attracts 1–2 million demonstrators in London

PROJECTS

1. Collect what information you can from books, articles, and newspaper reports about the fuel tax protests of 2000, and the campaign against genetically modifed food, and the Countryside Alliance. What does this information tell us about the conduct of modern pressure group campaigns?

2. Make a list of all the groups mentioned in this chapter and classify them into their different types listed in Briefing 13.2. What do you learn from this exercise?

3. Carefully read a good national daily newspaper for one week, and list all the pressure groups and pressure group issues mentioned in the news reports. What does this tell you about the pressure group world in Britain?

FURTHER READING

A recent comprehensive book is W. Grant, *Pressure Groups and British Politics* (Basingstoke: Palgrave, 2000). Slightly older is R. Baggot, *Pressure Groups Today* (Manchester: Manchester University Press, 1995). A good study of environmental pressure groups and movements is G. Jordan and W. Maloney, *The Protest Business* (Manchester: Manchester University Press, 1997). On business groups, see W. Grant, *Business and Politics in Britain* (London: Macmillan, 2nd edn, 1993) and, on trade unions, D. Marsh, *The New Politics of British Trade Unions and the Thatcher Legacy* (London: Macmillan, 1992). A good account of European pressure groups is found in S. Mazey and J. J. Richardson, *Lobbying in the European Community* (Oxford: Oxford University Press, 1993).

Useful shorter articles include N. McNaughton, 'Populist movements: a new development in the politics of pressure', *Talking Politics*, **14**, 2001, pp. 18–21; W. Grant, 'Outside in!: Insider groups under challenge', *Politics Review*, **11**, 2001, pp. 10–13; and W. Grant, 'Pressure politics: from "insider" politics to direct action?', *Parliamentary Affairs*, **54**, 2001, pp. 337–48. On pressure groups in Europe, see S. Mazey and R. Richardson, 'Pressure groups and the EC', *Politics Review*, **3** (1), September 1993, pp. 20–4. H. Margetts, 'Political participation and protest', in P. Dunleavy et al (eds), *Developments in British Politics* (Basingstoke: Palgrave, 2002) discusses protest politics.

For a collection of articles on recent pressure group issues (road building, airport extensions, abortion, calf exports, nuclear energy, gun control, animal rights and Europe), see *Parliamentary Affairs*, **51** (3), 1998, pp. 329–96, 445–85.

USEFUL WEB SITES ON PRESSURE GROUPS

Hotlinks to these sites can be found on the CWS website at http://www.booksites.net/budge.

Before visiting specific pressure groups web sites, you might want to log into www.historylearningsite.co.uk/pressure_groups.htm where you can find basic answers to questions such as: what are pressure groups? How do they influence democratic performance? What is pluralism?

There are literally thousands of pressure groups in Britain. In the following list you can find samples of those with particularly good web sites and those mentioned in the chapter. Each site will provide basic information about the group, like history, objectives, activities and ways in which you can become involved.

Action on Smoking and Health www.ash.org
Amnesty International www.oneworld.org/amnesty/index.html
Animal Concerns http://animalconcerns.netforchange.com/
Black Information Link www.blink.org.uk
British Medical Association www.bma.org.uk
Campaign for Nuclear Disarmament www.cnduk.org
Campaign for an Independent Britain www.bullen.demon.co.uk
Charter 88 www.charter88.org.uk
Child Poverty Action Group www.homelesspages.org.uk

Chronicle World (changing Black Britain) www.chronicleworld.org
Commonwealth Foundation www.commonwealthfoundation.com
Compassion in World Farming www.ciwf.co.uk
Confederation of British Industry www.cbi.org.uk
Conservation International www.conservation.org/xp/CIWEB/home
Country Landowners' Association www.cla.org.uk
Countryside Alliance www.countryside-alliance.org
Friends of the Earth www.foe.co.uk
Greenpeace www.greenpeace.org/homepage/
International Council for Local Environmental Initiatives www.iclei.org
League Against Cruel Sports www.league.uk.com
Local Government Association www.lga.gov.uk
Mind www.mind.org.uk
National Farmers' Union www.nfu.org.uk
National Society for the Prevention of Cruelty to Children (www.nspcc.org.uk)
National Trust www.nationaltrust.org.uk
Nexus www.netnexus.org/nexus/
Press for Change www.pfc.org.uk
Royal National Institute for the Blind www.rnib.org.uk
Royal Society for the Protection of Birds www.rspb.org.uk
Shelter www.shelter.org.uk
World Conservation Monitoring Centre www.unep-wcmc.org
World Council of Churches www.wcc-coe.org

14 The mass media and pluralist democracy

The mass media have a special place in politics because they are the main channels of communication in modern society, and therefore the main way in which governments, pressure groups, parties, politicians, and voters talk to and learn about each other. On the one hand, they reach audiences in the tens of millions every day, and, on the other, they are carefully watched by the politicians. In other words, the mass media inform voters about politics and politicians, and they inform politicians about politics and voters.

But the mass media are not merely channels of communication. They are also significant political actors in their own right: they help to create news as well as report it; and they give the news a slant, or perspective, by reporting it in certain ways. In this sense the mass media are no different from other pressure groups, pushing certain causes, pursuing their own economic interests, and supporting political parties. The question is how far they manage to balance their news-reporting function with their politics-influencing function, and what role they play in democratic politics as a result. This raises all sorts of questions about the nature and impact of the mass media, media bias, whether we should regulate the mass media or leave them to commercial forces, and the problem of increasing concentration of ownership and control.

This chapter, therefore, examines the nature and impact of the mass media, and its role in democracy. It covers:

- who uses what medium for what purpose
- the impact of the mass media
- media bias
- pluralist democracy and the mass media
  - the print media
  - the electronic media – regulation and the public service model
- commercialisation of the electronic media
- ownership and control
- the political consequences of market change
- e-media: digitopia or dystopia?

WHO USES WHAT MEDIUM FOR WHAT PURPOSE?

We take the modern media for granted in many ways, because we are totally immersed in them. Just as fish will be the last life form on earth to discover water, so we find it difficult to imagine what life would be like without TV, the radio, and the daily paper. A few contrasts between 1945 and modern times will help make the point:

- In 1945 there was no TV in Britain. The BBC resumed its post-war broadcasts in 1946 with 25,000 viewers and their tiny black-and-white sets clustered around the Alexandra Palace TV station. Now virtually every household has at least one TV set, with many channels to choose from, some operating round the clock. On average, the British now spend over 25 hours a week watching TV, and half the population watches TV news 7 days a week.

- In 1945 politicians communicated with voters mainly by newspapers, public meetings, and the radio. Newspapers were very slim (there were wartime and post-war controls on paper), had very little in-depth analysis of politics, and little commentary. There were no opinion polls. Reporting of Parliamentary debates was limited. Modern papers are fat and glossy, their political content is vastly larger, and they are far more critical and party political than in 1945. Some 32 to 35 million people read a daily or Sunday paper.

- In 1945 about 10 million households had a 'wireless', but political broadcasting was limited, and there was little coverage of the 1945 election. Now there are a great many radio stations, including commercial and local radio, and many have news programmes and headlines at regular intervals.

- In 1945 the terms 'spin doctor', 'photo opportunity', and 'sound bite' had not been invented. The government had press departments and officers, but nothing like the scale of modern operations. Spin doctors are now power players in government.

All this means that the mass media are vastly more important in politics, and are growing in power and influence all the time. But what exactly is their role in British democracy? To answer this seemingly simple question, we must first examine what sorts of people use what sorts of media for what sorts of reasons.

Tabloids, broadsheets, and TV

Broadsheets Serious national daily and Sunday papers, so called because of their size. Daily broadsheets are *The Times*, the *Daily Telegraph*, the *Guardian*, the *Independent* and the *Financial Times*.

Tabloids Less serious national daily and Sunday papers, so called because of their smaller size.

It has been said with some truth that all statements about the media are wrong: there are different mediums and different people use them for different purposes. There is a world of difference between the electronic mass media (radio and TV) and the print media, and a big difference again between the tabloids and broadsheets. We must be careful to distinguish between these different kinds of media and not talk loosely about them as if they were a single entity.

Broadsheet readers are usually better educated and more middle class (see Table 14.1). They spend more time with their paper than tabloid readers, trust their paper more than TV as a source of news, and know more about politics. Conversely, tabloid readers spend less time with their paper and more with the TV, although their TV diet is mainly entertainment and sports programmes,

Daily broadsheets	Sales (m)	Sunday broadsheets	Sales (UK)
Daily Telegraph	0.90	Sunday Telegraph	0.68
The Times	0.59	Sunday Times	1.30
Guardian	0.37	Observer	0.41
Independent	0.18	Independent on Sunday	0.18
Financial Times	0.41		
Total	2.45	Total	2.57
Number of titles	5	Number of titles	4
Average sales	0.49	Average sales	0.64
Daily tabloids		**Sunday tabloids**	
Sun	3.52	News of the World	3.86
Daily Mirror	1.96	Sunday Mirror	1.63
Daily Express	0.91	Express on Sunday	0.90
Daily Mail	2.35	Mail on Sunday	0.61
Daily Star	0.50	People	1.11
		Sunday Star	0.53
Total	10.15	Total sales	8.64
Number of titles	5	Number of titles	6
Average sales	1.69	Average sales	1.44
All national dailies		**All national Sundays**	
Total sales	12.60	Total sales	11.21
Number of titles	11	Number of titles	9
Average sales	1.15	Average sales	1.12

Table 14.1 *National newspaper sales and readership, 2003*

Notes: Sales are the same as circulation figures. Readership is the estimated number who read the paper. AB readers are those in professional, administrative, and managerial occupations – about 23% of the total population

Source: Audit Bureau of Circulations and National Readership Survey

not news and current affairs. However, because they watch so much TV, they also watch a lot of TV news – in fact they watch *more* TV news than broadsheet readers, and they trust TV news more than their tabloid paper (see Tables 14.2 and 14.3). But they are less interested in politics, and know less about them.

As Table 14.1 shows, more than three times as many tabloids are sold as broadsheets, but the tabloids have less political news and analysis, and tend to be more party political. Some media analysts argue that good newspapers are, in principle, better at conveying political news and comment than TV, which by its very nature tends to be superficial and entertaining. As a result, those who spend time with a good newspaper are usually better informed than those who watch TV news; but it is not always clear whether this is due to the inherent properties of different media or to the education of those who use them.

Table 14.2 *Different media, different uses, 1996*

	Educational qualifications		
	O level/GCSE or less	A level (percentages)	Further or higher
Newspapers	%	%	%
Irregular readers	43	47	43
Regular tabloid	54	41	31
Regular broadsheet	4	13	27
(Total)	(101)	(101)	(101)
Television hours per week			
Up to 3	28	46	58
3–4	41	39	32
5 or more	30	15	9
(Total)	(99)	(100)	(99)
TV news per week			
3 or less	27	32	28
4–6	14	24	22
Every day	59	44	50
(Total)	(100)	(100)	(100)

Note: Columns total more than 100 per cent because respondents mention more than one source. Broadsheet readers mention more than tabloid readers

Source: British Social Attitudes Survey, 1996 as reported in R. Jowell et al (eds), *British Social Attitudes: The 14th Report*, Aldershot: Dartmouth, 1997, p. 156

Table 14.3 *Main sources of political information*

Main source of political information	Broadsheet readers (percentages)	Tabloid readers
TV	32	62
Papers	57	28
Radio	25	14
(Total)	(114)	(104)

Source: Calculated from R. Negrine, *Politics and the Mass Media in Britain*, London: Routledge, 1994, p. 2

Knowledge gap
The result of the process whereby those with a good education and high status acquire knowledge faster than those with a poorer education and lower status.

Social scientists refer to this growing division between tabloid and broadsheet readers as the 'knowledge gap'. Educated people and those interested in politics read quality newspapers and magazines, listen to serious radio and watch serious TV, and talk more about politics with their friends, thereby accumulating a broader and deeper understanding of politics. Less well-educated people, who read the tabloids and watch a lot of entertainment TV, are likely to know less and understand less about politics. In other words there is a tendency for the information rich to become information richer. But whether this is due to the impact of different media, or to the qualities of media users is a different matter, and one that raises the crucial question of the impact of the mass media on society.

IMPACT OF THE MEDIA

Many people have strong and diametrically opposed views on the impact of the media. Some claim that media effects are strong and self-evident; others argue, with equal conviction, that the media have no direct effects of their own. In spite of these strong views it turns out to be remarkably difficult to demonstrate media effects, even more to measure them. There are three main problems:

1. It is difficult to untangle the effects of the media from other influences, such as family life, education, work or the community. The media are only one set of influences among many, and sorting out their distinctive impact is a tricky matter.

2. It is not possible to generalise about 'the impact of the media', when there are different kinds of media with different impacts. Moreover, different media may push and pull in different directions: Labour and Conservative papers, and neutral TV, for example.

3. There is an acute problem of establishing causes and effects. People pick the sorts of media that suit their tastes and opinions – they self-select themselves. At the same time, the media shape themselves to appeal to particular sorts of people and markets, so they reflect rather than create the views of their audiences. This makes it difficult to know whether the chicken or the egg comes first.

Consider the simple figures in Table 14.4. They show that people who read Conservative papers generally identify with the Conservative Party, compared with those who read Labour papers who generally identify with Labour. This is scarcely surprising, but which causes what? Do papers create the party sympathies, or do people usually select a paper to suit their politics? Or is it a bit of both?

Given these difficulties it is scarcely surprising that experts disagree fiercely about the impact of the mass media on politics. There are four main schools of thought on the subject: reinforcement theory claims minimal effects; agenda-setting theory and framing theory claim indirect effects; and media impact theory claims direct, though not necessarily strong, effects.

Table 14.4 *Politics of daily papers and their readers, 1997*

Party identification of reader	Politics of newspaper		
	Conservative	Labour	Other
	(percentages)		
Conservative	46	10	22
Labour	31	75	46
Other	23	15	32
(Total)	(100)	(100)	(100)

Source: MORI polls

Reinforcement theory and minimal effects

Reinforcement theory (media effects)
Argues that the media do not create or mould public opinion so much as reinforce pre-existing opinion.

Reinforcement theory argues that the media can only reinforce attitudes that already exist. There are two reasons:

1. **Markets**   In a competitive market the media are forced to give consumers what they want, just as supermarkets sell what their customers demand. They seek out tastes and try to appeal to them by reflecting and satisfying them. The modern media are bound by the golden chains of the market. Moreover, the media market is competitive. It presents a great diversity of political opinions, allowing customers to pick and choose what suits them.

2. **Personality**   Research shows clearly enough that individuals have a strong propensity to preserve their beliefs, even if they are forcefully challenged. They start by picking the media that best suit their predispositions (self-selection), and if unwanted messages get through they then tend to ignore, forget, distort, misinterpret, or simply refuse to believe them. Even if the mass media tried, they cannot shift entrenched opinion.

In sum, reinforcement theory argues that individual psychology, on the one hand, and consumer sovereignty in a competitive market, on the other, renders the media all but powerless to influence mass political opinion. Media effects are minimal.

Reinforcement theory does not fit all the facts about the British media, however. First, the British media do not operate in a free competitive market. As we will see, radio and TV are regulated in non-market ways, and the print media form an oligopoly rather than a free, competitive market. Second, individuals may adhere strongly to their core values – religion and morality – and to attitudes based upon their own experience, but politics are fairly remote for most. Few have first-hand experience of, say, the Iraq War, EU affairs, or economic policy, and they may be more open to media influence on these particular matters as a result.

Agenda setting

Agenda-setting theory
Argues that the media cannot determine what people think, but can have a strong influence over what people think about.

Agenda-setting theory claims that the media cannot determine what we think, but they can strongly influence what we think about, and so they help set the public agenda. In recent years in Britain we have seen waves of media interest in such things as football hooliganism, road rage, dangerous dogs, the monarchy, Princess Diana's death, and an ever-rising high tide of news about crime. Political issues highlighted by the media include:

- the foundation of the Social Democratic Party
- Labour's tax plans in the 1992 election campaign
- Conservative government sleaze in the 1997 election.

Widespread media attention to these topics has helped concentrate the public's attention on them.

Early agenda-setting theory tended to assume a pliant public that responds to the media's agenda. Some even claimed that the media barons could keep serious politics off the popular agenda by feeding the general public with an endless stream of distractions in the form of soap operas, game shows, Hollywood films, sport, gossip, trivia, and sensationalism. Critics of the theory argued that most issues will get a hearing in a pluralist system, and that there is much more about politics in the mass media than there ever used to be. At any rate, later agenda-setting theory now accepts that the public has its own agenda, while claiming that the media can still influence its priorities, especially on matters about which the public knows little.

Priming and framing

Framing theory goes one step further than agenda-setting theory and argues that the *way* in which the modern mass media present politics has a strong influence on how citizens see them and evaluate them. It is not the news content that is so important, but the mass media's basic approach to the news:

Framing effects (of the media) The argument that the media can exercise a subtle but strong effect on how public opinion thinks about political issues according to how it presents (frames) the issue in the first place.

- **Framing** Some media stories present issues in a general way, while others present it in human interest terms. For example, the issue of homelessness can be analysed with the help of statistics and explained in terms of social forces such as unemployment, the housing shortage, and mortgage interest rates. Or else it can be made into a human interest story by interviewing homeless individuals about their life stories. In the former, political and social forces are foremost, especially government policy, but in the latter, the homeless are more likely to be held individually responsible (laziness, drunkenness, stupidity).

- **Priming** Parties and candidates are usually strong in some areas of politics, weaker in others, and simply by focusing on a strong or a weak area, a news report can help or hinder their campaign. In most post-war elections, the Conservative Party has been thought more competent on the issue of law and order, whereas Labour has had a better rating on unemployment. By concentrating on one or other of these issues, the mass media can prime people to think about a party's strong or weak points.

- **Bad news** The mass media concentrate on bad news, conflict and violence, because these sell papers and hold TV audiences. This is said to create 'videomalaise' – cynicism and disillusionment with politics, distrust of politicians, and political apathy.

Videomalaise The attitudes of political cynicism, despair, apathy and disillusionment (among others) that some social scientists claim are caused by the modern mass media, especially television.

- **The 'fast-forward' syndrome** In Victorian times political events and news about them moved slowly. Nowadays, the mass media are constantly searching for the latest story to attract the public's attention, so news moves fast. In fact, new news breaks so quickly that the public is increasingly bewildered by an ever-changing flow of unconnected events.

- **Personalisation and trivialisation** The mass media concentrate not on policies or issues, but on personalities and appearances. Election campaigns are not presented as a struggle between party policies, but as a horse

Plate 14.1 Sun *cover on the day of the 1992 election: 'Will the last person to leave please turn out the lights.' Repeated attention to the Labour Party's tax plans led the* Sun *to claim it had won the election for the Tories*

race between party leaders, illustrated by the sound bites and photo opportunities of the spin doctors. Many politicians now go to TV 'charm schools' that train them to speak, smile, and dress correctly. Packaging and presentation, not content, is what matters.

Cross-pressures
Cross-pressures occur where political forces or influences push in opposite directions – for example, where someone with Labour sympathies reads a Conservative paper.

Direct effects

The most recent school of thought argues that the mass media directly influence attitudes and behaviour, including voting behaviour. Direct effects include:

Mobilisation There is evidence to show that higher levels of education combined with increasing media coverage of politics is associated with greater political awareness and interest – at least among the better educated sections of the population.

Reinforcement
Reinforcement occurs where political forces push in the same direction – eg where someone with Labour sympathies reads a Labour paper.

Voting behaviour Although many people pick their newspaper to fit their politics, a large minority of newspaper readers in Britain do not do this, especially tabloid readers. The evidence suggests that those who are politically cross-pressured by the paper they read are less likely to follow their own political inclinations than those who are reinforced by their paper. Differences in voting between the cross-pressured and the reinforced suggest that daily newspapers do have a direct effect on voting patterns, albeit a small one.

CONTROVERSY

Conflicting theories of media effects

Reinforcement theory

- The media do not create opinions, they reinforce existing ones.

- Market competition ensures that the mass media adapt to their audiences and give them what they want.

- In a pluralist system, many views have a way of making their voice heard.

- Different media with different messages compete. There is no single or dominant voice.

- Individuals select their media to suit their opinions and tastes. They tend to suppress, distort, forget or misinterpret what does not suit them.

- The effects of the modern mass media are minimal, they confirm what people already believe rather than creating or influencing political life and attitudes.

Agenda-setting theory

- The media cannot exercise much influence over what people think, but they can influence what they think *about*.

- Only a few issues can be important at any one time and the media play an important role in sifting and sorting issues for public attention.

- Different media often focus on the same events or issues. Journalists live in echo chambers (they talk among themselves most of the time) and indulge in 'feeding frenzies', taking cues from each other about what is important and topical.

- Concentrating media attention on a few issues at a time pushes them up the political agenda.

Framing politics

- The way in which the modern mass media treat politics subtly, but strongly, affects political life, and how people view it. This is a matter of presentation not content.

- By concentrating on bad news (wars, deaths, disasters, conflicts, incompetence, and corruption) the media give politics a bad name, and so create alienation, political cynicism, and distrust.

- The 'fast-forward' syndrome speeds up political life, and makes it difficult to understand.

- In order to provide human interest the media tend to trivialise and personalise politics. They emphasise style and appearance, sound bites and photo opportunities, rather than policies and programmes.

- By focusing on particular issues the media favour the politicians and parties that 'own' those issues ('priming' effects).

- Reports that concentrate on episodes, particularly individual human interest stories, tend to emphasise individual causes. News that deals with themes tends to emphasise 'the system' and the actions of governments.

Direct effects

■ Reinforcement theory was mainly a product of 1950s' social science before the creation of the powerful modern media, especially TV, so it underestimates media impacts.

■ The mass media now saturate society. In particular many people now spend a large proportion of their leisure time in front of the TV.

■ TV has powerful effects: it encourages passivity (the 'couch potato'), it entertains rather than explaining or informing, and it isolates people socially.

■ Media effects go beyond agenda setting, priming and framing. The media influence the way in which people think about politics – the videomalaise thesis.

■ There is some evidence that newspapers influence the voting patterns of their readers. Allowing for the effects of background characteristics and political attitudes, readers of Conservative papers are more likely to vote Conservative than readers of Labour papers, and vice versa.

MEDIA BIAS?

Many people are convinced that the media are biased. The problem is that right-wingers are convinced that the bias is left wing, and left-wingers are equally convinced that it is right wing! British governments of all persuasions usually feel that the press is unfair to them. We are unlikely to get far in this debate unless we go back to basics.

Bias in the mass media is most likely to originate in two sources: political authorities, especially the government, and the media themselves.

Government bias

The government is only one source of political information, but it is a particularly important one that can try to shape the news in two different ways:

1. **The suppression of news?** On the one hand, freedom of information is rather weakly protected in the UK and, on the other, the Official Secrets Act is powerful. Compared with many democracies, these two together give British governments rather more room for manoeuvre in controlling news flows and information. The governments of the 1980s were strongly critical of both the BBC and ITV for their treatment of some political issues, and there were whispers that this might affect both the renewal of the BBC Charter in 1994 and the price of the TV licence (the BBC's main source of income), which the government controls.

2. **The manipulation of news?** Government provides a large proportion of the daily news through its press releases and tries to shape the news ('give it a spin') in its own interests. Government efforts to market itself increased substantially in the 1980s under Thatcher and again in the late 1990s under Blair. The Whitehall and Downing Street public relations

machine now employs over 1,000 people, and at £141 million a year, it is the country's largest advertiser. At the same time both journalists and voters alike have become suspicious and cynical of attempts to manipulate the news. Trust in politicians has declined accordingly.

Newspapers

The main concern with media bias is probably not government manipulation of the media, but rather the bias of the media itself. In this regard, however, it is essential to distinguish between print and electronic media. The electronic media are required to be balanced and impartial, while newspapers can be as partial and partisan as they like. We will deal first with the easier case of the print media. There are four main reasons why British newspapers have had a particular ideological leaning for most (but not all) of the post-war period:

1. The press (and commercial TV) is owned and controlled by multimillionaires and multinational companies, often (not always) with the same economic and political interests.

2. Generations of British press barons have pursued not money, but power. They have frequently controlled the editorial policy of their newspapers, and even written the editorials themselves: Northcliffe, Rothermere, Astor, Beaverbrook, Thompson, King, Matthews, Maxwell, Rowland, Black and Murdoch have all followed this practice.

3. At the same time newspapers and commercial TV rely heavily on advertising income, and are unwilling to bite the hand of the business interests that feed them.

4. Since the late 1950s the British press has tried to carve out a media market that is distinct from television's. TV is required to be balanced and impartial, so the tabloid press has increased its party political bias, and the quality press has increasingly presented in-depth commentary and analysis of the news.

The result is that the British press as a whole is strongly party political compared with most other western countries, and for much of the post-war period (1945–92) it has been heavily Conservative. As Figure 14.1 shows, the circulation of Conservative newspapers outnumbered Labour or Liberal papers, 1951–97, and from the 1970s to 1997, they dominated. During these decades a large majority of people read a Conservative paper, including about 70 per cent of the working class people who traditionally provide Labour with most of its support. Three of the largest circulation mass tabloids (*Sun*, *Mail*, and *Express*) were strongly Conservative, and the fourth (the *Daily Mirror*) offered Labour only lukewarm support at times. Moreover, the pattern in Figure 14.2 shows that Conservative papers have a higher proportion of Conservative voters than one would expect from the social class of their readers. Labour papers have a similarly high proportion of Labour voters. Given what we know about self-selection, and how papers adapt to markets, Figure 14.2 proves nothing; but it is

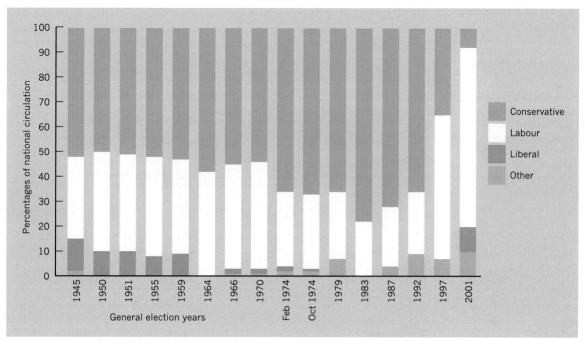

Figure 14.1 *Party politics of the press: percentages of national circulation*

Source: Calculated from figures provided by C. Seymour-Ure, *The British Press and Broadcasting since 1945*, Oxford: Blackwell, 1992, pp. 196–7 (1945–87); Audit Bureau of Circulations for more recent elections

circumstantial evidence that the Conservative nature of the national press may have helped the party in the war of words.

In the 1997 and 2001 elections the scene was totally changed. The Conservative government of the 1990s came under increasing attack and criticism, to such an extent that by 1997 the *Sun*, a strongly Conservative paper in the 1980s and early 1990s, switched support to Blair. For the first time, Labour had a newspaper advantage. Not only that, but *The Times*, *Telegraph* and *Financial Times* were not as staunchly Conservative as usual. By the election of 2001 the balance had swung even more to Labour. In that election the Tories were supported by only one national Fleet Street daily paper (the *Telegraph*).

Did this contribute to Labour's mammoth victory? We cannot be sure. Labour scored a remarkable win in 1945 with minority newspaper support, and won in 1964, 1966 and 1974 with most papers against it. Besides, it has been estimated that about 60 per cent of *Sun* readers would have voted Labour in 1997 even had the paper not switched. So many people had firm voting intentions of their own in 1997 and 2001 that the newspaper effect may well have been small, if it helped Labour to win at all.

Perhaps the main concern about the national press since 1950 is not that it supports this or that party, or that it has changed its support in the last two elections. The concern is that it has given heavy support to only one of the two main

Figure 14.2 *Party voting among newspaper readers: actual voting compared with typical class voting of readers*

Source: D. McKie, 'Fact is free but comment is sacred', in I. Crewe and B. Gosschalk (eds), *Political Communications: The General Election Campaign of 1992*, Cambridge: Cambridge University Press, 1995

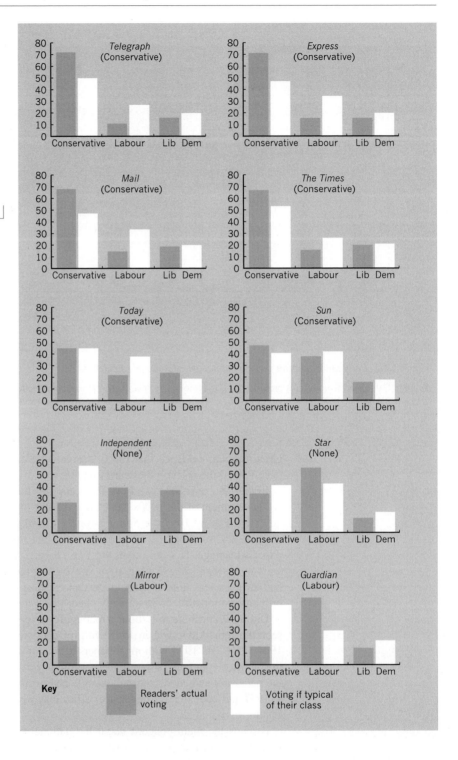

parties at any given time, and virtually none to the third party, the Liberal Democrats. It is not a pluralist press.

Radio and TV

The electronic media are an entirely different matter so far as party or political bias is concerned. Commercial TV is legally required to be politically neutral and balanced particularly in its handling of election campaigns, and the BBC voluntarily follows the same code of conduct. As a result a large majority of viewers trust both BBC and ITV news. A minority of between 15 and 20 per cent believe the BBC has a Conservative bias, and a smaller minority of about 5 per cent think it has a Labour bias. About 5 per cent believe that ITV has a Labour bias, while about the same proportion perceive Conservative leanings.

Nevertheless some research argues that TV news is systematically prejudiced. The Glasgow Media Group (GMG) has published a series of books (the main ones are *Bad News*, *More Bad News*, *Really Bad News*, and *War and Peace News*) which claim there is a pervasive elitist and conservative bias in the BBC's news. The Glasgow team has been criticised, in turn, by those who argue that their work is sometimes wrong or exaggerated, and ignores contradictory evidence. The controversy about broadcasting bias continues and is likely to generate more heat than light for some time to come.

PLURALIST DEMOCRACY AND THE MASS MEDIA

The mass media are an essential part of modern democracy. The reasons are easy to understand. Democracy requires, at a minimum, informed and politically educated citizens who can make decisions for themselves. In turn, they need balanced and reliable news and access to a wide variety of opinion so that they can make informed and sensible choices.

BRIEFINGS

14.1 **Pluralist democracy**

Pluralist democracy is based on the idea that modern societies contain all sorts of competing groups, interests, ideologies and ideas, which have a right to be heard and to defend themselves in the public arena. Democracy is seen as a peaceful struggle between political interests, ideas, and values – often expressed by parties, pressure groups, and social movements. The best arguments will win the day if there is a genuinely 'free market place of ideas' (J. S. Mill).

This is an attractive ideal. Unfortunately Britain, along with other modern societies, may fall short of providing a free market of ideas. Powerful groups and interests – including the party in power – may try to control the channels of communication and manipulate the news so that their views tend to shape discussion. Consequently, there is a controversy between those who want (a) market competition for the mass media, and (b) media regulation to protect the public interest.

Figure 14.3 *Sources of world news*

Source: Calculated from R. Negrine, *Politics and the Mass Media in Britain*, London: Routledge, 1994, p. 2

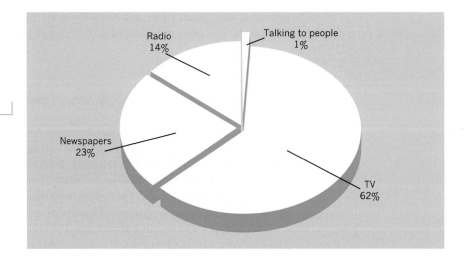

At the same time, most of us have to rely on the media for our news and opinion because we have little first-hand experience of politics – we know few politicians personally, and we rarely hear their speeches for ourselves or witness political events with our own eyes. Most citizens have neither a detailed knowledge nor a deep interest in politics. Most rely on the media to keep them informed, mainly TV news. Indeed, the great merit of television is that it brings political leaders and events into our own living rooms where we see and hear them for ourselves, and form our own judgements.

The first democratic requirement of the mass media, then, is to provide us with a full and fair account of the news and opinion so that we can play our role as informed citizens in a democracy. The news media, however, are far more than mere channels for the communication of facts. We expect them to comment, analyse, criticise, investigate, and evaluate – to tell us what is really happening, not just what politicians tell us is happening. For this reason the mass media are sometimes described as 'the fourth estate of the realm', or 'the watchdog of the constitution'. The problem is that the media role is a demanding and complex one, which requires them to perform a number of tasks, some difficult to achieve, and others not easily combined:

- The news must be accurate, but it is often difficult to get facts right in the rushed world of news deadlines.

- The media must present a full account of the news, but they cannot possibly report all the news. There is too much of it, and the media must select and impose their subjective judgement about what is important.

- It is impossible to be completely neutral about political news. Facts do not speak for themselves; they must be interpreted, and the language we use is sometimes loaded, especially about dramatic political events.

- The news should be objective and detached, but also critical and engaged: it should report what politicians say in their own words, but also hard hitting and dig beneath the surface (investigative journalism).

- The news media should present a wide variety of opinion, not just the views of government leaders. But it is quicker and easier to rely on neatly packaged government press releases than hunt for alternative views and information.

- The news media must resist the pressures of spin doctors who want to manipulate the news, but in doing so they are often attacked by political leaders who feel they have been unfairly treated.

- Perhaps most important of all, democracy requires the media to provide a full and comprehensive coverage of the news, but research shows clearly that citizens are bored by this. TV news audiences are falling and in 2001 voters got more news of the election than they wanted. The media are trapped between the demands of democracy and the market.

For these reasons alone, it is clear that the mass media would have a tough job playing its proper role in democracy, even in an ideal world, but the world of the British media is also far from a pluralist ideal, as we will see.

Pluralist theory and the media

It is clear that no single newspaper or TV news programme can possibly cover all news and opinion. What is important is that the news media as a whole present the important news and a diverse range of opinion, so that citizens can choose in a free market of ideas and opinions. This places great importance on a diversity of news sources that cover the news from different political perspectives.

In the late nineteenth century the newspaper market roughly met these conditions. It was relatively easy and inexpensive to publish a paper or newssheet to serve small, local markets, and there was competition between different publications advocating different political positions. The industry was fragmented and run by different people with different political positions, several of them independent of large political parties and major economic interests.

Nowadays the news media have an entirely different appearance and market. On the one hand, there are many more forms of communication – not just the papers and pamphlets of Victorian times, but radio, television, films, videos, tapes, CD-Roms, DVDs, email, and the net. In this sense the media are more pluralist because there are many more forms of communication. On the other hand, the modern media are now a capital-intensive big business with world wide markets. The question is whether they still represent a pluralist and competitive market.

Plate 14.2 *The internet is an increasingly important source of news and information. During the May 1997 general election campaign all the major parties used the internet to publicise their policies and recruit members. The most striking use of the medium was seen on the Labour Party's special election web site, created by The Wire Station*

Source: The Wire Station

THE PRINT MEDIA

In theory anyone can set up a newspaper or a magazine, especially in the age of desktop publishing. In theory there is no limit to the number of producers who can compete in this market. Thus there is no more theoretical need for state regulation of the print media than there is, say, for soap powder. Moreover, it can be argued that the principle of freedom of speech means that the less regulation of publishing there is the better. Therefore, the print media should not be subject to any political controls: they should print the news as they see fit, and publish whatever editorials and political advertisements they wish.

Since 1945, and the lifting of wartime restrictions, the State has intervened in the newspaper industry only in exceptional circumstances when market failure has threatened competition. In this sense the newspaper market is the same as any other that attracts the attention of the Monopolies and Mergers Commission when there is a danger of market failure.

In practice, however, the British newspaper industry has long shown strong oligopolist tendencies toward concentration of ownership in the hands of a few big publishing companies, and attempts to prevent further concentration have been no more than half-hearted. In 1981 Rupert Murdoch was allowed to buy

The Times and *Sunday Times*, although this, with the *Sun*, gave him 30 per cent of the national daily market and, with the *News of the World*, 36 per cent of the Sunday paper market. The national press in Britain does not show the pluralist market structure that is required for democracy.

In recent years another problem has been added; namely, the content and standards of tabloid journalism, including bias, inaccuracy, sensationalism, cheque book journalism and invasion of privacy. Press standards have been a long-standing source of complaint in Britain, but they seem to have fallen to a new low in the 1970s and after.

Because the principle of a free press is so strong, governments have been unwilling to impose outside regulation, and have placed their faith instead on self-regulation by the industry, in the shape of a Code of Practice drawn up by newspaper editors, and adjudicated by the Press Complaints Commission. The Commission has little power and few sanctions. The Calcutt Report (1990) and the Calcutt Review of the Press Complaints Commission (1993) recommended stronger action, but this was rejected by the government. Tabloid press standards remain a difficult and unresolved issue. Few outside the newspaper industry believe that self-regulation has worked, but State regulation is a minefield of political problems.

THE ELECTRONIC MEDIA: REGULATION AND THE PUBLIC SERVICE MODEL

Spectrum scarcity
The shortage of broadcasting frequencies for radio and TV caused by the fact that the wavelengths available for public broadcasting on the spectrum are limited.

Until quite recently, radio and television markets were entirely different from newspaper markets. Only a limited number of wavelengths were available for broadcasting, only one broadcaster could use a given wavelength, and wavelengths had to be reserved for 'narrowcasting' (special purposes such as shipping, air traffic control, police, fire, ambulances and radio taxis). Consequently, the electronic media were natural monopolies quite unlike the theoretically open market of the print media. Spectrum scarcity meant that the airwaves were regarded as a public good, and closely regulated by the State in the public interest.

Market regulation
Regulation of the media market by public bodies.

Content regulation
Regulation of the content of the media by public bodies.

State regulation of the electronic media takes two forms: market regulation, in which the State controls the allocation of broadcasting licences and divides them between public and private (commercial) organisations; and content regulation, in which the State tries to ensure that the electronic media broadcast in the national interest. Among other things this means that the radio and TV news should achieve 'balance . . . accuracy and impartiality' and that political parties and candidates are treated fairly during election campaigns. Paid political advertising is not permitted on radio or television in Britain (as it is in the USA, for example), except under the carefully controlled conditions of party political and party election broadcasts. Neither may radio or TV broadcast political editorials of the kind that newspapers print every day.

14.2 Market and content regulation of the electronic media

Market regulation

Because broadcasting wavelengths are limited in number (spectrum scarcity), the State controls the electronic media. Initially it gave the British Broadcasting Corporation (BBC) a monopoly over radio and TV, but as technology developed more channels became available and commercial TV and radio stations were legalised. There are still only a few terrestrial broadcasting wavelengths, so the State continues to control broadcasting licences.

In order to prevent monopoly or oligopoly emerging in the limited market the State also regulates cross-media ownership of TV, radio and newspapers. Market regulation is found mainly in electronic media, but it is also supposed to apply to the print media as well. In Britain, however, market regulation of the print media has not been conspicuously successful, and market regulation of all media has been relaxed considerably, starting in 1993.

Content regulation

Because the airwaves are public property it is argued that they should be used in the public interest. For example, the number and the content of TV and radio commercials is controlled, and programmes unsuitable for children are not broadcast until the late evening. News and election programmes are closely regulated by the Television Act of 1954, which established independent (commercial) TV, and which was amended by the Broadcasting Act of 1981:

- Political and religious advertising and editorialising are banned.

- Political programmes are required to maintain 'proper balance ... accuracy and impartiality'.

- Election candidates and parties must be treated fairly and impartially.

- Party political programmes and election broadcasts, made and financed by the parties, are broadcast free of charge, with time allotted to parties in proportion to their voting support.

The BBC is not legally bound by the 1954 or 1981 Acts, but voluntarily observes their codes of practice.

Content regulation by the European Union

The European Union has also begun to regulate the media and advertising. It has banned cigarette advertisements on TV, and controls other advertising. The advertising of alcohol and products aimed at children are also regulated. Other press, advertising and broadcasting restrictions are being introduced, and the EU is likely to play a bigger role in the regulation of broadcast content in the future.

Initially, market regulation of the electronic media in Britain meant that the British Broadcasting Corporation (BBC) had a monopoly of broadcasting, which it used according to 'the public service model'. Given a state-granted monopoly and funded by licence fees paid by radio and TV owners (later TV owners alone) it did not have to make a profit, and consequently was able to provide high-quality news and entertainment for the nation as a whole. The public service model of television operated from 1946 (when the BBC resumed its post-war TV broadcasting) until 1955, when commercial TV went on the air. In radio the BBC's monopoly lasted from 1926, when the BBC was founded, until commercial radio was legalised in 1971.

Radio and TV broadcasting is still carefully regulated in Britain by an alphabet soup of agencies, and news and current affairs programmes are closely regulated in order to achieve balance, accuracy, and impartiality. As a result, most people believe that the BBC and ITN (Independent Television Network) are reliable and impartial sources of news. Whereas about two out of three trust BBC and ITN 'a great deal', and about half say the same of their broadsheet newspaper, fewer than one-third of tabloid readers trust their newspaper.

Public service model
The idea that radio and TV should not be commercial but used in the public interest to educate, inform and entertain.

BRIEFINGS

14.3 The public service model

The main aim of the public service model of broadcasting is not to use the media to make money in a commercial market, but as a national resource for the public good. Lord Reith, the founding father of the BBC, saw it as 'the voice of the nation' with a duty to 'educate, inform and entertain', in that order of priority. The main features of the British public service model are:

- **Market regulation** As natural monopolies the electronic media are regulated by the State, which issues broadcasting licences under specific conditions.

- **Content regulation** If broadcasting wavelengths are public property then they should be used for the public good: programmes should appeal to a wide range of tastes, majority and minority; news and election programmes should be balanced, accurate and impartial; political advertising and editorialising are not allowed.

- **Accountability** The electronic media should be accountable to the public, not to market shareholders or the government.

- **Self-regulation by quango** To avoid the dangers of State interference the media should be controlled and regulated by their own bodies or quangos.

- **National broadcasting** Broadcasting should serve the entire nation, including remote areas, not a particular territory or section of the population.

- **Public funding** Broadcasting should be financed mainly from public funds, not commercial sources. Public funds may take the form of general subsidies from the government, or licence fees, or some combination of the two.

BRIEFINGS

14.4 **The alphabet soup of media agencies**

BBC (British Broadcasting Corporation)   Established in 1926 as a public radio monopoly, the BBC now runs local, national and international radio and TV channels, as well as the largest web site in Europe. The Home Secretary appoints its board of governors, which appoints the director-general, who has day-to-day authority. Its charter is periodically renewed, the last time in 1994 until 2006. It is funded mainly from the TV licence fee, which is set by the government.

ITC (Independent Television Commission)   The Broadcasting Act of 1990 created the ITC in place of the previous controlling body (the Independent Broadcasting Authority). The ITC licenses and regulates commercial TV stations, which have been auctioned since 1990. Commercial broadcasting is funded by advertising revenue.

BSC (Broadcasting Standards Commission)   The Broadcasting Act of 1996 replaced the Broadcasting Complaints Commission with the Broadcasting Standards Commission (BSC). The BSC is the statutory body dealing with codes of practice, standards and fairness, and complaints for all forms of broadcasting in the UK – BBC and commercial, text, cable, satellite and digital broadcasting.

The Radio Authority   The Radio Authority licenses and regulates all independent radio in accordance with the Broadcasting Acts of 1990 and 1996.

Oftel   Oftel was set up in 1984 to regulate the UK telecommunications industry when British Telecom (a nationalised industry) was privatised.

Radiocommunications Agency   This is an executive agency of the Department of Trade and Industry that manages the non-military radio spectrum and keeps it clean of unauthorised users.

OFCOM (Office of Communications), created by the Communications Act 2003.

Given the convergence of the TV, radio, phone, and computer communications sectors, a single new regulatory body (OFCOM) is planned for late 2003 that merges the ITC, BSC, Oftel, the Radio Authority, and the Radiocommunications Agency.

Friends of the BBC point out that it is widely admired throughout the western world for its high-quality broadcasting, especially its news and current affairs programmes. Critics say that as a public service monopoly it was notable for elitist or paternalistic broadcasting that gave people not what they wanted but what the BBC thought they should have. Since commercialisation, however, the BBC has had to pay more careful attention to its audience ratings, and 'backdoor commercialisation' is the result. The public service model of political reporting still applies to all radio and TV, but commercial pressures have changed almost everything else. Commercialisation of the media has been a fiercely controversial issue in British politics and it is likely to remain so for some time to come.

Public services versus free media markets

Public service model

- There is no market for ideas or for political news as there is for soap powder or motor cars. News programmes cannot be put to the same tests as consumer durables, neither can political ideas be subject to the same sort of tests as soap powder.

- The market does not ensure that truth will prevail, or even that the best ideas will survive, only that popular demands are satisfied. If people want sound bites, gossip, trivia, racism, sexism, prejudice, chauvinism, that is what the market will deliver.

- The news is far too important to be left to commercial forces that are only interested in profits. Only public regulation can ensure balance, accuracy, and impartiality.

- State control of the electronic media (market and content) should remain as long as there is no competitive market in the electronic media as there is, in theory, in the print media.

- There are dangers in the state regulation of the media, but these are avoided in some western countries where there is no state control or influence over the political content of the media.

- In the commercial media the bad drives out the good, and market competition forces the best to adopt the standards of the worst.

- The state has to step in when the market fails and the media market shows clear signs of oligopoly, not pluralistic competition.

- Media oligopolies are increasingly driven by conservative ideologies, which renders their content politically biased.

- The state will have to continue its regulation of such things as pornography, racism, and children's programmes.

- Self-regulation of the newspapers has produced low journalistic standards, cheque book journalism, sensationalism and the invasion of privacy.

- Probably the most commercial media market in the western world is in the USA, which also has one of the worst news services.

Free market model

- There is no difference, in principle, between the market for goods and services and the market for news and ideas. We should turn news and ideas over to the market, like other goods and services.

- The market ensures that people get what they want, which is more democratic than BBC directors broadcasting what they think people need.

- Regulation of the media is inconsistent with free speech, and government by quango still gives the government too much influence. The media should be completely independent of government.

- Cable and satellite TV, local radio, and the convergence of media sectors have virtually eliminated spectrum scarcity, and there is little difference between the markets for electronic and print media. State control is no longer necessary.

- Some claim that market competition between ideas will ensure that the 'truth will out', others that truth is relative, and only media competition will deliver a multiplicity of truths.

- The state can regulate cases of media market failure as it does other cases of market failure, but this means occasional intervention, not control.

- Content regulation of the media should go no further than dealing with the conditions for public order and the protection of those unable to protect themselves, especially children. Libertarians even argue that the state should not regulate pornography.

- Low journalistic standards are better than repression or manipulation by governments.

COMMERCIALISATION OF THE ELECTRONIC MEDIA

Post-war Conservative governments were persuaded by technical developments in radio and TV broadcasting to introduce commercial radio and TV, so ending the BBC monopoly and progressively diluting the public service model. The Television Act of 1954 created commercial (Independent) TV, which went on the air a year later, the first in western Europe. Then, pressured by pirate radio (illegal commercial radio broadcast from ships outside territorial waters), commercial radio was authorised in 1971. A second commercial TV Channel (Channel 4) was set up by the Independent Broadcasting Authority Act of 1979, and it went on the air in 1982. Meanwhile, cable TV was introduced in 1972, and satellite TV (first broadcast in 1962 from Telstar) expanded rapidly in the late 1980s, vastly increasing the total number of TV stations.

By 1986 the Peacock Report on funding the BBC stated that technological developments would soon end spectrum scarcity, and so create a consumer market in broadcasting. Although the report opposed advertising by the BBC at the time, it anticipated that there will soon be no need for state regulation; everything can be left to the 'free market'.

The arguments for commercial radio and TV, as against the public service model, are complex and many sided, and ultimately they are political rather than technical or economic. Advocates of the market claim that only full commercialisation can guarantee pluralist competition, and the absence of state regulation that freedom of speech demands. They argue that the British media can only compete with the main European players, never mind the giant media corporations of America, if media ownership restrictions are lifted. Defenders of public service media point out that the media market is an oligopoly, and likely to become more so. They fear that commercialisation will produce the worst kind of 'tabloid TV', just as the print market has produced the worst kind of newspaper journalism. Further commercialisation may result in American-style media that delivers poor news and current affairs coverage.

Although the British government may well introduce more commercialism into the media in the future, state regulation of broadcasting is not likely to disappear altogether:

- The European Union wants to impose greater regulation on the media market and its content.

- Those who most strongly advocate a media market are often most strongly opposed to some of its commercial products: pornography on TV and the net, for example.

- The requirements of balance, accuracy and impartiality for TV and radio news are still in place, as are the restrictions on election campaigning and reporting.

In other words the deregulation of the electronic media in some respects is likely to result in regulation and reregulation in others, as in other areas of public policy. At the same time, there is cause for concern about the democratic role of the mass media (print and electronic) that derives not only from its content but also from the structure of its ownership and control.

OWNERSHIP AND CONTROL OF THE BRITISH MEDIA

The history of the British mass media in the twentieth century is marked by five related features:

1. nationalisation
2. a declining number of newspaper titles
3. concentration of ownership and control
4. the growth of multimedia conglomerates
5. internationalisation.

Nationalisation

Britain is a small, densely populated and highly centralised country, so it is not surprising that the media have a centralised and nationalised market. There are still many local and regional daily and Sunday papers, but two-thirds of the adult population regularly see a national daily paper, and 70 per cent a national Sunday paper. As a result, the national newspaper market in Britain is very large by most standards. In round figures, 180 million newspapers a week are sold in Britain, of which 93 million are national dailies or Sundays. The national dailies have a total circulation of 13 million a day, and the national Sundays sell 12.5 million. Since each paper is read by between two and three people the readership of the national dailies is around 31 million, and of the national Sundays around 35 million. National newspaper sales have dropped substantially since their peak in the late 1950s because of competition from TV, and more recently because of unemployment and a shift of the small advertising to the net, but the two best sellers – the *Sun* and the *Daily Mirror* – still sell over 6 million daily between them. All national newspapers have their headquarters in London, even if they print regional editions in Manchester, for example, or in Scotland.

Radio and TV are also highly centralised, with a few national organisations dominating the market. ITV is based on regions, and there has been a rapid expansion of local and community radio stations, but most viewers and listeners still tune to national programmes and national news broadcasts.

Declining number of newspaper titles

In the same way that the market for cars has produced an ever-increasing need for capital investment, and so an ever-decreasing number of mass manufacturers, so the newspaper market has less and less room for competing titles. In 1900 there were 21 national daily papers, now there are 11 (including the *Financial Times*). In 1923 there were 14 Sunday papers, now there are nine. In the 70 years after 1920 the number of provincial morning papers declined from 41 to 18, of provincial evening papers from 89 to 76, and of national and provincial Sunday papers from 21 to nine. There were about 1,400 local and regional daily and Sunday titles in 1947, only 550 in the early 1990s. In 1975 18 per cent of British towns had competing papers run by different owners, half the percentage of 1921. In 1900 London had 11 evening papers; now it has one.

Concentration of ownership and control

Concentrated ownership and control of the British newspaper business is by no means new. In 1910 the biggest press magnate of the day, Lord Northcliffe, controlled 39 per cent of national daily circulation. In 2003 his modern equivalent, Rupert Murdoch, has 35 per cent of the daily and almost 40 per cent of the Sunday market. However, in 1910 the three best-selling national dailies accounted for two-thirds of total circulation. In 1983 the biggest three (Murdoch, Maxwell and Matthews) took 75 per cent. In that year the five biggest companies accounted for 84 per cent of national daily and 96 per cent of national Sunday sales.

Plate 14.3 *A meeting of moguls. Rupert Murdoch (centre) with the late Robert Maxwell and Lord Rothermere*

Source: Popperfoto

The big five have also increased their control of the local and provincial press. In 1947 they had 44 and 65 per cent of provincial evening and morning circulation. In 1983 the figures had risen to 54 and 72 per cent respectively. Over the same period they increased their share of the local weekly market from 8 per cent to almost one-third.

BRIEFINGS

14.5 Media moguls

Robert Maxwell

When Maxwell died in mysterious circumstances in 1991 his newspapers (*Mirror/Daily Record*, *Sunday Mirror*, *Sunday People*, and *Sporting Life*) sold close to 12 million copies a week, accounting for one-quarter of the daily tabloid market. Maxwell also had financial interests in TV (Central, Border, SelecTV, MTV and Rediffusion Cable), books (EJ Arnold and Pergamon Press), magazines and journals, computer software, transport and plastics.

Rupert Murdoch

Rupert Murdoch, an Australian with US citizenship, owns newspapers and TV stations on three continents. In Britain his companies own the *Sun*, *News of the World*, *The Times*, *The Sunday Times* and *The Times'* supplements with sales of over 10 million copies, including one-third of the daily and Sunday tabloid market and almost half the Sunday broadsheets. His financial interests include London Weekend TV, BSkyB (the largest satellite company in Britain), cable TV, films (Metromedia and Fox), recording, magazines and journals, general publishing (Collins, Fontana and Granada Books), the Reuters news agency, property, land and air transport (TNT trucking), computer software, gas and oil, and shares in Manchester United, Leeds United, and Chelsea football clubs.

Lord Matthews

The main Matthews company, Trafalgar House, ran the Express Group (sold to United Newspapers in 1985), which published, among others, the *Daily Express*, *Sunday Express*, *Star*, and *Standard*, and 11 local papers (a circulation of over 7 million). At various times his companies have had interests in TV-AM, Capital Radio, publishing houses in Britain and abroad, Cunard shipping and hotels, and in property and insurance.

Lord Rothermere

Rothermere's Associated Newspapers publishes the *Daily Mail*, *Mail on Sunday*, and *Weekend*, which have a circulation of around 5 million. It also has financial ties with Northcliffe Newspapers in companies on three continents that cover publishing, broadcasting, theatre, oil, transport and investment finance.

United Newspapers

When United Newspapers (Lord Stevens) absorbed the Express Group it controlled one-quarter of daily tabloid and 10 per cent of Sunday tabloid circulation. In the 1990s it published eight regional dailies, over 100 weeklies, and controlled two large publishers of magazines and directories as well as the Extel news agency.

The policy of regulating the market to preserve competition has not been effective in Britain. The Royal Commissions on the press of 1949, 1962 and 1977 all expressed concern about increasing concentration of ownership and control. As a result of a recommendation of the 1962 Commission it was decided in 1965 that large companies should get the consent of the secretary of state for the Department of Trade and Industry before acquiring more newspaper holdings. Between 1965 and 1977 50 such applications were made. None was refused. In 1981 Rupert Murdoch was allowed to buy *The Times* and *Sunday Times*, increasing his share of national daily sales to 30 per cent, and of national Sunday sales to 36 per cent.

In 1990 Murdoch's Sky company merged with its main rival, British Satellite Broadcasting (BSB) to form a satellite monopoly, BSkyB, although this was inconsistent with the 1990 Broadcasting Act. The companies did not consult the Independent Broadcasting Authority before the merger, but the IBA approved it after the event. In 1992 there was a moratorium on mergers of commercial TV stations, following the first franchise auction of the previous year. Nonetheless Yorkshire Television absorbed Tyne Tees Television and the Independent Television Commission agreed to the merger.

The concentration of ownership and control is likely to speed up over the next decades, because of economic pressures and because controls were loosened in 1993 by allowing companies to hold two licences, which some promptly did. In 1995 controls of cross-media ownership were further loosened, although large newspaper groups continued to have restricted rights to TV ownership.

Cross-media ownership
When the same person or company has financial interests in different types of mass media – radio, TV, newspapers, magazines, films, recording etc.

Multimedia conglomeration
When the same company has financial interests in different media and (usually) in a range of other economic activities as well.

Multimedia conglomeration

What makes the current situation different from the earlier times of press barons, such as Lords Northcliffe and Rothermere, is that the concentration of ownership and control now extends far beyond the press to publishing and other media forms. The largest multimedia conglomerates now include newspapers, journals, books, films, recording, radio, TV and entertainment. They also extend into commerce and finance of other kinds, such as property, banking, insurance, oil, transport and computers. As the Press Commission of 1977 wrote: 'Rather than saying that the press has other business interests, it would be truer to argue that the press has become a subsidiary of other interests.' This is even truer now. In short, the media have been absorbed into the general world of business and finance.

Internationalisation – the borderless world

In the last decades multimedia moguls and corporations have emerged that span not just countries but continents. The most conspicuous examples include Ted Turner in the USA, Berlusconi in Italy, the Bertelsmann and Springer groups of Germany, and Rupert Murdoch, whose companies operate in Australia, Asia, Europe and the USA. While newspapers usually cater for national (that is, specific language) markets, they are increasingly controlled by multinational companies, and some journals and magazines are increasing their international circulation (the *Financial Times*, the *Economist*, *Time*, *Newsweek*). The inherently international nature of films and TV is being strengthened by the spread of cable and satellite, which is creating a global, or borderless, television network. The result is that a few international news channels, such as Cable News Network (CNN) and BBC World TV, are chasing the global news market hard.

There are two dangers in increasing ownership and control, and of growing multimedia, multinational conglomerates. First, such companies are increasingly beyond public accountability or regulation, and represent growing power without responsibility. Second, by controlling large market shares they weaken media competition that pluralist theory says is essential for democracy.

POLITICAL CONSEQUENCES OF MARKET CHANGES

Changes in the media market seem to have contradictory consequences for news and current affairs reporting, some good and some bad.

Smaller media: specialisation and diversity

As ownership and control of the mass media becomes increasingly consolidated and centralised, so the mass media become progressively homogeneous. At the same time technology also makes it possible for the smaller media to become increasingly specialised and varied. Local TV and radio, satellite and cable TV, the increasing number of magazine titles, and the communication possibilities of the World Wide Web and email are a few examples of media differentiation. However, a closer look at these media sectors reveals a more complex situation of progressive consolidation of mass markets, and increasing fragmentation of minority markets.

MAGAZINES

A visit to any high street newsagent will reveal a pluralist heaven of magazine titles catering for a huge diversity of tastes. A closer look shows that many of the big circulation magazines in Britain are published by a few of the largest companies. Between 1966 and 1974 over half of the new consumer magazines with sales of 30,000 or more were launched by four major publishing groups. The largest, the International Publishing Corporation, has over 200 titles.

NEWSPAPERS

New computer methods of newspaper production have not weakened the Fleet Street empires, as they were predicted to do. It is true that two new national papers were launched between 1960 and 1985, whereas eight were created between 1986 and 1992, but few survive. Even Eddie Shah's attempt in 1986 to use the latest colour printing technology to break into the national market, with *Today*, failed when he was forced to sell the paper to Tiny Rowland's multimedia, multinational company, Lonrho. The *Independent*, also launched in 1986, was the first successful new national daily in the country since 1873, but with daily sales of around 180,000 (less than 2 per cent of the national total), it has barely disturbed the mass-circulation papers.

TV

BBC had a monopoly of TV with its single channel in 1955. Now it fights with an ever-growing number of terrestrial, cable, and satellite channels. In spite of this fragmentation of the market, however, the BBC keeps a 40 per cent share of the market, and the four main terrestrial channels account for 80 per cent. Moreover, following the auctioning of commercial TV licences in 1990 and the weakening of market regulation, three companies (Granada, United News, and Scottish Media Group) now control 10 of the 15 regional channels, and Murdoch's BSkyB has a virtual monopoly of satellite broadcasting. A large number of small channels account for a small percentage of the total TV market.

Sensationalism and investigative journalism

Commercialisation means that profit and dividends for shareholders has become an overriding imperative. This has two effects on news content; sensationalism and investigative journalism. These are different sides of the same coin, in the sense that both are intended to attract readers and viewers in a commercial media market. The tabloids turned to more cheque book journalism and sensationalism in the 1960s and 1970s, partly to combat TV competition. TV, faced with commercial pressures, has increasingly 'dumbed down' its programming and cut its news and current affairs coverage.

Investigative journalism In-depth and often critical journalism that involves research which is usually time consuming and expensive.

At the same time both newspapers and TV have turned to more investigative journalism. It could be argued that the media now do a much better job of questioning leading politicians than Parliament. The trend, started by Robin Day in the 1970s, has been sharpened by John Humphrys and James Naughtie on radio, and Jeremy Paxman on TV. Paxman once asked the Home Secretary, Michael Howard, the same question 14 times, to make it clear that he could not get a straight answer. Newspapers, for their part, are increasingly involved in investigative journalism (sometimes called 'attack' journalism). Recent examples involve the MPs Neil Hamilton and Jonathan Aitken.

Softening partisanship?

A recent trend that may be emerging, although it is early days to tell, is the softening of Fleet Street partisanship. Not only did the national press swing behind Blair in the 1997 and 2001 elections, but it also changed its previously strident party position to a more muted and balanced one. The failings of the Major government (sleaze, internal division, indecision, and unpopular EU policies) were fully reported rather than repressed by the Tory press, and support for both the main parties was more qualified, selective, and balanced. Possibly this is a short-run trend caused by New Labour's popularity, but it may be a longer term consequence of national papers trying to appeal to a broader range of readers in a declining newspaper market.

Plate 14.4 Guardian cover of Neil Hamilton: 'A liar and a cheat.' The Guardian's investigative journalism is a rarity, partly because of Britain's libel laws

Source: The *Guardian*

Less politics and current affairs?

Whether because of citizen political fatigue or commercialisation, or both, there are signs that political and current affairs reporting has been cut in recent years. The tabloids showed rather little interest in the election campaign of 2001 (perhaps because it was dull and a foregone conclusion), ITV cut its news programmes compared with 1997, and it was left largely to the BBC to do its public service duty. The best and most extensive election news tended to be 'ghettoised' in the specialised news channels that have small audiences. In other words, the political content of the mass media may be declining, but that of the more specialised media is increasing.

E-MEDIA: DIGITOPIA OR DIGITAL DYSTOPIA?

By the start of the new millennium, technical change had already transformed the electronic media market, and was set to revolutionise it again within another decade or so. The arrival of satellite and cable television, and of community radio and TV, has created an abundance of broadcasting stations and eliminated spectrum scarcity. Digital broadcasting means the convergence of media sectors (TV, radio, newspapers, and computer communication) so that sound, pictures, and words can be transmitted and received across media sectors, blending them into one. The potential of the 'wired nation' with information superhighways, smart buildings, and smart cards will introduce cheaper and more accessible communications with more competition and variety.

Some regard this as a huge potential benefit to politics, making direct democracy a reality by means of interactive, push-button communication. Others regard it is a threat, making it easier for global business empires to consolidate their control of communication technology, enhancing the cultural imperialism of American corporations, widening the knowledge gap and creating new information inequalities, and further commercialising and dumbing down the mass media.

It is certainly the case that new media in the shape of the World Wide Web and email have spread like wildfire. There were no web pages in 1988 but an estimated 200 million of them in 2000, and growth is exponential. Some 40 per cent of the population is predicted to be online by 2003. Acutely conscious of this, New Labour has set up special units within government to promote both e-government and e-commerce, but it looks as if it will fail to meet its targets for e-government by a wide margin. The difficulty is not technology but social attitudes and adaptability. In Parliament itself in 2000 fewer than 20 per cent of MPs had their own web site and only 50 per cent had publicly available email addresses. We can see the slow pace of change of e-politics most clearly in the 2001 election.

2001 – the first e-election

Email, the net, and the mobile phone could revolutionise political communication by (a) making it more interactive than ever before, and (b) replacing the crude mass audience approach of TV and papers with a refined marketing strategy tailor made for individuals. Although the 2001 election was called 'the first internet election', it conspicuously failed to live up to its (no doubt grossly exaggerated) claims. It is estimated that the two main parties together spend around 1 million pounds on web sites, email, and text messaging, and all the main parties had their web sites. The Labour Party was the most active, sending 32 daily e-bulletins and email messages to 35,000 addresses. It also text messaged 100,000 younger voters, enticing them to vote Labour with the promise of longer licensing hours. The mass media also had their election web sites, most notably the superb BBC News Online, as well as the daily press, and various private organisations.

All told, the e-campaign was modest and had little impact. Web sites were used mainly as electronic notice boards, and there were few attempts to use its interactive capacities, although there were an estimated 8,000 vote-swap agreements between tactical voters in marginal seats. Barely 3 per cent of the population used the net or email for election purposes. Perhaps the fact that the youngest generation of voters used them most tells us something about its future? And the fact that by the general election of 2009/10 we will have full digital interactivity may also help to bring about a political communications revolution. Meanwhile we seem destined for neither digital utopia nor dystopia, but for an adapted version of the TV/newspaper form of political communication.

ESSAYS

1. The British media are often said to be biased. Explain how and why this bias may reach beyond simple party political bias in the shaping of the news.

2. What impact have the new means of communications (notably the World Wide Web and email) had on British government and politics, particularly on election campaigning?

3. What has been the impact on news reporting of the commercialisation on the British media?

SUMMARY

■ The mass media have been transformed out of all recognition since 1945, and now play a hugely important role in British politics. We are in the 'media age', but exactly what this means is a controversial matter.

■ Different people use different media for different purposes. Well-educated people tend to read a broadsheet, and watch comparatively little TV. Poorly educated people tend to read a tabloid and watch a lot of TV, including TV news. The result is a 'knowledge gap'.

■ It is exceedingly difficult to pin down what sort of medium has what sort of impact on what sorts of people. The four main opinions on this topic are: reinforcement theory/minimal effects; agenda-setting theory; framing theory, which claims indirect and direct effects; and direct effects theory.

■ The matter of media bias is also highly controversial, but content regulation reduces party political bias in the electronic media, which, as a result is trusted much more than the tabloid press. Until 1997, Fleet Street leaned heavily towards the Conservatives.

■ Spectrum scarcity in the past resulted in both market and content regulation of the electronic media, and the BBC conformed closely to the public service model, but technological developments in broadcasting have changed this, and commercialisation and deregulation of the electronic media have followed.

■ The result is conflicting patterns in the media market and its coverage of politics: (a) concentration of ownership and control of the mass market, (b) greater variety in the specialised media, (b) the growth of sensational and of investigative journalism, but (c) a decline of political coverage in the mass media, an increase in the specialist media.

■ For all the speculation about them, e-media seem to have had little impact on politics so far.

MILESTONES

Milestones in British media history

1945–6 BBC Radio resumes normal peacetime broadcasting with the Light Programme, the Home Service, and, in 1946, the Third Programme

1946 BBC TV starts again

1950 First TV coverage of general election results. First political programme on TV (*In the News*)

1951 Beveridge Committee on broadcasting recommends public service TV similar to radio

1953 First edition of BBC *Panorama* programme. Press Council set up

1954 Television Act establishes commercial TV (ITV)

1955 ITV goes on the air

1956 Anthony Eden makes first Prime Ministerial TV broadcast (about Suez). Labour opposition insists on a reply

1959 First TV election campaign coverage

1962 First Telstar TV satellite broadcast

1964 BBC 2 goes on the air, as does Radio Caroline (pirate radio)

1967 First colour TV (BBC 2). First BBC local radio station

1969 Rupert Murdoch (News International) buys the *Sun* and *News of the World*

1970s Investigative journalism spreads as a feature of all newspapers and television

1971 Commercial local radio authorised

1972 First cable TV

1974 First election phone-in on radio

1975 Trial radio broadcasts of the House of Commons

1979 Independent Broadcasting Authority Act gives Channel 4 to IBA

1981 Murdoch buys *The Times* and *Sunday Times*

1982 First Channel 4 broadcasts

1983 Breakfast TV on BBC and ITV

1984 Maxwell buys Mirror Group

1985 Lord Stevens (United Newspapers) buys Express Group

1986 Peacock Report on financing the BBC recommends only minor changes. BSB wins contract for direct satellite broadcasting. Eddie Shah launches *Today*, then sells to Lonrho ('Tiny' Rowland). The *Independent* launched

1987 *Daily* and *Sunday Telegraph* bought by Conrad Black

1988 Broadcasting Standards Council established to regulate radio, TV and video standards. Rupert Murdoch announces Sky TV (satellite TV)

1989 House of Commons televised

1990 Commercial TV franchises auctioned amid much criticism. Sky TV merged with BSB to form BSkyB. BBC Radio 5 launched

1991 BBC launches World TV. Press Council transformed into Newspaper Press Complaints Commission with stronger powers

1992 Classic FM goes on air. Mirror Group passes to creditor bank when Maxwell dies. The *Sun* claims it won the election for the Conservatives

1993 Channel 4 sells airtime. TV ownership rules relaxed to make multiple ownership possible

1994 BBC Charter renewed until 2006

1995 Increasing concern about press invasion of privacy and 'cheque book' journalism

1996 Murdoch establishes monopoly over digital TV, but required to provide access to other broadcasters

1997 Channel 5 TV goes on the air

1997 The *Sun* switches support to Blair

1997 New Labour expands news management (spin doctor) staff in Downing Street and Whitehall

1998 *News at Ten* ends. Digital widescreeen TV starts. The ITC fines Carlton TV £2m for breaches of its code

2000 *News at Ten* reinstated. The Political Parties, Elections, and Referendums Act imposes tighter restrictions than ever on election spending and campaigning

2001 Fleet Street continues its strong support of New Labour. The BBC wins contract for new, 28-channel digital terrestrial TV

2003 The Communications Act creates OFCOM

PROJECTS

1. Playing the role of a national newspaper editor, explain how you would reconcile (a) your democratic obligations to inform your readers fully and fairly about politics, and (b) the demands of your shareholders to maintain your circulation figures.

2. (Class project). Debate the merits and deficiencies claimed for public service and commercial broadcasting.

FURTHER READING

Among the best general books are C. Seymour-Ure, *The British Press and Broadcasting since 1945* (Oxford: Blackwell, 1991), R. Negrine, *Politics and the Mass Media in Britain* (London: Routledge, 2nd edn, 1995), B. Franklin, *Packaging Politics* (London: Edward Arnold, 1994), and J. Watts, *Political Communication Today* (Manchester: Manchester University Press, 1997).

For good recent articles on the political media see J. Stanyer, 'Politics and the media: a loss of political appetite?', *Parliamentary Affairs*, **55**, 2002, pp. 377–88, and M. Scammell, 'New media, new politics', in P. Dunleavy et al (eds), *Developments in British Politics 6* (Basingstoke: Palgrave, 2002). For a short, general review of the media and democracy see B. Jones, 'The media and democracy', Parts 1 and 2, *Talking Politics*, **13** (1), pp. 17–21, and **13** (2), pp. 103–8. On e-government see R. Silcock, 'What is e-government?', *Parliamentary Affairs*, **54**, 2001, pp. 88–101.

USEFUL WEB SITES ON MASS MEDIA

Hotlinks to these sites can be found on the CWS website at http://www.booksites.net/budge.

There is sound evidence of the enormous influence that mass media has on every aspect of contemporary British politics. In this section, you will find links to Britain's most important media sites as well as links to academic and professional associations engaged in the analysis of the effects of mass media in contemporary Britain. The government's Office of Telecommunications is the UK's regulator for the Telecommunications Industry (www.oftel.gov.uk). There are other web sites for Britain's chief media regulators, these include the Broadcasting Standards Commission (www.bsc.org.uk), the Advertising Standards Authority (www.asa.org.uk), the Information Commissioner who is responsible for data protection and freedom of information (www.dataprotection.gov.uk), the Independent Television Commission (www.itc.org.uk), the Internet Watch Foundation (www.iwf.org.uk), and the Press Complaints Commission (www.pcc.org.uk). OFCOM's new site is www.ofcom.org-uk.

There are also independent associations aimed to improve the quality of media coverage, some of them include the Campaign for Freedom of Information (www.cfoi.org.uk), the Campaign for Press and Broadcasting Freedom (http://keywords.dsvr.co.uk/freepress/index.html), the Community Media Association (www.commedia.org.uk), the Different Voices Network (www.differentvoices.org.uk), The Presswise Trust (www.presswise.org.uk), Indymedia (www.uk.indymedia.org), and Media UK (www.mediauk.com). Some of the Unions representing media workers include Unison (www.unison.org.uk), the National Union of Journalists (www.nuj.org.uk), and BECTU (www.bectu.org.uk).

You also might want to visit www.newscorp.com where you can find useful information on media ownership in the UK. Interesting insights are also available from The Press Association (www.pa.press.net). At www.cultsock.ndirect.co.uk/MUHome/cshtml/ you can find an impressive number of links and resources for all issues related to mass media.

A very comprehensive and fully updated list of Britain's newspapers, magazines, TV and radio stations can be found at www.rapidtree.com.

Although we may be unclear about the details of media influence, few would deny that they play a major part in shaping the outcomes of elections, and thus the control of the government by one party and ideological tendency or another. The general elections of 1997 and 2001 changed the face of British politics by substituting a Labour government for the Conservative one which had ruled for almost 20 years. Now it looks as if Labour may last almost as long. Television and newspapers derive their power from the influence they are commonly assumed to have over political opinions, which ultimately get translated into votes. As British governments have to face elections every four or five years, everything that might affect their chances of winning or losing is important, and that gives them a strong motivation to control coverage or to seek the support of newspaper proprietors.

However, many factors in addition to the media shape election results. Voters' opinions can be influenced by family and friends; by their special background and the organisations to which they belong, such as churches, trade unions, firms and professional bodies; and by personal experiences that may have occurred many years earlier. The campaign strategies adopted by the parties may also have a considerable effect.

The exact number of votes a party receives may be less important than the way these votes are 'converted' into Parliamentary seats by the counting rules of the electoral system. British governments depend on being able to control Parliament by means of an overall majority of seats in the House of Commons (currently at least 330 out of the 659), not on winning 50 per cent of the popular vote. Labour's 2001 landslide victory, which netted the party 413 out of 659 seats in Parliament, was achieved with only 40.7 per cent of the vote. The Conservatives won ample majorities in 1979, 1983 and 1987 with 42–44 per cent of the vote.

This chapter will review all the factors affecting election results. Accordingly it will:

- give an overview of elections and parties since 1945

- examine the political effects of the current 'first past the post' system and of the alternative forms of electoral system that have been introduced by the Labour government for European and regional elections since 1997

- analyse the factors that cause votes to change and thus give electoral victory to one or other of the main parties

- review the reasons for some voters always voting for the same party, which gives Conservative and Labour a 'core support' of over a quarter of the vote, on which they can build – in sharp contrast to the Liberals

- consider Tony Blair's strategies for electoral success

- cover the reasons for declining turnout in elections and 'disengagement' from parties and the political process in general.

Elections	Conservative			Labour			Liberals			Others			Total number of MPs
	Seat no.	Seat %	Vote %	Seat no.	Seat %	Vote %	Seat no.	Seat %	Vote %	Seat no.	Seat %	Vote %	
1945	210	32.8	39.6	393	61.4	48.0	12	1.9	9.0	25	3.9	3.4	640
1950	298	47.7	43.4	315	50.4	46.1	9	1.4	9.1	3	0.5	1.4	625
1951	321	51.4	48.0	295	47.2	48.8	6	1.0	2.6	3	0.5	0.6	625
1955	345	54.8	49.7	277	44.0	46.4	6	1.0	2.7	2	0.3	1.2	630
1959	365	57.9	49.4	258	41.0	43.8	6	1.0	5.9	1	0.2	0.9	630
1964	304	48.3	43.4	317	50.3	44.1	9	1.4	11.2	0	0.0	1.3	630
1966	253	40.2	41.9	364	57.8	48.0	12	1.9	8.6	1	0.2	1.5	630
1970	330	52.4	46.4	288	45.7	43.1	6	1.0	7.5	6	0.9	3.0	630
1974 (Feb)	297	46.8	37.9	301	47.4	37.2	14	2.2	19.3	23[a]	3.6	5.6	635
1974 (Oct)	277	43.6	35.8	319	50.2	39.2	13	2.0	18.3	26	4.1	6.7	635
1979	339	53.4	43.9	269	42.4	36.9	11	1.7	13.8	16	2.5	5.4	635
1983	397	61.1	42.4	209	32.2	27.6	23[b]	3.5	25.4	21	3.2	4.6	650
1987	376	57.8	42.3	229	35.2	30.8	22[b]	3.4	22.5	23	3.5	4.4	650
1992	336	51.6	41.9	271	41.6	34.4	20	3.1	17.8	24	3.7	5.9	651
1997	165	25.0	30.7	418	63.4	43.2	46	7.0	16.8	30	4.5	9.3	659
2001	166	25.2	31.7	413	62.6	40.7	52	8.0	18.3	28	4.2	9.3	659

Table 15.1 *Election results, 1945–2001*

Notes: [a] Northern Irish MPs are counted as 'others' from 1974. [b] In 1983 and 1987 'Liberal' includes the SDP/Liberal Alliance

Source: Computed by authors

ELECTIONS AND PARTIES SINCE 1945

British elections register the popular standing of parties, using an electoral system that enables the party with a 'plurality' of the vote (ie the largest single vote) to win an absolute majority of seats in the House of Commons and thus form the government on its own. The next chapter will discuss how political parties came to dominate elections in the first place. In practically all democracies, elections involve a choice between party alternatives, not between individual candidates locally or party leaders nationally. In Britain, where one or other of the two main parties normally wins a majority of the seats, elections are unusually focused on the question of whether the country will have a Conservative or Labour government. Generally, the Conservatives favour less government intervention in the economy and Labour favours more, so the party choice carries with it a general policy choice: do voters want freer markets, more social inequality, lower taxes and lower public spending; or more state intervention, redistribution, taxes and public spending? This is the main ground on which the post-war elections listed in Table 15.1 have been fought and won.

Three major points emerge from the table. First, the winning party normally wins a proportion of Parliamentary seats that is higher than its proportion of the popular vote. For example, in each of the four elections from 1979 to 1992 the Conservative Party won over 50 per cent of the seats – and thus enough to form a government – even though its vote fluctuated around the 42 to 44 per cent level. Second, with roughly the same overall vote, the Conservative majority fluctuated from 51.6 per cent of the Commons seats in 1992 to 61.1 per cent in 1983. This demonstrates that under the current electoral system a party's Parliamentary strength depends not only on how many votes it gets but also on how its vote – and how the vote of opposing parties – is distributed across the constituencies. Small shifts in the distribution can produce major fluctuations in Parliamentary majorities. For example, between 1987 and 1992 the Conservative government's Parliamentary majority fell from a comfortable 100 to a slender 21 even though its share of the popular vote only shifted by a tiny 0.4 percentage points.

Under Britain's electoral system a concentration of support in a few areas penalises large parties but benefits small parties. Conversely, a relatively even spread of the vote benefits large parties but penalises small parties. A telling example of the latter is the Liberal Democrats, whose vote tends to be thinly spread across the country. In 1983, for example, they took 25.4 per cent of the vote (as the Liberal–SDP Alliance) but won a mere 3.5 per cent of seats.

The third feature to emerge from Table 15.1 is that, despite the distortions produced by Britain's first past the post system, the party that wins the most votes – even if less than half – normally wins an outright majority of seats. In this respect the electoral system usually dispenses a rough justice by giving the largest party a bonus of seats large enough to form a stable government over a full Parliamentary term. In the 15 elections since 1945 only two – 1950 and February 1974 – have failed to provide the winner with a large enough majority of seats to sustain it in office for a full term. And only two – 1951 and, again, February 1974 – produced the 'wrong' result, in which the Conservative and Labour parties respectively won slightly more seats but slightly fewer votes than their rival. The capacity of first past the post voting rules to convert a plurality of votes into a majority of seats for the leading party is its most distinctive characteristic, illustrated dramatically in the last general election when 41 per cent of the vote gave Labour 63 per cent of seats.

COUNTING VOTES INTO SEATS: ELECTORAL SYSTEMS

The method of counting votes into seats is thus crucial for the determination of election results and the Parliamentary strength of political parties. It can also affect the way people vote in the first place. This is particularly true of the impact of first past the post on the Liberal Democrats. Because the party fails to win many seats under the system, and is therefore perceived to have no realistic chance of taking or sharing office, many potential supporters consider a vote for the Liberal Democrats 'wasted' and vote, often reluctantly, for whichever of Conservative and Labour they dislike the least. First past the post doubly penalises the Liberal Democratic Party, first by awarding it disproportionately few seats, and, second, by discouraging sympathisers from voting for it.

Supporters of the current system including Tony Blair claim that unfairness to Liberal Democrats and other minority parties is more than counterbalanced by the fact that it ensures a majority government, thereby offering electors a real and focused choice between alternative governments with distinct programmes. If Britain adopted a system of proportional representation, which gave seats in a

First past the post
Also known as the single-member simple plurality system, this counts votes into seats by awarding each seat to the candidate who gets most votes (a plurality) inside a small constituency.

Proportional representation (PR)
A voting system that uses an allocation formula (of which there are many) for distributing seats among parties in proportion to their vote.

strict ratio to votes, it would be very rare for any one party to win a majority of seats. Two parties would always have to join to form a coalition government, and in effect the British electorate would be offered a choice of a Conservative–Liberal Democrat or Labour–Liberal Democrat coalition. The Liberal Democrats would find themselves permanently in government, even though they are the third-ranking party in terms of votes, which is just as unfair as their permanent exclusion from government. Moreover, voters could never be clear in advance what combination of parties would form a coalition and what programme the government would have. In spite of its unfairness, therefore, the present electoral system at least offers electors real choice and direct accountability.

BRIEFINGS

15.1 Main electoral systems: plurality and proportional representation

Free elections are the backbone of modern democracy, and although at first sight they appear to be a simple matter – expressing a preference for one party over others – they turn out to be complex affairs. There are two main types of electoral system (ie procedures for translating votes into seats): simple plurality voting and proportional representation (PR).

Electoral system
A set of procedures for translating votes received by party candidates into shares of Parliamentary seats.

Simple plurality systems

The single-member simple plurality system (SMSP)

Sometimes called 'first past the post', SMSP only requires the winning candidate to obtain more votes than any other candidate, no matter how many candidates there are, and no matter how small the winner's share of the total vote is. In a three-way contest the winner may get little more than one-third of the total, and in a four-way contest little more than one-quarter. Simple plurality voting is usually linked with single-member constituencies. In Europe it is used at present in the UK, and outside Europe in the USA and Canada. The advantage of the system is simplicity. The disadvantage is the probability of disproportionate election results in which the proportion of seats in the Parliament won by each party does not match the proportion of votes it won in the election. The simple plurality system unfairly penalises minority parties, including large minority parties such as the Liberal Democrats, which have widespread rather than concentrated support.

Single-member simple plurality (SMSP)
Also called first past the post, the electoral system used in British general elections in which the country is divided into constituencies, each returning one member of Parliament, who only needs more votes than any other candidate in that constituency to win the election.

Second ballot system

The second ballot system tries to avoid the worst flaws of SMSP by requiring the winning candidate to obtain an absolute majority (50 per cent + 1) of the votes cast in the first round of elections. Failing this, a second (run-off) election is held for the strongest of the first-round candidates. This system is currently used in France for both its Parliamentary and presidential elections.

▶

Additional member system (sometimes termed the supplementary vote)

Again this attempts to redress extreme disproportionality in the results from SMSP by having additional 'list' members elected in larger constituencies in a way which favours parties losing out in the constituency-based voting. A majority of MPs are still elected under SMSP, however. This is the system used for election to the Scottish Parliament and Welsh and London Assemblies, where it has reduced but not eliminated the bias in favour of Labour and led to their coalitions with Liberal Democrats. This is the system which the Labour Party would be most inclined to adopt if it changed from pure SMSP.

Alternative vote system

Another variation on the simple plurality system allows voters to indicate their first and subsequent preferences among candidates, so that if no candidate receives a majority of first preferences, second (and subsequent) preferences may be brought into play in second and subsequent counts. A version of this system was adopted for the election of the mayor of London.

Proportional representation systems

Proportional representation is not itself an electoral system but a principle by which different electoral systems can be judged. The principle is that the distribution of seats between parties in the elected legislature should correspond to the national distribution of votes cast for the parties in the election. In other words, minorities as well as majorities should be represented in proportion to their voting strength. The main ways of doing this are the party list system and the single transferable vote.

Party list system

This is the simplest way of ensuring that seats are proportional to votes. Parties draw up a list of candidates in order of preference, and the candidates are elected in proportion to the number of votes their party receives in the nation as a whole (as in the Netherlands) or in large regions, starting from the top of the party lists. This system puts a lot of power into the hands of the party leadership, which decides where candidates are ranked in the list. The system is used in most European countries and in the European elections in Britain.

Single transferable vote (STV)

This system is used in the Irish Republic and for the Northern Irish Assembly and is preferred by the Liberal Democrats for the UK. It requires multimember rather than single-member constituencies. Voters rank order their preferences for all the candidates, so that their second, third, or subsequent preferences can be taken into account. A minimum quota of votes for election to the Parliament is calculated (the quota depends on the number of votes cast divided by the number of members to be elected for the constituency). The first preferences are counted in the initial round of counting. In the second round the surplus votes (ie those over the number required by the quota) obtained by candidates elected in the first round are redistributed according to the second preferences of voters for unelected candidates. Once the redistribution of surpluses ceases to elect any further candidates the votes of the least preferred candidate are redistributed according to second and subsequent preferences. Counts continue in this fashion until all seats are filled. There are many minor variations on STV, and different ways of calculating the final result, but the system usually leads to close proportionality at the national level, especially if most of the multimember constituencies elect five or more members of Parliament. Because voters can rank order all the candidates they do not regard a vote for a minor party candidate as wasted.

A central feature of the SMSP system is the impact of constituency boundaries. Changing the boundaries – which is necessary to keep up with shifts of population – can deprive the sitting member by excluding districts with concentrations of supporters or including new districts with concentrations of opponents. The precise boundaries of a constituency are so crucial for the result that responsibility for drawing them up is given to an independent commission rather than to the political parties or the government.

Even so, the national pattern of Parliamentary boundaries can turn out to favour one party at the expense of another. The new constituency boundaries drawn up for the 1997 election helped the Labour Party. The average size of the electorate was 65,708 in Labour-won seats but substantially more – 72,021 – in Conservative-won seats. Thus Labour could win more seats with fewer votes. One reason for the discrepancy is the legal requirement to create smaller sized constituencies in Scotland and Wales, where Labour is strong, than in England. A second is that even new constituency boundaries are based on population figures five years out of date. They do not take fully into account the constant movement of population from Labour-dominated inner city areas to the Conservative suburbs and country towns. This creates the pattern of small-sized Labour seats and large-sized Conservative seats, which becomes more marked at subsequent elections until the boundaries are revised again. The extent of the pro-Labour bias is revealed by calculating a 'reverse result' for the 2001 election. The actual result was: Labour 40.7 per cent, Conservatives 31.7 per cent, Labour overall majority of 167. But if the result on the identical constituency boundaries had been: Labour 31.7 per cent, Conservatives 40.7 per cent, the Conservatives would not have had an overall Parliamentary majority though they would have been the largest single party! The major bias that boosted the size of Labour's majorities in both 1997 and 2001 will, if anything, grow until the constituency boundaries are redrawn.

IMPACT OF NEW ELECTORAL SYSTEMS

In 1999, for the first time, systems of proportional representation were introduced for elections on the British mainland. (In Northern Ireland the single transferable vote had been in operation for elections to the Assembly and to the European Parliament for some time.) The additional member system was used for the elections to the Scottish Parliament and Welsh Assembly in May 1999 and to the Greater London Assembly in May 2000. The party list system was adopted for elections to the European Parliament in June 1999.

The impact of the new systems both on the outcome and the way people decided to vote was marked. In the Scottish case it resulted in no single party commanding an overall majority in the Scottish Parliament. Had the election been held under the traditional first past the post system Labour would have won two very comfortable majorities. As it was Labour was forced to enter into coalition with the Liberal Democrats (the first time they had formed part of a regional or national government since the early 1930s) and, as a result, change some of its policies, notably on university tuition fees. In Wales, too, proportional representation deprived the Labour Party of the overall majority it would undoubtedly have secured in a first past the post system. Although it formed a minority administration it was constantly hampered by the threat of votes of no confidence, which eventually forced the resignation of Alun Michael in favour of Rhodri Morgan as party leader and first minister of Wales and the formation of a Labour–Liberal coalition.

The onset of proportional representation also had a predictably favourable effect on the fortunes of the smaller parties. In Scotland the Conservatives have become a small minority party. They won only a single seat in the 2001 general election, despite winning 17.5 per cent of the vote. But the provision for additional members drawn from the regional lists in order to ensure a roughly proportional Scottish Parliament allocated 18 seats to the Conservatives, and thus saved the party from extinction in Scotland.

The European elections provide dramatic examples of how proportional representation – in this case the regional party list – benefits the smaller parties. In the previous European elections of 1994, held under first past the post, the Liberal Democrats won 17 per cent of the vote but only 2 of the 84 seats. In 1999 their share of the vote fell to 13 per cent, but they were allocated 10 of the 84 seats – a direct consequence of proportionality. The smaller minority parties benefited too. The Greens and UK Independence Party each gained their first Parliamentary representation with two and three seats respectively, seats they could not have won under the old electoral system.

Proportional representation not only changed the way votes were translated into seats but changed the way votes were *cast* in the first place. The share of the vote going to minor parties – notably the Greens and UKIP – increased from 5 per cent in 1994 to 19 per cent in 1999. Proportional representation encourages electors to vote for the party, however minor, that they genuinely prefer. Simple plurality systems, by contrast, discourage voters from 'wasting' their vote on no-hope smaller parties and encourage them instead to cast a tactical and negative vote for whichever party has the best chance of keeping out the party they like the least.

Tactical voting

Tactical voting
The practice of voting for a candidate who is not one's first preference in order to keep out a less preferred candidate.

Tactical voting increased gradually in the 1980s and 1990s and was particularly evident in the 1997 and 2001 elections, when it boosted the strength of the non-Conservative parties. In the case of the Liberal Democrats it was particularly important, helping to more than double their tally of seats from 20 to 46 in 1997, despite a small decline in their share of the vote. The best estimate is that 25–35 seats were lost by the Conservatives in 1997 through tactical voting alone. Given the size of the Labour majority this did not determine the election result. But tactical voting might well swing a future election where the contenders are more evenly balanced. Some tactical voting continued in 2001, particularly between Labour and Liberal supporters. Whichever of these two parties had previously

Plate 15.1 *Dick Graham cartoon in the Manchester Evening News, 28 April 1997: 'I like to think of myself as a tactical abstainer.' While Labour got only 43 per cent of the vote in the 1997 election, tactical voting meant that they gained seats. The Liberals have also benefited from tactical voting with Labour*

Source: Manchester Evening News

shown they could win the seat, or mount the most effective challenge to the Conservatives, benefited from 'Lib–Lab' switching.

However, the degree of tactical voting should not be exaggerated. The majority of voters with an opportunity to vote tactically choose not to do so, either because they are unaware of the tactical situation or because they choose to vote positively for their party of first preference, however hopeless its prospects. Moreover, tactical voting only occurs on a significant scale where supporters of two of the parties feel much closer to each other than they do to the third. This was true for Labour and Liberal Democrats both in 1997 and 2001 and may continue if the two parties continue to propose similar policies and especially if there is the prospect of a coalition between them. Continuing convergence and co-operation could have major effects in future general elections:

- It could further increase the number of Labour and Liberal-held seats through tactical voting, at the expense of the Conservatives, reversing the advantage the latter had from a split opposition in the 1980s.

- Increasing numbers of Liberal seats make the party more and more credible and dispose of the 'wasted vote' argument.

- This in turn promotes prospects for a Labour–Liberal Democrat coalition, with major consequences for constitutional change and the party balance especially since the Liberals' main demand would be for change towards a more proportional vote–seat balance.

Targeting seats in 1997

Targeted electioneering
The practice of parties of concentrating resources on those marginal seats that they think they have the greatest chance of gaining from another party, or of losing to another party.

Another consequence of a small-constituency electoral system is the temptation for parties to concentrate money, volunteers and resources on those constituencies they think they have a good chance of winning. Such 'targeted electioneering' was very prevalent – again among both Labour and Liberal Democrats – in 1997. Indeed, it has been a long-standing Liberal tactic to 'target' constituencies where they have done well in local elections. In 1997 this tactic seemed to work for them in southwest England, their region of traditional strength, and to a lesser extent in southeast England. Labour, however, picked up only a few extra seats, possibly no more than four or six, through this strategy. In view of the massive concentration of resources involved and the resentment felt by local Labour parties elsewhere, this strategy was not repeated with the same ruthlessness at the election of 2001. Only the Liberals, who limited the number of targeted seats drastically, seemed to gain from the tactic.

EXPLAINING ELECTORAL SUCCESS

Electoral systems do not determine election results. But, in conjunction with the territorial distribution of the vote, they can strongly influence both the outcome and the way voters and parties act, as the examples of tactical voting showed.

Whatever its other effects, the first past the post system does tend to reward the party gaining the plurality of votes with the majority of Parliamentary seats and thus produce a decisive result. But how does one party rather than another manage to win the most votes? What explains why the Conservatives led Labour by 42 to 35 per cent of the national vote in the 1992 election but trailed Labour by 32 to 44 per cent in the 2001 election?

So many factors can influence voting that the task of selecting the most important to explain the overall result seems almost impossible. Voters are influenced by where they live; by their social class, religion and other social characteristics; by their personal experience going back to childhood; by their opinions on particular issues and their image of the parties; by tactical considerations; and a host of other factors. Moreover, these influences vary in their relative importance for different voters.

A vast amount of research has been done on the relationship between social, economic and political factors and the actual election result. It has identified the central processes that explain the overall election result and, as we shall see, is even capable of predicting it fairly accurately in advance.

What first needs to be explained is the *change* in the result from one election to another. Why do some voters switch parties, or move to and from abstention, between one election and the next? Ultimately, of course, we also wish to know why some people always vote for the same party, since they too contribute to the overall result. But clearly change between two elections will not be caused by them, even if their support for a party gradually erodes over the long term. We examine this possibility later.

BRIEFINGS

15.2 How voters explain their choices

General analyses of voting and elections can get too abstract and statistical, dealing as they do with mass movements of opinion. It is easy to lose sight of people's *own* individual reasoning about why they voted as they did, even though it is this that lies directly behind their choice. Here are some examples of the reasons voters gave to pollsters for their decision to change their vote:

'Give young people a chance.'
'Just decided at the last minute – we needed a change.'
'I work in social housing... Labour were offering a better alternative policy.'
'I didn't think the Liberal Democrats had much chance of getting in.' (so voted Labour)
'I voted Lib-Dem for tactical reasons – the Tory candidate didn't stand a chance and I didn't want Labour.'
'I always have voted for Lib-Dem... I went back to where my heart is.'
'I voted SNP because it was obvious the Conservatives were not going to win.'
'Labour... offered more policies to help education.'

Shifts in party support over a five-year term are much more likely to be caused by changes in public opinion and in the public's attitudes towards the parties than by underlying social factors, as these are unlikely to alter dramatically in the short term. But which from among the vast range of potential issues might be the most relevant to voting decisions?

One answer can be found in the factors that historically have influenced the policies and ideology of the political parties. It is, after all, the parties – particularly the Conservative and Labour parties – that set the election agenda and between which the voters choose when casting their votes. The great historical dividing line between these parties is the degree to which the state as opposed to the market should determine economic and social conditions. Under Margaret Thatcher Conservative policy shifted markedly from a belief in state intervention to reliance on the free market. Labour policy, although undoubtedly influenced by her ideas, remains more favourable to direct government action where it is felt to be needed. A good example is New Labour's 'welfare to work' programme, which was initially financed by an additional tax on the privatised utility companies.

The central concerns that people have in mind when voting are therefore likely to be economic in nature. It is natural to think of one's own well-being and that of one's family and ask whether it would be served best by direct government action or by the government standing aside and letting things take their course. When voters feel insecure about their jobs they may well feel the need for direct government action. When they feel more confident about their job security, and are more concerned with maintaining the value of their wages and savings, they may well want lower taxes and less government intervention.

Opinion polls provide direct evidence about British voters' main concerns. Since 1960 the Gallup Organisation has regularly asked a cross-section of the

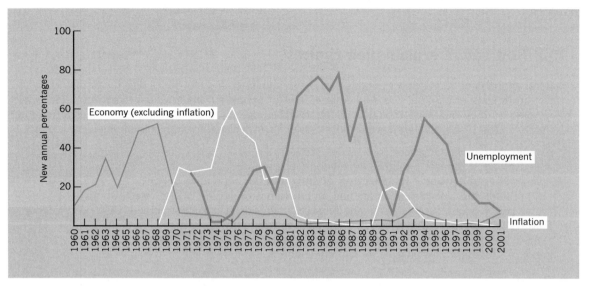

Figure 15.1 *Electors' perceptions of important problems facing the country*

British public: 'What do you think is the most important problem facing the country at the present time?' The three highest ranking answers to this question, averaged for each year from 1960 to 2002, are shown in Figure 15.1. They are unemployment, inflation and the economy: no other domestic issue had a significant number of mentions, and foreign affairs ceased to concern people very much as the Cold War faded in intensity in the late 1960s. From about 1970 the public became increasingly concerned about inflation and unemployment. This is not surprising in view of the very high inflation in the 1970s, associated with the sharp rise in oil prices, and a marked increase in unemployment that resulted from the restructuring of the economy and the end of industrial subsidies under the Thatcher governments of the 1980s (Chapter 3). In the late 1990s, after a sustained period of economic prosperity, public service issues – the NHS, schools and transport – began to assume more importance than economic issues.

Some people do worry about other issues such as pensions, law and order and the environment. But the major issues are economic in nature and related to very immediate concerns about jobs and money: personal economic well-being in short.

As economic conditions can change quite rapidly, particularly over the four or five years separating elections, financial concerns provide a dynamic for voting change. Of course, economic factors are not the only circumstances influencing voters. Dramatic political events such as the petrol price demonstrations of autumn 2000, or the smooth running of the government, also affect popular judgements.

These influences are incorporated in a simple explanatory model of the results of the 2001 general election which was used successfully to predict the results in advance – the sternest test of an explanatory model. We can therefore take it as the best available account of why the results of this British election turned out as they do. This explanation is known as the 'Essex Model', after the Department of Government at the University of Essex, where it has been developed over

Figure 15.2 *The Essex Model of the factors shaping British election results, 1997–2001*

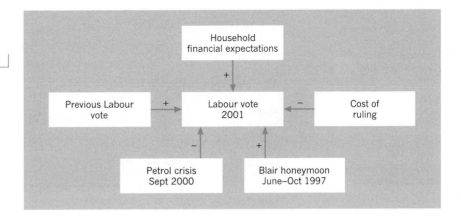

Essex Model
A method of explaining past election results and predicting future ones based on a statistical analysis of the changing economic influences on government support and the impact of dramatic political events.

the last 17 years. It is summarised in Figure 15.2 and incorporates many of the influences on voting that we have just discussed.[1]

The long-term underlying influences on the vote from 1979 to 1997 were:

- personal expectations about the family's economic situation in the months ahead. This summarises the worries about inflation and unemployment, which we saw were at the forefront of electors' minds after 1970 (Figure 15.1)

- 'cost of ruling' (reactions to what the government does) which gradually erode its lead between elections.

It would be very surprising if dramatic political events and issues had no effect on voting. The explanation in Figure 15.2 shows that they do, but also shows that their impact is confined to a particular time compared to economic considerations, or the steady erosion of support which comes from governing.

The political effects in the model are:

- **The petrol demonstrations (Sept 2000)** This was a short-term effect, felt only as a temporary fall in Labour support at the time. But it has to be taken into account in understanding the fluctuations in support over the period that includes it.

- **The Blair 'honeymoon' period** when there was exceptional enthusiasm for Labour after the change in government of 1997.

All these influences, as well as levels of Labour support, can be measured statistically. We can therefore relate them to each other through the equation shown in Table 15.2.

---

[1] A 'model' is a concise representation of a theoretical explanation, often statistical in form. What the Essex Model shows is that, as electors become generally more optimistic about how well off they are going to be in the months ahead, the government vote goes up (presumably because it is credited with producing more prosperity). Conversely, if more people become pessimistic about this they blame the government and withdraw their vote. Raising taxes also reduces the government vote as it takes money directly away from people.

Table 15.2 *Statistical relationship between economic conditions, political issues, and the Labour vote, 2001*

Overall regression equation

$$\text{Labvote}_t = 47.97 + 0.15\ \text{Labvote}_{t-1} + 0.15\ \text{Aggeconexp}_t$$
$$- 0.22\ \text{Costrule} + 2.73\ \text{Blair} - 9.38\ \text{Petrol}$$

A tabular presentation of the regression equation follows

Abbreviation	Full description	Numerical value attached to each factor given by full equation
Labvote$_t$	Labour voting support in the current month	
Constant	Base figure for Labour support	47.79
Labvote$_{t-1}$	Labour voting support in the previous month	0.15
Aggeconexp$_t$	Balance of positive over negative household financial expectations	0.15
Cost of ruling	Time in months since May 1997	−0.22
Petrol crisis	Sept 2000 scored 1, 0 otherwise	−9.38
Blair	Blair honeymoon effect (scores 1 for June–Oct 1997, 0 otherwise)	2.73

Notes: Economic considerations affect the government vote all the time. But there are also political influences, although these are shorter lived. The petrol demonstrations and reactions (often negative) to what the government does day to day also count.

The 'vote' which is explained by all these factors includes voting intentions that Gallup asked about every month over the period, between 1997 and 2001. What the model does is relate fluctuations in the explanatory factors to the ups and downs in voting intentions and actual vote for Labour. The Conservative vote can be explained in the same way simply by reversing the 'plus' and 'minus' effects in the figure.

Of course, the explanation leaves out many influences that might be thought to have had an effect on the vote. Why should the countryside demonstration not have had an effect on votes when the petrol ones did (if only for a short time)? Why did 'devolution all round', arguably the most important political reform of the period, not have an effect?

Various arguments can be made about this. From a statistical point of view, however, none of them improves the performance of this model in predicting the vote if they are added to it, and therefore they are not strictly needed to explain the results. The equation should be read as saying that Labour support in the present month is:

- a base figure of 47.97 per cent
- plus 0.15 multiplied by the percentage of Labour support there was last month
- plus 0.15 multiplied by the difference between the percentage of poll respondents with positive financial expectations and the percentage with negative ones
- minus 0.22 multiplied by the number of months after the May 1997 election (costs)
- plus 2.73 per cent in May–Oct 1997 (Blair honeymoon)
- minus 9.38 per cent in September 2000 (petrol crisis)

Source: David Sanders et al, 'The economy and voting', in Pippa Norris (ed.), *Britain Votes 2001*, Oxford: OUP, 2001, pp. 225–38

The table shows how the impact of each factor on the Labour vote can be estimated. Thus each 1 percentage point increase in the overall balance of positive over negative financial expectations will produce an increase of 0.15 in the percentage declaring their intention to vote Labour. This can be added to the increases or decreases in the vote produced by other factors in the equation to formulate a numerical prediction of the Labour vote, given specified changes in the factors affecting it. In April 2001 the Model predicted that the Labour vote would be 43.00 per cent (using Great Britain, not the United Kingdom as the base), acceptably close to the 40.7 per cent that the party actually obtained on 7 June.

BRIEFINGS

15.3 Regression equations

A regression equation is a numerical description of the relationship between the phenomenon you wish to describe (such as votes) and the factor(s) used to explain it (such as costs of governing). You start from a graph of the type with which everyone is familiar, relating these two variables.

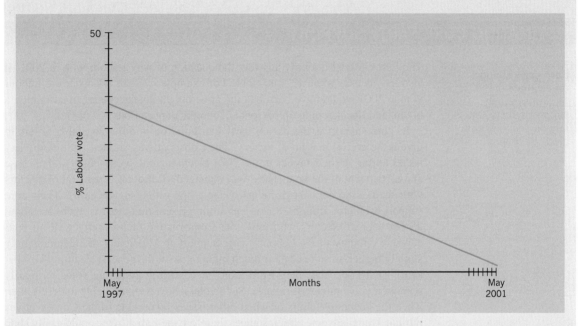

The line starts from a base of 47.79 percentage vote. It shows that for each month after the 1997 election the Labour vote goes down by 0.22 per cent. This can be expressed numerically as a 'regression equation' as follows:

$$LABVOTE_t = 47.79 - 0.22 \ COSTS$$

That is, the Labour vote equals 47.79 minus 0.22 times the number of the months after the last election. Each regression equation is thus a summary of a corresponding graph. The one in the example is a 'bivariate' equation because it relates two 'variables': percentage of vote and costs of governing.

It is possible to think of (but difficult to picture) a graph of four, five or higher dimensions, relating a number of factors simultaneously to the Labour vote. This can be described by a multivariate regression equation just as two-dimensional graph was described by a bivariate regression equation. The multivariate regression equation in Table 15.2 describes a five-dimensional graph. This cannot be portrayed in a picture but it can be described by the equation, just as a two-dimensional one is here.

The Conservative vote can be explained and predicted by the same equation (with the signs reversed, of course). Over the period it has been almost the reverse image of the Labour vote, so the same factors must influence it.

The story of the 2001 election told by the Essex Model is set against a background of economic prosperity following the severe recession of the early 1990s. By the time of the election economic prosperity was gently boosting Labour support. This was eroded, however, by a steady loss from negative reactions to what Labour was doing in government and (temporarily) to the increase in petrol prices. Tony Blair's popularity lasted a while but had little effect after the government got into its stride. The electoral factors working for and against Labour broadly balanced out, however, keeping their support at roughly the same level in 2001 as in 1997.

ESTIMATING CORE PARTY SUPPORT

Core party support
An estimate of the minimum voting support a party can rely on securing at a given election.

The Essex Model not only answers the question of why Labour won in 2001. It also lets us ask 'what if?' questions. For example, we can ask what the Labour vote in 2001 would have been had the government not succeeded in sustaining a boom, and thus keeping up personal economic expectations?

Its core support is the base a party can build on in attracting other voters to give it the crucial margin of victory. The Conservatives, in fact, with hardly any issues telling in their favour in the 2001 election came pretty close to their base at 31.7 per cent of the vote. They only managed to attract 2–3 per cent of electors with their issue appeals (principally their opposition to the euro). Their core support oscillates around 28 per cent at the present time: that is, there are about 28 per cent of electors who will vote Conservative under pretty well all conceivable circumstances. Labour's core support at 32 per cent of electors is only slightly higher, in spite of their much higher vote at the general election (41.7 per cent). That is because they *were* more successful at attracting votes, primarily with their economic performance. Such voters, however, are liable to desert them when the economy falters or when other issues favourable to the Conservatives intrude. Under adverse circumstances therefore the Labour vote could easily slide to round about 30 per cent as it did in the 1980s.

At least both Conservatives and Labour have a sizeable base of steady voters. The Liberals' great weakness is that they have very few of these and instead depend almost exclusively on their own issue appeals, and even more on what the other parties are doing, to attract voters. There is evidence to show that if Labour goes left and the Conservatives right (see Figure 16.1), while Liberals stay in the centre, moderate voters will be attracted and their overall vote will go up. However, when one or other of the major parties moves back to the centre such voters tend to return to their previous choice.

This need not be a total disaster for the party, however, as being close to Labour in policy terms encourages tactical voting which brings them more seats. These may be more important than sheer numbers of voters in boosting the party's credibility and bestowing more political power than total vote, particularly in a hung Parliament.

The fact that over half of all British voters support the Conservative and Labour parties even when there is almost nothing to commend them suggests that these are people who are impervious to election issues, the government's record or changing economic conditions. Whatever the political situation they will go on voting for the same party, election after election. This 'core vote' is important because it provides a stable basis for the fluctuations in party support discussed in the previous section. It ensures that the main parties will not disappear even when they do badly, and gives them the ability to 'wait out' such situations until circumstances change in their favour, just as Labour did between their resounding defeat in 1983 and their resounding victory in 1997. The following section explains why some voters remain loyal to 'their' party, and explores whether the characteristics that make them so may be slowly eroding.

CHARACTERISTICS OF CORE SUPPORTERS

Class Among the many and varied definitions of class, the most useful ranks the social and economic status of individuals according to their occupation, most notably into manual (working class) and non-manual (middle class) groups, and then into subgroups or strata of these categories.

By definition core support is not affected by the issues of the day, the government's performance or changing economic circumstances. Voter loyalty is embedded in factors that do not change, or change only very slowly. These factors consist largely of the enduring social characteristics of voters, such as their social class, religion, region and race.

To see why this might be so, consider the circumstances of a pensioner who lives in council-owned housing in a northern inner city, who had a manual job and belonged to a trade union. Such a person has been pushed by all the circumstances of his or her life into voting Labour. The Labour Party has historically been the party of the trade unions and council house building and has supported public expenditure, services and welfare, on all of which the voter is highly dependent. Neighbours, former workmates and fellow trade unionists are, in the main Labour supporters. Whether it is boom or bust, therefore, and whatever the political circumstances, this person is likely to go on voting Labour, election after election.

The same thing in reverse is true of the wealthy company director living in suburban Surrey, all of whose social circumstances push him or her into voting Conservative, whatever the state of the economy and however poor the Conservative government's record. To explain the considerable degree of stability in voting, therefore, we need to turn from the Essex Model of short-term fluctuations to the social characteristics that lead some voters into permanent support for the same party.

The single most important social factor for explaining party loyalty in Britain is social class: as Peter Pulzer famously put it: 'all else is embellishment and detail' (*Political Representation and Elections in Britain*, London: Allen & Unwin, 1997, p. 98). This is an exaggeration, as we shall see, but social class undoubtedly remains a significant influence in voters' enduring party choice.

The relationship between social class and the vote is shown in Table 15.3. In the period before 1970 it was quite strong: almost two-thirds of non-manual workers voted Conservative and a similar proportion of manual workers voted

	Conservative	Liberal/other	Labour	Non-manual Con + manual Lab as % of total vote
1945–1970 (mean)				
Non-manual	65	10	24	63%
Manual	30	8	62	
1979				
Non-manual	55	19	26	51%
Manual	36	17	46	
1983				
Non-manual	51	31	18	45%
Manual	35	28	37	
1987				
Non-manual	49	31	20	44%
Manual	37	23	40	
1992				
Non-manual	49	25	26	47%
Manual	35	20	45	
1997				
Non-manual	39	27	34	47%
Manual	24	19	55	
2001				
Non-manual	31	31	38	44%
Manual	19	22	60	

Source: Harris/ITN exit polls 3 May 1979, 9 June 1983, 11 June 1987, 9 April 1992; MORI polls in 1992 and 1997 adjusted to actual result. BES for 2001

Table 15.3 *Social class and the vote, 1945–2001*

Labour. However, this relationship has eroded over time. Between 1945 and 1970 63 per cent of all voters voted for their 'natural' class party – manual workers for Labour, non-manual workers for the Conservatives. That figure declined to just over half, 51 per cent, in 1979 and dipped further, to between 44 and 47 per cent, between 1983 and 2001. In the last 20 years, therefore, fewer than half of all voters have supported their 'home' party in class terms. In 2001 the proportion of the non-manual class voting Conservative (31 per cent) was less than the proportion voting Labour (38 per cent). For the first time more than half of the Labour vote was middle class.

However, Table 15.3 places all voters in one of two very broad class categories (manual versus non-manual). It is the voters in purer class situations, where all the social influences reinforce each other, who are likely to be the unswerving party loyalists. Thus it is not all manual workers, but manual workers in council houses on low incomes belonging to trade unions who are likely to vote Labour from one election to the next whatever the circumstances – if they vote at all.

Social class interacts with region as an influence on voting: people living in the geographical peripheries are less likely to vote Conservative than those in the

Region	Labour	Cons	Lib Dem	SNP/PC	Swing from Lab to Con
Scotland	44 (+4)	16 (–2)	16 (+4)	20 (–2)	–3.0%
Wales	49 (–6)	21 (+1)	14 (+2)	14 (+4)	3.5%
North	56 (–5)	25 (+2)	17 (+4)		3.5%
Yorks and Humberside	49 (–3)	30 (+2)	17 (+1)		2.5%
Northwest	52 (–2)	28 (+2)	17 (+2)		2.0%
West Midlands	43 (–3)	35 (+1)	15 (+1)		2.0%
East Midlands	45 (–3)	37 (+2)	15 (+2)		2.5%
East Anglia	36 (–3)	42 (+3)	19 (+1)		3.0%
Southeast	32 (0)	43 (+1)	22 (+1)		0.5%
London	47 (–2)	31 (–1)	18 (+3)		0.5%
Southwest	26 (0)	31 (0)	39 (+2)		0.0%

Note: 'Swing' is the sum of two parties' gain and loss divided by two

Source: Figures calculated by the authors

Midlands and southeast. Table 15.4 demonstrates this for the last two elections. The significant regional differences in party support are partly accounted for by differences in class structure between the regions. For example, the traditional working class is more prominent in Scotland, Wales and the northern regions of England than in the south, and the prosperous professional and business classes are found in the largest numbers in outer London and the southeast.

However, region has an impact on the vote independently of class. Some of these effects can be *indirectly* attributed to class. Areas that are predominantly middle class have a culture and way of life that reflects middle class values and influences the minority of manual workers living there too. The famous 'Essex man' of the late 1980s – a manual worker with a lower middle class lifestyle and Thatcherite values – is an example of this diffuse influence.

But, as we have seen, there are other regional influences – minority nationalism, language differences and so on – that are not attributable to class, and exert an enduring influence on voters that is impervious to short-term factors. A Welsh speaker in rural Wales, even if affluent and middle class, is unlikely to vote Conservative.

Ethnicity also influences votes. A large majority of Indians, Pakistanis and Afro-Caribbeans vote Labour. This is partly because many are in badly paid manual jobs living in poor conditions in the big cities; but it remains true irrespective of their social class or region. Asian and Afro-Caribbean people generally support Labour for historical reasons, because the Labour Party was more sympathetic towards immigrant minorities during the peak period of post-war immigration in the 1960s and early 1970s. At that time some Conservative MPs campaigned on an anti-immigration (and sometimes racialist) platform in their constituencies, and in 1968 a leading Conservative, Enoch Powell, made his notorious speech predicting 'rivers of blood' flowing from racial tensions in a mixed society.

Among all the groups we have mentioned the Labour vote is highest in the ethnic minorities, as Figure 15.3 and Table 15.5 both demonstrate. The ethnic minorities are a prime example of a relatively 'pure' social group that provides

	1974 (Oct)	1979	1983	1987	1992	1997	2001
Lab	81	86	83	72	81	85	74
Con	9	8	7	18	10	9	9

Source: Shamit Saggar, 'Racial politics', *Parliamentary Affairs*, **50**, 1997, p. 696; data held in the Data Archive, University of Essex (data set SN 3887). 2001 figures from BES 2001

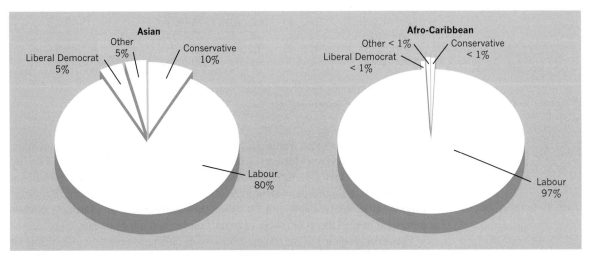

Figure 15.3 *Per cent vote for given parties among Asians and Afro-Caribbeans, 2001*

Source: Data set of the British Election Study 2001: www.essex.ac.uk/bes, September 2001

strong and stable support for one of the parties. Simply knowing that a voter is an Asian or Afro-Caribbean is to predict with a 0.74 probability of being right that he or she votes Labour. These are the kind of voters who generally offer unswerving support for Labour, largely unaffected by the particular circumstances of the election.

A combination of mutually reinforcing social characteristics is the most probable explanation for why many voters go on voting for the same party regardless of the state of the economy or the topical issues of the day. There are many different combinations of such characteristics, even when a vote for the same party is concerned. We can illustrate the general point here with a simplified 'Index of Social Predispositions' (Table 15.6). This shows how the pure combinations of characteristics (shown at the extremes of the table) push electors towards a vote for Labour or the Conservatives respectively, leaving people with 'mixed' social characteristics in the middle, who are 'cross-pressured' to respond more readily to short-term influences such as those in the Essex Model. For the same reason people with mixed social characteristics are more likely to vote for non-class political parties, such as the Liberal Democrats and the Nationalists in Scotland and Plaid Cymru in Wales.

		Manual factory worker		Other manual		Professional public employee		Other non-manual	
		Trade unionist	Not TU	TU	Not TU	TU	Not TU	TU	Not TU
Public housing									
Periphery	Ethnic minority	L	L	L	L	L	L	L	M
	White	L	L	L	L	L	M	L	M
Centre	Ethnic minority	L	L	L	L	L	M	L	M
	White	L	M	L	M	L	M	L	M
Private housing									
Periphery	Ethnic minority	L	L	L	L	L	M	L	M
	White	L	L	L	L	L	C	L	C
Centre	Ethnic Minority	L	L	L	M	L	C	L	C
	White	L	C	L	C	M	C	M	C

Table 15.6 *Index of Social Predispositions towards voting Labour or Conservative*

Notes: 'L' indicates high probability of voting Labour and 'C' of voting Conservative. 'M' is a group which is more likely to split its vote

ELECTORAL VOLATILITY

Electoral volatility
Large and rapid changes in voting behaviour from one election to another.

Modernisation and globalisation are creating an increasingly fluid and mobile society in Britain, in which distinctions of class, religion, region and even ethnicity are diminishing. The number of people belonging to 'pure' social groups is in steady decline while the number with socially 'mixed' characteristics is constantly growing. The 'purer' social groups are not immune from these deep-seated trends: for example, intermarriage, economic success and upward class mobility within some Asian minorities are already exposing a growing proportion of ethnic minorities to 'mixed' political influences. Manual workers are much more likely to own their houses and not belong to a trade union than their parents were and thus be more 'cross-pressured' between Labour and Conservative cultures. Such developments have already been discussed in Chapters 1 and 2 and are illustrated in terms of social class in Table 15.3, which reveals the weakening relationship between social class and party preference.

As fewer and fewer people are insulated from short-term economic and political influences so increasing numbers are likely to switch their vote (or, more likely, move to and from abstention) and the 'core' support on which parties can rely will gradually contract. Some of these effects are apparent from the gradual long-term decline in the level of support for the two main parties between the earlier post-war period of 1945 to 1970 compared with the later post-war period of 1974 to 2001 (Table 15.7). The average share of the vote fell for both parties, by 7 percentage points for the Conservatives, and by 10 percentage points for Labour. In both cases, moreover, their vote fluctuated more from one election to another in the later period. These trends were largely caused by the substantial

Table 15.7 *Means, ranges and fluctuations of the parties' share of the UK vote, 1945–70 and 1974–2001*

	1945–1970	February 1974–2001
Conservative		
Mean %	45.2	38.3
Range	39.6–49.7	30.7–43.9
Fluctuation	44.8 +/– 5.2	37.3 +/– 6.6
Labour		
Mean %	46.0	36.3
Range	43.1–48.8	27.6–43.2
Fluctuation	46.0 +/– 2.9	35.4 +/– 7.8
Liberal		
Mean %	7.1	19.1
Range	2.6–11.2	13.8–25.4
Fluctuation	6.9 +/– 4.3	19.6 +/– 5.8

Note: Liberal/SDP Alliance in 1983 and 1987; Liberal Democrat from 1992

rise in the Liberal vote (now the Liberal Democrats'), from 7.1 per cent to 19.0 per cent, a resurgence partly but not entirely produced by the ability of the Liberals to field candidates in all constituencies at each election after February 1974. Nevertheless the Liberals' vote fluctuated more from election to election in the later period, as did that of the two main parties.

Another indicator of decreasing stability is 'partisan dealignment' – the weakening sense of identification that British voters have with their preferred party (Figure 15.4). It began in response to the successive failures of Harold Wilson's Labour government of 1966–70 and Edward Heath's Conservative government of 1970–February 1974, but was underpinned by two parallel trends – the weakening of class-based voting discussed earlier and the growing ideological gulf between the Labour Party and its working class base. As Figure 15.4 shows, partisan dealignment has continued unremittingly since. Without exception each election has recorded a slightly weaker attachment of electors to the parties than in the previous election. The most noticeable weakening occurred at the elections that ushered in long-lasting changes in the shape of the party system – February 1974, 1979 and 1997. The cumulative effect over the whole period amounts to a pronounced change in the partisan character of the electorate. In 1964 and 1966 fully 44 per cent of the British public described themselves as 'very strong' party identifiers (almost all Conservative or Labour) and only 18 per cent said that they were 'not very strong' identifiers or identified with no party at all. In 1997 and 2001 the proportions were almost exactly reversed: only 14–16 per cent declared themselves to be 'very strong identifiers' while 42–46 per cent acknowledged having a weak identification or none. By 2001 not only had the numbers of weak identifiers increased but massive abstention from voting signalled the irrelevance of the parties to almost half the population.

Over three decades the British electorate has moved from committed partisanship to semi-detached preferences. In these conditions of volatility the prospect of further major changes in the party system – whether in the balance between the Conservatives and Labour, or in the rise of minor parties – is greater than a generation ago.

Figure 15.4 *Strength of party identification, 1964–2001*

Source: British Elections Studies

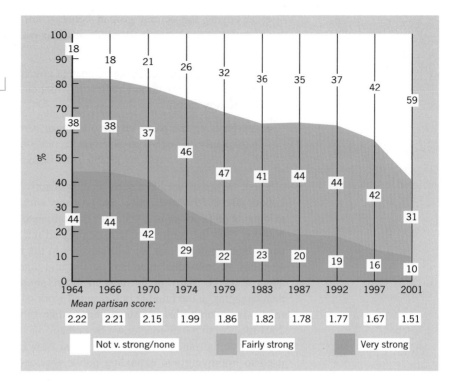

NEW LABOUR: A STRATEGY OF DEALIGNMENT?

The evidence just cited on electors' decreasing attachment to any of the main parties suggests that the Labour victories of 1997 and 2001 do not mark a fundamental redistribution of support between the parties, but rather the ability of Tony Blair and his entourage to attract the floating vote to Labour. Blair is unusual among British politicians and certainly among Labour ones in having set out to win not just one election but a series of them. The fundamental policy of the Labour government from 1997–2001 was to win next time. This explains their very orthodox financial and economic policies, designed to reassure business and persuade it not to rock the boat. It also explains its obsession with managing news about its activities and maintaining good relationships with media tycoons such as Rupert Murdoch.

Blair's basic calculation was that Labour's traditional voters (situated anyway in constituencies with massive Labour majorities) would continue to vote Labour as they had nowhere else to go. From this base vote however he could reach out to the affluent middle classes of southeast England to attract many of them with policies which favoured their interests – above all economic prosperity. His strategy can be summarised as:

- creating a cross-class coalition of support – a new social basis for the Labour Party

- occupying the central ground between left and right, neither too interventionist nor excessively hands off. This was glorified as the Third Way, a new ideological basis for New Labour

- establishing a reputation for competent government – hence a disinclination to rock the boat with any radical new policies (after getting devolution out of the way early)

- reorganising the party machine to make it more centralised and efficient, particularly in regard to electoral tactics such as lobbying the Boundary Commission to create favourable constituencies and managing the press.

These tactics as we have seen were brilliantly successful in building up the Labour vote in 1997 and 2001 – and probably with the impetus of these victories, in hanging on to power in 2005. They do nothing to build up a stable loyalist vote, however – on the contrary, this is eroding all the time. One symptom of this is party membership which we will consider in the next chapter. Labour attracted an influx of individual members in the mid-nineties, to push up numbers to about 400,000. Many of the new members simply gave cash however rather than engaging in the humble but essential work of canvassing voters, organising rallies, maintaining lists of supporters (unlike Liberal Democrat members). By 2001 membership had gone down by perhaps one-third.

It will be the same with voters now that New Labour, after 2001, committed itself to improving and extending public services (transport, health, policing). The petrol crisis of September 2000 showed how rapidly a government can lose support if it does not deliver, and New Labour is no exception to this. Its electoral support is mostly built on sand, which it has constantly to keep from shifting.

ELECTORAL TURNOUT

Strategies which aim at keeping the politics out of politics are hardly calculated to build up enthusiasm for voting or elections. This became obvious in the unprecedentedly low turnout of the election of 2001 – four electors in every ten chose not to vote. This was not however a one-off phenomenon. Figure 15.5 shows a general decline in turnout from the early 1950s to the 1980s and a dramatic drop between 1992 and 2001.

Turnout – the proportion of the registered electorate who vote – fluctuates, but the underlying trend has been downwards. It has fallen from almost 84 per cent in 1950 to 59.4 per cent in 2001. Turnout at secondary elections has also been low. In the 1999 local elections it fell to 29 per cent, the lowest on record, and in the European elections of that year fewer than one in four electors – a mere 23 per cent – bothered to vote.

Physical difficulties do not seem to have played a large part. The fall in turnout was fairly uniform throughout mainland Britain. Certain social groups, particularly ethnic minorities and young people turned out less than others (and fewer of them may have been registered in the first place). However these are fairly constant differences which have been observed in other elections as well. What accounted for the general drop between 1997 and 2001?

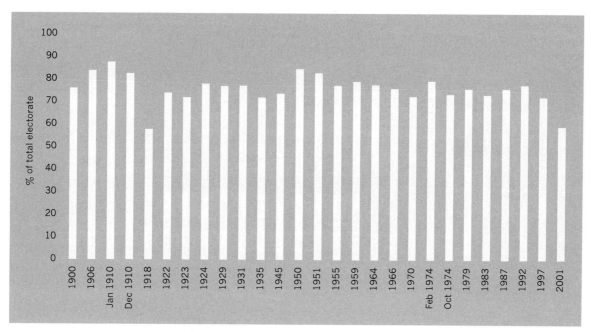

Figure 15.5 *Turnout in British general elections*

Four possible reasons have been suggested for large numbers of people deciding not to vote:

1. **General apathy** a total lack of knowledge, interest, or involvement in politics ('I don't know anything about politics'). Apathy may be on the increase. However it is more likely to produce a long gentle decline in turnout (certainly evident in Figure 15.5) than the sharp fall between 1997 and 2001.

2. **Alienation** people who resent the failure of politicians and parties to address their personal problems are often well informed but antipathetic at least to politics as they are today. Cautious New Labour government between 1997 and 2001 may well have turned off some people, particularly among Labour's own radical supporters. Again, however, one would expect steady growth over time rather than a dramatic surge in the numbers of such electors between 1997 and 2001.

3. **Indifference** where the main parties are seen as so similar that the election result will make no difference to the way the country is run. New Labour's studied cultivation of the middle ground, and actions like sticking to the Conservatives' spending plans from 1997–99, might well have convinced many electors that the outcome would make no difference to them, so they need not vote.

4. **Rational abstention** electors who calculate that their vote would make no difference to the result, so they see no reason for casting one. The many constituencies with entrenched party majorities (now heavily Labour) and the endless media predictions of a Labour landslide, probably encouraged a big increase in such thinking between 1997 and 2001. To a considerable

Plate 15.2 *Labour campaign poster from the 2001 general election*

Source: www.paphotos.com

extent it was New Labour's 'spin' to encourage these expectations, partly to depress turnout among Conservative supporters.

If indifference and rational abstention account for most of the fall between 1997 and 2001, both big parties carry a lot of blame for it. The Conservatives under William Hague distanced themselves from most electors by making opposition to the euro the centre of their campaign – even though polls showed that the public thought it a minor issue. And Labour, by dampening down interest certainly encouraged most people to think the result was a foregone conclusion and might not matter much anyway.

Elections are the essential institution of democracy in fulfilling its central purpose of making public policy conform to popular preferences. If less than half the people vote, however, the real popular preferences may get distorted or lost. Low turnout is also a sign that many people do not value democratic processes and may be disinclined to defend them forcibly if they are threatened. For both reasons there has been much discussion of how to encourage more people to vote in forthcoming elections. Suggestions range from civic education in schools to reforming the electoral system to make votes count more – as well as switching to electronic means to make it easier to vote.

These measures will probably all help but not enough to raise turnout to over 70 per cent again. Political circumstances are likely to play a bigger part – above all if the parties seem to have major policy differences and the election outcome carries important consequences for public policy. New Labour's strategy however seems to go against this, playing down differences and seeking to make non-controversial stands. Thus we should not really expect any dramatic rise in turnout in the near future.

CONTROVERSY

Turnout and compulsory voting

One way to stop worrying about turnout percentages would be to legislate for compulsory voting. This might be opposed on the grounds that it restricts freedom of choice. Just as we have to pay taxes however the act of voting could be seen as a civic duty we owe to the democracy we live in. It would not restrict voting choice once we got to the polling booth (or signed in electronically).

We could even spoil our ballot paper! But we would have expressed our preferences, which is essential to democracy. Countries such as Australia have had compulsory voting for a long time and nobody has ever accused them of being less democratic than the UK. Compulsory voting is not seriously being considered as an option at the moment but may be if turnout continues to decline.

ESSAYS

1. Why did Labour win the 2001 election? Why did it win by a landslide for the second time in succession?

2. What does the 'Essex Model' of voting tell us about British electors?

3. Is Britain's first past the post electoral system fair?

4. How much do election campaigns affect an election result?

SUMMARY

In seeking to explain the results of recent general elections, and the underlying pattern of voting behaviour, this chapter has raised the following questions:

- What are the effects of the electoral system? We have shown that Britain's first past the post system has the advantage of virtually ensuring an overall majority in Parliament for the winning party but the disadvantage of unfairly penalising small parties with widely distributed support, such as the Liberal Democrats.

- This makes for strong government but also means that the majority of voters actually voted for other parties than the one which gains office, which may produce cynicism and reduce turnout.

- Are there alternative systems? We have examined the way other electoral systems work and shown how the small single-member constituencies of Britain's first past the post system encouraged tactical voting in 1997 and to a more limited extent in 2001.

- To explain the outcome of particular elections we used the 'Essex Model', which relates party vote to aggregate economic expectations and cost of governing, on the one hand, and contemporary political issues, on the other. The 2001 result was explained largely by economic factors plus the perceived irrelevance of the Conservatives.

- To explain stability in the Labour and Conservative 'core vote' we looked at social characteristics such as class, region and race, and showed how they could be combined in an 'Index of Social Predispositions' that induce some electors to vote consistently for the same party over many elections.

- The exceptionally low turnout of 2001 can be explained largely by New Labour being expected to win and being deliberately non-controversial.

This chapter's account of elections and voting has focused on the question of which party wins most votes and why. Part of the explanation lies in the parties themselves. In the next two chapters we look directly at the parties and the ways they seek to organise and define themselves, so as to attract voters and members.

MILESTONES

Milestones in post-war elections

1945 Labour wins landslide, helped by army votes, on the basis of an ambitious programme of social reconstruction

1950, 1951 Conservatives accept most of Labour's social and economic reforms, including the Welfare State. On this basis, they reduce Labour majority to six in 1950 and take over government with majority of 17 in 1951

1955 Conservatives consolidate their majority on the slogan 'Conservative freedom works'

1959 Under Harold Macmillan the Conservatives win a substantially increased majority of 100. In a campaign speech he says, 'Let's face it, you've never had it so good.' The Liberals reorganise and put forward a programme of social reform, doubling their vote. Labour tries to abandon large-scale nationalisation as a policy

1964, 1966 Under its new leader, Harold Wilson, Labour wins a small majority in 1964 and increases it substantially in 1966, with promises of planning for the 'white heat of technology'

1970 Rising price inflation enables the Conservatives under Edward Heath to win the election unexpectedly, with promises of regulating trade unions and letting the 'lame ducks' of industry go

1974 Conservatives fight February election in midst of a miners' strike and power shortages (the three-day week) on the slogan 'Who governs Britain?'. Inflation, however, is the more important issue for voters. In a hung Parliament Labour forms a minority administration on a promise of 'getting Britain back to work'. In the October election Labour wins small overall majority, promising a 'social contract' with the unions. Liberals and Scottish

Nationalists win unprecedented support but few seats

1979 'Winter of discontent' – strikes and industrial unrest – lose election for Labour. Mrs Thatcher becomes Conservative Prime Minister

1983 A Conservative landslide victory of 144, helped by the Falklands War, economic recovery and a divided opposition. Disunited under its left-wing leader, Michael Foot, Labour proposes full-blooded socialism, unilateral nuclear disarmament and withdrawal from the European Economic Community. Its support plummets to a little over one-quarter of the vote. The Liberal/Social Democratic Alliance takes 25 per cent of the vote (but only 23 seats), the best third-party performance for half a century

1987 Labour's new leader, Neil Kinnock, achieves internal reform but pushes up the Labour vote only marginally. Alliance vote slips slightly. Conservatives retain their vote on the basis of an economic boom and the taming of the trade unions

1992 Conservatives present themselves as a totally new government under John Major and attack Labour as a high-tax party. Labour's attempt to concentrate election campaign on welfare fails. However, they increase their vote to 34.4 per cent while Liberal Democratic support falls

1997 New Labour wins a massive Parliamentary majority of 177 with 43.2 per cent of the vote. Conservatives reduced to their lowest share of the vote since 1832. Liberal Democrat seats double to 46, their largest number since 1929, as a result of tactical voting

2001 The results of 1997 are repeated, owing to economic prosperity and irrelevance of Conservative campaign on the euro. Liberal Democrat seats rise to 52

PROJECTS

1. In the light of its two successive defeats what advice would you offer the Conservative Party on how to win the next general election?

2. The alternative vote, the additional member system and the single transferable vote are considered possible alternatives to Britain's existing electoral system. Explain how each would work, and which party would benefit most from its adoption.

3. Design a research project for finding out the impact of party bias in the press on the way people vote.

FURTHER READING

Post-war elections and models of voting behaviour are clearly and comprehensively covered in Pippa Norris, *Electoral Change since 1945* (Oxford: Blackwell, 1997). The 2001 election is reported in David Butler and Dennis Kavanagh, *The British General Election of 2001* (London: Macmillan, 2001); 'Britain votes', a special issue of *Parliamentary Affairs*, **54** (4), 2001; and Anthony King (ed.), *Britain at the Polls, 2001* (London: Chatham House, 2001). Useful summaries of the 2001 election result include: John Curtice, 'General election 2001: repeat or revolution?', *Politics Review*, **11** (1) 2001, pp. 2–5. On the Essex Model of Voting, see David Sanders et al, 'The economy and voting', *Parliamentary Affairs*, **54** (3), (2001), pp. 784–802. On core voting, see Ian McAllister and Richard Rose, *The Nationwide Competition for Votes* (London: Pinter, 1984). On electoral systems, see the useful review by Matthew Shugart in Ian Budge et al, *The Politics of The New Europe* (Harlow: Addison Wesley Longman, 1997); B. Outhwaite, 'UK electoral systems', *Politics Review*, **11** (2), 2001, pp. 32–3; Lisa Boal, 'Electoral reform in the UK', *Talking Politics*, **12** (2), 2000, pp. 228–32.

USEFUL WEB SITES ON ELECTIONS AND VOTING

Hotlinks to these sites can be found on the CWS website at http://www.booksites.net/budge.

We strongly recommend that you visit the government's Electoral Commission web site (www.electoralcommission.gov.uk). Among other important aspects here you will find an ongoing consultation on the way elections are financed. The UK Politics site (www.ukpol.co.uk) has over 200 pages on election-related material. The British Elections site (www.club.demon.co.uk/Politics/elect.html) maintains coloured maps of Britain depicting its partisan composition across a range of national, local, and European elections. The Election Page (www.election.demon.co.uk) offers thorough coverage of all British elections with additional links. As the next general election approaches all the political parties will publish their manifestos on the web (see Chapters 15 and 16 for site details, or consult Richard Kimber's Political Science Resource Pages at www.psr.keele.ac.uk). The Democratic UK site (www.democratic.org.uk) has information on alternative electoral systems, including online election demonstrations for the devolved assemblies.

For more general information on British voting behaviour and public opinion see Market and Opinion Research International (MORI) (www.mori.com) which includes a digest of polls published by other companies and the Gallup Organisation (www.gallup.com). For data sets on British attitudes and public opinion see the UK Data Archive (www.data-archive.ac.uk) at the University of Essex and the Inter-University Consortium for Political and Social Research (ICPSR) at the University of Michigan (www.icpsr.umich.edu).

For comparative information about elections, voting patterns, electoral systems and electoral administration in other countries consult the excellent web site of the Institute for Democracy and Electoral Assistance (IDEA) (www.idea.int). See also www.pippanorris.com for papers and data on many aspects of elections and links to other sites and www.electionworld.org for information on elections in many countries.

http://dodgson.ucsd.edu/lij/, the web site of the Lijphart Election Archive at the University of California, San Diego, has information about elections in 26 countries.

For Scottish elections results and analysis, visit www.scottishelections.co.uk; for Northern Ireland www.ark.ac.uk/elections, and for Wales www.wales.gov.uk and www.election.demon.co.uk/wales.html.

There are also many sites engaged in analysis and proposals for electoral reform, some of these include Direct Democracy Campaign (www.homeusers.prestel.co.uk/rodmell/index.htm) and Direct Vote http://freespace.virgin.net/jamesimac.mcglynn/.

PART 5
Representation by Parties

The new Greater London Authority offices

Political parties and party factions

The parties, particularly the Conservatives and Labour, link together all the political processes and organisations we have examined up to this point. Their influence is obvious in elections, where they provide the alternatives for voting and stimulate popular participation. But they also form a central focus for the media, which they continuously try to manipulate in their own interest. The ultimate aim of vote seeking is to control government, so as to inject party policies and personalities into the decision process. In government the parties interact with civil servants, business and pressure groups in the ways already described.

The parties' external relations with other political institutions are thus the subject of almost every chapter of this book. Here we concentrate on the parties' internal structures and relationships, leaving the core of party identity – party ideology – to Chapter 17.

We look at internal relationships because we cannot take party unity and discipline for granted. Parties have to unite to win elections and run government (although, as we have pointed out, collegiality competes with ministerial autonomy in the Cabinet). But as the deep Conservative divisions on Europe show, virulent internal disputes can give rise to more or less institutionalised factions within the party. For most of the time party factions can live together; otherwise they could not form a party. Yet if disagreements become too extreme disaffected factions may split off to form a new party, as the Social Democrats did from Labour in 1981, and as the 'pro-Europeans' have in effect done in regard to the present-day Conservatives (a splinter pro-European Conservative Party fielded candidates in the 1999 European elections). We consider the history of party factionalism in this chapter, along with the ways in which party organisations and structures have adapted to counter it and put overall control in the hands of the leadership.

This chapter therefore covers:

- the functions of British political parties
- the evolution of the modern parties and the various groups and interests attracted to them over time
- factions and factionalism within the parties
- how they are organised
- what the parties stand for
- who joins the different parties.

FUNCTIONS OF PARTIES

The evolution of modern British parties cannot be understood without an appreciation of the general role they are called on to play. Democratic parties are associations of (generally!) like-minded people who, by means of popular election, compete for state power to further their common goals. A unique characteristic of parties is that they serve the dual function of government and representation. As instruments of government they form an executive that seeks to steer the state.

Party An organisation of ideologically like-minded people who come together to seek power – often to fight elections with a view to gaining representation in decision-making bodies.

They recruit and groom politicians, they implement policies and they mobilise popular support. As instruments of representation they promote the interests and values of sections of the electorate, translate their demands into government policies and give them a sense of place within the wider society. Most important of all, they form the government or the opposition, the 'ins' or the 'outs', thereby rendering the government of the day ultimately accountable to the electorate. Parties offer the public a scapegoat for government failure (or, more rarely, a totem of government success) enabling it to 'throw the rascals out' or 'keep the winning team'.

As instruments of government and representation the major parties therefore perform a third function: political integration. To win elections parties must attract support from many different groups. By aggregating their separate interests parties identify and create consensus across large segments of the population. They must also respond to expectations or persuade electors to modify them, magnifying or minimising ideas about what government can do. Horizontally, parties act as a bridge across groups; vertically, as a ladder between citizen and state.

In their governmental and electoral activities parties therefore have to concern themselves with interests and needs beyond those of their core supporters, because they need to legitimise themselves and attract other votes. They also aim to form governments that will make policy for the country as a whole. They cannot just pursue a narrowly sectional programme but have to reach out to as many groups as possible by varying their appeals as New Labour has done. It is this feature of parties that makes factionalism and internal disputes an ever present possibility. To be national and representative British parties have to be coalitions of interests; but such interests often come into conflict, particularly if there is no strong leadership. We can see concretely how this has worked out by looking at the growth of British parties from the mid-nineteenth century onwards.

PARTY UNITY AND INTERNAL DISSENT: CONSERVATIVES, LIBERALS AND LABOUR, 1868–1979

Emergence of modern parties: Whig and Tory, Conservative and Liberal

Like most other political institutions in Britain parties took on their modern form in the mid-nineteenth century. The shift produced by the Second Reform Act of 1867–8 from a small, restricted electorate to a large one numbered in millions meant that local 'notables' could no longer rely on their own resources and efforts to secure election. These had to be supplemented, and were quite soon replaced, by a central party organisation that fostered local clubs and associations in every constituency and provided funds and supporters for local campaigns. Members were drawn into them not by personal ties to the candidate but by support for the national party's principles and policies, which local MPs were pledged to support in Parliament. Soon it became immaterial whether the candidate was a local person or not. Anyone pledged to the national leadership and policy was acceptable because essentially the job of an MP was to support and serve the party. MPs thus owed their election to their endorsement by the central organisation and were therefore dependent on leadership approval for (re)election, a powerful factor enforcing party discipline in Parliament and ensuring that MPs there voted as members of a party bloc.

BRIEFINGS

16.1 Cadre and mass political parties

Cadre parties
Parties of like-minded and wealthy 'notables' who use their own money to fight political campaigns and rely on their own personal supporters.

Mass parties Are financed and organised with the help of a mass membership that both pays membership subscriptions and provides the human resources to conduct political campaigns.

The first recognisable political parties were 'cadre' parties, based primarily on Parliament. They grouped like-minded 'notables' who had organised their own election as MPs, using their own money and supporters. Such men could take a critical independent line if they wanted. They owed little to the party, having secured election by their own efforts, and could secure election again even if they crossed to another party.

The Conservative and Liberal parties in Britain between 1833 and 1867 were examples of 'cadre' parties, whose MPs frequently split off from one side and joined the other. But after the Second Reform Act (1867) widened the franchise beyond its narrow middle class base MPs could no longer be personally known to all electors. Consequently, their views and policies were identified by most electors with those of the party. If MPs lost their party affiliation their former supporters would cease to vote for them. At the same time financing mass campaigns became more expensive, so individual MPs became more dependent on, and hence obedient to, the central leadership. Mass parties, as the name implies, financed themselves by recruiting a large membership, up to a million or more, and collecting dues from them. In contrast, cadre parties were simply composed of MPs with their personal followers.

In theory, this arrangement should have ensured internal agreement within the parties, in place of bickering personalities. So, up to a point, it did. But because national principles and policy were now the focus of party cohesion, splits over these caused more widespread party disruption than continual but diffuse bickering. Thus the history of modern British parties alternates between tremendous unity and enthusiasm around some cause at certain points in time, which attracts new support; and splits and ebbing morale as the different groups within the party quarrel over implementation and emphasis or even attempt to redefine the basic principles themselves. One can see this process at work in both the Conservative and Liberal parties, which emerged from the old Tories and Whigs at the end of the 1860s.

The Conservatives redefined themselves as defenders of traditional institutions such as the Crown and Church, and as supporters of Empire and imperial expansion, but at the same time as social reformers concerned to improve poor living conditions, all in the general name of national unity but with the practical aim of attracting new working class votes.

Liberals emphasised free trade at home and abroad, and hence were not much interested in the Empire. They pushed political reforms, particularly ones opening careers to the lower middle class, Nonconformists and Roman Catholics. Most Catholics originated in Ireland. Both for electoral and tactical reasons the Liberals sought an alliance with the Irish Nationalist Party in Parliament, which led them to advocate Home Rule (a form of devolution) for Ireland in 1886. This was a measure that split the party, driving out self-made manufacturers who saw this as a first step to dissolving the Empire and its markets, and old Whig aristocrats who saw Home Rule as the latest of a series of attacks on Irish property rights.

The early twentieth century: Conservative, Liberal and Labour

The Conservatives suffered a similar split in 1905 when the new influx of Unionist businessmen supported tariffs to protect British markets in the Empire. The Liberal Party meanwhile united around the Irish Home Rule project and a programme of social reform, with an eye both to Catholic working class voters and their political representatives, the Irish Nationalist and the Labour parties. With their Parliamentary support legislation was passed from 1908–11 setting up a rudimentary Welfare State; the House of Lords was limited to a three-year delaying power over legislation, and Irish Home Rule was projected for 1914. Both this and the party were overtaken by the First World War, which split the Liberals over military strategy and foreign policy. A section of the party formed a coalition government with the Conservatives (1916–22), but the breach between the two factions was never completely healed during the inter-war period.

Party factions
The sections or tendencies within parties that emphasise different features of party policy while subscribing to the overall aims of the party and its organisation.

This provided an opening for the Labour Party. Unlike the other two leading parties this was not formed by Parliamentarians seeking a mass base, but by mass movements, primarily the trade unions, seeking Parliamentary representation to obtain greater recognition of their rights and limited social reforms. They allied with existing socialist parties with a constituency-based organisation to form a party in 1900. From its beginnings Labour existed as an uneasy coalition of committed socialists and pragmatic reformers. It rapidly attracted its 'natural' working class constituency, eroding the Liberals' electoral base. The weakening of both Liberal and Conservative parties resulting from divisions between 'coalitionists' and 'anticoalitionists' helped Labour form minority governments in 1923–4 and 1929–31.

The last of these coincided with the financial crisis of 1931 caused by the world depression. Labour split over the question of cutting Unemployment Benefit as part of a package of financially orthodox measures to restore banking confidence. Four members of the Cabinet, including the Labour leader and Prime Minister Ramsay MacDonald, joined a national government dominated by the Conservatives and supported also by a Liberal faction, the 'National Liberals'.

This split, regarded as betrayal by the majority of the Cabinet, damaged and haunted the Labour Party throughout the 1930s, and reduced the mainstream Liberals to political impotence up to 1959.

The national government's conversion to protectionism, government intervention and limited social reform as ways of dealing with economic crisis (Chapter 3) gave Labour a chance to adopt their recommendations, along with Keynesian economic policies, as its own during the wartime coalition government (1940–5). These gave Labour a comprehensive package of reforms round which it could unite and obtain a sweeping electoral victory in 1945.

Post-war developments: Conservative, Labour, Liberals and Liberal Democrats

Unilateralists
People who hold that Britain should renounce nuclear weapons on its own (unilaterally), without waiting for multinational agreement to do so.

While it remained reasonably united on its social reforms, the Labour Party split on two issues during the 1950s. One was on attitudes to the British nuclear bomb, where a powerful section recommended 'unilateral' renunciation on the grounds that the British bomb added nothing to the NATO deterrent and that British nuclear disarmament would set a moral example to the rest of the world. The other was on 'Clause 4' of the party constitution: whether Labour should retain a commitment to taking industry into state ownership (nationalisation) or not. Both attitudes tended to go together, the traditional 'left' advocating both unilateralism and nationalisation, the reformist right avoiding both positions.

The Labour splits of the 1950s were exacerbated by Conservative electoral success. The evident popularity of the post-war Labour government's reforms gave the upper hand within the Conservative Party to the 'one-nation' social reformers led by R. A. Butler and Harold Macmillan, who took up the 1870s' idea that national unity and stability depended on reasonable living conditions for the lower classes, through government intervention if necessary. This pointed to Conservative acceptance and indeed extension of the Welfare State but not to nationalisation, which was reversed in some industries during the 1950s.

This was not enough to challenge the 'social democratic consensus' between the dominant factions in both major parties, and among the 1960s Liberals. Harold Wilson, Labour Prime Minister 1964–70 and 1974–6, in fact fudged his internal party differences by promising to extend the government economic planning introduced by the Conservatives. Real planning rapidly broke down and the Wilson governments, followed by the Callaghan administration (1976–9), simply lapsed into pragmatic crisis management. This powered the growth of an 'alternative economic strategy' supported by the 'hard left' of the party, for full-blooded nationalisation and protectionism (including withdrawal from the EU) 'to save British industry'.

The Conservatives in the meantime were in hardly better shape. The defeat of the 'one-nation'-dominated party in the election of 1964 prompted a rethinking of its ideas and policies. This produced a more radical right-wing policy in the late 1960s, which advocated the ending of government intervention in industry but its imposition on the trade unions. As Prime Minister (1970–4), however, Edward Heath proved to be almost as pragmatic as Harold Wilson. Even so,

BRIEFINGS

16.2 The social democratic consensus, 1950–79

This is the label given to the broad set of ideas that the mainstream sections of all parties broadly shared in the period 1950–79. Factions of the Conservative and Labour parties always stood outside this consensus and, even where there was agreement by the parties on fundamentals, disagreement remained on details and emphasis.

The consensus consisted in:

■ acceptance of the Welfare State and the National Health Service, which included a commitment to financing a gentle expansion in these services as national prosperity grew

■ acceptance of a 'mixed economy', consisting both of private companies and of nationalised industries, particularly where there was a 'natural monopoly' of supply (coal, electricity, telephones etc)

■ acceptance of the powers and roles of the main pressure groups (particularly finance, business and trade unions)

■ a Keynesian economic policy aimed at balancing inflation against unemployment

■ a managed withdrawal from colonies and overseas territories, retaining links with Britain where possible

■ support for NATO in the Cold War with Russia, at the same time seeking to calm down confrontations (détente).

The Conservative 'New Right' under Mrs Thatcher broke dramatically with all but the last two of these ideas in the 1980s. Their success in doing so appears to have created a new, neo-liberal consensus in the 1990s with the incorporation of many Thatcherite social and economic policies into New Labour's 'Third Way'.

Plate 16.1 For many years Europe has been the most common cause of factions within British political parties, as illustrated here in this Michael Cummings cartoon in the Daily Express, 4 August 1961: Harold Macmillan tells Charles de Gaulle: 'Already, mon General, we've discarded our two-party system and got lots of extra new parties... like France!'

Source: Daily Express

"Already, mon general, we've discarded our two-party system and got lots of extra new parties --- like France ! "

energy shortages leading to a three-day working week, brought about by a miners' strike, brought him down in the election of February 1974. Convinced that Heath's mistake had been to abandon his free market programme and yield too easily to the unions, the 'New Right' won the party leadership election with Margaret Thatcher in 1975. As strict adherents of the new free market and monetarist doctrines, the 'dries' (as they were called) remained in a minority compared with the 'wets'. The latter had no very clear beliefs beyond a general feeling that the old social democratic consensus should be modified only as and when necessary. They confidently expected a return to compromise and pragmatism once the Conservatives returned to power, which they did in 1979.

FACTIONS AND FACTIONALISM SINCE 1979

What they got instead was Margaret Thatcher, a self-described 'conviction politician' and New Right ideologue who set about enforcing strict financial and fiscal orthodoxy, sales of state industry, rigid controls on trade unions, cuts in local government, a contraction of the Civil Service and administrative reform. She faced down her opponents both at home and abroad, whether the Argentines in the Falklands War (1982) or the miners in the Yorkshire coalfields during the bitter strike of 1984–5.

Although Mrs Thatcher and her supporters began in a minority in both Cabinet and party, she was able to get her way, usually by publicly committing the government to contentious policies that left it no choice but to back her, whatever the private murmurings among colleagues and backbenchers. Her unparalleled run of election victories gave her the prestige and authority to get rid of the more powerful 'wets' from the Cabinet and to win over the survivors to most of her own policies. Thus by the end of the 1980s the 'wet–dry' opposition had been superseded. Most Conservatives accepted the principle of the 'free market, strong (but slimmed-down) State' that Thatcher aimed at (even though she achieved them only patchily).

The election victories on which this acceptance rested were, however, due as much to splits within their main rival, Labour, as to the positive attractions of New Right policies. The Conservatives won only around 42 per cent of the vote in the elections of the 1980s. But with a divided opposition the 'first past the post' electoral system gave them substantial Parliamentary majorities. The left of the Labour Party blamed their electoral defeat of 1979 on the failure of Wilson and Callaghan to implement full-blooded socialist policies. These were incorporated into the 'alternative economic programme' supported by the new leader of the party, Michael Foot. Internal attempts to make MPs more responsive to left-wing pressure included the possibility of deselection of constituency MPs by local meetings dominated by left-wing activists.

The social democratic right of the Labour Party felt threatened by these developments. This provoked a major secession of some of the most prominent party figures: Roy Jenkins, a former Chancellor of the Exchequer, Shirley Williams and David Owen, both possible leadership contenders and ex-Cabinet ministers. This

'Gang of Four' (with another former Cabinet minister, Bill Rodgers) founded an alternative party, the Social Democratic Party (SDP) which aroused great enthusiasm in 1982–3 with its general commitment to a reformed social democratic consensus.

The Social Democrats were natural allies of the Liberals who, after 20 years of drift, gradually recovered from 1959 onwards with a non-doctrinaire but radical reform programme. The 'Alliance' formed between the two parties gained a quarter of the vote in 1983, driving Labour down to an unprecedented 27.6 per cent.

The Alliance held on to most of its ground in the election of 1987, winning 22.6 per cent of the vote to Labour's 30.8 per cent. By that time, however, bitter clashes between the leaders, provoked by the abrasive Owen, and the low ratio of seats to votes under first past the post voting, destroyed the morale of the SDP and produced a merger with the Liberals in 1988. The new 'Liberal Democratic Party' has been surprisingly cohesive, although the issue of co-operation with the Labour Party at national level has the potential to divide the party.

The Social Democratic secession, and the miserable performance of the party in the 1983 election, produced immediate internal effects in Labour. A 'soft left' co-operated with the surviving 'Campaign for Social Democracy' to elect a compromise leader, Neil Kinnock (1983–92). Convinced that the only way to retrieve their vote was to offer moderate policies and assert strong leadership, the party dumped the alternative economic strategy and gradually moved to accepting many Thatcherite reforms. Even so, votes returned only gradually (30.8 per cent in 1987 and 34.4 per cent in 1992).

These disappointing results were seen as pointing towards even further moderation in terms of accepting financial and, above all, fiscal orthodoxy, with restraints on government spending and low direct taxation. Strong internal leadership was also seen as a necessary element in Labour's appeal. This both produced and was buttressed by internal reforms aimed at purging local parties both of leftist 'entryists' and traditional, municipal bosses. It also produced changes in the balance of power at the expense of trade unions and constituency party activists and in favour of individual party members and MPs (see later).

Tony Blair, from the time of his election as party leader, following the death of Kinnock's successor John Smith, in 1994, has benefited from and built on these changes, largely by utilising them to impose strong discipline on MPs and constituency parties. His 'New Labour' has put its policy emphasis on attacking 'social exclusion' rather than promoting equality, thus neatly avoiding many of the more contentious issues associated with wealth redistribution and government intervention in the economy: most people, including Labour Party members, can agree with this. His overwhelming electoral successes in 1997 and 2001 (42 per cent of the vote and almost two-thirds of Commons seats) gives him great authority in enforcing party unity similar to that achieved by Mrs Thatcher in her time.

However, Thatcher's legacy to the Conservative Party in the 1990s has been two edged. The potential ambiguity of her support for a strong state, on the one hand, and a free market on the other, has been cruelly exposed on the European issue. Thatcher accepted the Single European Act (SEA) of 1986 because of

Europhiles Those who are generally well disposed to the further integration of Europe within the framework of the European Union.

Europhobes Those who are not generally well disposed to the further integration of Europe, at least within the framework of the European Union.

its promotion of a complete single market in the EU. The political institutions necessary to promote and support the single market were, however, also very important in boosting integration and limiting national sovereignty, a tension then exacerbated by the Treaty of Maastricht and subsequent agreements.

From 1993 these tensions between the sovereignty of the British state and the free European market came out into the open and produced overt confrontation inside the Conservative Party between 'Eurosceptics' and 'pro-Europeans'. Essentially, the Eurosceptics believe in defending British sovereignty, either by limiting the powers of the EU to what they were in the early 1980s, before the Maastricht Treaty or the SEA, or if necessary by withdrawing altogether. They strongly oppose European Monetary Union (EMU) and the adoption of the euro. A growing majority within the Conservative Party, they have carried the post-election Conservative leader, Iain Duncan Smith with them, even though he has de-emphasised the issue for strategic reasons.

The pro-Europeans believe that Britain cannot stand aside from currency union because it is already so heavily involved in the single market. In this they agree with many of the business and financial interests that have traditionally supported the Conservative Party.

The fact that euros are circulating on the Continent means that the Conservatives can hardly avoid the issue until it goes away. It seems likely to continue to weaken the party. Labour lacks the same depth of internal feeling on the issue and can recommend joining in its promised referendum if it feels there is a strong case that it can carry. The prospect of driving a wedge through the Conservatives and possibly provoking the full scale secession of the 'pro-Europeans' is obviously an attractive one for Labour. However, the party may face its own problems after splitting over the war on Iraq (2003) and Tony Blair's unquestioning support for the right-wing American President Bush.

Plate 16.2 *Matthew Pritchett cartoon from the* Daily Telegraph, *21 April 1997. From 1993 the Conservative Party split between 'Euro-sceptics', who believed in defending British sovereignty, and 'pro-Europeans', led by Kenneth Clarke*

Source: *Daily Telegraph*

'Scientists think they might one day be able to produce two Conservatives who agree about Europe'

PARTY STRUCTURE AND ORGANISATION

Iron law of oligarchy
The 'law' propounded by Robert Michels in 1911 whereby mass organisations cannot, by their very nature, be democratic, and will always and of necessity be controlled by a small elite – the oligarchy.

Factional disputes are thus capable of destroying political parties, or of blasting their hopes of re-election for many years. They are obviously situations leaders would like to avoid. One way of controlling or dampening confrontations is through organisation. We have already seen how Kinnock and Blair rooted out dissenting tendencies in constituency Labour parties by tightening central control. In this section we look at British party organisations, both in terms of how they enable the party to function generally and in terms of how they allow leaders to exercise control.

BRIEFINGS

16.3 Michels' iron law of oligarchy and the British parties

In 1911 the German sociologist Robert Michels published *Political Parties* (New York: Dover Publications), in which he formulated the famous 'iron law of oligarchy'. This states that mass organisations, by their very nature, cannot be democratic, but will always be controlled by a small elite. The modern world, he said, was faced with an insoluble dilemma. On the one hand, modern life requires large-scale institutions and organisations: parties, interest groups, churches, trade unions. On the other hand, large organisations will always be in the hands of a few leaders, no matter how strongly they aspire to internal democracy. There are two sets of reasons for this. First, leaders know all the business of their organisation, control the means of internal communication, and usually have greater political skills than ordinary members. Second, the 'incompetence of the masses': few know much about policy matters, or turn up to meetings, while most feel the need for 'direction and guidance' provided by leaders.

According to Michels leaders develop their own particular interests and goals, which differ from those of members. They control organisations, and use them for their own purposes, not those of the members. Thus leaders of mass movements inevitably become members of the power elite. Leaders of revolutionary movements always betray their cause.

The political scientist Robert McKenzie applied Michels' analysis to the Conservative and Labour parties in the 1950s. He detailed the various devices used by the leaders of both parties to make sure that the party conference, for example, always passed supportive resolutions and that their general control of party policy and activities was left undisturbed. In spite of Labour's claims to internal democracy, with the elected conference having ultimate control, an alliance of moderates made sure the trade union block vote was always used to support the Parliamentary leadership and to keep the more left-wing constituency parties in check.

Things changed, however, after McKenzie's book was written, when left-wingers came to power in some unions. Internal reforms have reduced union voting power in the 1980s and 1990s. However, party leaders seek other means of obtaining support, by using 'policy forums' and referendums of members to bypass conference. Contrariwise, if leaders were seriously out of step with the majority of their party they would clearly have to go.

The organisational ladder contains four main rungs. At the top is the party leadership, a group of no more than 20–30 MPs occupying, or hoping to occupy, senior government positions as Cabinet ministers. Their primary interest is in their party winning the next election. A little further down is the Parliamentary party of elected MPs and peers in the House of Lords, from whom the party leadership is drawn. They too place enormous importance on electoral success, but their priorities are subtly different from those of the leadership. Most MPs represent safe seats and have more to fear from deselection by their local parties or from an unfavourable redrawing of their constituency boundaries than from an adverse national swing against the party. Much further down the ladder is the party in the country – the unpaid officers and active members of local associations – many of them elected councillors on the local authority. For most activists the reward is not career advancement – indeed, there are no tangible rewards at all – but furtherance of the party's broad goals, on which they tend to take a more principled stand than the party's leaders and MPs. On the bottom rung is the 'party in the electorate': stalwart supporters who, while not formally members, can be relied on to vote for the party in elections and to accept the party line on most political issues (see Figure 16.1).

Superficially, all British parties are organised in the same way. A branch of the party exists in each Parliamentary constituency and, where support is strong

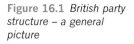

Figure 16.1 *British party structure – a general picture*

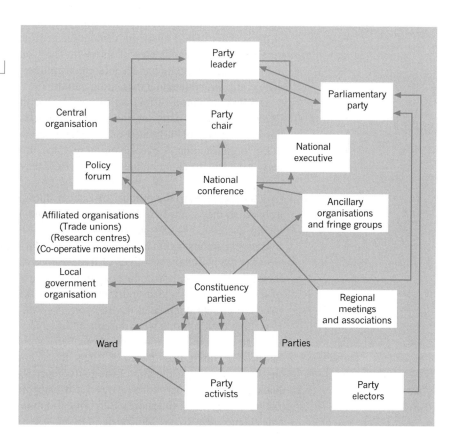

enough, in each local ward making up the constituency. Its main function is to contest elections by raising campaign funds, engaging in electioneering and, most important of all, selecting the candidate who, in the 500-plus safe seats, will become the MP. Political education and policy debates are intermittent and secondary: in most parties political agreement is taken for granted and politics is not discussed much!

The local parties send delegates to the national party's annual conference, whose role is ostensibly to discuss party policy but whose real purpose nowadays is to display the party, in particular its leadership, to best effect on television. The conference elects a national executive that oversees the day-to-day running of the national party. Policy is formulated by specialist groups recruited from party headquarters, sympathetic research institutes and the leaders' personal contacts: MPs, let alone ordinary party members, have less and less say. The leader of the Parliamentary party is the effective party leader in the sense of being the party's spokesperson, its chief campaigner at elections and the Prime Minister if the party wins. The Conservative leader is now elected by MPs and party members; the Labour leader by Labour MPs and the annual conference (on behalf of the wider Labour movement); the Liberal Democrat leader by the party members.

Despite these superficial similarities, the Conservative and Labour parties differ significantly in their constitutions and ethos. The contrasts owe something to the two parties' very different historical origins. The Conservative Party began in the nineteenth century as a Parliamentary faction that gradually built up a party in the country. The Labour movement existed outside Parliament before it put up Parliamentary candidates of its own. The Conservative Party has a unitary and hierarchical structure and a deferential culture; the Labour Party a federal and democratic structure and a dissenting culture.

The first structural difference to note is that the Conservatives (and Liberal Democrats) are a party of individual members whereas historically Labour has been a party of 'affiliated organisations' as well as of individual members. These organisations – overwhelmingly trade unions – are entrenched in the party's decision-making bodies and until 1990 they exercised a vote at the annual conference and in local parties roughly proportionate to their membership (strictly speaking, to the number of Labour dues-paying members they claim to have when they contribute to Labour Party funds). In the 1980s affiliated trade unions accounted for 89 per cent of the vote at the annual conference and the five largest unions commanded a majority (55 per cent of the vote) among them. Because the national executives of trade unions cast a 'block vote' on behalf of their members, usually without consulting them about their views, the leaderships of the big unions wielded enormous power in the Labour Party. Moreover the trade union vote dominated the election of 18 of the 28 places on the National Executive until reforms were introduced in 1993.

Trade union influence in the Labour Party was less obvious before 1970 and has been declining from the early 1980s. It was not obvious before 1970 because the Parliamentary leadership of the party generally agreed on policy with union leaders, so their block votes were cast to support them. Such support enabled the party leadership to ignore often critical opinion in the constituencies. It was this alliance that Robert McKenzie in his classic *British Political Parties* cited to support his point that both major British parties operated in roughly the same way, under leadership control, in spite of the façade of Labour Party democracy.

The alliance between the Parliamentary leadership and trade unions broke down in the 1970s as left-wingers gained more ground in the big unions, notably the Engineers and the Transport and General Workers. However, their control was never secure or extensive, so the Left pushed through reforms in the early 1980s, which put more power in the hands of constituency parties, where their real base lay. Thus it was agreed that the party leader would be elected by an electoral college, in which unions, constituency parties and MPs would all have a share (by the 1990s an equal share). The block vote was also eroded in 1990 by providing for union votes to be split in proportion to the distribution of opinions in the union.

A further reform in 1981, designed to make MPs more responsive to their local activists, was the reselection of the Parliamentary candidate or sitting MP for each election, instead of letting them stand again automatically.

The centralising leaderships of the 1990s paradoxically built on these left-wing reforms to open up the party to the influence of rank and file members. The leadership judged that it could mobilise more support from rank and file members than from either the unions or the party activists running the constituency parties, who tended to be on the Left. Thus local and national referendums have been held on the abolition of Clause 4 (which committed the party to nationalisation) and on the 1997 election programme. Annual elections for the National Executive Committee (NEC) on a one-member one-vote basis have also helped the leadership to get rid of opponents, although it could work against the New Labour leadership if voters turned against the Labour government. One example of increasing central control was the imposition of all-women shortlists for the selection of Parliamentary candidates (until struck down by judicial review!).

BRIEFINGS

16.4 New Labour focus groups – greater democracy or greater control?

From the mid-1990s New Labour leadership made much of consulting the public on its policies. The Prime Minister appeared at question and answer sessions with a (selected) audience in various parts of Britain. The main vehicle of consultation were, however, focus groups, some selected from the public outside the Labour Party, many composed of party members inside the party.

One can see such groups in two ways. On the one hand, they do give leaders a feel for what members are thinking and how they would react to policy proposals – which also gives a chance of adapting them at an early stage to make them more popular. On the other hand, such groups are formed on the initiative of the leadership and asked to react to proposals it has prepared rather than starting their own initiatives.

One can contrast this 'top-down' approach with the 'bottom-up' ideals of the classical Labour party where the members organised their own meetings to formulate policy which was then debated and accepted at the annual conference – independently and sometimes against the Parliamentary leadership's wishes. As Robert McKenzie pointed out, things did not usually work out like that. But one can see in focus groups a way to circumvent the membership organisations and get policy accepted without extensive debate.

All these changes empowering individual members, on the one hand, and the central leadership, on the other, have brought Labour closer in its structure to the Liberals and Conservatives. In the Liberal Democratic Party, for example, the leader is elected by the vote of all party members, and in early 1998 the Conservative Party adopted new rules for the election of its leader, by which Conservative MPs determine by election the two leading contenders, who are then subject to election by the party membership on the basis of one member one vote.

Important constitutional differences still distinguish the Conservative Party, however. Much greater power is given to the Conservative leader. In the Conservative Party the shadow Cabinet, the party chair and vice-chairs, the chief whip and deputy whips are all in the leader's gift. In the Labour Party the shadow Cabinet and chief whip are elected by Labour MPs and on becoming Prime Minister Labour leaders are required by Labour Party rules to include the 16-member shadow Cabinet in their full Cabinet, although it is the PM who determines their ministerial responsibilities. The general secretary of the Labour Party (the closest counterpart to the Conservative chairperson) is appointed by the NEC while the treasurer is elected by the annual conference.

The Conservative leader's policy making powers are equally extensive. The leader is solely responsible for the party's election manifesto and can incorporate or veto specific proposals without consulting the rest of the party, as Margaret Thatcher's 1983 manifesto commitment to abolish the Greater London Council testifies. The Labour manifesto is drafted by a joint subcommittee of the National Executive Committee and the shadow Cabinet (themselves elected bodies) and must incorporate any policy passed by a two-thirds majority of the annual conference.

A second, related difference lies in the formal powers accorded to the party in the country. The annual Labour conference is the electoral college for the party leader and deputy leader (with trade unions and the constituency parties and Parliamentary Labour Party allocated 33.3 per cent each). It is also the sovereign policy-making body with the right to determine party policy and incorporate provisions in the manifesto. The annual Conservative conferences have no such rights. They can pass policy motions or resolutions critical of the leadership (although they rarely do) but these have no constitutional power. Labour conferences decide; Conservative conferences confer.

A parallel difference exists at the constituency level. Local Labour parties can instruct their delegates to the annual conference on how to vote in elections for the NEC or the leadership and increasingly do so on the basis of ballots of local individual members. They not only choose the local Parliamentary candidate but, if their constituency has a Labour MP, require the MP to submit to a formal process of annual reselection. Conservative associations do not mandate those attending the conference and Conservative MPs are automatically reselected unless their relationship with the local party has badly deteriorated.

These constitutional differences were reinforced by quite distinct party cultures that endured until the late 1980s. Conservatives have traditionally valued party unity and loyalty above all else, and until recent years their conferences resembled rallies more than debates. Most resolutions from the constituencies were paeans of praise for the party leadership or, if critical, expressed in muted and deferential terms. The Labour Party, by contrast, took ideological principles ('socialism') more seriously and most activists accorded them priority over party unity, loyalty to the leadership or even electoral success. For most Conservative activists Conservatism was an instrument for winning elections; for most Labour activists elections were an instrument for implementing socialism. This is now changing. The Conservative Party is now ideologically riven, especially over Europe, and grumbles about the lack of internal democracy. In contrast the 'New Labour' leadership has succeeded in muffling ideological debate and uniting the party around a new will to win: as a result its annual conferences have turned into televisual rallies, largely free of serious policy debate, to which local constituency parties are increasingly reluctant to send delegates. This may however change now that serious internal divisions have opened up over British relationships with the USA.

Ironically, however, 'democratisation' of the election of the Labour leader has made it more difficult for a challenger to succeed. Selection by an electoral college requires three months' notice, the convening of a special conference and a campaign by the challenger, not only among MPs but among trade unions and local parties. Moreover, Neil Kinnock's leadership between 1983 and 1992 and Tony Blair's record so far demonstrates how powerful a determined leader can be. In the early 1980s the fundamentalist Left was in the ascendant, internal conflict was rife and the party was unelectable. In the space of nine years Kinnock and his personal allies expelled the Militant faction, marginalised the socialist Left, jettisoned the party's long-standing (but unpopular) policies of nationalisation, trade union legal immunities, withdrawal from Europe and unilateral nuclear disarmament, and reunited the party behind a pragmatic, mild, social democratic programme. Blair abandoned the hallowed Clause 4. The other constitutional reform of the early 1980s, mandatory re-election, has not led to its intended democratic consequences either. Very few Labour MPs have been deselected, and an increasing number of constituency parties in Labour-held seats have re-elected their MP from a shortlist of one.

However, to dismiss the Labour Party's democratic reforms as inconsequential would be premature. Kinnock and Blair could not have transformed the Labour Party without the support of sympathetic trade union leaders. Desperate to see the return of a Labour government, they turned a blind eye to the autocratic practices of the leader's personal office and used their influence to ensure a pliable NEC and an acquiescent annual conference. But such support would not long survive a period of Labour government that presided over a recession or serious inflation. Without economic success the Labour leader, and individual Labour MPs, would be threatened by an alliance of left-wing activists and dissatisfied trade unions exploiting the democratic reforms.

WHAT THE PARTIES STAND FOR

Social democratic consensus
The agreement, which was strongest in the 1950–79 period, whereby governments of all parties should accept the broad principles of the Welfare State, the mixed economy, Keynesian economic policies and a NATO-based alliance against the USSR.

Neo-liberal consensus
Agreement among different political groups and parties about neo-liberal beliefs that individual rights should be protected, freedom of choice maximised and government powers limited in favour of market economics.

We have seen how different factions struggle for ideological and policy control of British parties. This does not mean, however, that the party does not speak with a clear voice, particularly at elections, but also over long periods of time when it is enjoying reasonable electoral success under a strong leadership. The organisational structures we have just examined enable all factions in the party to endorse a general public statement about party priorities and commitments: the party manifesto. We shall look at manifestos in more detail in the next chapter. Here we need only note that they give a general programme for government after the election and constitute an agreed statement about what the party stands for, on which, except in extreme cases, all factions concur.

As we have noted, both major parties underwent ideological reconstruction in the 1980s and have emerged sharing a 'neo-liberal' consensus that has replaced the earlier 'social democratic' one. The key elements of the new consensus are:

- acceptance of a privately owned economy in which the government role is limited to ensuring fair competition and protecting consumers

- acceptance of the present powers of the main pressure groups

- an orthodox economic policy aimed more at low inflation than high employment

- ceilings on state expenditure on welfare and other public services

- support for NATO as the main defensive alliance and hence for US leadership in the New World Order, although divisions over this may be appearing inside Labour.

A point at issue between the parties remains the degree of integration in Europe. This is also an issue within the Conservative Party, as we have seen. Whether or not the Labour government goes into the euro, it will remain much more favourable to the EU for the foreseeable future.

The other major point dividing the parties is political reform. This extends from territorial devolution from the Westminster Parliament and government (Scotland, Wales, London) to entrenchment of individual civil and political rights and freedom of information.

These developments have moved the Liberal and Labour positions more closely together, which may have implications for future electoral and Parliamentary alliances against a Eurosceptic and nationalist Conservative Party. In Scotland the two parties together formed a coalition administration after elections to the Scottish Parliament resulted in no single party gaining an outright majority. However, the New Labour strategy has dangers for the Liberal Democrats too, as Labour has moved to being a non-doctrinaire, moderate, reforming party, the role previously played by the Liberals since 1959.

Plate 16.3 *Conservative Party manifesto for the 2001 general election*

Source: Conservative Party web site, www.conservative-party.org.uk/

CHARACTERISTICS OF MPS AND PARTY MEMBERS

Many of these tendencies are reflected in the social composition of party MPs, members and voters. As Table 16.1 shows, the Parliamentary Conservative and Labour parties are unrepresentative of both their members and voters. The MPs of both parties at the end of the 1990s were overwhelmingly middle class, university educated and male. MPs of both parties in fact resembled each other much more than they did their party supporters.

This resemblance was due above all to the fact that the Parliamentary Labour Party has ceased to be working class. The proportion of manual workers on the Labour benches steadily fell from 72 per cent between the wars to 36 per cent in the 1950s and fell further to 29 per cent in the 1980s and to a mere 13 per cent by 1997. Over the same period the proportion of graduates rose from 17 per cent between the wars to 66 per cent today. In 1997 four times as many Labour MPs were school teachers as miners. The Conservative Party has also lost some of its patrician

	Conservative Party			Labour Party		
	MPs	Members	Voters	MPs	Members	Voters
Social class						
Employers, managers, professional (upper middle class)	88	55	29	61	49	15
Intermediate and junior non-manual (middle and lower middle class)	11	31	32	26	20	23
Working class	1	14	38	13	31	62
Education						
Independent schools	66	23	21	16	5	8
University	81	19	11	66	30	10
Oxbridge	51	n.a.	n.a.	15	n.a.	n.a.
Women	8	49	54	24	39	52
Ethnic minorities	0	n.a.	3	2	n.a.	8

Table 16.1 *Social composition of MPs, members and voters of the Conservative and Labour parties (%), 1997.*

Source: D. Butler and D. Kavanagh, *The British General Election of 1997*, London: Macmillan, 1998, pp. 202, 204; Robert Worcester and Roger Mortimore, *Explaining Labour's Landslide*, London: Politicos, 1999, p. 243; Patrick Seyd and Paul Whiteley, 'Labour and Conservative party members compared', *Politics Review*, February 1995, pp. 2–7

element, although only very gradually. In the 1950s 75 per cent went to public schools and 22 per cent to Eton alone; in 1997 the figures were 66 per cent and 9 per cent.

Thus the two Parliamentary parties do not so much comprise two social classes as two strata within the middle classes. Most Labour MPs come from the less privileged and moneyed middle classes: compared with their Conservative counterparts they are more likely to be first rather than second-generation 'bourgeois', educated at state rather than private schools, at the 'new' rather than 'old' universities, at 'red brick' universities rather than Oxbridge, and to have worked in the public sector and the new professions rather than the private sector and the traditional professions. At a lower level the Labour Party is now more middle class than the Conservatives: a development of the past two decades is the steady replacement of working class party members by the professional and well-educated middle classes. The growing dominance of the middle class among Labour MPs and members may have strengthened the party's appeal to 'Middle England'. But of course the bulk of the party's voters are, as ever, working class and live in the geographical peripheries and the northern half of England. The majority of Conservative voters are middle class and live in the southern half of England.

One difference that has opened up between the parties in Parliament is in proportions of women MPs, who now constitute 24 per cent of Labour MPs, 101 in number, possibly a critical mass. Women constitute only 8 per cent of Conservative MPs and 7 per cent of Liberal MPs. Minority ethnic groups – Asian and Afro-Caribbean – remain substantially under-represented, just over 1 per cent of the membership of the House of Commons. The more conspicuous minority figures are on the Labour side, however.

The social gap that has opened between the parties in Parliament and the parties in the country perhaps accounts for the sharp decline in Conservative and Labour Party membership over the years since the war. In the 1950s the

Conservatives claimed to have about 2 million members and Labour 1 million. This slumped to a half and a quarter million respectively by 1992. Membership of the Liberal Democratic Party is much smaller, at about 80,000–90,000. However, developments in the late 1990s brought membership numbers much closer to each other, around 300,000 in all parties.

The general decline in membership of political parties was due not only to social trends but also to leaders' lack of interest in a mass membership, which was seen as a potential source of trouble. Party leaders fear that members might try to impose their own policy views on the party or support dissent. Moreover, having masses of members to canvass and campaign has seemed less necessary in an age of universal television, when parties could appeal over the heads of members directly to electors.

In the 1990s leaders began to realise that the foot-slogging electoral work done by party members should not be dismissed as insignificant. Important research by Patrick Seyd and Paul Whiteley (in *Labour's Grass Roots* and *True Blues*) showed that dynamic local constituency parties with a large and active membership had the capacity to mobilise the party's own natural supporters on a sufficiently large scale to make a crucial electoral difference in marginal seats. As part of its renovation and modernisation the Labour Party aimed at recruiting new, younger members. By the election of 1997 it had returned to a level of 400,000 members, helped by the initial popularity of the New Labour agenda, although numbers declined thereafter. The Conservative Party claimed a larger membership but informed estimates put the real figure at between 300,000 and 350,000, the majority aged over 60. The party's new leader, William Hague, introduced reforms designed to give ordinary party members more say over policy making and the election of the party leader, but these have not yet produced a revival of party membership. In 1998 and 1999 the Conservative Party proved unable to mobilise itself on the ground in local elections and in the Scottish and Welsh Parliamentary elections, an ominous sign for the future. The Labour Party, too, should be concerned for the future: as its membership has become overwhelmingly middle class it is likely to have growing difficulties in mobilising supporters in its working class strongholds, as reflected in the dismally low turnouts recorded at the general election of 2001 particularly in Labour's heartlands.

Declining memberships have been interpreted as a symptom of general party decay. They reflect other political and social trends too: the narrowing of party differences and weakening of ideological intensity, the erosion of identity with the local community and the growth of alternative and more attractive leisure pursuits. At the same time the politicisation of local government has meant that the most active members are now local councillors, sometimes controlling a municipal budget greater than that of some central ministries. Of the new MPs elected in 1997, two-thirds on the Labour and Liberal side had previously been elected at local level. This was true of only a quarter of newly elected Conservatives, but that figure may grow as more Conservatives get elected locally to counterbalance Labour success in central government.

The changes in the social base of its MPs and members strengthen Labour's capacity to broaden its appeal beyond its traditional working class base to all voters, particularly to those in the political centre. In Chapter 17 we shall examine this, and the corresponding policy adjustments made by the other parties, in more detail.

ESSAYS

1. How far are British political parties 'umbrella' organisations covering a loose alliance of factions and tendencies, and how far are they basically united?

2. Does Michels' 'iron law of oligarchy' still hold for British political parties?

3. Are party activists inevitably more extreme than party leaders? Why or why not?

4. Does the fact that MPs are socially different from their supporters make them unfit to represent them?

SUMMARY

Textbooks conventionally depict political parties as disciplined armies moving in perfect order on the political battleground. Reality could hardly be more different. As with all voluntary organisations, people join with dissimilar objectives and protest or quit if these are not met. Parties have an inner life, marked by ideological divisions, personal rivalries, and tensions between the leadership and the rank and file. All parties are uneasy coalitions.

This is clearly evident in the recent struggles within both Conservative and Labour parties and goes back a long way, as shown by our earlier discussion and by the milestones section that follows. We have emphasised not only party divisions, however, but also the way in which strong leaders can use their organisational advantages to pull the party together and stake out an electorally winning position that endures over a considerable period of time. Besides covering internal disputes this chapter has charted the overall development of the parties, their internal structure and the social sectors from which leaders and members come. Specifically it has discussed:

- inner tensions and ideological developments from 1868 to 1979

- factional and leadership initiatives of the 1980s and 1990s

- the way in which parties link grassroots and leadership through their organisational structures

- the leverage this gives to party leaders in pulling the party together

- changes in social representation in Parliament, particularly the increasingly middle class nature of Labour and the new influx of women MPs, which points to a possible modification of the overall style of party politics in the future.

MILESTONES

Milestones in the development of British political parties

	Conservatives	Liberals	Labour
1867–8	Second Reform Act transforms franchise from a small, propertied basis to a mass electorate		
1870s	Primrose League promotes mass organisation of party, with a branch in every constituency. Party promotes Empire, monarchy and social reform	Joseph Chamberlain and the 'Birmingham Caucus' pioneer a mass party organisation emulated in other parts of Britain	
1868–86	Alternation of Conservatives and Liberals in government		

	Conservatives		Liberals		Labour
1886	Accession of Liberal Unionists initiates 20-year dominance of Conservative Party in national politics		Gladstone's First Home Rule Bill for Ireland splits Liberal Party		
				1900	Labour Representation Committee brings together socialist parties and trade unions
1905	Under influence of Liberal Unionists, party advocates imperial preference and protection, is defeated in the general election, and remains divided	1905–14	Liberal governments introduce social reforms and push for Irish Home Rule Parliament Act 1911, National Health Insurance Act 1911, Irish Home Rule Bills 1912, 1913, 1914	1905–14	Labour supports reforming Liberal governments
				1914–18	Labour internally divided over whether Britain should fight First World War
1922	Break-up of coalition. Bonar Law propels Conservatives to office	1922–9	Liberals split between 'Lloyd George' and 'Asquith' Liberals	1923–4	First minority Labour government legislates for public housing programmes
1926	General strike broken by Conservative government with implicit support of Liberals and Labour				
				1929–31	Second minority Labour government
1931	Financial crisis related to world slump leads to split in Labour and Liberal parties, and formation of Conservative-dominated 'National government'				
1932	Government intervenes to impose protection, tariffs, industrial mergers and rudimentary planning		Split between mainstream opposition and 'National Liberals' who are absorbed by Conservatives	1932	Split between mainstream Labour and 'National Labour' who are absorbed by Conservatives
1940–5	Wartime Coalition government, in which Labour basically runs home affairs				
1946–51	Conservatives accept Welfare State and most nationalisations		Liberals drift without clear leadership		Reforming Labour governments establish 'Welfare State', nationalise large industries and decolonise India
1951–59	They win elections of 1951, 1955 and 1959 on basis of abolishing controls and freeing economy			1951–64	Party divides increasingly between left and right

▶

	Conservatives		Liberals		Labour
1962–4	Government shifts to idea of indicative economic planning	1964	Gain votes with advocacy of electoral reform, civil rights and European integration	1964–6	Wins 1964 and 1966 elections on basis of 'making planning work'. Devaluation of sterling leads to financially orthodox policies. Trade union reform fails. Strengthening of the Left
1965–70	Shift to the Right – support for free market and trade union reform				
1970–4	Heath government imposes legal framework on trade unions and joins European Union				
1973–4	'Three-day week' and miners' strike precipitate election, which brings government down	1974	Liberal vote increases to 18–19% at the two general elections that year	1974	Wins elections but with reduced vote. Wage and price controls lead to trade union revolt in 1979 ('winter of discontent'). Loses 1979 election
1975	Margaret Thatcher wins party leadership election on a 'New Right' programme				
1979–90	Margaret Thatcher wins a series of elections on a programme of financial orthodoxy, privatisation of state industry, strict regulation of trade unions, cuts in public expenditure, a cautious attitude to EU, and full support of NATO	1983–7	Alliance with Social Democrats nets one-quarter of the vote in general elections of 1983 and 1987	1979–83	Ascendancy of 'Hard Left'. Alternative economic programme and internal reforms lead to breakaway Social Democrat Party and to heavy election defeat in 1983
				1983	Election of Neil Kinnock as leader. Centralising reforms and adoption of 'neo-liberal consensus' fails to avert election defeats of 1987 and 1992

	Conservatives		Liberals		Labour
1990	Thatcher ejected as leader to avert election defeat				
1992–7	Split between 'Eurosceptics' and 'pro-Europeans' weakens party by continual controversy. Series of financial and sexual scandals. Go down to record defeat in 1997			1992	Kinnock resigns as party leader
				1992–94	John Smith carries on internal reforms as party leader
				1994	Tony Blair elected party leader, imposes strong central discipline, abolishes Clause 4, loosens ties with the trade unions and evolves image of 'New Labour', which wins 1997 election
		1997	Liberals win 46 seats in Parliament, their largest number since 1929	1997	Government initiates programme of political reform starting with devolution. Cautious pursuit of 'neo-liberal consensus' aids stability and economic prosperity
1998	System for electing party leader changed to include party members	1998–9	Coalitions with Labour in Scotland and Wales		
2001	Eurosceptic, right-wing leader William Hague loses election. He is replaced by the very similar Iain Duncan Smith	2001	New leader Charles Kennedy increases vote and seat numbers	2001	Landslide victory in general election consolidates Tony Blair's leadership
2002	Main party division shifts to efficiency and delivery of public services				
2003					Serious internal dissent over Iraq War

PROJECTS

1. Document with examples the major ways in which *either* Tony Blair or Charles Kennedy can control their respective parties.

2. Update Robert McKenzie's analysis of power relationships within the Conservative and Labour parties.

3. What influence do *either* Euro MPs (MEPs) or local councillors have within the Conservative and Labour parties? Base the project on actual newspaper accounts of how they have exerted influence.

FURTHER READING

Valuable historical material is contained in R. T. McKenzie, *British Political Parties* (London: Mercury, 1964). A graphic account of New Labour's management and electioneering, and of Conservative divisions, is found as background in D. Butler and D. Kavanagh, *The British General Election of 2001* (London: Macmillan, 2001). Earlier books in this series chart fluctuating party fortunes over the post-war period. On party membership, activists and organisational structure see Patrick Seyd and Paul Whiteley, *Labour's Grass Roots* (Oxford: Clarendon Press, 1992) and Paul Whiteley et al, *True Blues* (Oxford: Oxford University Press, 1994). The best accounts of the internal democratisation of parties are Paul Webb, 'Parties and party systems: modernisation, regulation and diversity', *Parliamentary Affairs*, **54** (2), 2001, pp. 308–21; Richard Kelly, 'Farewell conference, hello forum: the making of Labour and Tory policy', *Political Quarterly*, **72** (3), 2001, pp. 329–34 and 'The party didn't work', *Political Quarterly*, **73** (1), 2002, pp. 38–45; Justin Fisher and Philip Cowley, 'The Labour Party', *Politics Review*, **10** (1), 2000, pp. 27–9; 'The Conservative Party', *Politics Review*, **10** (2), 2000, pp. 2–5 and 'The Liberal Democrats', *Politics Review*, **10** (3), 2000, pp. 2–5. For the SNP and Plaid Cymru, see *Politics Review*, **11**(3), 2002, pp. 22–5.

USEFUL WEB SITES ON POLITICAL PARTIES AND PARTY FACTIONS

Hotlinks to these sites can be found on the CWS website of http://www.booksites.net/budge. (For further study aids on this subject, please see the self-assessment test for this chapter on *The New British Politics* web site at http://www.booksites.net/budge.)

The main political parties in Britain include, in alphabetical order:

Conservative Party www.conservative-party.org.uk/
Democratic Unionist Party www.dup.org.uk
Labour Party www.labour.org.uk/
Liberal Democrats www.libdems.org.uk/
Plaid Cymru www.plaid-cymru.wales.com
Progressive Unionist Party (NI) www.pup.org/
Provisional Sinn Fein sinnfein.ie/index.html
Scottish National Party www.snp.org.uk/
Social Democratic and Labour Party www.sdlp.ie/sdlp/
Ulster Unionist Party www.uup.org
United Kingdom Unionist Party www.ukup.org

On each web page you will find the parties' main aims and objectives, policy pronouncements, official manifestos, and lists of current officeholders (see Chapter 17). The party web sites also have links to other groups and movements that support their policies and political goals.

Other parties and factions of the main parties

The parties are listed in alphabetical order:

Alliance Party of Northern Ireland www.allianceparty.org
Britain in Europe Movement www.britainineurope.org.uk
British Democratic Dictatorship Party www.come.to/bddp
British National Party www.bnp.net
Communist Party of Britain www.communist-party.org.uk
Cymru Goch (Welsh Socialists) www.fanergoch.org
Democracy Movement (formerly Referendum Party)
   www.democracy-movement.org.uk/
Democratic Left www.democratic-left.org.uk
Democratic Unionist Party www.dup.org.uk
Green Party www.greenparty.org.uk
Independent Labour Network www.iln.labournet.org.uk
Irish Republican Socialist Party www.irsm.org/irsm.html
Labour Left Briefing www.llb.labournet.org.uk
Labour Reform www.cix.co.uk/~ecotrend/LR/index.htm
Liberal Party www.libparty.demon.co.uk
Monster Raving Loony Party freespace.virgin.net/raving.loony
Natural Law Party www.natural-law-party.org.uk/
Northern Ireland Labour Party www.labourni.org
Northern Ireland Unionist Party www.niup.org
Pro-Euro Conservative Party www.proeuro.co.uk
Progressive Unionist Party www.pup.org
Scottish Labour Action, a Home Rule faction of the Scottish Labour Party
   www.holyrood.org.uk/sla/
Scottish Liberal Democrats www.scotlibdems.org.uk/
Scottish Republican Socialist Movement www.glaschu.freeserve.co.uk
Scottish Socialist Alliance www.wkweb1.cableinet.co.uk/diblake
Socialist Equality Party www.socialequality.org.uk
Socialist Party www.socialistparty.org.uk
Tribune Group (voice of the Left) www.rost2000.abel.co.uk/tribune/uklinks.htm
Ulster Democratic Party www.udp.org
United Kingdom Independence Party
   www.independenceuk.org.uk/cgi-bin/ukip.pl
Welsh Distributist Movement
   www.dspace.dial.pipex.com/third-position/wdm.html
Whig Party www.home.clara.net/gamestheory/whigs.html

Party ideologies and political representation

Parties are at the heart of British politics not only because of what they are but because of what they do. The last chapter showed how their organisations span the various levels of British society, linking members and electors to a set of leaders who form the government or government-in-waiting.

Parties not only seek to run the country, however. They also seek to run it along certain lines, either as a free market economy or as a 'mixed' system, in which market competition is regulated and the state intervenes to protect losers. This is only one of the issues that divide the two main parties, but it has been a central one over the last 20 years, and has deep historical roots.

Other policy differences exist notably over the European Union (EU). However, parties tend to shift positions on these issues from time to time. Labour was split on the EU in the 1970s but is much more supportive today, while the Conservatives totally changed from support to opposition between the mid-1970s and the late 1990s.

On central questions such as the management of the economy and provision for the weaker members of society the parties are more consistent in the policies they adopt. This is partly because their position is embedded in their very identity and ideology, as well as in the expectations of core supporters and members. The Conservatives would not be the Conservatives, for example, if they were not sceptical about the extent to which governments can or should directly help people.

This chapter will accordingly:

- examine the concept of 'party families' and the development of party ideologies

- explore the idea of 'left' and 'right' in British politics and in the ideologies of British political parties

- examine party programmes and see how these reflect left–right ideologies

- ask whether ideology is still as important as it was in the past and whether differing party ideologies give voters a real choice

- question the importance of political parties in Britain and ask whether there is an alternative way of running the country.

PARTY FAMILIES

Party family
Groupings of parties with similar beliefs and support groups, even though they operate in different countries.

British political parties are the second oldest in the world (the Americans had them first). But they are not wholly unique. Labour falls into the general 'family' of socialist and social democratic parties, the most numerous of all party families. The Liberals belong to the rather small family of radical liberal parties. In recent years the Conservatives' natural home has been the conservative–liberal, free market grouping.

Even the smaller British parties have counterparts in other countries with whom they form a broad transnational grouping. The Greens, for example, resemble environmentally minded parties elsewhere; and parties such as Plaid Cymru (the Welsh nationalists) and the Scottish Nationalist Party (SNP) belong to a broad spectrum of minority nationalist parties. The Northern Irish Social Democratic and Labour Party (SDLP) can be classified with the Christian party family, given their Catholic basis. Ulster Unionists are in the rather unusual position of being a regional party upholding the central state. Their belief in the indissolubility of the Union groups them with straight Conservative parties elsewhere in Europe.

Representation
The process whereby one person acts on behalf of, or in the interests of another. Representative government entails the selection of representatives (usually by election) to make decisions, rather than direct participation of those represented.

Left–right continuum
The straight line on which it is often convenient to locate parties. It stretches from the left-wing parties that believe in radical or revolutionary change, through the socialists and centre parties, to parties of the moderate right that oppose change, and on to extremist parties espousing a Fascist or Nazi ideology.

Ideology A system of ideas, assumptions, values and beliefs that help us to explain the political world – what it is and why, and what it should be.

BRIEFINGS

17.1 Ideology and the concept of 'party families'

'Ideology' is a system of ideas and assumptions that help us understand and interpret the political world. It is a set of values and beliefs, factual assumptions and ideas, that point towards the appropriate political action to take in given circumstances. The term is often restricted to a fairly explicit, coherent and elaborate set of ideas: a theory of politics. In this sense few people have real ideologies, not even political leaders. But many do subscribe to looser and less explicit ideologies such as socialism, liberalism or conservatism. Parties are built around these conflicting political principles ('political principles' is a positive name for 'ideology', in its broader sense). Parties in different countries that share a similar ideology are usually grouped together as a 'party family' because they share the same beliefs, principles, policies and often win electoral support from the same social groups.

Table 17.1 shows the general 'family' to which each British party belongs. More than that it summarises which groups their supporters come from, what their core values and policies are and where they stand on the extent of government intervention in economy and society, which is the central issue in the left–right differences we discuss later. 'Families' are, in fact, roughly ordered in left–right terms (the left–right continuum), from radical environmental groupings to socialists and radical liberals to conservative liberals devoted to the free market and as little governmental intervention as possible.

State intervention versus the free market is not the only way in which to think of 'left' and 'right'. The terms are also used to distinguish between internationalist and nationalistic outlooks in foreign and defence policy and between libertarian and authoritarian outlooks on regulating private behaviour. Parties (and individual politicians) can be on the left on one dimension but in the centre or on the right on another. For example, New Labour might be described as left of centre on the classicial social and economic dimension but right of centre on

'Family' ideology	Support groups	Core values	Characteristic policies	Attitudes to government intervention	British 'family member'
Ecological and communitarian	Young, well educated	Environment participation, peace	Encourage sense of community, protect environment, help minorities, disarmament	Support more intervention to achieve objectives	Green Party
Socialist	Workers, public employees in social and service sectors, intellectuals	Equality of wealth and opportunity	Extend welfare protection (health and pensions), regulation of capitalism, peace	Government provision in all areas where market does not provide	Labour Party
Minority nationalist	Territorial minorities	Cultural diversity, regional devolution, autonomy	Decentralisation, devolution and autonomy	Intervention necessary to uphold minority cultures in the modern world	Scottish National Party, Plaid Cymru
Radical liberal	Anti-authoritarian elements of the middle classes, religious minorities, some peripheral regions	Liberty and a minimum standard of living to enjoy it	Safeguards for political and social rights	Against 'big' government but favour intervention to safeguard weaker sectors	Liberal Democrats
Christian democratic	Churches, especially the Catholic Church, the Catholic middle class, country and small towns	Fraternity, community, human dignity	Strengthen traditional morality and family, extend welfare, mixed economy	Intervention where necessary to ensure welfare and family stability	Social Democratic and Labour Party (SDLP) (Northern Ireland)
Conservative	Traditionalists of the state church, upper and middle class, 'loyal' members of working class, country and small town areas	Order, security, social hierarchy	Uphold established state structures and national boundaries, maintain armed forces	Intervention as and when necessary to ensure stability	Ulster Unionist Parties, British Conservatives 1868–1979
Conservative (neo)liberal	Business and professional middle classes	Liberty, individualism	Freedom from controls, free markets, efficient limited government	Government limited to upholding free market	Conservative Party (post-1979)

Table 17.1 European 'party families' and their British members

many aspects of the libertarian–authoritarian dimension, such as punishing private use of drugs. British party politics in the twentieth century largely revolved around the roles of the state versus the market in economic and social affairs and it is therefore in these terms that 'left' and 'right' are usually defined.

Of course, a summary table like this inevitably simplifies. The British parties have already been described in greater detail in Chapter 16. Nevertheless, the comparison shows what a lot in common they have with European parties, where the same groupings appear.

PARTY IDEOLOGIES

The three major British parties clearly differ in terms of all the factors listed in Table 17.1. Labour has traditionally drawn its members and most faithful supporters from the working class and public employees, has been dedicated to equality as a core value and has advocated extensive government-supported welfare to ensure this. This was played down in 'New Labour' manifestos but has been increasingly stressed in recent government pronouncements.

The Liberal Democrats, who are quite radical and reformist by general European standards, come close to Labour on these matters but historically are more inclined than Labour to set limits on what governments do. As we shall see, recently the two parties have crossed these ideological lines.

The legacy of Margaret Thatcher, Conservative leader from 1975 to 1990, was to change the Conservatives decisively. To the values of order and stability she added the principles of economic freedom and individualism, as represented above all by the free market. Traditional Conservatives had often been inclined to accept social welfare and economic intervention for the sake of political and social order (as with the 'social democratic consensus' over policy from 1950 to 1979). Mrs Thatcher, however, would have none of this and seriously set about reducing 'welfare dependence' during her years as Prime Minister (1979–90).

Recent years have thus seen political and ideological shifts on the part of both the New Right and New Labour. One could also say this of the Liberal Democrats, who have turned themselves into a mildly radical alternative to Labour. How significant are these changes? Are they likely to last? And do they mean that the parties are coming together? Are we seeing both convergence and an end of distinguishing party ideologies?

Ideologies and political cleavages

To answer these questions we need to put today's ideologies in historical perspective. All parties date to the beginning of the twentieth century or earlier and many of the traditional differences between them also derive from that time. Parties adapted their ideology to the needs of particular supporters, both building on and emphasising certain lines of political 'cleavage' in the country. Seeing how they did this helps us appreciate how enduring ideology can be.

BRIEFINGS

17.2 Social and political cleavages

A political cleavage has two elements:

1. A social division in the population (as between working class and middle class), that is, a cumulation of differences in lifestyle, social characteristics and material advantages that differentiates one group of people from another.

2. A political emphasis on one side of that division, usually by political parties, who aim to take up and advance the interests of 'workers' or the 'middle class' or whatever group is involved. By doing so the parties aim to mobilise them politically, recruit them as members, and win their votes. A first step historically was thus to enfranchise the relevant group so that they could cast votes in favour of the party.

Political parties are thus as important in the creation of cleavages as objective social divisions are. An illustration is that the division between town and country never turned into a cleavage in Britain, because all parties lined up with urban interests in accepting free trade after 1850. The divisions that did become cleavages in the nineteenth century were religion, region and class (in that order).

(For more on the relationship between cleavages and parties in Western Europe read the classic account, Seymour Martin Lipset and Stein Rokkan (eds), *Party Systems and Voter Alignments*, New York: Free Press, 1967.)

BRIEFINGS

17.3 Classical liberalism

The essence of liberalism (with a small 'l') is the belief that individual rights should be protected by maximising freedom of choice and by limiting the powers of government. Historically, liberalism represents a rejection of the absolute powers of a monarch, or other ruler, and seeks to establish limited government, tolerance, and freedom under the law. In Britain classical liberalism is built on the writings of John Locke (1632–1704) and John Stuart Mill (1806–73). In *Two Treatises of Government* (1690) Locke defended the Glorious Revolution of 1688 that established the dependence of the monarch on Parliament and was thus a first important step towards limited, constitutional government. In his *Letter Concerning Toleration* (1693) Locke makes the case for freedom of religious conscience, and so lays out the case for freedom of thought and belief in general, which is a fundamental tenet of liberal theory. In *On Liberty* (1859), Mill argues that the only justification for government interference with the liberty of individual citizens is to prevent them doing harm to others. His great fear is the tyranny of popular opinion (tyranny of the majority), which can threaten individual freedom no less than paternalistic or authoritarian government. In this sense classical liberalism is opposed both to the absolute powers of the monarchy, and to the broad-ranging powers and functions of a socialist state.

Classical economic liberalism is expounded by Adam Smith (1723–90) in his book *The Wealth of Nations* (1776), which argues that the 'invisible hand of the market' succeeds in making individual economic self-interest work for the common good. In this way Smith lays out the arguments for capitalism, individualism and free trade.

BRIEFINGS

17.4 **Neo-liberalism**

In the twentieth century some of the ideas of classical liberalism have emerged in 'neo-liberal', or 'New Right', form. Neo-liberals also place supreme importance on the freedom of the individual and on rolling back the frontiers of the state. They argue that market competition is the best way of guaranteeing both political freedom and economic growth. In *The Road to Serfdom* (1944), for example, F. A. von Hayek (1899–1992) argues that socialism and the Welfare State inevitably lead to loss of individual freedom. In a similar way, the 'Chicago School' of economics, led by Milton Friedman in the 1970s and 1980s, rejects Keynesian theory in favour of a form of classical economics that strongly favours competitive markets and low public expenditure. The main economic function of government is to regulate the money supply (monetarism) in order to control inflation. The ideas of Hayek and Friedman strongly influenced Margaret Thatcher. Two right-wing think tanks, the Centre for Policy Studies (established in 1974) and the Adam Smith Institute (established in 1977), were formed to promote and develop neo-liberal policies in British government.

BRIEFINGS

17.5 **Conservatism**

Conservatism (with a small 'c') is a general tendency in politics rather than a clearly worked out ideology such as Marxism or socialism. It believes in preserving what is thought best in traditional society and opposes radical change.

Conservatives believe that society is hierarchically organised and should be regulated by a strong state. The classical British work of conservative theory is Edmund Burke's *Reflections on the Revolution in France* (1790), which doubts the capacity of people and governments to plan an ideal society and therefore argues for slow change rather than radical transformation. Old institutions and practices, wrote Burke, often have great, though hidden, virtues, and should be allowed to adapt slowly to changing circumstances. The ideas of conservatives have usually been strongly represented in the policies of the Conservative Party.

British conservative thought has varied over the years. Strongly opposed to socialist ideas in the first half of the twentieth century, conservatism and the Conservative Party moved towards a social democratic consensus in the 1950–75 period when they were inclined to accept the broad principles of the Welfare State, the mixed economy, Keynesian economic policies and a NATO-based alliance against the Soviet Union. The consensus was also known as 'Butskellism' after the moderate Conservative Chancellor of the Exchequer R. A. B. Butler, and his moderate Labour counterpart Hugh Gaitskell, who agreed on broad policy issues, although not necessarily the details. The social democratic consensus was eroded during the Labour government led by James Callaghan in 1976–9 and was decisively broken by Margaret Thatcher in the 1980s. Her politics were closer to the neo-liberal ideas of the New Right than to traditional conservatism.

The Conservative and Liberal parties trace their origins to the 'cadre' parties operating under the very restricted middle class franchise from 1832 to 1867 (when the Second Reform Act transformed the situation). From today's perspective the differences between the leading figures of these two parties do not seem very great. Many (including Gladstone, the dominating figure of nineteenth-century Liberalism) switched between them. Starting from the effective introduction of free trade in 1846–7, however, the Liberals gradually developed more progressive policies, pressing for political reforms and the extension of the franchise. Because of this they attracted the support of minority groups who felt disadvantaged by the old set-up: the Scots, the Welsh and religious nonconformists (both Protestant and Irish Catholic).

With the actual achievement of a mass franchise it became even more important for the Liberals to attract the votes of these groups to gain power. To do so they took up the causes dear to them: removal of state support from the Anglican Church in Ireland and Wales; and wider political reforms, particularly of the patronage system in government appointments and of the Church's hold on education. Representing above all the nonconformist middle classes of Wales, Scotland, and northern and western England, the Liberals could not, however, appear as effective defenders of the working class interest. This left an opening for Conservatives and, by the early twentieth century, the newly formed Labour Party, which both parties took.

> **Patronage** The giving of favours – office, contracts or honours – to supporters of the government.

In the mid-nineteenth century the Conservatives, like other such parties in Europe, defended the traditional state structures – monarchy, army and church – against the increasingly reformist Liberals. With the advent of the mass male franchise in 1867–8 they developed an appeal to the new working and lower middle class that built on these themes, stressing national unity, British military strength and the Empire. Particularly after the Liberals backed Home Rule (a strong form of devolution) for Ireland in 1886, the Conservatives consolidated their new support, above all in the southeast and Midlands of England. The crisis over Irish Home Rule, which the Conservatives opposed, also shook out traditionalist elements from the Liberals (the Whigs), rendering them more than ever a party of nonconformists on the geographical peripheries and in the urban areas of northern England.

The peripheries were based economically on manufacturing and so were dominated demographically by the urban working class (Chapters 1 and 2). This left the Liberals vulnerable to a class-based party that could unequivocally put the interests of industrial workers first. The rise of Labour, which did just that from the beginning of the twentieth century, eroded Liberal support. The Liberals suffered from a double haemorrhage, losing working class support to Labour, while the business classes fled to the Conservatives, who offered stronger opposition to welfarist and protectionist demands.

The consequences were:

- A steady decline in Liberal importance. From one of two major parties they became one of three in the 1920s and saw their vote drop to below 10 per cent in the 1950s.

- As a result Labour became the main party of opposition to the Conservatives.

- The Conservatives themselves became divided between the traditionalists, still disposed to concede welfare demands for the sake of national unity, security, hierarchy and order, and the newly acquired ex-Liberal supporters of free trade and the free market.

This group progressively took over the party, a process finally completed in the 1980s under Mrs Thatcher. Of course, free markets depend on the state maintaining order and security. The two sides could compromise on the need for both. But in terms of political priorities, order and security began to take second place to economic freedom, both at home and abroad.

The Labour Party, unlike the Liberals, has always been ambivalent towards free trade, and wanted protection for workers and the weaker elements at home, secured by government intervention. It parted company with the increasingly radical Liberals (now Liberal Democrats) on this last point. The Liberals developed the argument that to take advantage of economic freedom people needed the resources to implement their choice. To have a choice of medical services, for example, is of no benefit if one cannot afford to buy any of them. However, unlike 'old' Labour, they did not see state intervention as a good in itself but as a means to giving individuals economic freedom. As in the case of the other two parties, these ideas spring out of older concerns, modified to fit modern conditions. The question asked later in this chapter is, how far have their older ideas been modified?

First, however, we should comment on the relationship between cleavages and ideologies. Just how does the social base of a party relate to its political ideas?

The two intermesh because parties aim their appeals at certain social groups in order to gain their votes and support. It is easier to target social groups with identities and interests in common. Trying to appeal to the electorate as a whole on the basis of their common interests is more difficult because of a large degree of uncertainty about what their common interests actually are and how they are responding. With a distinctive social group, politicians can talk to their leaders and communicate more easily.

Of course this is a two-way process because, by appealing to group interests, the party is helping to define them. The working class was much more conscious of itself as a separate sector of society, with distinct and sometimes conflicting interests from other sectors, once the Labour Party was launched. The Labour Party also helped develop other organisations to represent them (eg by strengthening trade unions).

In the books, articles and pamphlets that set out the Labour and working class case, a systematic analysis of the position of workers in contemporary society appeared, linking together the appeals for more welfare, housing, minimum wages and equality that Labour made at elections. Labour, like other European socialist parties, had the advantage of being able to draw on the immensely influential and comprehensive work of Karl Marx, who wrote from the mid-nineteenth century onwards, and his intellectual followers; but it drew much more on other traditions, in particular religious nonconformity and radical liberalism such as the Chartism of the 1840s.

Marxist theory sees all events in terms of the class struggle. Nationalism, religion and individualism are simply bourgeois weapons to create 'false consciousness'

False consciousness
The emphasis on individualism or nationalism as opposed to their collective class interests induced in the workers by capitalist ideology in order to conceal the real nature of capitalism.

and delude the workers about where their real interests lie. These are in essence to struggle against their employers, and eventually to overthrow the capitalist system that allows the latter to control the means of production such as factories and land. Their monopoly over the means of production enables them to exploit workers by forcing them to sell their labour (their only resource) very cheaply and thus creates gross inequalities of wealth and social conditions in society.

BRIEFINGS

17.6 **Marxism and socialism**

Developed by Karl Marx in the mid-nineteenth century, Marxism is probably still the best known political ideology. Although it has developed many different branches, Marxism essentially states that economic relations, particularly those between the classes created by the system of production, directly or indirectly determine all forms of political and social life. In the late capitalist system there are only two classes of political importance: the capitalists (or property owners or bourgeoisie), who are increasingly rich; and the workers (or proletariat), who are exploited, and become increasingly poor. Economic conditions and an informed political leadership encourage workers to develop a revolutionary class consciousness, overthrow the system and, after a period of state socialism, establish the conditions for a society without state or property.

According to Marx, history can only be understood in terms of class, and capitalist politics can only be understood as a constant class struggle between the bourgeoisie and the proletariat. Other ideas, such as religion or nationalism, might seem important, but are simply different manifestations of class interests, which are used by the ruling class to mask political reality and create the false consciousness that conceals the real class struggle. A Marxist, therefore, reacts to events by asking whose class interests are being served. Foreign wars, for example, may appear unconnected with the class struggle but, according to Marxist theory, they are actually a means of promoting capitalist interests.

Almost no parties in contemporary Europe support the whole of the Marxist argument. Democratic socialists such as British Labour may, however, agree that class relationships are the most important ones and that the central issues in politics are those concerned with the distribution of resources between classes. But they would argue that the working class – like others – has an interest in preserving peace and stability and that redistribution achieved through negotiation and argument is much better than imposed solutions supported by force, since these can always be reversed by greater force.

A similar acceptance of non-violence and democracy occurs among the adherents of the other party ideologies. In practice, this means accepting the policies chosen by the elected government, no matter how much one may criticise them as unfair or unjust. Indeed, if an opposition party can persuade enough electors that government policies are unfair, it can hope to reverse the electoral decision next time and thus modify government policies. Because of this possibility, most governments will tend to compromise with the parties out of government so that the projects they initiate will have some chance of permanency and do not get repealed once there is a change of power.

BRIEFINGS

17.7 **Social and social democracy**

Socialism takes from Marxism the ideas of class interest, equality and the Welfare State. It differs from Marxism, however, in stating that political and social change can and should be achieved by means of peaceful reform and democratic action rather than revolutionary violence. The British Labour Party is a social democratic party, as are the mainstream labour movements in Scandinavia and Germany. Like most ideological schools of thought – including Marxism and liberalism – socialism has many variations, including anarcho-socialism, Christian socialism, Fabianism, guild socialism and market socialism. Fundamentally, socialist theory argues for the collective ownership or control of key parts of the economy, for state economic planning, and state provision of basic services such as health care, education and social welfare. But it opposes complete state control of the economy (the command economy) of communist systems, and favours the retention of large areas of social, political and economic life that are outside the state and independent of it. It is therefore opposed to economic liberalism, on the one hand, and to communism, on the other.

British socialism has not been strongly influenced by West European socialist thought, and has drawn heavily upon the work of British writers such as Beatrice Webb (1848–1943), Sidney Webb (1859–1947), George Bernard Shaw (1856–1950), R. H. Tawney (1880–1962), John Maynard Keynes (1883–1946) and C. A. R. (Anthony) Crosland (1918–77). The writings of the 'Fabians' (the Webbs and Shaw) put faith in the 'inevitability of gradualness' rather than revolution, and concentrated on practical schemes of reform (sometimes called 'gas and water socialism'). Fabians assumed that a democratically elected central government had the means and will to ensure greater equality and eliminate poverty. Tawney's book *Equality* (1931), based on a Christian ethic, also argued for state action and progressive taxation, in the interests of economic stability and growth, and political equality and democracy. But it was Keynes who had a particularly strong influence on political thought and government policy in Britain and throughout the western world. In his book *The General Theory of Employment, Interest, and Money* (1936), Keynes advocated some government economic intervention and planning in order to achieve economic stability, growth and full employment. Keynesian demand management and a mixed economy replaced classical, liberal (market) economics as the orthodoxy of economic theory and practice between 1945 and 1975.

In the 1960s British socialist thought went through a period of change under the influence of Anthony Crosland's book, *The Future of Socialism* (1956). This argued that socialist goals of freedom and equality require some government economic planning but a large measure of private economic activity. State control and regulation of key sectors of the economy was necessary, but not further nationalisation.

Within this broad acceptance of democracy, party ideologies differ from each other in terms of which groups are considered to be the important ones in society and how their interests should be served. Are classes so pervasive and central that the interests of the workers should always come first? Or are workers' interests only part of a more general, societal interest, as 'bourgeois' parties tend to argue, and hence better served by strengthening the free market that will create more wealth for all? Or, on the contrary, is economic growth the force that is destroying the natural world in which we all have a common interest, as Greens argue, and so should it be resisted? Also, perhaps, should economic growth be resisted because through uncontrolled development it ravages the countryside and threatens the culture of minority groups, which need to be defended by setting up their own state or substate institutions, as in Scotland and Ireland?

There is thus rich ground for controversy and argument among the adherents of different ideologies. This is particularly so because no one can say, scientifically or objectively, which ideology is right. Assertions that class is the most important of social relationships, or that the world would suffer an irreparable loss if Welsh ceased to be spoken, are not subject to 'scientific' or 'objective' proof. They spring out of an identification with or immersion in a particular group in society. One function of an ideology, indeed, is to buttress that identity, as most people belong actually or potentially to many different overlapping groups. For example, is a Polish-born secretary working in northeast England primarily a worker, British, English, Polish, European, Roman Catholic, an immigrant or a woman? In a situation of multiple individual identities parties struggle to make one identity predominant and thus to mobilise support for their policies and general point of view.

Ideologies are thus important not only in telling leaders what to do but in telling voters who they are and so making them receptive to leaders' diagnoses of the political situation. Ideology is particularly important for political parties, which have to operate across different levels of society. It helps to link up often complex governmental decisions with the broadly defined interests of a party's supporters and voters.

'LEFT' AND 'RIGHT' IN BRITISH POLITICS

Specific party ideologies can also be distinguished in terms of how far they are to the 'right' or to the 'left'. This is because differences over the extent of government intervention in society – whether to leave things to the free market or to limit its often disruptive workings – are a central and permanent political issue in modern societies. Intervention is sought by all sorts of groups that feel themselves weak in social and economic terms: not just the working class but also ethnic minorities, women and environmentalists. They want the government to restrict the power of the purely economic interests privileged by the market.

Idealism The view of politics, especially international relations, that emphasises the role of ideals and morality as a determinant of state policies, and hence the possibility of peaceful co-operation.

These differences appear in attitudes to foreign affairs as well as inside Britain. The left-wing parties (Greens, Labour, Liberals) are generally more sympathetic than the right towards supranational bodies such as the EU and UN designed to regulate what states and multinational corporations do (although the Labour left opposed NATO and the European Economic Community, as it then was, in the 1980s). They tend to be 'idealists' in international terms, with a strong belief in the possibility of peaceful co-operation at international level and a commitment to building institutions to encourage this.

In contrast the 'right' adopts more 'realist' views, seeing the international arena as a form of free market, where states and firms pursue their own interests, and often maximise the general well-being by doing so. To prevent the pursuit of national interests getting out of hand, however, strong military alliances are

17.8 Left–right differences in British politics

The terms 'left' and 'right' originated from the location of supporters and opponents of political change in France at the end of the eighteenth century. Supporters of reform sat on the left of the legislative chamber while supporters of the Crown and established institutions sat on the right. The terms have kept their connection with those who urge change on the one hand, and those who oppose it on the other. However, this connection is often more rhetorical than real, as right-wing parties often in practice introduce greater changes than left-wing ones (one example would be the Thatcherite reforms in Britain in the 1980s).

In the twenty-first century the core distinction is defined in terms of support for more government intervention, on the left, and opposition to it, on the right. Left-wing parties want to extend the Welfare State and apply more regulation and planning to the economy. Right-wing parties want government to refrain from interfering in society and the economy as far as possible, in order to extend individual freedom of choice. But they do support strong government measures to guarantee law and order internally, and national security externally. Thus they support a strong, but limited, state. In contrast left-wing parties want peace through international co-operation. Left-wing positions have generally developed out of some variant of Marxist ideology.

Centre parties tend to mix these positions and support limited government intervention in most policy areas, but specifically oppose the Marxist analysis of society.

The fact that parties consistently take up these positions means that their election programmes and manifestos can be statistically analysed to see how they 'move' in left–right terms from election to election (as in Figure 16.2).

(For more detail, see Ian Budge, H. D. Klingemann, Andrea Volkens, Judith Bara and Eric Tanenbaum, *Mapping Policy Preferences: Estimates for Parties, Electors and Governments 1945–1998*, Oxford: OUP, 2001, p. 22.)

Realism The view of politics, especially international relations, that emphasises the role of self-interest as a determinant of state policies, and hence the importance of power in these relations.

necessary to create a 'balance of power' where no one side can dominate. The Cold War of 1948–89, when the US and Soviet alliances confronted each other, was an example of such a balance, where each side deterred the other from taking over the world. Now that the Russians have voluntarily accepted capitalism and free markets new threats may arise, such as Islamic fundamentalism, which make continuing military preparations necessary. 'Idealists' would be much happier seeing the old alliances dismantled and substituted by world or regional development bodies. The fact that all parties take a position on these questions allows us to place them on a single line running from left to right, as shown in Figure 17.1.

To be sure, left–right differences are not the only ones that exist between parties, and probably not the most important ones for minority nationalists, for example. They are central to British politics, however, so it is interesting to look at them across the whole political spectrum.

The point that leaps out from Figure 17.1 is that the three main British parties are not, on average, so very distant from each other in terms of the full range of ideological difference (at least in left–right terms) that could exist. Labour is far from wanting to have everything regulated and the Conservatives do not want to

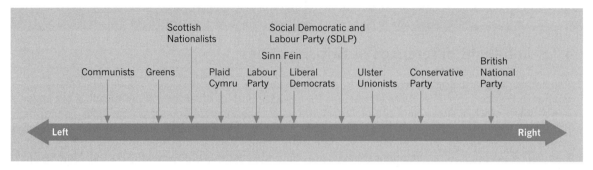

Figure 17.1 *Location of United Kingdom political parties on the left–right ideological spectrum*

leave everything to the free market or (internationally) to only what can be agreed through interstate negotiations. (They, after all, formed the government that joined the EU in 1973.) The Liberals are the most centrist of all, seeking to balance the general efficiency of the free market with necessary government intervention in favour of weaker groups.

Of course, these positions summarise what the parties have said and done over the whole post-war period from 1945 to 2000. A more interesting question is how they have changed recently: have they moved closer together or drifted further apart? Below we analyse more precisely what has happened recently and whether these left–right differences still remain.

It is also worthwhile looking at the smaller parties' position in these terms. Often smaller parties are thought to be more extreme because they are more 'pure' ideologically than the big parties can afford to be in case they put off voters. However, none of the regional parties takes positions very far (in left–right terms) from those of the main parties. The Scottish Nationalists are somewhat to the left of Labour, a good strategic position to take in left-leaning Scotland. Plaid Cymru is less radical, partly because it is the Welsh-speaking middle class who form its backbone. The Northern Irish SDLP are even more centrist than the leftist Sinn Fein, and (in left–right terms) are not too far from their local opponents, the Ulster Unionists. The last are traditional conservatives who believe above all in order, security, and the integrity of the British state. But they are not averse to financial aid and government-directed development in Northern Ireland. Further to the right are small single-issue British nationalist and racist parties. The Democracy Movement (formerly the Referendum Party) and UK Independence Party define British nationalism in terms of independence from the European Union (and in particular European Monetary Union); and the British National Party in terms of extreme hostility to immigrants and to their descendants, especially Asians and Afro-Caribbeans.

The most extreme left-wing parties are those that have a 'cause' and no regional base, the Communists and the Greens (the party that wants government intervention to save the environment). Both are small parties with limited political support.

With the collapse of communism in Russia and eastern Europe, and its dilution in China, British Communists, who were always weak electorally but wielded influence in some trade unions, are unlikely ever to win much support. However, a small 'socialist left' has emerged, with evidence of some strength in Scotland, and might gain growing support from traditional Labour supporters disillusioned with the New Labour government's shift to the centre right. In addition, the steady deterioration of the environment, both in Britain and the rest of the world, may well provoke a crisis that will give the Greens more votes and influence. At the moment, however, they are electorally weak, although they won two seats in the 1999 European elections, three seats on the Greater London Assembly and environmentalist pressure groups have been effective on many issues (see Chapter 23).

Left–right differences in the major parties' ideologies

At the British level, therefore, it is the three traditional parties that are the real contenders for power. The next sections examine how they have changed their policies and ideologies over the post-war period. Have they moved closer together recently, or moved further apart, or all moved in the same direction? Seeing how the main parties have changed from election to election, in terms of the left–right differences illustrated in Figure 17.1, provides a way of answering this question.

It is true, of course, that such a 'single-line' representation gives only a very summary idea of the full range of party policies. There is more to political life, and ideology, than just left and right. As Table 17.1 showed, parties on the left have significant differences of opinion among themselves, on the importance of devolution for example, or the primacy of environmental issues. These do not show up in simple left–right terms.

Left–right differences thus do not cover all of British politics. But they are central to them for the following reasons:

- Political discussion – in the press, on television, in Parliament – is structured in terms of left and right. An important question for commentators is always whether a party is moving towards the centre or the extremes, particularly in the context of elections. A party that has 'seized the centre ground' is usually considered to have a better chance of winning the election, as most electors are thought to be in the 'middle' (ie somewhere between the left and right positions).

- The question of how far governments should intervene – in welfare and the economy above all – is and always has been central to British politics. Chapter 2 showed how it defined politics in the late nineteenth century and it has remained the crucial dividing line between the major parties ever since.

- Because of their centrality, the positions parties take in their election programmes on this range of issues are more likely to carry through into actual government policy than others. This is important because the measure we use to trace left–right ideological shifts in party positions is derived from the party election programmes (manifestos), as explained in the next section.

ELECTIONS, MANIFESTOS, AND PROGRAMMES

Party manifesto
The document parties publish at the start of election campaigns outlining the policies they intend to implement if elected to government.

A major feature of each general election in Britain is the programme published by each party at the beginning of its campaign (a month or five weeks before the election). This is termed the party manifesto. In it the leaders set out their views on how British society should develop and how the country should be run for the next five years. Setting out a reasonably detailed overall plan for national development is something only the parties do, and it distinguishes them from other organisations in Britain.

Its practical use is that it gives electors an indication of what would be done if the party were elected into government, and thus enables voters to choose between them on grounds of policy. Manifestos enable ordinary voters to exert some influence over which policies the incoming government will pursue. The ability of electors to influence government in this way is, however, dependent on the existence of parties with alternative programmes.

Plate 17.1 *Labour Party manifesto for the 2001 general election*

Source: www.paphotos.com

If elections simply involved selecting individuals who came together in Parliament after the election in order to form a government, nobody would know in advance what their policy would be and electors would lose their opportunity to influence government policy. It is no coincidence, therefore, that the slow extension of democracy in Britain over the last century and a half has been bound up with the consolidation and growth of parties and the intensification of their competition for office. Democracy in Britain is indissolubly linked to the political parties; and electoral influence over public policy is linked to the programmes the parties offer.

Manifestos are prepared under the direction of party leaders. But many of the documents on which they are based have been approved by party conferences and other official bodies. They thus constitute a unique and authoritative policy programme to which the party as a whole is publicly committed.

Despite their importance in setting out a national five-year plan, and offering a choice, party manifestos are not widely read by electors. Their contents are, however, extensively reported in the newspapers and on the television and radio and so they are known to voters, although at second hand. Electors who want to choose between parties in terms of their policies will, in the course of the campaign, be able to acquaint themselves with the main policies the parties lay out.

What do the manifestos actually say? On first reading they seem rather woolly and far from offering a precise programme for government. New Labour was exceptional in 1997 and 2001 in making relatively precise pledges about Scottish and Welsh devolution and about limiting tax increases. Usually the manifesto makes precise commitments in only a few areas, often peripheral ones, such as restoring trade union rights at the Government Communications Headquarters (they were abolished by Margaret Thatcher), which are relatively easy to keep. About 70 per cent of these pledges are carried through if the party gets into government. But this is less impressive than it seems if the promises do not cover central areas of policy.

Much of the document consists of rambling discussions of various topics such as 'youth', 'unemployment', 'the economy', and so on. Topics like these constitute its main sections. Typically the sections state how important the problem is and give an analysis of past developments and of the present situation, stressing party concerns and achievements in the area, but not committing it to very much. This vagueness is due to a well-founded fear by party leaders that tying themselves down to specific actions while in government might give too many hostages to fortune. Changed circumstances or a financial crisis might result in their not being able to do what they promised, and thus lead to accusations of bad faith and to their loss of credibility.

From the viewpoint of parties it is better to emphasise the importance of a particular policy area rather than state what exactly it is they will do about it. This does not render the manifesto valueless as a statement of future policy. Its main purpose is to set priorities for government action rather than to tie the government in advance to specific things it must do. Talking a lot about a particular area such as 'youth' implies that the party would do more and spend more in the area, without saying exactly what it would do or how much it would spend. Setting priorities in this way actually makes it easier for electors to choose between the parties on broad general grounds relating to what they would like to see done, rather than having to decide on the feasibility of particular courses of action in areas where they have no expert knowledge.

There is often scepticism about the extent to which parties do carry through their programmes in government. Many feel that promises made at the election are simply not kept once the party takes office. Research by Klingemann et al (*Parties, Policies and Democracy*, Boulder, CO: Westview, 1994) has shown however that not only are the majority of pledges carried through by the winning party but also that the priorities stressed in the manifesto are strongly related to subsequent government expenditure in the different policy areas. Electors choosing between parties on the basis of their policy priorities can thus have some confidence that they will try to put them into effect in government.

Party manifestos and party ideology

Manifestos are programmes for government action so it follows that they are strongly influenced by party ideology. This is apparent from the manifestos issued by different parties at the same election. These often give such dramatically opposed accounts of the situation that one would think they were talking about two quite different countries! Thus in 2001 the Labour manifesto painted a glowing picture of a Britain with an expanding economy and prosperity trickling down to all, while the Conservative document talked of a crisis in the public services and threats to freedom.

Such differences occur in part because ideologies lead parties to focus on different groups and developments. The Conservative reference point is the English middle class, in particular in the southeast, with their concerns with financial markets, order and opportunity. Labour is more focused on the peripheries and their problems of economic stagnation, bad housing and health.

Differences in the party programmes also occur because the parties' ideologies and history make them 'proprietors' of different issues. A voter who wants free markets and an emphasis on individual opportunity and law and order knows from what the Conservative Party has done and said in the past that it is more likely to provide these than any other party. If these issues are the ones people think important in an election more are likely to vote Conservative. If, however, more people are concerned about education and welfare, these are 'Labour issues', that will promote support for that party.

Issues such as these become important partly because of developments outside the political arena. But the parties can also try to focus on them by emphasising 'their' issues in the manifesto and in their campaign. Differences in emphasis thus arise partly from the imperatives of competition, building however on the pre-existing ideological differences between the parties and their reputation for competence in different, ideologically defined, issue areas.

Measuring left–right ideology in manifestos

The fact that party programmes stress different kinds of issues according to their ideology gives us an opportunity to measure the ideological distance between

Policy areas	Labour		Liberal Democrat		Conservative	
	% of sentences in manifesto					
	Rank	% emphasis	Rank	% emphasis	Rank	% emphasis
Government effectiveness and authority	1	14.0	1	11.4	1	17.3
Social services expansion	2	10.2	3	7.3	2	9.0
Law and order	3	8.7	4	6.9	4	6.4
Education expansion	4	7.2	5	5.7	5	3.3
Non-economic groups	5	6.1	7	5.6	3	7.0
Technology and infrastructure	6	5.9	6	5.7		
Internationalism: positive	7	3.6	8	4.2		
Environmental protection	7	3.6	2	7.4		
Decentralisation: positive	9	3.0			6	4.4
Economic goals	10	2.8				
European Union: positive			8	4.2		
Government efficiency			10	4.1	9	2.8
European Union: negative					7	4.0
Art, sport, leisure, media					8	3.6
Agriculture					9	2.8

Table 17.2 *Top ten issues, 2001*

Note: The entries in the table are percentages of sentences in each party manifesto for 2001 devoted to the policy areas listed down the side, together with the rank order position of each area for each party. Percentages are given only for the leading ten issues in each manifesto. Where these do not coincide, no entry is given for the party or parties for which they do not come in the top ten

Source: Judith Bara and Ian Budge, 'Party policy and ideology: still New Labour?' in Pippa Norris (ed.), *Britain Votes 2001*, Oxford: OUP, 2001, p. 28

them at each election, by estimating the amount of attention each document pays to the characteristic issues of the left and right. As noted earlier, its position between left and right is not the whole of a party's ideology but it is a major part of it. It covers the most central issues in British politics and the ones on which electors are most likely to assess parties, and governments to take action.

The emphasis parties give to different issue areas can be measured very simply and directly, by counting the number of sentences in each manifesto devoted to each issue area. Table 17.2 shows how the parties differed on the 'top ten' issue areas in the 2001 election, that is, the ten most often mentioned categories in each party manifesto, to which most sentences were devoted. From this it can be seen that Labour put more relative stress on technology and peaceful internationalism. The Conservatives were distinguished by their opposition to the European Union and support for decentralisation – more autonomy to institutions such as schools than devolution, however. The Liberal Democrats were particularly distinctive in their support for the environment.

In the 2001 election the Labour and Conservative parties came unusually close by stressing many of the same topics such as government effectiveness and authority, traditionally a Conservative issue – and social service expansion – traditionally a Labour one. That was because debate focused on the running of

Figure 17.2 *Left–right movements of the three major British parties, 1945–97*

Source: Judith Bara and Ian Budge, 'Party policy and ideology: still New Labour?', in Pippa Norris (ed.), *Britain Votes 2001*, Oxford: Oxford University Press, 2001, p. 32

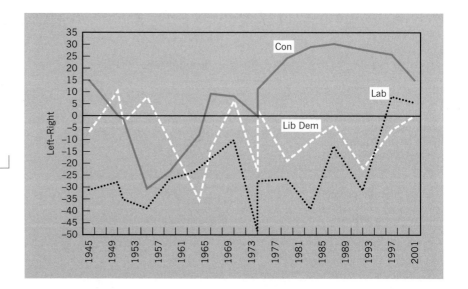

the public services – Labour saying that much had been done but much more remained to do (so vote Labour to ensure this!). The Conservatives said services were in crisis because of bureaucratic inefficiency so we had to turn to them and to the private sector.

Unusually, in the last two elections, the Labour and Conservative parties did converge on some of the same topics, such as government effectiveness and authority, traditionally a Conservative issue. Here Labour felt it could attack the government record of division and scandal, while the Conservatives felt they had to defend it. In Figure 17.2, which traces the ideological progression of the British parties over the post-war period, we can see how this affects their ideological positions in relation to each other. To do this one can look at left–right differences more directly. All one needs do is group 'left-wing' issues together and add up percentage references to them. Then one groups 'right-wing' issues together and adds up their percentage score. Finally one can take the combined percentage for left-wing issues and subtract this from the combined percentage for right-wing issues. That gives us a 'scale' running from +100 per cent (all references in a manifesto are to right-wing issues) to −100 per cent (all references in a manifesto are to left-wing issues). In practice, of course, each manifesto will contain references both to left- and right-wing issues, so they will never be totally right-wing or totally left-wing. Neither will all topics mentioned by parties fit into this particular ideological distinction. This means that on average the main British parties fall near the middle of the left–right space, as we have already seen in Figure 17.1. The positions they take in specific elections vary more, of course, but only within a range of +30 towards the right and −50 towards the left.

Table 17.3 lists left- and right-wing issues. As the essence of the left-wing position is support for government regulation and intervention domestically and the creation of governmental bodies to do the same internationally, the topics

Table 17.3 *Creating a left–right scale from party manifestos*

Negative items (left wing)	Positive items (right wing)
Nationalisation	Free enterprise
Controlled economy	Economic orthodoxy
Welfare: positive	Social services expansion: negative
Regulation of capitalism	Incentives
Economic planning	Freedom
Protectionism: positive	Protectionism: negative
Military: negative	Military: positive
Peace	Effective authority
Education expansion: positive	Constitutionalism: positive
Internationalism: positive	National way of life: positive
Decolonisation	Traditional morality: positive
Labour groups: positive	Law and order
Democracy	Social harmony

Source: Budge et al, *Mapping Policy Preferences*, Oxford: OUP, 2001, p. 22

picked out as leftist all have a bearing on these questions. They include national-isation (takeover of businesses by government), regulation and control of the economy, provision of welfare and education (again by government) and peace and international co-operation. The right opposes these emphases and puts a stress on freedom from government. The free market needs some government support to keep it going, which is provided by law and order at home and military alliances abroad. All these elements can be seen in Conservative policies up to 1997 which have been characterised as 'free market, strong state'.

Measuring left–right differences in this way enables us to trace the ideological progression of the three main British parties over the whole of the post-war period. In Figure 17.2 left–right positionings are measured on the upright dimen-sion (from +35 – relatively right wing – to −50, relatively left wing). The horizon-tal dimension is time. Each election can be identified by its particular date: 1945, 1950, 1951 and so on until 2001.

Left and right – convergence or divergence?

Differences between the parties started by being very large in 1945, the post-Second World War election in which Labour won a large majority and started a programme of intervention and reform in all areas. The Conservatives realised that the reforms, particularly the creation of the Welfare State, were popular and that to win elections they had to accept them. By emphasising such left-wing positions they came very close to Labour from 1955 to 1964, the heyday of the so-called social democratic consensus between the main parties. This meant that both parties accepted the Welfare State and a mixed economy, in which the gov-ernment owned large sectors of industry. However, the two-party convergence was due partly to Labour's own move to the right as it tried to tone down the unpopular emphasis on nationalisation in its proposals. Meanwhile, the Liberals wandered about between the other two parties with no very fixed principles or positions.

All this changed after the 1966 election as the Conservatives, with some minor deviations, moved to the right; up to 1997, in fact, they remained relatively far to the right. The gap between the two main parties widened as Labour moved dramatically left in 1974 and again in 1983. Only in 1997, as 'New Labour', did it make a dramatic shift to the right, largely by playing down economic intervention in its programme while continuing to support welfare and education. This move to the right paralleled that of the Conservatives leftwards in the 1950s: 'If you can't beat 'em, join 'em!' Unlike the earlier Conservative change, the move did not bring Labour close to its main rival as the Conservatives still remained much further to the right. So the 1997 election saw ideological convergence only up to a point. 2001, however, consolidated these tendencies – the Conservatives moved more to the centre and Labour stayed where it was. As compared to 1997 the Liberal Democrats moved closed to Labour, but without much altering the slightly left of centre position they have held ever since 1964. What we are seeing in the manifestos is the emergence of a 'neo-liberal consensus' which has taken the place of the 'social democratic consensus' of the 1950s (for more on this, see Chapters 3 and 27).

THE END OF IDEOLOGY?

Ideology is a term with highly negative connotations for many people. It has associations with Marxism and thus with sterile debates among fanatics and extremists about abstract principles. Alternatively, it is associated with totalitarian regimes that murdered millions in the name of 'racial purity' or 'the victory of the proletariat'. Even when manifested in democratic politics ideology is seen as preventing agreement and maintaining artificial party differences, which get in the way of national unity and successful problem solving.

No wonder, then, that many commentators have eagerly predicted an 'end of ideology' at various times in Britain's post-war history. 'Ideology' has been particularly associated with the left. Thus the electoral defeat of Labour and its modification of socialist principles have been seen by many as necessary to creating a more rational and balanced society in Britain.

In reality, however, the positions taken up by the parties, even in 1997 and 2001, are still quite sharply divided in ideological terms. If any of the parties are close to each other, they are Labour and the Liberal Democrats, who could conceivably come together at some point to form a centre left coalition against the Conservatives.

Past experience suggests that convergence is a temporary phenomenon. Convergence is normally followed by divergence. There is no 'inevitable' trend towards general agreement. If this did come to pass the parties would lose their identity and with it their separate existence, and would cease to offer alternative choices to electors. For all these reasons a drawing together is always likely to be followed by a drawing apart to traditional policy positions. No 'end of ideology' seems in view, no matter how much party squabbles irritate the public.

17.9 **Conditions for electoral control over public policy**

To summarise the relationship between party representation and electoral choice, one can specify four conditions for electoral control over future government policy:

1. Parties must offer voters a choice.

2. Voters need to be aware of the choice.

3. People must vote on the basis of the choice.

4. The party in control of the government follows policies consistent with the options it placed before the electorate (party accountability).

All these conditions require that the parties subscribe to different ideologies to generate policy choices for voters, and to give them an incentive to carry through their programme in government.

The positive contribution of party ideology to electoral choice

Is this necessarily a bad thing? Although 'ideology' has bad connotations it can be regarded as the same thing as holding to firm political principles. Having principled politicians rather than self-servers and office seekers is generally regarded as good. If the 'end of ideology' amounts to the 'death of principle' it appears in rather a different light.

As the discussion at the beginning of the chapter also indicates, it is impossible to operate in politics without an ideology. People need to have a set of beliefs and assumptions about the way the world works in order to understand it at all. Socialism could only be abandoned by replacing it with another ideology. Neo-liberalism and free market beliefs are in this general sense just as much ideologies as Marxism. Indeed, far and away the most ideological politician in recent British politics has been Margaret Thatcher, the right-wing Conservative prime minister from 1979 to 1990.

We cannot escape having ideological parties, so the only question is whether parties should have different ideologies or all share the same one. The general conclusion we can draw from our examinations of party programmes is that they are likely to remain different.

This has positive advantages for the role parties play in representing the views of the British electorate. Consider what would happen if parties did all share the same ideology and offered electors the same policies in their programmes. This would mean that whichever party electors voted into government the same policy would be pursued. Voters would then have no opportunity to choose between policies appropriate to the current situation. Differences in ideology guarantee that different solutions will be offered by different parties and that electors can weigh them up and decide between them with some probability of determining which will actually be pursued.

The constitutional doctrine of the party mandate rests on the idea that electors are able to choose between programmes in this way. The core of the argument is that a majority or plurality vote for a party in the general election can also be interpreted as an endorsement of that party's policy programme. This gives the party the authority to put its policies into effect when in government. If all parties offered the same programme governments would lack the authority of a mandate, because no one would know whether electors had really endorsed their programme or had simply been deprived of the opportunity to express an opinion.

BRIEFINGS

17.10 **The party mandate**

The idea of a party mandate assumes that the party winning most votes in an election will form a government that will carry through its electoral programme, because this has been supported by a majority or plurality of electors. The details of the argument are:

- Electors choose between parties at least in part on the basis of their programme.

- Such programmes are distinguishable from each other, so they offer electors a basis for choice.

- The party which gains most votes forms the government.

- The party or parties that form the next government have a responsibility to carry out their programme in government, because this is a major basis on which they were elected.

- They also have the authority to carry out their programme in government, as it has been selected by the largest number of electors as the best.

- Parties do carry through their programmatic priorities in government.

Ideology has another positive contribution to make in a party democracy such as Britain. It gives parties an incentive to carry through their programme when they get into government. Many voters are cynical about whether governments will actually carry out election promises, or will simply ignore their commitments as soon as they take office. The Wilson governments (1964–70, 1974–6) were particularly criticised, having gained office with the promise of economic expansion through state planning and ending by restricting economic activity and creating high unemployment.

In contrast, no one could say that the highly ideological Margaret Thatcher did not vigorously carry through her programme of restricting government and promoting the free market. Thatcher did this because, as well as promising such measures to the electorate, she actually believed in them very strongly.

In theory, governments could be punished retrospectively for breaking earlier election pledges. Some analysts argue that electors would not vote for such a government because they could not trust it to carry through policies they otherwise find attractive. In practice, however, this seems a rather weak sanction because of the lapse of time involved and the many circumstances that will have intervened to make earlier pledges irrelevant or incapable of fulfilment.

While external sanctions or election penalties may be weak, ideological imperatives to carry through the programme may be quite strong, as the case of Thatcher shows. Ideology can thus play a very important role in promoting party accountability. It might be preferable to have 'conviction politicians' saying and then doing what they believe rather than opportunists following the changing whims of public opinion or doing the minimum they think they can get away with.

ALTERNATIVES TO PARTY DEMOCRACY

Party democracy
Either (1) the widespread distribution of power within a political party and/or (2) a system of national democracy resting on competitive parties.

At the start of the third millennium, parties seem to be exerting a more pervasive influence on general debate than ever. Thanks to the media they totally dominate government and politics. Our evidence shows that they are still divided in ideological terms, and that this situation is likely to continue. It clearly has many advantages in presenting electors with sharp policy choices and guaranteeing that most governments will carry them through.

Many, however, find the constant squabbling between parties deeply dispiriting. It is epitomised by televised debates from Parliament, where Labour and Conservatives appear to shout each other down, with no attempt to debate the merits of the case or to find agreement. Surely things would be better if the good people on all sides came to a problem without party prejudices and found the best solution that genuinely served the national interest?

The problem lies in discovering what *is* in the national interest and how best to achieve it. Does it exist at all or is it simply a projection of the interests of one group, for example the City of London or the southeast 'Establishment', at the expense of others? The national interest is perhaps most easily identified in foreign affairs – keeping Britain strong and influential in the world. Even here, however, there has been much criticism of Britain's subservience to the United States and of the costs an overextended world role has imposed on manufacturing industry and internal welfare.

The 'best people' coming together outside their parties would still, therefore, face policy dilemmas, and divide and argue over them. There are no easy or obviously 'best' solutions to political problems. That is why parties and their ideologies have evolved, to ensure that no major interest or grouping in society lacks an advocate to promote its views on any problem about which it is concerned. As Winston Churchill remarked of democracy in general: 'It seems unattractive until you look at the alternatives.' The same can be said of parties and their ideologies. If they did not exist today they would rapidly re-emerge, as they are so essential to democratic debate and choice and to the control of electors over government. In that sense, British democracy cannot do without them, whatever their incidental defects.

ESSAYS

1. What is ideology? Why is it useful to have one?

2. What is a party family? What different 'families' are represented in Britain?

3. What does it mean to say that a party is to the 'left' or to the 'right' in politics?

4. Why is it important that British electors should be presented with different party programmes in an election?

5. What are the essential characteristics of 'party democracy' in Britain?

PROJECTS

1. Read three party manifestos without their identifying labels, analyse them and try to guess: (a) which party they belong to; (b) whether they were published at the same election. Give reasons for your judgement.

2. Analyse the reasons for ideological change on the part of the British parties with reference to Figure 17.2.

SUMMARY

This chapter has examined the different party ideologies that exist in Britain today and how they help maintain party identity and distinctiveness. In particular it has looked at:

- the different 'families' to which British parties belong and how they have evolved over time

- the way in which party families can be 'placed' in terms of an underlying left–right ideology, centred on differences about the nature and extent of government intervention in society

- how the left–right positions of the main parties can actually be measured from their election manifestos and used to track changes in their ideological positions over time (Figure 17.2)

- the boost this gives to electoral choice between alternative programmes for society and to electoral control over government actions, and hence to the general functioning of representative democracy in Britain.

FURTHER READING

The nature of political ideologies in general is discussed in A. Heywood, *Political Ideologies* (London: Macmillan, 1992) and A. Dobson, 'Ideology', *Politics Review*, 1 (4), April, 1992. Applications to British election manifestos are made in Ian Budge et al, *Mapping Policy Preferences: Estimates for Parties, Electors and Governments 1945–1998* (Oxford: OUP, 2001) and in Judith Bara and Ian Budge, 'Party policy and ideology: Still New Labour?' in Pippa Norris (ed.), *Britain Votes 2001* (Oxford: OUP, 2001) pp. 26–42, reproduced in *Parliamentary Affairs*, **3**, 2001, pp. 590–606. A review of party families and ideologies, as well as of other aspects of British parties, can be found in Paul Webb, *The Modern British Party System* (London: Sage, 2000). Two useful articles on the ideology of New Labour include Michael Freeden, 'The ideology of New Labour', *Political Quarterly*, **70** (1), 1999, pp. 42–51 and J. Buckler and B. Voldwitz, 'New Labour's ideology', *Political Quarterly*, **71** (2), 2000, pp. 101–4, which criticises Freeden. On the Conservatives, see J. Garnett and P. D. Lynch, 'Bandwagon blues: the Tory fightback fails', *Political Quarterly*, **73** (1), 2002, pp. 29–37. For a comparison of the British party system with other European parties see Ian Budge et al, *The Politics of the New Europe* (Harlow: Addison Wesley Longman, 1997).

USEFUL WEB SITES ON PARTY IDEOLOGIES AND POLITICAL REPRESENTATION

Hotlinks to these sites can be found on the CWS website at http://www.booksites.net/budge.

In the previous chapter we provided an extremely comprehensive list containing links to the main political parties as well as the more important party factions (see Chapter 16).

There are a number of political ideology sites that cover Britain and the world. The Keele Guide to Political Thought and Ideology on the Internet (www.keele.ac.uk/depts/por/ptbase.htm) is an A–Z guide to political thought, theory and ideologies. In addition to this you can also visit the Social Science Information Gateway (www.sosig.ac.uk/roads/subject-listing/World-cat/polideol.html) for a general introduction to the leading currents in political thought.

In more specific terms, the LockeSmith Institute offers an excellent account of the formative years and historic development of classical Liberalism (www.belmont.edu/lockesmith/), on the same topic, very interesting insights can be found in the Stanford Encyclopaedia of Philosophy (http://plato.stanford.edu/entries/liberalism/). With regard to neo-liberal theory, a brief historical account of its evolution can be found at www.globalissues.org/TradeRelated/FreeTrade/Neoliberalism.asp and a more academic approach is available at www.globalpolicy.org/globaliz/econ/histneol.htm. The main trends within Conservatism and its potential evolution are described and critically assessed in www.ukconservatism.freeuk.com. A very insightful analysis of the main currents within Marxism is available from the above-mentioned web site of Keele University.

Concerning the specific ideological features of the main British parties a good deal of information can be obtained from a careful reading of the political speeches given by their respective leaders. We suggest you visit http://politics.guardian.co.uk/speeches/story/0,11126,666146,00.html where you can find the full text of Tony Blair's definition of New Labour's 'third phase'. Concerning the Conservative Party, visit http://politics.guardian.co.uk/speeches/story/0,11126,635027,00.html for the full text of Iain Duncan Smith's definition of conservatism. Material on the Liberal Democrats may be accessed at http://politics.guardian.co.uk/libdems/story/0,9061,753601,00.html where Charles Kennedy also offers a detailed approach to the past, present and future of the Liberal Democrats. A complete list of party manifestos since 1945 is available at www.psa.ac.uk/WWW/elections_uk.htm.

Data collected by the party manifestos project (Budge et al) which codes and counts party policy commitments is available from the book *Mapping Policy Preferences* (Oxford: OUP, 2001) and its associated CD-Rom.

Parties and Parliament

The last two chapters have emphasised the fact that Britain is a party democracy rather than a Parliamentary democracy. That is, elections decide which party is to form the government rather than what individual is going to represent a constituency in Parliament. MPs get elected because of their commitment to a particular party rather than on their own merits. Once elected they are expected to vote with the government or opposition, except on the rare occasions when their party does not take a position on an issue, or they are given leave to dissent on what the party managers define as a matter of conscience.

MPs have little scope to act collectively, independently of parties. This raises in acute form the question of whether Parliament can or should be much more than a forum in which the government mobilises public opinion in favour of its policies, and the opposition mobilises opinion against them. Such confrontations are designed to influence the result of the next election rather than formulate good laws or scrutinise administrative action. This chapter therefore discusses whether Parliament can have a useful role independent of party and, if so, whether this would improve the quality of democracy in Britain.

The chapter covers:

- the structure and procedures of the two Houses of Parliament
- Parliamentary scrutiny of administration (as distinct from legislation) and the work of select committees
- MPs' interests and business links
- party discipline in Parliament and backbench rebellions
- third parties, coalition government, and ritual 'shadow boxing' between government and opposition.

GOVERNMENT AND PARLIAMENT

To administer the country, Her Majesty's Government must have the support of the majority of elected members of the House of Commons and be confident of retaining that support for the duration of the Parliament. Usually, but not invariably, a single party wins an absolute majority of seats at the general election and thus forms the government on its own. The growth of third parties (Liberal Democrats, Welsh and Scottish Nationalists, Ulster Unionists and Social Democrats) means that a 'hung' Parliament, where no clear Conservative or Labour majority exists, is an increasing possibility. However, since 1945 the government of the day has lacked an absolute majority only in 1974, 1977–9 and November 1994–April 1995 (when the whip was withdrawn from eight Conservative Euro-rebels) and an adequate majority in 1950–1 and 1974–7. The more usual situation is that of 1997 when Labour won the election with a majority of 179 overall, only slightly reduced in 2001.

The varying size of the government's majority clearly affects the balance of power between government and opposition and between the leadership of the government party and its own backbenchers. In addition to providing stable support for the government, and to being the pool from which almost all government ministers are recruited, Parliament has the equally important role – at least in constitutional theory – of scrutiny, debate, criticism, amendment and, if necessary, defeat of government proposals, whether legislation or executive action. It is on this aspect of Parliament that this chapter concentrates. The obsessive secrecy of British governments, and their desire to manipulate information to their own advantage, undermines Parliament's role as a forum for informed criticism and constructive debate. Together with the majority party's (ie the government's) firm control over procedures and legislation, governments deprive ordinary MPs of any significant political influence at all, except at times of crisis. To understand how governments exert such control we turn first to the structure of Parliament and the nature of its business.

STRUCTURE OF PARLIAMENT: THE LORDS

'Parliament' is frequently equated with the elected House of Commons, but it also includes the nominated House of Lords. Before 1999 the bulk of its members were hereditary peers. Britain is the only country in the world to have had such a chamber within a democratically elected Parliament for the whole of the twentieth century. Its inappropriateness was already clear in 1911, when the Preamble to the Parliament Act (which restricted its previous power of veto to one of delay over legislation) stipulated: 'It is intended to substitute for the House of Lords as it at present exists a Second Chamber constituted on a popular instead of a hereditary basis, but such substitution cannot be immediately brought into operation.' This turned out to be the constitutional understatement of the last century. Not until 1999 did the House of Lords lose its largely hereditary character, and it remains for the moment a non-elected body.

The Lords' powers are limited by the Parliament Acts of 1911 and 1949. The House of Lords has no power to amend or delay a 'money bill' (ie any financial measure) and can delay other legislation for up to a year, which does give it power in the final year of a government. In addition, it abides by a convention that it will not oppose measures that were included in the government's election programme. Formally, it has retained the power to reject secondary legislation (ie rules and regulations made by ministers in the form of statutory instruments or orders in council by authority delegated to them by acts of Parliament) but it treats such legislation no differently from primary legislation. Like the Commons the Lords has a scrutinising function but currently operates only two regular committees, on science and technology and the European Union; all other legislation is scrutinised in full chamber.

Although it is not uncommon for the government, especially a Labour government, to be defeated in the House of Lords, it is unusual for the government to allow the defeat to stand, unless it is in its final year. (For example, the

18.1 How to reform the House of Lords?

Reform of the Lords is usually thought of in terms of who is to be in it and how members are to be selected. The question of membership, however, is bound up with the question of its powers.

An elected body would have greater legitimacy and authority in investigating government or challenging its proposals. For this reason government proposals favour nomination or appointment of its members while opposition parties favour election.

There is less argument about what its powers should be. The consensus is that it should retain its delaying powers under the existing Parliament Acts. More importance is placed on its powers of scrutiny over the executive and an extension and strengthening of its committee system for this purpose, in line with similar proposals for the Commons. Few have suggested that the Second Chamber should be abolished, although regional assemblies and Parliaments seem to get on without one and scrutiny and expert debates (the Lords' most important functions) could be undertaken by a strengthened House of Commons.

With the departure of hereditary peers, members are either nominated by a non-political Appointments Committee or by the political parties (with party nominees scrutinised by the Committee). The government at the end of 2001 proposed a 600-member chamber with more than half nominated by the parties and only 20 per cent elected by nations and regions. The Liberals and Conservatives (and most Labour backbenchers in the Commons) want most or all of the House elected (the Liberals by PR within nations and regions, the Conservatives by first past the post within the historic counties). Either the government will now have to move towards a largely elected Second Chamber or – a more likely outcome given the history of Lords' reform – the current system will stay in the absence of agreement.

Conservative government of 1992–7 could not reverse the defeat of the bill to give police increased rights of covert surveillance.)

Except when entering the final few months of a full Parliament, the government nearly always returns the measure unamended to the Lords, having again passed it in the Commons, and the Lords nearly always accepts the measure that it previously defeated. On only two occasions since the 1949 Parliament Act has the government invoked the Act to override persistent defeat in the Lords: the War Crimes Bill in 1990–1 and the European Parliamentary Elections Bill in 1999, after the Lords had rejected the proposal for a 'closed regional list' system of proportional representation for elections to the European Parliament on no fewer than six consecutive votes.

Largely hereditary in composition and permanently pro-Conservative, the House of Lords before 1999 was self-evidently an anachronism in a democratic age. It also appeared to be ineffective: very rarely did it change the government's mind or expose serious maladministration. Did it, in fact, serve a useful purpose?

Supporters of the old House of Lords made a number of points in its defence. First, it was argued, the Lords was never as pro-Conservative as the party affiliation of members implied, because, being unelected members for life, they were not beholden to the party whips or to local constituency associations and thus were much more independent than MPs. Moreover, defenders pointed out, the majority of hereditary Lords, who accounted for the nominally Conservative predominance of the House, were inactive attenders or debaters. Second, it was argued that the House of Lords was not as undemocratic as it appeared. Peers may be unelected, but the very randomness of their selection and their sheer number resulted in a cross-section of society with an expertise on almost every aspect of life. The quality of debate in the Lords can be very high (partly because many life peers, as well as the Law Lords and the bishops and archbishops of the Church of England are distinguished people in their own right) and is always less predictably partisan than in the Commons. However, the overwhelming majority of Lords were educated at private schools, a mere 8 per cent are women and a tiny 1 per cent are from the ethnic minorities.

Third, it was argued that the old House of Lords performed a valuable scrutinising role, filling gaps and making up for weaknesses in the performance of the Commons. Although the two Lords committees perform their scrutinising functions more thoroughly and professionally than Commons select committees, their limitation to two reflects a fundamental weakness of the Upper Chamber. It has to be selective about the legislation it scrutinises because its procedures are antiquated, its committee attendance too sparse, its professional staff too few, and even its active members too part time to take on more.

Some of the defects of the old House of Lords – the predominantly hereditary composition, the pro-Conservative bias and the social imbalance – have been rectified in its new incarnation. However, its undemocratic character will remain for so long as its membership depends on the patronage of the Prime Minister (and, to a much lesser extent, the other party leaders): a legislature packed by the government of the day is the very antithesis of a Parliamentary democracy. Moreover, for as long as the powers and resources of the House of Lords continue as now – no significant changes are currently proposed – the Upper Chamber will continue to exert only a nuisance effect on government measures. Its role will continue to be peripheral, if occasionally colourful. It is in the House of Commons that governments are formed and major debates take place.

STRUCTURE OF PARLIAMENT: THE COMMONS

Standing committees
Committees of the House of Commons that examine bills after their second reading in order to make them more acceptable for their third reading.

The House of Commons (now 659 members) meets for about 200–250 days of the year, on a reasonably continuous basis from late October to July or August. General debates, questions to and statements from ministers, and certain stages of legislation take up full meetings of the House, normally from mid-afternoon to around midnight (reforms will make this 11.30 a.m. – 7.30 p.m.). Much work is done in specialised committees, which meet both in the mornings and later in the day, in tandem with meetings of the whole House.

Such committees are of two general kinds: standing committees and select committees. Standing committees consider the technical details of legislation. Each government bill put before Parliament receives a formal first reading and then a second reading on its general principles. This involves the whole House of Commons.

Since the government party normally commands an overall majority of the House of Commons and can count on party discipline, government bills are almost always approved, although often after amendments are made in the course of the bill's passage through Parliament. After the second reading the bill goes to a standing committee for a clause-by-clause review of its details. Occasionally, the whole House of Commons may constitute itself as a committee for this purpose, for example, for bills of constitutional significance or those that need to be passed into legislation urgently. Some of the standing committees are specialised (for example, the Scottish and Welsh standing committees, to which Scottish and Welsh legislation is referred) and have a relatively permanent membership. Generally, however, the question of which standing committee a bill goes to is arbitrary, and membership shifts, sometimes because MPs have a direct or indirect interest in the details. Each committee is selected to reflect the balance of parties in the House of Commons so that the government party normally has a majority.

After the technical parts are approved the bill goes back to the full House of Commons for its report stage and subsequently its third reading. All bills pass through the Commons; bills can be introduced first in the Lords but this is not usual. If the Lords amend the bill then it returns to the Commons, which considers those amendments but can override them, unless the Lords go to extremes and throw out the legislation altogether.

Private members' bills
These are introduced in Parliament by backbench MPs or peers on their own initiative.

Private members' bills, which are introduced by backbench MPs, sometimes with government backing, and private bills, which are sponsored by an outside body (normally a local authority) also go through these general stages. Without government support, however, such bills are unlikely to reach the statute book.

Since the government so strongly dominates legislative proceedings, and is so concerned to 'get its business through', the process of passing legislation does not provide much of an opportunity for Parliament to improve legislation independently of what the government will accept. By and large legislative bills pass as originally drafted by the government: most amendments are initiated by the government itself, sometimes in response to strong pressure from its own backbenchers, but very rarely in response to the opposition or the House of Lords. The capacity for the government to get its way is revealed by Table 18.1, which shows how an exceptionally contentious bill in 1999, the Welfare Reform and Pensions Bill, survived fierce opposition from both the Lords and many Labour backbenchers almost unscathed over a period of nine months.

Select committees
Committees of the House of Commons and the House of Lords that consider general political issues which are wider than a particular piece of legislation. The Public Accounts Committee of the House of Commons, which considers all accounts of money appropriated by Parliament, is a major example.

The major instrument through which the legislature independently scrutinises the executive is the other main type of committee, the select committee. These are bodies whose membership is selected to serve for the length of a Parliament. They are sometimes chaired by an opposition MP, and are expected to produce non-partisan reports on detailed aspects of government administration. They may concentrate on the financial side (as with the Public Accounts Committee) or on a particular region (Scottish or Welsh affairs). Mostly, however, they are organised so as to cover the functions and responsibilities of the major ministries on a departmental basis or of major policy areas that cut across departments, such as European legislation and public administration. Select committees examine

Table 18.1 *Passage of the Welfare Reform and Pensions Bill, 1999*

House of Commons

First reading: 10 February 1999

Welfare Reform and Pensions Bill introduced into the House of Commons by Alistair Darling, the Social Security Secretary

The bill contained provisions for compulsory interviews for benefits claimants, the extension of widow's benefit to men, introduction of stakeholder pension schemes, reform of benefit for the long-term sick, children and young people

Second reading: 23 February 1999

Standing Committee (25 sittings): 2 March–27 April 1999

Money resolution debate: 14 April 1999

Report stage: 17 May 1999, continued on 20 May 1999. The bill passed by 310 votes to 270, with 67 Labour MPs voting against the government. Another 67 did not vote; at least half of the absentees were believed to have abstained deliberately, including 15 who stayed in their seats and abstained in person

Third reading: 20 May 1999

House of Lords

First reading: 21 May 1999

Second reading: 10 June 1999

Committee stage (5 sittings): 24 June–20 July 1999

Report stage: 11 and 13 October 1999

Lords defeat government on two proposals in the bill:

- the two-year rule (benefits only available to people who have worked for the two previous years), by a majority of 156

- means testing, by a majority of 108

Third reading: 27 October 1999

The government proposes two amendments to the bill to placate the rebels in the Commons:

- raising the threshold of losing some incapacity benefits with an occupational pension from £50 to £85

- anyone who had not made National Insurance payments in the previous 2 years being denied benefit was extended to 3 years

House of Commons

Considers Lords' amendments: 3 November 1999

53 backbench Labour MPs rebel against the government on 3 votes on Lords' amendments to the bill, although all are passed:

- restricting entitlement to incapacity benefit (325 to 265)
- means testing of incapacity benefit (320 to 262)
- abolition of the severe disablement allowance (326 to 253)

▶

Table 18.1 (continued)

House of Lords

Considers Commons amendments: 8 November 1999

The Lords defeat the government on two aspects of the bill:

■ for an amendment restricting entitlement to incapacity benefit to those who have not worked for 7 rather than 3 years (260 to 127)

■ to let war widows with children keep their war pension if they remarry (153 to 140)

House of Commons

Considers Lords' amendments: 9 November 1999

Despite 43 Labour MPs voting against the government the Lords' amendments are defeated:

■ the amendment restricting entitlement to incapacity benefit to those who have not worked for 7 years (314 to 234)

■ restricting entitlement to incapacity benefit for those with occupational pensions from 50 per cent to 23 per cent (312 to 234)

■ raising the threshold of entitlement to incapacity benefit for those with occupational pensions from £85 to £128 (361 to 178)

The *Welfare Reform and Pensions Act 1999* received the Royal Assent on 11 November 1999

Source: HMSO

documents and witnesses and issue reports on aspects of policy, which sometimes attract widespread newspaper and television comment.

The role of committees in scrutinising administration is supplemented by oral or written questions that individual MPs can put to ministers, including the Prime Minister, in meetings of the full House. Written questions in particular, to which answers are published in *Hansard*, can be useful for extracting factual information from the government. Oral questions, by way of contrast, tend to be framed to make – or extract – a partisan point, and often involve point scoring. It is not unknown for the party managers on both sides to supply questions to their own backbenchers in order to bolster or embarrass a minister. Government ministers may well be evasive and occasionally downright misleading: in autumn 2001 the Labour Secretary of Transport denied he was taking over Railtrack while he was actually doing so. On certain days backbench MPs can also raise urgent questions for a short 'adjournment debate' at the end of the day's proceedings.

The opposition parties can initiate debate on aspects of government policy on the 'supply' days allotted to them in the Parliamentary timetable. These are used to criticise selected aspects of policy, and to promote the opposition party's alternatives, although at a very broad level. Given the secretiveness of both government and Civil Service and the influence of party rivalries, it is unusual for these set debates to be influential or informed.

BRIEFINGS

18.2 Two examples of a Commons question and reply

Mr Michael Fabricant (Conservative, Lichfield): *'Will the Secretary of State make a statement on tuition fees for tertiary education in Scotland?'*

Dr John Reid (Secretary of State for Scotland): *'The policy on tuition fees, announced in July 1997 by my Right Honourable Friend the Secretary of State for Education and Employment, remains throughout the United Kingdom. From 1 July, education – and so the conduct and outcome of the review being conducted at the Scottish parliamentary level – will be a matter for the Scottish Parliament.'*

In his supplementary question **Michael Fabricant MP** said: *'First, I congratulate the Right Honourable Gentleman on his promotion to the Scottish Office. I hope that it will not be too long before he is promoted to the position of Secretary of State for Defence – which is where, I suspect, his true interests lie. However, before he gloats too much at the victory of his Right Honourable Friend the member for Glasgow Anniesland [Donald Dewar MP] over the fawning Liberal Democrats in Scotland, does he think that, while the United Kingdom is still the United Kingdom, it is fair that some students studying at United Kingdom universities should be disadvantaged in comparison with other students studying at United Kingdom universities?'*

Dr Reid replied: *'I think that we strengthen the unity of the United Kingdom by recognising our diversity, which is precisely one of the reasons why we have devolved decision making to Scotland and to Wales, and why we are on the verge of doing so in Northern Ireland and to London. Perhaps, in future, we shall do so also to other areas. I think that the vast majority of people across the United Kingdom will be gratified that the government are ensuring that local decisions affecting local people are being taken at a more local level.'*

Sandra Osborne (Labour, Ayr): *'I join in welcoming my Right Honourable Friend to his first Question Time in his new role as Secretary of State. Will he confirm that it is estimated that as many as 40 per cent of students will pay no tuition fees at all?'*

The **Secretary of State** replied: *'I thank my Honourable Friend for her congratulations. I can also tell her that although it was estimated that about 40 per cent of those entering Scottish higher education would not pay any tuition fees at all, according to the latest figures that we have, more than 50 per cent will pay no tuition fees at all. She will know that the entire purpose of our policy is to extend higher education in Scotland to a far greater number of people than has hitherto been the case. Moreover, the fact that more than 50 per cent will pay no tuition fees demonstrates that a greater number of people from low-income groups will now have access to education, which surely must be one of the priorities of any decent, civilised government.'*

Hansard, London: HMSO, 24–27 May 1999

Government and party

The presence of both the actual government and of the alternative government (the official opposition) in the House of Commons has both advantages and disadvantages. It means that the chief policy makers directly face elected representatives for most of the year, which makes for close and intimate communication. Contrariwise, it also means that proceedings are dominated by ritual quarrels between government and opposition, which make it difficult for the House of

Commons to organise itself as an entity distinct from government and to express an independent point of view.

Almost all members of a British government must be members of one or other House of Parliament (the exceptions are certain law officers) and in practice the large majority are MPs. The government continues for as long as it commands the confidence of a majority of MPs, in effect the support of the majority party. Party cohesion is therefore central to the functioning of Parliamentary democracy as it currently operates in Britain. It is the responsibility of the party managers (whips) to secure party cohesion; they apply a variety of sticks and, more frequently, carrots to maintain discipline. The emergence of some 80 MPs belonging to minority parties whose support government may need in a close Parliamentary situation also undermines the major parties' dominance of proceedings. The basic reality, however, is tight control by the majority party leadership.

BRIEFINGS

18.3 Organisation and management of Parliamentary parties

There are two aspects to the way MPs are organised in Parliament. One is the methods by which the party leadership keeps control over its followers. This is particularly important for the party in government: with a disciplined party majority the government can do almost anything. Dissent gives an impression of disunity and weakness and at worst leads to humiliating defeat for the government. The same consideration holds, less forcibly, for the opposition parties.

The second aspect is the question of how backbench MPs (ie those who do not hold office in the government or the 'Shadow Cabinet') organise themselves to take action independently of the leadership, so making the House of Commons more of an autonomous body and less of a mechanical register of the strengths of the parties. The most significant of such backbench bodies is the Conservative Private Members' Committee, better known as the '1922 Committee', so called because of the year of the election of the MPs who first formed it. The Committee is open to all Conservative MPs, who elect their own executive committee and chair, but is in effect a sounding board for Conservative backbenchers. Meetings are an obvious focus for party discontent, as in 1992–7 over the issue of Europe. There is no real equivalent in the Labour Party.

Both major parties also have large numbers of policy committees, and eight to ten regional groupings, all for backbench MPs. In addition all-party backbench committees on numerous, usually non-contentious, subjects provide a 'Commons voice' on policy issues but are usually rather muted.

The leadership controls its party in two ways:

1. **The meeting of the full Parliamentary party to agree policy** Members of the leadership and the government attend. As the latter generally consists of over 100 MPs anyway, all of whom are bound to support official policy, the party leadership typically needs to secure the support of an additional 100 MPs to decide party policy, which all members of the Parliamentary party are then bound by party rules to support. With the support of no more than 200–250 of all MPs, therefore (of whom about 100 are on the government payroll), the government can dominate the full Commons.

2. **The whips** (the name comes from whippers-in of foxhounds at a hunt, hardly flattering for backbench MPs!). There is a whips' office in each of the major parties, with a chief whip, deputy and four or five others, who are each assigned to a regional grouping of backbench MPs.

> **Whips**
> Officials appointed by Parliamentary parties in the Lords and the Commons to promote party discipline and manage party business in Parliament.

The whips' job is complex. They have to ensure that all MPs turn up for important votes (their summonses are also confusingly called 'whips': a 'three-line whip' is underlined thrice to indicate its importance). Primarily, however, they have to maintain party loyalty and discipline. They do this in three ways:

1. By passing information about party morale and opinion up to the leadership and by passing reassuring messages from the leadership down to backbenchers.

2. By rewarding loyalty, nominating favoured MPs for desirable committee assignments, trips abroad and other 'treats'. Most importantly, they advise leaders on promotion to junior ministerial office when the party is in government.

3. By punishing disloyalty. Whips prefer rewards to sanctions but they can punish dissenters by withholding patronage and, in serious cases, by 'withdrawing' the whip, that is, suspending or expelling dissenting MPs from the party. If suspension becomes permanent MPs will lose their party's endorsement at the following election and thus, in all probability, fail to be re-elected. But this sanction is like the nuclear bomb, damaging the user as much as the target, and is rarely deployed.

Labour has supplemented these Parliamentary arrangements by creating a general Party Disciplinary Committee, which can suspend MPs, as it did in the case of Thomas Graham (Renfrewshire West) and Mohammed Sarwar (Glasgow Govan) shortly after the 1997 election. Sanctions and rewards only work, of course, because MPs stand or fall together as a party and are strongly motivated to support 'their' opposition or 'their' government. Discipline is much less effective when deep ideological divisions occur.

Party unity in the Commons

Even when a minority of MPs disagree with their party leadership they normally vote loyally for them against the other party or parties for the sake of party unity and in order to keep 'their' government in office. Most ministers are MPs. This means that, out of the 350 or so MPs belonging to the majority party in a typical Parliament, a proportion approaching one-third actually form the government. The presence of so many ministers actually in the House of Commons clearly encourages party unity. Conversely, it acts against the House developing views independent of the government in office. Although the position of the leaders of the other main party (recognised as Her Majesty's Official Opposition) is more akin to that of an ordinary MP, their enforcement of a united front against the government also inhibits the House from developing a 'Commons' view of most matters.

Within the government there is a hierarchy. On the lowest rung stand the Parliamentary private secretaries who act as 'bag carriers' for the more important ministers. Further up are Parliamentary undersecretaries; on the next rung up are ministers of state, who are normally second in command in a large department, and non-Cabinet ministers, who head their own departments. Above them are Cabinet ministers, who normally run important departments or ministries and also participate in discussions of overall government policy. Whatever their status or role in the government, all its members are formally bound by the doctrine of collective ministerial responsibility. This means that ministers must publicly defend any government policy as if it were their own, even if they privately disagree with it; their only alternative is to resign office. Internal party disputes, with occasional spectacular exceptions, are fought out in interdepartmental memoranda and in Cabinet committees, rather than in public debate in Parliament. The last thing parties want is the political embarrassment and electoral damage of internal clashes aired in a general debate. Collective responsibility and party cohesion operate to maintain at least the semblance of a united, effective government and opposition and, in doing so, they reduce the possibility of MPs expressing independent points of view in Parliament.

PARLIAMENTARY SCRUTINY OF GOVERNMENT

Parliamentary scrutiny of government actions means a critical review of what ministers have done, or intend to do, and is important for two reasons. First, the wider discussion accompanying the review, sometimes conducted by experts, may improve the quality of the policies being pursued. Second, in constitutional theory Parliament is the main national institution that represents the views of the population. Potentially, at least, it can express these views more freely than press and television, not being constrained by censorship and libel laws. In other words, the government is accountable to the people through Parliament.

The winning party at the general election is assumed to have had its policies approved by voters, and is therefore said to have a 'mandate' to use its majority in the Commons to carry them through in government. However, many problems

Electoral mandate
The idea that a party whose policies are approved by a majority of voters has the duty and authority to carry them through as a government.

unforeseen at the time of the election campaign emerge in the three to five years separating most elections. Many of these could be raised and examined in Parliament. But there is an ongoing tension between the government's claim to an electoral mandate and Parliament's claim to the right of scrutiny.

Electoral mandate versus continuing Parliamentary scrutiny

There are major obstacles to informed Parliamentary debate about policy alternatives. The first is the way in which Parliamentary procedures are designed to facilitate set-piece Conservative–Labour battles. The domination of business first by the government, and second by the leadership of the next largest party, constitutes the major obstacle to independent initiatives by the House of Commons as such.

This institutional monopoly is buttressed both by constitutional doctrine and the entrenched attitudes of many MPs. A common Parliamentary view is that the government's ultimate responsibility to serve popular wishes is guaranteed by exposure to a general election at the end of its term. The task of the majority Parliamentary party is therefore to support the government and of the opposition parties to maintain opposition morale, and sap the government's, by ceaselessly criticising ministers. As the House of Commons is simply an arena for partisan encounters it can have no collective and independent role vis-à-vis the government. Neither *should* it, since that would blur the responsibility of the majority party for government policy, on which it will be judged at the next election.

This belief is in turn linked to a broader idea, also embedded in constitutional theory, that the government is in the best position to understand the public interest, and should be left to get on with the task of governing unhindered between elections. This outlook colours opinion on a wide range of constitutional issues that extend beyond the character and procedures for Parliamentary debate. For example:

- **government secrecy** desirable, because it discourages too much outside intrusion into government business

- **reform of the current electoral system** undesirable, because the current first past the post system, although unfair to many smaller parties, generally allows one major party to take clear responsibility for the policies and record of the government

- **accountability of the leadership to party members** undesirable, because it renders leaders, who may become ministers, less able to act decisively on their own initiative.

Support for strong, unfettered government thus militates against effective day-to-day scrutiny in Parliament. The justification is that 'the public interest' (a term often used to justify government action) can only be served in this way. Governments should not be put under pressure to meet immediate demands, for to do so might result in an inability to govern in the longer term interest and to plan for the future. In turn the opposition should set out an alternative government programme for the next election, supported by its MPs. Nobody in the major parties should engage in independent action outside the party line.

The case for MPs adopting a more independent and critical attitude towards the government is that most of what gets done during its term of office is only tenuously related to the broad lines of policy presented at the preceding election. The implementation of the main commitments in the government's party manifesto requires many intermediate decisions, some of which may be debatable. Moreover, much of the business of government is unrelated to electorally endorsed party policies and is carried out by unelected civil servants. Wider and more informed discussion might improve rather than hamper the business of government. A growing belief that this is so has spurred MPs to develop procedures for discussing the justification, and likely outcomes, of government policy, on a broadly non-party basis. We discuss these procedures later in the chapter.

Government and journalists

Lobby system
The name given to specially selected correspondents of the main newspapers, TV and radio stations who are given confidential information by the government on a non-attributable basis. Not to be confused with 'the lobby', or pressure group system in Parliament.

The obstacles to even establishing simple facts about what the government is doing are hard to exaggerate. The selective management of information by government is best illustrated in the Parliamentary context by the 'lobby system' of specialist journalists attached to Parliament. (Incidentally it is significant that British political reporters, almost without exception, are concentrated within Parliament rather than in the executive offices, where no official place is assigned to them, but which all have press offices now tightly co-ordinated by the New Labour Director of Information.)

The Parliamentary 'lobby' is a name given to specially privileged Parliamentary correspondents of the main newspapers and television and radio channels who spend most of their time in the 'lobbies' of Parliament. They are given confidential information and have ready access to ministers, but rarely to civil servants. It is understood that in return they will reveal only what they are expressly authorised to publish. Failure to observe the understanding leads to exclusion from the lobby's privileges. Thus much of the political information that is published is divulged at the initiative of the government, and consists of what the government wants to reveal rather than what journalists think it ought to reveal.

Two recent developments have undermined this traditional way of managing the news. The first is the increasing practice by ministers and civil servants of privately 'briefing' selected journalists, usually in order to resist or promote policy proposals within the government. This is a common tactic by departments wishing to resist budget cuts, and is pursued even by figures such as the joint chiefs of staff, the military commanders. Such briefings can shade into the unauthorised 'leak' of news by nominally subordinate officials or junior ministers opposed to policies backed by their superiors. Briefings always represent selective management of information in the briefer's (if not the government's) interest.

The other process undermining the lobby system is the development of a more independent stance on the part of a minority of political journalists. This is linked to the spread of 'investigative journalism' where stories are pursued at the initiative of the newspapers or, more rarely, television editors (see Chapter 14). Journalists and newspapers have been prepared to risk prosecution either under the Official Secrets Act, under the D-notices circulated by governments to prevent discussion of topics relating to national security, or under the severe British libel laws, for refusing to reveal the sources of their information. The editors of some newspapers have withdrawn from the lobby (notably the *Independent* and *Guardian*) and now explicitly quote their official sources.

In spite of this, the ethos of the lobby system still predominates in British government. Information is for insiders rather than outsiders and the government (or at least its constituent ministers and administrators) determines who shall be insiders. MPs depend heavily on published material for their own information, to supplement erratic personal contacts and the selective confidences of party leaders. The government's management of news deprives MPs of a major source of information just as much as it deprives the general public.

Live radio and television coverage of Parliamentary proceedings has not changed this situation. What is broadcast tends to be the set debates (on the Queen's Speech, or the budget, for example) and the weekly Prime Minister's Question Time, which have become ritual gladiatorial contests between the government and opposition leaderships. Only if Parliament itself develops procedures for uncovering and evaluating important information will broadcasts be more illuminating.

This accepted, the set-piece exchanges typical of the big debates or of Prime Minister's Question Time do perform a democratic function. They oblige Prime Ministers and ministers to state their positions clearly and to defend them. They have to convince their own supporters, and the wider public to whom they are exposed through the mass media, as well as put up a defence against the attacks and taunts of the opposition parties. For most of the time these exchanges are simply theatre; but it reflects the importance attached to such occasions that Tony Blair (and his predecessors as Prime Minister) typically spend the morning before Prime Minister's Question Time closeted with their officials second-guessing the questions that will be asked and rehearsing answers. Occasionally, a single speech can make a difference, as Sir Geoffrey Howe's thinly veiled attack on Margaret Thatcher following his resignation as Foreign Secretary did in 1990, and as Ann Widdecombe's criticism of Michael Howard ('there is something of the night about him') did in 1997.

Scrutiny through select committees

One way to extract information from government is for Parliament to use what investigatory powers it has to examine important policy areas and to publish the findings. Attempts to do this in the last 20 years have concentrated on extending the remit, and strengthening the organisation, of an old Parliamentary institution, going back to the mid-nineteenth century, the select committee. In these, if anywhere, a Parliamentary view can be expressed, and the facts discovered.

In 1979 the number of select committees was significantly increased in order to 'shadow' the main government ministries. There are now around 40 select committees, most of which are listed in Table 18.2. This also reports on who chairs them (a government or opposition MP) and what kind of inquiries they undertake.

Table 18.2 *Main select committees in the House of Commons, 2002*

Committee	Chair	Notable past inquiries
Culture, Media and Sport*	Gerald Kaufman, Lab	National Lottery management
Defence	Bruce George, Lab	Gulf War syndrome
Deregulation*	Peter Pike, Lab	
Education and Skills	Barry Sheerman, Lab	
Environment, Food and Rural Affairs	David Curry, C	
Environmental Audit*	John Horam, C	
European Scrutiny*	Jimmy Hood, C	All aspects of European legislation
Foreign Affairs	Donald Anderson, Lab	Pergau Dam, arms for Sierra Leone
Health	David Hinchcliffe, C	London Ambulance Service
Home Affairs	Chris Mullin, Lab	Judicial appointments
Human Rights**	Jean Corston, Lab	
International Development	Tony Baldry, C	Aid programmes
Liaison*	Alan Williams, Lab	
Modernisation*	Robin Cook, Lab	Organisation of business of the House
Northern Ireland	Michael Mates, C	
Procedure*	Nicholas Winterton, C	
Public Accounts*	Edward Leigh, C	Ferranti contract; sale of County Hall
Public Administration*	Tony Wright, Lab	Next Steps' reforms
Science and technology	Ian Gibson, Lab	Scientific education
Scottish Affairs	Irene Adams, Lab	Food poisoning (e-coli) epidemics in Scotland
Standards and Privileges*	Sir George Young, C	'Cash for questions'; MPs interests
Statutory Instruments**	David Tredinnick, C	
Trade and Industry	Martin O'Neill, Lab	Export credits
Transport	Gwyneth Dunwoody, Lab	Financing of the London Underground
Treasury	John McFall, Lab	Collapse of Barings Bank
Welsh Affairs	Martyn Jones, Lab	Welsh colliery closures
Work and Pensions	Archy Kirkwood, Lab	

*Non-departmental committee. In addition, there are a number of 'domestic' committees of the House of Commons, eg Accommodation and Works, Administration, Catering and Information.
** Non-departmental joint committees with House of Lords

Source: House of Commons Library, 22 August 2002: www.parliament.uk.commons/lib/selmen.htm

BRIEFINGS

18.4 European Scrutiny Committee

This is a centrally important area for Parliament to exert its authority, given the ever-increasing policy areas dominated by EU directives and legislation. The weakness of the Committee illustrates the difficulty faced by Parliament in asserting itself against governments. We have already discussed the difficulties of this Committee – part of the general 'democratic deficit' of the EU – in Chapter 9. The best that Parliament can hope for in attempting to control and scrutinise EU legislation is to influence the British government's negotiating position within the various European bodies. In practice, this has been extremely difficult. All the Committee can do is recommend that a matter be referred for debate to a standing committee or, in certain important cases, to the House as a whole. With 30–40 documents arriving at the Committee every day few can be given any further consideration.

Once an issue is earmarked for debate there remains the problem of how Parliament is to influence the government's negotiating position at the European Council. No specific amendments are allowed to be made to the Commission proposals, and the House or standing committee may only debate on a 'take-note' motion. Additional problems arise from the fact that a maximum of 90 minutes is allowed for a debate, and even this small amount of time is not made available until two hours before midnight.

The Committee faces further scrutiny problems when the House of Commons is in recess. No debate can be called and the Committee cannot even meet. The fact that the Parliamentary timetable is not co-ordinated with the timetable of the Council of Ministers means that the Committee is often unable to carry out its functions. When an instrument is adopted in Council before it has reached the Committee, the limit of the government's obligation is 'that the Committee should be informed, by deposit of the relevant document and by submission of an explanatory memorandum, of instances where fast-moving documents go for adoption before scrutiny can take place'.

Parliamentary approval is not required for European legislation. The government *may* take it into account but can also ignore it if it wants.

Despite their impressive coverage their role is limited. Committees derive their power from the House of Commons, and governments try to ensure that select committee membership reflects the balance between parties, as well as influencing the choice of chair and subjects of inquiry. The traditions of government secrecy also mean that ministers and departments rarely invite committee inquiries into areas where they experience difficulties. Rather they seek to fob off investigations and 'cover up' for mistakes where they can.

However, the government must at least *seem* to co-operate with the select committees. By refusing to allow civil servants to appear before them it would publicly appear to be engaged in a cover up. In principle committees not only have general powers to choose their area of inquiry but they also have a right to see the relevant documents and to summon persons to appear before them, and to make them answer all questions that the committee puts. Witnesses cannot constitutionally excuse themselves by claiming that this may subject them to civil (legal) actions.

Practice is sometimes different from theory. Ian and Kevin Maxwell (newspaper proprietors and sons of the late Robert Maxwell, who were suspected of massive embezzlement of company pension funds to prop up their own business) success-fully deflected inquiry by pleading that answers would damage their defence in an impending trial. Two Conservative government ministers successfully refused to answer select committee questions – Lord Young over the privatisation of Rover cars and Sir Leon Brittan over the sale of Westland helicopters.

The ability of committees to extract information from civil servants is also limited by the 'Armstrong memorandum', which was adopted by the Head of the Civil Service, Sir Robin Butler, when he appeared before the Treasury and Civil Service Committee in 1988. He explained that the duty of civil servants to their ministers was similar to that owed by military personnel to their com-manding officer. Thus civil servants could only respond to committees (or indeed appear before them) on behalf and with the approval of their minister.

The issue of what evidence civil servants may give to select committees is cru-cial, because MPs generally lack any professional expertise or research backing of their own and depend on witnesses or expert evidence for their information. The major exception is the oldest committee, the Public Accounts Committee (PAC) (established in 1862), which has a large and well-qualified staff and backup from auditors and accountants. However, the PAC can only pass judge-ment on whether money has been spent as authorised by Parliament and cannot comment on policy as such. Much of the work of select committees is like this, necessary but dull.

Only certain MPs are regarded as suitable for particular committees. Thus ap-pointment to the Foreign Affairs Committee is restricted to backbenchers whom the whips trust not to leak information to the media and who endorse current defence policy. This ensures that important committees share a sense of cohesion, but at the expense of policy controversy. In contrast, less favoured committees – for example, Environment and Education – are less cohesive. They have fewer secrets, commitment is less robust and there is a higher turnover of members. They are also the committees where established policy has been more strongly challenged.

Following elections a long period has often been spent in reconstituting the committees – quite possibly a benefit from the government's point of view as it relieves it from scrutiny during that period. However, Robin Cook, new Leader of the House, took credit for setting up committees in only three weeks after Labour's election victory of May 2001.

This achievement was marred by the Labour whips' attempt to keep two former convenors – Gwyneth Dunwoody and Donald Anderson – from the nomination lists for committee members. Their crime was to have been too independent minded in the past. Over 100 Labour backbenchers rebelled over this and forced their inclusion. Ms Dunwoody subsequently proved her independence by criti-cising Labour's Private Finance Initiative for London Underground in her role as Chair of the Select Committee on Transport, and releasing a scathing report by the Committee on its details.

Robin Cook himself, as New Labour Leader of the House of Commons (ie chief government manager of business there) showed himself sympathetic to

Plate 18.1 *Commons Treasury Select Committee in session*

Source: www.paphotos.com

strengthening the role of committees – for example, by giving them freedom to appoint subcommittees and also joint subcommittees with other select committees. There have also been discussions about linking committees and other bodies with their counterparts in the Lords, independently of the government and the parties. A Liaison Committee of Select Committee Chairmen provides another independent Parliamentary platform for developing a 'Commons view' of policy as distinct from purely party ones. However, just mentioning these improvements makes it clear how limited committee powers were before.

Another limitation select committees face is in making policy recommendations stick. At present their major strategy has to be leaks to the press and interviews on the media. A current proposal is to institute weekly half-hour debates in the House of Commons on topical reports, which should enhance their impact so far as government or Civil Service response to reports is concerned. There is, however, no indication that any of these measures will have any real effect. Typical is the Transport Committee's scathing condemnation in 2002 of part-privatisation of the London Underground. In common with the Mayor of London and practically all the other authorities involved, the report anticipated that the separation of track maintenance from actually running services would bring all the problems which caused Railtrack to collapse in the case of mainline railways. The government, however, pressed on with its proposals totally unchanged.

This is the norm rather than the exception with select committee reports. The Public Accounts Committee, the best resourced and in many ways most respected committee, has for many years criticised the basic accounting procedures and massive cost overruns, often billions of pounds, incurred by the Ministry of Defence. No heads have rolled and costs have routinely exceeded estimates. In most cases ministries ignore critical reports or delay replying to them for several years by which time there may be a general election, possibly another party in power and a membership change in the committee itself.

Hampered by internal party divisions, lack of support, and largely ignored by governments and Civil Service, select committees mirror the position of Parliament itself. Nevertheless they represent a quantum advance on the inert and disorganised state of the Commons, and particularly backbenchers, in the earlier part of the post-war period. Then their function was to give unwavering support to their party and wait to be called to higher things if indeed they ever were. The slightest criticism could blast their political career. Now select committees provide an opportunity for backbenchers to participate, even in a limited way, in government. Inexperienced newcomers have an ideal opportunity to learn about policy making and administration and, perhaps, to start making a name for themselves. The 'has-beens' or 'never-will-bes' are able to participate actively and are more likely to take independent positions. And all backbenchers have the potential to put forward the views of particular interests. Thus committees offer a forum for various groups whose views might otherwise not get a hearing, even if action after that is problematic.

MODERNISATION OF PROCEDURES

To some extent Parliamentary ineffectiveness is its own fault, so mired is it in archaic procedures, abstruse debating rules, anti-social working hours (mid-afternoon to midnight), inadequate accommodation and rudimentary infrastructure. The new assemblies and the Scottish Parliament have shown Westminster up with reform in all these areas, although still hampered by inadequate resources. Major innovations in the new legislatures have been their strong and decisive committees and a deliberate attempt to tone down party hostility. This of course has been aided by all of them being multiparty, with coalition executives, which require agreement across party lines.

Major changes at Westminster would certainly follow if the Liberal Democrats held a balance between the two major competitors. With the growth in third-party support, and certainly after any change in the method of electing MPs, this is a possibility. The confrontation between Conservatives and Labour has certainly militated against any attempt to change the procedures which facilitate it. The expectation by both that they will eventually form a strong majority government militates against any change which might make Parliament more effective in scrutinising them.

Nevertheless New Labour has its image as a reforming party to consider and thus has been unable to totally ignore the more glaring inefficiencies in Parliamentary procedures. A Modernisation Committee has considered such changes as reform of working hours and a legislative process in which bills are not lost if they fail to be passed in one Parliamentary session, but can be carried over. This, in turn, would mean more rational planning of the government legislative programme and possibly more time for considered debate.

These ideas will be implemented because they make life easier for governments too. By enabling backbenchers to plan their time better they may also give them more scope. Like select committee activities, however, they are slightly marginal. Domination of the Commons by the big parties is likely to continue until the political balance itself changes.

INTERESTS: PROPER AND IMPROPER REPRESENTATION

The representation of interests lies at the heart both of constitutional theory and of the actual practice of Parliamentary and party politics. As Chapter 13 pointed out, an immense variety of groups and organisations are affected by government policy and therefore seek to influence it in their favour. Their most common and effective means of lobbying is by direct contact with government ministers and officials rather than with MPs, which underlines the general predominance of the executive over Parliament in Britain.

However, sometimes a specific piece of legislation can have very important consequences for particular groups. For example, even such a seemingly boring and technical matter as regulation of hygiene on caravan sites could gain or lose site owners millions of pounds: it all depends on whether they or the water companies are legally obliged to provide the requisite water facilities. Water companies will therefore also be drawn into this debate.

Throughout the nineteenth century (and indeed before then) it was taken for granted that MPs should not only represent outside interests but be personally linked to them, particularly land, commerce, industry, the City of London and the professions. Far better, it was assumed, that MPs have personal experience of the 'real world' than be full-time parliamentarians, and that they depend on inherited wealth or paid employment for their livelihood rather than on the taxpayer.

This generally relaxed attitude towards MPs' links with outside interests had gone into reverse by the end of the twentieth century. One reason is that most MPs have become full-time political professionals: they have no outside employment; devote all their time to committee work and (increasingly) to constituents' problems; and depend on a fairly modest Parliamentary salary and permitted expenses for their livelihood. This is particularly true of Labour MPs, who are drawn mainly from the 'talking professions' of teaching, law and journalism, but is increasingly true of Conservative MPs too, who are less likely than a generation ago to have inherited or accumulated significant private wealth. The advantage of MPs having private means or significant outside earnings (as a barrister, for example) is that it confers a degree of personal political independence; the danger of relying on a Parliamentary salary alone is that it exposes MPs to the temptation of accepting an often generous fee for lobbying on behalf of a particular interest.

A second reason is that the scope of governmental and Parliamentary action broadened immensely in the course of the twentieth century. When governments regulated only a few aspects of the economy, and firms could act much more freely and independently, the business interests involved in Parliament were few in number and clearly defined. Now almost everything the government does has financial implications for some companies and interests. Even when it decides to disengage from part of the economy, by privatising a state-run industry, for example, the way it chooses to do so (the nature of the share offer or the new regulatory regime) can have enormous financial implications for City interests and private companies. In these circumstances it can be very beneficial for the affected interests to have MPs quietly interceding on their behalf.

Third, as the culture of political deference has gradually declined, so the mass media have become less reticent and trusting about the connections between MPs, especially ministers, and outside interests. Clear evidence of explicit corruption is rare; the details of any situation are usually fuzzy and the motives of the people involved ambivalent and complex. It is difficult to know whether a wealthy businessperson makes a substantial gift to the Labour Party in the hope of a legislative favour, a knighthood, an invitation to Number 10 or out of genuine ideological sympathy – it may be all of these. It is equally difficult to tell whether a government decision that happens to benefit the donor was taken in gratitude for or anticipation of a donation or entirely irrespective of it in the public interest. What has changed is the media's assumptions: they no longer automatically give politicians the benefit of the doubt as 'honourable' members but presume selfish motives unless the contrary can be proved. For example, during the Conservative governments of the 1980s and 1990s a number of ex-ministers and senior officials joined the boards of major companies (eg Lord (John) Nott became a director of the merchant bank Lazards in 1983; Lord (Jim) Prior became chairman of GEC in 1984). Even though the ministers and officials abided by the Cabinet Office rules regulating such practice, the media would ask whether the prospect of such appointments affected the decisions of the minister when they were still in office. Similarly, the media, encouraged by the Conservative opposition, sought to imply that the businessmen appointed to the New Labour government by Tony Blair in 1997, such as Lord Simon and Lord Sainsbury, were subject to conflicts of interest even though they had dispensed with the shares they held in their companies.

In order to deal with the problem, Parliament in 1975 required MPs (and Lords) to register their interests and financial links in writing (the Parliamentary Register of Interests) and to declare their interest before participating in a debate or committee. However, by the 1990s this provision appeared to be ineffective. Some MPs failed to declare all their interests in the Register, whether through genuine inadvertence or deliberate concealment, and the Register did not stop

MPs from declaring a connection with a public relations company specialising in Parliamentary lobbying and accepting a 'consultancy fee' or favours for lobbying on behalf of an undisclosed particular interest. It also transpired that in the 1992–7 Parliament some MPs were being paid (at £1,000 per question!) by outside organisations to ask Parliamentary questions on their behalf. Neil Hamilton's failure to declare his connection with Mohamed Al Fayed, the owner of Harrods, and other paid activities on behalf of Ian Greer Associates (a Parliamentary lobbying company) is but one notorious example.

Individual links with special interests are to some extent legitimised by the fact that the parties to which they belong have institutionalised links with the same or similar interests. The Conservative Party has historically received substantial donations from major companies such as Hanson, Dixons and Marks & Spencer and from business associations such as Aims for Industry seeking to promote free enterprise. It has also accepted more dubious donations from wealthy overseas businessmen. A substantial proportion of Labour MPs have been sponsored by trade unions, which have contributed to their election expenses, although the practice is declining. Successive Labour leaders, including Harold Wilson, James Callaghan and Tony Blair, have relied on donations from wealthy but initially anonymous sympathisers to pay for their private office, general election campaign headquarters and for policy research.

A run of minor Parliamentary scandals and dubious practices during the 1992–7 Major administration led to the impression that Parliament and politicians were becoming 'sleazy'. This hit the Conservatives harder than Labour, because of their more extensive business links and their ability while in government to do more for their sponsors. In response to widespread disquiet, John Major as Prime Minister took the unprecedented step of setting up an extra-Parliamentary permanent committee under an Appeal Judge, Lord Nolan, to investigate. In 1996 the Conservative government, despite fury among some of its backbenchers, reluctantly accepted most of its recommendations for much wider disclosure of interests and for a prohibition against MPs accepting payment for lobbying. Under the Labour government, the Neill Committee (which succeeded the Nolan Committee) reported on party finance. Its recommendations for much greater transparency (for example, that all donations of more than £5,000 are to be declared, and that the state should fund both sides in a referendum equally) have been accepted by the Labour government, although again with a degree of reluctance. Although plausible allegations of 'sleaze' have somewhat abated since 1997 the Labour government has not avoided them altogether: its exemption of the ban on tobacco advertising in sport for Formula One Racing appeared to be due to the influence of Bernie Ecclestone, a Formula One Racing millionaire who had made a substantial donation to the Labour Party and had direct access to Tony Blair. The government has also been criticised by the commissioner for public appointments for favouring its political sympathisers in appointments to quangos, in particular to NHS trusts. The tenuousness of the arrangements in force for checking improper links between MPs and special interests was illustrated by the effective sacking in 2002 of the Parliamentary Commissioner for Standards, Elizabeth Filkin, because she had been too active in investigating MPs' and ministers' interests.

Sleaze A popular term, much used in the mid-1990s, referring to the corrupt and improper behaviour of public officials, initially mainly members of the Conservative government.

BRIEFINGS

18.5 **The arms to Iraq scandal (and war on Iraq, 2003)**

One example of the lengths governments can go to to conceal facts from Parliament is the arms to Iraq scandal. In the 1980s Iraq and Iran fought an eight-year war. To avoid exacerbating the situation most western governments, including the British, agreed not to export arms to either side. Government ministers assured Parliament in the late 1980s that the policy had not changed. But in fact the relevant Cabinet committee had decided to allow Iraq to be supplied with arms from 1987 onwards – ironically in terms of subsequent events, as it was considered more pro-western! Ministers deliberately misled Parliament by concealing the change of policy. To compound the scandal, executives of one of the companies encouraged by the government to export arms to Iraq were then charged with illegal export in the early 1990s. Their conviction at trial could have led to heavy prison sentences. The defence claim that the executives' action was officially authorised relied on documents that the solicitor-general and other ministers tried to withhold from the court by signing a 'public interest immunity certificate', which stated that their disclosure would endanger national security. In fact, disclosure to the court would not have endangered security at all – one minister, Michael Heseltine, refused to sign the certificate – but would have embarrassed the government. Only disclosure of the facts by an eccentric ex-minister, Alan Clark, led to the collapse of the trial and prevented the wrongful imprisonment of the executives. The disclosure provoked a judicial inquiry, the Scott Commission, whose report strongly condemned the government and various ministers. However, the Conservatives argued that the government was fully absolved by the Report and in February 1996 won the heavily whipped vote in the Commons by a majority of one. No ministers resigned. In September 2002 Parliament was urged by Tony Blair to support an invasion of Iraq on the basis of a highly selective report prepared by the government to show that Iraq was 'developing weapons of mass destruction'. The complex report was issued two hours before the Parliamentary debate. The New Labour government sought to avoid a vote, as the decision was strongly opposed within the party and the government could declare war without Parliamentary approval under the royal prerogative!

PARTY DISCIPLINE IN PARLIAMENT AND ITS RELAXATION

The major reason for Parliamentary weakness in the face of the executive is the loyalty given by MPs to their party, particularly when their party is in power. This raises two crucial and related questions. What mechanisms are available to secure MPs' loyalty? And under what circumstances does loyalty break down? The rights and wrongs of party loyalty are bound up with issues of democratic theory. On the one hand, party discipline is a prerequisite for strong and effective government and for communicating to the electorate the principles and policies of the parties. It enables the electorate to know where the parties stand and on that basis to make a rational choice between them. On the other hand, the individual MP was elected by the voters of his and her constituency and has obligations to represent their interests and views. MPs sometimes defy party discipline, therefore, in order to vote with their conscience or with the wishes of their local constituents. This tension between the electoral mandate for the party and the individual MP's duty to conscience and constituency has increased in recent years.

Maintaining party cohesion

Parties maintain cohesion by a variety of strategies and mechanisms. The leader of the majority party is also Prime Minister and can therefore appoint MPs to ministerial office – or, just as important, offer the prospect of office in the future – as a reward for loyalty. The Prime Minister can also award honours and make appointments or nominations to outside bodies (for example, to the European Commission) as to a lesser extent can the leader of the opposition. The Prime Minister has the power to dissolve Parliament and call a general election through a formal request to the Queen. The uncertainty of the result prevents this threat being made very often – after all, it could lead to electoral defeat and the Prime Minister relinquishing office – but it can promote cohesion on a particular issue. Edward Heath, the Conservative Prime Minister from 1970 to 1974 – widely unpopular among backbenchers for his lack of personal warmth and failure to distribute honours more widely – still secured a majority of 309 to 301 on the second reading of his much opposed bill to join the European Community (February 1972). He made the issue a vote of confidence, and thus indicated his willingness to hold an election if defeated. Similarly, in July 1993, the day after the Conservative government's defeat by 324 to 316 on the Social Policy Protocol of the Maastricht Treaty, John Major declared the issue a vote of confidence and secured a reversal of the decision by 339 to 301.

The party leadership is supported by party officials known as whips, selected from MPs not in the government (or in the shadow Cabinet, in the case of the opposition party). One of the whips' powers is withdrawal of the 'whip' from a dissident, with resulting loss of access to Parliamentary order papers and backbench party committees. The ultimate sanction is expulsion from the Parliamentary party, involving loss of the party's endorsement at the next election and near-certain electoral defeat.

The whips allocate backbench MPs to standing committees on government bills, recommend them for select committee appointments and choose MPs for Parliamentary and party delegations abroad. They can provide a host of small favours for MPs with health, family or financial problems. Such incentives improve the atmosphere on the backbenches and encourage loyalty. Prime Ministers rely on whips for advice about appointments to junior government posts, which are the stepping stones to more senior positions. Margaret Thatcher's failure to select ideologically 'sound' whips contributed to the emergence by 1990 of a Cabinet that was out of tune with many of her own policy positions, and helped to undermine her at a crucial point.

Ironically 'ideology' (adherence to a particular doctrine or programme) is more likely to lead to party division than unity. 'True believers' are more likely than pragmatists to put doctrine before party and to reject the compromises that all governments have to make. From the 1950s to the mid-1980s this posed more problems for Labour than the Conservatives because the Labour Party was divided between doctrinaire 'socialists' and pragmatic 'social democrats' over a wide range of issues (but particularly Britain's relations with the USA, Europe and the Soviet Union; nuclear defence; nationalisation and internal party democracy). However, Conservative MPs became noticeably more ideological under

Mrs Thatcher's premiership and by the 1992–7 government dissent became endemic within the Parliamentary Conservative Party. This coincided with the influx of new-style Tories in the 1980s who, like Mrs Thatcher herself, did not come from the traditional male, public school, armed forces and colonial service stereotype, in which acceptance of authority and loyalty to the institution was paramount. The new-style Conservative MPs were more likely to be upwardly mobile meritocratic individualists for whom loyalty to party was less important, and they were encouraged in this view by Margaret Thatcher's sporadic disloyalty to John Major after she ceased to be Prime Minister. They chose the issue of 'British sovereignty' against 'Europe', which symbolised 'Thatcherism' versus 'Majorism', as the cause for rebellion. Meanwhile Labour, desperate to avoid a fifth election defeat in 1997, preserved an uncharacteristic unity despite the reservations of many on the Left about Tony Blair's abandonment of traditional positions. The Labour leadership tightened the standing orders that regulate backbenchers' freedom to dissent and the electronic pager issued by the whips to each Labour MP became a symbol of the leadership's 'control freakery'. However, major revolts occurred over Social Security, over select committee chairs and, in early 2003, on the war in Iraq. After 1997 and particularly after 2001, the Conservative Party regained cohesion by eliminating 'Europhiles' from its ranks.

Dissent within Parliamentary parties

All governments are vulnerable to backbench rebellions if they persistently ignore the views of their MPs and appear to be heading for defeat at the next election. Local constituency parties will be less inclined to disown rebels if they themselves are critical of the party leadership for deviating from party principles or for governmental incompetence. Ideologues with an 'all or nothing' approach ignore the danger that public dissent might weaken the government in the eyes of voters and enhance the prospect of defeat.

As Table 18.3 shows, party discipline was strong under both Labour and Conservative governments during the 1950s and 1960s. It began to crumble during the 1970–February 1974 Conservative government led by the aloof Edward Heath. Internal tensions grew after the government's economic U-turns on its manifesto and as a result of its commitment to joining the European Economic Community (now the EU) – consistently the most divisive issue in post-war British politics. An identifiable body of Conservative MPs emerged with a hard line on monetary policy and social issues. They gradually took over the leadership of the party with the election of Margaret Thatcher as party leader in 1975 and Prime Minister in 1979. Semi-public dissent by the 'wets' from the prevailing monetarist orthodoxy then became common, and increased in extent after 1980.

Backbench rebellion became almost epidemic during the 1974–9 Labour governments of Harold Wilson and James Callaghan. It reflected growing disillusion with the economic performance of the government and rooted objections to devolution to Scotland and Wales. No less than 45 per cent of all whipped divisions in the 1978–9 session saw some Labour MPs voting against the government. What is more, only 62 Labour MPs (19 per cent of the total) cast no

Table 18.3 *Rebellions by government backbenchers, by end of two full Parliamentary sessions, 1945–2001*

Parliament	Number of rebellions	Average size of rebellions	Average size of rebellions as % of Parliamentary party
1983	137	8	2%
1970	135	8	2%
1992	119	12	4%
Oct 1974	**115**	**23**	**7%**
1987	111	7	2%
1979	64	6	2%
1959	52	5	1%
1945	**38**	**14**	**4%**
1997	**96**	**15**	**4%**
1966	31	22	6%
Feb 1974	**8***	**35**	**12%**
1955	7	4	1%
1950	**5***	**13**	**4%**
1951	2	12	4%
1964	**1***	**1**	**0%**

Note: *Short-lived Parliaments that did not last for as long as two sessions
  Bold indicates a Labour government

Source: Data provided by Philip Cowley, October 2002

dissenting votes, while 40 cast more than 50, and 9 more than 100. The secession of the Social Democrats in 1981–2 can be traced to these increasing factional tensions among Labour MPs in the late 1970s.

The watering down of Thatcherite policies under John Major (1990–7) left the more diehard members of the party disgruntled. They found a cause to rally round in opposition to 'Europe'. The government's progressive loss of its modest majority through by-election losses meant that even small groups of determined opponents within the party could force its hand. The limit to the leadership's power to impose party discipline was demonstrated when it withdrew the whip from eight Eurosceptic rebels in November 1994 (a ninth resigned the whip in sympathetic protest). The withdrawal gave the rebels publicity, underlined the party's divisions, and left the government even more vulnerable to defeat in the House of Commons. Within a year it was forced to readmit them without guarantees of their future compliance.

The Labour government elected in 1997 was far more united than its Conservative predecessor. In its first two full Parliamentary sessions there was less rebelliousness than in any full-length Parliament since the 1950s. In the 703 divisions one or more Labour backbenchers rebelled in a mere 35. Perhaps surprisingly, the large cohort of newly elected women Labour MPs were particularly loyal, contrary to the assumption that they might shake up both Parliament and the Labour Party and introduce a new agenda into British politics. This exceptional Parliamentary cohesion was assisted by tougher party management but also by an acute awareness of Labour backbenchers of the role played by disunity in keeping the party in opposition for 18 years after 1979. An even more important factor was the government's relatively successful record of economic management and consequently its high standing in the opinion polls. However, it was not entirely immune particularly on various aspects of welfare reform (see Table 18.1). Stronger backbench dissent is evident in the 2001 Parliament, particularly over war in Iraq and relations with the US in general. A further point of tension are government proposals for more private involvement in public services.

ROLE OF THIRD PARTIES

The House of Commons is so dominated by the battle between the two big parties, representing Her Majesty's Government and Her Majesty's Loyal Opposition, that so far we have given little attention to third parties. Yet if Parliament is to develop a function beyond sustaining the government and official opposition, the part played by the smaller parties is crucial. Because they are structurally placed outside the main struggle between government and opposition they can make criticisms that are not simply directed at doing the government down or which may be overlooked.

Third-party representation in Parliament has grown, if somewhat erratically, since the 1950s, as Figure 18.1 shows. Seventy-five MPs were elected in 1997, the largest number since 1931, of whom 30 were regionalist MPs, particularly concerned with issues affecting their own part of Britain. The Ulster Unionists, the largest single group, are also a 'single-issue' regional group in the sense that they are overwhelmingly concerned with government policy on Northern Ireland. The 2001 Parliament has 80 third-party MPs.

Regionalist MPs will not be strongly interested in general British issues, or at any rate will be willing to trade support on these for regional concessions if the government is in a tight corner (as the dying Major administration found to its

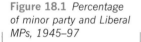

Figure 18.1 *Percentage of minor party and Liberal MPs, 1945–97*

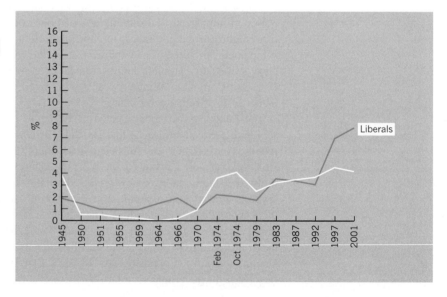

cost when dependent on the votes of a few Ulster Unionists 1995–6). The Liberal Democrats are the party most likely to act as a genuine third voice on questions of general British concern. It is for this reason that their Parliamentary growth is shown separately in Figure 18.1.

Liberal Democrat strength in Parliament has grown in fits and starts since their initial recovery in the early 1960s. The electoral system, however, prevents them from translating their substantial share of votes into Parliamentary seats. This creates a vicious circle. The number of Liberal Democrat MPs has been too limited to break the hold of Conservatives and Labour over Parliamentary procedures and the adversarial style of debate it engenders. This culture also extends to select committee proceedings and appointments. For example, only one Liberal Democrat chaired a select committee in the 1997 Parliament although in many ways Liberals would be ideal in forging a 'Commons view' outside the main party battle. The Parliamentary weakness of the Liberals means that they cannot force through the electoral reforms that would end it. Thus the 'third force' that might help to develop a genuinely autonomous role for Parliament is normally disadvantaged by the latter's institutional bias towards the two main parties.

POSSIBLE REFORMS OF PARLIAMENT

Political reform is rare but not impossible in Britain, as Scottish and Welsh devolution shows. However, the government must perceive reform to be in its interest to carry it through. No government voluntarily transfers some of its power to other parties or institutions to the detriment of its own position. The electoral importance of Scotland and Wales to Labour, and the ability of regional nationalism to threaten its dominance, accounts for devolution. Only if the Liberal Democrats could carve out a similarly powerful position might a Labour government carry through the crucial change to a more proportional election system. Such a change would normally produce a strong bloc of about 100 Liberal Democrat MPs, usually sufficient to deprive both major parties of an absolute Parliamentary majority. At one stroke this would give the Liberal Democrats powerful leverage in Parliament because they would normally be the 'kingmakers', deciding whether the Conservatives or Labour should govern with their support in a coalition government.

Such a change would also make individual MPs more important, because their immediate voting decisions could affect the survival of finely balanced governments. MPs would have a more independent standing with ministers and civil servants, which would enable them to strengthen their inquiries and investigations and compel more attention to them. This applies particularly to the role of select committees. Precisely because such changes would make life more difficult for governments and the major parties they are likely to be strongly resisted. The key reform, proportional representation for elections to the Commons, is only likely to emerge from inter-party bargaining in a 'hung' Parliament with a sizeable Liberal Democrat presence, or if a Labour government believes that it is the only way to save itself from defeat at an imminent general election.

BRIEFINGS

18.6 **A really useful reform of Parliament?**

Usually the idea that Parliament might be reformed is opposed on the grounds that its main function is to support the government. Mandate theory assumes that a party is elected on the basis of its programme and is accountable to voters at the next election for its success or failure. From this perspective any exercise of autonomous power by Parliament simply blurs government and party accountability.

If one accepts that government policy is subject to 'party democracy' rather than 'Parliamentary democracy', one can still envisage a role for both Houses of Parliament outside central election issues. A convention could be adopted that independent Parliamentary action should not be taken in regard to these (rather as the House of Lords currently accepts that it must pass legislation embodying election pledges, no matter how distasteful). However, there could be no objection to Parliament:

■ obtaining and publishing information about central election policies, how they are being implemented, whether they have been changed, and what their cost is

■ making recommendations and even taking action about policies and decisions not covered in the manifestos.

A prerequisite to both of these activities is to compel witnesses to attend and give evidence. The House of Lords could concentrate more on information gathering and evaluation and the Commons on action, as is appropriate, given their different constitutional status.

ESSAYS

1. Could we still have a democracy in Britain without Parliament? If so, how would it function? If not, what is the irreplaceable contribution that Parliament makes?

2. Why do MPs nearly always vote as the whips instruct them, even when they have doubts about their party's line?

3. What can a Parliamentary select committee do that an investigative journalist cannot?

SUMMARY

This chapter shows that:

■ Parliament at the present time is dominated by the two major political parties. The mass of MPs owe their election to party support and thus tend to support their party and shield it from criticism, whatever their private doubts.

■ This means that Parliament's main role is to sustain the government and provide a forum for the opposition to criticise it.

■ However, some weakening of major party cohesion and increased third-party representation have allowed backbench MPs to assume a slightly more independent role in questioning aspects of government policy.

■ This has been expressed by voting against some government legislation, and by more vigorous questioning and investigation by select committees.

■ Scrutiny and questioning of the administration is probably a more important and justifiable activity for Parliament than querying legislation. Important legislation has been given a 'mandate' through the government party's electoral success. The details of implementation, however, have not, neither have the many major administrative decisions made by the Civil Service. A useful role of committees is simply to provide more information about the workings of British government.

- Parliament plays only a peripheral part in government. It could play a modestly useful role in scrutinising the administration, if it were better organised to do it. Most reform will have to wait until third parties or dissident MPs are in a position to force change out of the leadership of one of the major parties. In spite of rhetoric, the New Labour government is no more anxious to diminish its present or prospective power than any other government. Thus major reform of the House of Commons is not on the immediate horizon.

MILESTONES

Milestones in Parliamentary development

1295–1306 Edward I summons representatives of boroughs and counties, as well as Lords, to consent to taxation. In return he redresses grievances they complain about

1306–1532 This practice continues and the Parliament clearly divides into two Houses (Lords and Commons). The Commons establishes itself as the more active House, with power to grant taxation

1532–59 Parliament confirms the Royal Succession and sanctions the major religious changes

1640–51 Parliament fights civil war against the Crown and wins. It establishes its supremacy over the law courts

1688–9 The Glorious Revolution. Parliament transfers Crown from James II to William and Mary and establishes exclusive power to raise money and sanction military forces. Members given personal immunities

1701 Parliament settles Protestant succession

1715–1832 The 'eighteenth-century constitution'. Government has to be acceptable both to the King and the Commons majority. From time to time party caucuses ('Whigs', 'Tories') form to manage the majority

1832 Great Reform Act. Election becomes the clear and exclusive basis of membership of the House of Commons. Government is now totally dependent on a Commons majority. Monarch withdraws from active politics

1867–8 Second Reform Act institutes mass male franchise. Mass-membership parties impose discipline on MPs in return for sponsoring their election. 'Elective dictatorship' of government commences

1874–86 Imposition of procedural devices to ensure government legislation passes in spite of filibustering by Irish nationalists ('guillotine' to curtail debate on clauses etc)

1911 Lords cannot oppose financial legislation and can only delay legislation for three years

1922 Government of Ireland Act sets up Northern Irish government and Parliament

1949 Parliament Act limits delaying power of House of Lords to one year

1970 Growth of dissent from the party line among backbench MPs

1972 European Communities Act significantly limits Parliamentary sovereignty

1973 Abolition of Northern Irish Government and Parliament

1979 Creation of system of departmental select committees to scrutinise administrative actions

1994–6 Scott Committee reveals extent to which governments may mislead the Commons

1994 Government sets up Committee of Inquiry into Standards in Public Life, under Lord Justice Nolan

1995 Nolan Report recommends public disclosure of MPs' interests and party donors

1996 MPs obliged to register all details of outside contracts with a new Parliamentary commission

1998 Devolution to Wales, Scotland and Northern Ireland

1999 House of Lords Act: hereditary peers lose their voting rights, except for 92 who retain them during a transitional period

2001–3 Debate over how Lords' members should be selected: Liberals and Conservatives come out for largely elected House with same general powers

1. On the basis of the 2001 Labour Party manifesto and the Queen's speeches made in the present Parliament, estimate the extent to which the government has fulfilled its election pledges up to this point.

2. On the basis of newspaper accounts and *Hansard* (the report of Parliamentary proceedings) calculate the amount of dissent within the Parliamentary Labour Party and the Parliamentary Conservative Party during the present Parliament.

3. 'Shadow' two select committees in this Parliament on the basis of newspaper reports. Do you feel that one is more effective than the other? Why?

4. Outline the reforms that you think are necessary for the Commons to operate better.

FURTHER READING

General works on Parliament are P. Norton, *Does Parliament Matter?* (Brighton: Harvester Wheatsheaf, 1993), especially Chapter 10, 'The role of party'; and Stuart Weir and David Beetham, *Political Power and Democratic Control in Britain* (London and New York: Routledge, 1999), Part 3. The latter is particularly strong on the incapacity of Parliament to scrutinise the executive and hold it accountable. For a longer study of parties in Parliament, see J. Brand, *British Parliamentary Parties* (Oxford: Oxford University Press, 1992), and for the work of party whips see K. Alderman, 'The government whips', *Politics Review*, **4** (4), April, 1995, pp. 23–4. Committees are discussed in T. Morgan, 'Teeth for the Commons watchdog', *Politics Review*, **8** (4), 1999, p. 6–10. For recent discussions of the reform of the House of Commons, see the Hansard Society Commission Report, *The Challenge for Parliament: Making Government Accountable* (London: Hansard Society, 2001) and the Constitution Unit's *Monitor* (quarterly). New Labour's attempts to reform the House of Lords are summarised in M. Baldwin, 'Reforming the Second Chamber', *Politics Review*, **11** (3), 2002, pp. 8–12. A series of general overviews of proposals for reform are 'What's new? Parliamentary reform and political parties', *Politics Review*, **11** (2), 2002, pp. 6–7; Michael Rush, 'A summary of the Wakeham Report on the House of Lords', *Talking Politics*, **13** (1), 2000, pp. 134–9; Philip Cowley and Mark Stuart, 'Parliament: a few headaches and a dose of modernisation', *Parliamentary Affairs*, **54** (3), 2001, pp. 442–58; Lord (David) Puttnam, 'A democratic and expert House', *Political Quarterly*, **70** (4), 1999, pp. 368–74; Chris Ridsdill-Smith, 'Do we have Parliamentary government?', *Politics Review*, **11** (1), 2001, pp. 26–9.

USEFUL WEB SITES ON PARTIES AND PARLIAMENT

Hotlinks to these sites can be found on the CWS website at http://www.booksites.net/budge.

For a complete list of political parties' web sites see Chapter 15 of this book. The Westminster Parliamentary structure is described thoroughly in www.parliament.uk, which also provides general information on representative democracy in the UK as well as in-depth information on both chambers and their members. Acts of the UK Parliament are available at Her Majesty's Stationery Office (www.hmso.gov.uk/acts.htm). POLIS is the Parliamentary Online Indexing Service (www.polis.parliament.uk); they provide an excellent database on all sorts of issues related to Parliamentary activities in the UK. Other useful information about Parliament may be obtained from the Committee on Standards in Public Life (www.public-standards.gov.uk) and the Royal Commission for the Reform of the House of Lords (www.lords-reform.org.uk).

For information on the Scottish Parliament visit www.scottish.parliament.uk. Information on the Welsh Assembly is available at www.wales.gov.uk; for data on the Northern Ireland Assembly visit www.ni-assembly.gov.uk. The institutional structure and the list of members of the European Parliament are available at www.europarl.eu.int; for a more specific search visit the UK Office of the European Parliament at www.europarl.org.uk/uk_meps/MembersMain.htm.

In addition to the parties themselves, there are many institutions devoted to the design of the parties' political agendas and their implementation through

Parliament. In this respect, it might be worth looking at some of the issues raised by some of the most prestigious think tanks in the UK. The Centre for Policy Studies is closely related to the Conservative Party. On their web site you will be able to find a wide range of academic articles combining policy making and conservatism; visit them at www.cps.org.uk/start.htm. For the case of the Liberal Democratic Party, we suggest you visit the Centre for Reform at www.cfr.org.uk; finally, the Fabian Society (www.fabian-society.org.uk/int.asp) and the Institute for Public Policy Research (www.ippr.org) are quite representative of the ideological conformation of New Labour.

PART 6

Law, Order, and Security

The Royal Courts of Justice

Politics and law

Legislation and scrutiny of the executive are not the monopoly of Parliament. Increasingly these powers are shared with the higher courts (including the European Court of Justice). Central and local government in Britain are, in fact, complemented by the legal system. This not only scrutinises and reviews their decisions but in many ways functions as a parallel line of administration on its own, processing and deciding a variety of matters that would otherwise need to be handled directly by the political authorities. As it is, governments can express their general intentions through Parliamentary legislation, which judges then apply to specific cases in the courts.

Unfortunately, governments do not always express their wishes clearly, and are even deliberately ambiguous on certain matters for political reasons. This gives considerable scope for judges to interpret or even to modify law, even where they are not formally reviewing it. Their powers make the question of who the judges are, and how the courts operate, of considerable political relevance.

This chapter accordingly:

■ describes the court systems of England and Wales, Scotland and Northern Ireland
■ comments on the way law is interpreted in the courts and the consequences this has for their political role
■ examines the appointment, background and outlook of the judges
■ describes the nature of legal procedures and the way in which they require political judgements to be made in some cases.

COURT SYSTEMS

The court structure of England and Wales (it differs in Scotland and Northern Ireland) has not changed since a major reorganisation in 1972. Its main components are summarised in Table 19.1. In the localities are the magistrates' courts, which outside the main conurbations are staffed by part-time, unpaid laypeople. These are local notables, appointed by secret committees nominated by the Lord Chancellor. There are over 30,000 magistrates, known as justices of the peace (JPs) roughly half of whom are male and half female. Although magistrates' courts are sometimes described as 'the people's courts', JPs are in no sense representative of the populations in their areas, and there is no direct public participation in their selection. Contrariwise, JPs have more contact with local communities than professional, full-time judges. They deal with most minor crime and also decide whether more serious cases should be sent for trial by judge and jury in the Crown Court. The crimes they deal with are minor but they have, and very often use, the power to imprison for up to six months. Although they are

Court	Functions		Number of courts	Annual caseload	Composition	Additional comments
	Criminal	Civil				
Magistrates' courts	Minor crime	Very limited	Several hundred	Vast	Part-time lay JPs, except in major conurbations	Apart from trying minor crime, these courts vet all prosecutions to check whether there is a case to be heard before judge and jury in the Crown Court
County courts	None	Extensive caseload for all civil law cases subject to financial limits	260	Approximately 2.5 million cases started each year; less than 5% come to trial	Circuit judges and (more than 500) district judges	Most civil cases start and finish here, and much of the work is small claims business
Crown courts	All	Some limited areas	Technically one court, with 90 centres	Approximately 100,000 cases put down for hearing[1]	High Court (QBD) and circuit judges and recorders	This is the main criminal court. It has three tiers: in the first, High Court judges sit to try the most serious crimes; in the other two circuit judges try less serious offences. It also hears appeals from magistrates' courts and passes sentence on certain cases where conviction has taken place before magistrates
High Court[2] A: Chancery Division	None	Trusts, wills, tax law, company law, property etc		Approximately 700 trials	17 High Court judges under the Vice-Chancellor	
B: Family Division	None	Family law in general		2–3,000 defended cases	15, under the President	All divorce cases start in the county courts but defended ones may come here, as with adoption procedures

C: Queen's Bench Division (including its divisional court)	Some appeals, mainly in public law from tribunals and magistrates' courts	All civil law not dealt with elsewhere, specially contract and tort	1,500–2,000 full trials	63 judges under the Lord Chief Justice
Court of Appeal				Lord Chief Justice, Master of the Rolls and 17 Lord Justices
A: Criminal Division	Most criminal appeals	None	6–7,000	It sits in benches usually of one or two judges from the Court of Appeal sitting with judges from Queen's Bench Division
B: Civil Division	None	Appeals from High Court, county court and certain tribunals	c. 1,000	Usually sits in three-person benches
The House of Lords	Appeals from any court in England and Wales on any matter, and from Scotland and Northern Ireland in many cases. Most of the work consists of civil appeals from the Court of Appeal		c. 200	Between 10 and 12 Lords of Appeal, under the Lord Chancellor (who will very rarely sit). Usually works in five-person benches

Table 19.1 *The modern English court system in outline*

Notes: [1] Caseloads are very difficult to estimate because the bulk of civil cases are resolved either before coming to trial at all or before the trial is over. The figures given are rough estimates of the number of cases that actually do come to trial, whether they are brought to judgment or not.
[2] The various divisions of the High Court all play some role in appeals over cases in their areas from lower courts and from tribunals. This is particularly so for the QBD, which has an overall responsibility to supervise all inferior courts and tribunals

aided by legally trained clerks the biggest problem about the magistrates' courts is the enormous variation from area to area in their sentencing practices.

England and Wales is the only jurisdiction in the world to rely on lay magistrates in this way. It is a fourteenth-century relic, which has enormous power because it handles so much of the work. Magistrates only handle minor crime, but the huge bulk of crime is minor. Two million cases a year – 98 per cent of all criminal cases – start and end with magistrates.

A peculiar anomaly of English law makes the fact that one can appeal from the magistrates' decision almost irrelevant. This is because convicted people sentenced to prison start their sentence immediately, even if they are appealing. The

BRIEFINGS

19.1 Law and different kinds of law

The essence of law is that it is a general rule backed by sanctions against those who break it. Who decides and applies such sanctions (international bodies, state or substate governments) may vary. There is debate about whether law could take the form of customs and conventions backed by public opinion in societies without government. However, in the modern world law is generally defined by having the backing of some authority that issues the rule in written form.

The general nature of law consists in the fact that it specifies appropriate behaviour for everyone under a particular set of circumstances. These circumstances are likely to arise, however, only for particular groups or types of people. Thus laws will have more relevance for some groups and individuals than others, which is why these are more involved in lobbying the executive and legislature and in court actions designed to change existing rules.

The body of law is divided up according to the area of life it regulates. Thus there is a body of criminal law, commercial law, private law, family law, public, constitutional and administrative law, and so on. The borders between these are fluid and often depend on rather arbitrary definitions: for example, whether sharp practice in business comes under commercial law or criminal law depends on whether it can be classed as a fraud (illicit deception). Legal cases are often defended on the grounds that an inappropriate charge has been brought.

Some practices, such as making contracts, cut across a number of fields, so that the law of contract has a general applicability, as does the law of evidence. Laws about procedures (such as how valid laws must be made) thus have a more general impact than most substantive law, since they affect the whole process of law making. This is why constitutional courts generally have a higher status than ordinary courts. Very often the outcome of a particular case depends on whether the relevant laws under which it is brought are valid or not. Ultimately, therefore, decisions about political and legal procedures will affect us all.

Law A body of rules enforced by the power of the state.

slowness of appeal means that anyone serving a sentence of a month or six weeks, the most common sentence, will have served at least half before the appeal is heard. And as Crown Court judges often increase the magistrates' sentence it is seldom rational to appeal, however innocent one feels.

As well as the magistrates' courts, there are two sorts of professionally staffed local court: the Crown Courts for criminal law and the county courts for civil law. There are 90 Crown Court centres in England and Wales, and about 260 county courts. Crown Courts are staffed, for most trials, by the most junior type of judge, the circuit judges, or by part-time recorders. There are about 500 circuit judges drawn from the legal profession, most being barristers. Although solicitors can be appointed, no more than 10 per cent of circuit judges come from that branch of the profession, even though solicitors outnumber barristers by ten to one. In the county courts most of the work is done by circuit judges and district judges.

Crown and county courts are the workhorses for more serious crime and for the overwhelming bulk of civil cases. Each year over 2.5 million civil cases are started in the county courts, most for the recovery of money. Very few of these are actually tried, most disputes being settled out of court. The Crown Courts try all serious criminal offences; the more serious the crime the more senior the judge, but almost all crime will end at the Crown Court level. The number of criminal cases dealt with in the crown courts is about 120,000 per annum. In only 34,000 or so do defendants plead not guilty, thus requiring the case to be fully tried. Only 8,000 of those found guilty appeal, and the bulk of appeals are against the severity of sentence, not the verdict itself.

Above these courts we enter the world of the real legal elite. The first step up in the legal system is the High Court. This is a very complex institution that handles more substantial and difficult cases. The High Court is divided into three divisions, the Queen's Bench Division (QBD), Chancery Division and the Family Division. The QBD handles the most complex tort and contract cases. It is headed by the Lord Chief Justice and staffed by approximately 63 High Court judges. As well as dealing with civil cases in the QBD these judges also spend some of their time on circuit hearing the most serious criminal cases in Crown Courts.

The principal business of the Chancery Division is insolvency disputes, trade and industry disputes, disputes over intellectual property and trusts. It is staffed by approximately 17 High Court judges. Family disputes of various types are dealt with in the county courts, the magistrates' courts and the Family Division of the High Court. The Family Division can hear all cases involving children and is the only court that has jurisdiction in wardship matters. It is staffed by approximately 15 High Court judges.

Confusingly, each of these divisions has its own divisional court that filters out cases before they come to the main court. The most important of these is the Divisional Court of the Queen's Bench Division, which deals with applications for judicial review of decisions of public bodies. Many of these are appeals by immigrants against deportation orders made by the Home Office.

The Court of Appeal is divided into the Criminal Division and the Civil Division. It is staffed by the Lord Chief Justice who heads its Criminal Division, the Master of the Rolls who heads its Civil Division, and by 27 Lord Justices of Appeal. (Lord justices are not Law Lords. Law Lords sit in the Judicial Committee

Plate 19.1 *The High
Court of Justice, London.
Its architecture is gothic,
corresponding to the
medieval origins of
English law*

of the House of Lords (see later.) The Criminal Division hears appeals from the
Crown Courts and handles in the region of 7,000 appeals a year, most of which
are appeals against the sentence imposed rather than the verdict itself. The Civil
Division hears approximately 1,000 appeals a year from decisions of the High
Court, county courts and certain tribunals.

Most jurisdictions have only one court of appeal, but Britain has two. Above the Court of Appeal itself is the (Judicial Committee of) the House of Lords, a different entity from the Parliamentary House of Lords. The Judicial Committee of the House of Lords consists of 12 specially created life peers – the Law Lords (technically, Lords of Appeal in Ordinary) who have reached the summit of the legal profession. By convention, two of the Law Lords will be Scots lawyers. The House is also the ultimate Court of Appeal from Scotland but only on civil matters. On criminal cases the High Court of Justiciary in Edinburgh gives the final rulings.

The Judicial Committee of the House of Lords is very senior indeed. It handles fewer than 200 cases a year and there is no automatic right of appeal to it; this has to be granted either by the Lords themselves or by the Court of Appeal. The doctrine is that it will only handle cases that have far-reaching implications for the impact of law on the whole society.

There are, in addition, two other legal structures that have a potential impact on politics. At a level lower than the High Court are innumerable tribunals and appeal tribunals, which handle a massive and diverse range of disputes between individuals and public bodies. There is also the Judicial Committee of the Privy Council, which is essentially the Law Lords under another name. This Committee acts as a final court of appeal from certain Commonwealth and colonial countries. As such it often acts as a fully fledged supreme court interpreting a written constitution. The Privy Council has, for example, decided on the constitutionality of the death penalty in Singapore. With reform of the House of Lords, suggestions have been made (eg by the current Lord Chief Justice), that the two judicial committees – of the Lords and of the Privy Council – should be merged to form a Supreme Court.

Courts in Northern Ireland, although separate, closely resemble the English, with less emphasis on lay magistrates and juries. The law administered there derives largely from English common law, modified for Irish conditions and shaped to some extent by acts of the former Northern Irish Parliament between 1922 and 1972. There is an Appeal Court in Belfast, but the judicial House of Lords has ultimate jurisdiction.

The Scottish system is more distinctive. While there are district courts with lay magistrates, the major court is the Sheriff Court, with jurisdiction over a considerable population and area, and powers to try all but major criminal and civil cases. The sheriff is a professional lawyer. At the centre of the system are the 18 senators of the College of Justice in Edinburgh, who staff both the chief civil court, the Court of Session, and the chief criminal court, the High Court of Justiciary. Other senators than those who tried the original case sit as a Court of Criminal Appeal, which is the final authority here. There are also appeals in civil cases from the Outer to the Inner House of the Session, but the final authority is the Judicial Committee of the House of Lords, sitting with two Scottish Lords of Appeal.

These institutional differences are reflected in the different nature of the law administered in Scottish courts. This diverges from the English system in two major ways. The actual law, in the sense of the legal rules applied by courts, often differs from equivalent rules in England. Property law, for example, retains much more of the feudal inheritance than does the English law of real estate. These differences are becoming greater now that separate legislation for Scotland is produced by the new Scottish Parliament. It seems likely, for example, that there will be greater freedom of information than in England under new Scottish legislation. Second, the sources of Scots law, and the general theory of law are different. Although this difference can be exaggerated, Scots lawyers operate under a system heavily influenced by Roman law, as is true in Continental Europe. There is no room here to discuss Scotland separately. Much of what is said here will still be true of Scottish courts and judges, but not all. It will certainly be the case, however, that any conclusions about the autonomy and political importance of English judges will apply equally, if not more, to Scottish judges (and for that matter to Northern Irish judges).

A last general point about all the legal systems is the exceptional degree of autonomy that lawyers enjoy. With regard to the practice of their profession and

BRIEFINGS

19.2 Differences between English and Continental European law

In the modern world national legal systems are converging because: (a) businesses often operate in many countries; (b) many national systems now come under the same higher authority (eg the EU); and (c) various international committees and lawyers' associations are trying to bring together the different systems.

The major differences between the English law and legal system, and the Continental law and court systems are:

■ **Sources of law**   Continental law generally bases itself on written codes influenced by Roman law. English law is mainly based on previous decisions (precedents) of higher or parallel courts, although these can be modified by Parliamentary statute. The difference, though real, can be exaggerated, as Continental judges use previous judicial decisions to decide how the written code applies in a particular case. Scots law actually combines these processes of reasoning, as does the European Court of Justice.

■ **Handling of cases**   English courts rely on adversarial encounters between the two opposing sides, represented by their lawyers, and often trying to persuade a jury of laypeople of the justice of their case. Continental courts take over the case themselves on the basis of a report prepared beforehand (in criminal cases by an investigating magistrate).

■ **Personnel**   English judges are overwhelmingly barristers who have had some success in their profession. They are thus weighty figures in their own right who attract much respect. Continental judges are a branch of the Civil Service who specialise in this side of legal work direct from university. The idea of having lay judges, for example JPs, is quite alien in Continental Europe. Juries are also rarer.

■ **Systems of law**   Almost all Continental countries have two separate kinds of courts: 'ordinary' ones handling civil and criminal cases and administrative ones handling disputes involving State bodies. The English system has traditionally fused the two, particularly at the higher court levels (eg from the Queen's Bench Division of the High Court upwards).

its ethics, they are totally self-regulating under their elected councils. Since legal ethics determine the conduct of business in court, and much of the interpretation of law, the self-government of lawyers is even more important politically than the self-government of other professions such as doctors.

It reaches out to the substance of law in the proceedings of the (separate) Law Commissions for England and Scotland. These are quangos charged with revision of law, and composed wholly of lawyers. Formally they deal with technical revisions – cleaning up obscure language, consolidating and codifying branches of law, repealing obsolete statutes – and everything they recommend has to be approved by Parliament. In practice, the matters being technical and politically non-controversial, their recommendations are usually accepted with little debate. Although technical, such revisions can have enormous importance for individuals, as when they changed the basis of Scottish landholding to freehold from a form of tenure where the superior tenant still retained certain rights (such as mineral rights) and could prohibit development, for example. In some areas the Law Commissions act as a mini-legislature, except that they are nominated, not elected bodies, and are responsive to legal opinion much more than to any other. One very good example of the influence of the English Law Commission is the 1986 Public Order Act. This was the cause of much Parliamentary furore and lobbying by such bodies as the Police Federation and the NCCL (National Council for Civil Liberties). Looked at closely, however, the Act hardly deviates at all from the draft bill published by the Law Commission in 1983.

BRIEFINGS

19.3 Attempted reform of the English legal profession in the 1990s

In 1989–90 Mrs Thatcher and her reformist Lord Chancellor, Lord Mackay (significantly, a Scottish lawyer) put forward proposals for the most far-reaching reform of the English legal profession since the nineteenth century. This involved abolishing the distinction between barristers and solicitors, simplifying court procedures and throwing open the selection of judges to the whole of the legal profession.

The proposals, although they had the support of solicitors representing the vast majority of lawyers, were fought tooth and nail by judges and the barristers' associations. They were diluted more and more until only minor changes remained. Legal reform then changed direction, in sympathy with the government's value-for-money concerns, by cutting down on legal aid (which assists persons of up to middling incomes with the high legal costs of any court action) and expanding administrative discretion in such areas as appeals by immigrants against deportation. Sentencing, which involves enormous prison costs, remained unaffected.

The changes the government made in the end thus adversely affected solicitors rather than barristers and made no difference to judges. Similar changes proposed by the Labour Lord Chancellor Irvine ended up the same way.

It is a sign of its entrenched power that the Bar managed to fight off nearly all proposed legal reform during the 1990s and seems well able to continue its successful resistance over the next decade. Given the autonomy of the legal profession and its influence over the substance of the law, this is of great political significance.

POLITICAL ROLE OF THE COURTS

The growing recourse to legal action to resolve political disputes means that the higher courts have an important mediating role between central and local government, on the one hand, and between both of these and European Union institutions on the other. Conservative legislation of the 1980s, particularly the laws regulating industrial relations and trade union activities, extended the supervisory and decision-making powers of the courts into new areas, where they often find themselves in conflict with powerful political interests.

All this has happened in a system where the courts lack what has often been taken as the distinguishing mark of a 'political' jurisdiction, that is, the power of 'constitutional review'. Constitutional review in its layperson's sense means a system in which laws and other acts of the legislature can be overruled by a court if they are held to conflict with constitutional rules, basic human rights, or any other laws treated as superior to ordinary legislation. In the United States of America the Supreme Court can invalidate acts of the federal Congress or the state legislatures if they contradict the constitution. Courts with similar powers exist in Canada, Australia and Germany among other countries and, as we have seen, the European Court has similar powers in countries of the EU, including Britain.

Constitutional review
The process by which laws and other acts of the legislature can be overruled by a court if the court holds them to conflict with constitutional rules, human rights or other laws treated as superior to legislation.

When this sort of power belongs to a court its judges are clearly of political importance. Until recently most experts would have agreed that no such power belonged to English courts: no act of Parliament could be brought before a court and challenged as to its basic lawfulness (Scottish courts have asserted vague claims to do this on occasion, but have never actually done so). This is part of the general doctrine that Parliament is supreme and, ultimately, knows no constraint at all (Chapter 4).

This formal supremacy of Parliament also applies, of course, to governments, quangos, local government, and all other public bodies. Nonetheless these can by their actions render Parliamentary or even governmental action ineffective, and sometimes a dead letter. Thus it does not follow that, because courts cannot overrule state law, they therefore lose their political relevance. It is useful in this regard to note a seldom-mentioned fact about other national courts that have traditionally had the power of constitutional review – they seldom use it! Only a handful of congressional acts have been overruled in the USA since the 1930s, and in Canada, Australia and Germany the use of a court to veto legislation is even rarer. But no one will try to argue that these supreme courts are not politically important.

Of course, in recent years there has been a significant growth in the political importance of the English courts. The judges have developed the principles of judicial review to a point where they are now prepared to scrutinise the actions of all public bodies to ensure that their decisions are legal, fair and reasonable. Where fundamental rights or other important interests are at stake, this scrutiny may extend to examining the substance of decisions – as distinct from the legislation under which they are taken – made by ministers and other governmental bodies, even where it is claimed that Parliament has conferred complete discretion on the minister or body concerned. Moreover, where EU law is involved judicial review may even extend to acts of Parliament. This is not constitutional review in the strict sense of the term because the courts will not declare acts of Parliament unlawful as contrary to the constitution. But they may declare provisions of an act to be unlawful in so far as they deprive individuals of rights created by EU law (eg *Factortame*, see Chapter 8). In this sense it can no longer be assumed that primary legislation is legally unassailable. Now the Human Rights Act has come into force, the courts have the power to declare primary legislation to be incompatible with the provisions of the European Convention on Human Rights and to refuse to enforce it on these grounds.

EU law The treaties, legislation and case law of the European Court of Justice, which are the legal basis of the European Union.

The way in which the HRA operates in the English context is as follows:

- The HRA requires courts to interpret legislation in such a way as to be compatible with the ECHR if this is possible.

- If it is not, the court must issue a 'declaration of incompatibility'.

- Ministers will then come under political pressure to remove the incompatibility by using a 'fast-track' Parliamentary procedure.

- Ministers are required to issue 'certificates of compatibility' when bills are brought before Parliament stating that their content is compatible with the ECHR. The courts have stated they can give only limited weight to such statements since they are for political, rather than judicial consumption, and not based on detailed technical analysis in most cases.

- The HRA therefore increases the likelihood of disagreements between the executive and the judiciary. Indeed David Blunkett, the Home Secretary, speculated aloud as to whether it would be necessary to 'suspend the HRA' (in the wake of the terrorist attacks on New York of 11 September 2001).

- The courts have already made declarations of incompatibility in respect of provisions affecting individuals' human rights under the 2001 Consumer Credit Act (denying a court hearing if all its provisions were not exactly complied with) and the 2001 Mental Health Act (it is not for patients to prove they should not be detained but for those detaining them to show just cause).

- Of course, much of the exercise of power and control by the state in Britain does not involve the application to a citizen of statutes passed by Parliament. The courts exercise political influence in a variety of non-legislative ways, including the following:

  - Local authority bylaws are controllable by the courts, which may overrule them if they do not fit with the Parliamentary legislation authorising them. One example is the series of important cases in England during the 1960s that involved the 1961 Caravan Sites Act. Under this, local authorities were given great powers to plan and control the development of caravan sites. But their effective power to do so was severely limited by the Judicial Committee of the House of Lords, which used the empowering legislation, the Parliamentary act, to curtail and alter what the local authorities wanted to do.

– We should note that many Parliamentary acts do little more than empower ministers to reach decisions in conformity with often vague and general Parliamentary intentions. This discretionary power is entirely subject to control by the courts, with the effect that, though an act may not be overruled, most of the steps necessary to make the act do anything can be. In 2001, for example, the Home Secretary used his statutory power to designate Pakistan a country which did not pose a serious threat of persecution to refugees. This order was subsequently approved by an affirmative resolution of the House of Commons. A deportee challenged this in the courts. The minister claimed that a successful appeal would defy Parliamentary sovereignty. The Court of Appeal disagreed, arguing that the courts were able to overturn the minister's decision as the question had not been thoroughly debated in Parliament and was clearly wrong on the facts before the court.

– Although courts cannot formally overrule an actual act of Parliament that does not mean that acts are not considered by the courts. The vast majority of legal cases, whether they are between private citizens or between a citizen and the state (either as criminal cases or otherwise) involve statutes. No one asks a judge to say a law is not a law at all in Britain, as they sometimes do in the USA. What they ask is what the law actually means. This process is called interpretation, or 'construction'. It is in interpreting the meaning of the act, often a matter of dealing with very vague or general phrases, that judges have most of their power. The whole thrust of a piece of Parliamentary legislation can be changed, bent, reduced or increased in impact in this way, and all entirely legally. For example, the 1976 Race Relations Act was very considerably reduced in its ability to prevent discrimination between citizens of different racial backgrounds by two decisions of the House of Lords, which were presented as simply matters of 'interpreting' what the words in the act actually meant. In one case a local authority was allowed to refuse to give a council house to a man who had the legal right to live permanently in Britain, and who had done so for 20 years, and who was otherwise entitled to a house, simply because he was, in origin, a Pole. The court 'interpreted' the word 'race' to mean only colour, not nationality, so it was acceptable to discriminate between whites from different countries.

Constructionism
The practice whereby the courts define and interpret the meaning of acts of Parliament, especially where they are vague or general.

– In another case a political club was allowed to refuse membership to a card-carrying member of the relevant party because he was black. The Lords 'interpreted' a clause that forbade discrimination by anyone 'providing services to the public or a section of the public' in such a way as to allow this discrimination, although no one could possibly have thought Parliament wanted to let political clubs off the duty to be unprejudiced.

– Finally, our courts have enormous influence over the rules we all have to obey in our relations with each other, because much of criminal law and most of civil law does not come from Parliamentary acts at all, but from what is known as 'common law'. Common law is overtly made by the

19.4 Judicial autonomy: sentencing and dealing with criminals

The biggest problem, intellectual and practical, about crime, is what should be done about the sentencing of criminals. In the last 20 years it has become ever more clear that orthodox penalties imposed by courts have an entirely negligible impact on crime, either in terms of deterring criminal behaviour or reforming those convicted and imprisoned. This worldwide criminological finding is known as the 'nothing works' thesis. Research in many countries has shown that *recidivism* (the probability that someone once convicted will offend again) is completely uncorrelated with the sentences imposed. If there is any pattern, it is a social–psychological one related to offenders' age and sex: most crime is committed by males aged between 15 and 30. 'Nothing works' is a very strong finding, and it rubs against the 'common-sense' assumptions of many people, and of most Conservative politicians.

In particular, research shows that lengthy prison sentences have only one effect: to increase the probability that prisoners will reoffend, because they will have been further socialised by prison life into a criminal lifestyle. This general idea has been accepted by the Home Office for years, and efforts have been made to reduce the rate of imprisonment and substitute other sentences. Community service orders, for example, have been operative in Britain since the mid-1970s, and have been copied in most other common law countries. Probation services have been expanded and encouraged to find more sophisticated ways of dealing with criminals.

Although community service is doubtless preferable on humanitarian grounds to prison, research again suggests no real impact. Community service recidivism is neither better nor worse than recidivism from any other sentence.

All of this has long been accepted by professional criminologists, including those in the Home Office. Combined with their concerns about prison overpopulation it has led to increased efforts to reduce the use of prison sentences. These have all come to nothing, with prison populations rising inexorably year after year, and the recidivism rate staying constant.

The first effort was the idea of a suspended prison sentence. This simply increased the imprisonment rate, because so many reoffended that they ended up serving both the new sentence and the suspended sentence. Community service was introduced to replace prison at the 'lower end' of imprisonable crimes. However, the courts used such orders for people who would not have gone to prison anyway, and happily continued sending down everyone they would have sentenced to prison before.

Britain continues to have the highest per capita prison population of any major western democracy except the USA. Why do these reforms fail to reduce the number imprisoned in the face of indubitable evidence that prison does not work? Because the criminal justice system, once it gets to the courts, is completely out of the government's control; the judges simply will not take on board the government's, or anybody's, belief that imprisonment is useless in the vast majority of cases.

To the judiciary, sentences must follow, and only follow, the seriousness of the crime, and not the utility of the sentence. The most recent attempt by the government to restrict prison sentences and replace them with 'community correction', the 1991 Criminal Justice Act, is ineffective because it plays into the judges' hands by making 'seriousness' the test of what sentence is appropriate. It is drafted so loosely that no judge who wants to send someone to prison could possibly be prevented from doing so.

Precedent A decision or practice of the past that is accepted as a guide for the present. In the law, precedents are past decisions of the courts that are thought to apply to similar legal problems or situations in the present.

judges. It was the original law of the country before Parliament existed or bothered much about regulating private activities. It is a matter of tradition, a slow developing of rules based on previous cases known as 'precedents'. Most of the law of contract, for example, which regulates business activities, is still common law; what rule shall govern a contract drawn up between two private parties is essentially up to the judges and their ability to understand or to change the rulings in previous similar cases.

The principles of judicial review are all judge made. What is a fair procedure? When will a minister be held to have acted unreasonably? The answers to questions such as these cannot be found in any statute. Parliament has never legislated on the matter. But hundreds of judges over the centuries have made decisions that can be seen as containing rough and changeable rules.

All these powers go together to suggest that courts and judges are very important indeed. If the judges can create rules that we have to obey, alter rules created by Parliament or control the exercise of powers given to ministers and authorities by Parliamentary acts, are they not actually governing us, or at least influencing the way we are governed? Who then are the judges?

APPOINTMENT AND IDEOLOGY OF JUDGES

According to John Griffith: 'The most remarkable fact about the appointment of judges is that it is wholly in the hands of politicians' (*The Politics of the Judiciary*, London: Fontana, 1997). High Court, circuit judges and magistrates are appointed by the Lord Chancellor, who is a member of the government; the most senior judges are appointed by the Prime Minister after consultation with the Lord Chancellor. Almost all High Court judges are appointed from the ranks of QCs (Queen's Counsel), who are senior barristers. (The Lord Chancellor also decides which barristers are to become QCs.) An outside appointments commissioner now sits in on the process, and in September 2002 issued a highly critical report on its arbitrary nature, which favours older white males.

It is now unlikely that senior judges will be appointed because of their political allegiance to the Prime Minister of the day. Certainly, since Lord Haldane was Lord Chancellor (1912–15) appointments are believed to have been based on legal and professional qualities rather than political affiliation, as was the case in earlier years. Today 'being a known supporter of a political party seems to be neither a qualification nor a disqualification for appointment' (Griffith, op cit, p. 16). Senior appointments may nonetheless be politically controversial. For example, it is known that in 1996 the right wing of the Conservative Party 'strongly resisted' the appointment of Lord Bingham as Lord Chief Justice and Lord Woolf as Master of the Rolls following the retirement of Lord Chief Justice Taylor.

Because senior judicial appointments tend to be made from the most experienced barristers, the choice of candidate at any one time is extremely limited, possibly not extending beyond five or six suitable people. Officially no regard is had to gender, race, religion, secular orientation or political affiliation. But the fact that the potential number of candidates is so small inevitably means that the vast majority of judges are white, middle-aged or older males. Since they have spent their professional lives working as barristers they are overwhelmingly likely to have come from privileged backgrounds. There have been many studies of the social background of senior judges over the years. Overall these show that about 80 per cent of the senior judiciary are the products of public schools and of Oxford or Cambridge; that they have an average age of about 60; that 95 per cent are men; and 100 per cent are white.

Clearly, such a socially restricted group are likely to share particular attitudes and social and political orientations. How far does this affect their interpretation of the law?

Ideology of English judges

Because the courts have autonomy and political power, the legal culture in which they operate – that is, the implicit and informal criteria by which judicial decisions are made – is important. A significant question is whether the legal culture reflects or ignores popular attitudes and interests in society.

Judges themselves conceive the courts as neutral appliers of law, thinking of their function as 'deciding disputes in accordance with law and with impartiality'. The law is regarded as an established body of principles that prejudges rights and duties. Impartiality means not merely an absence of personal bias or prejudice in judges but also the exclusion of 'irrelevant' considerations such as their religious or political views. In contrast it has been claimed that judges in the United Kingdom:

> [C]annot be politically neutral because . . . their interpretation of what is in the public interest and therefore politically desirable is determined by the kind of people they are and the position they hold in our society; [and because] this position is part of established authority and so is necessarily conservative, not liberal.

Griffith, op cit, p. 336

This assertion is supported by the fact that the family and social background of judges is extremely privileged and atypical of the population. With a more formal training system for barristers, and with adequate incomes to be earned soon after admission to the Bar, the system of recruitment should be less exclusive in the future. But even then most barristers, and hence most judges, will not be ordinary citizens.

The same can be said of the personnel of most key institutions in Britain, including the Labour Party. So a more exclusive background is not necessarily associated with Conservative opinions. However, Griffith's main thesis is not that judges are conservative because of their upbringing and training. Judges are conservative because they are judges. The judiciary in every society, whatever the background of its individual members is bound to be conservative (with a small 'c'), since its task is to maintain order and the stability of the state. This implies respect for precedents and the established way of doing things.

Judges do not see themselves as free, and often give decisions that go against the grain. An example is Lord Hailsham who, as a member of several Conservative Cabinets, was unambiguously party political. He was giving judgment in a case where a woman was being prosecuted for breaking regulations on overcrowding in boarding houses, although actually she was running a refuge for battered wives:

> At the beginning of this opinion, I said that my conclusion, though without doubt, was arrived at with reluctance . . . This appellant . . . is providing a service for people in urgent and tragic need. It is a service which in fact is provided by no other organ of our much vaunted system of public welfare . . . When people come to her door, not seldom accompanied by young children in desperate states and at all hours, because, being in danger, they cannot go home . . . the appellant does not turn them away . . . but takes them in and gives them shelter and comfort. And what happens when she does? She finds herself the defendant in criminal proceedings at the suit of the local authority because she has allowed the inmates of her house to exceed the permitted maximum, and to that charge, I believe, she has no defence in law. My Lords, this is not a situation that can be regarded with complacency by any member of your Lordships' House, least of all by those who are compelled to do justice according to the law as it is, and not according to the state of affairs as they would wish it to be.

He then cast his vote against the side he undoubtedly favoured.

Similar examples are too numerous to mention. The extent to which judges believe that they are restricted by precedent and by a duty to follow Parliament is something that could not be exaggerated were it not that the orthodox view in English law, unfortunately, has exaggerated it. Perhaps there is no better example of this role belief than the voting in one case in 1972, *Jones* v *Secretary of State for Social Services*, which, as far as the facts went, was a nearly identical replay of a case in 1967. In the *Jones* case at least two Law Lords voted for Jones in order not to overrule the earlier case, even though they felt that both Jones and the earlier plaintiff were not entitled to win, and even though they acknowledged that the House has the right to reverse itself; so strong was their adherence to the principles of certainty and *stare decisis* (letting previous decisions stand).

The law, however, is often not clear, and judges have wide areas of discretion. What legal values guide them in this case, and are they systematically biased towards one political side rather than another? It is certainly the case that judges (and lawyers generally) are professionally trained into notions of restraint, caution, restriction, respect for property and family, and obedience for law. They also have a leaning towards conventional moral values. These are attitudes congenial to Conservatives in Britain but they are also values cherished by most Labour supporters. In other words, to equate generally conservative attitudes with politically Conservative attitudes on the part of judges also implies categorising the British population as a whole as Conservatives, which is obviously not correct.

One can put the idea of a politically Conservative bias on the part of judges to a partial test by examining their actual decisions in a number of cases. Judges who regularly vote in a way that, for example, protects individuals against state intervention by ruling against tax inspectors and planning bodies and so forth, but who very frequently vote to uphold criminal law convictions, might be seen as revealing pro-Conservative sympathies. If most judges voted in this way the bench collectively might be seen as Conservative. In fact even a partial check on the decisions of a few leading judges reveals considerable differences between them. It is hard to explain why these should exist if we have a consistently pro-Conservative bench. If judges divide among themselves (or incline to different sympathies on different issues) they are doing no more than reflecting general tendencies among the population and can hardly be singled out as politically biased on that ground.

Moreover, the great expansion of judicial review occurred during a period of Conservative government. In recent years the most controversial legal situations have involved conflicts between judges and Conservative ministers. Michael Howard, Douglas Hurd, Kenneth Baker and Margaret Thatcher all found themselves criticised by the courts. The experience of the last Conservative government does little to suggest that the courts are prejudiced towards the Conservative Party and much to suggest otherwise. But here again it may well be that seeking party political prejudice is beside the point.

More often judges decide on the basis of their own values and these are generally conservative. However, rather than seeing this as a deliberate attempt to impose their own views on the rest of us, it can more usefully be seen as evidence of weakness in the structure of our laws. When a judicial decision is not strictly determined by the legal/factual material before a judge, the judge is not only free, but forced, to give a decision that will have ideological undertones. There is no such thing as a 'neutral' decision in these circumstances.

Consider, for example, the decision mentioned earlier in which the Law Lords allowed discriminating practices on the part of political clubs. The judgment was criticised for using a restrictive definition that curtailed the reach of the Act. It has often been asserted that they should instead have extended the scope of the legislation. Perhaps they should. But had they done so they would not have been acting neutrally, but demonstrating another ideological bias. Wherever choice exists the choice made will be representative of some set of values. Neutrality in any absolute sense is hardly to be obtained.

JUDGES' VALUES AND COURT DECISIONS

From what has been said it is clear that judicial political values, often conservative in a general sense, slip into the system via structural weaknesses in the law.

The following are the most important situations in which judges are forced to exercise choice or discretion and in which judicial 'values' will play a part:

- interpretation of statutes where they are unclear

- inclusion within statutes of concepts that call for judges to decide an essentially unknowable thing, such as what a reasonable person would do, or whether a minister 'is satisfied that', or whether (more rarely) something is 'in the public interest'

- statutes that require judges themselves to use discretion with little in the way of guidelines, for instance family law cases where judges must decide themselves what is in the interest of a child.

We will now look at each of these in turn.

Statutory construction

This is the most important, because the most frequently found, of these situations. When a statute is unclear on what it requires a court to decide, the judge must find some way of removing what is unclear. Although there exist a host of rules for statutory interpretation they provide little real help. As with 'interpretation acts', they are best seen not as telling judges how to decide, but how to express what they have decided.

Basically, what judges have to do in such a situation is to try to work out what Parliament really intended when it passed an act. Until recently they were supposed to work only from the text of the act itself and, in theory, not supposed to take account of what was said in the relevant debate.

Although some of the difficulties of discovering Parliamentary intent are pragmatic, in that it is probable that Parliament had some intention relevant to the case and expressed itself badly, most cases are not like this. The worst problems of statutory construction arise because no one ever thought of a particular problem at all during the legislative phase, and so there is no intention there to be discovered! And, of course, the whole idea of Parliament's intention is often metaphysical: who is Parliament? The best approximation is probably that 'Parliament' means the people who actually composed the text and the secretary of state responsible for the bill's progress through Parliament.

These combined pragmatic and logical difficulties mean that, where lack of clarity exists in a statute, judges may resolve it only by putting themselves in Parliament's place and deciding what they would themselves have intended to do about a problem had they been the legislators. Indeed, this is precisely what judges are told to do by the Swiss rules for interpretation, which gain at least in honesty in that respect.

Other rules of interpretation, notably the 'plain words' rule, help to point out a further essential weakness in the structure of statute law. One must follow the literal meaning of a statute unless to do so would either be clearly unjust or lead to a situation that Parliament would not have intended. This is tantamount to saying that not only must judges use their own initiative where there exists a lack of clarity, but also that it is up to them to decide whether there is a lack of clarity. Remembering, of course, that the judge's task is to decide between two sides of an argument, both sides will often have plausible but very different views of what the legislation means. Statutory lack of clarity is not a practical problem that can, hypothetically, be got round. The judgement of when a statute requires interpretation is itself a political judgement. The law reports are full of cases where a statute that is the very model of linguistic clarity is deemed to require interpretation, not because it is hard to see what Parliament intended but because a judge was unable to believe that it *could* have intended what it did.

It is in the decision to use such interpretative powers that political ideology can most often be seen to invade judicial impartiality. Consider the two following examples of statutory interpretation. The first demonstrates a conflict between judges where there does appear to be genuine uncertainty about the meaning of a phrase. In the second the conflict is really not about verbal confusion but about whether Parliament could possibly have meant what it said.

In *Suthendran* v *Immigration Appeal Tribunal* the Lords had to decide the meaning of a clause of the 1971 Immigration Act, Section 14(1), which allows an immigrant 'who has a limited leave to stay' in the country to appeal against a decision of the Home Office not to extend that leave. Mr Suthendran, having entered as a student with a 'limited leave to stay' while he underwent a training course, defied the terms of his leave, took a job, and overstayed his permit. Various efforts were made, by him and by his employers, to get his leave extended and to get him a work permit, although none of these actions was taken until his original one-year permit had expired. He appealed against the Home Office's refusal to let him stay. Originally his appeal was upheld but later was rejected by the Immigration Appeal Tribunal on the ground that the Act clearly only granted the right of appeal to those who have, not to those who no longer have, 'a leave to stay'. Suthendran's appeal had not been lodged until some time after his permit had expired.

Is the Act unclear here? Can one say that 'has a leave to stay' automatically includes those who 'have had' but do not now have a leave to stay? The Lords were divided three to two on the issue, the majority denying Suthendran's appeal and upholding the Home Office's right to deport him. Divorced of context it might seem that the debate is trivial, but the political context introduced on both sides of the case important reasons for finding one way or another. The minority were worried at the potential injustice of the 'literal reading', for it would allow the Home Office to win dubious cases by delaying their decision on a request to remain until the original leave had expired and thus save themselves from a potentially embarrassing appeal. The majority felt it necessary to stick to the literal words of the Act. Although they did not say so, there was a political reason here too, in all probability. The reason is demonstrated by a case going on in the Court of Appeal at almost the same time: if immigrants manage to remain in Britain for five years they win an automatic right to permanent residence. The court clearly feared that, by indefinite delay and by using up all the various rights of appeal given in the Act, immigrants could prevent themselves ever being deported.

The majority in this case were what Americans term 'strict constructionists' (ie those who interpret constitutional law strictly). Lord Simon, one of the majority, said, for example:

> Parliament is prima facie to be credited with meaning what it says in an Act of Parliament . . . The drafting of statutes, so important to people who hope to live under the rule of law, will never be satisfactory unless the courts seek . . .

to read the statutory language . . . in the ordinary and primary sense which it bears in its context without omission or addition.

He goes on to admit that this must not be done were it to produce injustice but that 'it would be wrong to proceed on the assumption that the Secretary of State would act oppressively'.

The minority simply invert this last argument. Lord Kilbrandon said: 'Faced with two interpretations of this somewhat perplexing statute . . . neither of them altogether convincing, I prefer that which . . . at least avoids giving a statutory sanction to a possible injustice which I do not believe Parliament would knowingly have countenanced.' One thing is certain: no decision in this case would have been neutral, and nothing, other than a private feeling about what one would have done as a legislator oneself, can solve the problem presented.

Strict construction may, on occasion, require the more liberal of two possible readings. The next case demonstrates this, since three of the judges – Wilberforce, Dilhorne and Kilbrandon – heard both cases. Whereas Dilhorne was a strict constructionist and conservative in the *Suthendran* case, in *Davmond* v *SW Water Authority* he insisted that the words of the Act could not mean what they said and again produced a conservative judgment. Wilberforce, in the minority on Suthendran, now turns into a strict constructionist so as to render a liberal judgment.

Mr Davmond complained that he ought not to be required to pay a sewerage charge in his water rates because he was not connected to mains drainage. The statutory clause in question provides that water authorities can fix such charges 'as they think fit' and Dilhorne said: 'This section is silent as to the persons from whom water authorities can obtain payment of their charges. I find this most astonishing.' After insinuating that the government deliberately left this section unclear so as to avoid controversy in Parliament, Dilhorne went on to say that it was unthinkable that the intention was to allow water authorities to tax anyone in the UK, and proceeded to demonstrate that Parliament could only have intended to make those pay who actually benefit from a service. In so doing he rejected the argument, persuasive to Wilberforce and Diplock in the minority, that as local authorities had always had the right to pay for sewerage from a general rate, Parliament could not be seen as intending to remove this vital public health power from the new authorities, unless they said so. This second case, as the first, demonstrates that statutory interpretation necessarily involves private belief. How else could a judge first decide whether a clause was in need of interpretation and then go on to interpret it?

Inconclusive concepts

A second structural feature of the law is that statutes often require judges to interpret such notions as 'reasonable care'. In some other cases laws that appear to be 'hard' are, in fact, quite empty. A good example is the task set by the law on negligence when the courts have to decide whether people have exercised reasonable care. In public law the vital questions refer to a minister's judgement of a factual situation. Courts may hold ministers to be acting *ultra vires* where a statute empowers them to act 'if they are satisfied that' something is the case. Judges have to decide whether ministers considered anything they ought not to have considered, or failed to consider what they ought to have done. By their own testament, judges may not replace the minister's judgement with their own; they are entitled only to decide whether or not the minister could be satisfied of something.

These examples are even more pernicious than statutory interpretation because they pose problems only soluble by judges in fact doing what they are supposed not to do, that is, replacing a minister's judgement with their own. The Tameside case is one of the best known examples. The 1944 Education Act authorises the Secretary of State for Education, where he or she is satisfied that a local education authority (LEA) is acting unreasonably, to instruct them to desist. When a minister had been to court to enforce a decision that an LEA was acting unreasonably the House of Lords had a double inference problem: what constitutes 'unreasonable behaviour' by an LEA, and could the minister be satisfied in this case that these constituent elements existed?

The case centred round the cancellation, by a newly elected Conservative education authority, of plans to introduce comprehensive education due to go into effect in September 1976, the authority not being elected until the spring of that year. In particular the controversial point was whether the hastily reintroduced selection procedures would be fair, given the shortage of time to implement them, and a strike on the part of teachers who were angry at the abandonment of the comprehensive plans.

The Lords unanimously argued that 'unreasonable' must be taken not to refer to mistaken behaviour but only behaviour so guaranteed to create chaos that no reasonable LEA could possibly undertake it. On these grounds it was further argued that the Secretary of State, who only had 'to be satisfied' that the authority was acting unreasonably, could not have been considering the situation correctly, because there were no grounds on which he could possibly believe Tameside's new plan to be literally unreasonable in this way. It had to be borne in mind that the council had recently been elected with a mandate to maintain selection, despite the fact that the LEA in the end had to plan on doing the assessment of several hundred children, for only 200-odd grammar school places, in a few weeks, with a team of only a few teachers not joining the strike; and where, though there was testimony by some experts that it was possible, there was testimony by others that it was not.

Here the Lords had no choice but to put themselves in the minister's place. The only way they could possibly come to the conclusion that he was misdirecting himself in law was by considering the evidence available to him (and, actually, evidence not then available to him) and deciding that they did not think the authority was acting unreasonably.

This, naturally, is not the only case raising similar problems. In the past the courts' tendency has been to treat ministers' statements that they were satisfied with something as sacrosanct except when there was objective evidence that they had cheated. So in the classic case of *Padfield* v *Minister of Agriculture*, in the mid-1960s, a minister required to use his discretion in allowing or refusing a special investigation into the Milk Marketing Board was held to be acting *ultra vires* in refusing an investigation only because he had stupidly written a letter admitting that his action was dictated by party political motives. However, over the last decade, courts have increasingly felt able to say that a minister could not be reasonably 'satisfied', while at the same time insisting that they were not applying their own reasoning but objectively testing the minister's process of reasoning.

Often statutes as well as common law rules involve the idea of 'reasonable behaviour', or rest on what a 'reasonable person' would do in some situation. For example, one branch of family law entitles a court to dispense with the consent of a parent to the adoption of a child where that consent is 'unreasonably' withheld. On this criterion the Lords, in a case in 1976 concerning a homosexual father, felt entitled to ignore the father's objection to the adoption of his son. Although he wished only to be allowed to visit the boy for a few hours a week, in the mother and stepfather's home, they argued that no reasonable person could agree that a homosexual has something to offer his son. Certainly a conservative judgment by much modern opinion.

Discretionary judgments

In a vein generally similar to the last case considered, one must separately add those cases where the courts are not so much called on to vet another's decision as to make their own first-order decision. The second example discussed later is again taken from family law because it is an area where cases most richly demonstrate the inevitability of judicial ideology having a role. But the first example is more directly political.

This is no dramatic case of the overthrow of a Parliamentary statute by a powerful and independent judiciary, merely the 'automatic' application of a written law in a civil case against a local authority. In 1979 elections to the former Greater London Council (GLC) were won by the Labour Party, which campaigned on one issue above all others: it would introduce cheaper fares on London Transport. It was, therefore, a manifesto commitment. As soon as possible after its election it introduced an extensive flat-rate policy of cheaper fares under the general label of 'Fare's Fair'. But in order to cut the fares they had to increase the property tax on London residents. The GLC did this by telling the London borough councils to apply a supplementary rate. Most obeyed without question, and public transport fares in London dropped dramatically, although rates did go up. One Conservative borough council rebelled and appealed to the courts. The case did not come up until the London Transport Executive (LTE), under the instructions of the GLC, had completely restructured its transport plans and fare structures to fit the Labour Party manifesto.

When the borough council's case came to the High Court it failed, but they went on to the Court of Appeal under the presidency of Lord Denning. This upheld the appeal on an interpretation (ultimately accepted by the Law Lords) of one word in the governing act, the 1969 London Transport Act. This had a phrase which said that the LTE, under conditions set by the GLC, must organise transport 'economically'. Nobody in the country knows what, if anything, that was really supposed to mean. Most probably it was there as a caution against rampant inefficiencies. However, the courts saw it as very simple. It meant that London Transport must be run on a breakeven basis. It could not adopt any policy known ahead of time to be sure to incur a deficit, even if the relevant political elected authority asked it to do so and guaranteed to make up the deficit by a grant, financed from local taxation, which they had every right to levy. Whether or not such a policy is just, sane, politically admirable or whatever is no decision for us to make. But no more is it a decision for eight senior lawyers to make. This one decision had immediate and direct effects on a travelling population of nearly 10 million people. It also involved, in the estimate of the transport experts, an average fare rise of 150 per cent, in a world where almost no mass public transport system breaks even and during a period when it would throw a large number of newly employed transport workers out of a job in a city that already had more than 300,000 on the dole. Right or wrong, this was an enormous power to be exercised by an odd interpretation of one word.

But cases of less public importance can also reveal the extent of the power wielded by judges through their interpretations. In one typical family law dispute a father wanted custody of his daughter as his former wife, her mother, had died. He could offer a home with a perfectly adequate income, a wife (the daughter's stepmother) and a stepsister for the daughter, with a generally suitable background in terms of parental and sibling age. But he was challenged by his wife's

Plate 19.2 *MAC (Stan McMurty) cartoon in the* Daily Mail, *10 September 1996. A 12-year-old boy, beaten by his stepfather with a cane after he tried to stab another child with a kitchen knife, takes his case to the European Court of Human Rights*

Source: *Daily Mail* (Atlantic Syndication)

'Before you decide what action to take over my smashing up your car, father, I'd like you to meet my lawyer, my social worker and a bloke from the European Commission of Human Rights . . .'

mother, the girl's grandmother, known to the social services as bitterly opposed to the father and determined to make the child hate him. The father, by the same token, was accepted by social services as doing his best to help the daughter continue loving her other relatives. The job of a judge in such a case is to choose whatever is in the child's best interest. The High Court and the Court of Appeal both decided that the grandmother should have custody because the stepmother, now in her late twenties, admitted having been promiscuous as a teenager. Although most readers will agree with the social services' report in this case, firmly on the side of the father and stepmother's right to custody, no one can complain that the judges unfairly exercised a biased opinion. Yet again they were given no choice but to rule as their private attitudes required because there is no other solution.

Instead of this harrowing family law case we might have quoted a more traditionally 'political' example from, say, the Restrictive Practices Court, where judges are required, off their own bat, to decide whether some complicated trade arrangement is or is not in the public interest. We chose the family case only because it has an immediate subjective meaning for most of us. The problem remains the same in that judges are required to decide what is or is not in X's interest, in a political system that supposedly decides 'interest' questions through a pluralist electoral representative system. It is hardly surprising that they consult their private views and decide, in the family case, that the grandmother should have custody, and in restrictive practices cases readily accept high unemployment rates. Still, if Parliament insists on judges answering problems that legislatures and executives fight shy of, it can only blame itself if the answers are not always to their taste.

JUDGES' ATTITUDES AND THEIR POLITICAL ROLE

The political importance of the judges grew tremendously during the 1980s as they become involved in many facets of central–local relations as well as industrial relations. Conservative legislation created a whole corpus of new law in this area. It was no accident that the restrictions on trade unions, such as the prohibition of secondary picketing and the obligations to ballot their membership through a secret vote before undertaking strike action, were imposed as laws and given to the courts to enforce. By so doing the government intended to distance itself from actual enforcement of its constitutional victories over the trade unions, and give the provisions the aura of non-political technical expertise that judges enjoy. The current Labour government, with its policy of constitutional reform and the incorporation of the European Convention on Human Rights, has strengthened the political role of the courts further.

In enforcing the new labour relations restrictions in the 1980s the courts certainly did not act to reduce their impact. In imposing financial penalties on SOGAT 82, a print workers' union in dispute with Rupert Murdoch, owner of *The Times*, over his dismissal of many of their members, the Court of Appeal did not take into account, for example, that Murdoch had deliberately split up

BRIEFINGS

19.5 How has the EU affected English judges?

On the face of it the increased power of the European Court of Justice (ECJ) might seem to threaten the powers of English courts and judges, by limiting their independence of action and autonomy of judgement. In fact the opposite seems to be true. The activity of the ECJ has impinged on the higher English courts in three ways:

- It has encouraged them to take a stronger stand on judicial review of legislation in general, not just on EU matters.

- It has given English courts the power to suspend Parliamentary legislation if they think it runs counter to the EU treaties. While they have to refer the final decision to the ECJ, delaying the effects of legislation (often till after the next general election) could be tantamount to nullifying it.

- On specific interpretations of law the ECJ's often 'progressive' attitudes have nudged the English courts into a more supportive attitude towards, for example, gender equality.

It should be noted, however, that in most matters the ECJ simply enunciates general principles, in keeping with the practice of Continental supreme courts. It leaves to national courts the responsibility of deciding, for example, whether discrimination has actually taken place. This leaves ample scope for construction, interpretation and the other practices which give the courts their power.

his newspaper's holdings into separate companies. By picketing his distribution company (engaged exclusively in distributing *The Times* and its companion newspapers), SOGAT 82 were only technically engaged in illegal secondary picketing. They were actually carrying on their primary dispute against *The Times* by one of the few means at their disposal. Courts have emerged as strict constructionists on union legislation. If they have not sought to mitigate their consequences they have not sought to extend them either. This rather passive interpretation of their role paid off in terms of avoiding the overt hostility of trade unions. These concentrated on political support for the Labour Party, in hopes of getting the legislation modified, rather than on the tactic (counterproductive electorally) of attacking the courts that apply it.

In the less constrained field of local–central relations the courts' record was more mixed, sometimes upholding Conservative governments and sometimes Labour authorities. In the 1990s, however, the extension of judicial review increasingly involved them in conflict with the Conservatives, to the extent that they were openly criticised by leading members of the Major government. Such overt conflicts have not been so evident under New Labour, where the government itself is acceding to majority judicial opinion by incorporating the European Convention on Human Rights into English (and Scots) law. However, clashes have occurred with Labour Home Secretaries, notably on immigration and terrorist cases.

While the HRA enhances the political role of courts and judiciary it hardly creates it from new. If this chapter shows nothing else it demonstrates that the courts must take a political stance because: (a) it is inherent in many decisions they have to make; and (b) it is thrust on them by politicians in most pieces of ordinary legislation, let alone through the Human Rights Convention or the accession to the EU and the European Court of Justice, which force them to assess the 'compatibility' with them of British Parliamentary legislation.

In the absence of any other guidance, judges are prone to making judgments in line with their own class and career socialisation. The best ways of improving this situation are by, first, removing some ambiguity by writing down the constitution and taking more time on the wording of statutes; and, second, opening up recruitment to wider groups, particularly minorities and women. Lord Irvine, the New Labour Lord Chancellor, has taken a cautious step in this direction by making appointment criteria more transparent, but shrank from radically reforming the system. Thus it is likely that judges will continue to be drawn from a relatively narrow group, and continue to make conservative judgments (but with a small 'c').

ESSAYS

1. To what extent do judges want to make political judgements and to what extent are they forced into making them?

2. How would judges' decisions be different if they came from different social backgrounds?

3. What is meant by the 'political role of the judiciary'? Why is it increasing?

4. To what extent is the court system in England and Wales efficiently organised for the work it must do?

SUMMARY

This chapter has discussed the workings of courts and the thinking of judges, mainly with reference to the situation in England and Wales, but with applications elsewhere in the United Kingdom. It has concluded that:

■ Courts handle an enormous volume of work that would otherwise need political decisions. They thus substantially ease the general task of administering Britain.

■ The general political role of the courts has been growing. This is not just due to constitutional changes such as the superiority of EU law over British, and the adoption of the Convention on Human Rights. It also stems from the volume of politically related legislation (for example, the trade union laws) passed in the last 30 years.

■ In interpreting this and other legislation judges are often thrown back on their own reasoning because laws are ambiguous or unclear. Hence they have to use their own personal opinions as a guide.

■ Since judges are drawn from a narrow and exclusive social and professional group the criteria they apply are likely to be cautious and rooted in respect for precedents, property and established rights.

■ Recruitment patterns are not likely to be changed much in the foreseeable future so we may expect judgments also to continue along the same lines.

MILESTONES

Milestones in legal development 1846–2004

1846 County courts established for small civil disputes

1873–5 High Court established for major civil disputes. Court of Appeal established

1876 House of Lords becomes highest court of appeal

1949 Civil legal aid established

1953 UK becomes party to European Convention on Human Rights but the treaty is not incorporated into UK domestic law

1966 Law Lords decide that the House of Lords is no longer strictly bound by previous decisions

1972 Crown Courts replace assizes and quarter sessions

1972 European Communities Act incorporates EU law into UK law

1974 Juries Act abolishes property qualifications for jurors, who are to be drawn from the electoral register

1981 Supreme Court Act lays down current jurisdiction of the High Court and its three divisions

1985 Solicitors lose their monopoly over conveyancing

1990 Courts and Legal Services Act: barristers lose their monopoly of arguing cases in court; cases involving less than £25,000 to go to county courts; cases involving more than £50,000 to the High Court. *Factortame* case – European Court of Justice rules that UK courts can suspend the provisions of acts of Parliament that appear to contravene European law until a definitive ruling can be made

1994 Barristers' monopoly to appear in High Court abolished. Woolf Report, Access to Justice, recommends radical streamlining of civil litigation

1997–9 Substantial reforms of civil legal aid scheme imposed by government, cutting financial support to claimants and litigants

1998 Incorporation of the European Convention for the Protection of Human Rights into UK law

2000–3 Courts increasingly assert powers of judicial review of administrative decisions

FURTHER READING

The classic work on English courts and judges is J. A. G. Griffith, *The Politics of the Judiciary* (London: Fontana, 5th edn, 1997). Other useful books are R. Stevens, *The Independence of the Judiciary* (Oxford: Oxford University Press, 1993), and P. Madgwick and P. Woodhouse, *The Law and Politics of the Constitution* (Hemel Hempstead: Harvester Wheatsheaf, 1995). David Robertson in *Judicial Discretion in the House of Lords* (Oxford: Clarendon Press, 1998) deals in depth with the highest court in the system. On relationships between English (and Scots) law and Continental systems, see, for a specific review, Chapter 14 of Ian Budge et al, *The Politics of the New Europe* (London: Addison Wesley Longman, 1997).

Two useful articles on the changing relationship between politics and law, and politicians and judges in Britain are L. Foster, 'The encroachment of the law on politics', *Parliamentary Affairs*, **53** (2), 2000, pp. 328–46; D. Woodhouse, 'The law and politics: in the shadow of the Human Rights Act', *Parliamentary Affairs*, **55** (2), 2002, pp. 254–70.

PROJECTS

1. Find law reports for Scotland and for England and Wales that deal with a similar kind of case. On the basis of the law reports, determine the extent to which the different legal systems of Scotland and of England and Wales produce different results.

2. Analyse the reform of the English legal profession attempted by Lord Mackay of Clashfern under the Major government. Examine the reasons for its failure. Decide whether these would have applied to any attempt to reform the system or were peculiar to this attempt.

USEFUL WEB SITES ON POLITICS AND LAW

Hotlinks to these sites can be found on the CWS website at http://www.booksites.net/budge.

As a first step we suggest you visit the British Council web site, as it offers an excellent introduction to all the relevant aspects of the British legal system (www.britishcouncil.org/governance/jusrig/uklaw/system/). For more specific information on legal issues visit the Government Legal Service at www.gls.gov.uk. It might also be worth looking at the web site of the Law Commission for England and Wales (www.lawcom.gov.uk). In addition, The Government's Court Service (www.courtservice.gov.uk) is an executive agency of the Lord Chancellor's Department. It covers policy, legislation and the magistrates' courts' activities. The Crown Prosecution Service is responsible for prosecuting people in England and Wales charged by the police with a criminal offence; visit them at www.cps.gov.uk.

The process of European integration has strengthened the influence of the European Union in the functioning of the legal systems of all its country members. Visit the European Court of Justice at www.curia.eu.int. On the web site of the Council of Europe (www.coe.int) you have access to the full text of the European Convention for the Protection of Human Rights; the Human Rights Act is available at www.hmso.gov.uk/acts/acts1998/19980042.htm. The International Court of Justice represents a crucial step towards juridical globalisation; their web site is available at www.icj-cij.org.

A great deal of information and critical analysis is available from the Judicial Studies Board (www.jsboard.co.uk) and the Law Society (www.lawsociety.org.uk). Justice is one of the UK's leading legal and human rights organisations. You can visit them at www.justice.org.uk.

The police and policing

As the other institutional upholder of law and order, the police service to some extent share the same dilemmas as the courts, being forced back on their own judgements of priority since they do not have enough resources to enforce the entire (vast) body of existing legislation. The police in Britain link with both local and central government and the courts. Officially they are under the supervision of police authorities, composed in part of local councillors and in part of other local people and magistrates. Britain is almost unique in Europe in not having a national police force directly under the Ministry of the Interior (the Home Office). Instead it has many different, mainly local, police forces. The question of who actually controls them is ambiguous, as we shall see. But there is no doubt that control of the police is more dispersed than it is on the Continent.

The relationship of the police to courts and judges is more straightforward. The police uphold the law and work with the Crown Prosecution Service (CPS) to bring criminals to trial. However, since there is much legislation and only limited power to enforce it, the police are forced to set priorities about what laws they will act on, just as judges are forced to fall back on their own opinions. The police are not therefore just executors of policy made by local or central government or judges. They also make day-to-day policy decisions themselves, partly to pursue their own priorities but also because they may be forced to do so in the absence of clear guidance from elsewhere.

This chapter focuses on police in England and Wales and considers:

■ the principles, pressures and politics underlying and shaping modern policing
■ the history of the British police and how this influences the way they operate today
■ police accountability: for what are they responsible and to whom?
■ police procedures and the individual citizen
■ the politicising of policing
■ law and order legislation
■ EU legislation and policing
■ New Labour and the police.

WHAT ARE 'THE POLICE' AND WHAT DO THEY DO?

Police The civilian organisation established to enforce criminal law. The creation of the Metropolitan Police in London in 1829 marks the beginning of the British police force.

'The police' have been variously regarded as a key social and political institution, a law enforcement agency, a social service and a symbolic site of power. They can be regarded as homogeneous and treated as a complex organisation of hierarchical command, or as pluralist and as harbouring many conflicting goals and interests. Our own encounters with the police are primarily as individuals or groups. This chapter focuses on the organisational aspects and their relationships with other organisations. The chapter also focuses on policing in England and Wales, because the legal system in Scotland is rather different.

20.1 The police in Scotland

The development of policing in Scotland illustrates the original breadth of the term 'police'. Thus, from 1833, various nineteenth-century statutes authorised 'burghs' to adopt a 'code of "police", covering watching, lighting, paving, cleansing and water supply, and thereby to become "police burghs"' (Walker, 1992, p. 131). Authority was given to police magistrates and police commissioners. In the counties, paid police were established under Acts of 1839 and 1857.

The Home and Health Department of the Scottish Office oversees the eight police forces of Scotland. Walker (1992, p. 367) summarises the function of the police in Scotland as being to 'preserve law and order, to enforce a great volume of legislation, to search out and apprehend criminals and to report crimes detected to the appropriate procurator-fiscal'. In Scotland, the latter takes on the process of prosecution under the Lord Advocate. Hence the function of the police in Scotland does not differ greatly from that in England and Wales; however, the legal system within which it works is significantly different (Walker, 1992).

D. M. Walker, *The Scottish Legal System: An Introduction to the Study of Scots Law*, Edinburgh: Green/Sweet & Maxwell, 6th edn, 1992

Policing
The processes and arrangements, usually but not always involving the police, established to maintain social order. All societies have to maintain order and so all engage in policing, although not all do so through a civilian police force.

Legitimation
The process of making something morally acceptable in the view of the population.

It is important to distinguish between 'police' and 'policing'. 'Police' refers to a particular, established organisation found in some but not all types of society. 'Policing' is about the creation of arrangements for maintaining social order. All societies have to maintain order, so policing is an activity they all engage in, but not necessarily through 'the police'.

There are three major influences shaping modern 'policing' in Britain:

1. **Function** The police have to maintain order and prevent and detect crime. Doing this makes them highly visible participants in the community through their characteristic activities of patrol and surveillance. Their duties here also include control of crowds, gatherings, and other potential sources of disruption.

2. **Legitimation** The police have a great need to keep what they do acceptable to the public. Prevention of crime is difficult and the detection of offenders even more so. Both rely heavily on the goodwill and assistance of the public. Detection, in particular, relies on witnesses, confessions, informants, the general gathering of intelligence and, increasingly, the use of technology (eg matching databases, DNA testing and so on). These order-maintaining and investigative activities have to be seen to be legitimate and agreed to reflect the exercise of power on behalf of an elected body. The legitimated use of force by the police must be seen to be used on behalf of the community and at the behest of its elected representatives. It must not be seen to favour particular social or political interests above others.

3. **Autonomy** The police themselves seek to influence their own development. As a key institution of the state and as a large-scale organisation, the

BRIEFINGS

20.2 **Social workers and 'policing'**

Many organisations other than the formally constituted 'police forces' are concerned with 'policing' in a broad sense, ie surveillance of society and maintaining social order. The probation service is an obvious example but it is only one of the array of social services – usually local government departments – which not only provide for individuals but keep an eye on them. One good example is the concern of social workers with problem families and particularly the well-being of children. A wide interpretation of their powers of intervention led to scandals over a too-zealous use of these during the 1980s – often leading to children being arbitrarily taken away from parents whom social workers disapproved of.

This has led to a much more cautious approach in recent years, where action has been confined to enforcing specific legal provisions involving their clients. This has also followed from chronic under-staffing of social work departments. Their limited resources and high staff turnover result from bad pay and conditions. Social workers are, of course, as much subject to criticism, particularly from the media, for underuse as well as overuse of their powers, particularly on a retrospective interpretation of certain harrowing cases. Like the police and judges they are often forced to make difficult personal judgements because of the lack of clarity of the legislation and rules governing what they do. The fashionable stress on service delivery and efficiency has, in practice, put pressure to do more in less time and forced them into defining priorities on the basis of bureaucratic rather than client-oriented needs.

police seek to maximise their resources, power and status. This is not to say that 'the police' are a wholly unified body: there are conflicts and contradictions within the police service overall, between the 43 different forces, between ranks, between officers and so on.

These three underlying influences can be seen at work in all aspects of police activity we shall examine in this chapter.

BRIEF HISTORY OF BRITISH POLICING

Historically, policing was regarded as a communal responsibility and every adult male had an obligation to play his part. During the eighteenth century a wide variety of private and voluntary forms of policing flourished and initiatives to establish a formally administered system were rather piecemeal. By the mid-eighteenth century the system of watchmen was being criticised by many as inadequate, and in 1750 two magistrates, Henry Fielding (author of *Tom Jones*) and his brother John, sought improvements by creating a small force of their own, the Bow Street Runners. In 1798 another magistrate, Patrick Colquhoun, established a police force for the Port of London and in 1800 this became a statutory force, recognised and part-funded by the government. The Fieldings and Colquhoun were prolific social commentators on the problem of crime and the need for a police force, and their views were greatly influenced by the work of the Italian legal philosopher Cesare Beccaria and his 1764 *Essay on Crime and Punishment*. Beccaria's ideas were influential within the 'vigorous branch of political economy known as the "science of police"' (R. Reiner, 'Policing and the police', in M. Maguire et al (eds), *The Oxford Handbook of Criminology*, Oxford: Oxford University Press, 1994, p. 705). This 'science' embraced broader concerns about the governing and good order of the community than are conveyed by our modern and narrow notion of policing, and was promoted by political philosophers of such stature as Jeremy Bentham and Adam Smith.

Parliament was less enthusiastic, indeed hostile, toward such proposals, and Parliamentary committees considered and rejected the idea of a police for the capital in 1770, 1793, 1812, 1818 and 1822. Opposition to the proposal reflected a mix of concerns, including those of the landed and merchant classes wary about what a police force might do and the need for higher taxes to pay for it. There was also a general mistrust of the Continental model of state-controlled police and their association with spies and informers. The 1822 Committee thus argued that: 'It is difficult to reconcile an effective police force with that perfect freedom of action and exemption from interference which are the great privileges and blessings of society in this country.' Nonetheless, the Home Secretary of the day, Sir Robert Peel, finally saw his Policing Bill for the creation of a Metropolitan Police Force succeed in 1829. The foundations of modern British policing were laid by that bill and its provisions.

Among these were guiding principles that remain pertinent today. They emphasised the independence of the police from direct political control or interference, and strict internal disciplinary systems to prevent the unconstitutional abuse of authority. The police were also encouraged to develop friendly relations with the public, to be 'civil and obliging to all people of every rank and class', although never so far as to compromise their authority. The important legacy of this mix of the 'helping hand' and 'figure of authority' was the image of the 'benign British bobby'. A further consequence of earlier mistrust was the local nature of the forces set up outside London. These were created by local authorities to police their own area and were under the supervision of a local 'watch committee'. Despite amalgamations, the tradition of local forces with supervision by local representatives still survives and accounts for the patchwork of local forces that we have in Britain today.

From 1945 to the 1970s: consensus and controversy

As Reiner observes:

> The 1950s were the heyday of cross-party consensus on law and order, as on other social issues. The police were generally regarded as national mascots, totems of patriotic pride, routinely referred to as role models for the world. The pedestal on which the police stood is illustrated by the popularity of the TV series *Dixon of Dock Green*, in which the central character was a kindly, avuncular PC who captured the cosy stereotype of the British bobby which then prevailed in the public imagination.

R. Reiner, op cit, p. 710

BRIEFINGS

20.3 **Police powers**

The legal status of police powers has developed in a peculiar way. It is derived less from Parliament than from two typically British oddities of legal judgment: a 1930 High Court case concerning mistaken identity (*Fisher* v *Oldham Corporation*), and a controversial decision by Lord Denning in 1968. Under the former, it was held that a police officer is not the servant of the watch committee (ie of the representatives of the local council) but that police officers act on their own 'original' authority and are answerable only to the law. In the latter case, Lord Denning made a judgment regarding the Metropolitan Commissioner, which he clearly implied was equally applicable to all chief constables, defining their principal duty as being to 'enforce the law of the land' and arguing that the Commissioner:

> is not the servant of anyone, save of the law itself. No Minister of the Crown can tell him that he must, or must not, keep observation on this place or that; or that he must, or must not, prosecute this man or that one. Nor can any police authority tell him so. The responsibility for law enforcement lies on him. He is answerable to the law and the law alone.
>
> (*R* v *Metropolitan Police Commissioner, ex parte Blackburn* [1968] All ER 769)

This is regarded as a notoriously unsound judgment, with the legal commentator Lustgarten (1986, p. 64) remarking that 'seldom have so many errors of law and logic been compressed into one paragraph'. Nonetheless, this is where the law stands, and the outcome is that police officers wield great powers of discretionary decision making. These powers are facilitated by vague and ambiguous rules that have frequently been inadequate to specify appropriate conduct properly (Reiner, 1994, p. 725).

L. Lustgarten, *The Governance of the Police*, London: Sweet & Maxwell, 1986; R. Reiner, op cit

As the decade came to a close this cosy image was challenged by a series of scandals involving officers of high and low rank. Although by today's standards these incidents seem unremarkable, it was felt that public confidence in the police had been damaged. The Home Secretary established a Royal Commission in 1960 and its report in 1962 provided an overdue review of the role, organisation and accountability of the police. The result was a major piece of legislation, the 1964 Police Act. With regard to the question of accountability and restoration of public confidence, the most enduring contribution of the 1964 Act proved to be the tripartite mechanism for supervision of the police, involving the local authority police committee, chief constable and Home Secretary. For some time this seemed a reasonably effective structure, and it was only as society and policing changed that the inherent weaknesses of the model became abundantly apparent. Calling the police to account is far from being a straightforward matter; this stems from the distinctive basis of their constabulary powers that have been defined by the courts as inherent to the police themselves and not subject to scrutiny by outside bodies.

Perhaps more stringent requirements concerning accountability and appropriate conduct were seen as unnecessary while consensus reigned and the 'British bobby' was still a folk hero in the national consciousness. In fact we now know

Plate 20.1 *Peter Schrank cartoon in the* Independent on Sunday, *23 February 1997. Three men, jailed 18 years previously for the murder of Carl Bridgewater, were freed amid allegations of 'serious, substantial and widespread police malpractice' after new methods proved that the confession used to condemn the three had been obtained under false premises*

Source: *Independent*; Schrank

from autobiographies and archive research that, even in the 'golden age' of the 1950s, some members of the police service were rather flawed heroes. However, it was the exposure of corruption within the Metropolitan Police in the late 1960s and 1970s that truly tarnished the image, with members of specialist squads being charged with receiving bribes and corrupting the course of justice. 'Dixon' was laid to rest as journalists charted, in the title of a famous book on this period, *The Fall of Scotland Yard* (B. Cox, J. Shirley and M. Short, Harmondsworth: Penguin, 1977).

New structures

The first moves at post-war reform were not, however, procedural but organisational in nature, and were more related to the concurrent restructuring of local government than to burgeoning scandals. They stemmed from the report in 1962 of the Royal Commission mentioned earlier, the first since 1919. Their recommendations were effected through the 1964 Police Act, which, as a first step, combined many of the smaller forces.

Before the amalgamation consequent on the 1964 Act Britain had a very large number of local police forces – over 170. Apart from the Metropolitan Police covering London, and a few forces in the other larger cities, most forces were small by today's standards, some tiny. Their average size was probably around 600, and some were as small as 150. The small size and small area they policed made these forces very local, and local politicians had, one way or another, a good deal of influence over them.

There was, in fact, a sharp distinction historically between two sorts of police force: those in towns and cities, called the 'borough forces', and those covering non-urban areas, the 'county forces'. The borough forces were ultimately governed by local watch committees, essentially committees of the town or city council, while the county forces were controlled, much more loosely, by the county's magistrates. In fact, because there was a tendency to appoint upper class, ex-army officers as the chief constables in the county forces, there was little need for direct control. The concerns and attitudes of the magistracy and the chief constables coincided to a very large degree, and county force policy represented these interests.

The borough forces were nearly all commanded by professional police chiefs who had come up through the ranks, and there were occasional tensions between them and the watch committees, with the police wanting to take a more independent line. London has always been policed in a different way, with the Metropolitan Police and the City of London Police being commanded by commissioners directly appointed and controlled by the Home Secretary.

By the early 1960s the sheer inefficiency of having many small forces, combined with a growing concern about lack of uniformity, led to the appointment of a Royal Commission. This prompted an often impassioned debate about whether the entire structure should be thrown away and replaced by one national police force, accountable to Parliament, as is the model throughout the rest of Europe. The debate was often confusing because the key issue, which was accountability to political control, could be argued in several ways. Opponents of a national police force feared political intervention and the thought of a highly partisan police under government control. At the same time, many of the proponents of a single national force argued that there was far too little democratic control in the current system, and a single force would be more democratic because of its accountability to Parliament. The Metropolitan Police, it was argued, had never been politicised, even though controlled by the Home Secretary.

The legislation that followed in 1964 was a compromise, picking up ideas from both the majority and minority reports. The number of forces was to be cut enormously by amalgamations that ran across the old county–borough distinction. This happened in several stages, and there are now only 43 police forces in England and Wales. The smallest forces have at least 1,500 officers, and the average is around 3,000. A few, like the West Midlands Police, are much bigger than anything that existed before; one of its chief constables is on public record as saying he could not control it. Similarly, the Thames Valley Police, with nearly 5,000 officers, covers three entire counties.

POLICE ACCOUNTABILITY AND CONTROL

The question of control of these forces immediately became a serious problem, and has remained so. The 1964 Act envisaged a three-cornered control system, with political authority (and budgetary obligations) shared between the Home Office, chief constables and new bodies, called 'police authorities', consisting of both local magistrates and local councillors. However, the old question of how far these authorities could extend their control to details of police policy was left essentially as it had been in the county, rather than the borough, forces. The basic doctrine is that no one can give chief constables any orders about how to carry out their job. They can be sacked for incompetence, but not directed. As noted, the courts have held in subsequent case law that they cannot intervene to order a police force to do anything particular in the carrying out of their functions.

In fact, the police authorities have almost no powers. They need Home Office approval to appoint a chief constable; they can be ordered by the Home Office to dismiss their chief constable; and, because so much of the finance comes from the government, directly or otherwise, they hardly even have financial power over the police. (In fact it is also the Home Office that sets minimum and maximum staff levels, equipment tables and so on.) This situation finally became clear in 1988 in a major case where the Northumbria Police Authority tried to get the courts to forbid the Home Office from interfering with their own preferred policy. The case in question (*R* v *Home Secretary, ex parte Northumbria Police Authority* [1988] 2 WLR) is probably the most significant legal ruling on police and politics in the twentieth century.

The Home Office decided that it would authorise the acquisition of plastic bullets (technically 'baton rounds') for use by police forces, and hold these centrally for distribution to any force that convinced the Home Office inspectors of constabulary that they might need them. The chief constable of Northumbria decided that he might have a need for such weapons, but his police authority took the policy decision that he should not have them, and refused to approve his purchase of plastic bullets out of funds he was granted. The Home Office authorised him to have them. The police authority, outraged that their view of what was acceptable in Northumbria had been flouted, went to court, asking for an order to quash the Home Office decision. The court held that the Home Office did have the power to provide weapons to a police force against the wish of that force's own police authority. Even more, they held that the Home Office had this power, not because of the 1964 Police Act, but under the 'royal prerogative'.

What this means is that the central government has an automatic right to fix local police policy, whether or not Parliament has specifically given it this right! The only control on weaponry, and probably on any policy question where a chief constable wants something is, therefore, the central government. The powers of the police authority are simple: they are entitled to one yearly report by the chief constable on the activities of the force. They are also entitled to ask for other reports on specific matters. But chief constables can refuse to make these reports if they feel they should not give them! In contrast, the Home Office can demand any report or investigation it likes, and the chief constable must then report.

So the situation is that police forces are entirely under the control of the chief constables, subject to the Home Office. There are only 41 chief constables of English and Welsh forces. There are about a dozen inspectors of constabulary, and perhaps 50 policy-level civil servants controlling the use of police throughout the UK. This is a significant level of elite power.

The question arises whether this situation constitutes a move towards a national police force. The debate on a national force has never been properly resolved. Most chief constables themselves do not wish for one, and no government has ever suggested its creation. But it is often suggested that a de facto national force already exists. Some critics have even argued that the government prefers to have a system that operates effectively as one force but with the formal trappings of a series of separate forces. This way, it is argued, Parliamentary control is avoided, making the police force even more independent of democratic control than it would otherwise be.

The basic argument behind the thesis that Britain has a de facto national force rests on the fact that there is a small national police elite from whom all senior police officers are recruited. Apart from chief constables themselves, there are two other ranks – deputy chief constable and assistant chief constable – that make up the membership of an extremely powerful pressure group, the Association of Chief Police Officers, usually known as 'ACPO'. These senior officers, and junior colleagues aspiring to membership, share a closely integrated set of experiences. They have all been on senior officers' courses at the police college in Bramshill; they all have some sort of national experience, for example, being a staff officer to an inspector of constabulary or being seconded to the Home Office; and they have all served in several forces, almost certainly including a stint in 'the Met'. Their career patterns are interesting. Although they have all started as constables, and will usually have taken seven or eight years to become sergeants, they will have gone through the next five ranks, to assistant chief constable, at the rate of about two years per rank. They are high-flyers, and the need to move from force to force in order to fly so fast leads to a much more national outlook. As with any small elite, these officers know each other well, have attended endless courses and seminars together, and have formed their ideas and attitudes in concert. Most important of all, they are members of ACPO. (ACPO membership is open to those of assistant chief constable rank upwards and equivalent rank in the Metropolitan Police.)

As is typical in Britain, ACPO is not an official governmental organisation, and technically is simply the professional organisation of senior police officers, part-trade union, part-club, part-official representative for professional views, something like, say, the British Medical Association. However, it is funded by the Home Office and it is ACPO that selects delegates to Home Office conferences and committees. The importance of ACPO became particularly apparent during the 1984–5 miners' strike. The problems of policing the picket lines were beyond the capacity of any one force so ACPO invoked the use of an established agreement providing for a National Reporting Centre (NRC) to co-ordinate demand and supply of support to forces policing the dispute. Although technically chief constables could refuse to co-operate with other forces, the Home Office made it quite clear that they would use legal powers to enforce co-operation if the NRC did not work. The felt need to co-operate was intense, and at least in terms of staff supply the British police became effectively a national force, under ACPO control, for over a year.

The arrangement produced a nationally co-ordinated policy of providing police support to colleagues under pressure and putting up roadblocks to prevent convoys of pickets rushing to particular collieries from all over the country. Effectively, this meant that operational decisions in some areas far from the crisis points were being made in the light of operational needs hundreds of miles away. (The policy was, incidentally, of very dubious legality.) Chief constables deny that ACPO and the NRC constituted a national force. But significantly, what they have also argued is that if they had not organised themselves unofficially the government would have created an official national force. It is unclear that saying there is no de jure national force because there is a de facto one means very much. This combination of independence from local control, dependence on the Home Office, a small national elite of common-minded professionals, and ACPO's co-ordinating role, adds up effectively to a national force. Other factors, such as the increasing importance of specialised units, nearly all run by the Metropolitan Police, and a serious concern for a uniform position to be taken in Europe as the frontiers go down, encourage this move to centralisation.

POLICE PROCEDURES AND THE INDIVIDUAL CITIZEN

There have been two crucial changes enforced by recent legislation that have materially affected police work. The most important was the passing of the 1984 Police and Criminal Evidence Act, known universally as 'PACE', which was partially based on the report of the Royal Commission on Criminal Procedure published in 1981. This Act is hard to assess objectively because it managed to offend both civil libertarians and the police. Civil libertarians object, for example, to the general power the Act gave to stop and search people or vehicles where an officer has reasonable grounds for suspecting possession of stolen or prohibited objects. In fact, to a large extent, this part of the Act just formalised a mass of separate stop and search powers and probably did not change police procedure very much (although the impact of the MacPherson report (see later) was to increase the degree of caution in use of stop and search). Civil libertarians remain critical of the Act because ACPO's evidence to the Royal Commission stressed the need for new legal powers for the police and in many ways PACE provided these. However, PACE also introduced measures that the police did not welcome.

Civil liberties
The freedoms that should not normally be constrained by others, whether private individuals or the state.

PACE enormously changed procedures for questioning suspects and for taking down what they say and any statements they make. Police critics of the Act argue that they are seriously hampered by the need to tape record all interviews, and to have a complete and contemporaneous account of the entire interview process. Second, a suspect's rights to have a solicitor present, and to say absolutely nothing to the police, mean that police cannot risk detaining and interrogating anyone until they already have enough evidence to win a committal in a magistrates' court. In other words, they have had to abandon the practice of relying on getting a confession because they do not have enough evidence otherwise. (There is still pressure to make a conviction impossible merely on the basis of a confession, which is already the law in Scotland.)

In fact, PACE has simply put into a formal statute rights that already existed in judges' rules, making them very much more effective. In the words of one expert: 'The old informal procedures for crime control, based on fabricating evidence, have had to go.' It is interesting to note that the post-1980 series of acquittals in the Court of Appeal of people wrongfully convicted years earlier nearly all stem from the days before PACE.

PACE had an interesting side-effect on statistical measures of police effectiveness. The 'clear-up rate' for crime declined substantially. In part this is because, before PACE, detectives could often persuade offenders to confess to a series of other crimes that they would ask to be 'taken into consideration' (TIC) in court. Criminals are very much less willing to co-operate with police in this way now, and 'TIC' clear-up has dropped considerably. The fact that police were so dependent on these admissions, and the question of just how people were persuaded to co-operate in this way (against their interest, because a court was likely to increase the sentence if there were a number of TICs) suggest PACE was very much needed.

The second statutory restriction on the police to come out of the 1981 Royal Commission was the creation of the Crown Prosecution Service (CPS) by the Prosecution of Offences Act 1986. This is, constitutionally, a more radical change than PACE, which (at least in theory) simply gave statutory recognition to received practice. Before the setting up of the CPS England and Wales had a system quite unlike that of any other western democracy. Everywhere else in the world there was a sharp distinction between the job of detecting crime and the task of deciding whether or not to prosecute and handling the prosecution. In Continental Europe the decision to prosecute (as well as the supervision of much of the investigation) is in the hands of a member of the judiciary called an examining magistrate. In Scotland an official rather like the examining magistrate, the procurator-fiscal, plays this role. In the USA these decisions are taken by an elected district attorney (or a politically appointed one in the case of federal jurisdiction).

But in England and Wales the police themselves decided whether or not to prosecute. In the magistrates' court they themselves handled the prosecution and in higher courts they instructed counsel themselves. Now all such decisions are made by solicitors who are full-time salaried officers of an independent service, organised regionally but under the ultimate control of the Director of Public Prosecutions, a central government officer who had always had this power for certain very serious crimes.

The previous fusion of responsibilities mattered principally because there is always a considerable element of discretion involved in the decision to prosecute, and in what evidence will be used by the prosecution. Discretion covered both which crimes to prosecute and when to prosecute any particular offender. There may be some value in discretion in the first sense, because community standards on, say, pornography, do vary. In fact, the police can still exercise some discretion in this area by simply refusing to investigate crimes they do not want prosecuted, given that the police authority cannot order them to act. The police also used their discretion not to prosecute cases that were simply not worth taking to court.

This use of discretion was effectively using court appearances as a method of social control, as a policing activity, rather than as a legal consequence of clear guilt. For example, police often merely cautioned, or simply talked to, young offenders guilty of minor affrays or disturbances of the peace. But if there were complaints about behaviour on a certain housing estate they would suddenly start to prosecute instead. It was an inappropriate use of the discretion to prosecute. The CPS uses objective, nationally determined guidelines in this sort of case.

Discretion on whether to prosecute really depends on how high a probability of conviction there should be before a prosecution is launched. The rate of conviction in a jury trial where there is no plea of guilty often surprises people, because it is only around 70 per cent. As the cost and suffering of going to trial can be devastating, even for those acquitted, no prosecution should be launched lightly, however certain the police may be in their own minds that they have the right person. There is no doubt that the Crown Prosecution Service demands a significantly higher probability of conviction before they will prosecute than the police used to expect. The CPS is also keener to check that evidence is reliable and all police procedures watertight, thus further enforcing civil rights against police enthusiasm.

THE POLITICISATION OF POLICING

During the 1970s the police and their role became increasingly politicised, reflecting a broader social context of tension and conflict. Political and industrial protest, and the anxieties provoked by rising crime rates, led to a new strategy put forward in the Conservative 1979 election campaign. Suddenly, providing more policing was given equal (if potentially contradictory) priority with the promise of reducing taxation. As Mrs Thatcher declared (28 March 1979): 'The demand in the country will be for two things: less tax and more law and order.' The support of the 'rank and file' Police Federation was immensely valuable in making 'law and order' a vote-winning issue for the Conservatives. Deeply hostile toward Labour after a pay dispute in 1977, the Federation provided a well-publicised, openly political endorsement of Tory policy.

Once elected to government, the Conservatives delivered what they had promised to the police: greatly enhanced pay awards and increased budgets for recruitment and resources. In turn, the police were supposed to deliver their part of this bargain. They had been given the rewards in advance; now there could be no excuses for losing the 'fight against crime'. Of course, once mutual admiration and rhetoric were put aside, it became apparent that the practical problem of crime control could not be reduced to a simple formula of 'more police equals less crime'. Crime rose and, with fluctuations here and there, it continued to do so throughout the 1980s, although the statistics improved somewhat in the 1990s.

While this suggested that 'more policing' was not working, two key and symbolic episodes of the first half of the 1980s kept the police high on the Thatcher government's list of 'favourites'. These were, first, the inner city riots of 1981, and, second, the miners' strike of 1984–5.

In urban riots then and since the police have first contained disorder and then moved in to enforce order. Their efforts at 'community policing' after rioting, in line with the Scarman Report of 1981, helped prevent further outbreaks of protest

20.4 Political aspects of policing

Discrimination, minorities and the police

Prejudicial treatment of minority groups has long been a key issue for critics of the police. Considerable evidence suggests that, while police policy has belatedly but increasingly sought to stamp out sexual and racial discrimination and increase recruitment of ethnic minority officers (Holdaway, 1991), prejudice nonetheless remains part of what is known as the 'canteen culture'. In everyday policing, the disproportionate 'stop and search' of black youths has been one expression of this.

Tensions between black youths and the police were the volatile background against which the inner city riots of 1980–1 flared, first in Brixton, south London, and then in Toxteth, Merseyside; Moss Side, Manchester and Handsworth, Birmingham. The first event was investigated by a senior judge, Lord Scarman, whose Report on the Brixton Disorder (1981) made recommendations concerning the need for police and community consultation. The government expressed gratitude to the police for their efforts in containing such outbreaks of inner city disorder.

The miners' strike: the police in a political dispute

The miners' strike is significant for what many saw as the political use of the police by the government and for the operation of a national command and control strategy through the National Reporting Centre (NRC). The NRC has no statutory basis but arises out of agreements first reached in 1972 within the Association of Chief Police Officers (ACPO) and can co-ordinate all 43 forces of England and Wales in combined operations. This agreement was in place before the miners' strike but it was its employment in this context that suggested to some that it provides a de facto national riot police (after the dispute the NRC was renamed the Mutual Aid Co-ordinating Centre). Home Office ministers and chief constables have traditionally argued that Britain does not and should not have a national police force but should be responsive and accountable to local interests; that this renders them less susceptible to central and politically inspired direction by national government.

The legacy of the miners' strike was to expose the emptiness of such an argument, given a government that was prepared to use the police in pursuit of its political objectives.

S. Holdaway, *Recruiting a Multi-ethnic Police Force*, London: HMSO, 1991

(though 20 years later controversy again rose around police and community relations leading up to and following riots in Asian communities in Bradford and elsewhere).

Financial scrutiny and the push for reorganisation

Inevitably, however, the police came under financial scrutiny. As crime rose, despite high investment in police pay and resources, the yardstick of 'value for money' was introduced. The first step in this direction was the 1983 Financial Management Initiative requiring the setting of objectives and priorities, efficient allocation of resources, and the planning of policing. After a period of relative immunity from public expenditure cuts the police now experienced the push

20.5 Police effectiveness and 'value for money'

Just how effective are the police? In recent years the adequacy of government policy concerning law and order has become more and more politically sensitive. The increase in the importance of the issue has come about largely because, until the 1997 general election, the Conservative Party had always been able to present itself as much more concerned about law and order than Labour, and Conservative governments since 1979 considerably increased resources for crime control.

It is necessary first to get some sense of scale on the problem. Talking to the Police Superintendents Conference in 2002, the Home Secretary, David Blunkett, announced that police numbers in England and Wales were the highest on record and now totalled 129,603. This included 20,000 in the Metropolitan Police, but not around 40,000 civilian employees. This makes the English police roughly half the size of the French police, and not much more than one-third the size of the Italian forces; that is, Britain has roughly one police officer for every 450 inhabitants, France one for every 250.

Second, unlike their European counterparts, the British police are a general duty and entirely civilian force, handling every aspect of policing. Elsewhere in Europe, the police are more functionally specialised, usually with a paramilitary organisation like the French gendarmerie or the Italian carabinieri who are primarily responsible for public order. It is a predominantly (although decreasingly) unarmed force, and one that has always tried to police consensually.

In this last respect the British police have probably improved since the severe criticisms of heavy-handed tactics in the 1981 Scarman Report. Usually senior officers will avoid using serious force to contain ethnic rioting in case it exacerbates the situation, although this has not been the policy in industrial disputes. On the whole this has paid off, and public order policing is fairly effective without being too oppressive. In the other sense of use of force, the use of deadly force with firearms, there has been a clear rise in the number of criminals, or disturbed people, shot to death by the police in recent years. But the total numbers are too small to constitute a significant rise.

Assessing how effective the police are in detecting and 'clearing up' crime other than public order offences is a methodological nightmare. Crime statistics are unreliable. Taking an uncritical view, property offences continue to dominate recorded crime, accounting for 91 per cent of all notifiable offences recorded by the police in England and Wales in 1997. Over half of theft offences and one-quarter of all recorded crime are vehicle-related theft; 23 per cent of recorded crime are burglaries; 1 per cent are drug offences (including trafficking and possession) and public order offences. Violent crime (including violence against the person, robbery, sexual offences) accounted for around 8 per cent. The detection rate, however, remains very low: roughly one-third of crimes are cleared up, with the rate dropping marginally every year.

It should immediately be noted that, even were these figures reliable, they do not justify the use that some politicians make of them. Nine-tenths of all crime is crime against property, and the overwhelming bulk of that is very minor, where the cost of the stolen or damaged property is less than £200, and often very much lower.

toward centralisation and privatisation already applied to most other public services. The language of accountancy became paramount, with HM Inspectorate of Constabulary (HMIC) being given a more substantial and critical remit to monitor efficiency (as measured by a 'matrix of performance indicators'), and the Audit Commission and National Audit Office also evaluating aspects of policing.

20.6 **Should policing be privatised?**

The 1996 Home Office Review was widely expected to take the privatisation agenda pursued elsewhere and push it firmly and radically into the province of policing. With relative ease the government had already accomplished the previously unthinkable feat of (partially) unhitching the State from the administration and delivery of punishment. It had done this by contracting out the building and/or the management of some prisons to the private sector and turning the prison service into an 'agency' with a director appointed from outside the sector. On this basis the idea of privatising criminal justice still further seemed a highly likely reality. Indeed the police had always seemed a more likely candidate for the privatisation agenda than prisons. There was little twentieth-century precedent for the latter. Yet a key feature of the provision of police services in western societies since the 1960s has been the phenomenal growth in private security companies. Policing is now provided by a mixed market but the question remains: how much further can the privatisation of policing go?

T. Jones and T. Newburn, *Private Security and Public Policing*, Oxford: OUP, 1998

The police responded with hesitant and small-scale reforms but not to the satisfaction of the government. By the 1990s more far-reaching changes were envisaged, first through the 1993 Sheehy Report on pay, conditions and rank structure, and then through a 1996 Home Office Review of Police Core and Ancillary Tasks. This raised the question of how far 'public' policing could be privatised.

Both initiatives were embarrassing failures for the government. The Sheehy Report attracted derision in the press, criticism from a significant alliance of Labour and police, and faced a highly organised and high-profile opposition from the united police ranks. The result was serious dilution of Sheehy's recommendations.

The second initiative, the 1996 Review of Core and Ancillary Tasks, was supposed to fit in with the government's drive to push services into the market sector wherever possible. However, the promise of a 'big bang' actually resulted in little more than the 'whimper' of transferring various minor tasks to local authorities and private companies. In hindsight the fate of these two attempts to reshape policing in Britain were signals that the Tory law and order engine was running out of steam.

As relations between the police and the Conservatives deteriorated, so they warmed with Labour. The culturally conservative character of the police might have reacted strongly and adversely against the 'loony left' of the old metropolitan administrations but the sound bites of emerging 'new realism' in the Labour Party were rather more palatable.

Across the floor

Views of the police from Labour and the left have varied over time and their history under the Blair governments is now of particular interest. In the 1960s some on the left argued that changes in the strategy of policing, with moves to patrol cars and 'firebrigade policing' (ie responding to calls rather than being on the beat), meant that the police were increasingly remote from the communities they served. The corruption cases of the 1970s, followed by revelations about the number of deaths in police custody (274 between 1970 and 1979), sparked further distrust (even though most – but not all – deaths arose from natural causes). Police confrontations with demonstrators and strikers created 'a suspicion in the Labour Party and the trade union movement that the real function of the police is to maintain the inferior and subordinate status of the working classes' (Howard Elcock, in Philip Norton (ed.) *Law and Order and British Politics*, Aldershot: Gower, 1984, p. 157). The local elections of May 1981 were particularly significant, with the councils of all of the (then) metropolitan areas now being dominated by radical Labour. These provided critical power bases for the questioning of police policy, generating acrimonious but important debates about the actual nature of police accountability and leading to several high-profile clashes between police authorities and chief constables. Given this history of Labour antipathy towards the police, post-1979 Conservative administrations had good reason to think that their stance on the police and 'law and order' was far more appealing to the voters. There were some in the Labour Party who took note.

In terms of the recent realignment of British politics it is interesting (although unsurprising given who was involved) that it was the issues of crime and policing that provided an early indication of new Labour thinking on social policy. In early 1993 the Home Secretary, Kenneth Clarke, was in debate with his 'shadow', Tony Blair, on *The World This Weekend*. An apparently 'off-the-cuff' (but actually well-rehearsed and polished) proposition from Blair encapsulated a new Labour approach to policing and crime control. The sentence 'We need to be tough on crime and tough on the causes of crime' surprised Clarke, and immediately passed into the newspeak of New Labour. As Home Secretary, both Jack Straw and David Blunkett, among the closest associates of the PM, have been responsible for the 'being tough on the crime' (and terrorism) parts of the package. Both have been much criticised by human rights groups for their restructuring of immigration policy and in particular for proposals to streamline court procedures, limit jury trial and restrict the rights of defendants. At the same time the government's particular stress since 2001 on efficient service delivery has also led to confrontations with the police, as with other public sector workers, on unpopular changes in working practices in return for pay increases. All this seems not dissimilar from the experience of previous, Conservative, Home Secretaries.

POLICE, PUBLIC, AND THE LAW

In reviewing the law relating to the police since the 1980s the first point to make is that there has been a great deal of it! This is partly related to the stamp that successive Home Secretaries wished to make on policy, but was also driven by electoral strategy, the need to be constantly producing 'new ideas'. The key piece of legislation is undoubtedly the Police and Criminal Evidence Act 1984 (PACE), already discussed. Subsequently legislation on police powers was produced at a furious pace, from the Public Order Act 1986 to the Police and Magistrates'

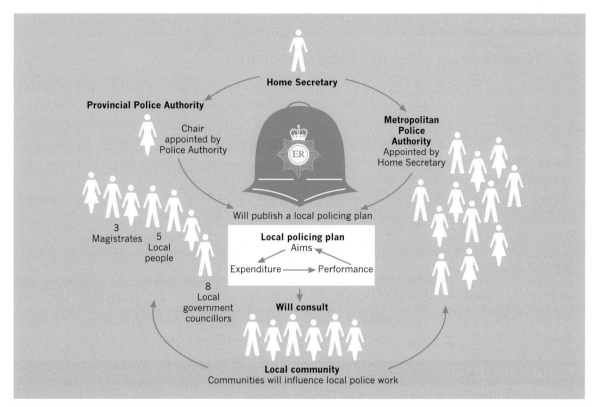

Figure 20.1 *The new police authorities of April 1995*

Courts Act 1994 and then the 1998 Crime and Disorder Act which placed a responsibility on the police to work with the local political authority and other services with the aim of reducing crime.

The 1994 Act, in particular, reshaped the tripartite structure of police account-ability noted earlier, reducing membership of the police authorities, giving them wider powers within a 'business-oriented' brief, and making them accountable to the Home Secretary. Critics say that these committees are now little more than mini-quangos and are far from being democratically representative of local people. Figure 20.1 shows the structure of the new police authorities.

Clearly the strengthening of police powers was one of the dominant motifs of 'law and order' legislation since the 1980s. Some obviously felt that the wisdom of this trend was highly questionable as another and darker theme emerged in parallel. This concerned the misuse of police powers and the miscarriage of justice. A dramatic sequence of appeal cases, from the early 1980s through to the mid-1990s – and continuing – has revealed serious police malpractice (eg sup-pression or falsification of evidence and wrongful arrest) resulting in appalling miscarriages of justice. Earlier disclosures of corruption had, it seemed, produced few enduring lessons for the police. As David Rose remarks: 'If police detectives could steal or take bribes, it did not take a vast leap of the imagination to consider

BRIEFINGS

20.7 Recent cases of wrongful imprisonment

The *Birmingham Six* were imprisoned for causing explosions in Birmingham pubs in 1974 in which 21 people were killed and 162 injured. The six were freed from jail in 1991 and cleared of charges.

The *Bridgewater Four* were found guilty of murdering 13-year-old Carl Bridgewater in 1978. The four were later released and cleared because police evidence against them was found to be wrong.

The *Guildford Four* were found guilty in 1975 of causing an explosion in a Guildford pub frequented by British soldiers. They were freed in 1989.

Stephan Kiszko was found guilty of murdering a young girl and imprisoned in 1976 but was released in 1992 when it was found that evidence of his innocence had been withheld.

Stephen Downing, 44, was freed in 2001 after being jailed for life in 1974 for the killing of typist Wendy Sewell. He was then 17 but had the reading age of an 11-year-old. He was convicted mainly on the basis of a confession obtained after he had been interrogated by Derbyshire police for more than seven hours, during which time he had to be shaken awake and officers took bets on whether he would confess. He was never informed by police that he was under arrest or in custody and was not told of his right to consult a solicitor.

BRIEFINGS

20.8 The 'Ways and Means Act': canteen culture and police deviance

Police accountability always faces the problem of balancing strict application of rules with the need to allow operational flexibility. This is generally accepted within reasonable limits. However, such limits may be unacceptably stretched by the informal police culture (often called the 'canteen culture'), and invocation of the fictitious 'Ways and Means Act' as a form of justification. An important investigation of police culture and police perceptions of the public was a study commissioned by the Metropolitan Police and undertaken by the Policy Studies Institute (PSI) in the early 1980s (Smith and Gray, 1983). The research found evidence of disturbing levels of racism and sexual discrimination (still a problem according to recent reports of Her Majesty's Chief Inspector of Constabulary (HMCIC), 1998, 1996) (the 1999 Macpherson Report on 'institutional racism' within the police service is discussed later). The PSI report also distinguished between three types of 'rule' within police culture: the 'working', the 'inhibitory' and the 'presentational' (ibid, pp. 169–72). The first type represents the 'accepted' way of working but is by no means always in line with formal regulations. Inhibitory rules are formal rules that carry organisational weight and must therefore be followed, even if seen as unnecessary by officers. Presentational rules highlight the disparity between how the police are supposed to act and how they actually act. As Reiner (1996, p. 730) summarises: 'Presentational rules are those official rules which have no bearing on police practice, but which none the less provide the terms in which accounts after the event must be couched.' The continued existence of such organisational sources of resistance to management supervision and public accountability is a strong reminder that the internal politics of the police are far from transparent.

D. J. Smith and J. Gray, *The Police in Action*, London: Policy Studies Institute/Gower, 1983); Reports of HMCIC, London: HMSO, 1998, 1996 that they might also present evidence produced by fabrication or duress' (*In the Name of the Law*, London: Jonathan Cape, 1996, p. 43). The cases exposed present a dismaying picture of dishonesty, impropriety and callousness on the part of some police officers. Notable were those of the Birmingham Six, the Guildford Four, Stephan Kiszko, the Bridgewater Four and Stephen Downing in 2001, all judged to have been wrongly convicted.

Unsurprisingly, a recurrent concern for reformers and critics of the police is the question of how to detect and prevent police deviance, corruption and prejudicial mishandling of cases. It was hoped that the calling of an inquiry into the criminal justice system under Lord Runciman would offer a programme for sweeping reforms. In the event the Report of the Royal Commission on Criminal Justice (1993) suggested very few. New Labour proposals for relaxation of controls on the police (eg suspension of rights in cases of suspected terrorism) may exacerbate the problem.

THE POLICE AND EUROPE

The so-called 'Third Pillar' of the Maastricht Treaty on European Union (1991) is concerned with justice and home affairs, including provisions for co-operation between police and customs services of the EU Member States. Such co-operation has a long history but is accelerating. Organised crime, smuggling, drug trafficking, terrorism and international fraud have all stimulated mutual assistance through treaties, secondments, intelligence sharing, joint training and so on. However, the Maastricht summit accepted a proposal that takes co-operation a stage further with the creation of a European Police Office, or 'Europol'. This is an agency for the collation, analysis and exchanging of information. Some states, notably Germany, support the idea of making Europol an operational police force, but most others are unenthusiastic. Anderson et al make several important points here:

> The absence of a federal structure in Europe, a common criminal justice system, and a supranational accountability mechanism, makes operational powers for Europol extremely unlikely. However, even a Europol without operational powers may grow into a powerful institution, a prospect which may strengthen the argument against such powers.

M. Anderson et al, *Policing the European Union*, Oxford: Clarendon, 1995, pp. 282–3

Since the terrorist attacks of 11 September 2001 on the USA, both the agenda and support for international police co-operation have changed. The 'war on terrorism' now increases the likelihood that Europol will develop as an operational agency and certainly some European partners such as Germany are strong advocates of this.

Successful and acceptable progress toward a 'borderless Europe' is highly dependent on the ability of the police and customs services to ensure that transnational crime and the movement of illegal immigrants are not advantaged by the removal of frontier controls. In response, from the 1985 Schengen Agreement onwards, the shift in national and now pan-European policing has been toward

20.9 Europe and harmonisation: two subjects of controversy

One question that the 'Europeanisation' of policing raises is whether Britain will adopt practices that are common in other European states but that remain controversial here? Two topics for discussion suggest themselves.

The first is the case of identity cards. Of all EU members, currently only Britain, Ireland and Denmark do not have ID card systems. One argument for mandatory carrying of ID cards is the suggestion that this would help prevent terrorism and smuggling. The idea of a national scheme for Britain was endorsed by the then Home Secretary at the 1994 Conservative Party conference. Such a system is not without precedent within living memory: national registration cards were introduced during the Second World War and only abolished in 1952. Two possible public reactions were well (if inconsistently) provided by the *Sun*:

> Why not? No law-abiding citizen should object to carrying them. ID cards will be a big weapon against crooks, illegal immigrants and terrorists.
>
> *Sun*, 10 August 1994

> If we ever get identity cards they will be used to bully, nanny, and harass us. We are being suffocated by the State, treated as imbeciles, to be herded and prodded and controlled.
>
> *Sun*, 11 August 1994

This subject obviously invites cautious debate! In 2002, in the wake of the 11 September 2001 attacks, the Labour Home Secretary, David Blunkett, raised the ID proposal again, only to withdraw it in the face of widespread criticism, not least from senior members of the Conservative Party.

The second concern relates to firearms. Other European police forces are routinely armed. In Britain there has traditionally been a great reluctance on the part of government and senior police officers even to contemplate (at least in public) moving toward arming the police beyond the minimal arrangements currently in place. Since the Dunblane tragedy, when a class of 5-year-old children were shot by a gunman in Scotland, public opinion has swung against firearms. At present Britain is unlikely to 'harmonise' in this respect. Will it ever do so?

intelligence-led methods relying on surveillance, informants and exchange of information. While there are serious and convincing arguments about the desirability of such developments if policing is to keep pace with the threats of transnational crime, nonetheless the accompanying threats to civil liberties and the need for systems of accountability are also very real.

CURRENT AND FUTURE ISSUES

Whether because they have been placed on a pedestal, or because of the importance of their powers, the police attract a great deal of attention and criticism. It should, of course, also be emphasised that the police perform an unenviable and difficult task and receive a great deal of deserved praise, and public and political support. However, there are areas for future development and reform.

Police forces have faced recurrent criticism for being predominantly male and white. Forces have sought to improve recruitment of women and ethnic minority officers (see Figures 20.2 and 20.3), but the issue will remain important, raising the question of the representativeness of the police. According to figures published in the latest available report from HMCIC, less than 16 per cent of officers are women and only 2 per cent are from ethnic minorities. A related question is, who actually 'polices' society? In fact, 'the police' make only a particular kind of contribution to this. The general public do a great deal of 'police work', regulating young people, providing surveillance and intelligence (Neighbourhood

Figure 20.2 *Percentage of female police officers, England and Wales*

Source: HMSO

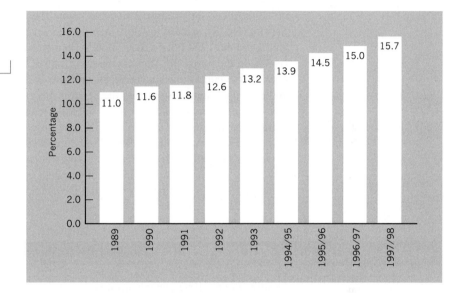

Figure 20.3 *Percentage of ethnic minority police officers, England and Wales*

Source: HMSO

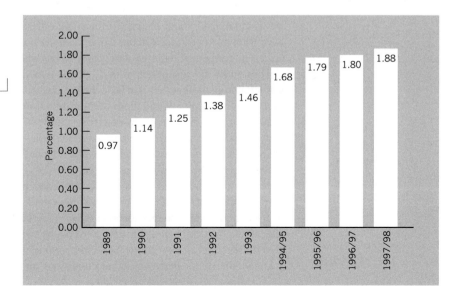

Watch, Crimestoppers). Various public and private bodies employ inspectors, investigators, wardens and guards. The 'boundaries of policing' are increasingly blurred, most significantly because of the unrelenting growth of the private security sector. A mixed market now flourishes and readers might note some interesting echoes of eighteenth- and nineteenth-century arrangements for policing society.

The future of policing is likely to raise (once again) the issues of centralisation of control and amalgamation of forces. The run-up to the European 'single market' of 1992 concentrated some police and policy minds on the idea of centralised policing and the creation of six 'superforces' created by amalgamation. The different views of successive Home Secretaries, as well as the radical changes and costs that would be involved, eroded enthusiasm for this proposal. However, it will almost certainly reappear at some point. The National Criminal Intelligence Service (NCIS), created in 1992, incorporates several formerly distinct databases and under the 1997 Police Act is now supported by a new National Crime Squad (NCS). In the post-Cold War era the involvement of the security services, first in operations against domestic terrorism, and now in relation to the 'war on terrorism and on drugs' (authorised under the Security Services Act 1996), has also been a development to note. This represents the involvement in criminal investigation of a highly centralised yet largely invisible and unaccountable agency. In the future co-operation between NCIS, the NCS and the security services will create a very powerful, centrally directed police establishment. Does all this represent an Orwellian vision of Big Brother police agencies, or is it simply a practical response to the increasing diversity and incidence of serious organised crime?

NEW LABOUR: NEW POLICE POLICY?

Shortly after the 1997 general election, Labour's new Home Secretary, Jack Straw, enjoyed a warm reception on his first visit to a Police Federation annual conference and in October that year he told delegates at his party conference: 'We said we would make Labour the party of law and order. And we did.' So what policies have been pursued since Labour came to power – are they new or do they largely represent continuity with the 'old' party of law and order, the Conservatives?

Those who are disappointed that Labour is no longer identified with the radical left complain that they see little difference between the crime control policies of the new government and those of their predecessors. Prior to the 1997 election there did indeed emerge a new consensus between the parties on several relevant matters and clearly there is some continuity today. However the 1998 Crime and Disorder Act also illustrates significant differences between the new and previous governments. The Act placed particular emphasis upon the prevention and reduction of crime, linked to a requirement that the police develop closer working partnerships with local authorities to implement community safety strategies. In these new arrangements for interagency co-operation the police become just one among several agencies that must work together and, importantly, local government has a key role. While the previous government had refused to acknowledge links between social conditions and crime, the new government readily adopted the connection as a target for policy, creating a Social Exclusion Unit, introducing proposals to prevent and tackle juvenile crime and announcing a new strategy to reduce the misuse of drugs. All three initiatives reflected both compromise and tension between old-style Labour welfarism and New Labour's policy of being tough but showing compassion where appropriate. Action against social exclusion includes creating opportunities for employment and education but also commitments to regenerating social and community life in deprived areas. Policing and community safety play significant roles here and the 1998 Act also created a framework for intervention that coupled prevention with deterrence. Relevant measures include: anti-social behaviour orders, under which police or a local authority can apply to magistrates for an order requiring a young person (or persons) to cease acting in ways causing distress to others; parenting orders, requiring parents to take responsibility for the behaviour of their children; and curfew orders, which are temporary, apply to children under the age of 10 and are designed to prevent young children frequenting the streets after a designated time, thereby seeking to divert them from trouble at an early age. All these community measures require the involvement and support of the police if they are to be effective. A preventive agenda is evident here and central to it is a concern to help young people and families. However, we can also hear quite clear echoes of the tough 'zero tolerance' approach that has been borrowed from the politics of US policing. This was exemplified in Jack Straw's stance as shadow Home Secretary when he declared: 'We have literally to reclaim the streets for the law-abiding citizen from the aggressive begging of winos, addicts, and squeegee merchants; make street life everywhere an innocent pleasure again.' As Joyce (1999, p. 21) observed, these themes were also evident at the 1998 Labour conference when:

> Prime Minister Tony Blair proposed the introduction of 'order maintenance' into 25 crime 'hot spot' areas throughout Britain. This included a more targeted use of police patrols, based on the belief that random patrols were largely ineffective in deterring crime or catching criminals. This blended the reactive aspects of zero tolerance with crime prevention.

This proposal became part of a promise to increase the number of police officers on the street, delivered to the party conference of the following year, 1999, but the pledge quickly became the subject of a political dispute. In 1995 John Major had made a similar promise to his party conference but chief constables used their discretion over budgets to spend money on new technology. Labour's idea was for a fund to which specific bids must be made to constrain chief officers and ensure the money was used for recruitment. In itself this seemed an imaginative way to compel police chiefs to spend funds as government intended. However, the question then arose of just how many extra police officers would actually be recruited? Mr Straw insisted the plan was to recruit 5,000 officers 'over and above' the recruitment plans of the police service. A leaked memo and questions from the shadow Home Secretary, Ann Widdecombe, cast doubt on this, suggesting the effect would merely be to stabilise current total numbers by replacing officers leaving and retiring. Three years later the Police Federation was still complaining about shortages of regular officers forcing 'rookies' onto the beat. It accused government of a 'boom and bust' policy.

POLICING, CIVIL LIBERTIES, AND HUMAN RIGHTS

Human rights
Western ideas about 'rights' are traceable through the English Magna Carta, the United States Declaration of Independence and the French Declaration of the Rights of Man. The 1948 United Nations 'Universal Declaration of Human Rights' proposed a number of fundamental rights, including those of 'life, liberty and security of the person', 'freedom of movement' and 'of thought, conscience and religion'.

The government has passed a Human Rights Act, intended to signal a commitment to equal treatment, justice, and freedom from unwarranted interference. Clearly sensitive to such trends, the report of HMCIC (1998) noted that equal opportunities training for police officers was in need of improvement and suggested that impressive-sounding policy and strategies still have a long way to go before they make a real impact on the predominantly white police organisation.

At the same time critics continue to see some developments in policing as endangering civil liberties and human rights. The record of deaths in police custody continues to give rise to concern, attracting the attention in 1998 of the United Nations Committee Against Torture; the use of CS gas spray by the police is increasingly controversial following reports of deaths said to be connected to improper use of the weapon; and further cases of police misconduct and corruption have come to light. One recent Commissioner of the Metropolitan Police acknowledged that there may be up to 250 corrupt officers serving in this force, suggesting that the pursuit of an unknown number of criminal investigations may be compromised.

The extension of police powers is worrying. For example, the capacity for police surveillance was increased under the 1997 Police Act, which gave police similar powers to the security services to employ hidden cameras and microphones ('bug and burgle' powers) during the investigation of serious crimes. A new national database holding over 3 million DNA samples from active criminals has been promised by Mr Blair, and both he and the Home Secretary have stated they wish to see the extension of drug testing of people arrested and charged by the police. Unsurprisingly, such developments are strongly criticised by civil liberties commentators.

Critics also point to the difficulty of making the police accountable for their actions or, in some important cases, their inaction. There have so far been fewer revelations of miscarriages of justice than in the 1980s and early 1990s. However, some have surfaced, particularly related to police mishandling of cases involving ethnic minorities. Such cases have included wrongful arrest and prosecution. In October 1999 the Metropolitan Police paid compensation of £50,000 to Winston Silcott, a black man, wrongly prosecuted for the murder at the Broadwater Farm riot of a white police constable, Keith Blakelock. Significantly, while this out-of-court settlement was welcomed by Silcott's family, support groups and the liberal press, news reports of the award also described a 'backlash' among rank and file police officers, who saw the award as 'pandering to the race lobby' (*Independent on Sunday*, 17 October 1999, p. 8). This defensive reaction reflects a new context in which the police find themselves under scrutiny. The very poor record of the police in recruiting ethnic minority officers, and their inadequate handling of offences against black people, have now become major issues for police, political and media attention.

THE STEPHEN LAWRENCE MURDER AND THE MACPHERSON INQUIRY

On 22 April 1993 Stephen Lawrence, a young black teenager, was murdered in an unprovoked attack carried out by white assailants. The police investigation into his death was grossly inadequate and the racist nature of the attack given little attention. A long campaign by Stephen's family and supporters called for an official inquiry into the police handling of the case, failure to follow up important information available at the start of the investigation, and lack of success in providing evidence that could lead to the prosecution of identified suspects. The call for an inquiry was resisted by the Metropolitan Police and rejected by Conservative Home Secretaries. In 1998 the new Home Secretary asked Sir William Macpherson, a former High Court judge, to chair an official inquiry into the case. Sir William examined three specific allegations against the police – that they were incompetent, racist and corrupt. Macpherson (1999) did not find evidence of corruption but firmly concluded that the police investigation had been 'marred by a combination of professional incompetence, institutional racism, and a failure of leadership by senior officers'. He was clearly frustrated to find some senior officers unable to agree their accounts of conversations about the early part of the investigation, coldly concluding of one instance that one or the other of two officers who appeared before the inquiry was 'palpably wrong and cannot be telling the truth'. This highly critical report could not be lightly dismissed by the police. As Cathcart (1999) observed, its author is 'no Tom Paine', being a Scottish aristocrat in his seventies, chief of his clan, and a member of the Queen's ceremonial bodyguard! Hence the impact of the Macpherson Report has been considerable.

Naturally comparison was made with the report prepared by Lord Scarman in 1981 (described earlier), which found evidence of racism within the police and made important recommendations concerning police–community relations and the need for racism-awareness training for the police. Macpherson's reminder of the intervening lack of progress in improving police recruitment of minorities and changing police culture has been disturbing. HMCIC had acknowledged these particular problems in its 1998 report and noted the 'continued and disturbing evidence of racist, sexist and discriminatory behaviour within forces'. However, Macpherson went further than either Scarman or HMCIC and argued that racism was a problem that could be viewed as pervasive throughout the Metropolitan Police (and, by implication, throughout the police service nationally). The Report referred to the idea of institutional racism to describe this state of affairs, defining it in the following way:

Institutional racism The collective failure of an organisation to provide an appropriate and professional service to people because of their colour, culture or ethnic origin.

> The collective failure of an organisation to provide an appropriate and professional service to people because of their colour, culture or ethnic origin. It can be seen or detected in processes, attitudes and behaviour which amount to discrimination through unwitting prejudice, ignorance, thoughtlessness and racist stereotyping which disadvantage minority ethnic people.

Sir William Macpherson of Cluny, *The Stephen Lawrence Inquiry: Report of an Enquiry*, London: The Stationery Office, 1999, para. 6.34

Plate 20.2
*The Metropolitan Police
sheds crocodile tears over
the failure to convict the
murderers of Stephen
Lawrence. Cartoon in
the* New Statesman,
26 February 1999

Plate 20.2
*The Metropolitan Police
sheds crocodile tears over
the failure to convict the
murderers of Stephen
Lawrence. Cartoon in
the* New Statesman,
26 February 1999

Plate 20.3 *Stephen
Lawrence inquiry suspects
leaving the court and
gesturing at Lawrence
family supporters*

The Macpherson Report made 70 recommendations and the Home Secretary accepted most of these (see Joyce 1999 for fuller discussion). At the 1999 Labour Party conference Stephen Lawrence's father spoke from the podium and highlighted the issues raised by the case and the Report, thanking the Home Secretary for initiating the inquiry. The occasion received an emotional response from the conference floor and considerable media coverage.

Clearly, the agenda for the government and, more than ever, for the police, now includes serious initiatives for a change in institutional culture. Such change needs to be more sensitive to the problem of racism, to civil liberties and to human rights issues. This is, of course, an 'ideal' agenda and readers will by now be fully aware that the police service is a rather conservative organisation. In coming years the politics of policing will partly revolve around tackling police resistance to fundamental change. At the same time it must be emphasised that since the 1980s, it has not been only domestic issues that have shaped the police agenda but also international pressures such as the 'war on drugs' and now the 'war against terrorism'. Critics argue that the latter has given rise to a new era of policing of 'suspect' groups as 'risk populations', such as immigrants and Islamic minorities who have come under scrutiny for possible terrorist connections. Labour has adopted a tougher anti-immigration stance and supported the extension of police and security service powers in the face of a terrorist threat. In such a climate, fundamental change, in the sense of increasing police sensitivity to racism and human rights issues, may be harder to accomplish than previously hoped.

SUMMARY

Government ministers and students of politics alike would do well to remember that the police are not 'apolitical' and that the politics of policing are a complex business. This has been amply demonstrated by the questions and problems raised in this chapter, chief among them:

■ the scope of 'policing' as distinct from 'police'

■ police organisation and accountability: who is really in control?

■ moves from a local to a national organisation

■ procedural reforms and individual rights in relation to the police

■ the politicisation of policing

■ the privatisation of police functions

■ Europeanisation

■ the police and New Labour

■ the issue of institutional racism

■ the impact of the new international terrorism.

ESSAYS

1. Are 'the police' a police 'force' or a police 'service'? What are the implications of these different terms?

2. One conclusion of the Scarman Report was that: 'public tranquillity should have a greater priority than law enforcement if the two conflicted' (Reiner, 1994, p. 725). Discuss in relation to the policing of either: (a) minority communities, making reference to the Macpherson Report; or (b) environmental protests.

3. 'The fact that the British police are answerable to the law, that we act on behalf of the community and not under the mantle of government, makes us the least powerful, the most accountable and therefore the most acceptable police in the world' (Sir Robert Mark, Metropolitan Commissioner, *Policing a Perplexed Society* (London: Allen & Unwin, 1977), p. 56. Debate this argument.

MILESTONES

Milestones in the development of British policing

1829 Sir Robert Peel's Metropolitan Police Act

1830–60 Establishment of county and borough forces under local control

1856 County and Borough Police Act establishes home office inspection of, and grants for, local police authorities

1960 Establishment of the Royal Commission on the Police

1962 Report of the above

1964 Police Act amalgamates 117 police forces into 43. Tripartite control by chief constables, police authorities and Home Secretary

1972 Bains Committee recommendation that chief constables should be as accountable as local authority chief executives is rejected

1976 Police Complaints Board (PCB) established

1979 Central government controls over local government expenditures also mean central control over police expenditure

1981 The Brixton disorders (10–12 April) and the Scarman Report, which criticised aggressive tactics used by the Metropolitan Police

1984 Police and Criminal Evidence Act (PACE) consolidates police powers but introduces better safeguards for suspects

1984 Police Complaints Board replaced by Police Complaints Authority (PCA)

1984–5 Miners' strike. Employment of national co-ordination and control of local police forces

1986 Creation of Crown Prosecution Service (CPS)

1988 Court of Appeal gives the Home Secretary powers to override the police authorities on matters of equipment and expenditure

1993 Royal Commission on Criminal Justice (Runciman Report)

1994 Police and Magistrates' Courts Act reduces police authorities to agents of Home Secretary

1995 First woman chief constable appointed. Metropolitan Police Commissioner states that some police routinely carry firearms

1997 Police Act created a new National Crime Squad and gave the police enhanced powers to mount surveillance operations

1998 Crime and Disorder Act places emphasis on co-operation between police, local authorities and other agencies; introduces various 'orders' available to the police and courts to curb anti-social behaviour

1999 The Macpherson Report follows an Inquiry into the murder of Stephen Lawrence and concludes that the police investigation was incompetent, marred by institutional racism and failure of leadership from senior officers

2001–03 International terrorist attacks spark US-led 'war on terrorism' and suspension of human rights in cases of suspected British terrorists

FURTHER READING

P. Joyce, *Law, Order and the Judiciary* (London: Hodder & Stoughton, 1999) is a good overview of this general area, well written and comprehensive; R. Reiner, *The Politics of the Police* (Oxford: OUP, 3rd edn, 2001) is generally regarded as the best introduction to the study of the police and policing; see also C. Elmsley, *The English Police: A Political and Social History* (Hemel Hempstead: Harvester Wheatsheaf, 1991) on the history of the police; L. Lustgarten, *The Governance of the Police* (London: Sweet & Maxwell, 1986) is the classic study of the police and the constitution. B. Cathcart, 'The police force we deserve?', *New Statesman*, 26 February 1999; A. Travis, 'Home affairs: crime and prisons', in M. Linton (ed.), *The Election: A Voter's Guide* (London: Fourth Estate, 2001); D. Woodhouse, 'Politicians and the judges: a conflict of interest', *Parliamentary Affairs*, **49** (3), 1996, pp. 423–40, are recent specialised discussions.

PROJECTS

1. Using newspaper reports, contrast the priorities of any two local police forces in enforcing specific laws.

2. Is the idea of a 'private' police an anomaly? Write a discussion document on the issues raised by the privatisation of the police.

3. Review and discuss the Stephen Lawrence case and the Macpherson Inquiry and Report.

USEFUL WEB SITES ON THE POLICE AND POLICING

Hotlinks to these sites can be found on the CWS website at http://www.booksites.net/budge.

There are a number of very good web sites that cover key aspects of police, policing and crime in the United Kingdom. The first stop for students is the web site for the police services of the UK (www.police.uk). The Metropolitan Police web site is available at www.met.police.uk.

The Home Office offers a comprehensive account of the guiding principles of criminal law and police reform, a great deal of information can be obtained from www.homeoffice.gov.uk/new_indexs/crim_jus.htm. In addition, the government maintains an individual web site on police reform (www.policereform.gov.uk). The government's Criminal Policy Group (http://www.homeoffice.gov.uk/cpg/cpg.htm) works in conjunction with the Home Office aiming to ensure the effective delivery of justice, through efficient investigation, detection, prosecution and court procedures. Police Law (www.policelaw.co.uk) is an independent organisation that provides insightful information and analysis of all aspects of British criminal law.

Rethinking Crime and Punishment (www.rethinking.org.uk) is an independent organisation that aims to raise the level of public debate about the use of prison and alternative forms of punishment in the UK. You can also obtain useful information on crime and the strategies oriented to prevent it at www.crimeconcern.org.uk. The Police Complaints Authority web site is available at www.pca.gov.uk.

As noted in the last chapter, police efforts to maintain order have been increasingly supplemented over the post-war period, most spectacularly by private security firms. Related groups such as Customs and Excise and various bodies of inspectors also operate to detect crime in their specialised areas. Ordinary citizens have been drafted in, notably through Neighbourhood Watch schemes, and have been encouraged to use 'hotlines' to denounce social security frauds. Many major roads, high streets, and shopping centres are now covered by 24-hour camera surveillance.

Wherever we go and whatever we do in Britain therefore we may be under surveillance and scrutiny by someone, even our neighbours. Much of this activity is initiated by the security and intelligence services, whose functions have been expanded in recent years to combat serious crime, such as international terrorism and drugs trafficking.

All modern states have security services to protect themselves against terrorism, subversion and violence, but they present democracies with dilemmas nonetheless. First, one of the most important principles of democratic government is that no person or organisation is above the law. Yet the British security services are constitutionally outside, if not above, the law. Second, all branches of a democratic state should be publicly accountable, but the security services are under a blanket of secrecy, for obvious reasons. Third, to be effective the security services must have powers necessary to operate secretly and effectively against the enemies of the state, but they must not be used by the government against its own citizens. In other words, governments must use the security services for the public interest, not for their own political purposes. Nor, protected by secrecy, must the security services be able to take the law into their own hands and act against either the government or its citizens.

Every modern state faces these dilemmas and none has an easy solution. Yet the British State appears to be unusually secretive, by western democratic standards, and gives its security and intelligence organisations broad and unaccountable powers. How and why this is the case is discussed in this chapter. It is divided into six parts, as follows:

- the rise of security and secrecy as a political issue
- the security and intelligence services
- laws and conventions about secrecy
- accountability
- freedom of information and open government
- motives and opportunities for state secrecy.

Throughout the chapter it must be kept in mind that the security and intelligence services are secret, by definition, and it is not possible to say much about them with any certainty.

RISE OF SECURITY AND SECRECY AS A POLITICAL ISSUE

In the 1950s and 1960s national security was not a major issue. On the contrary, the importance and success of wartime intelligence, and the fear of communism during the Cold War, helped to sustain the security services and their secrecy. The issue grew, however, as a result of a sequence of events in the 1970s and 1980s, including:

- IRA action in Northern Ireland and the mainland

- international terrorism: events of 11 September 2001 in the USA raised anxiety to an altogether new level

- rising crime, including large-scale international drug and crime rings

- a long series of revelations about high-level failures of the security system, to the extent of personnel acting as Soviet spies – among others, the double agents Guy Burgess, Donald MacLean and Kim Philby, as well as (Sir) Anthony Blunt, Sir Maurice Oldfield (former head of MI6), George Blake (an officer of the Secret Intelligence Service), the Portland Spy Ring, John Vassall, and Michael Bettaney. The names of Melita Norwood, Robin Pearson and John Symonds have recently been added to the list. Sir Roger Hollis (a former Director-General of the Security Services) and John Cairncross of MI6 are believed by some experts to have been Soviet double agents, although Hollis was cleared by an official inquiry in 1974 and later by evidence of the Soviet defector, Oleg Gordievsky.

This long list of names contributed to a growing concern about state security. Contrariwise, there was also mounting concern about growing government power, and threats to individual rights and civil liberties. Fears were fuelled by:

- the growing power and centralisation of the police force, and its apparent lack of accountability (Chapter 20)

- the growing power of central government, especially the Prime Minister and Cabinet, and the apparent weakening of the legislature (the Commons) and local government

- the growing power of the security services as a result of legislation increasing their responsibilities

- new technology for surveillance and the centralisation of computer records

- an increasing awareness of the secretive nature of the British State, and of the ways in which the Official Secrets Act has been used; between 1945 and 1974 34 people were prosecuted under the Official Secrets Act – between 1978 and 1986 the number was 29

- a ruling by the European Court of Human Rights in 1985 stating that Britain's laws on phone tapping were insufficiently clear (about 1,500 phone lines a year are tapped in the UK)

BRIEFINGS

21.1 **Operations of the secret State**

Arms sales to Nigeria, Jonathan Aitken, 1971   Aitken (then writing for the *Sunday Telegraph*) and a retired general were prosecuted under the Official Secrets Act for reporting that arms sales to Nigeria were much larger than the government claimed. Both were acquitted, and the judge said that the Official Secrets Act was in urgent need of reform.

ABC trial, 1977   Two journalists, Crispin Aubrey and Duncan Campbell, were tried with John Berry, a former member of Signals Intelligence, for disclosing defence information. Although this information was in the public domain already, they were found guilty, but given only light sentences.

Tisdall and Cruise missiles, 1984   Sarah Tisdall, a clerk at the Foreign Office, believed her minister, Michael Heseltine, was deceiving the public about the arrival of Cruise missiles at Greenham Common in order to minimise public opposition. She released information to the *Guardian*, was prosecuted, and received a six-month prison sentence.

Ponting and the *Belgrano* affair, 1985   Clive Ponting was a high-flying civil servant who released information suggesting that the government had concealed the true circumstances of the sinking of the Argentine battleship *General Belgrano* in the Falklands War. Ponting defended himself in court on the grounds that he was acting in the public interest, and was acquitted by the jury.

Political vetting in the BBC, 1985   It was revealed that MI5 had an office in the BBC in order to vet job applicants. It was promised that the practice would stop.

Phone tapping, 1985   A former member of MI5, Cathy Massiter, claimed in a TV documentary that MI5 routinely tapped the phones of trade union officials and CND (Campaign for Nuclear Disarmament) leaders.

***Spycatcher*, 1987–8**   The government tried to ban the book by Peter Wright, formerly of MI5, even though it was easily available abroad. The government sent the Cabinet Secretary, Sir Robert Armstrong, to an Australian court to try to ban publication there. This was itself a controversial political use of a civil servant, and Sir Robert caused more criticism by admitting that the government had been 'economical with the truth'. Among other things Wright claimed that some members of MI5 tried to destabilise the Wilson Labour government, and that MI5 'bugged and burgled its way across London'.

Zircon, 1987   A film about the British spy satellite, Zircon, made by the journalist Duncan Campbell (also of the ABC case), was seized by the Special Branch from the Edinburgh offices of the BBC, together with five other programmes in the same series. The government claimed that the film was a danger to state security, but critics argued that the government wanted to conceal the fact that the Zircon project was behind schedule.

Defending the realm, 1991   Evidence from an ex-security services official, Robin Robison, was presented in a *Guardian*/ITN *World in Action* inquiry, claiming that the security services regularly engage in unauthorised spying on, among others, Britain's EU partners, to discover their negotiating positions, on commercial companies both at home and abroad, and on trade union leaders. Robison claimed that the security services keep some of this activity from their ministers.

Surveillance of MPs and ministers The memoirs of ex-minister Alan Clark suggested that MPs and ministers are under MI5 surveillance. Before him, MPs Jonathan Aitken and Sir Richard Body made the same claim.

The Scott Inquiry (1996) The official inquiry into arms to Iraq revealed how secretive the British government is at the highest levels, and how little is known even by MPs.

State censorship Examples of government censorship of TV include among others, *Yesterday's Men* (1971), *Real Lives* (1985, about politicians in Northern Ireland), *The War Game* (1965), *A Question of Ulster* (1972) and the Zircon affair (see earlier in this briefing). The government also strongly criticised the BBC for its reporting of the Suez War, the Falklands War, and the US bombing of Libya, and the Independent Broadcasting Authority for showing *Death of a Princess* (1980) and *Death on the Rock* (1988).

- a series of events involving the security forces and government secrecy with allegations about either government misuse of secrecy, or security services abuse of power. Almost all these claims have been officially denied.

As a result of this the security services have been drawn into the political limelight, and the problems they pose for democracy have become a political issue. While the need for effective security is more urgent than ever after 11 September 2001, there is a strong suspicion that governments have sometimes enforced secrecy, not in the public interest but to protect their own political reputations. There are also fears that the powers of the security services have been used by governments to spy on citizens, and claims that the security services themselves have engaged in covert operations against citizens and even the government. To understand how this might be so it is necessary to understand the nature of the security services and the laws and conventions under which they operate.

SECURITY AND INTELLIGENCE AGENCIES

Little is known for certain about the British security services, and it is difficult to sort out fact from fiction about them – contrary to rumours, however, we are allowed to know that MI5's carpets in the headquarters in Thames House are blue (Briefing 21.2).

From 1993 some official information has been released, and web sites opened. The UK has three main intelligence and security agencies – the Secret Intelligence Service (SIS – better known as MI6), the Security Service (better known as MI5), and the Government Communications Headquarters (GCHQ). They were placed on a constitutional basis by the Intelligence Services Act 1994, and two Security Service Acts of 1989 and 1996. Collectively they are known as the agencies. Their combined budget for 2002/3 was projected to be £893 million.

21.2 **Blue carpets and chicken Madras at MI5**

'Members and former members of the Security Service are prohibited by Section 1 of the Official Secrets Act 1989 from disclosing without lawful authority information relating to security or intelligence which came into their possession while in the Service.

'It is clearly important that security and intelligence information is protected from unauthorised disclosure. But section 1 is sometimes criticised as prohibiting disclosures even about such matters as the colour of the Thames House carpets and the menu in the staff restaurant. These criticisms are misguided: such matters do not fall within the scope of the Act. It is therefore not an offence for a member of the Service to disclose that the Thames House carpets are blue, or that the staff restaurant serves a particularly good chicken Madras!'

http://www.mi5.gov.uk/myth12.htm

Plate 21.1
MI5 headquarters on the River Thames

Source: Stockwave, Central Office of Information

To the three agencies we should add three more with a different status and paid for from different funds, namely the Defence Intelligence Staff, the Special Branch, and the National Criminal Intelligence Service. All six are concerned in one way or another with the security of the nation, and the intelligence this requires.

21.3 The security services

The Security Service (MI5)

The domestic intelligence service concerned with covertly organised threats to the nation, primarily terrorism, espionage, and the proliferation of weapons of mass destruction. Since the Security Service Act 1996 its role has been expanded to cover work against serious crime. It employs 1,832 full-time equivalent staff, and its 1998/9 budget was almost £140 million, of which £30 million was spent on terrorism relating to Northern Ireland, and £22 million on international terrorism. In 1992 it took over from the police the responsibility for gathering intelligence about the IRA on the British mainland. MI5 is also engaged in political vetting, and with 'the preventing and detection of serious crime, and for connected purposes'. It co-operates closely with SIS and GCHQ, and with foreign police and intelligence agencies. Its headquarters are in Thames House, Millbank, London SW1, and it has a web site (listed at the end of the chapter).

The Secret Intelligence Service (SIS, better known as MI6)

A government report on the national intelligence machinery states that the main job of the SIS is to produce secret intelligence on Britain's interests in the fields of security, defence, and foreign and economic policies. Less is known about it than the Security Service, but its annual budget was estimated at about £150 million in the mid-1990s, and its headquarters are at Vauxhall Cross, London. It is thought to employ about 2,300 staff. Its role has also been expanded to cover the war against drugs. The Chief of the Secret Intelligence Service, Sir Richard Dearlove, is known simply as 'C'. The SIS has no web site.

Government Communications Headquarters (GCHQ)

The existence of GCHQ was officially acknowledged in 1983 as the result of a spy scandal. It is famous for its wartime work on decoding German messages enciphered by the 'Enigma' machine. It is mainly concerned with government coding and decoding, and with the use of satellites and listening posts to monitor world communications. It works closely with its equivalents in the USA, Canada, Australia and New Zealand. Its British headquarters in Cheltenham employs 7,000 people and its estimated annual budget is £500 million. It was the subject of political controversy in 1984 when the government banned its workers from trade union membership (allegedly under pressure from the Americans after a spy scandal). Trade union rights were restored by the Labour government in 1997. Its web site is listed at the end of the chapter.

Defence Intelligence Staff (DIS)

Part of the Ministry of Defence and funded from the defence budget, the DIS is mainly concerned with foreign military threat assessment and intelligence, but also with the internal security of the armed forces. The DIS is estimated to have a total staff of about 4,600 civilians and military people.

Special Branch

As Branch 12 of the Special Operations of the Metropolitan Police, Special Branch is especially concerned with gathering and analysing intelligence on extremist political and terrorist activity. Under the direction of a senior officer of the Metropolitan Police, and therefore accountable to the Home Secretary, the Special Branch works closely with MI5. Its responsibilities include intelligence work, enforcing official secrets laws, the security of VIPs, watching ports and airports, and making arrests for MI5. It employs about 2,000 people in its central and local offices. The Metropolitan Office of the Special Branch has a budget of over £20 million.

The National Criminal Intelligence Service (NCIS)

The youngest of the intelligence agencies, it was set up in 1992 in order to collect and analyse intelligence about serious and organised crime. It is mainly concerned with economic crime, drugs, illegal immigration, vehicle crime, West African organised crime, serious sex offenders, counterfeits, football hooliganism, kidnap and extortion, and wildlife crime. It works closely with foreign intelligence agencies and contains the UK division of Interpol. Outside its headquarters in London it has offices in Birmingham, Bristol, Glasgow, London, Manchester, Wakefield, and Belfast. It has a staff of 900 and an annual budget of £93 million. It falls under the authority of the Home Secretary.

ACCOUNTABILITY

The Prime Minister is responsible for intelligence and security matters overall. For day-to-day operations the services are under the control of their respective heads, who, in turn, are personally responsible to their minister (see Figure 21.1). Two main committees of central government are responsible for the work and co-ordination of the various branches of the security services.

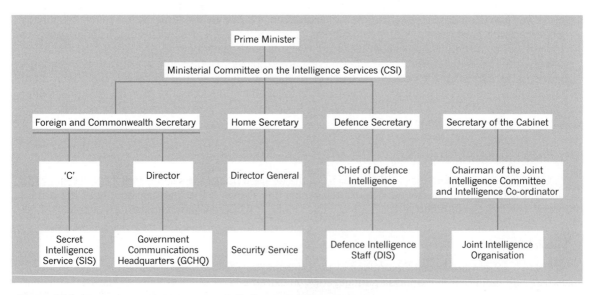

Figure 21.1 *Ministerial and Cabinet responsibility for the intelligence services*

The Ministerial (Cabinet) Committee on the Intelligence Services (CSI)

The terms of reference of the Committee are to 'keep under review policy on the security and intelligence services'. It is chaired by the Prime Minister and its members are the Deputy PM, the Home, Defence, and Foreign Secretaries, and the Chancellor of the Exchequer.

Joint Intelligence Committee (JIC)

This is part of the Cabinet Office and under the authority of the Cabinet Secretary. It is chaired by a senior member of the Cabinet Office and is the main body for advising on intelligence priorities, and for gathering and assessing results that are provided to ministers and other senior officials.

Intelligence and security agencies are not accountable to Parliament, and ministers can refuse to answer any Parliamentary question related to national security. The House of Commons has a Parliamentary Intelligence and Security Committee that issues a brief annual report, and other reports on specific matters. The reports are not very informative, and select committees of the Commons have not been successful in recent attempts to interview security officials, or in attempts to scrutinise the security police. The heads of the intelligence and security agencies themselves are not subject to a public complaints procedure, as are the police with the Police Complaints Authority, but are monitored by a security service tribunal that works entirely in secret. Between 1989 (when it was set up) and 1996 the tribunal considered 187 complaints against MI5, rejecting them all. MI5 documents are protected from scrutiny by the courts and when MI5 officers have appeared to give evidence in court they have always been unidentified and hidden. MI5 is not required to tell the police about its operations. The Security Service, the Secret Intelligence Service and GCHQ are exempt from the provisions of the Freedom of Information Act 2000.

In effect, no more than the dozen people who are members of the Cabinet Committee on Intelligence Services and of the Joint Intelligence Committee have first-hand information about the security services. Half of these are unelected and unaccountable and the other half are the busiest politicians in the land, with little time to spare. In short, the security services seem to be largely 'self-tasking': they set their own goals, choose their own means and monitor their own activity. They are beyond the scrutiny of all but a few overworked politicians, and perhaps even beyond that. According to Peter Wright in *Spycatcher*, and Robin Robison in the TV programme *Defending the Realm*, the PM and the Cabinet do not know half of what goes on.

Some hoped that the role and size of the security services would be reduced after the collapse of the Soviet Union, but instead its activities were expanded to include 'the prevention and detection of serious crime, and for connected purposes'. It is no longer only concerned with national security but also with duties that were previously reserved for the police. At the same time MI5 is charged with vague duties – serious crime and connected purposes – but unlike the police is not subject to democratic accountability.

THE SECRET STATE

The British State as a whole, not just its security and intelligence agencies, works within a framework of laws and conventions that give it substantial powers to protect itself from public scrutiny. The centrepiece of the system is the Official Secrets Act of 1989, which replaced the 1911 Act after many years of pressure and debate. Section 1 of the 1911 Official Secrets Act made it an offence to engage in conduct contrary to the safety or interests of the state, including the disclosure of information of use to enemies. In most cases this section has been uncontroversial. It was Section 2 that caused trouble. This made it a crime for anyone employed by the state to pass on official information to those not authorised to have it. The section was so broadly and vaguely worded that it included almost any information: the number of paper clips used by a government department or the number of cups of tea it drinks.

It is widely held that Section 2 suppressed legitimate discussion about British government, a belief supported by a series of incidents. The judge who tried the journalists who revealed that the government was supplying large quantities of arms to Nigeria (1971) said that the section should be pensioned off. The 1972 Franks Committee on Official Secrecy recommended repeal. A string of events in the 1970s and 1980s brought the issue to the surface again, but nothing was done until 1988 when a private member's bill to reform the act was defeated by the government, which then passed its own Official Secrets Act of 1989.

BRIEFINGS

21.4 Instruments of the secret State

Privy Counsellor's oath

Since the year 1250 members of the Privy Council has been required to swear, in the presence of the monarch, an oath dealing with secrecy, among other things. Only senior government and opposition members are Privy Counsellors, but membership is for life.

Royal prerogative

Powers inherited by governments from the Crown that are held constitutionally to be independent of Parliamentary approval or scrutiny. They are, as is the rest of the 'unwritten constitution', vague and undefined, so give governments and their security advisers great scope to do what they want (see Chapter 4).

D-notices

The job of the D-notice system ('D' is for defence) is to prevent the publication of information that is not in the public interest. The old D-notice Committee, made up of representatives from the Ministry of Defence and the media has been reconstituted as the Defence, Press and Broadcasting Advisory Committee. It no longer issues D-notices but what are called Press and Broadcasting Advisory Notices. It recently caused controversy when it advised the media not to publish the address of a web site that listed members of MI6.

Government Directive, 1952

This directive stated the convention that ministers 'do not concern themselves with the detailed information which may be obtained by the Security Service in particular cases but are furnished with such information as may be necessary for the determination of any issue on which guidance is sought'.

Public Records Act 1958 – the 30-year rule

Under the Public Records Act certain government papers are not publicly available until they are 30 years old, or longer in some cases.

The Act covers about 40 categories of document including those about living people, confidential government information, state security, and Ireland.

The Interception of Communications Act 1985

This Act made it possible to issue warrants to bug, phone tap, or open mail in the interests of national security, the prevention and detection of serious crime, and to protect the economic well-being of the UK.

The Official Secrets Act 1989

- The Act covers the following subjects: security, defence and international relations; crime and its investigation; warrants issued under the Interception of Communications Act (1985) and the Security Services Act (1989) and information that these warrants produce; secret information provided by foreign governments and international agencies.

- Release of information that is deemed 'harmful' to the public interest is a criminal offence. It is no defence to argue that public disclosure of the information is in the public interest, or that the information is publicly available abroad.

- Disclosure of information covered by the Act is harmful in itself; the prosecution is not required to prove that disclosure has probable or actual harmful effects.

- The Act covers Crown servants, members of the security services, government contractors and journalists. Editors who encourage journalists to disclose such information are liable to prosecution.

Security Services Act 1989

The 1989 Act gave MI5 (not MI6) a statutory basis, and a broad range of rather vaguely defined functions. These were expanded in 1997 to include the prevention and detection of serious crime and connected purposes. It also provided for a security services commissioner to review phone-tapping warrants, and a tribunal to revoke improper warrants. Critics argue that the commissioner and the tribunal are weak and ineffective.

Regulation of Investigatory Powers Act (RIPA) 2000

This updates the Interception of Communications Act of 1985 to cover electronic communications. The Act gives law enforcement organisations (that is police forces, intelligence services, Customs and Excise and the Inland Revenue) blanket powers to intercept, monitor, and track all electronic communications (email and internet). It can do this secretly (it cannot be revealed in court) in the interests of national security, preventing or detecting crime, preventing disorder; public safety; protecting public health, and 'in the interests of the economic well-being of the United Kingdom'.

Section 1 of the 1911 Act remained unchanged in the 1989 Act, which concentrated on Section 2. The government claimed to have liberalised the law by dropping many of the items covered by the 1911 Act. Critics claim that the new Act simply excludes harmless information that has not been a problem in the past, while at the same time increasing secrecy in other areas, including those raised by the *Spycatcher*, Tisdall and Ponting cases, all involving officials who leaked information about government activities that they thought harmed the public interest. Critics also argue that the definitions of what is 'harmful' are both broad and vague: it is estimated that the Act creates about 2,300 offences. In short it was said that the 1989 Act increased rather than decreased state secrecy by tightening the government's grip on a range of broadly and vaguely defined matters, by expanding the range of people to whom they applied, and by eliminating the most important grounds that might be used in defence by those prosecuted under the Act.

FREEDOM OF INFORMATION AND OPEN GOVERNMENT

Freedom of information
Free public access to government information and records as required by citizens.

Open government
The relatively unconstrained flow of information about government to the public, the media and representative bodies. In open government it is the government, not the citizen, who decides what information to release, but under freedom of information it is citizens, not the government, who decide what information they want.

Critics of the Official Secrets Act and of the broader apparatus of state secrecy in Britain do not deny the need for some secrecy. What they argue is that Britain is unnecessarily secretive compared with most other western states, and that it needs legislation that positively requires the government to release certain sorts of information to citizens, if they require it. This is not a matter of military information, espionage, or the war against terrorism, but information the state holds about its citizens and organisations relating, for example, to individual health records or tax payments, or to issues such as mad cow disease or the arms to Iraq affair. In recent years the matter of freedom of information has become one of the most controversial in the UK.

Many western democracies have freedom of information acts that guarantee citizens the right to see a wide variety of documents, both state and personal. State secrets in these countries are exempt, of course, but they are more narrowly and precisely defined than in Britain. Although there are many practical difficulties with freedom of information acts (documents can be 'lost', destroyed or suppressed), countries such as the United States of America and Sweden have operated them successfully for many years. The UK, however, did not get its Freedom of Information Act until 2000, and even then, the critics claim, it got an inadequate one.

Freedom of information

Pressures for freedom of information provisions have increased over the past decade, prompted by the tightening of official secrets legislation in the 1989 Official Secrets Act, although Major's Conservative government did promote open government in 1992 by making public some government documents, such as the rulebook on procedures for ministers, the list of Cabinet committees, some records not previously released under the 30-year rule, and even information about MI5. The Citizen's Charter of 1991 also promised more open government and information. A code of practice was introduced in 1994 that promised: (a) secrecy only where there is good reason for it; and (b) increasing amounts of information.

Major's initiative did not satisfy the freedom of information lobby, especially since the government rejected two private member freedom of information bills in 1992 and 1993 and then expanded the powers of MI5 with the Security Service Act of 1996. The Scott Report on the arms to Iraq affair, published in 1995, and the government's handling of the BSE (mad cow) scare revealed a deep-seated culture of secrecy at the highest levels.

Two pressure groups took the lead in campaigning for freedom of information:

Charter 88   a broad alliance of people and organisations to press for a range of constitutional changes including freedom of information and open government

Campaign for Freedom of Information (CFOI)   created in 1984 with the backing of some leading, all-party politicians and senior ex-civil servants. It now has 90 supporting and observer organisations.

Some progress was made with the Data Protection Act (1984), and the CFOI was able to promote private members' bills that resulted in the Local Government (Access to Information) Act 1986, the Access to Personal Files Act 1987, the Environment and Safety Information Act 1998, and the Access to Health Records Act 1990.

Labour came to power in 1997 with freedom of information as a manifesto commitment. Blair had promised an end to obsessive and unnecessary government secrecy, and to work on the presumption that information should be, rather than should not be, released. In the event, the Freedom of Information Bill was delayed, and when it was presented to Parliament by the Home Secretary, Jack Straw, it turned out to be a noticeably watered-down version of what had been promised. After controversial and hurried progress through Parliament the Act was passed in 2000.

Freedom of Information Act (FOI) 2000

The main provisions of the Act are:

- Individuals already had the right of access to their own personal information held on computers and some paper files, under the Data Protection Act 1998. The FOI act extends these rights to all types of information, whether personal or not.

- Approximately 70,000 'public authorities' and 'publicly owned companies' are covered by the Act.

- The Act is enforced by a newly created Information Commissioner, who combines responsibility for freedom of information and data protection, and a new Information Tribunal.

- There is a duty laid on authorities that do not disclose information to show that this is in the public interest.

- There are many exemptions to the Act. It does not cover any of the intelligence and security agencies, and information will not be released that will cause harm to:

  - national security

  - internal discussion of government policy

  - law enforcement

  - personal privacy

  - business activities or information that could unfairly damage a company's commercial standing

  - the safety of individuals, the public and the environment

  - references, testimonials, or other matters given in confidence.

Critics have concentrated on the Act's 23 exemptions that ministers can use to preserve secrecy, including one 'catch-all' clause that enables ministers to withhold information that is not in the public interest or that prejudices the conduct of public affairs. And under a 'right-to-silence' provision, ministers can refuse to acknowledge whether the information they had been asked for even exists at all. Almost exactly a year after the Act was passed the Home Secretary recorded the first refusal to release information about a minister's private business interests. The full implementation of the Act has been delayed several times, and it will not now come wholly into operation until 2005. It is difficult to see quite how it will work until then. Meanwhile, both the Scottish and Welsh governments have made more radical provisions for freedom of information. It is possible, for example, to read the minutes of meetings of the Welsh Cabinet on the net.

STATE SECRECY: MOTIVES AND OPPORTUNITIES

Enough has been said to suggest that Britain well deserves its reputation as one of the more secretive states in the western world. Secrecy is tightest around the security services, but it extends into all areas of central government. Why is British government so secretive? One way of answering the question is similar to the procedure in murder mysteries. To solve the case, one must first establish a motive and then an opportunity. British government has both in abundance.

Some of the motives for secrecy are:

- **Government accountability** one of the great strengths of the British system of government is said to be the clear chain of responsibility that runs directly from the electorate through the majority party in Parliament to the Cabinet and Prime Minister. Because it is not easy for the PM to escape this, there is a motive for suppressing information that might cause problems, as noted in many previous chapters.

- **Broadening scope of government activities**   the more a government spends and does, the greater the chances that something will go wrong, and the bigger the incentive for secrecy.

- **Geopolitical role**   Britain continues to play an important political role in the world – the United Nations Security Council, NATO, the G7 nations, the EU, and the Commonwealth – and has state secrets of corresponding importance.

The UK also has plenty of opportunity to impose secrecy because of:

- **the unitary state**   the more powerful the central government, the greater its ability to maintain secrecy. In Britain it is difficult for any branch of government or any other body to challenge central government.

- **Partial fusion of executive, legislative and judiciary**   giving central government substantial powers to protect itself with secrecy (we have noted how party control of the Commons operates to stifle inquiry and debate).

- **No written constitution**   which would place clear legal limits on the powers of government.

- **Not having a bill of rights** (as yet)   which clearly states the rights of citizens, although the incorporation of the EU's Convention for the Protection of Human Rights fills part of this gap (see Chapters 5 and 19).

- **No effective freedom of information act**   to guarantee open government.

- **Having an elitist political culture** (as claimed by some)   which gives governments a good deal of independence.

By western standards this is a rather unusual combination of factors. They create an unusually strong and centralised form of government with both motives and the opportunities to maintain tight government secrecy. The government has security services to match.

SUMMARY

- By definition it is difficult to draw any hard and fast conclusions about the secret state, but Britain has a reputation for being one of the most secretive of western democracies.

- The security services present democracy with a dilemma: to be effective they must be secret, but not so secretive that they are unaccountable. There are no simple solutions to this dilemma.

- The main agencies of state security and intelligence in Britain are the Security Service (MI5), the Secret Intelligence Service (MI6), the Special Branch, the

ESSAYS

1. Is it true that Britain is one of the most secretive democracies in the world, and, if so, why?

2. Is the Freedom of Information Act 2000 fundamentally flawed, as some claim?

3. The public interest is the basis of government powers to monitor private communications and the basis for it withholding information. What is the public interest and who should define it?

Defence Intelligence Staff (DIS), the Government Communications Head-quarters (GCHQ), and the National Criminal Intelligence Service (NCIS).

■ The main laws and conventions governing state secrecy are the Privy Counsellor's oath, the D-notices system, the Public Records Act (1958), the Interception of Communications Act (1985), the Security Services Acts (1989, 1996) and, most important, the Official Secrets Act (1989).

■ While some small steps have been taken towards open government and free-dom of information, recent legislation has been criticised for being inadequate and creating too many exemptions.

■ The high level of secrecy in the British State, particularly in its security services, is best explained in terms of central government having an unusual combination of motives to exercise secrecy, and opportunities to do so.

MILESTONES

Milestones in British security and secrecy

1958 Public Records Act. Designated documents not available for 30 years after the event, or longer if the Lord Chancellor decides

1968 The Fulton Committee on the Civil Service argues that it is too secret and recommends more openness

1972 The Franks Report on Section 2 of the Official Secrets Act recommends its repeal and replacement with a new, and narrower, official information act

1977 ABC trial: journalists tried and sentenced for disclosing defence information

1984 MI5 officer Michael Bettaney sentenced to 23 years' imprisonment for spying

1984 The Tisdall case about disclosing arrival of US Cruise missiles. Data Protection Act

1985 The Ponting case about the sinking of the Argentinian battleship, *General Belgrano* – Ponting claimed the Government lied

1985 PM states that security service members will not appear before select committees of the House of Commons. The European Court of Human Rights states that British law about phone tapping is insufficiently clear. This results in the Interception of Communications Act

1986 Local Government (Access to Information) Act

1986–7 The *Spycatcher* affair

1987 The Zircon affair: TV film impounded by security services

1989 Security Services Act; Official Secrets Act

1990 Access to Health Records Act. MPs Jonathan Aitken and Sir Richard Body claim that MPs are under MI5 surveillance

1991 A TV programme, *Defending the Realm*, claims that MI5 routinely spies on EU partners, commercial organisations and trade union leaders, and keeps much of this secret from ministers

1991 Citizen's Charter promises more open government

1993 Home Secretary states that the head of MI5 will not appear before the Home Affairs Select Committee of the Commons. Ex-minister Alan Clark claims that ministers are under MI5 surveillance. Limited official information released about MI5

1996 Scott Inquiry shows how secretive British government is at the top levels, and how little Parliament knows. Security Services Act

1999 Proposals for new freedom of information and anti-terrorist acts

2000 Regulation of Investigatory Powers Act (RIPA). Freedom of Information Act

2002 Freedom of Information (Scotland) Act passed by the Scottish Parliament

PROJECTS

1. Using official and private web sites, find out what is known for certain and what is only rumour and hearsay about the security and intelligence services.

2. Debate the merits and deficiencies of the Regulation of Investigatory Powers Act 2000 and the Freedom of Information Act 2000.

FURTHER READING

Little is known and not much has been written about the security services in Britain. Most textbooks barely even mention them. Books on the subject include P. Birkinshaw, *Reforming the Secret State* (Milton Keynes: Open University Press, 1991), S. Dorril, *The Silent Conspiracy: Inside the Intelligence Services in the 1990s* (London: Heinemann, 1992), and R. Norton-Taylor, *In Defence of the Realm? The Case for Accountable Security Services* (London: Civil Liberties Trust, 1990).

More is written about freedom of information – see M. Rathbone 'The Freedom of Information Act', *Talking Politics*, **13** (3), 2001, pp. 165–70 and M. Flinders, 'The politics of accountability: a case study of the freedom of information legislation in the United Kingdom', *Political Quarterly*, **71** (4), 2001, pp. 422–35.

USEFUL WEB SITES ON SECURITY AND SECRECY

Hotlinks to these sites can be found on the CWS website at http://www.booksites.net/budge.

In the wake of the terrorist attacks of 11 September 2001, issues related to intelligence and security have become more important than ever before. Global security provides an excellent introduction to the organisation and the different institutions of Britain's intelligence agencies at www.globalsecurity.org/intell/world/uk/index.html. The official web site of MI5 can be found at www.mi5.gov.uk, and the GCHQ at www.gchq.gov.uk. A great deal of information about the National Criminal Intelligence Service is available from www.ncis.co.uk. It is worth consulting the United Kingdom mission to the UN at www.ukun.org. Official documentation on the national intelligence machinery can be obtained from www.archive.official-documents.co.uk/document/caboff/nim/natint.htm. The full text of the Anti-terrorism, Crime and Security Act 2001 can be obtained from www.hmso.gov.uk/acts/acts2001/20010024.htm, the Official Secrets Act 1989 is on www.hmso.gov.uk/acts/acts1989/Ukpga_19890006_en_1.htm and for the Security Services Act 1996 visit www.hmso.gov.uk/acts/acts1996/1996035.htm.

A visit to the Lord Chancellor's Department web site on freedom of information at www.lcd.gov.uk/foi/foidpunit.htm would also be useful. The Freedom of Information Act 2000 is available at www.legislation.hmso.gov.uk/acts/acts2000/20000036.htm. The Information Commissioner (www.dataprotection.gov.uk) enforces and oversees the Data Protection Act 1998 and the Freedom of Information Act 2000. The Campaign for Freedom of Information monitors existing access rights and provides practical guides to help people use them; visit them at www.cfoi.org.uk. Liberty is an independent organisation devoted to the protection of civil liberties and human rights; their web site is available at www.liberty-human-rights.org.uk.

SISG is the Security and Intelligence Studies Group (www.rdg.ac.uk/SecInt/), a specialised group of the UK Political Studies Association. We suggest you also visit the International Centre for Security Analysis (Department of War – King's College London) at www.icsa.ac.uk.

PART 7
Policy

The Ministry of Defence

Foreign and defence policy

A major justification for keeping the extensive, and expensive, security apparatus described in the last chapter is Britain's position in world affairs. Its role as a major power means that it is vital for hostile states and interests to know about government intentions and policies. By the same token, it is important for Britain to know about theirs. This justifies large investments in decoding and intelligence gathering (spying) abroad, and placing some restrictions on freedoms at home to prevent foreign spies doing the same things here.

This rather chilling picture of Britain being unable to trust its allies and of countries constantly surveilling and undermining each other rests on a particular view of states. This defines them by their possession of a particular territory that they have to control and defend against aggressive neighbouring states. States are thus always in potential conflict with each other, no matter how united and friendly they seem. But it is not only states that present a threat to Britain. As the events in Ireland over many decades and on 11 September 2001 showed, terrorist groups can operate almost anywhere in the world and do not necessarily depend on any one state for support. This dimension to British and world politics adds further complexity to the business of making defence and foreign policy.

This chapter will:

■ describe the main actors and institutions in British foreign policy making

■ outline the 'realist' and 'idealist' views of foreign policy

■ briefly review the major events and developments in British foreign policy since the 1950s and examine the way in which these have been influenced by Britain's structural and geographical position half-way between Europe and overseas

■ trace the changes in the world that have influenced Britain's post-war foreign policy

■ analyse the motivations and assumptions governing Britain's foreign policy under New Labour and the consequences of these for its antiterrorist capacity and military role and capabilities

■ ask how successful Britain has been in achieving a world order to its government's liking and assess whether Britain really does remain a 'big player' in international affairs.

FOREIGN AND DEFENCE POLICY MAKING IN BRITAIN: ACTORS AND INSTITUTIONS

Even more than with other areas of public policy, foreign policy making in Britain is dominated by the executive. The two key Whitehall departments – the Ministry of Defence (MoD) and the Foreign and Commonwealth Office (FCO) – implement policy. The responsible Cabinet secretaries make policy, although the Prime Minister is always closely involved both with foreign policy and with strategic defence decisions. Within the Cabinet, the Overseas and Defence Policy

Committee is the main forum for foreign policy discussions. Parliament plays virtually no role in the actual formulation of policy, although via select committees and debates it can act as a focus for criticism and advice.

The FCO is unusual among Whitehall departments in having few direct constituents. Instead, it oversees the Diplomatic Service, which in turn protects and advances British commercial and diplomatic interests in embassies and consulates throughout the world. As with most other diplomatic services, it operates (at least in part) according to a set of externally agreed international rules governing the behaviour of foreign governments and international organisations such as NATO and the United Nations. In most international political contexts there is, therefore, a foreign policy 'line' that puts negotiation, tact and compromise first, and confrontation second. Nonetheless, the FCO can be subject to pressures both from within government and from societal interests. Relief organisations may work to change the government line in Afghanistan, for example, or human rights groups may call for an embargo on arms sales to autocratic regimes.

The MoD is a very different political animal. It directly serves the very important constituency of the armed services and, indirectly, arms manufacturers and suppliers. Often there is potential or actual conflict of interest between the two departments. At the time of the Falklands War, for example, it was the obligation of the FCO to seek a political solution, while the MoD was obliged to continue its preparations for armed conflict should diplomatic initiatives fail. The Falklands episode also demonstrates just how intimately involved are Prime Ministers when Britain engages in armed conflict overseas. At some stages of the crisis Prime Minister Thatcher was taking decisions almost on her own.

Other departments including the Department for the Environment, Food and Rural Affairs (DEFRA), the Department of Trade and Industry (DTI) and the Treasury can also be closely involved in foreign policy, and liaison committees, interdepartmental groups and exchanges of personnel help facilitate policy co-ordination.

As we saw in Chapter 8, the EU increasingly impinges on foreign and defence policy. Joint projects such as the 'Eurofighter' have a clear EU dimension. And, generally, the moves towards a common defence and foreign policy have crucial implications for the future of the whole policy area.

REALISM AND IDEALISM

The view that states need to be on perpetual guard against each other is the so-called 'realist' view of international relations. It is termed 'realist' because its proponents claim to be able to see beyond governments' protestations of good intent and desire for the common good to their 'real' motives, which on this view are always selfish and aimed at material and territorial gain at the expense of their neighbours.

As most other states are too small and weak to hurt Britain, historically this analysis has mostly concerned the 'big players', that is, France, Germany, Russia, the USA, Japan and China, although most recently it has also included 'rogue' states such as Serbia (until 2000) and Iraq (until 2003). 'Realist' assessments of the world are most influential in regard to military affairs, where decision makers are usually obliged to adopt a 'worst case' view in order to know what their capabilities should be to ward off the worst threats. Of course, it also dominated assessments during the Cold War (1948–90) when the US-led NATO alliance (of which Britain was a leading member) confronted the Soviet Union and its allies, sometimes violently but never in full-scale war.

BRIEFINGS

22.1 The Soviet Union (USSR) and the Warsaw Pact

The collapse of the Russian Empire in the First World War (1917) led to a political takeover by the Communist Party after a civil war (1918–22). The Empire was reconstituted within a reduced territory as the Union of Soviet Socialist Republics (USSR). The republics were created as political units to satisfy the aspirations of the minority peoples of the old Empire who had been conquered by the Russians. However, the Russian Federal Socialist Republic (RFSR) remained the largest and predominant republic. In any case, all the republics and the USSR as a whole were effectively ruled by the Communist Party, which was the real centre of power.

The USSR was attacked by Nazi Germany in 1941 and bore the brunt of fighting over the next four years. Soviet troops gradually pushed the Germans back and occupied eastern Germany and east–central Europe. Communist regimes modelled on the Soviet one were forcibly installed in all these countries while the Soviet frontier was extended to take in all the territory of the old Empire.

These actions led to a break with the USA and Britain. Hostility and frontier incidents prompted the formation of a western military alliance in 1949 (NATO, the North Atlantic Treaty Organisation) covering the USA, Canada, Britain and most countries of western Europe. NATO left troops in Europe, notably in Germany and Britain, which were confronted by the forces of the Warsaw Pact, dominated by the USSR.

The confrontation between those opposing sides was known as the Cold War and lasted from 1948 to 1990. The inefficiency of the Soviet system brought it to an end, as the USSR was unable to sustain a high-technology arms race with the USA. The countries of east–central Europe instituted democracy while the minority republics of the USSR broke away to become independent, leaving Russia itself as the successor state.

With the end of the Cold War and the growth of intergovernmental co-operation channelled through organisations such as the United Nations and the European Union, another analysis of international relations has gained support. Termed 'idealism', this sees countries as having many common interests that they can maximise only through full co-operation. Often such co-operation involves the setting up of international regimes and organisations that may even take over sovereign power from states in certain areas. To a considerable extent these 'idealist' assumptions are the ones that led to the formation of the EU. They also have a considerable affinity to the nineteenth-century idea that countries could attain peace and prosperity by opening themselves to each other through free trade, as described in Chapter 2. Indeed, an alternative label for the idealist position is (international) liberalism.

22.2 The United Nations

The First World War (1914–18) killed around 20 million people through fighting, famine and disease, mostly in Europe. To help avoid conflict in the future, the victors hoped to create a world body that would bring nation states together and help them resolve disputes peacefully. This was the League of Nations. The League held regular assemblies but became increasingly ineffective as national conflicts intensified in the 1930s. It was also weakened by the fact that the USA and USSR were never members. It did, however, do useful work through its specialised organisations, particularly for refugees in the 1920s and was associated with bodies such as the International Labour Organization (ILO), which tried to get world agreement on working conditions.

Such bodies were inherited by the League's successor organisation, the United Nations, set up in 1946 after the Second World War (1939–45). This tried to avoid the weaknesses of the League by having, besides a General Assembly in which all States had a vote, a Security Council of major powers: USA, USSR (now Russia), China, Britain and France. Each of these can veto UN action, but if they agree they control forces that other States cannot resist. The UN has proved a useful umbrella both for intervention where order has broken down and to police disputed borders. The intervention in Bosnia (1992–5) was a mixture of both. The UN has been relatively ineffective in stopping fighting, however, because Member States often disagree on objectives and are reluctant to pay for costs.

Like the League, the UN does much useful work through specialised agencies for refugees, education, children and health, and also works for international agreements on the environment. The Secretary-General appointed by the Assembly has become a world figure but as a result is often controversial and opposed by one or other of the superpowers. The activity of the UN marks another breakdown in the traditional view of the state as a sovereign entity controlling everything that happens within its own borders.

As we shall see, both 'realism' and 'idealism' have influenced British foreign and military policy. Like most general ideas, however, they do not give complete answers to the practical decisions faced by governments. For example, the concepts have but limited application in the fight against international terrorism. Terrorism is often inspired not by state-based nationalism but by broader religious or ideological causes that cut across nations and continents. Thus, increasing terrorist threats require different military and diplomatic tactics from those appropriate to fighting the Cold War and other 'traditional' conflicts involving nation states.

POST-WAR DEVELOPMENTS IN BRITISH FOREIGN POLICY

A summary of major events and developments is given in the milestones section at the end of the chapter. For convenience they are grouped under three headings: general international developments involving Britain; decolonisation – the process of disengagement from the colonial empire that in 1945 covered almost a quarter of the globe; and the European Union, already discussed in Chapters 8 and 9.

The problem of decolonisation was a major preoccupation of the first half of the post-war period, as it carried potential threats to British investment and trade

Decolonisation
Colonies are foreign territories dominated by stronger states by means of military and economic power. Decolonisation, therefore, is the process of withdrawing from colonial relations with foreign countries so that they gain the autonomy of an independent sovereign state.

Cold War The state of international relations between the West and the communist bloc, which stopped short of outright war but involved intense hostility, the stockpiling of arms and the maintenance of large armies in case war should break out.

and might involve the army in unwinnable colonial wars. As the colonies became independent, however, Britain's direct involvement diminished and government attention shifted to the accelerating moves towards economic and political union in Europe, culminating in the 'deepening and widening' of the European Union in the 1990s.

Some have seen this shift of attention from overseas to Europe as evidence of the decline of Britain from a world power to a regional, European power. But this is to ignore the major preoccupation of British governments throughout the post-war period, which was neither the Empire nor the European Union but the Cold War, the standoff between NATO (led by the USA and backed heavily by Britain) and the USSR. This involved a state of constant military readiness on both sides, the stockpiling of huge nuclear and other military weapons, and the maintenance of large armies. As part of their commitment to NATO the Americans maintained important air and army bases in Britain and Germany, to confront the Soviet forces stationed in central and eastern Europe.

The Cold War sometimes erupted into local conflicts, although the Americans and Russians never confronted each other directly. Thus in Korea (1950–3) US troops, supported by Britain and other NATO allies, fought North Korean and Chinese troops backed by the Soviet Union. In Vietnam (1964–75) US troops with local support fought local communist troops backed by the Soviet Union. In Afghanistan (1979–89) Soviet troops fought local guerrillas armed and financed in part by the USA.

With the collapse of the Soviet Union and communism in eastern and central Europe between 1989 and 1991, British foreign policy has been redirected towards maintaining stability and peace in a multi-polar world. Hence, the major foreign engagements of the last ten years have involved Bosnia, Kosovo, East Timor, Afghanistan policing Iraqi belligerence in the Middle East and fighting international terrorism.

CHANGING WORLD CONTEXT

Clearly, the developments we have traced have not taken place in a vacuum. British politics and interests have changed in response to other events taking place around them. For example, the British would hardly have abandoned their Empire of their own volition. They got out because they sensed their presence would no longer be tolerated by the colonised populations, or even perhaps by the two superpowers, the USA and USSR. In this section, we outline the major changes in the world context that influenced British responses in the post-war period. These policy changes in the post-war period are reflected in a changing climate of ideas as to how foreign policy should be conducted.

Changing climate of ideas

Ideas are often discounted as a source of influence in politics, in part because of the realist view that what matters are resources and power. No matter what governments say, they will always try to do each other down because all they 'really' care about is maximising their own state interests.

Such a 'hard-boiled' view of international relations often attracts people because it cuts through the pretence and hypocrisy with which governments often mask their own self-interest. It is true up to a point and in many situations, but, by the same token, ideas and ideals often exert an independent influence on events. For example, in order to understand how subsistence farmers were mobilised throughout the third world against well-equipped colonial armies, one needs to appreciate the force of nationalism and calls for social justice.

Not surprisingly, therefore, material changes in global economics and politics have been accompanied in the post-war period by changes in the overall climate of ideas. Four of these are worth highlighting. One was that the 'white man's burden' view of Empire – in which the colonising powers claimed to be on a civilising mission that would grant independence to colonial peoples 'when they were ready for it' – became increasingly unacceptable. It was replaced by embarrassment about the domination and exploitation of the third world that colonialism implied. Unfortunately for the newly liberated colonial populations, however, this change in attitude was not accompanied by much of a willingness on the part of the ex-colonial powers to make up for earlier exploitation.

A second change in the climate of opinion after 1945 was the apparently increasing appeal of communism as a mobilising ideology of the dispossessed. Anti-imperialists throughout the third world frequently saw the economic and political difficulties that their countries faced, even after decolonisation, as deriving from the global capitalist system of production, distribution and exchange. Between 1945 and 1975 over 30 countries 'succumbed' to the attractions of Marxist–Leninist ideology (and, as we saw, the British were often combating it in the colonies). After 1980, however, this seemingly inexorable tide of socialism went into rapid reverse. With the success of the Islamic revolution in Iran after 1978, with Moscow's conflict with Islamic forces in Afghanistan after 1979, and with the collapse of socialism in eastern Europe and in the Soviet Union (1989–90), communism's appeal as a vehicle for mobilising deeply felt grievances declined significantly. A third major change in the post-war climate of international opinion was an increased interest in, and commitment to, the promotion of individual human rights. In part this emphasis reflected a conscious rejection of the 'collective rights' stressed by communism. But it also reflected a genuine humanitarian effort on the part of western governments and non-governmental organisations (such as Charter 88 and Amnesty International), that sought to extend internationally the protective cover of human rights legislation.

A fourth set of ideas emerged in the 1990s around the goal of establishing a New World Order based on spreading freedom and democracy to all nation states. Although agreement among the leading democratic powers on exactly *how* this was to be achieved was never established, international forces did fight wars in Bosnia, Kosovo, Afghanistan and Iraq that resulted in the overthrow of aggressive regimes. In the case of Afghanistan, of course, the intention was to eliminate a regime that directly succoured international terrorism. In all these cases, Britain played a crucial role either directly through military action or as a key ally of the United States. By 2003, the toppling of regimes that harbour terrorists became the main goal of the New World Order led by the United States with strong support from Britain.

BRIEFINGS

22.3 The international human rights movement

The United Nations launched a Universal Declaration of the Rights of Man [sic] when it was founded. Although another of its principles was mutual non-interference in the internal affairs of states, in practice gross breaches of rights have led to UN or NATO intervention (for example, in Bosnia from 1992 onwards).

Mutual policing of rights was, in fact, institutionalised by the Helsinki Accords of 1975, signed between the NATO and Warsaw Pact countries. Britain and the USA have also made protests about violation of human rights in China. Under the auspices of the Council of Europe Britain and other members have submitted themselves to the jurisdiction of the European Court of Human Rights to which individuals and groups in Britain can appeal against the British government. The European Court of Justice, in practice, applies the European Convention on Human Rights in its own jurisdiction, and Britain has incorporated it into its domestic legislation (see Chapter 19).

Supplementing these governmental initiatives, voluntary organisations such as Amnesty International, with headquarters in London, have policed each country's own observance of basic rights and procedures, publicised abuses and sent observers to trials to monitor what is going on. Britain has been reasonably supportive of their efforts, though sometimes subject to criticism itself.

Globalisation

Nationalist movements in the old empires were not, of course, fuelled wholly by ideas. European rule produced economic development, which in turn brought social and political tensions. The process of urbanisation, together with the expansion of education and mass communications, fragmented old social networks, rendering the indigenous populations of the colonies much more susceptible to the new, radical ideas. By developing the colonies the imperial powers created the very conditions in which anti-colonial oppositions could thrive.

The British were astute enough to realise this early on, concentrating on putting the more congenial members of the opposition in power and integrating them and their newly independent countries into the western political and trading system. In doing so, they contributed to the process of 'globalisation' that has transformed the world over the last 50 years. Globalisation relates primarily to the process whereby all parts of the world, even the most remote and isolated, have been linked up by western trade and communications. Therefore, the way people live and work, the way they dress, the food they consume, the things they do – even the way they think – has become more similar. There are very few subsistence economies left that produce only for themselves. Even the largest western economies are not self-sufficient any more but dependent on networks of traders and producers in other parts of the world.

Before 1945 countries with relatively powerful economies tended to use their economic and military muscle to extend their direct political influence beyond their current national boundaries. European imperialism in the nineteenth century, and German and Japanese expansionism in the 1930s involved precisely this sort of extension. Since 1945, however, nation states have increasingly recognised

Imperialism
The practice of one nation controlling or dominating another state or territory, usually by military and economic means, and to the advantage of the imperial power.

that economic security and global influence can be achieved without direct or indirect political control, as the cases of post-war Germany and Japan have demonstrated.

A related change in the international system has been the massive increase in world trade and financial exchanges. These increases have both reflected and reinforced the revolutions in transport technology and global communications that have occurred since 1945. Although direct comparison is difficult, the available figures suggest that the volume of world trade in goods and services in 1999 was more than 25 times greater than it had been in 1950. The volume of currency exchanges and capital transfers, spurred on by trade liberalisation and deregulation, was so great by the late 1990s that it was beyond the capability of national governments even to monitor them effectively. This expansion of the financial sector, in particular, has served to increase the significance of international markets and market forces. Economists sometimes speak about the permeability of national economies, meaning the extent to which capital, labour, goods and services can be either introduced into or extracted from a given country. There can be little doubt that, over the last 50 years, the average level of permeability has increased considerably. The consequence of this has been a corresponding decrease in the decision-making autonomy of national governments, which have found their economic policy strategies increasingly vulnerable to international market pressures.

Reflecting economic globalisation and integration one can observe a parallel growth of 'international regimes'. Regimes are sets of international 'rules of the game' accepted by states because of the importance of joint rather than independent decision making in many areas. States are prepared to accept regime-imposed restrictions on their decision-making autonomy on two conditions: first, that the benefits of any co-operation sponsored by the regime more than outweigh the costs entailed by any loss of autonomy; and second, that the regime is able to ensure that states which fail to co-operate (or which 'free ride' on the concessions made by others) are suitably penalised.

In the post-war period international regimes have proliferated to such an extent that we cannot even attempt to describe them all here. Three examples, however, indicate the wide range of contexts in which international regimes have developed. In the economic sphere, the General Agreement on Tariffs and Trade (GATT) (now the World Trade Organisation) has been remarkably successful, through a series of negotiating rounds that culminated in the Uruguay Round in the early 1990s, in bringing down trade barriers and in expanding world trade. In the security sphere, the Conference on (now the Organisation for) Security and Co-operation in Europe made an important contribution to the softening of east–west relations in the years immediately before the end of the Cold War. Finally, in the ecological sphere, the Vienna Convention (1985), and the Montreal Protocol (1987) established and extended guidelines for reducing CFC production in order to protect the earth's ozone layer and the Kyoto Protocol on Climate Change (1997) proposed a reduction in the emission of 'greenhouse' gases.

Ensuring compliance with a regime's rules is always a difficult matter in practice and in some instances, for example the Kyoto Protocol, a major country such as the United States withdrew its support with the coming of the Bush Presidency

Trade liberalisation
The process whereby international trade is increasingly opened up to market forces (free trade) by reducing trading tariffs, import and export controls, and other forms of protection.

International regimes
Sets of international institutions and 'rules of the game' that are created and accepted by states in order to promote international co-operation and integration, as opposed to independent decision making and national competition.

in 2001. Nonetheless, the enormous growth of regime-like organisations and practices since 1945 represents an important change in the international environment in which Britain now operates. To a lesser extent this also reflects the commitment of successive UK governments to the construction of regimes that would themselves facilitate further international co-operation (a practical application of 'idealist' principles).

MOTIVATIONS AND ASSUMPTIONS OF BRITISH FOREIGN POLICY

Foreign policy is largely constrained by developments in the surrounding world. No country can simply devise a policy and carry it through, unaffected by external events. Any attempt to ignore these would be self-defeating.

British foreign policy is no exception and has clearly had to respond to the developments traced earlier. The real question is whether it has been a good or bad response. Has it succeeded in advancing British interests as well as could be expected within the inevitable constraints or has it squandered resources while not achieving its objectives? We will be able to judge this better after analysing policy in this section and considering British capabilities, both general and military, in the following one.

The key question with regard to foreign policy, as with any other policy, is whose interests are being served? It is a mistake to assume that there is any readily identifiable general British 'national interest' to be served by its foreign policy. Usually there are competing interests, one of which successfully asserts a claim to be the 'national interest' while the others lose out.

It is only fair to say, however, that the major motivation behind post-war policy, to defend liberal democracy and the capitalist system against communist attempts to subvert it, enjoyed widespread support among all sections of the population. Thus, on the major lines of British policy – managed decolonisation, staunch membership of NATO, support for international organisations and regimes operating on broadly democratic liberal lines (the UN, WTO) – there was broad agreement.

On some of the more detailed implementation of policy, there might naturally be dissent. Three major areas are the European Union, nuclear deterrence and the relationship with the USA.

European Union

The decision to join the European Union, taken by a Conservative government in 1972, was attacked by the trade unions and Labour Party as a sell-out to European capitalist interests that would thwart left-wing plans for a radical overhaul of British society. Paradoxically, by the 1990s the EU was seen by the Conservative right in exactly parallel terms, as a leftist constraint on radical free market reform in Britain! Both reactions demonstrated the structural and cultural difficulties the British had in coping with the capitalist–protectionist traditions of France and Germany, so alien to support for a totally free market in Britain.

Nuclear deterrent
The threatened use of nuclear weapons to prevent aggression on the part of foreign states, on the grounds that the aggressor nation will suffer too much damage to make the venture worthwhile.

Nuclear deterrence and unilateral disarmament

Few groups in Britain advocated a pullout from NATO. There was considerably more support for giving up the independent British nuclear deterrent, which was seen as expensive and unreliable in light of US capabilities. Protests against British nuclear, and to a lesser extent chemical, weapons reached a head in the 1960s, when the Campaign for Nuclear Disarmament could muster up to half a million people in its protest marches. In the 1980s there were other protests against the stationing of US nuclear missiles on British soil.

The 'special relationship' with America

British leaders (including Tony Blair) have long argued that Britain has a special relationship with the USA, based on a common language and traditions and a history of opposing common foes (Germany, Japan, the Soviet Union). The relationship took its most concrete form inside NATO, where Britain actively backed up the US leadership. Most other NATO members were content to let the USA carry a disproportionate share of common defence costs. Britain, in contrast, allocated a significantly higher proportion of its GDP to defence. In 1979, for example, the UK spent 4.7 per cent of GDP on defence compared with Germany's 3.9 per cent. In the 1990s the purchase from the USA of Trident submarines to carry nuclear missiles still went on, even under Labour, while the new government reaffirmed its commitment to development of a Eurofighter, estimated to cost £15 billion.

In the post-Cold War era Britain has consistently supported American policy in the Gulf War (1991), Bosnia (1995–7), Kosovo (1999), Afghanistan (2002) and Iraq (2003) even when American actions have been given at best a lukewarm reception from other EU states such as Germany and France. In 2002–3, the British gave the strongest support to the Bush administration to topple the Saddam Hussein regime in Iraq. This almost unquestioning loyalty to the Americans has led many to argue that the UK is America's 'poodle' or is still trying to emulate its imperial past by slavishly supporting the exercise of American power. This critique raises the question of British defence and foreign policy capability. Why should a mid-sized power with a mid-sized economy play such a prominent role in global affairs?

BRITISH CAPABILITIES IN THE POST-COLD WAR ERA

Britain has always had a large 'defence establishment' made up of arms producers, the armed forces and supportive officials in Whitehall. For many years it was argued that an overemphasis on defence industries was 'distorting' the economy by starving 'civilian' industries such as car manufacturing of capital and technological help. Whether or not this is in fact true, the high priority given to defence industries has resulted in the development of arms manufacturing into one of the more successful and largest areas of the British economy. Britain is one

Plate 22.1 *Michael Cummings cartoon in* The Times, *26 July 1997: the government grants export licences for more Hawk jets to Indonesia and sponsors an international arms fair – after Labour pledges that it 'would not permit the sales of arms to regimes that might use them for internal repression or internal aggression'. More than 200,000 innocent people have died in East Timor and internal dissent has been ruthlessly suppressed in parts of Indonesia*

of the three leading arms exporters in the world (along with the USA and France). British armaments firms such as British Aerospace depend heavily on British taxes to provide a protected market where they can recoup costs on weapon development and subsidise overseas sales. Their close relationships with the civil servants of the Ministry of Defence have meant that massive cost overruns and delays on weapons development have not only been tolerated, but paid for, by British taxpayers. Often these have escalated to five or six times the original cost of a project. The Ministry of Defence has been astonishingly tolerant of this and has never been held closely to account for its expenditures, even in the most cost-conscious and cost-cutting days of Conservative government. The argument that national security is involved seems to silence critics, who may also be under pressure from the security services mentioned in the last chapter.

The argument that military investments have distorted economic ones does seem to have some validity but these effects are not unique to Britain. Exactly similar subsidies to arms firms and the blurring of civil and military expenditures have occurred in France and the USA. It seems that any country with a sizeable military force is liable to run into these problems.

The armaments industry is powerful partly because it has protectors and supporters right up to the highest levels of government. High-ranking ministers have had past links with arms firms or taken up positions with them after leaving office. So also have retired civil servants, particularly from the Ministry of Defence. Their technical expertise may have some market use but they are more likely valued for their political and administrative contacts.

22.4 The career of Jonathan Aitken, journalist, arms dealer, politician, criminal

Jonathan Aitken is a nephew of one of the pre-war media moguls, Lord Beaverbrook (Max Aitken). He was prosecuted under the Official Secrets Act in 1971, when he reported in the *Sunday Telegraph* that arms sales to Nigeria were much larger than the government claimed. After he was acquitted he went on to engage in the arms trade himself, becoming particularly involved in the huge arms deals of the 1980s with Saudi Arabia.

At the same time he became a Conservative MP and rose rapidly, becoming Chief Secretary to the Treasury – second in command of finances – in the 1990s. He continued to accept hospitality from Saudi Arabians engaged in the arms trade. Mohamed Al Fayed, who was pursuing a personal vendetta against the British Establishment, leaked receipts to the *Guardian* from a stay of Aitken's at the Ritz Hotel in Paris that had been paid for in this way. Government ministers are not supposed to accept such hospitality in case they are influenced improperly.

The case contributed to the accusations of sleaze facing the Major government and Aitken resigned from his post in a reshuffle in order to pursue a libel charge against the *Guardian*. This had to be abandoned in 1997, amid accusations of perjury against him. Aitken's final disgrace came in 1999 when he was jailed for this perjury offence.

Aitken's career illustrates the close connection between the arms trade, politics and journalism in Britain, and the role of the Official Secrets Act and severe libel laws in suppressing relevant political information. It is still unclear what the influence of arms dealers over government policy really is, but their ability to gain high level political representation and to influence aid-for-trade deals, such as the Pergau Dam, in Malaysia, indicates that it is great. What facts we have come mostly from investigative journalism to which, paradoxically, Aitken contributed at the beginning of his career.

There is also an institutionalised pressure group right at the heart of government that will always speak up for defence contracts. This is the Joint Chiefs of Staff Committee, representing the high commands of the army, navy and air force. Naturally the generals, air marshals and admirals are anxious to see their forces well equipped. They have two reasons for this: first, a genuine concern that the military should have the capability for what is demanded of them; and second, the more that is spent on the armed forces the more important they and their commanders become in the governmental structure. Influence correlates with budgets, so budget cutting constitutes a major threat.

By the same token, decisions about what weapons to buy generally sets off a struggle within the armed forces. Is money to be invested on ships for the navy, new fighters for the air force or tanks for the army? Each service desperately tries to ensure that it is not downgraded relative to the others. Withdrawal 'east of Suez' in the late 1960s meant that the navy was no longer so important for guarding extended communication routes to India and southeast Asia. It was compensated to some extent, however, by the shift in delivery systems for the nuclear bomb from aircraft to submarines. The expeditions to the Falklands and the Gulf again demonstrated the importance of the navy in carrying troops to where they were needed. However, airlifts were also very important, and air offensives were

	1994/5 outturn	1995/6 outturn	1996/7 outturn	1997/8 outturn	1998/9 outturn	1990/00 outturn	2000/01 plans	2001/02 plans
					(£ million)			
Cash provision[1]	22,562	21,517	22,345	21,610	22,475	22,863	22,820	22,981
As percentage of GDP[2]	3.3	3.0	2.9	2.7	2.6	2.6	2.5	2.4
Cash provision in real terms[3]	26,075	23,791	24,315	22,878	23,037	22,863	22,318	21,927
Year-on-year change in real terms (%)		−8.8	+2.2	−5.9	+0.7	−0.8	−2.4	−1.8

Table 22.1 *Trends in defence spending*

Notes: [1] Figures exclude the element of receipts arising from the sale of the married quarters estate that were appropriated onto defence votes in 1996/7 and 1997/8. [2] Based on the latest available GDP assumptions. [3] At 1999/2000 prices, based on the latest available GDP deflators

Source: The Government's Expenditure Plans 2000/2001 to 2001/2002, Ministry of Defence, Cm 4608, April 2000, Table 6

a crucial element in both these cases as also in Bosnia, Kosovo, Afghanistan and Iraq. That is one reason why the Royal Air Force (RAF) has managed to retain political support for an expanded rapid deployment capability for moving troops and equipment around the world.

The need for an effective army is unchallenged, whether to fight off a large-scale invasion of Europe or, more recently, to undertake limited war or peace-keeping operations (which often in fact develop into low-intensity conflicts). The question, as always, is what kind of army with what kind of equipment? Should it be equipped to fight at all levels, even if some possibilities are less likely than others are? The concern of governments in the twenty-first century is to get as much value for money as possible – especially given the pressure to increase spending in such areas as health and education. In one sense, the demise of the Cold War and the emergence of a war on terror and on small but aggressive states such as Iraq has made these choices easier. For what is needed today is a highly trained, well-equipped and highly mobile defence capability. This need not involve a large army (Britain has one of the smaller armies in relation to its size in Europe). Neither does it have to be very expensive. As can be seen from Table 22.1 defence spending has in fact been slowly declining in recent years – especially if expressed as a percentage of GDP. None of this is to argue that the defence establishment is happy with the contraction of the armed forces. But recent events do show that even with relatively small forces, Britain can still play a major international role.

Following the terrorist attacks of September 2001, the Americans became much more willing to use troops abroad in order to establish domestic and international peace. Given the vast size of their armed forces it is likely, therefore, that as in Afghanistan and Iraq, they will provide the main force supported by smaller British (and other) forces. Britain may in fact be establishing a 'niche' role in the New World Order as a seasoned peacekeeper and loyal ally of the Americans.

BRITISH FOREIGN AND DEFENCE POLICY: THE PARTY POLITICAL DIMENSION

One of the most interesting aspects of the foreign and defence policy area is that Labour and Conservative governments have broadly adopted the same strategic stances. It was the 1945–50 Labour government that first took up a realist confrontational stance towards the Soviet Union – a stance that, in spite of opposition from the Labour left, was adhered to by all governments right until the collapse of the Soviet Union in 1991. Indeed, apart from contrasting attitudes on the EU, it is very difficult to discern major differences between Labour and Conservative governments in any area of foreign policy in the last 50 years. They may criticise each other in opposition and Labour, in particular, may promise to deliver a foreign policy that pays more attention to considerations of human rights than do the Conservatives, but once in office these differences usually diminish or even disappear.

This certainly applies to the Labour government elected in 1997. On coming to office Robin Cook declared that foreign policy would have a strong 'ethical dimension' and not one where 'political values can be left behind when we check in our passports to travel on diplomatic business' (cited in Hamill, 1997, p. 29). Indeed both Robin Cook and Prime Minister Blair promised to change the values of the 'foreign and defence policy establishment' by ensuring that, among other things, Britain would not sell arms to undemocratic states that then proceeded to use them against their own people. On 21 May 1997 the government signed up to the 'Ottawa Process' – a Canadian-led initiative to ban the production and stockpiling of anti-personnel mines. In addition, the government did not stand formally in the way of the extradition of former dictator General Pinochet to Spain to face prosecution for war crimes.

In spite of these initiatives, however, the fundamentals of foreign policy, including the pattern of arms sales, remained the same as under the Conservative government. By the late 1990s, Britain had become the second largest defence exporter in the world after the USA. In no instance did it reverse a past pattern of major arms sales, including the sale of Hawk jets to Indonesia – a country known to have used force of arms against dissident citizens. In effect, the commercial imperatives of the arms industry have taken precedence over humanitarian concerns. To be fair, Britain does not sell arms to a number of countries on strategic and political grounds. And these states (including North Korea, Iraq, Iran and many African countries) usually have very poor records on human rights.

The absence of fundamental differences between the parties also applied to the events following the terrorist attacks on the United States in September 2001. Tony Blair together with his Foreign Secretary, Jack Straw (who replaced Robin Cook in the second Labour term), gave almost total support to the American actions in Afghanistan and Iraq, thus strengthening further the special relationship with America. Iain Duncan Smith and other Tory leaders fully supported the government's position. Indeed most of the opposition to British engagement initially came from within the Labour Party and the trade union movement, although as events in Iraq came to a head in 2003, the anti-war coalition broadened to include a large cross-section of society.

Support for the USA fits well with Tony Blair's belief in a world order underpinned by democracy and the rule of law. The policies that result from this, including support for American leadership, often carry with them considerable risks. These include not only the loss of life and suffering that goes with military action, but also intra-party support and the loss of prestige and influence that can result from military and diplomatic failure. So, in spite of the relative decline in Britain's forces and in the domestic economy, Britain continues to play for very high stakes on the world stage. No other European country has taken on such a role. In this regard, Britain's international influence remains far greater than could be expected from a medium sized European power.

ESSAYS

1. Does the Blair government's role in Bosnia, Kosovo, Afghanistan and Iraq demonstrate that the 'special relationship' with the USA really does exist?

2. What accounts for the differences in approaches to foreign and defence policy among the countries of the European Union?

3. Outline Britain's role in the conduct of the Cold War, 1948–90.

4. 'In foreign policy there have been more differences *within* British political parties than *between* them.' Discuss.

SUMMARY

Following a brief outline of the major actors and institutions in foreign and defence policy, this chapter has reviewed British foreign and military policy over the post-war period. This has been dominated by three developments:

1. decolonisation (1945–64)

2. increasing involvement with the European Union, culminating in the possibility of economic and monetary union at the start of the millennium

3. European and world security, seen by British governments as best secured by a close alliance with the USA inside NATO.

In the light of these:

- British governments have been criticised for trying to do too much abroad in support of the USA (the 'special relationship').

- Although money could have been saved on costly defence projects it is difficult to see what else, broadly, Britain could have done. Major mistakes have been avoided and the NATO alliance 'won' the Cold War.

- Overlaying this strategic need is the question of the protection of human rights and the pressures to pursue an ethical foreign policy. However, such objectives often conflict with commercial imperatives as the experience of the Blair government shows.

- As the major US ally, Britain under Tony Blair has taken a highly interventionist stance in world affairs since the terrorist attacks in September 2001. The Conservatives supported him in this stance. Such a strategy carries with it a risk not only of domestic opposition to the use of military force, but also from abroad and especially the European Union.

MILESTONES

Milestones in post-war foreign policy

	World		Decolonisation		European Union
1945	Defeat of Nazi Germany and Japan				
1946	Foundation of UN				
1946–8	Growing tensions between USA and USSR initiate Cold War. US Marshall aid stabilises economic situation in UK and western Europe	1948	Independence of India, Pakistan, Burma, Ceylon and Palestine		
1949	Communist takeover of China	1950–4	Mau-Mau war in Kenya		
1949	Foundation of NATO, the US-dominated military alliance against USSR. UK leading initiator and member	1951–60	Guerrilla war in Malaya	1951	Treaty of Paris: the six – Belgium, the Netherlands, Luxembourg, France, Italy and West Germany – form European Coal and Steel Community (ECSC)
1950–3	Korean War: NATO confronts China				
1948–55	Britain develops nuclear bomb	1956	Abortive invasion of Suez by UK with France and Israel	1957	Treaty of Rome: European Economic Community aims at free market of six countries
1950–73	World economic growth and liberalisation of trade under GATT	1956–62	Guerrilla war in Cyprus		
		1960	Ghana becomes first African colony to gain independence		
1962	Attempt by USSR to place missiles in Cuba brings USA and USSR to brink of nuclear war	1960–2	Peaceful independence of most African, Caribbean and Pacific colonies	1962–3	British application to join EEC rejected
1964–75	US defeat in Vietnam War, tensions within NATO. UK stays aloof	1960–3	Breakdown of British rule in South Arabia	1966	De Gaulle establishes right of national veto within the EC (Luxembourg compromise)
1962–79	US–USSR relaxation of Cold War, mutual arms limitation	1962–4	Successful confrontation with Indonesia in Borneo		

	World		Decolonisation		European Union
1967	Devaluation of sterling	1964–94	White regimes in Rhodesia and South Africa first consolidate power, then negotiate handover to African majority	1968	British application rejected
1972	Discovery of oil in British North Sea	1968–72	British military withdrawal from east of Suez		
1973–7	Steep rise in world oil prices initiates inflation and periodic economic recessions	1970–96	Northern Irish terrorism	1973	UK, Ireland and Denmark join EEC
1979–88	Renewed arms race provokes economic crisis in USSR and ends Cold War on US terms	1982	Falklands War: sea-borne British expedition reconquers islands from Argentina	1979	Direct elections to European Parliament
1989	Central and eastern European regimes democratise and create free markets			1985–6	The Single European Act undermines national veto by introducing qualified majority voting on measures to achieve a single market
1989–93	World economic recession				
1991	USSR splits between Russia, Ukraine and other successor states			1986	Spain and Portugal join EC
1991	Gulf War: NATO against Iraq			1992	Treaty of Maastricht plans for economic and political union. UK 'opts out' of Social Chapter
				1992	Black Wednesday: UK forced out of European Monetary System
1992–5	Bosnia crisis ended by NATO intervention			1993	EMS reorganised with broader exchange rate bands
1993	Further liberalisations of world trade under GATT			1994–7	Plans for single currency and closer union increasingly attacked by UK Conservative government
1993–8	Gradual world recovery from recession			1995	Finland, Sweden and Austria join EU

▶

	World		Decolonisation		European Union
		1997	UK returns Hong Kong to China	1997	Amsterdam Summit fails to move to closer union. New Labour government accepts Social Chapter and welcomes EMU
1999	War in Kosovo provokes a NATO military response			2000	EU moves haltingly towards a common defence and foreign policy
2001–2	Terrorist attacks on the United States provokes strong British backing for American action in Afghanistan. Taliban regime toppled			2002	EU supports action in Afghanistan but is more cautious than UK and US
2002–3	US and UK military intervention in Iraq			2002–3	Germany and some other EU states initially oppose intervention in Iraq

FURTHER READING

For a critical overview of British foreign policy, see David Sanders, *Losing an Empire, Finding a Role: British Foreign Policy since 1945* (London: Macmillan, 1990). Bernard Porter, *The Lion's Share: A Short History of British Imperialism* (Harlow: Longman, 1988) gives the background to decolonisation. On arms sales, see Mark Phythian, *The Politics of British Arms Sales since 1964* (Manchester: Manchester University Press, 2000). On the special relationship, see John Dumbrell, *A Special Relationship: Anglo-American Relations since 1960* (Basingstoke: Macmillan, 2000). On ethics and New Labour, see James Hamill, 'New Labour, ethics, foreign policy', *Politics Review*, November 1997, pp. 29–33. David A. Baldwin (ed.), *Neorealism and Neoliberalism: The Contemporary Debate* (New York: Columbia University Press, 1993) gives an overview of these contrasting views of international relations, on which so many evaluations of British foreign policy depend. Accessible articles on foreign policy in general with an emphasis on the British role can be found in *International Affairs*, the quarterly journal of the Royal Institute of International Affairs.

USEFUL WEB SITES ON FOREIGN AND DEFENCE POLICY

Hotlinks to these sites can be found on the CWS website at http://www.booksites.net/budge.

A general introduction to some of the landmarks in British foreign relations is available from http://britishhistory.about.com/cs/foreignpolicy/. For a more

PROJECTS

1 Write a Foreign Office briefing for a new government on how it can successfully fight the 'war on terrorism'.

2 In what ways are defence contractors privileged in British politics? Answer with respect to *one* major weapons system.

3 Provide a statistical review of British defence spending since 1960. Comment on any patterns found with respect to:
  (a) spending as a % of GDP
  (b) spending in relation to other government programmes
  (c) spending between the different armed forces.

specific site, we suggest you start by looking at the Ministry of Defence site at www.mod.uk; in their 'about us' section you can find a full list of links to all the main defence institutions in the UK. In addition the Foreign and Commonwealth Office (www.fco.gov.uk) provides insightful information on global and regional foreign relations. The Department for International Development (DFID) is the UK's government department working to promote sustainable development and eliminate world poverty; visit them at www.dfid.gov.uk. The British Foreign Policy Resource Centre at King's College London (http://foreign-policy.dsd.kcl.ac.uk/index.htm) offers an extraordinary range of useful material, they have sections covering issues from academic essays on British foreign policy to the war against terrorism. The 2001–2002 publications of the Foreign Affairs Select Committee can be obtained from www.publications.parliament.uk/pa/cm/cmfaff.htm. The Department of Trade and Industry has a useful section on world trade (www.dti.gov.uk/worldtrade/).

Britain has always been substantially involved in a series of international organisations. Currently the process of European integration occupies a privileged place on the agenda; the Foreign and Commonwealth Office has an excellent section on the relations between Britain and the EU, you can find it at www.fco.gov.uk/servlet/Front?pagename=OpenMarket/Xcelerate/ShowPage&c=Page&cid=1007029391674. The Organisation for Security and Co-operation in Europe (OSCE) is the largest regional security organisation in the world. It is active in early warning, conflict prevention, crisis management and post-conflict rehabilitation. Visit their web site at www.osce.org.

It is also worth visiting the web sites of the major international organisations in which Britain participates. The European Union (www.europa.eu.int), NATO (www.nato.int), the Council of Europe (www.coe.int) and the United Nations (www.un.org). We suggest you also visit the Royal Institute of International Affairs (www.riia.org).

Environmental problems raise important questions about the capacity of modern governments to solve difficult dilemmas. This chapter begins with an example of how environmental policies can lead to major domestic and international disputes. It then goes on to look at:

■ changes in the character of environmental problems

■ the leading policy actors and institutions in the UK

■ the long-standing British philosophy of pollution control

■ new pressures, especially from developments within the EU

■ the difficulties that confront the New Labour government in any attempt to implement its ambitious environmental goals.

During the spring and summer of 1999 what had, up to that point, been a relatively quiet backwater of public policy erupted into intense and prolonged front-page headlines. The subject was genetically modified (GM) foods. In February the *Daily Mirror* ran THE PRIME MONSTER as a headline, when Tony Blair said that he would be prepared to eat genetically modified food. Other newspapers, previously noted more for their Conservative Party sympathies than anything else, started to refer to 'Frankenstein foods' and published lists of common supermarket items that were genetically modified. The Prince of Wales, long known for his support of organic farming, publicly challenged supporters of genetic modification to defend their stance. With memories of the food scare surrounding BSE and the eating of beef fresh in their minds, retailers began withdrawing stocks that had previously sold well. By July Greenpeace was organising raids on farm trials of genetically modified crops, pulling them up and claiming to be acting according to the popular will. The European Union began to reform its own policies on the control of genetically modified organisms.

Although the eruption of intense public debate took place between May and August 1999, the issues had surfaced the year before when in August Dr Arpad Pusztai, a scientist working at the Rowett Institute in Aberdeen, had made a public statement saying that the growth of rats experimentally fed on GM potatoes had been stunted. This claim immediately sparked enormous scientific controversy, with august bodies such as the Royal Society establishing a committee to investigate – and ultimately reject – its scientific validity. But whatever its scientific merits the incident sparked enough concern to lead the government to review the arrangements for controlling the development of biotechnology and to ask its chief medical officer and chief scientist to review the evidence on the safety of genetically modified foods.

The events of 1999 could not have been more badly timed from the government's point of view. In May the joint report from the chief medical officer and chief scientist argued that there was no evidence that eating GM food was unsafe but proposed new public bodies to regulate biotechnology developments. That report coincided with one from the British Medical Association, which argued that there should be a moratorium on the planting of GM crops following the publication of a paper in the scientific journal *Nature* which claimed to show that in the USA monarch butterflies were killed by eating pollen from GM maize. The leaking of a government paper to the *Independent on Sunday*, advocating the establishment of a 'central co-ordinated rebuttals strategy' did not help the government's cause. Suggesting the need to enlist eminent scientists to explain the government's point of view, it could be read as the government being partial towards the biotechnology industry.

The problems lay deeper than these coincidences, however. On coming to office New Labour needed tangible ways in which it could demonstrate that it was the party of production rather than redistribution. Just as Harold Wilson had referred to 'the white heat of the technological revolution' to show that Labour was the modernising party in 1964, so New Labour after its election victory in 1997 began explicitly to support the development of biotechnology as the engine of economic growth for the twenty-first century. When it found itself out of step with public opinion on biotechnology issues it did not know whether to persist in its original strategy or to retreat to a point where it could portray itself as a guardian of public safety impartially regulating a technology that might be useful but which could be discontinued if it were shown not to be safe.

However, even if the government had consistently presented itself as the neutral regulator of public safety, it would still have had difficulties, since the safety and environmental hazards associated with modern technology pose risks that are inherently difficult to control in ways that make sense to members of the public. The problems involved in handling the issues associated with GM crops are simply examples of the central problems of environmental policy. In particular, there is a whole range of issues, spanning food safety, the control of chemicals or the control of climate-changing gases, that pose significant but unquantifiable risks to human health and the environment in ways that are bound to cause political controversy. In a situation in which uncertainty is high and public concern intense, how can a British government strike the right balance between environmental protection to the high standards expected of it and a commitment to prosperity and economic competitiveness?

Behind this problem lay others. How should the UK deal with the pollution legacy of past industrial activity, which left hazardous chemicals in the environment? How best can the complex and difficult choices be made between policy options, all of which, in the light of that legacy, involve environmental damage? How far can these policy choices be made in ways that pay attention to the technical/scientific aspects of the issues without also engaging with broader issues of public opinion and sentiment? What role is there for European institutions in providing a forum within which international differences can be discussed and resolved? How well adapted, in short, are British political institutions in dealing with the politics of the environment?

ENVIRONMENTAL PROBLEMS

Environmental problems arise in many different ways and from many different sources (see Table 23.1). Sometimes the problem is local, as when a person's bonfire pollutes the neighbouring environment. Sometimes it occurs on a regional scale, as when a river basin is polluted. And sometimes it is worldwide, as is the case with global climate change. Human activity has had effects on the environment for centuries. At one time northern Europe was covered in forests before they were cut down for agriculture, a process of deforestation that is mirrored in developing countries today. Moreover, environmental issues inevitably arise from a large number of social activities and government policies. Industrial development causes problems of landuse and pollution. Boosting agricultural crop production through incentive payments leads farmers to an increased use of pesticides and fertilisers that, in turn, cause the pollution of rivers and chemical residues in the food chain. Transport provision takes land for road building, and causes air pollution through the burning of fossil fuels. The specification of building regulations has implications for energy consumption, and tax law can affect how people consume resources. Environmental policy is both a separate sphere of government activity and a dimension of many government activities.

The term 'environmental policy' in the UK covers a wide field of government activity, including pollution control for discharges to air, water or land; the control of nuclear power; the release of genetically modified organisms into the environment; landuse planning; building conservation; the protection of the countryside, including plants and wildlife; and urban regeneration. Within the UK there is a long history of public policy measures directed at some of the most

Table 23.1
Environmental problems, characteristics, and causes

Environmental problem	Main sources	Related human activities	Expected effects
Protecting wildlife	Pesticides, landuse development	Agriculture, transport, house building	Loss of species
Global climate change	Carbon dioxide, methane, CFCs	Power generation, transport	Temperature rise, unpredictable weather
Ozone depletion	CFCs	Aerosol use, refrigerators	Loss of protection against sun's radiation
Increase of acid in environment	Sulphur dioxide, nitrogen oxides, ammonia	Fossil fuels	Crop and building damage, ill health
Over-enrichment of waterways	Phosphates, nitrates	Fertiliser, sewage	River pollution
Dispersed dangerous substances	Chemicals	Most modern production processes	Damage to human health, eg, lower fertility

serious environmental problems. Industrial air pollution in the nineteenth century led to pressure from landowners for controls, and in 1865 the Alkali Inspectorate was formed to regulate major industrial sources of pollution. In the late nineteenth and early twentieth centuries legislation led to slum clearance and the rebuilding of housing to higher environmental standards. In 1947 the post-war Labour government passed the Town and Country Planning legislation, which imposed restrictions on developments and created green belts around British towns. In 1956 clean air zones were established to prevent the recurrence of the urban smog that had caused 4,000 deaths in London in 1952. In 1969, in the wake of a worldwide upsurge of public concern and interest in environmental matters, a permanent Royal Commission on Environmental Pollution was established to help formulate policy. And in 1974 the Control of Pollution Act was passed, which brought together previous pieces of legislation. In the 1980s the UK began to move towards the establishment of a separate Environment Agency, a move that was completed in 1995, and in the 1990s major policy initiatives began to develop in a context in which European and global concerns were becoming prominent.

In terms of the control of pollution, modern environmental policies typically involve regulation, that is to say the specification by government or a government agency of the standards of pollution control that a product or a process has to meet. For example, there are regulations governing car exhaust fumes that manufacturers have to conform to, and on the volume of gases that can be emitted from a major electricity generating plant. Bathing and drinking waters are subject to quality standards, and factories are not allowed to discharge unauthorised pollution into rivers. There are controls on where waste can be dumped, as well as bans on the use of certain chemicals. Building and other forms of development are subject to planning controls, and certain areas may be designated as national parks or sites of special scientific interest because of the plants or animals they contain. The regulations may not always be enforced stringently, and there are many disputes about the standards. But the point remains that the most important policy instrument of environmental policy is regulation, and much of the substance of environmental policy concerns the content and strength of those regulations.

However, in recent years influential voices have been urging that effective environmental policies require a wider set of instruments. In particular, many policy analysts have argued for a greater use of economic instruments to tax environmental 'bads' and encourage environmental 'goods'. The same analysts have often pointed out that in practice political systems already have economic incentives in place that have implications for the environment, but they may not always be beneficial. For example, agricultural subsidy programmes may encourage intensive farming with consequent use of fertilisers and pesticides that may be environmentally harmful. So the need is not only to devise new economic instruments but also to scrutinise the effect of those already in place. In comparative terms the UK has not been a leader in the adoption of economic instruments or the scrutiny of potentially harmful economic incentives to wasteful use of the environment. During the 1990s, as we shall see, this pattern began to change – with political consequences.

POLICY ACTORS AND INSTITUTIONS

Around the politics of environmental regulation has grown up a varied policy community of those who take an interest in the way that standards are set and enforced (see Briefing 23.1). Until 1997 the Department of the Environment was the principal ministry in England and Wales, with its counterparts located in the Scottish and Northern Ireland Offices. The New Labour government of 1997 merged the environment department with transport and regional planning, to create a new superministry (the DETR). After the 2001 election, there was a further reorganisation, with the creation of the Department of Environment, Food and Rural Affairs (DEFRA), which combined the environment section of the DETR with the old Ministry of Agriculture, Fisheries and Food (MAFF). Transport, which in 1997 has been identified as a major environmental issue, was hived off from the Department of Transport, Local Government and the Regions. It was re-designated as the Department for Transport.

Environmental policy in the UK is embedded in a network of specialist advisory groups and committees, of which the most important is the Royal Commission on Environmental Pollution. Within Parliament there is a great deal of environmental interest and expertise in the House of Lords. Two Lords committees in particular, that on science and technology and an environment subcommittee of the European Union Committee, have been especially active. Successive environment committees in the House of Commons have also played an important role on various issues. The Labour government also established a new House of Commons committee, the Environmental Audit Committee, in December 1999.

Environmental policy is an area in which there are well-established pressure groups, many with a high degree of skill and extensive resources, making them well able to take political action. Some have a long history, with large and influential memberships. For example, the Royal Society for the Protection of Birds is the largest wildlife protection group in Europe with an active, vocal and persuasive membership. As well as managing its own reserves it also has a campaigning arm. It became increasingly active from the late 1970s on issues to do with pesticide use, farming practices such as the rooting out of hedgerows encouraged by the Common Agricultural Policy, and the need to provide international protection for migrating species. Other organisations, such as Friends of the Earth and Greenpeace, campaign on issues of air pollution, water pollution and waste disposal. Friends of the Earth, which started as a radical outsider group in the 1970s, has since been incorporated into the world of routinised government consultation and discussion. In addition to these formal organisations, there are now many local and informal groups, some of which are mobilised by what they see as threats to the environment. Protesters building tree houses and tunnels to stop the Newbury Bypass or the new runway for Manchester airport fall into this category.

Other actors who should also be included as members of the environmental policy network include think tanks, journalists and other opinion formers, including various scientific researchers whose work bears on policy questions. Some of

Environmentalism
A concern with the natural environment (including many things from the physical environment affecting 'the quality of life') and the belief that its protection should be given more importance and economic growth less.

BRIEFINGS

23.1 Main actors in British environmental policy institutions

Department of Environment, Food and Rural Affairs Incorporating an environment component and an agriculture component. The Department is the main policy-making department, although the Department for Transport, and the Department of Local Government and the Regions has some environment responsibilities, as do the territorial ministries. The Secretary of State is assisted by ministers responsible for specific aspects of environmental policy.

Environment Agency Created in 1995 by a merger of the National Rivers Authority and Her Majesty's Inspectorate of Pollution. Responsible for detailed standard setting and implementation of pollution control measures and river basin management.

Parliamentary committees The Environment, Food and Rural Affairs Committee of the House of Commons shadows the department. There is also an Environmental Audit Committee, which examines how far general government policy is consistent with environmental concerns. The Commons Committee on Science and Technology has taken an interest in environmental questions, as has its counterpart in the House of Lords. A subcommittee of the House of Lords European Union Committee is also concerned with scrutinising EU environmental legislation. All these committees have produced important reports on issues of environmental policy.

Royal Commission on Environmental Pollution The major advisory body on matters of pollution control policy. Responsible for introduction of major concepts of environmental policy, most notably integrated pollution control, and for some influential reports on lead in petrol and transport policy.

Other advisory bodies The Sustainable Development Commission; Advisory Council on Business and Environment; Genetic Manipulation Advisory Committee. Two new advisory bodies created at the end of 1999 include the Human Genetics Commission and the Agriculture and Environment Biotechnology Commission.

Local authorities Important responsibilities for solid waste regulation (county and unitary authorities) and for local environmental controls (district authorities).

European Union Important source of pressure to raise standards (see Briefing 23.4).

Environmental groups Friends of the Earth, Greenpeace, Council for the Protection of Rural England, the Royal Society for the Protection of Birds, World Wide Fund for Nature, Surfers against Sewage, National Society for Clean Air, Transport 2000, GeneWatch.

Affected interests Electricity supply industry, water industry, road hauliers, farmers and the general public as consumers and drivers of private cars.

Think tank
An organisation set up to develop public policy proposals and to press for their adoption by government.

the general think tanks, such as the Centre for Policy Research on the right and the Fabian Society or the Institute for Public Policy Research on the left, have published work on environmental policy from their own perspectives. In addition, there are specialist think tanks and research organisations (for example, the Institute for European Environmental Policy or the International Institute for Environment and Development) that have played an important role in diffusing knowledge and understanding of policy problems. During the 1980s there also grew up a significant body of specialist journalists in the media, many of whom were extremely knowledgeable about environmental issues, and who kept in touch with both the developing scientific research and the work of the pressure groups.

Environmental policy is something no one likes to be seen to be against. Consequently, opposition to measures to protect the environment usually takes the form, not of questioning the goal of environmental protection, but of questioning the costs, and in particular questioning whether the improvement in the environment justifies the costs that are incurred. During the 1980s the Central Electricity Generating Board, the nationalised industry responsible for electricity production, led the resistance to tighter international controls on air pollution (see next section). And in the 1990s doubts about the costs of water pollution regulation have been raised by Ofwat, the government body responsible for regulating water industry prices. In addition, at various times the Confederation of British Industry (CBI) has expressed doubts about the imposition of environmental costs. Perhaps more important, however, has been the structural power of those groups, such as farmers or the road construction industry, whose political clout makes it difficult to devise suitable policies to control pollution or modify existing landuse practices.

ISSUES IN ENVIRONMENTAL POLICY

Scientific uncertainty

Policies to protect the environment go back many centuries. The main lines of the British approach were laid down in the late nineteenth century with a series of measures to control air and water pollution (see the milestones section at the end of the chapter). During the last 20 years the modern politics of environmental policy has revolved around the question of how far the UK government can accept the new philosophy of environmental protection known as 'sustainable development'.

The traditional British way of thinking about pollution and environmental policy became firmly established among key policy makers from 1900 until the mid-1970s (see Briefing 23.2). Briefly put, this tradition placed a great deal of emphasis on the scientific understanding of environmental problems and on the need to ensure flexibility and informality in the imposition of environmental regulation. The key idea was that pollution and environmental risk were inseparable from human activity, so the task of the environmental regulator was to understand the risks and to control those that were most damaging to the environment. As Lord Ashby, the distinguished biologist who first chaired the Royal Commission on Environmental Pollution, argued in the 1970s, the task of environmental policy is not to eliminate pollution, but to optimise it. In other words, the traditional approach was to regulate effectively, but in such a way as to recognise the capacity of the environment itself to assimilate a certain amount of pollution. The traditional British philosophy of pollution control was therefore built on the principle of 'dilute and disperse'.

23.2 **Phases of UK environmental policy**

Nineteenth century to mid-1970s   The 'traditional philosophy' phase. Environmental control standards were entrusted to specialist inspectors, negotiating on a co-operative basis with industry.

Mid-1970s to 1988   Attempt by policy makers to hold onto the traditional philosophy in the face of domestic and international criticism. Domestically, groups such as Friends of the Earth questioned the closed nature of the traditional regulatory system. Internationally, there was criticism of the slow and hesitant response of the UK government to problems of pollution, and the UK was dubbed 'the dirty man of Europe'.

1988–97, the period of transition   In September 1988 Mrs Thatcher made a speech to the Royal Society emphasising the seriousness of the problem of global warming. In 1989 the European elections showed strong support for the Green Party. UK policy began to shift, accepting the need for a precautionary approach and stressing the importance of integrating environmental concerns with all aspects of public policy.

1997 onwards, implementation of sustainable development?   The New Labour government has committed itself to action on global climate change and to action to control the harmful environmental effects of car use. There have also been developments in environmental taxation. New bodies have been established to help control biotechnology and new forms of public consultation have been experimented with.

The record of pollution control that was built on this philosophy was impressive for its time. However, by the late 1970s, it was increasingly recognised that there were new problems that were not easy to deal with using the principle. The problem that came to symbolise these new challenges was that of 'acid rain'. When coal and other fossil fuels are burnt they give out a series of gases, most notably sulphur dioxide, which reacts in the atmosphere to form sulphuric acid. This sulphuric acid is then deposited in the form of rain, snow or mist, causing damage to crops, buildings, soils and fresh waters. As part of its policy to disperse pollutants from urban centres the UK government had favoured a policy of building tall chimney stacks. These stacks dispersed their plumes over long distances, crossing national boundaries and contributing to a generally worsening problem in Europe.

The difficulty with acid rain as an issue was that, unlike many of the traditional problems of pollution, the scientific understanding of the effects of acidifying pollution was uncertain and contested. For example, although sulphur dioxide is given off in the burning of fossil fuels, it is also given off naturally by volcanoes and some sea species. Determining how much was due to human sources and how much to these naturally occurring ones is a complex problem. It is equally complex to trace the effects of emissions. It was often thought, for example, that given its prevailing south-westerly winds the UK exported most of its acid pollution to northern Europe. But research in the late 1980s showed that, with complex air currents, some acid rain was carried from northern England to the Highlands of Scotland.

This story was repeated in a large number of cases throughout the 1980s and 1990s. It was clear that rivers were suffering damage from excessive nitrates, but was this due to fertilisers, plough patterns or sewage sludge? How far was it possible to say that sewage pollution caused health problems for swimmers, when those who did not go into the water when they went to the beach reported as many symptoms of gastric illness as those who did? Were very small quantities of pesticide residues in drinking water really a health hazard? How far was it correct to say that a significant rise in global temperatures could be predicted from observed trends? It was, of course, precisely this issue of scientific uncertainty that was at issue in the controversy over GM foods.

These scientific uncertainties and the contestable hypotheses to which they gave rise began to undermine the traditional UK philosophy of pollution control. Where cause and effect relationships are contested or uncertain it is difficult to base environmental regulation purely on scientific evidence. In the face of this difficulty a number of other countries, including Germany, the Netherlands, Denmark, Sweden and Norway, began to push for precautionary action to control pollutants even when the evidence of their damage was difficult to establish. The UK came under considerable political pressure especially in the EU (see later) to adopt the precautionary principle, which requires policy makers to take action against environmental risks, even when the causes of those risks are poorly understood.

Cross-cutting nature of environmental issues

Another important feature of the changing politics of the environment has been the recognition that environmental considerations cut across all aspects of public policy. One area this affected was the privatisation policies of the Thatcher governments. Both the water industry and the electricity industry were major sources of pollution. When they were nationalised they had the protection of their 'sponsoring ministries', which spoke up for them in government during the making of policy. They were also prevented from making investments in pollution control by Treasury spending limits that restricted capital spending by the nationalised industries. With privatisation, however, this constraint has been lifted. In the case of water in particular, large investments have been necessary to meet various international obligations. This has led Ofwat to question how far these pollution control measures are necessary. In other words, a new institutional tension has been built into the British policy system between those who favour environmental protection and those who stress the cost of stringent measures.

Another feature of this cross-cutting character of environmental issues has been the need to deal as much with problems of consumption as with problems of production. Since environmental damage arises often as the by-product of everyday activities, environmental policy also needs to deal with issues of lifestyle and the control of consumption. This is most obvious in the case of transport and the significantly increased use of cars in recent years. Mrs Thatcher favoured what she called 'the great car economy' and in the late 1980s significant increases in

Plate 23.1 *Sizewell B nuclear power reactor on the Suffolk coast north of Aldeburgh*

road building took place or were planned. Moreover, the deregulation of bus services and the withdrawal of subsidies to the railways made the car an economically more attractive option for many households. Public expenditure cuts, and a new thinking about the extent to which roads generate increased traffic, led to a serious reduction in the road-building programme under the Major government. A legacy has been laid down, however, that will make it difficult to develop alternative forms of transport to the car.

There have been important measures to control emissions from car exhausts and to limit the noise of vehicles, but the benefits of these measures are often offset by the increase in cars being driven on the road. The Royal Commission on Environmental Pollution, in an authoritative report, summarised the situation as follows:

> At present pollutants from vehicles are the prime cause of poor air quality that damages human health, plants, and the fabric of buildings. Noise from vehicles and aircraft is a major source of stress and dissatisfaction, notably in towns but now intruding into many formerly tranquil areas. Construction of new roads and airports to accommodate traffic is destroying irreplaceable landscapes and features of our cultural heritage. The present generation's cavalier and constantly increasing use of non-renewable resources like oil may well foreclose the options for future generations. This is doubly irresponsible in view of the risks from global warming.
>
> *Royal Commission on Environmental Pollution, 18th Report, 1994, p. 233*

However, the chief problem for any government in response to this sort of issue is how to implement any feasible changes in priorities and organisation.

The principal way in which the pressures to secure greater policy integration have been played out in practice is in terms of the machinery of government. The creation of the DETR in 1997 can itself be seen as an example of this tendency. Bringing environment and transport together (not for the first time: something similar was done in the early 1970s) reflected a policy perception that the solution to environmental problems lay in the better planning of transport provision. The splitting of environment and transport in the reorganisation of 2001 suggested to some observers a lowering of this priority. But it could also be seen as evidence that environmental issues cut across many fields of public policy, including the newly salient agricultural policy.

In addition, however, the Labour government had inherited from the Conservatives a commitment for all ministries to report on their environmental performance, together with a commitment that key Cabinet ministers would meet regularly to discuss the environmental implications of their work. Early in its period of office, in November 1997, the government set up a new House of Commons committee, the Environmental Audit Committee, to scrutinise the extent to which environmental concerns were being integrated into government policy. At the time, John Prescott described it as a 'terrier to bite our ankles'. With John Horam, a former Labour MP turned Conservative via the Social Democrat Party, the new committee quickly started biting. Having ascertained the information in one of its inquiries that the Cabinet Committee on the Environment had only met twice in its first year, it extracted the thought from Michael Meacher, the relevant minister, that this was a good sign because it indicated consensus on the major issues! It has subsequently gone on to highlight the extent to which there is a shortage of established procedure and environmental management information in the running of Whitehall.

Another topic to which the Environmental Audit Committee has turned its attention is the development of policy on the use of economic instruments for environmental goals. From its earliest days the committee started to press the Treasury on the extent to which taxes could be used to discourage the consumption of environmental 'bads' or encourage the consumption of environmental 'goods'. Although the Treasury refused to appear before the Committee in the run-up to the 1998 budget, subsequent policy developments were to mark one of the most important developments in environmental policy of the Labour government.

Development of eco-taxation

The turning point in using taxes for environmental purposes came with the budget of March 1999. Trumpeted by Patricia Hewitt, the economic secretary, as 'the largest and most radical package of environmental tax reforms ever announced in this country', the budget did indeed contain some significant proposals. The policy of increasing fuel taxation higher than the rate of inflation each year, which the Labour government had inherited from the days of Kenneth Clarke as Chancellor, was confirmed, as were higher tax rates for solid waste going to disposal in landfills. There was also mention of the possibility of introducing environmental taxes on pesticides and a planned tax on aggregates. However, the most important development was the introduction of a climate change levy that would introduce taxation on companies emitting greenhouse gases in their production processes. In March 1998 the government had asked Lord Marshall, the former president of the CBI and the chairman of British Airways, to chair a task force on the use of economic instruments to control greenhouse gas emissions. The task force reported positively in November of that year, and the budget intended to put a scheme into effect in 2001.

At this point we encounter a familiar pattern of environmental policy not only in the UK but throughout the developed world. The budget announcement set in train a predictable set of reactions from those adversely affected by the proposals. The proposals on the climate change levy allowed for a reduction in the rate of tax to be paid provided the industry in question undertook voluntary energy-saving measures. Industrial representatives therefore started to lobby to increase the scope of voluntary agreements, while energy-intensive industries also began to lobby for exemptions, on the grounds that the costs of the tax would be disproportionately heavy in their case. Coincidentally, a global rise in oil prices was taking place at that time, leading to increased complaints from commercial vehicle operators about the increased cost of fuel from the policy of increasing taxes faster than inflation, culminating in their taking direct action in September 2001 blocking the movement of fuel from depots. In other words, a political dynamic took over in which relatively small groups in society that bear concentrated costs from a measure have an incentive to lobby hard against its introduction and they meet little opposition because the potentially large number of beneficiaries are only affected to a small degree.

As a result of this lobbying activity the next major budget announcement of the Chancellor, Gordon Brown, conceded ground on the matter, and the policy was adopted that there would be greater flexibility in the application of the climate levy, while the fuel escalator policy was ended. Despite these concessions the introduction of environmental taxes on the scale proposed can still be seen as a major turning point in policy, even though other possible environmental taxes, including water pollution charges that have proved successful in the Netherlands and Germany, have also been quietly shelved. To have accepted a role for environmental taxes of the sort contained in the climate change levy is important and it is reasonable to expect that influential members of the environmental policy community will push for even more such measures to be adopted.

Sustainable development
Development that meets the needs of the present without compromising the ability of future generations to meet their needs.

Sustainable development

Another important element in the dynamic of policy is the rise of the principle of 'sustainable development' in international policy discourse. This is an idea that originated with a UN Commission on Environment and Development in 1987 chaired by Mrs Gro Harlem Brundtland, the Norwegian Prime Minister. The Brundtland Report defined sustainable development as development that meets the needs of the present without compromising the ability of future generations to meet their needs (see Briefing 23.3). The importance of this concept is that it challenged an assumption that was strongly built into much conventional environmental policy, namely that environmental improvements had to be bought at the expense of economic growth. The Brundtland Report pointed out that economic growth not only did environmental damage but also prevented economic development in the future, for example through overfishing or the depletion of natural resources.

BRIEFINGS

23.3 The idea of sustainable development

'Humanity has the ability to make development sustainable – to ensure that it meets the needs of the present without compromising the ability of future generations to meet their own needs.

'Sustainable global development requires that those who are more affluent adopt lifestyles within the planet's ecological means – in their use of energy, for example.

'The objective of sustainable development and the integrated nature of the global environment/ development challenges pose problems for institutions, national and international, that were established on the basis of narrow preoccupations and compartmentalised concerns. Governments' general response to the speed and scale of global challenges has been a reluctance to recognise sufficiently the need to change themselves. The challenges are both interdependent and integrated, requiring comprehensive approaches and popular participation.'

World Commission on Environment and Development, *Our Common Future* (the Brundtland Report), Oxford: Oxford University Press, 1987, pp. 8–9

The politics of sustainable development are intrinsically international. The most important manifestation of this was the Earth Summit in 1992 in Rio de Janeiro, at which governments signed up to a number of international agreements, including ones on biodiversity and climate change. In 2002 there was a high-level follow-up to Rio in Johannesburg, which was intended to produce implementation plans in several key areas of sustainable development, including energy use, corporate accountability, chemicals and the marine environment. The UK government's participation at first had an element of farce, when it was announced that the Environment Minister, Michael Meacher, would not attend on the grounds that members of the government did not wish to seem to be indulging in expensive overseas trips, only for this decision to change when Friends of the Earth offered to pay for Mr Meacher's expenses.

When at the summit the UK government, together with other European Union governments, pushed rather unsuccessfully for agreements in their key areas of concern. In particular, the EU states pushed for a commitment to increase to 10 per cent the use of renewable energy sources in the overall global mix by 2010. They were opposed by both a coalition of developed countries, including the USA, Australia, Canada and Japan, and a group of developing countries, including China, which objected to the proposal. Eventually, in the face of this opposition, the EU states had to back down, settling for a mere declaration of intent to promote renewable technologies. This particular instance represented a pattern across other areas of discussion, in which declaratory commitments replaced targeted action plans. Despite these setbacks, Mrs Margaret Beckett, as Secretary of State in DEFRA, hailed the summit as a new path.

Sustainable development is also an important topic of debate within UK environmental policy. The idea was first endorsed in the Conservative government's white paper, This Common Inheritance (Cm 1200, London: HMSO, 1990), which sought to examine how far the principle of sustainable development could form the basis for public policy measures. The problem of how to achieve sustainability in fields as diverse as agriculture, transport and energy consumption as well as the search for cleaner technologies that are compatible with the requirements for sustainability dominated much thinking and policy argument over the subsequent decade within environmental policy networks.

One important consequence of these debates is that many now argue there is no simple conflict between proponents of environmental protection and the business community. Business and industry are still responsible for a great deal of pollution. But there are segments of business, for example within the pollution control industries or in the field of mass transport, that have an interest in pushing the case for more stringent environmental protection. There is a lot of questioning as to whether proponents of more sustainable alternatives, for example the organic farming industry, are competing on equal terms, in respect of the public subsidies available, with their more established counterparts.

These issues – the need for precaution as well as scientific certainty, the integration of environmental policy with general public policies, the growing interest in economic instruments and the implications of sustainable development – have transformed the politics of the environment in the last 20 years. The traditional assumption that environmental regulation was largely a specialist affair, limited to engineers and civil servants negotiating about technical standards of control, has given way to the idea that environmental standards are part of social and economic life. The policy networks around environmental policy are therefore more crowded, with new actors emerging on the scene, and with issues in sharper dispute. The way in which the disposal of GM foods hit the national and international headlines is just one small illustration of the new politics of the environment. Moreover, these politics, as with others areas of public policy, are being increasingly carried out not only within the framework of the European Union, but also in a global international context.

ROLE OF THE EUROPEAN UNION

From the beginning of the 1980s the EU has been one of the principal forces operating on the British system of environmental protection, reshaping many of its main characteristics. Indeed, there is no other area apart from agriculture where the EU has been so influential in changing the assumptions and standard operating procedures of UK policy.

Environmental policy was not originally part of the Treaty of Rome and so was not one of the original functions of the European Economic Community (as it then was). There are two reasons why environmental policy came to occupy a central place in EU policies. First, there is often a connection between the creation of a single market and environmental regulation. For example, if one country imposes high standards on vehicle exhaust emissions, requiring that cars sold within its borders meet those high standards, this policy in effect erects barriers to trade in vehicles manufactured in other countries where standards are not so high. Indeed, some of the earliest EU legislation on the environment was concerned with harmonising standards on the permissible level of noise from vehicles.

The second reason for the EU's interest in environmental policy was that it could be seen as a way of securing greater legitimacy for the processes of European integration. EU leaders responded to the upsurge of public interest in the environment in the late 1960s and early 1970s, adopting a declaration on the importance of environmental protection in 1972. The declaration led to some policy developments during the 1970s and early 1980s, although environmental regulation was not formally included in the competences of the EU until the Single European Act of 1987.

There are a number of different actors within the EU (see Briefing 23.4). However, decisions on environmental policy have been crucially shaped by the policy stances of the Member States, and in particular, given its size and central-ity, by the position of Germany. Until the early 1980s Germany had a similar environmental policy to the UK, for example being sceptical of the international action to control acid rain that the Scandinavian countries had been proposing. For domestic political reasons this position began to change in 1982 and was consolidated by the conversion of the Christian/Liberal coalition government in 1983 on the acid rain issue. From then on, Germany began to use the EU as a major forum within which to press for the imposition of higher environmental standards on products and manufacturing processes. First, it pushed for measures to reduce acid rain by more stringent controls on sulphur dioxide emissions from electricity power stations and other large furnaces. This initial pressure was followed by support for a wide-ranging series of measures including higher stand-ards on vehicle emissions, tighter control of water pollution and reductions in the volume of packaging waste and measures to control the disposal of wastes in landfill sites. On these points the other 'green' Member States, Denmark and the Netherlands, often supported Germany in the Council of Ministers. This dynamic was particularly important in the 1980s, but was modified by the weakening of the German government's environmental commitment for much of the 1990s, a weakening that has recently been joined by Denmark.

In the middle of the 1980s the UK found itself in the position of opposing higher environmental standards in the EU, thus earning for itself the unenviable title of the 'dirty man of Europe'. From one point of view this was justified. The UK was always going to find it difficult to meet the high environmental standards demanded by countries that had a higher per capita income (and which therefore could afford to spend more) and that had, especially in the case of Germany, world-class engineering and pollution control industries. Moreover, the UK

BRIEFINGS

23.4 Main actors in EU environmental policy

The Commission The Commission has a Directorate with responsibility for environmental policy. Its principal concern is to draft directives that govern the use of resources and control permissible levels of polluting discharges into the environment. There are now some 300 pieces of environmental legislation.

The Council of Ministers All environmental measures have to be agreed by the Council of Ministers, representing the Member States. Since 1992 most measures can be agreed by qualified majority voting.

Over the last 20 years those Member States with the most positive environmental reputation have been Austria, Denmark, Finland, Germany, the Netherlands and Sweden. During the 1990s German interest weakened, as has Danish interest more recently. Those with concerns for economic growth and development include Greece, Ireland, Portugal and (especially) Spain. In between are France and Italy. The UK has often found itself in opposition to measures proposed by the environmental 'leader' states.

European Parliament The main actor here is the Environment Committee. It has the reputation of taking a strong 'pro-environment' line, for example on the control of car exhaust emissions or controls on landfill sites.

European Court of Justice The Court plays a role in enforcing compliance with environmental measures, and a number of its judgments, for example on the legality of measures taken by Member States to impose environmental regulations on products, have had a significant effect on policy.

European Environment Agency This was established in 1995 in Copenhagen. Its brief is to collect data and information, rather than implement environmental measures. However, some see it as the forerunner of a European environment inspectorate.

government did not enhance its reputation by its poor implementation of measures to which it had agreed. For example, when it came to implementing the bathing waters directive, the UK designated only 27 beaches in the whole of the UK as places of traditional bathing. Not only did the list exclude Blackpool and Brighton, it also meant that officially the UK claimed to have fewer bathing beaches than land-locked Luxembourg!

Yet in some ways the reputation of the UK as an environmental laggard in the EU is one-sided. On some issues of EU environmental policy the UK has been a pioneer; for example, it was the UK that pressed for important legislation on wildlife protection, most notably the protection of migrating birds. The UK also pioneered the policy of agricultural set-aside, by which farmers are paid to protect their land rather than farming it intensively. Similarly, the UK introduced the principle of integrated pollution control into EU environmental policy, by which emissions to air, water and soil are controlled as a whole. Moreover, on some questions, the UK was not alone in opposing proposed measures. Spain was hostile to the control of sulphur dioxide from power stations, neither France nor

Environmental impact assessment
A requirement of the European Union, which came into effect in 1988, requiring all public and private projects above a given cost to be subject to environmental appraisal in which the advantages and disadvantages from the environmental point of view are laid out.

Italy wanted catalytic converters on small cars and France was also opposed to the proposal for a carbon/energy tax.

Despite the conflicts over environmental policy in which Britain has been engaged there is no doubt that the effects of EU policy on UK law and practice have been considerable. For example, some of the main measures of the 1990 Environmental Protection Act conformed to the requirements of the 1984 EU directive on air pollution control. Much of the capital cost of water pollution control measures of the 1990s has been incurred through accepting EU standards on bathing and drinking waters. Over the next few years significant sums of money will be spent on replacing lead water piping in order to meet tighter standards on lead in drinking water.

Britain's future position in the environmental politics of the EU is more difficult to identify. The sharp antagonisms of the 1980s softened in the 1990s, not least because the EU itself lost momentum in the field of environmental policy after the difficulties of ratifying the Maastricht Treaty. With its own economic problems after reunification German environmental initiatives became less pressing, particularly after its committed environment minister Klaus Töpfer was replaced.

By way of contrast, the UK failed to regain environmental powers in a number of fields under the doctrine of 'subsidiarity', which it tried for in the wake of the 1992 Edinburgh Summit. Moreover, the accession of Sweden, Finland and Austria has augmented the pro-environment group of countries in the Council of Ministers, and led to changes in the Treaty of Amsterdam (1998), which strengthen environmental provisions. In large part, the position the UK takes in the EU and other international forums will depend on how it is able to deal with precautionary measures, integration of environmental with social and economic policy, and sustainable development.

By the beginning of the 1990s the issue of global climate change had come to dominate discussions of European environmental policy. Global climate change involves the prediction that over the next 50 years or so the earth's atmosphere would warm up with unpredictable effects. Ironically, the issue had been thrust into prominence by Mrs Thatcher's speech to the Royal Society in September 1988, when she appeared to accept the seriousness of the problem. Under the Conservative government the difficulty as far as the UK was concerned was that the solution seemed to involve a tax on carbon fuels or on energy more generally, in order to cut consumption. The UK was not prepared to cede more tax-raising powers to the EU, thus undermining the possibility of joint action by Member States.

The Labour government made the issue a priority, in part helped by the fact that the substitution of gas-fired energy production in place of coal-fired production promised to reduce greenhouse gas emissions anyway. The issue is an interesting one since it shows how the UK's relationship to global environmental issues is mediated through its membership of the EU. The most significant meeting took place in Kyoto in December 1997, when there was agreement among the nations present to cut emissions of greenhouse gases by 2008–12 to 5 per cent below their level in 1990 and 30 per cent below their projected levels. However, it was the EU that entered into this agreement on the part of its Member States, and subsequent bargaining was necessary in the Council of Ministers to share out the burdens of meeting this target. The UK was able to make the issue one of its priorities for its presidency in the first part of 1998.

NEW LABOUR: NEW ENVIRONMENTAL POLICY?

In its 1997 election manifesto the Labour Party offered the oft-quoted assertion that environmental policy 'is not an add-on extra, but informs the whole of government, from housing and energy policy through to global warming and international agreements'. This assertion suggests that those drafting the manifesto have some understanding that environmental issues could not be contained within one segment of public policy. The politics of the environment and of sustainable development challenge assumptions about the workings of the economy, the organisation of transport and communications, as well as the responsibilities that government owe to present citizens and future generations and the responsibilities that citizens owe to one another. After one term in office and a renewed general election success, how is the challenge of sustainable development likely to work itself out?

The most obvious and politically salient area of challenge is in the field of transport policy. The original merging of the ministries of transport and the environment in 1997 was intended to signal the priority to be given to dealing with congestion and transport pollution. The demerger in 2001 marks the failure of that strategy, as does the slowness of the Labour government in delivering on its aim of producing a workable integrated transport strategy. The failure of Railtrack and the difficulties of establishing its successor quickly on a sound basis has also contributed to the challenge. Without a feasible alternative, many people are forced into daily reliance on the car, in ways that are not ultimately sustainable. The Conservatives styled themselves the friend of the motorist at the 2001 general election, posing a political problem for the government. Less urgent, but in some ways more difficult to handle, are the environmental problems arising from the growth of low-cost air travel, which offer a growing market in cheap travel, using a fuel that remains untaxed. Whether the Labour government will be able to confront this new form of consumerism remains to be seen.

The brigading of environment and agriculture in the same ministry also points to areas of continuing challenge. So far the government has not been successful in its attempts within the European Union to secure fundamental reform of the Common Agricultural Policy, a policy that is both wasteful of resources and environmentally damaging. The growth of a political movement around the Countryside Alliance means that the issues of rural policy have in general become more difficult to handle. Also, there remains the issue of genetically modified crops and the decisions that will have to be taken once the current round of field-scale trials is complete. Such crops are inherently controversial with some arguing that they have the potential for environmental benefit, because they require a lower use of pesticides, and others arguing that their development is hindering the emergence of sustainable organic agriculture. Behind this particular issue there lies a more general question about the extent to which the government can manage the process of innovating in biotechnology.

The third area of political controversy may well be over landuse developments. Although the road-building programme is not extensive, the government launched a discussion document in 2002 on the expansion of airport facilities, containing suggestions of the need for a massive growth in runway capacity. Already these suggestions have prompted the mobilisation of opponents around some the main airports targeted for expansion, such as Stansted. Landuse planning issues are also raised by the reform of planning legislation announced in the Queen's Speech for the 2002–03 session of Parliament. Planning legislation, which protects land from uncontrolled development, remains, along with the National Health Service, one of the most lasting legacies of the post-war Labour government. Earlier proposals by the present Labour government to limit the right of individuals to challenge the development of large-scale projects, proposals that had run into stiff opposition from environmental groups, have been dropped in the current legislative proposal. But the pressure on land from commercial developments, especially in the southeast of England is considerable and could still provoke strong political opposition, perhaps in the form of direct action.

In short, environmental policy is not one item of policy but raises issues that challenge assumptions in many areas of policy. At present this is more recognised in the rhetoric of policy than in the reality. How far the British political system can adapt to the challenges is a open question.

ESSAYS

1. Explain the difficulties that a UK government would face in seeking to impose taxes on polluting activities. How best could these difficulties be overcome?

2. How important has the European Union been in the development of UK environmental policy?

3. What are the obstacles to a UK government pursuing policies promoting the goals of sustainable development? Can those obstacles be overcome?

SUMMARY

- Environmental policy raises important questions about the international dimension of public policy and the ability of the British political system to cope with the challenges of environmental management.

- Environmental policy covers a wide range of issues, but the usual way in which governments deal with environmental problems is by regulation. The politics of the environment is thus primarily concerned with the stringency of this regulation, but new instruments – such as the use of environmental taxation – are also coming into play.

- The UK's system of environmental regulation has a long history. But in some ways the perception of Britain's 'proud record' of environmental policy has inhibited adaptation to new issues and approaches, especially problems of scientific uncertainty, overall policy integration and sustainable development.

- The EU has been a major force in reshaping Britain's environmental policy. At one stage the UK stood out against EU policy making, but the picture is more subtle than a simple tale of British intransigence would suggest.

- The present government faces the challenges posed by the idea of sustainable development, especially in the areas of transport, agriculture and planning.

MILESTONES

Milestones in the development of UK environmental policy

1865 Alkali Inspectorate created. The world's first national pollution inspectorate, it was responsible until the 1980s for regulating air pollution from industry

1947 Town and Country Planning Act creates the framework within which local authorities can control building and other development with the aim of protecting the countryside and enhancing town life

1952 London smog, caused by the burning of domestic coal fires, responsible for 4,000 deaths, the event that triggered the move for the 1956 Clean Air Act, by which local authorities could create smokeless zones

1969 Harold Wilson as Prime Minister establishes the Royal Commission on Environmental Pollution, a standing Royal Commission to report on matters of environmental policy

1974 Control of Pollution Act, the first attempt to begin to codify national pollution control standards

1983 German government 'conversion' on the issue of acid rain. Germany begins to push for tougher pollution control standards in the EU, and the UK often seeks to resist the pressure

1986 The Alkali Inspectorate is merged with other pollution inspectorates to create Her Majesty's Inspectorate of Pollution, the beginnings of a separate environment agency

1987 Single European Act makes environmental policy a normal EU responsibility for the first time. Except when related to the single market, voting in the Council of Ministers is by the principle of unanimity

1988 Mrs Thatcher makes speech to the Royal Society in September referring to the problems of global warming

1990 Environmental Protection Act, the first major piece of legislation since 1974; aimed to introduce a modern regime of pollution control, particularly in respect of air pollution and waste management. Conservative government publishes This Common Inheritance, in September, a statement of its policies towards sustainable development. Stronger on machinery of government issues than on substantive policy

1992 Government pursues the policy of regaining some EU environmental powers to the Member States under the principle of subsidiarity

1995 Environment Act establishes the Environment Agency, bringing together the National Rivers Authority and Her Majesty's Inspectorate of Pollution

1997 Government creates new super department (Environment, Transport and the Regions), which should aid the co-ordination of environmental policy

2001 Newly re-elected Labour government abolishes Department of Environment, Transport and the Regions and creates Department of Environment, Food and Rural Affairs

FURTHER READING

Useful general books on environmental politics in Britain are Robert Garner, *Environmental Politics*: *Britain, Europe and the Global Environment* (Basingstoke: Macmillan, 2000); P. Lowe and S. Ward (eds), *British Environmental Politics* (London: Routledge, 1997); and T. Gray (ed.); *UK Environmental Policy in the 1990s* (London: Macmillan, 1995). On green political thought, see A. Dobson, *Green Political Thought* (London: Unwin Hyman, 1990) and the short article by B. Jones, 'Green thinking', *Talking Politics*, **2** (2), 1989/90, pp. 50–4. W. P. Grant, 'Are environmental pressure groups effective?', *Politics Review*, September 1995, and M. Robinson, *The Greening of British Party Politics* (Manchester: Manchester University Press, 1992) discuss the issue

PROJECTS

1. Compare and contrast the positions of the major party manifestos on the subject of environmental policy in the 1997 and 2001 elections.

2. Identify all the major interests affected by a policy of stressing public transport rather than the car, and say whether each interest would be for or against the policy.

3. Assess the impact of one major EU directive on environmental policy on the UK.

from the point of view of pressure groups and parties. R. Garner, 'How green is Labour?', *Politics Review*, **8** (4), 1999, pp. 26–8 assesses the Labour government's green credentials in its first term, and J. Callaghan, 'Environmental politics, the New Left and the New Social Democracy', *Political Quarterly*, **71** (3), 2000, pp. 300–8 compares the position of Labour on the environment with other European social democratic parties.

A good book on European Union environmental policy is A. R. Zito, *Creating Environmental Policy in the European Union* (Basingstoke: Macmillan, 2000), which can be usefully complemented by the essays in A. Jordan (ed.), *Environmental Policy in the European Union* (London: Earthscan, 2002). A. Weale et al, *Environmental Governance in Europe* (Oxford: Oxford University Press, 2000) provides coverage of the politics of environmental policy at both the EU and the member state level. T. O'Riordan and J. Jager (eds), *Politics of Climate Change* (London: Routledge, 1996) is a collection of essays on climate change, including a chapter on the UK.

USEFUL WEB SITES ON ENVIRONMENTAL POLICY

Hotlinks to these sites can be found on the CWS website at http://www.booksites.net/budge.

The protection of the environment has acquired a central role in the government's agenda in the last decades. There are many web sites of institutions dealing with environmental policies. The first stop is the government's Environment Agency (www.environment-agency.gov.uk) and the Department for Environment, Food and Rural Affairs at www.defra.gov.uk. The Institute for European Environmental Policy (www.ieep.org.uk) is an independent organisation dedicated to the analysis and development of European environmental policy. Environmental Data Services (www.ends.co.uk) is an independent publisher; on their web site you have access to daily information on a wide variety of topics related to environmental policies and strategies; they also provide excellent links to sites devoted to the analysis of issues such as air pollution, waste and recycling and environmental law. You can access it from www.ends.co.uk/links/index.htm.

The Policy Library (www.policylibrary.com/environment/index.htm) offers a very comprehensive section on environmental policies. The Chartered Institute of Environmental Health (www.cieh.org.uk) is a professional and educational body, dedicated to the promotion of environmental health.

The Centre for Social and Economic Research on the Global Environment (CSERGE) is based at the University of East Anglia. They work with the aim of mitigating environmental problems in both developed and developing economies; visit them at www.uea.ac.uk/env/cserge/. You can also visit the Environmental Change Institute at Oxford University (www.eci.ox.ac.uk). For information on legal aspects of environmental protection visit the US-based Environmental Law Institute (www.eli.org).

In Chapter 13 of this edition you can find a comprehensive list of web sites belonging to pressure groups in the UK, which includes a wide variety of non-governmental organisations, interest groups and social movements devoted to the protection of the environment. Some of the most important ones are Friends of the Earth (www.foe.org) and Greenpeace International (www.greenpeace.org).

Economic policy

Previous chapters showed how many aspects of security and foreign policy are insulated from democratic scrutiny and debate. This and the two following chapters will examine contrasting styles of decision making on the economy, social affairs and equal opportunities. Of all these, management of the economy is the 'master' policy area. Put simply, the level and quality of almost all government-provided services depend on public spending, and spending in turn is a product of the ways in which governments manage the economy. The chapter will first attempt to place spending in Britain in a comparative and historical context. It will then distinguish between macro and micro economic policy and move on to discuss the institutional context and the style and substance of decision making in this area. The chapter will conclude by pointing up the extent to which international events are now a major influence and how this will affect the likely direction that policy making will take over the next few years. It therefore covers:

■ the historical and comparative context of economic policy
■ the basics of economic policy
■ the institutional context, characterised above all by centralisation
■ the style and substance of policy making: a new orthodoxy?
■ the internationalisation of economic policy making.

ECONOMIC POLICY IN HISTORICAL AND COMPARATIVE CONTEXT

As was shown in Chapters 2 and 3, Britain has had an unusual and fascinating economic history. It was the first country to move from a feudal agricultural economy to one based on cash crops and modern farming methods. It was then, in turn, the first economy to industrialise. By the first third of the nineteenth century, Britain had established itself as the leading industrial nation and by the second third of the century the British economy was easily the largest in the world. It is important to know how Britain came to assume this position. Even today, the making of economic policy is influenced by this distinctive past.

Three key facts relating to Britain's economic history have affected the nature of policy making in this area:

1. Britain was – and, many would argue, remains – a world leader in the extension of free market principles. In marked contrast to such countries as France, Germany, Japan and Russia, Britain's industrialisation occurred with little direct intervention from the central government. Private capital was the driving force behind both the construction of infrastructure (canals, railways, roads, utilities) and the development of manufacturing and extractive (mining) industries. As a result, governments proved reluctant to

Plate 24.1 *Lloyd's, home of the famous insurance exchange – a symbol of the City's continuing importance in international finance*

Source: Lloyd's

intervene directly in economic affairs until the traumatic events of the great depression and the Second World War forced their hand (see Chapter 3). At the same time Britain was a champion of free international trade, so has long pursued policies that opened up export and import markets among all trading nations.

2. Britain's political system is highly centralised. From the very beginning, therefore, economic policy making has been directed from the centre. It has also been executive led. Unlike political systems with federal arrangements or the separation of powers, in Britain lower level governments, the courts and even Parliament have played a minimal role in economic policy. Until 1997 the central bank (the Bank of England), which in comparable systems plays a major role in economic management, was also subservient to the executive.

3. Since the First World War economic policy in Britain has been in almost continuous crisis. This has resulted in the elevation of economic policy to the top of the political agenda. Only very rarely have other policy issues overtaken economic affairs in importance. Hence it was economic questions rather than foreign policy or social issues that tended to make or break governments for most of the twentieth century.

When discussing public policy it is usual to distinguish between the institutional context and the style and substance of how policy is made. Before we examine these points, however, we need to provide some basic information on the nature of economic policy itself.

ECONOMIC POLICY: THE BASICS

Macro economic policy
The branch of economic policy that deals with total or aggregate performance of the national economy, including monetary policy (money in circulation and interest rates), inflation, exchange rates, capital, employment and labour.

Micro economic policy
The branch of economic policy that deals not with the total performance of the economy but with the performance and behaviour of individual economic actors, including firms, trade unions, consumers, and regional and local governments.

Fiscal policy A type of macro economic policy that uses taxation and public expenditure to manage the economy.

The most fundamental distinction in economic policy is between macro and micro economic policy. Macroeconomics is concerned with the total or aggregate performance of the economy, including monetary policy (how much money is circulating in the economy, interest rate levels or the cost of borrowing) and the exchange rate of the pound in relation to other currencies. Monetary policy is in turn one of the determinants of the general level of activity in the economy and in particular the level of inflation. Microeconomics is concerned not with aggregates but with the behaviour of individual economic actors such as firms, trade unions, consumers, and regional and local governments. Clearly the two are related. How firms and consumers behave greatly influences the amount of money circulating in the economy (the money supply) as well as the overall level of demand for goods and services and the savings rate. These in turn will inform macro economic management.

As far as policy is concerned, many free market economists believe that most of economic policy should be confined to macro economic management, and that governments should do as little as possible to interfere with individual firms and consumers. Such an approach implies minimal levels of taxation and of government spending and therefore a minimal level of government debt. Put another way, it implies that governments should be concerned with macro economic policy but not with the microeconomics of the economy. As we all know, however, governments in Britain have legislated to affect the behaviour of all economic actors and they are intimately involved in microeconomics. Manufacturing firms, for example, are taxed in several ways, their labour markets are regulated (employee safety, job security, equal opportunity); the safety and quality of their products are regulated by law, and government plays a major role in providing for or regulating their production environment (environmental controls, the provision of roads and utilities, planning law and so on). The EU and local governments as well as central government play some part in this process.

The policy universe covering this micro economic environment is highly complex and the product of numerous pieces of legislation enacted at a number of levels over a period of time. Often these laws are contradictory or incompatible. High 'on costs' (employer Social Security contributions) may conflict with job security. Competition or anti-monopoly policy and planning policy may result in reduced profits and therefore reduced government revenues. Much of the time governments are concerned to find a balance between these conflicting objectives, or they seek to find the optimal tradeoffs between them. Because micro economic policies affect the behaviour of individuals they tend to be highly politicised. Consumers, firms, taxpayers and workers are acutely aware of changes in taxation, competition policy or trade union law and are therefore likely to mobilise to protect their interests.

24.1 Characterising economic policy: institutions and actors in approximate order of importance

Monetary policy (interest rates, money supply, exchange rates)

Institutions	**Actors**
The Bank of England (the European Union, if Britain joins EMU) The Treasury International financial markets	Monetary Policy Committee chaired by the Governor of the Bank of England (European Central Bank, if Britain joins EMU) Chancellor of the Exchequer The Prime Minister The Treasury Market investors and speculators Organised interests

Fiscal and spending policy (taxation, government spending)

Institutions	**Actors**
The Treasury The Cabinet and Cabinet departments The Public Accounts Committee and Parliament The European Union International financial markets	The Prime Minister The Chancellor and First Secretary to the Treasury Treasury officials Cabinet ministers Spending department officials Members of Parliament Organised interests Local governments EU officials Market investors and speculators

Other micro economic policies (labour market, industrial, regional, environmental, health and safety, and competition policy)

Institutions	**Actors**
The Cabinet Cabinet departments The European Union Organised interests Parliament Local authorities	The Prime Minister and Cabinet Ministers Departmental officials EU officials Interest group spokespersons and officials Members of Parliament Local government councillors and officials

Macro economic policy is, by definition, an easier area both to characterise and to manage. Only central authorities can direct broad changes in the economy and in practice this means the executive branch of the central government. In addition, central banks are always closely involved in monetary policy, and the

Economic management
The process whereby governments assume, to varying degrees, the task of managing the national economy by means of macro and/or micro economic policies.

more independent they are of central control the less party political monetary policy becomes. This is a point we will return to later. This said, all aspects of macro economic management ultimately affect individuals, so they can be highly controversial. If, for example, the government decides that the economy is overheating then it is likely to raise taxes and and/or reduce government spending. Both decisions are likely to be resisted by a range of political and economic actors.

INSTITUTIONAL CONTEXT

As with so many other aspects of British politics, the most notable institutional characteristic of economic policy making is its highly centralised character. Part of this derives from the British Parliamentary system, with its dominant executive, and part from the inherent weakness of regional and local government in Britain. In many other countries lower level governments – for example, the Länder (federal states) in Germany – play an important role in micro economic policy. In others, for example the USA, national legislatures are intimately involved in the budgetary process.

Centralisation within the executive is also high in the UK, so the lead actors are the Prime Minister, the Chancellor and the Treasury. It is significant that the Prime Minister is also the First Lord of the Treasury, so emphasising the important historical role of the Treasury in British politics.

The pre-eminence of the Treasury stems from the fact that it is the institution responsible not only for providing the government with advice on general questions of economic policy, but also for enforcing government spending priorities and rules on all other departments. Hence, the so-called 'spending departments' negotiate over the detail of their budgets with the Treasury. Its civil servants have the highest status in Whitehall, and the Chancellor of the Exchequer is widely regarded as the most senior minister in the Cabinet bar the Prime Minister.

Of course 'the Treasury' is a building staffed with civil servants. Formally, it is not a decision-making body at all. Its job is to implement the policies of the government of the day. In this sense, the key institutional actors are the Prime Minister, the Chancellor, the First Secretary to the Treasury and the Cabinet. In reality, the Cabinet as a collective entity plays a relatively minor role in economic management. Even the key Cabinet committees in the area are not central players. In the Blair government, the Ministerial Committee on Economic Affairs, Productivity and Competitiveness is more an advisory than a decision-making body. Of course, individual Cabinet ministers will lobby hard for their departments in the appropriate Cabinet forum, and of course general questions of economic management are discussed in Cabinet. But the core decision making is done by the PM, Chancellor and First Secretary. They may work in ad hoc groups, or they may be influenced by outside advisers – much as Margaret Thatcher was by Sir Alan Walters – but they are unlikely to depend on the collective will of the Cabinet.

The Treasury will have a 'view' on economic management, whose influence is very hard to measure. Treasury officials have almost always been fiscal conservatives or averse to increasing government debt. Since the Thatcher era they have also become significantly more hostile to government intervention in industry and in the economy generally. What role Margaret Thatcher and her ministers played in this, compared with a changing intellectual mood on the role of government, is very difficult to say. But we do know that the Prime Minister made a number of key appointments to the Treasury that greatly helped her cause. She appointed an outsider, Terry Burns, as chief economic adviser (he was a professor at the London School of Economics rather than a career civil servant), and worked hard to get Peter Middleton appointed as permanent secretary. Burns and Middleton were both committed to fiscal orthodoxy and a reduction in the role of government and they dominated the Treasury for most of the 1980s.

Controversy on the policy role of the Treasury has waned significantly since the Thatcher era. The reasons for this relate to the rise of a new orthodoxy in economic policy that pervades not only much of British government but also governments elsewhere.

Central banks are key players in economic policy in almost all political systems, including the British. As the institutions responsible for setting interest rates, controlling the money supply and defending the national currency on the foreign exchanges, they are of obvious importance. Unusually among democracies, the Bank of England has traditionally shared with the government the responsibility for setting interest rates. Until the 1990s this was primarily the government's prerogative, although the Bank always gave advice. Under John Major the balance shifted towards the Bank. The Chancellor and the Governor of the Bank would meet monthly, the Chancellor would take the decision, but the minutes of the meeting were published later, so revelation of any rifts between the Bank and the

Plate 24.3 *The Bank of England. Chancellor of the Exchequer, Gordon Brown, gave the Bank freedom to set interest rates on New Labour coming to power in 1997 and set up a separate regulatory body for financial institutions*

government was delayed. Many previous governments used interest rate policy to manipulate the economy for political advantage (Chapter 3) and this innovation was designed to depoliticise the whole process.

On coming to power in 1997 the new Chancellor, Gordon Brown, announced that in future the Bank would be given the freedom to set interest rates, subject only to the advice of a group of experts appointed by the government (a group of eight economists and bankers known as the Monetary Policy Committee (MPC), most of whom are appointed by the Chancellor). This unexpected change – there was no reference to it in the Labour manifesto – effectively gave to the Bank the same freedom enjoyed by many other EU central banks. Only under emergency conditions can the government give instructions to the Bank on interest rates and then only for a short period. Most commentators agree that this move proved successful. The MPC is mandated to target inflation at 2.5 per cent and during its first two years of operation it acted swiftly to raise interest rates when the economy was seen to be overheating and to reduce them when the economy was slowing down. With inflation firmly under control after 2000, the MPC reduced rates to their lowest levels in 40 years during 2001 and 2002. Interestingly, the Chancellor, Gordon Brown, has broadly supported these decisions.

While the Treasury and the Bank of England are undoubtedly the core economic policy-making institutions there are numerous other institutional actors with some influence. All the major spending departments, and in particular those directly concerned with economic matters such as the Department of Trade and Industry (DTI), play some role. The DTI is concerned with micro rather than macro economic policy, although in its liaison with numerous private sector firms over such matters as competition policy and aid for small business it is, by definition, immersed in the concerns of individual economic actors. The same is true of the role played by local authorities. Although their spending powers have been greatly reduced over recent years (Chapter 18) they continue to plan landuse, which can greatly affect the investment decisions of companies.

Until the privatisations of the 1980s and 1990s the nationalised corporations were important economic actors. Often their pricing and investment decisions were used by central government as instruments of government policy. For example, if government wanted to rein in spending it would cut new investment in British Rail or British Steel. Similarly, the corporations were used as examples in incomes policy: pay rises for rail workers or miners might be held down to encourage restraint in the private sector.

The role that Parliament plays in economic policy is, in effect, a very small one. The Public Accounts Committee (PAC), which is the most important of Parliament's select committees, meets twice a week and is charged with scrutinising the government's accounts and ensuring that government spending provides value for money. Although important, this function does not relate directly to the formulation of economic policy. Generally there are clear limits to the ability of Parliament to keep the government accountable in any detailed way (Chapter 17).

Apart from the PAC, Parliament's role is limited – as it is with most aspects of public policy – to the collective power of backbench MPs. When they can muster

BRIEFINGS

24.2 Organised interests and government in economic policy making

In some countries peak associations (the equivalent of the British Trades Union Congress or Confederation of British Industry) are directly incorporated into the economic decision-making process. Such systems are usually labelled corporatist. Austria is usually identified as a corporatist system, and there are elements of corporatism in other countries such as Germany and Japan. Scholars agree that Britain has never had corporatist political arrangements. Major corporations or unions are rarely consulted before important decisions are taken. More often they will lobby to protect their interests, but there is no guarantee that their wishes will be heeded. For example, during the 1980s, Conservative governments systematically reduced the powers of trade unions. More revealing was the government's rejection of pleas by manufacturing industry during the early 1980s that its policies were leading to rapid de-industrialisation. The determination to continue with monetarist policies showed just how far removed industry was from central decision making.

The US political scientist Charles Lindblom has pointed out, however, that businesses – but not trade unions – are uniquely privileged in economic policy because they can always threaten that anti-business policies will lead to recession and unemployment. In other words, they do not need to be directly involved in decision making; instead they have a hidden veto on the policy agenda. Today this seems almost a truism, and it is certainly the case that all governments now talk in terms of maintaining a good environment for business investment and profits. Given Britain's status as a major trading nation over many generations, UK governments have been particularly keen to serve the interests of the City of London (see Chapters 2 and 3) which may however encourage short-termism so far as industry and manufacturing are concerned.

C. Lindblom, *Politics and Markets*, New Haven, CT: Yale University Press, 1977 a majority against the government they can be very effective, but this rarely happens. Indeed the only example in the last 20 years of a government's being defeated on a major economic question was when an alliance of opposition and dissenting Conservative MPs rejected the rise in VAT on fuel from 8 to 17.5 per cent in the November 1994 budget.

Finally, what role do organised interests play in economic policy? It is clear from earlier discussions that groups are rarely involved directly. Firms and unions may make comments on (say) a rise in taxation or interest rates, and they may lobby hard in favour of or against one policy or another. Sometimes their demands are heeded, as with the transitional relief from the uniform business rates granted to business during the early and mid-1990s.

Business, in particular, is privileged in relation to other organised interests as it has an indirect veto on a range of economic policies. Governments are very aware that policies that challenge the free market environment can lead to recession and unemployment. It is rarely necessary for business leaders to threaten such consequences should particular policies be adopted. All of the actors in the policy process are aware of it and this in turn helps mould a pro-business policy agenda. Because of Britain's history as a trading nation governments have been particularly deferential to the financial markets of the City of London. As will be discussed later, maintaining the value of the pound on the foreign exchanges was for long a major priority of successive governments.

STYLE AND SUBSTANCE OF POLICY MAKING

Monetarism
A revised version of neo-classical economics that, contrary to Keynesianism, argues that government should minimise its involvement in economic matters, except for controlling the money supply as a way of holding down inflation.

Economic policy making in Britain in the twentieth century has taken the form of almost continuous crisis management (Chapter 3). British efforts to sustain the free convertibility of sterling into gold, followed by the great depression, the Second World War and the near bankruptcy of the post-war years, were quickly followed by decades of 'stop–go' policies. Successive governments, intent on maintaining the value of the pound on the foreign exchanges, were forced into periodic bouts of deflation only to be followed by electorally inspired reflation.

By the late 1970s controlling inflation became the top priority and, with the election of Margaret Thatcher in 1979, the fight against inflation was seen as inexorably linked to the supply of money circulating in the economy. Monetarism, as it came to be known, dominated British politics during the early and mid-1980s. It was highly controversial, not only because of its uncertain intellectual pedigree but also because, if implemented fully, it could be highly deflationary. At a time when unemployment was in any case rising monetarism was viewed by many as involving increased unemployment as a deliberate tool of economic policy.

The monetarist experiment was abandoned once it became clear that the relationship between the money supply (which in any case was notoriously difficult to measure) and inflation was tenuous at best. What the episode demonstrates, however, is the extraordinarily centralised and closed nature of economic policy making in Britain. The Prime Minister, Chancellor (Sir Geoffrey Howe) and

BRIEFINGS

24.3 Monetarism and British politics

On coming to power in 1979 the Conservatives were already converted to the belief that the control of the money supply (the amount of cash and credit circulating in the economy) was the key to controlling inflation. Margaret Thatcher and her intellectual guru, Sir Keith Joseph, accepted the analysis of the Nobel Laureate economist Milton Friedman, who had long argued that rising inflation was linked to governments' neglect of monetary targets. Accordingly, the government adopted a medium-term financial strategy that set specific targets for one of the Treasury's broader money supply indicators (M3, which denoted cash and accounts at UK banks). In order to curb the money supply interest rates were raised and public expenditure cut. In addition the standard rate of value added tax (VAT) was almost doubled. The immediate effects of these changes was to fuel inflation and to depress the economy. Economists assured the government that this was a short-term phenomenon, or a necessary dose of medicine to guarantee long-term economic health. In the event the recession bottomed out in 1982 and a slow but steady recovery set in thereafter. By 1983 it was becoming obvious that the objective performance of the economy, including the inflation rate, was only loosely linked to the money supply. The Treasury set ever-higher monetary targets but these were almost always overshot. Meanwhile inflation was falling steadily. By 1985 monetary targets, although set, were no longer the main guiding principle of government policy.

Monetarism was important because it demonstrated how a determined Prime Minister could almost unilaterally change the direction of economic policy. Monetarism also became a catch-all phrase to describe 'Thatcherite' policies. In fact, by the end of the 1980s Thatcherite policies bore very little relationship to the strictly economic definition of monetarism.

Exchange Rate Mechanism (ERM)
The ERM is the first stage of a European Union plan for financial integration. As part of the European Monetary System (EMS) introduced in 1979, the ERM was designed to minimise currency exchange fluctuation among members of the EU belonging to the system.

personal Downing Street and Treasury advisers (Alan Walters and Terry Burns) decided on the policy and it was implemented. Many in Margaret Thatcher's Cabinet objected, as did many Conservative backbenchers. Many Treasury officials were sceptical, as were most economists.

Since the mid-1980s there have been two more major crises. One of them is a typically insulated instance of economic policy making and the other – British membership of the Exchange Rate Mechanism (ERM) and of the European currency – is highly atypical. The first crisis occurred after the stock market 'crash' in October 1987. The Chancellor of the Exchequer, Nigel Lawson, feared that the consequences would be deflationary and therefore stimulated the economy with interest rate cuts. The crash did not have the expected effect, however, and the fall in the cost of money further stimulated an already overheated economy. Credit became extremely easy to obtain and consumer debt soared. By mid-1988 the boom was widely recognised as inflationary; property prices were soaring and the government was obliged to take draconian corrective measures in 1989 and 1990. These events contributed to the deepest recession of the post-war era.

The second crisis grew in part out of a major rift between the lead policy makers in the economic policy arena: Prime Minister Margaret Thatcher and her Chancellor, Nigel Lawson. The issue was British membership of the ERM and of the European Monetary System (EMS). Lawson supported membership, while the Prime Minister was vehemently opposed. Lawson's resignation in 1989 was

Plate 24.4 *Nicholas Garland cartoon in the* Sunday Telegraph: *Kick-starting the economy. British membership of ERM was a failure, splitting the Conservative Party and causing the electorate to lose confidence in Conservative management of the economy*

KICK-STARTING THE ECONOMY

European Monetary System (EMS) The third and final stage of European financial integration, EMS provides for a single European currency (the euro), to replace existing national currencies, and a European central bank.

partly inspired by this disagreement. But the ERM supporters finally won the day and Britain joined in October 1990. Only the threat of a Cabinet revolt caused Thatcher to change her mind. This was, therefore, one of the rare instances when economic policy making moved beyond a small coterie of Downing Street and Treasury officials.

British membership of the ERM was a failure. In September 1992, the UK was forced out of the currency agreement. The issue continued to dominate economic debate for the next dozen years and more, but now in the form of Britain's position on the single European currency. The unusual nature of this policy issue is well demonstrated by the fact that the Conservative governments of John Major could not make a clear commitment one way or another on the question. So deep were the divisions in the Conservative Party that the government's hands were effectively tied. No other economic issue in recent British political history has been diffused into the rank and file of a party in this way. The typical mode, as with monetarism and the Lawson boom, is for decisions to be taken by a few lead actors and then implemented irrespective of the opposition.

While Britain's membership of European Monetary Union remains a vitally important issue it has not divided the Blair government as it did Major's. Blair's 'wait and join EMU only when the conditions are right' policy is broadly supported by the Cabinet and Parliamentary Labour Party. In addition, Blair is Prime Minister at a time when an unusual degree of consensus applies to the fundamentals of economic policy. There are a number of reasons for this, including the almost universal perception that the primary aim of economic policy should be the control of inflation. As a result, the controversial issues that dominated most of the post-war period – the proper economic role of the state, the extent of public ownership, the timing of stop–go policies, monetarism and the relationship between the trade unions and the government – have, at least for the time being, largely passed from the political agenda.

BRIEFINGS

24.4 The new orthodoxy in economic policy

When, in October 1997, the Deputy Prime Minister John Prescott announced to the Labour Party conference that he would not renationalise the railways, he was conforming to what is an almost universally supported orthodoxy in economic policy. This consists of the following assumptions:

- **The primacy of keeping rates of inflation low** over all other objectives. It used to be the case that low rates of unemployment and high rates of growth were governments' top priority, with low inflation a poor third. Now, with the internationalisation of capital, governments almost everywhere see low inflation as the prerequisite for economic well-being.

- **Fiscal responsibility** During the 1960s and 1970s some British governments believed that it was possible to 'spend their way out of trouble' or stimulate the economy through borrowing and spending to speed recovery. Today governments are convinced that the only way to spend responsibly is to finance expenditure with taxation. Government borrowing is permissible but should not rise to more than 3 per cent of gross domestic product (GDP). During periods of sustained growth, as in the late 1990s, it should be reduced well below this figure.

- **Low, preferably indirect, taxation** is a good thing; high direct taxation is a bad thing. At one time Labour governments supported the idea of high progressive personal income taxes and low indirect taxes (taxes on expenditure such as VAT). Today economists argue that high income taxes distort consumer preferences and undermine efficiency. Indirect taxes leave the consumer the choice to save rather than spend, or to spend on low tax rather than high tax items. The Blair government has broadly accepted this view, as did the Major government. The main difference between them is Labour's preference for a much lower starting rate of income taxes for the low paid, which was set at 10 per cent in 1999.

- If possible, **the market rather than the state should provide goods and services**. Until recently Labour governments believed in nationalisation and the Conservatives in privatisation. Today all parties accept the advantages of privatisation. Labour accepts the need for more regulation of companies previously in public ownership, but does not propose any major renationalisation. Even the failure of Railtrack in 2002 was not followed by outright nationalisation, but by a state-supported investment company, Network Rail. It is unlikely that the Conservatives would have acted differently.

- A major debate in the Labour Party used to be between supporters of an economy protected from outside competition and those who believed in **free trade**. Today this debate is all but over. All leading Labour politicians support open international markets, with only a very minimal state role in protecting British industry. Put another way, Labour governments are enthusiastic supporters of free and open competition at home and abroad.

This has almost certainly made Tony Blair's job easier. He was, of course, still obliged to operate in the same institutional environment as his predecessors. And on occasion 'traditional' economic crises, such as the public sector labour disputes of the winter of 2002–3 erupt to disturb the relatively benign policy environment. Let us look at the nuts and bolts of the most important part of this environment – the budgetary process – in more detail.

Budgetary process

Until the late 1960s, the budgetary process was conducted in much the same way as it was 100 years earlier. It consisted of an annual round of expenditure approved by the government on an ad hoc basis. No systematic survey of spending, or planning of future spending, was involved. On the recommendation of the Plowden Report in 1961 the government accepted the need for annual expenditure surveys, which were finally adopted in 1969. The system was known as the Public Expenditure Survey Committee (PESC). Over the years, and especially since the economic traumas of the 1970s, this process has become more thorough and more systematic.

Until the election of a Labour government in 1997 the system worked like this:

1. The process started with the estimates procedure whereby officials from the spending departments report to the Treasury on their spending needs over the next three years.

2. These estimates were then summarised in the PESC, which reported to the chief secretary to the Treasury. The chief secretary in turn reported to the Cabinet, which made an estimate on spending needs over a five-year period.

3. This was followed by a series of bilaterals or face-to-face negotiations between spending department ministers and Treasury ministers. This was the first phase of the spending round. It was characterised by horse trading, confrontation and intense negotiation. A great premium was placed on the quality of argument. Intellectually gifted and aggressive ministers were more likely to squeeze something out of the Treasury than their less gifted colleagues.

4. The results of these negotiations were passed on to Cabinet committees and thence to the full Cabinet for approval. If a minister failed to agree with the Treasury the request was sent to the 'Star Chamber'. This was a Cabinet committee made up of senior Cabinet members who hear the arguments and adjudicate disputes between the disagreeing parties. The Star Chamber's decisions were usually final. Ministers may have tried to appeal against their decision to the full Cabinet, but were unlikely to gain much satisfaction.

5. Predictably, most disputes involved the large spending departments – Health, Social Security, Defence and Education – that serve large and politically powerful constituencies. As can be seen from Table 24.1, spending has remained at a high level since 1971, accounting (today) for about 40 per cent of GDP. In comparative perspective over time, note that government spending is high in most countries, although there has been some levelling off and decreases in recent years. All governments are now committed to holding spending and government debt down. Given that the public continue to assign a high priority to health, education, housing and Social Security (see Table 25.1), the pressures for increases can be appreciated. Indeed, spending on Social Security, health and education now dominate

	1985	1990	1995	1999	2000	2001	Projections 2002	2003
Australia	37.3	33.0	35.7	32.4	33.0	33.1	32.5	32.1
Austria	50.3	48.8	52.5	49.9	48.8	49.6	48.8	47.8
Belgium	57.1	50.5	50.2	47.4	46.7	46.4	46.2	45.3
Canada	45.2	45.7	45.0	38.7	37.7	38.2	38.2	37.7
Czech Republic	–	–	43.9	43.8	46.1	45.0	47.9	47.7
Denmark	–	53.6	56.6	52.5	50.6	50.8	50.1	49.3
Finland	42.6	44.4	54.3	47.1	43.6	44.6	45.2	44.3
France	49.8	47.5	51.4	49.6	48.7	48.6	49.0	48.5
Germany	45.6	43.8	46.3	46.2	43.3	45.9	46.3	45.4
Greece	43.8	47.5	46.7	43.3	43.3	41.5	41.5	40.9
Hungary	–	–	56.2	50.0	47.5	49.3	49.7	48.8
Iceland	35.3	39.0	39.2	39.1	38.8	39.7	40.3	40.2
Ireland	50.7	39.9	38.0	31.9	29.2	30.6	31.8	31.9
Italy	49.5	52.9	51.1	46.7	44.8	45.7	45.5	45.4
Japan	29.4	30.5	34.4	36.1	36.8	36.9	37.9	37.6
Korea	17.6	18.3	19.3	23.3	22.9	23.6	23.2	22.8
Luxembourg	–	41.3	42.8	39.8	38.5	38.9	40.5	39.7
Netherlands	51.9	49.4	47.7	43.8	41.6	41.7	41.8	41.6
New Zealand	–	48.1	38.6	38.8	38.2	38.4	39.0	39.0
Norway	41.5	49.7	47.6	45.8	40.8	41.8	42.3	41.9
Poland	–	–	47.0	43.4	43.7	45.5	46.3	46.4
Portugal	39.3	39.3	41.0	40.6	40.3	41.1	40.8	40.2
Slovak Republic	–	–	41.0	54.2	52.2	52.9	52.2	51.1
Spain	39.7	41.6	44.0	39.6	38.8	38.5	38.8	38.4
Sweden	60.4	55.9	61.9	55.0	52.2	52.5	52.6	51.8
United Kingdom	–	39.1	42.2	37.1	37.3	38.3	39.1	39.4
United States	33.8	33.6	32.9	30.2	29.9	30.4	30.9	30.5

Note: *Estimates and projections

Source: *Economic Outlook*, **71**, 2002, Table 26, OCED, p. 232

the national budget (Figure 24.1). Note also the relatively low proportion of spending devoted to defence. Just £24 billion was spent on defence in 2002 – less than 6 per cent of total government spending. For most of the post-war period defence was one of the largest items in the government budget.

6. The budget was then consolidated in a finance bill that was presented to the House of Commons in November. Since 1993 both the expenditure side and the income (taxation) side have been combined in the November budget (previously, the taxation measures were announced in the spring). The finance bill is then referred to House committees, and individual measures are debated before votes are taken. While this process takes some time, major amendments are very rare. Indeed, we earlier noted that the government's defeat on the increase in VAT on fuel in 1994 was a very unusual event and one that can partly be attributed to the government's very small Commons majority at that time.

Figure 24.1
Central government expenditure, 2002

Source: HM Treasury,
www.hm-treasury.gov.uk

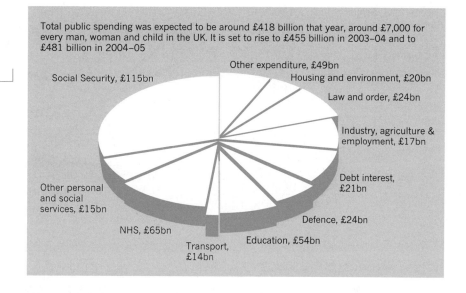

Total public spending was expected to be around £418 billion that year, around £7,000 for every man, woman and child in the UK. It is set to rise to £455 billion in 2003–04 and to £481 billion in 2004–05

Social Security, £115bn

Other expenditure, £49bn

Housing and environment, £20bn

Law and order, £24bn

Industry, agriculture & employment, £17bn

Debt interest, £21bn

Defence, £24bn

Education, £54bn

Transport, £14bn

NHS, £65bn

Other personal and social services, £15bn

While the fundamentals of this system remain in place, when elected in 1997 New Labour tried to make the system more amenable to longer term planning by guaranteeing the three-year departmental expenditure limits (DEL) thus eliminating the annual expenditure round which was used under the old system to secure ad hoc increases. Other changes included a shift to 'resource accounting budgeting' or an emphasis on counting expenditure when commitments are made rather when invoices are paid. As result it was hoped that value for money would be achieved. Finally, the government announced 'cross-sector co-ordination' or 'joined-up government' when allocating resources. As of 2003 the government continues to experiment with novel means of rationalising the public expenditure control system.

Within the machinery of Whitehall negotiations over spending are intensely political. But the same is rarely true of decisions affecting revenue. In the November budget the Chancellor announces, in a highly ritualised manner, forthcoming changes in taxation. These are deemed to be strictly confidential, with only the Prime Minister and the Treasury team privy to their contents. Indeed, it is rare for even senior Cabinet ministers to be party to these decisions. Of course, much speculation surrounds the process and leaks are not uncommon. Once announced, the decisions may prove highly controversial (as with the VAT on fuel case) but they are very rarely successfully challenged. Almost all the major changes in UK taxation, including the shift from direct to indirect taxation over the last 20 years, have been the result of a relatively closed decision-making process involving very few political actors. Such was the case with the 2002 decision to increase National Insurance contributions by 1 per cent from 2003 to fund large increases in health spending. In effect, this added 1 per cent to the marginal rate of income tax for those in employment. Almost certainly this decision was taken by the Chancellor and Prime Minister alone. Figure 24.2 shows the percentage distribution of tax revenues in 2002–2003.

Figure 24.2 *Central government income, 2002*

Source: HM Treasury, www.hm-treasury.gov.uk

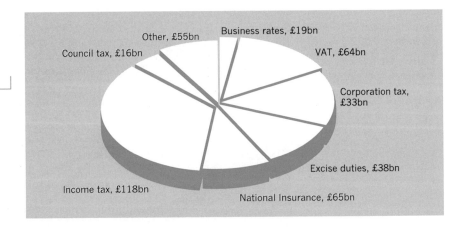

INTERNATIONALISATION OF ECONOMIC POLICY

Economic policy in Britain has been affected by external events for many decades. Recently, however, the constraints imposed by the international environment have grown in importance. Let us summarise these briefly.

European Union

The EU impinges on British economic policy in a number of ways. Most of these affect micro rather than macro economic policy. EU regulatory, environmental and competition policy have precedence over British law. In addition, should Britain join the single currency (or European Monetary Union, EMU) then all the crucial aspects of macro economic policy – interest rates, and exchange rate policy – would be set by a European central bank rather than by a government or the Bank of England. Only fiscal (taxation and expenditure) policy would be left in the central government's hands. Although even here it would be subject to the rules of the Stability and Growth Pact.

Stability and Growth Pact The Stability and Growth Pact was adopted at the Amsterdam Meeting of the European Council, 1997, to ensure smooth progress towards fiscal convergence (single monetary policy) and price stability within the EU.

International capital markets

Since exchange rate and other controls on the movement of capital were abolished in Britain and the other leading trading nations during the 1970s and 1980s the pressure on all economic authorities to follow certain policies has been intense. These policies include low levels of inflation and public (government) debt. If the markets sense that inflation or debt is out of control then investors will move out of what is considered a vulnerable currency. In order to maintain the value of currencies governments will be forced into taking drastic corrective measures, including cuts in spending and raising interest rates and taxation. The

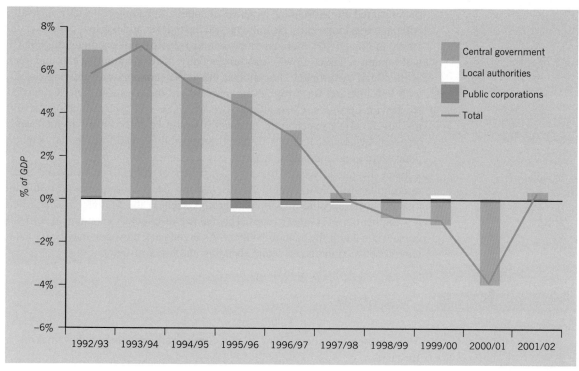

Figure 24.3 *Public Sector Net Cash Requirement, 1992–2002*

Source: House of Commons Library Research Paper 02142, 1 July 2002, p. 16

Public Sector Borrowing Requirement (PSBR)
The total amount borrowed by government to finance its annual expenditure.

alternative would be to let the currency fall which in an import-dependent economy would result in more inflation. As can be seen from Figure 3.1, the inflation picture is complex. Figure 24.3 shows the size of the Public Sector Net Cash Requirement (PSNCR) over the period 1992–2002. Generally, the PSNCR rises during periods of recession and falls during booms. As of 2002, the PSNCR was on the rise but to very modest levels compared with the early and mid-1990s. Most commentators agree that public debt is being held at a reasonable level in Britain. Generally, the centralised and unitary nature of economic policy making in Britain gives to incumbent governments all the tools necessary to control the level of government expenditure and income, and therefore the level of public debt.

Blair government and the public sector: the return of old Labour?

In the period from 2001 to 2004, the Labour government announced bold new targets for improving the quality of the public services. This included raising health spending to at least the average in the EU (around 7/8 per cent of GDP), easing transport congestion within ten years and raising the number of the 18–30-year-old age group going into higher education to 50 per cent. Naturally, this was accompanied by substantial increases in public spending especially in health. Although this looks like a return to the old 'spend, tax and borrow' policies of the 1960s and the 1970s, there are important differences. For one thing the PSNCR will remain relatively low – and substantially lower than during the mid years of the Major government. For another thing, the economy was growing steadily with low inflation for a full seven years before the increases were announced. No previous post-war Chancellor enjoyed the luxury of such a situation. Finally, the largest single expenditure (in health) would be financed by an increase in National Insurance. In terms of fiscal responsibility, therefore, the government plans were quite compatible with the new economic orthodoxy.

Even the public sector strikes of the winter of 2002/3, which looked like a return to the bad old days of the 1970s, had few fiscal consequences. Most of the disputes were specific to particular groups such as the firefighters which held few implications for other groups. The real test of Labour's economic record will come when and if the economy falters. As in the past, they then may be forced to choose between increased social spending and fiscal restraint.

ESSAYS

1. What is the new orthodoxy in economic policy? Why has it come about?

2. Why has economic policy dominated British politics over the last 30 years? What evidence is there that this special status is now changing?

3. Why is micro economic policy usually much more politicised than macro economic policy?

4. What are the differences between the Blair government's economic policy and that of the Conservative opposition?

SUMMARY

This chapter has shown how highly centralised economic policy making in Britain is:

■ Even within the executive, very few political actors are involved in the key decisions. This applies to both monetary and fiscal policy.

■ Until recently monetary policy was the shared prerogative of the Chancellor of the Exchequer and the Bank of England. Since 1997, however, the Bank has been the dominant influence in setting interest rates. The Prime Minister, Chancellor and the Treasury remain the key players in setting levels of government spending and taxation.

■ Other Cabinet ministers play a reactive rather than proactive part in this process. Parliament's role is usually confined to approving decisions and to a limited form of supervision. Other interests such as business and the unions play an indirect role, although they may be closely involved in the detailed implementation of aspects of micro economic policy.

■ Government options in this area are, however, greatly circumscribed by the need to maintain the confidence of business. This applies both domestically and, as far as the money markets are concerned, internationally.

■ In addition the European Union plays an increasingly important role in micro economic policy. Should Britain join the single currency then the EU's role in macro economic policy will become dominant.

■ Labour governments have adhered to a new orthodoxy in economic policy, although there are dangers that increased social spending in the 2001–2004 period will conflict with agreed borrowing targets should the economy falter.

MILESTONES

Milestones in recent economic policy making

1961 Publication of the Plowden Report on the need for more systematic control of public spending

1969 PESC (Public Expenditure Survey Committee) system introduced to plan expenditure in advance

1976 Introduction of the 'Star Chamber' to arbitrate disputes over departmental spending

1979–80 Margaret Thatcher's monetarist experiment begins

1983–5 Monetarism quietly dropped as a guiding principle in economic policy

1987 Stock market crash followed by over stimulation of the economy

1989–93 Deepest recession of the post-1945 period

1990 Britain joins the Exchange Rate Mechanism (ERM) of the European Monetary System (EMS)

1992 Britain is forced out of the ERM ('Black Wednesday')

1993 Spending and taxing side of the budget consolidated into one November budget

1994 Government defeated over further increases in VAT on domestic fuel

1997 New Labour Chancellor, Gordon Brown, announces that the Bank of England is immediately to be given the freedom to set interest rates

1999 Budget established a new 10 per cent income tax starting rate for the poorest working families

2002 Budget includes large increases in health spending announced to finance by a 1 per cent increase in National Insurance (in effect a 1 per cent increase in income tax for all those in employment). Budget surplus becomes a (small) deficit

PROJECTS

1. Catalogue the changing pattern of direct (income and corporate) taxes in Britain since 1960. What accounts for these changes?

2. Write a departmental brief from one of the major spending departments (defence, Social Security, health, education, transport, Home Office) justifying expenditure to the Cabinet Star Chamber. Write a Treasury reply arguing for reduced expenditure.

FURTHER READING

For a comprehensive statistical background and accounts of the policy-making process, see Peter Curwen (ed.), *Understanding the UK Economy* (London: Macmillan, 1997). Wyn Grant's *Economic Policy in Britain* (London: Palgrave, 2002) provides a good up-to-date introduction to economic policy making. On the Treasury and public spending, see Maurice Wright and Colin Thain, *Treasury and Whitehall: Planning and Control of Public Spending* (Oxford: Clarendon Press, 1995). A good summary of New Labour economic and social policies is provided by Gerald R. Taylor (ed.), *The Impact of New Labour* (London: Macmillan, 1999). See also Wyn Grant, 'The changing nature of economic policy', *Politics Review*, **10** (4), 2001. On the Thatcher years, see Andrew Gamble, *The Free Economy and the Strong State* (London: Macmillan, 2nd edn, 1994). For an account of recent changes in expenditure control, see Simon James, *British Cabinet Government* (London: Routledge, 2nd edn, 1999).

USEFUL WEB SITES ON ECONOMIC POLICY

Hotlinks to these sites can be found on the CWS website at http://www.booksites.net/budge.

In Britain, economic and fiscal policy is dominated by the Chancellor of the Exchequer; the main policy goals and achievements can be found at

3. How does the European Union affect British economic policy? Answer with respect to *one* of the following:
 (a) competition policy
 (b) interest rate and currency policy
 (c) labour market policy.

4. Explain the differences between Labour's first three budgets (1997–99) and the subsequent expenditures. Answer by providing statistics on changes between departments and on the overall level of spending.

www.number-10.gov.uk; there are other relevant sites related to economic and fiscal policies, these include the Treasury site www.hm-treasury.gov.uk, the Bank of England www.bankofengland.co.uk, and the Department of Trade and Industry www.dti.gov.uk. There is some useful information available at the government's Centre for Management and Policy Studies (www.cmps.gov.uk). It might also be worth looking at the British Chambers of Commerce (www.chamberonline.co.uk/index.jsp). The Confederation of British Industries is at www.cbi.org.uk. You can find the Trade Union Congress at www.tuc.org.uk.

There are a number of think tanks and research groups where economic theories receive critical assessment, some of them are: the Institute of Fiscal Studies (www.ifs.org.uk), the National Institute for Economic and Social Research (www.niesr.ac.uk), the Centre for Economic Policy Research (www.cepr.org), the Adam Smith Society (www.adamsmith.org.uk), and the Institute for Economic Affairs (www.ie.org.uk). The *Financial Times* (www.ft.com) and the *Economist* (www.economist.com) offer regular market, financial and economic analysis.

In the Policy Library web site, under the entry on economic policy, you can find an excellent set of resources on topics such as agriculture, employment, business and taxation. We strongly suggest you visit them at www.policylibrary.com.

Social policy

Few issues in Britain arouse as much controversy as social policy. The vast majority of the population support free health care provided by the National Health Service (NHS), free high-quality primary and secondary education, adequate old age pensions and unemployment benefits. Yet to a greater or lesser extent all of these benefits are perceived to have been reduced in value or quality by successive governments. Many of the problems associated with state social provision in Britain are related to the sometimes painful transition from the universal benefits promised at the inception of the Welfare State in the 1940s to the much more selective system that economic and political realities have imposed since the 1980s. Much of this chapter will be devoted to explaining why this transition has occurred and why the pressures for more selectivity continue to increase even when the public expect higher standards of social provision. The chapter will cover:

■ problems in defining 'social policy'

■ the Welfare State in Britain: its foundations and principles

■ the four main areas of social provision – income maintenance, housing, health and education – over the last 20 years

■ policy areas examined in their institutional context. A special emphasis is placed on the efforts by New Labour to improve the quality of the public services.

Universal and selective benefits Universal benefits are welfare benefits distributed to all groups and individuals who are eligible, irrespective of their particular circumstances, compared with selective benefits for which eligibility is determined according to individual circumstances such as income, age or disability.

DEFINING SOCIAL POLICY

What constitutes social policy depends on both historical and geographic circumstances. In some countries what we regard as social support is provided by families or the market. If social policy is defined as *state* support for people in need (a definition adopted by this chapter) it is clear that within countries, the definition changes over time as it does between countries. In Britain, for example, state support for housing has moved from a limited form of municipal provision before the Second World War, to near universal provision for 'general needs' housing after the war, back to a minimal level of support today. In many poorer countries state-provided benefits are limited to education. Even in rich industrialised nations such as the United States of America and Japan social policy means something very different from what it means in the UK. In the USA, for example, housing is rarely considered a part of social policy and there is no system of universal health care. Instead, the market is the major provider in these areas. In Britain today the definition is changing as the political and public support for state provision of housing has fallen.

BRIEFINGS

25.1 Universalism, selectivism, and the Welfare State

In many developed modern economies, for example the USA, most state welfare benefits are provided on a selective basis, that is, eligibility is determined by individual circumstances. Income, disability and age are the usual criteria employed when potential recipients' eligibility is tested. Benefits may be selective both in terms of the social group eligibility and in terms of the level of support. State pensions, for example, are obviously only available to the old and survivors (those widowed) and the amount of the pension may vary according to circumstance and past employment record.

In other systems, benefits are provided on a universal basis. All social groups may be eligible and the benefits may be distributed on a flat-rate basis, which means that the same benefit is given to everybody, irrespective of circumstances. Elements of both systems prevail in most countries. Even in the self-reliant USA, elementary and secondary education is organised on a universal basis.

The British Welfare State as implemented by the Labour government after 1945 was based more on universal than selectivist principles. Everybody was entitled to health care, including dental care. Public housing was for 'general need' and rents were unrelated to income. Family allowances were flat rate as were elements of the old age pension.

The founders of the system were not so naive as to believe that it could be introduced without considerable cost. How then would it be funded? Three devices would be employed to ensure the system was viable. First, Keynesian demand management would be the dominant tool of macro economic policy. As a result the country would enjoy full employment; the poverty, illness and dislocation associated with mass unemployment would be avoided. Second, much of the system would be self-financing through contributory national insurance stamps. Eligibility for unemployment benefit, for example, would be directly linked to this system. Third, although never explicitly stated, a system of rationing would reconcile the demand for, and the supply of, certain services. Waiting lists would prevail for some hospital treatments and for public housing.

In spite of numerous problems the Welfare State worked well for most of the post-war period. Even in the early twenty-first century elements of universalism – for example, in the NHS – persist.

Very generally, social policy covers those areas where the government (or the state), rather than the market, plays a major role in providing for the physical well-being of families and individuals. Governments came to play this role because of the failure of markets to provide acceptable standards of provision. Usually, although not always, it was electorally powerful socialist or Labour parties that legislated for social provision. Often they came to power following periods of serious economic dislocation.

In Britain, for example, the Labour government elected in 1945 legislated to create what became known as the Welfare State, or a system of social support designed to protect every citizen from the physical insecurities of life.

THE BRITISH WELFARE STATE

Welfare State
A system in which the state takes responsibility for providing at least the minimum conditions of social and economic security by providing public services such as housing, health care, sickness and unemployment benefits, and pensions.

The British welfare system was largely a product of the great depression of the 1930s and of the Second World War. Although the rudiments of a pension and unemployment insurance system were introduced by the Liberals soon after the turn of the century, it was not until the election of a Labour government in 1945 that the construction of the Welfare State began. The mass unemployment of the 1930s had demonstrated how inadequate social protection was in the absence of comprehensive state aid. Low levels of unemployment assistance (known as the dole) were means tested or available only to families close to destitution. Families whose means were above these low levels of income had to make do as best they could. Other services, including health, housing and secondary education, had to be paid for or were freely available only on a very limited basis.

BRIEFINGS

25.2 **Foundations of the British Welfare State**

Income maintenance

1942 Beveridge Report on social security

1945 Family Allowance Act: family allowances

1946 National Insurance Act: unemployment benefit, disability, old age and survivors' pensions

1948 National Assistance Act: income support for those not covered by national insurance

Housing

1946 Housing Act: central government subsidies for local authority housing

1949 Housing Act: council housing designated as 'general needs' and not just for the working class

Health

1948 National Health Service Act: creation of the National Health Service

Education

1944 Education Act: secondary education available to all, free of charge; 11-plus exam would select the academically gifted for grammar schools

Employment

1944 Employment Policy white paper: official recognition of Keynesian full employment policy; also recognised the need for regional policy to reduce economic disparities between the regions

By the end of the 1940s, an intellectual and political consensus was emerging in favour of a greatly enhanced role for government in economy and society. The Second World War had demonstrated how massive government spending could quickly remove the blight of mass unemployment, and politicians became convinced that Keynesian economics, or demand management, could be used to keep unemployment at acceptably low levels for the foreseeable future. During the late 1930s and early 1940s the government commissioned a number of reports into almost all aspects of social and economic life from landuse planning to education to employment. The most famous of these, the Beveridge Report, concerned social welfare.

BRIEFINGS

25.3 Aneurin Bevan on housing and health

The following extracts reflect the views of the Labour politician Aneurin Bevan who was Health Minister 1945–51 and introduced the National Health Service in 1948:

'I said that in my view it was entirely undesirable that on modern housing estates only one type of citizen should live. I referred to them then as "twilight towns", and said it was a reproach to our modern social planning that from one sort of township should come one income group. I said that, if we are to enable citizens to lead a full life, if they are each to be aware of the problems of their neighbours, then they should be all drawn from the very different sections of the community and we should try to introduce in our modern villages what has always been the lovely feature of English and Welsh villages, where the doctor, the grocer, the butcher and farm labourer all lived in the same street... I believe it is a necessary biological background for modern life, and I believe it leads to the enrichment of every member of the community to live in communities of that sort. We believe that it is essential that local authorities should also provide accommodation for single persons, for persons who are following a professional life, and that they should provide for old people.'

Bevan in 1949, recalling his intentions in 1945, quoted in D. McKay and A. Cox, *The Politics of Urban Change*, London: Croom Helm, 1979, p. 118

'Allowing for all sensible administrative measures to prevent waste, the plain fact is that the cost of the health service not only will, but ought to, increase. Most of the hospitals fall far short of any proper standard; accommodation needs to be increased, particularly for tuberculosis and mental health – indeed some of the mental hospitals are very near to a public scandal and we are lucky they have not so far attracted more limelight and publicity. Throughout the service there are piling up arrears of essential capital work. Also it is in this field, particularly, that constant new development will always be needed to keep pace with research progress (as, recently, in penicillin, streptomycin, cortisone, etc.) and to expand essential specialist services, such as hearing aids or ophthalmic services. The position cannot be evaded that a nationally owned and administered hospital service will always involve a very considerable and expanding exchequer outlay. If that position cannot, for financial reasons, be faced, then the only alternatives (to my mind thoroughly undesirable), are either to give up – in whole or in part – the idea of national responsibility for the hospitals or else to import into the scheme some regular source of revenue such as the recovery of charges from those who use it. I am afraid that it is clear that we cannot have it both ways.'

Bevan in 1950, quoted in R. Klein, *The New Politics of the NHS*, Harlow: Addison Wesley Longman, 3rd edn, 1995, p. 32

Beveridge argued that, with the new tools of economic management that would ensure that mass unemployment would never occur again, the government could afford to provide a complete system of social protection for those who, through misfortune, inadequacy or dependency, could not provide for themselves. The new system would be built on the principles of universal care: the state would provide flat-rate benefits irrespective of the ability to pay. Hence, public (or council) housing would be provided on a 'general needs' basis. Rents would be the same for all tenants irrespective of income. Health services and a flat-rate family allowance would be provided on the same basis. This comprehensive system of welfare would ensure that everybody was secure 'from the cradle to the grave'. The Labour government legislated to produce just such a system, which was fully in place by 1950.

Given its scope – some would say its utopianism – the Welfare State worked remarkably well and was widely copied in other countries. There are a number of reasons for its initial success. First, full employment was indeed established quickly after the war, so Keynesian demand management appeared to work. Not until the 1970s did mass unemployment re-emerge. Full employment kept the cost of the Welfare State down and government revenues up.

Second, benefits were established at modest levels. Unemployment benefits and old age, survivors' and disability pensions were to be self-financing. Employees would pay National Insurance stamps out of their wages; these stamps were to be stuck on to a National Insurance card that would act as proof of eligibility for benefits. And, initially at least, welfare benefits were low. In addition, the school leaving age was 15 and only a minority of pupils stayed on after 16, with a tiny minority going on to higher education. Health care standards were, by today's norms, low and inexpensive. Limited supplies of housing and health facilities ensured that the system worked. In effect a system of rationing prevailed that involved long waiting lists.

Third, a remarkable degree of consensus on the status of the Welfare State emerged. People from all regions, ages and social classes were agreed that it was a good thing. Almost everybody used the health service, the vast majority of children went to state schools, private pensions were available only to a minority of the middle classes. Even council housing attracted a wide social mix, at least during the serious housing shortages prevalent during the 1940s and 1950s.

The system worked adequately until well into the 1960s, and indeed Labour governments legislated to extend and improve benefits during this decade. By the 1970s welfare spending had become easily the largest item on the national budget. Politicians on the right were arguing that unless spending was curbed the system would become untenable. During the 1980s Conservative governments began to roll back the Welfare State, a process that continues in some areas such as income maintenance to this day. At the same time public support in the UK for welfare spending remained high, with health and education the top priorities for extra spending. Even by 2000 this support prevailed across all social classes (Table 25.1). A good way to understand how and why this transition has occurred is to examine each of the main components of social policy in turn. In addition, we will examine the main actors and institutions involved in these policy areas.

Utopianism A form of ideology that claims that it is possible to create a perfect or near-perfect society. Some utopias are constructed by their creators not as feasible societies but as models against which to compare the real world.

Table 25.1 *Priorities for public spending by class, 2000*

	Salariat*	Self-employed	Working class
First priority for extra public spending	%	%	%
Health	46	43	48
Education	37	33	30
Public transport	6	4	3
Roads	2	6	4
Housing	1	2	5

*Salaried employees

Source: *British Social Attitudes*, 17th Report, 2000, Table 3.2

INCOME MAINTENANCE

Almost certainly the greatest actuarial problems in the income maintenance area apply to old age pensions. The flat system created by Beveridge (all would receive the same pension having paid enough National Insurance contributions) was expected to become more expensive over time, but by the 1960s it was, in real terms, twice as expensive as envisaged. More people were living longer and the political pressures for maintaining or increasing the level of benefit proved considerable. By the 1970s governments were convinced that the system was in need of long-term reform. Poverty among the old remained a serious problem, which the flat-rate system could not solve except at huge expense. In 1975 the government compromised by introducing a State Earnings Related Pensions Scheme (SERPS), which added an earnings-related element to the system. However, this too was projected to become very expensive and in 1986, the Conservatives legislated to restrict the scope of the SERPS system.

By the 1990s governments were under even more pressure to reduce the real value of the old age pension. In 1980, the Conservatives linked pension increases to prices rather than to earnings, so the relative value of the pension declined over time, but even so the cost of state pensions could become prohibitive in the longer term. As can be seen from Table 25.2 the number of people in the UK likely to be dependent on the working population will increase substantially in the decades after 2020, and it is the old whose dependency will increase the most. As a result, politicians from all political parties are now committed to making the provision of state pensions selective by replacing them for most of the working population with private pension schemes. Given the special status that the flat-rate state pension has assumed in the minds of most voters, this proposal is bound to be politically controversial.

Family poverty was originally tackled through the provision of National Assistance or welfare payments available to all those past school leaving age not in receipt of unemployment benefit and who were in need. In addition a flat-rate family allowance was payable to second and subsequent children (it was assumed that the first child could be cared for if one parent was working). While National Assistance was selective (ie it was means tested), everybody from the Queen down was eligible for family allowances. Over the years, this system has been

Table 25.2 *Projected dependency ratios, 1994–2061*

	Child dependency	Elderly dependency	Overall dependency
1994	34	30	64
2001	33	29	62
2011	30	31	60
2021	28	30	58
2031	29	39	68
2041	28	43	72
2051	28	43	71
2061	29	44	73

Note: Table 25.2 shows 1994-based projections, for number of children and people over retirement age to every 100 people of working age. The ratios take account of the change in state pension age for women from 60 years to 65 years between 2010 and 2020

Source: *Social Trends 27*, London: The Stationery Office, 1997, Table A.2

Poverty trap
The idea that the Welfare State creates a vicious cycle of poverty for some social groups by imposing welfare systems that discourage people from taking responsibility for their own life or finding work. The cycle tends to continue, some claim, into the next generation of children who grow up in such a system.

modified, although, remarkably, the flat-rate element in Family Allowance (now called Child Benefit) remains. The main changes have been:

- In 1968 family allowances became taxable, but the 1975 Child Benefit Act actually strengthened the flat-rate principle by making the allowance payable to all children. One-parent families received a higher level of benefit.

- In 1966 National Assistance was replaced with Supplementary Benefits. These means-tested payments were available to all in need, including pensioners and the unemployed who could not manage on the flat-rate pension or unemployment benefit.

- By the early 1970s it was clear that many families were in a 'poverty or income support trap'. If an adult took a job the family income could fall, given that the earned income (net of tax) could be less than the state benefits forfeited once employment began. Legislation to reduce this disincentive to work was passed in 1971 (Family Income Supplement) and 1988 (Family Credit). These laws allow benefit recipients to work without losing all their benefits. While helpful for some families, a general consensus had emerged by the late 1990s that the disincentive effect of the benefit system remained considerable for many families. Given the array of benefits (including Housing Benefit) individuals and families have to make complex calculations when taking employment. The system also provides an incentive for benefit recipients to work while receiving benefits without declaring their income.

- In 1982 the government removed earnings-related supplements to unemployment benefit and made such benefits taxable. Gradually during the remainder of the Conservative period in office the relative value of benefits was reduced and eligibility criteria were tightened.

- In a 1998 green paper, A New Contract for Welfare, the Labour government stressed the need to 'empower' the poor and thus remove dependency. This and subsequent government publications have emphasised the mutual responsibility of the needy, government and the business community to tackle low incomes together. Labelled a 'New Deal' for younger people, lone parents and the disabled, this policy has been directed towards increasing opportunities to exploit the untapped resources of the under-employed. To this end businesses have been encouraged to provide work for this largely unused labour force. The 1999 budget introduced a new minimum income guarantee of £200 per week per working family with children, with tax credits and income tax reductions so that families at and slightly above this level would pay no income tax at all. Non-working adults in families would be required to seek work.

- The new system was labelled the Working Families Tax Credit (WFTC) which, together with similar tax credits for children and the disabled, removed most of the disincentive for the less well paid to work. In April 2003, the system was overhauled again and the scope of the benefits was widened. The new credits were known as Child Tax Credit (CTC) and the Working Tax Credit (WTC). For the old, the basic state pension (BSP) which is simply not enough to live on was supplemented by a Minimum Income Guarantee (MIG) or a system of welfare benefits to supplement the BSP.

Actors and institutions

Unlike economic policy, where key decisions can often be made by a few senior politicians and officials, income support policy tends to change incrementally and is often infused with interest group activity. This is particularly true of pensions policy. Given that almost all the population will eventually become pensioners the issue is politically highly salient. In the past politicians from all parties have expressed sympathy for poverty among the old. Groups such as Age Concern are active in keeping the issue in the public eye, and the vulnerability of the old ensures that any policy changes that occur have to be implemented over the longer term. Family support policy has a slightly different status. Public support for poor families is lower, and the Conservative legislation of the 1980s shows that relatively major changes can be wrought without serious political repercussions. This said, pressure groups (such as the Child Poverty Action Group) and individual members of Parliament are likely to be active in support of or against particular proposals.

Given the premium on expertise in this policy area, individual Cabinet ministers and their officials are usually closely involved in income support policy making. Indeed, by the early part of the twenty-first century, the more than 20 different benefits available to the needy, administered by several departments, required a high level of expert input to inform any future reforms.

New Labour policy

As noted, New Labour's stance on income maintenance is quite similar to that of the previous Conservative government. Labour accepts the need to supplement (or eventually replace) the flat-rate pension with a system of private pensions.

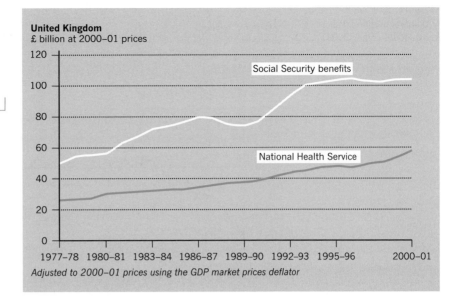

Figure 25.1 *Real growth in Social Security benefits and National Health Service expenditure, 1977–2001*

Source: *Social Trends 32*, 2002, Chart 8.3

More surprising is the Labour Party's conversion to 'workfare' or a system of family support designed to oblige parents, and particularly single parents, to work rather than depend on state help. Coupled to this objective is a commitment to expand both nursery education (which will enable single parents to take employment), institute training for the unemployed, encourage business to play a major part in providing employment and provide a minimum income guarantee for working families. During their first two terms Labour faithfully worked towards meeting these objectives, which they called a New Deal or welfare to work strategy. These policies do, of course, represent a sea change from the universalist welfare policies of the 1970s.

Related was the new emphasis on co-ordinating different aspects of social policy in what was called 'joined-up' government. Hence the creation of the Social Exclusion Unit in the Cabinet Office in 1997 represented an attempt to co-ordinate all those government departments, including Social Security and education, whose brief covered helping those such as the poor, homeless, truants and others excluded from the mainstream of British society.

As a result of these changes and a healthy economic environment, government spending on social security (all income maintenance including pensions) levelled off during the late 1990s and early 2000s (Figure 25.1).

HOUSING

In 1946 the Labour government legislated to provide a new system of housing subsidies channelled through local authorities. This and later legislation identified council (public) housing as 'general needs' accommodation. In other words, the

Figure 25.2 *House building completions by sector, 1951–2001*

Source: *Social Trends 32*, 2002, Chart 10.3

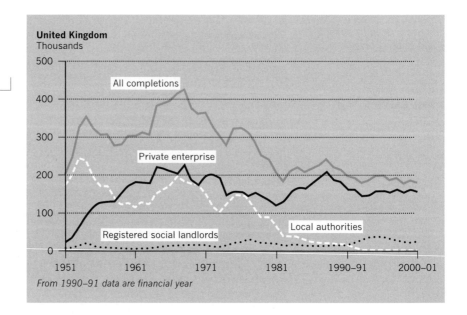

private sector was to be relegated to secondary status and most housing would be provided by local councils. Although the Conservatives later assigned a much more prominent role to the private sector, both parties accepted that council housing would be the source of new housing for the working class population. Serious housing shortages meant that during the 1950s and early 1960s Conservative and Labour politicians vied with each other over who could build the most houses.

Unlike income support, the housing policy system closely involved local authorities. They were the recipients of government housing grants but were left much on their own when making decisions about the location and management of housing estates. As housing was in short supply a 'waiting list' system was created whereby local government housing departments decided on eligibility for housing. Family size, income and job status were the main criteria employed. Only in 1972 did (a Conservative) government apply a systematic means test, whereby rent rebates were given to needy tenants both in the public and private sectors. Until that time everybody in council housing paid the same rent, irrespective of income.

As can be seen from Figure 25.2, public sector housing construction remained at a high level through to the mid-1970s. Generally, Conservative governments and local authorities favoured the private sector while Labour favoured the public sector. At the same time public housing was increasingly viewed as housing for the disadvantaged, a perception that was strengthened by the construction of large, anonymous housing estates during the 1950s and 1960s that were increasingly occupied by disadvantaged families. Figure 25.2 shows how council housing construction fell from the mid-1970s on. This was initially a result of fiscal emergency, but after 1979 it was the direct result of Conservative government policy.

Margaret Thatcher's administrations (1979–90) disliked publicly provided housing. They believed that it undermined self-reliance, encouraged local authority overspending and aggravated class divisions. As a result they progressively cut government housing grants and launched the largest single change in housing policy since the Second World War: the sale of council houses to tenants. The major changes in this and other areas were:

- In 1980 tenants were given the right to buy their houses. A system of discounts on the price was available depending on length of tenure.

- In 1982 Housing Benefits were introduced. Council rents had increased steadily although individual authorities retained some freedom to subsidise them. For those who could not pay these rents because of poverty or disability a system of rebates was available.

- In 1986 and 1988 the government provided further incentives for council house sales. Councils could sell to housing associations and private landlords. The discounts available to sitting tenants and council flat tenants, where the property was particularly hard to sell, were increased.

- In 1989 the government effectively ended local authority rent subsidies. In future they would have to charge an 'economic rent' with rebates available to the disadvantaged in the form of Housing Benefits.

- Throughout their tenure in office the Conservatives attempted to increase the role of private landlords. This was the smallest and least efficient part of the housing market and they believed that labour mobility would improve with a larger and more flexible private rental sector. A new form of 'regulated tenancies' was created with reduced security of tenure for tenants. Conservative efforts here were less than successful, however. Ultimately, the failure to stimulate this part of the market relates to underlying factors, including restrictive planning laws on landuse and public disquiet with private landlords, which even radical Conservative governments were not prepared to challenge.

In the late 1990s and early part of the twenty-first century social housing (as it is now called) is provided mainly by housing associations and through Housing Benefits. Indeed, housing associations have become the major providers of social housing in the system. Local authority housing remains important but it is declining rapidly and consists mainly of large estates occupied by disadvantaged families. Meanwhile, owner occupation has soared and now accounts for some 67 per cent of the total housing stock (Figure 25.3).

Actors and institutions

Unlike income maintenance, the key actors in social housing in Britain have been local governments. They remain important as administrators of the remaining council housing stock and of Housing Benefits, although their discretion over these policy areas is now quite limited. Central government decisions during the 1980s and the 1990s were taken with little reference to local government

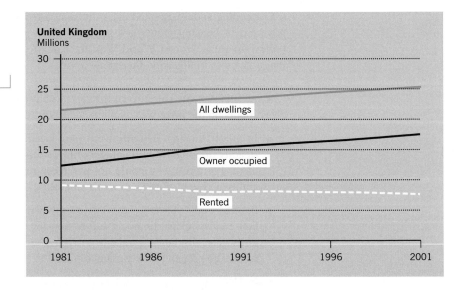

preferences. Organised interests in this area, including pressure groups representing the poor and homeless, have usually played a reactive rather than proactive part. In some ways it is easier to cut capital spending on social housing rather than current expenditure on such things as pensions or Housing Benefits. The latter have numerous recipients who are highly sensitive to marginal changes in their incomes. Capital spending cuts are felt in the longer term, involve few immediate victims, and are therefore politically easier to impose.

New Labour policy

Although housing shortages remain and many people live in poor housing conditions, the issue has slipped in political importance compared with health, education and pensions. Politicians from all parties believe the private sector should play the dominant role in housing provision. Housing Benefits are now the main means by which the State helps house the disadvantaged, and in this sense housing policy has become inseparable from income support policy. New Labour recognises this fact and has not proposed a reversal of council house sales and a return to traditional public housing. Instead, it supports an extension of owner occupation to the less advantaged through tax and interest-deferred mortgages together with the provision of social housing for those who are ineligible for mortgages.

HEALTH

State-provided health care has assumed a very special status in British society. As noted earlier, the utopian vision of the founders of the National Health Service (NHS) was that health care would be provided on a universal basis. Unlike housing and many aspects of income maintenance, much of the health care system in the early part of the twenty-first century, and in particular primary doctor and hospital care, remained free and universally available. However, the increasing cost has brought constant pressure for reform, and some aspects of provision, including dental care, are now provided on a selective basis. In addition, market-like mechanisms have been introduced into the system, changing what might be called the culture of health care in the UK.

The 1948 system

When the NHS was created in 1948 its administrative structure was a compromise between existing and new institutions. (The following description applies to England and Wales; Scotland had a separate system.) General practitioners (GPs) worked much as they had before the reforms, except that their revenue came from government rather than patients; many health services remained in the hands of local authorities. The major innovation was the creation of 14 new regional hospital boards. Within each region most hospitals were run by locally appointed hospital management committees but an elite of teaching hospitals were run by boards of governors with direct links to the Ministry of Health.

The 1974 reforms

During the 1950s and 1960s a number of serious problems emerged with this structure. Regions varied enormously in size, resources tended to move towards an elite of teaching hospitals, little in the way of planning for the whole system was possible. When, during the 1960s, a major hospital building programme was launched, every regional board required major new capital expenditure but there was no means whereby priorities could be set. Therefore, both Labour and Conservative governments agreed that reform was needed. What transpired was a new structure that was eventually implemented in 1974. The regional boards (now regional authorities) were given the job of overall strategic planning, and a new tier of 90 area health authorities was created to manage direct care. The rationale was to facilitate better management and control of the service from the centre. At the same time democratic accountability was enhanced through the creation of a system of advisory committees and community health councils. These were made up of laypeople and interest group spokespersons nominated by local governments, voluntary organisations and regional authorities.

The 1982 reforms

Among the problems with the 1974 structure was a perception that the system was run in the interests of the producers (the health care professionals) rather than the consumers (patients). At the same time, local government involvement seemed unnecessary. In 1979, the Conservative government published a consultative document, *Patients First*, which recommended a number of changes. These

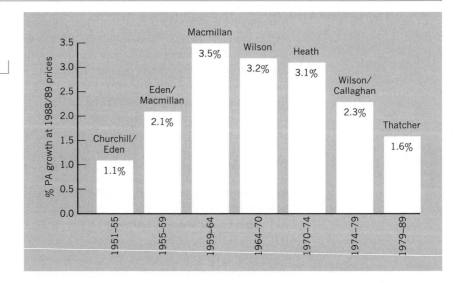

culminated in the 1982 reforms that abolished area authorities and created 192 district health authorities (DHAs). Local government participation in DHAs was reduced and that of local experts and notables increased. In addition, the government devolved greater management responsibility to the DHA level. In the ensuing decade government spending on health was reduced, at least in relation to the rest of the post-1955 period (Figure 25.4), and much of the pressure on spending was felt by the DHAs.

The 1991 and 1993 reforms

Organisational change during the 1970s and the 1980s was informed by what might be called 'managerialism', or the belief that improved managerial structures and lines of accountability would improve efficiency and therefore the quality of service provided to the public. However, during the 1980s a new administrative philosophy assumed that bringing in market forces rather than improving management structure would enhance efficiency. A white paper, Working for Patients (Cm 555, London: HMSO, 1989), argued that NHS institutions acted as both providers and purchasers of health care. In other words, they might provide hospital care but they would also have to purchase hospital supplies and services. Moreover, a conflict had arisen between these two functions because the health service was more producer than it was consumer oriented. Much as with the Civil Service before the Next Steps reforms, the white paper argued that the institutional structure of the service gave health care professionals (doctors, nurses and so on) an incentive to improve their status and conditions of service rather than to make patient care the top priority.

Again, as with the Civil Service, the answer was to change the incentive structure of the service by introducing market principles into the system. Accordingly, the government designated a system of providers (NHS trusts and general practitioners) who would bid for business (or draw up a contract) with a purchaser (district and family health authorities, GP fundholders).

The NHS reforms in perspective

Most commentators agree that the reforms of the 1990s had both desirable and unwanted consequences. By some measures (waiting lists, outpatient services) some improvement occurred, although measuring performance is notoriously difficult. The district health authorities, which were the key purchasers on behalf of consumers in the system, seemed to be more attuned to GPs than to patients. Critics also pointed to the rapid increase in the number of managers in the system. But the main problem was that the reforms did not significantly increase the quality and the quantity of health care delivery that the public expected. The economics of health care are such that some degree of rationing by price or availability is necessary in any system. The reforms of the 1990s recognised this. In effect, the rationing element that has always been present in the NHS was made more explicit. Not surprisingly, the public were quick to notice this and to demand more and better provision.

BRIEFINGS

25.4 The economics of health care

The search for increased efficiency in some social policy areas, and especially in health care, is beset by a structural economic problem that, unless checked, means that the cost of health care will spiral ever upwards. With most items we buy as consumers the more that is invested in the productive process the lower the unit costs of production become. Investment in a car factory, for example, reduces the labour input, increases productivity and ultimately reduces the real cost of the product. Capital investment in health, however, can have perverse results. New equipment bought by a hospital usually results in an increased demand for labour to operate it. Worse, the complexity of such things as dialysis machines and CAT (computerised axial or computer-assisted tomography) scanners requires highly trained operative staff. (In the car factory required skill levels typically fall as capital investment increases.) Given that labour is the most expensive item in most organisations, this means that increased investment in health results in increased costs.

This problem is compounded by the fact that, in the economists' parlance, the demand for health care is highly inelastic, that is, it responds only imprecisely to variations in price. If you have the money to pay for a life-saving operation you are likely to pay for it irrespective of the cost. In addition, the health professionals (doctors, nurses and so on) are in a good position to organise and negotiate higher wages. This is what has happened in the USA, where health care accounts for 17 per cent of GDP.

In Britain the government is, in effect, a monopoly supplier and employer of health services and labour, so it has been able to hold costs down through rationing and central financial controls. An ageing and more demanding public has, however, greatly increased the pressure for more spending on health, which will almost certainly rise steadily in the future (see Figure 25.1). Given the constraints on the NHS increasing numbers of the more affluent have turned to private health care.

These problems have shifted the emphasis in health care from curing illness to preventing illness.

Actors and institutions

As can be inferred from what we have said already, health care professionals have always been intimately involved in the politics of health care. Expertise is so crucial in this policy area that their involvement – and co-operation – is crucial. The Department of Health and its predecessors have also been a key actor, because of its intimate links with the institutional structure of the NHS. Until the 1990s change came only slowly to the system, in part because of the entrenched power of professionals and in particular hospital doctors.

The public's role has also been crucial, not in terms of the day-to-day management of the system, but in terms of what has always been a strong public commitment to free universal health care. Conservative reforms were condemned by the opposition as 'backdoor privatisation'. This was the worst possible criticism in the British context. In fact only dental care has effectively been privatised. Moves towards market-like transactions have changed the culture of the NHS but not who pays for NHS services (the taxpayer). The Labour critique was enough to disturb the electorate, however, and almost certainly contributed to the Conservative government's defeat in 1997.

As in so many other areas, the role of local governments in health care has all but vanished, while central financial controls have strengthened.

New Labour policy

In December 1997 the New Labour Government published a white paper, The New NHS: Modern, Dependable, which identified three themes for reform: partial abolition of the internal market, mandate GPs to join primary care groups (now called primary care trusts) and the improvement of clinical care. Although, in opposition, Labour promised to abolish the NHS internal market, they proved reluctant to implement a wholesale abolition. Instead, they concentrated on trying to reduce the transaction costs associated with the internal market by streamlining the relationship bweteen the purchasers of health care (health authorities and primary care trusts) and the main providers (the NHS hospital trusts). In some respects the Labour reforms went further than the Conservatives – and in the same direction. For now GPs are required to form conglomerates covering 100,000 people. They are governed by a board, a chief executive and an executive board. By 2001 481 such primary care trusts had been established. These in turn had set up long-term service agreements with the NHS trusts. The new structure is shown in Figure 25.5. Most commentators agree that the new system works quite well. In effect the Labour reforms endorsed the changed management and operating culture of the service and accepted the main change instituted by the Tories: placing GPs at the centre of a system based on 'buying' services from NHS trusts.

Further reforms were instituted with the publication of the NHS plan in July 2000. This followed a winter characterised by bed shortages and lengthening hospital waiting lists. Two features of the plan should be noted. First, it did not propose changing the NHS structure but instead concentrated on the identification of priorities through public consultation. Second, it was accompanied by a government pledge to double real growth spending on the NHS to reach the European

Figure 25.5 *The National Health Service since 1999*

Source: Robert Leach and Janie Percy-Smith, *Local Governance in Britain*, Basingstoke and New York: Palgrave, 2001, Figure 3.7

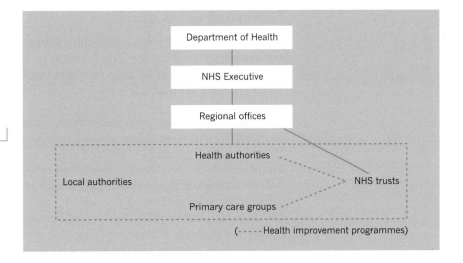

average of around 8 per cent of GDP by 2004. Yet further increases were announced in March 2002 which were to be funded by an increase in National Insurance contributions.

There can be no doubt that Labour was committed to maintaining free universal care for the vast majority of the population. The political salience of the issue is very high and Labour has made commitments in the area that are truly impressive – if they can be met. By 2003, the NHS seemed still to be in crisis. Hospital consultants – the group that traditionally has held most power in the system – refused to go along with new conditions of service that would require them to spend more of their time on NHS patients. Without their full co-operation, the government's plans for better hospital care were threatened. It is also interesting to note that the Conservatives have also changed their stance to one of supporting increased spending – although they continue to differ from Labour on the way the service should be managed.

EDUCATION

While, historically, Britain has long been regarded as a world leader in the public provision of health care, it has never been regarded as a great innovator in the provision of state education. Unlike many countries, including France and the United States of America, elite secondary education has traditionally been provided by the private rather than public sector (through the perversely named public school system). Not until the passage of the 1944 Education Act did the central government assume full responsibility for universal free primary and secondary education up to the age of 15 (16 from 1971). Since 1944, education policy has revolved around two related themes: comprehensive versus selective education, and the relationship between educational standards and the management and funding of schools. We will add a note on higher education following a discussion of these two points.

To select or not to select?

The 1944 Act formally recognised three different sorts of secondary school: grammar for the academically gifted, modern for the mass of the population and, in some areas, technical for those with vocational skills. Very soon, secondary modern schools assumed a low status and grammar schools high status. Critics pointed to the fact that entry to grammar schools, decided by an examination at the age of 11, was closely correlated with social class. Liberal-minded Conservative ministers and local politicians were among such critics. When elected in 1964, the Labour government pledged to reform the system by introducing one sort of school, the neighbourhood or community comprehensive, which would cater for all abilities. In October 1965 local authorities were instructed to draw up plans for the reorganisation of education by introducing comprehensive schools and, once re-elected in 1974, Labour made the change mandatory. The resulting change in school type is shown in Table 25.3.

While comprehensive schools made sense in rural areas where the provision of two sorts of school was not viable, the reforms proved highly controversial in many urban and suburban communities. Many Conservative-controlled authorities refused to comply, although the vast majority adopted the new system. In 1979, the new Conservative government removed the directive and later actively encouraged authorities to maintain grammar schools.

The crucial issues in this debate were parent choice and educational standards. On the right, commentators argued that comprehensive schools drawing on poorer communities tended to develop a culture of underachievement. Gifted children from such areas were not given the chance to develop their potential as

United Kingdom	1970/71	1980/81	1990/91	1994/95	1998/99	1999/00	2000/01
Public sector schools[3]							
Nursery[4,5]	50	89	105	111	109	144	152
Primary[4]	5,902	5,171	4,955	5,230	5,374	5,337	5,298
Secondary comprehensive[6]	1,313	3,730	2,843	3,093	3,207	3,266	3,340
Grammar	673	149	156	184	203	204	205
Modern	1,164	233	94	90	92	108	112
Other	403	434	300	289	291	282	260
All public sector schools	9,507	9,806	8,453	8,996	9,276	9,341	9,367
Non-maintained schools[3]	621	619	613	600	617	618	626
Special schools[7]	103	148	114	117	116	114	113
Pupil referral units	–	–	–	–	9	9	10
All schools	10,230	10,572	9,180	9,714	10,018	10,082	10,116

Table 25.3 *School pupils,[1] by type of school[2]*

Notes: [1] headcounts; [2] see Appendix, part 3: main categories of educational establishments and stages of education; [3] excludes special schools; [4] nursery classes within primary schools are included in primary schools except for Scotland from 1990/91 when they are included in nursery schools; [5] nursery schools figures for Scotland prior to 1998/99 only include data for local authority pre-schools. Data thereafter includes partnership pre-schools; [6] excludes sixth form colleges from 1980/81; [7] includes maintained and non-maintained sectors

Source: *Social Trends 32*, 2002, Table 3.1

they had no choice but to attend 'dump' schools. Worse, according to the right, a new cohort of teachers infused with egalitarian educational notions were aggravating this culture of underachievement by emphasising children's development as personalities rather than as individuals trained in essential skills. Right-wing think tanks such as the Institute for Economic Affairs and the Adam Smith Institute became increasingly vocal during the 1970s and were beginning to influence expert and political (Conservative) opinion.

The Conservatives were also keen to encourage private education and in 1980 introduced an Assisted Places Scheme that gave a small number of lower income parents a subsidised place for their child at an elite private school. Although highly controversial at the time the scheme remained small in cost and scope until its abolition by New Labour in 1997.

Standards and management

As with health care, debate moved forward rapidly during the 1980s to revolve around the question of the individual incentives of teachers and managers in the educational system. Local authorities were the traditional managers of education but the Conservatives became increasingly critical of their management standards. In two Education Acts, one passed in 1986 and the other in 1988, the government devolved the day-to-day management of schools to school governing bodies. It also allowed schools to opt out of local authority control altogether and be maintained directly by central government.

In combination, these laws increased the power of 'managers' over educational 'professionals'. Boards of governors, which include elected parent governors, hire and fire, and manage school finances. Increasingly they have to conform to central financial directives and to central performance indicators. A National Curriculum is now in place requiring pupils to study English, maths and science and seven foundation subjects. League tables on examination performance are widely published and classroom teachers are formally assessed and graded. Parents can now make comparisons between schools and, in theory at least, can choose which is best for their child. As with health care, these reforms have had good and bad consequences. By most criteria, educational attainment is improving. However the pressures on teachers have been considerable – many have taken early retirement – and the new school-level management structure has been used as an instrument of national policy rather than local discretion.

Higher education

Higher education escaped major reform until the 1990s. Since the Second World War, free higher education has been available to all those able to get a place at university, with maintenance grants available on a means-tested basis. Until the 1960s, when higher education was greatly expanded, this meant that a tiny minority (under 5 per cent) of 18-year-olds enjoyed university education. Expansion in the 1960s was not accompanied by any reform, so the system became increasingly expensive. Cuts in the real value of the maintenance grant helped, but were insufficient to prevent the system from experiencing a serious fiscal crisis when further expansion occurred from the late 1980s onwards. The government instituted much tighter central controls through a newly created quango, the University Funding Council (now the Higher Education Funding Council). By the mid-1990s it was clear that, for the system to survive in the absence of greatly increased funding, students would have to make some contribution towards the cost of their education. The Conservatives were already drawing up plans to this effect before their defeat in 1997. Once elected Labour promptly announced the introduction of tuition fees for all students with rebates for those on a low income. They also abolished what remained of the student grant system.

They soon accepted that this new regime disadvantaged students from poorer backgrounds and promised a complete overhaul of the system of student finances. At the same time, in 2001 the government set a target of 50 per cent of the 18-year-old age group to be in higher education. In 2003 the government finally produced a long awaited white paper on higher education that proposed the reintroduction of a (very limited) form of maintenance grant for those on low incomes. More importantly, universities were to be given the freedom to charge fees up to a maximum of £3,000. Most commentators agreed that this, together with a more targeted system of research resources, was likely to result in a two-tier system: an elite headed by Oxford and Cambridge and a large number of universities whose primary function would be teaching rather than research.

Actors and institutions

Education is not unlike health in that it is an area where expertise is at a premium. Therefore, educational professionals have always been important actors in the system. Local governments, too, were important players until the Conservative reforms of the 1980s. Today school boards of governors have assumed a new importance but they are subject to increasingly close central control. Teachers too are now more circumscribed both in the ways in which they teach and in their role in day-to-day management. Parents, in spite of the rhetoric of 'empowerment' contained in various educational reforms, remain more passive than active actors in the system. Unlike parents in the US system, for example, they have no direct say in the financing of schools.

Again as with health, the most important decision-making institutions operate in central government. For it is the Department for Education and Skills that sets the financial priorities and monitors school and teacher performance.

New Labour policy

It would be misleading to talk of a consensus between the major parties on educational matters, but much more agreement exists than might be expected. Labour has abolished the Assisted Places Scheme, but the scheme was a minor part of the system. The 1998 School Standards and Framework Act led to the creation of up to 25 education action zones consisting of two or three secondary schools together with their feeder primary schools. Action forums made up of parents, representatives from businesses and local education authorities were given the job of raising standards. Elsewhere in the system, selective schools remain but parental ballots determine whether grammar schools should continue on an exclusively selective basis. The new emphasis on standards reflects Labour's desire to persuade many middle class parents to shift from private to state education, which can only be done by improving some state schools.

Local governments were not given back their management role – although grant-maintained schools have been returned to local authority control – and performance indicators remained, so what distinguished Labour from Conservative? Most of the differences are in emphasis rather than substance. Substantively, Labour is more committed to nursery education than were the Conservatives and has promised nursery places for all 4-year-olds. But in most areas Labour governments have simply modified Tory policies. If anything they have been tougher on 'failing' schools and have given considerable support to the idea of specialist schools. But the main dilemma for Labour is the same one that faced the Tories: do you try and improve *all* schools or simply *most* schools? Labour governments have often been muddled in their thinking on this subject. Specialist 'beacon' schools seeking excellence in science, art or music, and the continuation of grammar education suggest a more elitist approach. At the same time ministers insist that they want to create a good educational environment for everyone. This dilemma extends to other areas of social policy, of course. In many ways, New Labour is meritocratic and market oriented. Yet it remains committed to helping the 'socially excluded' and working towards a society where everyone is educated and participating fully in social and community life.

ESSAYS

1. What accounts for the high level of support for universal state provision of education and health in Britain?

2. What are the advantages and disadvantages of 'workfare' programmes? Answer with specific reference to the changes introduced by Labour since 1997.

3. Outline the main reforms of the NHS since 1990. What have been the main objectives of these reforms?

4. In 1970 most people rented their housing. Today more than two-thirds are owner–occupiers. To what extent has public policy been responsible for this change?

SUMMARY

This chapter has summarised the major changes in social policy that have occurred since the inception of the Welfare State:

- In all the areas under discussion a move from universalism to selectivism has occurred. More recently, the main values underpinning reform attempts have shifted from those associated with managerial efficiency to those associated with the discipline of the market.

- More and more, policy takes heed of the personal incentives of individual actors and how reforms can harness individual incentives to particular ends, such as reduced costs and improved quality in health care or education. Even in income maintenance this transformation is under way, with the prospect that private pensions and workfare will replace universal flat-rate benefits in the longer term.

- While differences between Labour and the Conservatives remain there are few fundamental differences between the parties in most social policy areas. New Labour is committed to the state employing market-like solutions to a range of problems. In housing, the private sector is now accepted as the main provider. Income maintenance benefits have become increasingly selective. Education and health remain predominantly state-provided services for the foreseeable future, but in both areas market-like transactions have partly replaced hierarchical bureaucratic relationships.

■ In terms of the institutions and actors involved in policy, central government ministers and bureaucracies continue to dominate. The independent influence of professionals (doctors, teachers and so on) may, in turn, decline in relation to the 'users', 'customers' and 'clients' in the system – parents, patients, benefit recipients.

■ The unanswered question, however, relates to the power of the consumer, that is, the patient, client or parent. Reforms have promised consumer 'empowerment'. It remains to be seen whether reforms will empower the public or merely result in increased central control over the quality and price of services.

MILESTONES

Milestones in post-war social policy

1944–9 Foundation of the Welfare State

1952 Conservatives introduce charges for prescriptions and optical and dental treatment

1965 Directive calls for local authorities to draw up plans for comprehensive education

1966 Supplementary benefits replace National Assistance

1971 School leaving age increased to 16

1972 Means-tested rent rebate scheme provides assistance to tenants in public and private sectors

1974 National Insurance contributions are earnings related. Pension increases are linked to prices or earnings, whichever is the greater

1974 Health service reorganised. Regional and area health authorities created to co-ordinate family, hospital and community care

1975 Local education authorities directed to implement comprehensive school plans

1977 Child Allowances replaced with Child Benefit. Benefit is available to all children, with increased rate for single parents

1978 State Earnings Related Pension Scheme (SERPS) links pensions to earnings

1980 Pensions linked to prices only, thus reducing their relative value

1980 Assisted places scheme introduced. Local authorities given right to keep selective schools

1981 Local authority tenants given the right to buy their homes. Incentive to buy is further strengthened in 1986 and 1988

1981 Housing Benefit available to provide subsidies for rent and rates

1982 Earnings-related supplements to unemployment benefit abolished. Unemployment benefits taxable

1983 NHS reforms create district health authorities as main management units in the system

1986 and 1988 Education Acts Day-to-day management of schools devolved to school governors. Schools given the choice to opt out of local authority control. National Curriculum introduced

1988 Family Credit introduced to encourage families on income support to work

1989 Government ends subsidies for council housing. Local authorities required to set economic rents, with Housing Assistance for the needy

1991 and 1993 Major NHS reforms. Service divided into providers and purchasers. Regional authorities abolished. Central financial controls strengthened

1997 Labour government announces introduction of tuition fees in higher education. Social Exclusion Unit created in the Cabinet Office

1998 School Standards and Framework Act sets up education action zones and gives parents the right to change the admissions policies of grammar schools

1999 Budget announces a minimum £200 weekly income guarantee for all families with working parents and children. Major NHS reforms reorganise the service around primary health care groups

2001–2 Chancellor announces huge increases in NHS spending

PROJECTS

1. Provide an account of secondary educational provision in your immediate area. What are the differences between the various schools and how do these differences present a challenge for government policy?

2. Interview senior and junior medical and administrative staff at your local NHS trust hospital. From the responses, how would you characterise the main problems facing the NHS today?

3. Catalogue the ways in which since its inception the Welfare State has moved from universal to selective provision. Has this pattern been a good or a bad thing for us, the 'consumers'?

FURTHER READING

A good introduction to the subject is provided by Kenneth Blakemore, *Social Policy: An Introduction to Social Policy* (Milton Keynes: Open University Press, 1998). On New Labour and social policy, see Stephen P. Savage and Rob Atkinson (eds), *Public Policy under Blair* (London: Palgrave, 2001). On the relationship between spending constraints and social policy, see Nicholas Deakin and Richard Parry, *The Treasury and Social Policy* (London: Macmillan, 2000). On the redistributive effects of the Welfare State, see A. B. Atkinson, *Incomes and the Welfare State* (Cambridge: Cambridge University Press, 1996). On the politics of welfare, see Nicholas Deakin, *The Politics of Welfare* (Hemel Hempstead: Harvester Wheatsheaf, 1994). On health, see Judith Allsop, *Health Policy and the NHS: Towards 2000* (Harlow: Longman, 2nd edn, 1995). On the official current NHS Plan, see *Delivering the NHS Plan: Next Steps on Investment, Next Steps on Reform* (London: Stationery Office, 2002). The various publications of the King's Fund, a charity devoted to health policy research, should also be consulted. A historical account of housing policy is provided by Brian Lund, *Housing Problems and Housing Policy* (Harlow: Longman, 1996). On recent changes in education, see Michael Fielding (ed.), *Taking Education Really Seriously: Three Years Hard Labour* (London: Routledge Falmer, 2001).

USEFUL WEB SITES ON SOCIAL POLICY

Hotlinks to these sites can be found on the CWS website at http://www.booksites.net/budge.

In general, social policy concerns the health, education and welfare of British citizens. As an introduction you can visit the British Council, in particular their account of the transformation of the British Welfare State in the recent past at www.britishcouncil.de/e/governance/pubs/gerpp303.htm. The most important governmental institutions related to social policy are the Department of Health (www.doh.gov.uk), the Department for Education and Skills (www.dfes.gov.uk), the Department for Work and Pensions (www.dwp.gov.uk), the Social Exclusion Unit (www.socialexclusionunit.gov.uk), and the Office of the Deputy Prime Minister's Housing and Housing Policy section (www.housing.odpm.gov.uk). New Deal is a key part of the government's Welfare to Work strategy; its web site is available at www.newdeal.gov.uk. Information on social policies for children is available from the Child Support Agency (www.csa.gov.uk).

The Joseph Rowntree Foundation (www.jrf.org.uk) is one of the largest social policy research and development charities in the UK; their web site provides excellent information on housing, education, child support and other important areas. The New Policy Institute maintains a web site devoted to the monitoring of poverty in the UK; among other valuable sources they offer a good deal of statistical information on income distribution. Visit them at www.poverty.org.uk. There are a variety of other sites that can prove useful for a proper understanding of how social policy works in Britain, including the National Health Service (www.nhs.uk), the Social Security and Child Support Commissioners (www.osscsc.gov.uk), and the Pension Service (www.thepensionservice.gov.uk).

In addition, you can consult the National Health Service Confederation (www.nhsconfed.net), the Association of University Teachers (www.aut.org.uk), and the National Institute for Social Work (www.nisw.org.uk).

Equal opportunities

In contrast to the original objectives of the Welfare State, which emphasised equality of condition in the provision of a wide range of benefits, policies designed to provide equal opportunity for women, ethnic minorities and other disadvantaged groups must by definition be selective in scope. When legislation was first enacted in this area during the 1940s it was concerned with discrimination against disabled people. Since then it has been widened to embrace discrimination based on race, gender and sexual preference. The political salience of the issue has varied over time, and since the first legislation was passed the values underpinning public policy have changed very substantially. The chapter will outline the main legislative changes and will evaluate the effectiveness of the law in this important area. The actors and institutions involved will also be discussed and some basic data on inequality in Britain today are presented. The chapter examines:

- some problems of definition associated with equal opportunity
- inequality and discrimination in Britain
- equal rights for women
- legislation to help the disabled
- race relations and immigration
- sexual preference
- the future of equal opportunity legislation.

EQUAL OPPORTUNITY: A POLITICAL AND SEMANTIC MINEFIELD?

Discrimination
The practice of distinguishing (usually in order to disadvantage) between individuals or social groups on grounds or criteria (such as race, religion, gender or colour) that are not relevant to circumstances.

Equal opportunity laws are designed to reduce entrenched inequalities in society. They have come about because the income, employment, housing and educational conditions pertaining to certain social groups are persistently inferior to those of the general population. Such inequalities may result directly from discrimination that in turn may be overt, covert or structural. Typically, overt discrimination is easy to identify and to eradicate. Advertisements for rental housing stating 'no coloureds' – not unusual in the UK during the 1950s and early 1960s – can be identified quickly and proscribed by law. Covert discrimination is more difficult to deal with. Estate agents may have a stated policy of non-discrimination, but a tacit understanding between renter and agent might exclude minority applicants. Structural discrimination is the most problematical of all. To continue with the housing analogy, during the 1960s and 1970s many local authorities used 'housekeeping standards' as one of the criteria for eligibility for council housing. Some ethnic minorities failed to meet the prescribed standard, which was culturally biased in favour of white families.

Some feminists argue that a typical example of structural discrimination today applies in science education. Very few women enrol on engineering and science undergraduate courses and even fewer on postgraduate courses. As a result, there are very few female engineers and scientists in the job market. The problem stems not from discrimination at entry but from the fact that few women choose school or university courses in these areas. This may be the exercise of free choice or it may be that biases in the system discourage women from pursuing 'male' subjects and instead direct them into the more 'female' arts and humanities.

Problems with gender discrimination are sometimes rooted in biological differences. Until quite recently (and very recently indeed as far as the armed forces are concerned), pregnancy was an adequate basis for dismissal from a job. Thus few women were able to build continuous and successful careers unless they remained childless. In order to deal with such problems governments have legislated to ban discrimination and provide for equal opportunity – although it does not always work as intended. For example, pregnancy continues to affect women's career chances in spite of what looks like appropriate legislation.

Few subjects arouse so much passion. There are a number of reasons for this. First, policies designed to redress discrimination against the disadvantaged must focus on the circumstances of social groups as well as individuals. Because a group (eg women) as a whole is disadvantaged does not, of course, mean that all members of that group are disadvantaged. As a result, group-based anti-discrimination policies are often criticised for 'favouring' women or minorities over males or whites. This problem is particularly acute in a society where liberal, rather than collectivist, values are well established. Many of the values that make up our society are based on the value of the individual, whose merit or worth, not membership of a particular group, should, we believe, determine rewards. Equal opportunities policies, however well intentioned, are often difficult to reconcile with such beliefs (see Briefing 26.1).

A second and related problem concerns the nature and level of government response to inequality and discrimination. Laws may be designed to combat overt discrimination and they may also tackle structural discrimination. They may go even further and attempt to reverse the effects of a long-established pattern of discrimination. In the USA such laws are called *affirmative action measures*. Their objective is to allow women and minorities to 'catch up' with whites and males. Typically, they apply in employment and education and involve the use of quotas and 'balancing' to ensure that workplaces, schools and universities hire or enrol women and minorities in proportion to their numbers in the local or national population. British governments have eschewed affirmative action measures as unfair to equally qualified individuals who are not members of disadvantaged groups.

The Labour Party has, however, employed affirmative action through its use of 'Emily's List' or the idea that women-only shortlists for the selection of candidates should be adopted in some constituencies. In 2001 Iain Duncan Smith instigated reforms in the Conservative Party requiring measures to increase the numbers of women and ethnic minority candidates among those selected as Conservative candidates.

These intra-party reforms apart, British equal opportunities policy has developed incrementally. Even today it is incomplete, as the evidence on income and jobs shows. We examine this before proceeding to a discussion of the politics of equal opportunity legislation.

Affirmative action (positive discrimination) Policies designed to provide groups with redress for a past pattern of discrimination. Such policies often take the form of legal requirements that organisations should take positive steps to increase their numbers of minority groups.

26.1 Liberalism and equal opportunity

One of the most difficult problems associated with equal opportunity policy is reconciling rules and regulations designed to assist social groups with the fact that in liberal societies each citizen's worth is measured in terms of individual merit. When we apply for a job or a place at university we assume that what determines success is our qualifications or A level scores, not membership of a particular social group. Liberal values are offended by those collective notions of worth that prevail (or have prevailed) in some Muslim states where gender or religion determines access to employment and education, or in South Africa under apartheid where race determined access.

When there has been a long-established pattern of discrimination, however, some argue that society has a duty to seek redress for past transgressions through the use of affirmative action. Affirmative action can, however, mean a number of things. It can mean the use of race or gender quotas where a minimum number of places is reserved for, say, entry to a university. In such a situation it is possible that the best qualified of the minority group will have qualifications inferior to those of the majority group. In the USA the courts have effectively banned quotas of this sort, arguing that they constitute a violation of the equal protection of the law guaranteed by the constitution. As problematical are affirmative action measures that adopt a general policy of favouring particular social groups without specifying numbers. These too have been under attack from the courts, although their exact legal status remains unclear.

Affirmative action is often used interchangeably with the term positive discrimination, or the application of policies that discriminate in favour of some social groups. Generally, positive discrimination is used to create a 'level playing field' for the disadvantaged. It could apply, for example, to the provision of special English-language classes for non-native speakers, or special educational help for children from poor areas. In other words it involves policies that allow certain groups to 'catch up' with the general population through special training and education.

In Britain the use of affirmative action is rare. British anti-discrimination laws take the individual, not the group, as the basic unit, and the law's objective is to provide redress for demonstrable grievances against individuals, rather than reverse a pattern of discrimination against groups. However, there is a limited form of affirmative action for the employment of the disabled, and in one form or another positive discrimination has been a part of British social policy for many years.

INEQUALITY AND DISCRIMINATION IN BRITAIN

Equality of condition
The ideal objective of providing all citizens with equal access to income, wealth, education, employment and other aspects of social life.

All societies display a degree of wealth and income inequality. Equality of condition, or the same income and wealth for all, is clearly impossible to achieve. Most societies strive for equality of treatment, meaning that the same rules and standards apply to all social groups. Equality of treatment is similar to equality of opportunity, the main difference being the emphasis on rules guaranteeing equality of treatment rather than emphasising individuals' circumstances, which is implicit in equality of opportunity.

In fact, there can never be complete equality of opportunity given individuals' widely varying inherited, home and educational backgrounds. Equality

Equality of treatment
The application of the same rules and standards to all individuals and social groups.

Equality of opportunity
The practice of ensuring that individuals compete on equal terms for goods, benefits and life chances, such as education, employment or housing, even though the outcome may be unequal.

of opportunity should, therefore, be seen as an ideal goal rather than an absolute. Equality of treatment is more achievable. Rules and regulations can be standardised so that, in theory at least, all citizens are treated equally. This distinction helps us separate out all those economic differences and inequalities that derive from employment, educational and geographic factors, from those that derive from overt, covert or structural discrimination.

Of course, in reality, discrimination may be practised against almost anyone including poor whites and the old. But our natural sense of justice is most offended by systematic and institutionalised discrimination against ethnic minorities, women, the disabled and sexual minorities. Hence, the liberal conscience was outraged at apartheid in South Africa or segregation in the American South. Similar feelings are aroused by the treatment of women and homosexuals in some fundamentalist Muslim states.

Measuring discrimination is difficult, to say the least. By definition, covert discrimination is not measurable and, while we may be able to identify the rules and procedures that make up structural discrimination, we can rarely measure the effects of such rules accurately.

What we can do is identify income inequalities by social group. Britain has a sizeable ethnic minority community. As can be seen from Table 26.1, 8.4 per cent of the population of Great Britain (which excludes Northern Ireland) consists of ethnic minorities. While the definition of 'ethnic minority' is highly contentious, the categories itemised in Table 26.1 are those recognised by the government as constituting minority groups. Note that, the Chinese population apart, ethnic minorities in Britain are much younger than the general population. As a result their numbers are likely to increase proportionately over time irrespective of future immigration patterns.

	Under 16	16–34	35–64	65+	Total (millions)	Ethnic groups as a percentage of total population
White	20	25	39	16	53	92.9
Black Caribbean	23	27	40	10	0.5	0.9
Black African	33	35	30	2	0.4	0.7
Other black	52	29	17	–	0.3	0.5
Indian	23	31	38	7	1.0	1.8
Pakistani	36	36	24	4	0.7	1.2
Bangladeshi	39	36	21	4	0.3	0.5
Chinese	19	38	38	4	0.1	0.2
None of the above	32	33	32	3	0.7	1.2
Other ethnic minorities[1]	30	34	33	3	0.8	1.4
All ethnic minorities	–	–	–	–	4.8	8.4
All ethnic groups[2]	20	26	39	15	57.1	100%

Table 26.1 *Population of Great Britain by ethnic group and age, 2000–2001*

Notes: [1] Includes those of mixed origin; [2] population living in private households

Source: *Social Trends 32*, 2002, Table 1.4

BRIEFINGS

26.2 **Defining ethnic minorities in Britain**

Over the years both the official and unofficial labels attached to Britain's ethnic minority population have changed considerably. During the 1950s and 1960s 'immigrant' and 'coloured' were used almost interchangeably. Both are condescending. 'Coloured' has passed from the official vocabulary and 'immigrant' is obviously inappropriate for the majority of the ethnic population born in Britain. Later, the census used the coded term BPBNC or both parents born New Commonwealth to distinguish 'black' from 'white' immigrants and their descendants. The official labels in use today are reproduced in Table 26.1. While these are more accurate and sensitive, they remain very broad categories. The use of the term 'black' is gradually being replaced by the hyphenated 'Afro-'. Using 'black' as a shorthand for all ethnic minorities is also passing from the political vocabulary. Of course, no one is literally black, any more than anyone is literally white; in reality the minority population is extraordinarily heterogeneous in its origins. West Indian or Afro-Caribbean includes people from very different island cultures. Indian applies to all those from a vast and complex medley of cultures, religions and languages. Only the Chinese population is relatively homogeneous, the vast majority having originally come from Hong Kong.

Even these distinctions can be offensive, for most of Britain's ethnic minorities have been born in Britain and are as British as the royal family or anyone else. By many measures the Welsh, Irish and Scots are also 'minorities' but, Catholics in Northern Ireland apart, their treatment is not a political issue because they suffer from little discernible discrimination.

Labels are, however, a necessary evil. If discrimination and inequality are to be identified and dealt with it is necessary to collect the relevant statistics.

New Commonwealth
A coded term used to refer to non-white Commonwealth countries.

Disposable income
More often known as 'take-home pay', disposable income refers to income after taxes have been paid.

Table 26.2 shows the extent of income inequality among ethnic minorities in Great Britain. Note the very dramatic concentration of low incomes among the Pakistani/Bangladeshi population and the generally lower incomes of other ethnic groups. In fact, these figures are worse than they appear when geographic location is taken into account. Most of the British minority population is concentrated in London and the Midlands where incomes are relatively high. Very few live in some of the lowest income areas: Northern Ireland, the northeast, Merseyside and the Glasgow area. Only in what used to be the textile towns of Lancashire and Yorkshire is there a congruence of high minority population and generally low local incomes.

As far as economic activity rates are concerned (the percentage of each social group that is in the workforce) women are generally less active than men, and whites are generally more employed than ethnic minorities (Table 26.3). Note

Table 26.2 *Distribution of disposable income by ethnic groups, 1994–5*

| | Quintile group of individuals Percentages | |
	Bottom fifth	Top four-fifths
White	19	81
Black (African and Afro-Caribbean)	27	73
Indian	27	73
Pakistani/Bangladeshi	64	36
Other ethnic minorities	36	64
All groups	20	80

Source: *Social Trends 27*, London: Stationery Office, 1997, Figure 5.20

	Males				Females			
	Higher qualification	Other qualification	No qualification	All aged 16–64[5]	Higher qualification	Other qualification	No qualification	All aged 16–59[5]
White	89.9	81.7	58.4	80.4	85.1	72.5	47.7	70.9
Black	83.5	62.3	48.6	64.8	77.4	56.3	32.6	57.6
Indian	92.1	72.1	52.7	75.5	80.4	59.9	36.4	60.1
Pakistani/ Bangladeshi	82.9	57.7	49.5	59.7	68.6	30.2	7.2	24.7
Other ethnic groups[3]	85.4	56.9	50.9	64.4	68.2	42.5	28.1	47.7
All ethnic groups[4]	89.7	80.5	57.7	79.5	84.3	71.0	45.5	69.3

Table 26.3 *Employment rates[1] by ethnic group, gender, age and highest qualification, 2000–2001[2]*

Notes: [1] percentage of the working age population in employment; [2] combined quarters: spring 2000 to winter 2000–2001; [3] includes those of mixed origin; [4] includes those who did not state their ethnic group; [5] includes those who did not state their qualifications

Source: *Labour Force Survey*, Office for National Statistics

the particularly low participation rates among Asian and particularly Pakistani/Bangladeshi women. Note also the high rate of workforce participation for the more educated from all ethnic groups. These figures are, of course, different from unemployment rates, which measure the numbers of people actively seeking work. Unemployment is actually considerably lower among women than among men and during the recession of the early 1990s this gap widened considerably (Figure 26.1). The gender earnings gap is the inverse of this pattern – men earn more than women and the gap tends to widen with age (see later). These figures are for full-time employment. In fact many more women, around 5.1 million in 1998, are part-time workers compared with fewer than 2 million men. Hourly earnings in part-time work are typically lower than in full-time employment.

Data on income, employment, educational or housing inequality in no way proves the existence of discrimination. What it does show, however, is a pattern

Figure 26.1
Unemployment by gender

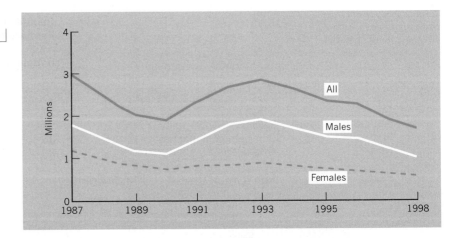

of inequality that persists over time and which almost certainly is related to discrimination in one form or another. This perception has led successive governments to legislate to reduce or remove discrimination, and to provide redress for aggrieved parties. The next section will provide an account of this legislation and the politics surrounding it as it has affected gender, disability and race.

GENDER

Unlike race, gender has been on the political agenda for many generations. Equal pay for men and women working in the same job has been a trade union demand since the end of the nineteenth century, but it was not until 1970 that legislation was enacted to achieve this end. The Equal Pay Act of 1970 allowed women to claim equal pay if their work was of 'equal value' to that of men. This law was amended in 1983 to comply with an EC directive on equal pay that required equality of remuneration without a formal job evaluation of the work concerned and without regard to physical differences between the sexes.

In 1976, the government acted to outlaw discrimination based on sex or marital status in employment, education, housing and public facilities. The law set up an Equal Opportunities Commission (EOC) to process complaints and refer them to industrial tribunals. As with the Commission for Racial Equality (CRE), the EOC has limited enforcement powers, although its provisions have gradually been strengthened by European Union directives, particularly in the areas of Social Security and welfare.

Two major omissions in the law have been partly addressed in recent years. The first concerns maternity and pregnancy. European directives on maternity leave and pay were issued during the 1970s and 1980s but it was not until 1996 that these were formalised in law. Under the 1996 Employment Rights Act women have the right to paid time off both for antenatal care and after the birth of their child, with the right to return to work. As of April 2003 pregnant employees were entitled to a minimum of 26 weeks leave with pay provided 21 days' notice is given. Benefit is paid at a rate of 90 per cent of full pay provided the employee has worked for a minimum period and earns at least £75.00 a week. Lower benefits are available for the lower paid and separate arrangements are in place for the self-employed. These provisions are an improvement on previous benefits and have been introduced as a result of EU directives – although benefits are not as good as in some EU countries. From April 2003 fathers were entitled to two weeks' paid paternity leave.

The second omission concerns pension rights, which relate to the date of compulsory retirement, that typically is lower for women than for men. The government has agreed to standardise these over time at 65. In addition, the law has been changed to allow a divorced spouse a share of the former partner's pension.

The political salience of equal rights for women has gradually increased over the years, although the women's movement in Britain has often been less vocal than in the USA and some Continental European countries. While overt discrimination in employment has been reduced, women continue to be at a disadvantage in relation to men in many workplace situations. Men hold most senior administrative and managerial posts and women are greatly over-represented in lower paid, part-time work. For many women pregnancy results in an interrupted career pattern even when those concerned have no wish to undermine their career prospects. Sexual stereotyping in employment remains. How many students reading this text would assume they had got 'the secretary' if they phoned a college department and a man answered the phone? As can be seen from Table 26.4

Battle of the sexes				
Profession	End of 19th century		End of 20th century	
	Men	Women	Men	Women
National government	88,894	11,666	143,370	206,120
Police	44,734	0	130,030	16,580
Armed forces	134,061	0	176,800	13,090
Barrister, solicitor, advocates	23,089	0	57,660	22,150
Medical practitioners	21,519	113	65,890	29,550
Veterinarians	3,725	3	5,090	2,080
Nurses, midwives and related	650	56,829	81,350	899,140
Teaching professional	57,772	157,358	325,230	530,890
Domestic housekeepers, cleaners etc	123,098	1,601,656	121,310	688,110
Chartered and certified accountants	9,129	50	83,220	22,670
Farming	1,043,780	74,695	356,170	91,530
Milliner, dressmaker, tailors, etc	145,755	566,943	12,060	17,570
Coalmine labourers	587,542	3,833	20,770	160
General labourers	659,124	3,022	91,660	7,740
Authors, writers, journalists	5,539	689	4,517	3,418

Table 26.4 *Women's employment over 100 years*

Source: *The Times*, 11 May 2000, p. 8

Figure 26.2 *Hourly earnings from full-time employment by gender and age, April 1998*

Source: Office for National Statistics

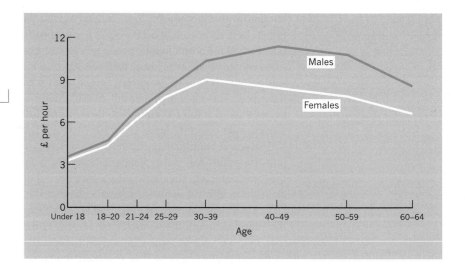

women have made some headway over the longer term, but in such professions as accountancy, the law and medicine they still have a long way to go.

The 'pay gap' between men and women remains at around 20 per cent and tends to grow during the middle years of life when earnings are typically at their highest (Figure 26.2). Moreover, in spite of the fact that Britain has had a Sex Discrimination Act for almost 30 years, employers continue to find ways of passing over women for appointment, and/or promotion, find cause to sack them if they are pregnant, and generally treat them unfavourably. Part of the reason for this is that there is no statutory body charged with the job of providing redress. As mentioned, the EOC, which was created in 1976, provides only a referral service to employment (formerly industrial) tribunals. Moreover, incomplete information on women's pay means that much discrimination goes undetected. Therefore, the EOC has repeatedly called for the creation of 'pay audits' or systematic audits by industrial and commercial sectors to find out how, exactly, different social groups are treated.

With the election of a Labour administration with the largest government and Parliamentary representation of women ever, it is likely that women's issues will be given greater prominence over the next few years. Certainly, both in its response to EU directives and its stance on relevant British legislation, Labour has been more supportive of sex equality than were the Conservatives. Of all women's issues, childcare and the position of working mothers are likely to head the political agenda. Labour has made changes to the welfare system to encourage single mothers to work (see Chapter 25). However, the effects of these reforms will be limited in the absence of universal state provision for childcare and training programmes for single parents. Although extra resources for nursery education have been allocated by Labour governments most commentators agree that it will be many years before the incentive structure for single parents is changed in ways that will remove their disadvantaged status.

DISABILITY

The 1944 Disabled Persons (Employment) Act defined a disabled individual as a 'person who, on account of injury, disease or congenital deformity, is substantially handicapped in obtaining or keeping employment'. Disabled people could, voluntarily, register under the Act and, as amended in 1958, the Act required employers of more than 20 people to employ a 3 per cent quota of registered disabled people. This law was widely flouted – employers could apply for exemption – and it was poorly enforced. Worse, the legislation did nothing to change the environment in which disabled people worked. Instead it assumed that disability was a permanent handicap and employers should patronise disabled people's condition by giving them 'suitable' work. Car park and passenger lift attendants were officially identified as the most appropriate work for the disabled!

By 1970 attitudes towards disability were changing and the Chronically Sick and Disabled Persons Act of that year placed on local authorities a duty to see to the general needs of the disabled. Under the Act authorities are obliged to identify the local disabled population and to provide them with help. The Act was well intentioned. But the actual provision of such things as suitable housing, home helps and the adaptation of facilities to the needs of the disabled was to be financed by limited local authority budgets. Local authority finances were increasingly hard pressed from the mid-1970s onwards and, as a result, provision was patchy and incomplete.

By the 1990s the pressure for more effective legislation was mounting. Disability was increasingly seen in terms of equal opportunity. In other words, people with disabilities should, as far as possible, be given access equal to that of the general population to jobs, housing, education and public facilities. In other countries, and notably in the United States of America and Australia, legislation had been passed requiring schools, universities, employers, and providers of transport and other public facilities to make special provisions for the disabled. In Britain, however, the Conservative governments of the 1990s proved reluctant to pass equivalent legislation. They argued that it would prove an expensive burden on employers and (perversely) would be resented by the disabled themselves. Instead they opted for legislation that, although it strengthened the rights of the disabled, fell far short of the mandatory provisions of the US and Australian legislation. Hence the 1995 Disability Discrimination Act makes it unlawful to discriminate on grounds of disability in employment; requires employers of more than 20 people to accommodate the needs of the disabled; and establishes a right of access for the disabled in transport, higher education and some other areas (see Table 26.5).

The law also created a National Disability Council to provide advice on freeing the disabled from discrimination. Crucially, however, a number of loopholes in the law made most of its provisions advisory rather than compulsory. For example, there is no requirement that newly built restaurants, pubs or cinemas provide access and toilet facilities for the disabled. Many do, but equally many do not.

This issue is likely to increase in importance during the next few years, partly because the number of disabled is increasing and because economic activity rates

Table 26.5 *Economic activity status of disabled people by gender, 2001*

United Kingdom	Males	Females	Percentages All
In employment[1]			
Working full time	43.5	22.9	33.8
Working part time	5.6	21.6	13.1
All in employment	49.1	44.6	46.9
Unemployed[2]	5.1	3.2	4.2
Less than one year	3.1	2.3	2.7
One year or more	2.0	0.9	1.5
Economically inactive	45.8	52.2	48.8
All disabled (=100%)(millions)	3.6	3.2	6.8

Notes: [1] males ages 16 to 64 and females 16 to 59 with current long-term or work-limiting disability. See Appendix, Part 4: Disabled people; [2] based on the ILO definition. See Appendix, Part 4: ILO Unemployment

Source: *Social Trends 32*, 2002, Table 4.8

among the disabled remains low (in particular for women) (Table 26.5). In addition, advocates on behalf of the disabled have become more effective and vocal. In the Parliamentary debates on legislation for the disabled the Labour opposition was always more supportive of compulsion in the law than were the Conservatives. Once in government New Labour did legislate to provide for better access for the disabled to public buildings and benefit levels were increased above the rate of inflation. In 2000 it created the Disability Rights Commission (DRC) whose job was to eliminate all discrimination against the disabled and to investigate complaints of discrimination. But the DRC lacks enforcement teeth and when it came down to hard choices between more state aid for the disabled and fiscal prudence, the government often chose the latter. For example, it was accused of discriminating against the disabled when it tried to make benefits more selective by reducing the amount available to those with other sources of income. This issue illustrates nicely one of the central dilemmas of Labour's social policy: how do you target benefits to the most needy without giving the impression that many existing recipients of benefits are scroungers and a burden on the state? For many disabled people, being denied benefits because they have other sources of income seems insulting because they believe that their benefits are a *right* that should be available irrespective of income. Interestingly, the European Union has been much less active in issuing directives in this area than it has over discrimination based on gender, although the 1997 Treaty of Amsterdam declared that it was EU policy to improve workplace and transport access for the disabled throughout the EU.

RACE

Race has been an important issue in British politics at least since the 1950s. For much of the nineteenth and early twentieth centuries Britain had the reputation as a haven for those subject to religious and political persecution in other European countries. Until the First World War immigration controls were minimal and successive waves of Jews, socialists and Marxists settled in Britain during these years. Their numbers were, however, relatively small. Overt discrimination against Jews, which had become commonplace in many Continental countries during the 1930s, was relatively rare in Britain. After the Second World War a further wave of refugees arrived in Britain from the Continent. Again, numbers were limited (by official policy) and again these groups of Jews, Poles and other eastern Europeans were assimilated with relative ease.

In 1948 the Labour government passed the British Nationality Act, which allowed Commonwealth citizens to settle in the UK. The assumption was that, with decolonisation, a new Commonwealth of Nations sharing a language and common traditions could move freely from one state to the other. At the time, it was not expected to result in mass immigration. The citizens of the 'White Commonwealth' – Australia, New Zealand, Canada – enjoyed high living standards and had little incentive to migrate to Britain. Citizens of the 'Black Commonwealth', including newly independent India, rarely had the economic resources to migrate to what was a very distant land. During the 1950s, however, the British economy suffered from shortages of labour and some employers such as London Transport actively recruited cheap, unskilled workers from the West Indies and elsewhere. By the late 1950s the numbers of immigrants from the West Indies and the Indian sub-continent had increased substantially. Racist attitudes were widespread, as was discrimination. In 1958 a race riot in the Notting Hill area of London raised the political salience of the issue.

Unrestricted entry of Commonwealth citizens ceased in 1962 with the passage of the Commonwealth Immigrants Act. Thereafter, all Commonwealth citizens were subject to immigration control except those holding British passports issued in Britain. A system of work vouchers was created that had to be issued by employers before entry was permitted.

Overt discrimination against ethnic minorities (at the time generally called 'coloureds') was commonplace and was not proscribed until the passage of the 1965 Race Relations Act. As amended in 1968, this law banned 'whites only' advertising, prohibited discrimination in housing and employment and set up a Race Relations Board to mediate disputes concerning discrimination. Most commentators agree that the 1960s' legislation was minimalist in scope. Conciliation rarely worked and large areas such as education were excluded from the law.

A much more effective law was passed in 1976 (the Race Relations Act) that banned direct and indirect discrimination in employment, education, public facilities and housing. The definition of discrimination was expanded to include nationality, citizenship and ethnic origin, and a Commission for Racial Equality was established to receive and process complaints. The CRE was instructed to tackle both direct and indirect discrimination and to refer unresolved complaints to an industrial tribunal for settlement.

Although the 1976 law was a great improvement on earlier legislation, the CRE's powers are quite limited. It cannot take on 'class' actions or complaints about discrimination against whole groups of complainants as opposed to individuals, its sanctions under the law are limited and difficult to enforce, and its operations have been consistently underfunded. Part of its brief was to advise governments on how best the law might be improved. This it has done, but none of the Conservative governments in the 1979 to 1997 period acted on its advice.

Against this background of anti-discrimination law the politics of race changed dramatically from 1968 to 1997. During the 1960s race became an important electoral issue, especially following the Conservative Enoch Powell's 'rivers of blood' speech in 1968. Powell likened the effects of immigration in Britain to the excesses of ancient Rome: 'As I look ahead I am filled with foreboding. Like the Roman, I seem to see the River Tiber foaming with much blood.' Although he was immediately sacked from the shadow Cabinet, Powell's views were not unpopular in many parts of the country. He persisted with his demagoguery and later called for a stop to all immigration, accompanied by compulsory repatriation.

During the 1970s and the 1980s a racial element emerged in electoral politics. In a number of West Midlands seats race was a factor in determining electoral outcomes. As leader of the opposition, Margaret Thatcher said in 1978 that she understood that the 'British character' might be 'swamped' by immigrants from different cultures. And although overt cultural nationalism – some might say racism – of this kind was rare in public life, it was apparent to most in the minority communities that Conservative governments were at best lukewarm supporters of an enhanced state role in fighting discrimination.

Racism The practice of discriminating between individuals or groups on racial grounds.

A further incident in 1992 confirmed in the minds of many minority voters that some local Conservative parties held unacceptable racial views. In Cheltenham, a highly qualified black candidate, John Taylor, was nominated to fight the Parliamentary seat. However, he was confirmed only after an unseemly row in the local party where overt racist views were expressed. Only national publicity and pressure from Central Office facilitated Taylor's nomination. He was subsequently defeated in the general election but was later appointed a Conservative life peer.

Although the Conservative Party has always been identified as anti-immigrant, it has never come remotely close to endorsing discrimination and has usually been quick to condemn overtly racist attitudes and actions. Far-right parties, such as the National Front, which have racist platforms, have had very limited success in British politics. In the post-war period they have never won a Parliamentary seat and have won only a few local elections. Indeed, in comparison with the major Continental states including France, Germany, Spain and Italy, Britain has no tradition of far-right political parties or far-right racist politics.

Most ethnic minorities in Britain vote Labour. There is a class and a race element to this pattern, in that minorities tend to have lower incomes. But more vote Labour than would be expected from this fact alone. In many inner city constituencies the ethnic vote has been crucial in swinging the result to Labour, so it is not surprising that as a party it has been more supportive of minority interests than have the Conservatives.

One major problem for the minority communities has been racially inspired harassment and violence by whites and a widespread perception that the police have been less than vigilant in stamping out racial incidents. Such incidents are common, especially in the London area, and should be considered a serious public order problem. As can be seen from Table 26.6, racial incidents are at a high and rapidly increasing level – although it is very difficult to find reliable statistics in this area. Many incidents go unreported and an apparent increase in attacks may be the result of an *improved* race relations environment when victims are more likely to trust the police to act and thus more likely to report incidents.

	1994/95	1995/96	1996/97	1997/98	1998/99	1999/2000	% change 1994–2000
England and Wales	11,878	12,222	13,151	13,878	23,049	47,814	330
Metropolitan police area	5,480	5,011	5,621	5,862	11,050	23,346	307

Table 26.6 *Racial incidents reported to the police in England and Wales, 1999–2000*

Source: *Statistics on Race and the Criminal Justice System*, 2000, computed from Table 8.1, Home Office 2000, available at www.homeoffice.gov.uk

During the late 1990s and early 2000s, the government made special efforts to raise police consciousness of the issue. In London the reaction to the failure by the police to catch the killers of Stephen Lawrence who was stabbed to death in a racial attack in 1995, led to accusations that the police force was infused with a culture of racism. This was precisely the finding of the Macpherson Report, which was set up to investigate police handling of the killing. Since then, efforts have been made to reform police attitudes and practice.

Antipathy towards police forces that have taken a less than firm hand in this area may help explain periodic outbreaks of rioting in British cities. These assumed serious proportions in the early 1980s and again in the early 1990s and in 2001. In almost all cases the rioting has centred around conflict between the police and ethnic minorities. These problems persist in spite of the fact that many forces have instituted racial awareness programmes and have made special efforts to recruit minorities.

The condition of minorities in Britain is certainly not one of unrelieved gloom. Educational standards among Asian and Afro-Caribbean British are generally high. Intermarriage and cohabiting – often an indicator of good race relations – is also high as regards the Afro-Caribbean and the white population. Indeed, around one-third of all Afro-Caribbean males have white partners. The 2001 intake of MPs included 1 per cent from ethnic minorities among their number, significantly up on the historic average. Perhaps most importantly, throughout the long history of immigration into Britain, governments have never created a separate category of immigrant labour with a status inferior to that of the 'native' population. Once admitted, immigrants and their children have similar rights and privileges to other citizens. This is in contrast to countries such as Germany and Switzerland that have made extensive use of temporary migrant labour, many of whom enjoy limited civil rights. This is not to deny the existence of serious flaws in British immigration laws (see Briefing 26.3). All sorts of anomalies and restrictions exist and over the years governments of all political complexions have made migration to Britain more difficult. It is merely to state that the citizenship status of legal immigrants is better than in many European countries.

The immigration debate took on a new relevance after 1999 when the number of people seeking political asylum increased substantially following the war in Kosovo and continuing economic and political dislocation in such countries as Afghanistan and Iraq. By 2000 the government received nearly 98,000 asylum applications, in 2001 over 76,000, and in 2002 around 100,000. This was more than in any other EU country – although not, in the case of some countries, in relation to population. Of these a relatively small number were successfully processed – most remained dispersed in the community in specially provided housing or, in the case of those awaiting deportation, in detention centres. All asylum seekers receive state benefits – although only because of a judicial ruling in 2003 that overturned a government ruling limiting some benefits.

Generally speaking, the British system of processing asylum seekers is one of the most legalistic in Europe. In some cases, the process can drag out for years. The popularity of Britain as a destination is not easy to explain, but is almost certainly related to the fact that communities of Kosovans, Afghanis and others already exist in the UK, especially in London. Britain also has a relatively relaxed 'official regime', There is no system of national identity cards (although all asylum seekers are issued with identity cards) and restrictions on freedom of movement and employment are minimal.

BRIEFINGS

26.3 Immigration law in Britain

Since the passage of the 1962 Commonwealth Immigrants Act, British immigration law has gradually been tightened. In 1968 the law was changed specifically to withdraw the rights of African Asians to migrate to Britain following the granting of independence to the black majorities in East Africa. However, British citizens not born in the UK but with a parent or grandparent born in Britain (ie whites) could migrate to Britain. The 1971 Immigration Act abolished the work voucher system, so restricting future immigration to spouses and dependants. The law also strengthened the government's powers of deportation.

The 1988 Immigration Act removed the right of men to be joined by dependants if they had entered the UK before the 1971 Act became effective in January 1973.

The British Nationality Act of 1981 effectively restricted immigration to those of British parents or parents settled in Britain. 'British' citizens not born in the UK and with no familial links to Britain were not permitted to settle in the UK. The vast majority of the population of Hong Kong were categorised thus.

The Refugee and Asylum Seekers Act 1996 made a distinction between 'economic' refugees, who were seeking a higher standard of living in Britain, and 'political' refugees fleeing political persecution. The Home Office draws up a list of countries eligible for political refugee status, which happens to exclude India and Pakistan. The Act also denies social security and other benefits to those seeking asylum in Britain. Immigrant welfare groups condemned the law as discriminatory and leading to the breakup of families, especially those from the Indian sub-continent.

The 1997 European Union Treaty of Amsterdam will standardise immigration rules for all EU borders by 2004. However, special provisions are allowed for the UK to retain some control over its own borders. By 2003 the government was prepared to further relax immigration controls in order to encourage immigration by skilled workers in such areas as health and education.

Finally it should be pointed out that, for all its flaws, Britain has a more extensive framework of anti-discrimination law than exists in most European countries. In marked contrast to its stand on gender and disability discrimination, the EU has taken few initiatives in this area.

SEXUAL PREFERENCE

It was not until 1967 that a Labour government voted to remove the ban on homosexual relations between consenting adults in England and Wales. (The ban remained in force in Scotland until 1980 and in Northern Ireland until 1982.) Until then, homosexuality was a criminal offence punishable by imprisonment. However, the new law applied only to consenting adults over the age of 21, although heterosexual relations were permitted at the age of 16. At the same time homosexuals received no protection against discrimination in employment or housing.

With changing attitudes towards sexuality in general, homosexuality became generally more acceptable during the 1980s and 1990s, although in some areas and notably in the armed forces and the police service, the subject remained taboo.

In 1994 the Conservative government reduced the legal age of consent for homosexuals to 18, and the pressure to standardise the law for all at the age of 16 was increasing. When elected in 1967, the Labour government pledged to do just that and after a long Parliamentary battle the law was changed in November 2000. Thus the age of consent for all is now 16 in England, Scotland and Wales and it is 17 in Northern Ireland. The government succeeded only after invoking the Parliament Act to overcome resistance in the House of Lords where a determined Tory peer, Baroness Young, led the opposition.

Another area of great controversy concerns Section 28 of the 1988 Local Government Act. This reads: 'A local authority shall not a) intentionally promote homosexuality or publish material with the intention of promoting homosexuality; b) promote the teaching in any maintained school of the acceptability of homosexuality as a pretended family relationship.'

Gay rights activists including such groups as Stonewall and Outrage quickly condemned Section 28 as a mandate to discriminate against homosexuals, and when elected in 1997 the Labour government promised to repeal it. However, as with the age of consent, the government at first faced considerable opposition from the House of Lords, and more recently has not found Parliamentary time to change the law. It has been established that the law does not apply to schools and most local authorities have not explicitly invoked Section 28. Paradoxically, in Scotland, where support for Section 28 has been high, the law was repealed by the new Scottish Parliament in June 2001. Given that the government remains pledged to repeal – and action under the European Convention on Human Rights may yet force repeal – a change in the law is almost certain.

By 2003 even the Conservatives were broadly supportive of an extension of gay rights and the first Tory MP to come out as gay (Alan Duncan) did so without losing his shadow ministerial post.

The European Court of Human Rights has already forced the government to act in the area of gays in the armed forces. In spite of a 1997 electoral pledge to lift the ban on homosexuals in the forces, the government refused to do so but was forced to reverse its decision by a unanimous European Court of Human Rights decision in September 1999. European law has been vital in producing the first ever ban on discrimination against homosexuals in Britain. The government acted in this area in 2003 in order to comply with an EU directive deriving from the 1997 Treaty of Amsterdam.

POLITICS OF EQUAL OPPORTUNITY: WHAT DOES THE FUTURE HOLD?

Political correctness
A controversial term to describe the use of language about socially sensitive matters, such as race or gender, in a way that is designed not to give offence. Often the implication is that politically correct language is silly or absurd.

ESSAYS

1. Outline the law protecting women from discrimination in Britain. How effective is it? What changes would you make to protect women from discrimination?

2. Do we need a new Race Relations Act? Answer by critiquing existing race relations law in the UK.

3. Why has legislation banning discrimination against homosexuals been delayed for so long? Should homosexuals be given the same rights as other minority groups?

4. 'Affirmative action policies are wrong because they undermine the essential liberal value that society is made up of unique individuals rather then broad social groups.' Discuss.

Our discussion demonstrates how attitudes have changed over time. Political discourse as it affects disability, race, gender and sexual preference is very different today from that prevailing in the 1970s, let alone the 1940s or 1950s. This is reflected in semantics – in that we use a different language to describe the issues – and in behaviour, in that discrimination is now relatively rare. Some argue that there has been a 'backlash' against tougher antidiscrimination laws. Certainly disquiet has been expressed at what are often viewed as the strident demands of the 'politically correct'. A number of leftist local authorities were much derided during the 1970s and 1980s for what were considered their extreme policies in support of the disabled and sexual and other minorities.

The reality of inequality and discrimination in Britain is, however, that a framework of law was laid down in the 1970s that, although updated and amended since, in no way compares with the reach of the law in a number of other countries including the United States of America, the Netherlands and Australia. Many loopholes in our laws exist and some forms of discrimination on grounds of age and sexual orientation remain lawful. Given the changes that have occurred in the disability, gender and race areas, it seems probable that these issues will assume a similar status in due course. As noted, governments have already been obliged to act in order to conform with EU directives.

Labour governments have extended opportunities and removed discrimination, but not if this has meant spending more money on social benefits available to large, undifferentiated categories of disadvantaged citizens. This was nicely demonstrated in late 1999 when, faced with a backbenchers' revolt, the government was forced to modify some of its reforms designed to make benefits for the disabled more selective. As part of the New Deal for the disadvantaged (see Chapter 25) the government announced that incapacity benefits would be increased for those most in need. The term 'need' was broadened to include not only the extent of disability but also potential recipients' financial circumstances. Although the government did accede to some of the backbenchers' demands, the principle that physical need alone would determine eligibility was effectively abandoned.

SUMMARY

■ The provision of equal opportunity for women and disadvantaged minorities has become an important issue in British politics over the last 30 years. All the political parties support equal opportunity, but the Conservatives have trodden more cautiously in this area than have Labour. Indeed, the framework of law that was laid down by Labour governments in the 1970s has remained largely unchanged.

■ Generally, the British have eschewed affirmative action as a form of redress for past discrimination and have instead opted for redress based on proven individual grievances. Both the Commission for Racial Equality and the Equal Opportunities Commission operate on this basis.

- The framework of protective laws provided for ethnic minorities and the disabled in Britain, although flawed in many respects, compares favourably with that of many European countries. Britain has tended to lag behind other EU states in the provision of equal opportunity for women, however.

- As far as sexual preference is concerned, Labour governments, although more liberal than the Conservatives, have been very cautious in instituting change. On such issues as gays in the armed forces, the European Court of Human Rights has forced their hand.

- The political salience of the issue is likely to increase in the years ahead, in part because the Labour government is likely to play a more proactive, if fiscally cautious, role, and in part because inequality and discrimination remain a serious disadvantage for many social groups.

MILESTONES

Milestones in equal opportunities policy

1944 and 1958 Disabled Persons Acts establish quotas for the employment of the disabled

1948 British Nationality Act allows access to the UK for Commonwealth citizens

1958 Notting Hill riots in London

1962 and 1968 Commonwealth Immigrants Acts restrict immigration, introduce work vouchers and deny access for African Asians

1968 Enoch Powell's 'rivers of blood' speech

1965 and 1968 Race Relations Acts provide limited redress for discrimination

1970 and 1983 Equal Pay Acts

1970 and 1976 Chronically Sick and Disabled Acts charge local authorities to see to the needs of the disabled

1975 Sex Discrimination Act outlaws sex discrimination and sets up Equal Opportunities Commission

1976 Race Relations Act outlaws race discrimination in employment, education and other areas and sets up Commission for Racial Equality

1981, 1985, 1991, 2000 Widespread race riots in British cities. British Nationality Act confines entry to UK to those with British ancestry

1986 Disabled Persons Act requires educational and other facilities to provide for the disabled

1996 Refugee and Asylum Seekers Act restricts asylum and denies social benefits to asylum seekers

1996 Employment Rights Act gives women the right to maternity pay and leave

1997 Record intake of women into the new Parliament

1998 Government announces a New Deal for the disadvantaged and those in need involving more training, and the targeting of benefits

1999 European Court of Human Rights outlaws British ban on gays serving in the military

2000 Legal age of consent for homosexual and heterosexual relations standardised at 16 (17 in Northern Ireland)

2001–3 Asylum seeker numbers increase greatly. Government encounters serious difficulties processing applications and toughens its rhetoric

2003 EU directive requires governments to act to end discrimination against homosexuals

PROJECTS

1. Research the pattern of asylum seeking in the UK compared with other EU states. What explains this pattern? Answer with respect to the role of public policy as well as cultural and economic factors.

2. Write a report on the state of race relations in the UK today. Answer with respect to *one* of the following:
  (a) housing
  (b) education
  (c) employment.
  How might public policy be changed to improve equal opportunity in your chosen area?

3. Taking your own school or college as an example, write a critical report on the facilities available to the disabled. Write a report on how policy might be changed to provide the disabled with a more equal opportunity to use these facilities.

FURTHER READING

A good account of racism in Britain is John Solomos, *Race and Racism in Britain* (London, Palgrave, 2003). See also Andrew Pilkington, *Racial Disadvantage and Ethnic Diversity in Britain* (London: Palgrave, 2003). On access of minorities and women to the British Parliament, see Pippa Norris and Joni Lovenduski, *Political Recruitment: Gender, Race and Class in the British Parliament* (Cambridge: Cambridge University Press, 1994). On the politics of gender equality, see Esther Breitenbach, *The Changing Politics of Gender Equality in Britain* (London: Palgrave, 2000). On citizenship and women's rights, see Ruth Lister, *Citizenship: Feminist Perspectives* (London: Macmillan, 1998). An excellent account of equal opportunity and social policy is provided by Barbara Bagilhole, *Equal Opportunities and Social Policy* (London: Longman, 1997). A comparative perspective on the Kosovo refugee crisis is provided by Joanne Van Selm (ed.), *Kosovo Refugees in the EU* (London: Continuum, 2000). Both the Commission for Racial Equality, the Equal Opportunities Commission and the Disability Rights Commission provide good up-to-date reports on inequality and discrimination.

USEFUL WEB SITES ON EQUAL OPPORTUNITIES

Hotlinks to these sites can be found on the CWS website at http://www.booksites.net/budge.

Equal opportunities for women, ethnic minorities, disabled people and those with alternative sexual orientations have become important issues for government and politics in Britain. A good starting point is the government's Commission for Racial Equality (www.cre.gov.uk) and the Equal Opportunities Commission (www.eoc.org.uk); it is also recommendable to check the Women and Equality Unit (www.womenandequalityunit.gov.uk), and the Women's National Commission (www.cabinet-office.gov.uk/wnc). Her Majesty's Stationery Office (www.hmso.gov.uk) has official statistics on labour force trends with respect to race, gender and disability. Funded through the European Social Fund, Equal is an initiative which tests and promotes new means of combating all forms of discrimination and inequalities in the labour market; visit them at www.equal.ecotec.co.uk. The TUC campaigns against discrimination at work and in wider society. They have a special section devoted to equality at www.tuc.org.uk/equality.

Citizenship21 (www.c21project.org.uk) is an independent organisation devoted to the protection of civil rights and the promotion of equal treatment for every British citizen; a similar line of camaigning is supported by Liberty (www.liberty-human-rights.org.uk). For the protection of people with disabilites visit the Disability Net at www.disabilitynet.co.uk. There are a variety of organisations aimed to promote equal treatment for gays, lesbians and transgendered people; some of them are the Lesbian and Gays Employment Rights web site (www.lager.dircon.co.uk), Stonewall (www.stonewall.org.uk), and Outrage (www.outrage.org.uk).

PART 8

A New British Politics?

The Angel of the North

New Labour:
A new politics for
a new millennium?

This chapter cuts across the detail of previous discussions to ask if the changes made at the end of the last century add up to a total transformation of the British political scene. Or have the political institutions and processes again proved resilient enough to carry on unchanged into the new millennium, just as nineteenth-century institutions and procedures underpinned much of twentieth-century politics?

New Labour certainly promised far-reaching changes when it came to power in 1997. How far have these been truly radical as opposed to an adaptation of the Thatcherite revolution that came earlier?

Most politicians like to present themselves as bold, innovative and radical. We do not need to take their assertions at face value. By evaluating the extent and nature of changes in the various areas we have discussed we can see if they really do add up to a wholesale transformation. If this has occurred, where is it taking the country? What are its implications for the quality of British democracy? This is the question posed at the beginning of the book, which we shall consider in Chapter 28.

This chapter therefore:

■ considers the later post-war period to see if there has indeed been fundamental political change in the areas of social and economic policy, government and Europe

■ evaluates the policies of New Labour and compares them with Conservative and Liberal alternatives

■ pays special attention to two issues – the public services and Europe – that now make up the main party battleground

■ assesses whether the individual changes add up to a fundamental transformation of British politics

■ asks whether the changes that have occurred are irreversible and, if so, where they are heading.

BACK TO THE FUTURE?

Neo-liberal consensus
Agreement among different political groups and parties about neo-liberal politics, that is the political belief that individual rights should be protected by maximising freedom of choice, limiting the powers of government and promoting market economics.

Society and economy

No one doubts that, in terms of ideology, New Labour broke with the 'social democratic consensus' of the earlier post-war years by adapting the neo-liberalism of the Thatcher era into what has been called the 'Third Way'.

This has little in common with the social democratic consensus and much in common with Thatcherism. Both Labour and the Conservatives now accept the market as the major mechanism for distributing resources. Both agree that bureaucracies and governments are best when they organise themselves as the markets do and limit their own role to upholding markets. The most characteristic policy of the Thatcherite period was the privatisation of government-owned services and industry, which fits beautifully into this set of ideas. Labour did not

BRIEFINGS

27.1 Views of the 'social democratic consensus' (1948–73) and the 'Third Way' (1997–)

Social democratic consensus

1. The government knows best so will frequently intervene in the market to secure optimal economic conditions and social justice.

2. This is also true internationally (the EU and UN should actively intervene to solve problems and prevent crises).

3. The economy must be 'fine-tuned' by government, above all to avoid unemployment, spread economic benefits all over the country and secure economic growth for its own sake and to support social expenditures.

4. For planning and control purposes governments need to work through large, hierarchically organised bureaucracies. If necessary, companies and sectors should be taken into public hands (nationalisation) in order to ensure acceptable levels of supply and appropriate prices.

5. Redistribution across social classes is essential for the good of society and should be achieved via progressive taxation and other means.

The Third Way

1. The free market is best at distributing resources. The government's role should be limited to guaranteeing and regulating markets so that they function efficiently.

2. A similar philosophy applies to international economic affairs (relations between states should be freely negotiated with bodies such as the World Trade Organisation (WTO) promoting world free trade).

3. Multilateralism should also be supported in pursuit of international security and justice. Hence Labour governments support the UN, NATO and international environmental treaties.

4. The government should get out of the economy as far as possible. Its main role is to provide stability and control inflation. Financial considerations should thus be central.

5. High standards of public services should be established and if necessary markets and market-like arrangements should be employed to deliver services. All public spending should be supported by appropriate levels of taxation.

6. The government should protect the weak and vulnerable in society through state benefits. But these should be carefully targeted. Redistributing income and wealth across social groups should result from economic growth and equality of opportunity and not through redistributive taxation and other policies.

7. The relationship between the state and citizen should be renewed through constitutional reform and novel forms of consultation including referendum.

renationalise one firm let alone a whole industry, and when forced to take over the failing Railtrack it replaced it not with a government-owned enterprise but with a hybrid company (Network Rail) that could eventually be returned to the private sector.

Of course, the Thatcher governments, like other governments, were limited by political realities and could not do everything they wanted. The vast social schemes of the Welfare State they inherited – social services, social benefits, the National Health Service – could not be abolished without provoking mass disorder, and their continued existence throughout the Thatcher period represents a basic continuity over the whole of the post-war period.

The real innovation of Thatcher and her supporters was, however, to reorganise these social bureaucracies on market lines. In addition, they responded to the fiscal crisis they attributed to open-ended social demands by limiting expenditure and encouraging a shift to private provision. The idea of changing to private pensions for old age, with state payments only for those unable to contribute, is a good example of neo-liberal thinking on the subject.

Limiting government spending and activity of course carries social costs. The reason social democratic ideas evolved in the first place was as a solution to the poverty, disease, crime and unemployment of the nineteenth century. Cutting down government intervention – even partially – in the 1980s and 1990s resulted in a sharp increase in those living below the poverty line to about 20 per cent of the British population, mostly in the larger conurbations. Poorer sections of the population were almost certainly better protected in the era of the social democratic consensus when benefits were provided more on a universal rather than selective basis. When welfare benefits were costed, however, and provided more selectively – and particularly when income support was being cut – they lost out.

All the main defenders of working class welfare, higher spending and greater government intervention were defeated or sidelined in the 1980s and the 1990s. The Conservatives won a famous victory in 1984–5 over the miners' union, the NUM, which prepared the way for the state coal industry to be dismantled. This allowed the government to weaken or restrict the trade union movement as a whole. (New Labour followed suit by keeping the unions at a distance.) Local government spending was controlled. The Labour Party was defeated in four successive elections and when it came back into power in 1997 it had taken on board many Thatcherite ideas and renounced the possibility of returning to the social democratic consensus.

Hegemonic In popular language the term refers to an idea or practice that is widely accepted as correct, but the term originally meant a social class (the capitalists) or nation state that is so powerful that its view of the world is accepted even by those whose interests are not served by such a world view.

Along with the Conservatives, New Labour took on the idea that real reforms take place only if the national finances are sound. So on coming to power in 1997 New Labour stayed loyal to the previous (Conservative) government's spending plans. In addition, the freeing of the Bank of England to set interest rates was a formal recognition that the government would not in the future manipulate rates for electoral advantage and thus damage the longer term prospects for the economy. The New Labour government in May 1997 took this action, however, not its Conservative predecessors. This fits nicely with Labour's general move to the right (Figure 17.2) and shows the extent to which neo-liberalism has become the hegemonic ideology, supported even by Labour, just as the social democratic consensus was in the 1950s.

It would be wrong, however, to brand New Labour's philosophy as merely a variant of Thatcherism. In many respects it is different, and by 2003 there were signs that it was developing into something quite distinctive.

New Labour: new policies?

What results has this change of underlying philosophy had on detailed party policy? Table 27.1 provides a general overview of the three British parties' general stance in each specific policy area at the start of the new millennium.

The Liberal Democrats have the most distinctive programme. They have an unequivocal commitment to joining the single currency of the EU (the euro) and they support the extension of some EU powers. They also support the delegation of central powers down to the English regions. They have a strong environmental wing advocating control of commercial agriculture and assuring access to the countryside for the general public. In keeping with this they are strong on the protection and extension of civil liberties, sceptical of the 'war against drugs' that would seek to restrict these liberties, and supportive of freedom of information. They want to spend more money on social services and education, partly to advance women and minorities. Finally, they appear to be more committed to an 'ethical' foreign policy, including controls over arms sales, than is the Labour government. In 2002 and 2003, Charles Kennedy and the Liberal Democrats were alone among the British party leaderships in voicing doubts about military action against Iraq.

Of course, the Liberal Democrats can afford to take a radical stance, as their chances of achieving power remain relatively remote. As long as Labour continues to enjoy a large majority, there is no prospect of a Liberal Democrat/Labour

Policy area	Labour	Liberal	Conservative
Foreign policy and defence	More favourable to EU but still committed to strong support for US leadership, NATO and free world trade	Very supportive of EU and would join single currency immediately. More suspicious of unqualified support for the US	Opposed to any extension of EU powers, very committed to US leadership, NATO and free trade measures
Environment	Cautiously scaling down support for genetically modified (GM) food and agriculture. 'Right to roam' – access to countryside. Supports multilateral international environmental treaties	Strongly in favour of environmental protection and access both at home and abroad	Strongly support commercial agriculture and other countryside interests (such as fox hunting and opposition to free access). More suspicious of multilateral treaties
Transport	Supports both improvement of public transport and new roads to ease congestion	Regulation of road building and motorists, improvements in public transport	Support for motorists and new roads; limit regulation of utilities and rail companies

Table 27.1 *Political party programmes for the new millennium*

Policy area	Labour	Liberal	Conservative
Economy	Balance finances, fight inflation, Bank of England free to regulate interest rates. Raise taxes only for specific purposes (such as the NHS)	More Keynesian and interventionist, but also supports sound finances	Get government out of economy. Favours balanced finances
Social	Intervene to help disadvantaged: tax credits for poor, introduce employment schemes. Retain major features of internal market in the NHS but spend more money on it	Intervention to fight inequalities. Strong support for state-funded public services	Cut taxes and privatise pension schemes. Favours support for the disadvantaged but highly targeted. Supports improved public services but favours a public/private mix to achieve this. Wants high standards maintained through competition
Equal opportunities	Some gender and racial quotas: anti-discrimination legislation extended to police and army. Higher but more selective benefits for disabled	Against all discrimination, strongly in favour of enforcement mechanisms	Opposes discrimination but also believes in upholding authority that is seen as too often challenged by minority groups. Views on homosexuality softening
Law, crime and rights	Combine social measures against 'causes of crime' with 'toughness on crime' itself. Rights of asylum seekers and 'criminals' restricted. Freedom of information only slightly extended. Has softened law on marijuana use	Strongly for individual and civil rights. Sceptical about 'war against drugs'	Strongly 'law and order', propose even more severe measures in 'war against drugs', against 'abuse of asylum' and social benefit frauds
Education	Improve state education through rigorous central inspection and control. Favours specialist and beacon schools. Promises 50% of cohort in higher education	Spend more on education through dedicated taxes	Supports more private education and 'opting out' from state sector. Standards in state sector should be maintained through testing and league tables
Constitutional	Limited reforms through more extended judicial review of administration and legislation: more proportional voting regionally and locally hereditary element in House of Lords abolished	Change 'first past the post' electoral system to proportional representation. Strong regional governments to be created	No more constitutional change
Devolution	Limited changes to regional and local democracy	Devolution to English regions	Oppose any further devolution
Administration	Joined-up government to make the present system work more effectively. Increased public consultation to act as a guide for policy	Subsidiarity – decentralise administration to devolved and local bodies	Privatise, 'hive off', deregulate, decentralise

Table 27.1 (continued)

Plate 27.1 *The Millennium Dome – a conscious parallel with the Festival of Britain promoted by Labour in 1950 (Plate 3.1). But are New Labour's policies as innovative?*

pact. At the same time, while they have made some inroads into Conservative electoral territory, there are few signs that they are about to replace the Tories as the main opposition party.

In contrast, Labour has the responsibilities of government, as Blair, Brown and Straw never tire of emphasising. New Labour's major policy might indeed be defined as replacing the Conservatives as the 'natural party of government' for the twenty-first century. To this end they have tried to conciliate big business – above all multinational firms and financial interests. In practical terms this has meant balanced budgets (or in times of economic downturn, controlled deficits) and low inflation – almost guaranteed by giving the Bank of England the power to determine interest rates autonomously.

Also promoting an atmosphere of internal stability are strong support for law and order ('tough on crime, tough on the causes of crime') and the 'war against drugs', combined with some restrictions on individual liberties and on access to information that might hinder authoritative government. The support given by Britain to the US-led police actions in the Balkans (1999), Afghanistan (2001–2002) and Iraq (2002–2003) could also be seen as part of an overall strategy of reassuring the main economic locomotive, the United States.

While these policies look similar to the Conservative policies that preceded them, they are different in important respects. There is no point in the Labour government selling out all along the line since that would provide electors with no motive for preferring Labour to the Conservatives. Indeed, voters might well reason that a Conservative government is better at administering purely Conservative policies than a Labour – possibly even a New Labour – one.

Quite apart from the ideological commitments that keep Old Labour (and a sizeable number of Labour MPs) minimally happy, it also makes sense for the government to appeal to core Labour voters in terms of traditional goals to which they are clearly attached – goals such as welfare and redistribution. There is little doubt that the employment schemes of 1997–8, financed by a levy on public utilities, or family credits covered by buoyant tax revenues, involve spending more money on families and the poor, not to mention the massive increases in NHS spending which add up to much more than Conservative governments would have done. 'Stealth' taxes and service charges have crept up under New Labour, whereas the Conservatives are committed to cutting them. Labour also appears to be more concerned with the general problem of 'social exclusion'.

Similarly, although both main parties agree that regulation rather than state ownership is the way to deal with 'natural monopolies' such as gas, electricity, water and transport, Labour is disposed to regulate them more vigorously. Labour's handling of the railways including its creation of a semi-public body, Network Rail, is more interventionist than earlier Tory policies. Labour has also proved more willing to protect and open up the environment in response to public demand. Consumer anxieties over genetically modified food have even overcome its reluctance to take on US multinationals such as Monsanto.

Labour interventionism is even more evident in education, where a concern to improve the state system has resulted in draconian inspection and centralisation of the curriculum. This certainly builds on previous Conservative policies, although it reflects Labour's concerns to improve state education (Blair has said that his priorities are 'education, education and education'), not to hive it off or privatise it piecemeal. Similarly, the government has been more willing than its predecessors to intervene on behalf of minorities, whether this has resulted in extending anti-race discrimination legislation to the police or incorporation of the European Convention on Human Rights into British law.

Devolution has, of course, been an area where Labour has led quite radically, compared to previous administrations. The Conservatives have had to accept it even in the case of London. However, plans for regional government in England have proceeded very slowly and little power has been returned to local government.

Indeed, on constitutional questions and the 'machinery of government' in general both major parties differentiate themselves quite strongly from Liberal support for 'subsidiarity' and decentralisation. Apart from minor differences over reform of the House of Lords they want to retain real power in the House of Commons, so effectively maintaining the 'elective dictatorship' that suits Blair and in the past has suited Conservative governments.

In spite of his administrative activism and New Labour's penchant for government intervention, neither Blair nor his ministers have undertaken a general

Elective dictatorship
The term used to describe the British political system as one in which, once elected, the leadership of the majority party in the House of Commons can do more or less what it wants without constitutional checks and balances, until it faces the electorate at the next general election.

reform of the Civil Service or the administrative machine. On the one hand, Labour policy on open government and freedom of information seems to be not so very different from previous Conservative governments. On the other hand, the Prime Minister's exhortations to create 'joined-up' government by cutting across traditional departmental boundaries remain, for the most part, just that – exhortations. Having said this, the Blair government has used ministers and permanent secretaries in a more programmatic way than did the Major or even the Thatcher governments. Officials are now directed to implement specific government policies and to co-ordinate objectives across departments. In addition, the Blair governments' use of special ministerial advisers who are effectively political appointees has made the job of full-time civil servants more problematical. As was shown in Chapter 9, such advisers as Jo Moore (Transport Secretary Stephen Byers' adviser until 2002) and Alistair Campbell (in the Prime Minister's Office until 2003) have proved to be highly controversial figures because they were seen to intrude into the territory traditionally reserved for permanent officials.

What *did* change under both the Conservatives and Labour was the ways in which central (and highly centralised) governments intervene in society. The old style of policy making was based on the assumption that all that was needed was the pulling of levers in Whitehall to be followed by smooth implementation by local governments, health authorities and so on. But the experience of the 1960s and the 1970s showed that central government could often lose control of what was going on at the grassroots level. Consequently, the Thatcher and Major governments greatly strengthened central control of the detail of policy implementation. Blair's governments continued or even strengthened that tendency.

Conservative and Labour governments 1979–2003: detailed intervention but no institutional transformation

Margaret Thatcher's bold social and economic initiatives of the 1980s were carried over to local government and bureaucracy, but not to the Core Executive itself, or to Parliament. There she was content to use the existing machinery, which gave her and her Cabinet great power over the detail of policy, so long as they retained control of the majority party.

This power was used to substitute quangos for local government in many areas, and to force the latter to sell off housing stock and contract out local services. Inside the central administration many services were either sold or hived off to semi-autonomous agencies. This compounded difficulties of controlling and checking administration, which forms a central part of our discussion of democracy in the next chapter. One has to say, however, that the old undivided ministries were hardly models of accountability and transparency either. In this respect, matters may not have been greatly improved by 'Next Steps', the Conservative programme of administrative reform, but they have hardly become worse.

It is also true that government organisations, particularly central government ones, are very resilient. The fact that prisons or payment of benefits are handled by separate agencies may not make much difference to the sponsoring ministry so long as it sets the terms of the contracts and makes overall policy. So far, at any rate, ministers and their civil servants seem to have retained their old policy-making functions. The major difference is that they are now more closely controlled and directed than before. If anything, the change to New Labour has increased central control by reducing somewhat the market-oriented 'hiving off' of administration replacing it with 'joined-up' government and a greater emphasis on the ministries.

The same may be said of the survival of local councils and their officials. Pushed out of many areas of local administration, obliged to follow national procedures in giving out contracts, marginalised elsewhere, they nevertheless emerged as vibrant centres of local opposition to Conservative policies. We see the same process under New Labour. With wider control over development and planning, councils may simply have exchanged declining functions for ones growing in importance. After the turbulent era of the 1980s and 1990s they are probably also in closer touch with their electorate, helped by the development of 'community politics', and with a new role as articulators of local grievances as well as facilitators of local services.

These, of course, were consequences not intended by Thatcher. But they were provoked by her policies. The same may well be true of the Scottish Parliament and Welsh Assembly. Thatcher herself was fiercely opposed to devolution, but her insensitive imposition of full-blooded neo-liberal policies on basically social democratic societies may have swelled support for a degree of independence from central government. Not only are Welsh, Scottish and Northern Irish legislatures now in place, but London has been given an executive mayor and an elected assembly with very limited powers in place of the Greater London Council abolished by Thatcher in the mid-1980s. Thus new institutions have been created that run counter to the policies of Conservatism in the 1980s and 1990s. Moreover, these institutions may well serve as entrenched centres of opposition to any future Conservative government.

The territorial decentralisation of power initiated by New Labour is matched to a limited extent by some central reforms. The main manifestation of this is the incorporation of the European Convention on Human Rights into British law. This extends the scope for judicial scrutiny of political and administrative decisions, thus strengthening a growing tendency developed by the courts in the late 1980s and the 1990s, again partly in reaction to the 'elective dictatorship' of Westminster (Chapter 10).

Other constitutional innovations under New Labour have been limited, however. Real access to information has hardly been extended despite an Act passed in 2000, which purports to do so. An enhanced role has been given to the security services. Tight party discipline has been enforced within the government and the House of Commons, and with respect to candidates for the Scottish, Welsh and London executives – although as we have seen (Chapter 11) this sometimes went disastrously wrong.

It seems that the 'elective dictatorship' of the majority party will be maintained as long as possible. The unwritten constitution that puts such power in the hands of a determined Prime Minister will remain in all its essential aspects, the main limitations on personal rule being the balance of personalities in the Cabinet.

Electoral reform could change this state of affairs almost overnight by ensuring that no majority party emerges to dominate Parliament and that governments must be coalitions. For that very reason no government with a Parliamentary

27.2 The 'elective dictatorship' in British government

The 'elective dictatorship' is the shorthand term (coined by Lord Hailsham) used to describe the situation whereby the leadership of the majority party in the House of Commons forms a government that can do more or less what it wants, with only weak constitutional and legislative checks. This is possible because of (a) tight internal discipline which ensures that the MPs of the majority Parliamentary party will always vote to uphold the government (Chapter 17); and (b) the unwritten constitution, whose conventions are more or less what the government says they are (Chapter 4).

Although some limitations have been placed on governments through EU legislation, devolution, judicial review and investigative journalism, these are relatively weak and ineffective at the present time.

majority is likely to change the present system of election very radically. Only if Labour and Liberal Democrat supporters continue to vote tactically can the Liberal Democrats hope to build up their Parliamentary strength under the present system. Only if they hold a balance between the parties will they have real power to bargain for some change. To the extent that they are effectively tied to Labour, however, change is likely to be limited and might only extend to changing the present voting system. Even limited electoral reform will not materialise until well into the first decade of the millennium.

Constitutional essentials have thus changed less than other aspects of politics over the post-war period. They still put massive power into the hands of the central government. Two minor but potentially important developments may be portents of greater flexibility in the future:

1. Greater use of referendums, whereby all or part of the British population votes on constitutional change (eg the European referendum of 1975; now also promised on any decision to adopt the single currency). Such exercises in direct democracy (ie voting directly on policy questions rather than electing representatives to decide them) are, however, largely limited to questions that the government of the day would like to avoid making itself, but nonetheless thinks it can win in a referendum. Thus referendums are still largely cosmetic; they do not constitute a serious change in the present system.

2. The same may be said of the select committee structure of the House of Commons, interestingly strengthened as one of the first acts of the new Conservative government of 1979. The committees do provide a potential channel for a Parliamentary voice to be asserted against a domineering government. Investigative committees in combination with investigative journalism have uncovered many abuses. They have rarely affected actual government policy, however, and are unlikely to do so while the 'elective dictators' can simply ignore them.

More administrative, constitutional and political changes thus took place after 1979 than before. They may form a basis for greater transformations to come, but they have not yet fulfilled that potential. Above all, most of the changes – with the notable exception of Scotland – have done little to limit the power of the central government in London. On the contrary, the increase in the use of monitoring, performance review, appraisal, 'value for money' and league tables have greatly increased the ability of the government to control even the minutiae of how the public sector interacts with the broader society.

Europe

Another major move towards change in Britain comes, significantly, from outside the country, from Europe. In the face of the vast potential transformations this entails, commenting on domestic reforms may seem like describing the decorations on the *Titanic* as it headed for the iceberg!

European Monetary Union (EMU) is not only about economics but also about political union. If economic and monetary policy comes to be managed at a European level, fiscal policy (taxation) may well follow. This addition to the existing powers concentrated at Brussels will finally tip the balance of power away from Member States such as Britain and towards the European institutions. Pressure will grow to make these democratically responsible and accountable, by redesigning the European Commission, Council of Ministers and the European Parliament along the lines of a real federal government and assembly.

If Britain becomes increasingly committed to EMU it will have to go along this path with its partners. Faced with the alternatives of withdrawing totally from the EU (on which it would still be economically dependent, however) or going along with the others, it is likely to go along, however virulent Eurosceptic opposition to the loss of sovereignty becomes.

Joining the then European Community in 1973 meant accepting its established powers, an act that immediately subverted British Parliamentary sovereignty. The European Court of Justice (ECJ) had established the superiority of European law over the law of Member States and, moreover, obliged British courts to review British legislation to ensure that British law was compatible with European law. This encouraged British courts to extend the scope of their judicial review, even where European law was not involved. Hence growing judicial activism is a feature of the last quarter-century of British government.

While the importance of the EU to British politics should not be underestimated, by 2003 there were signs that the issue was receding in importance – if only temporarily. Difficulties in finding an interest rate that suited all Member States led some in the British government – not least the Chancellor, Gordon Brown – to become increasingly cautious about EMU membership. Equally important, the EU Member States did not speak with one voice after events of 9/11 and the subsequent conflicts in Afghanistan and Iraq. Britain supported the American position while others, notably Germany and France, dissented. The EU Common Defence and Foreign Policy looked quite fragile in this context. Finally, having been badly hurt by the issue in the 2001 election, the Conservatives quietly sidelined the European question after 2002. Instead they joined battle with Labour over the question of the public services.

LABOUR, CONSERVATIVES, AND THE PUBLIC SERVICES

That the public services should have replaced Europe as the main issue on which the parties have joined battle is not surprising given the events of the early twenty-first century. In spite of the economic fallout from the September 2001 terrorist attacks and the global economic slowdown from 2001 to 2003, the British economy continued to grow at a moderate pace. Employment held up, inflation was low and, notwithstanding some deterioration after 2002, public finances remained essentially sound. This gave Labour the opportunity to make the most of an area in which it always had an electoral advantage over the Conservatives – the state of public services. Until 1992 the Conservatives were widely regarded as the party most likely to deliver on economic policy while Labour was viewed as the party that would let public spending spiral out of control. With Britain's withdrawal from the Exchange Rate Mechanism, the Conservatives' reputation as the party of economic competence was seriously damaged. After 1997, Labour's steady handling of the economy under Chancellor Gordon Brown enabled them to replace the Tories as the party of financial prudence. At the same time, although the electorate was unhappy at the way many of the public services were run, few regarded the Conservatives as more attractive in this issue area. On the contrary, following the Thatcher and Major experience, they were widely seen as uncaring. Labour, by way of contrast had always been a champion of better state provision in health, education, transport and the social services.

By Labour's second term, this issue dominated the policy agenda. Still smarting from two massive electoral defeats, the Conservatives moved on to Labour's ground by de-emphasising the European question and instead claimed that they too were champions of the public services. What then divides the parties on how best to deliver high-quality public services? In terms of the substance of policy, not a great deal (Table 27.2).

All political parties are agreed on the *ends* of public policy. Where there is disagreement is over the means to those ends, with the Conservatives favouring a more market-led approach and the Liberal Democrats a more devolved, community-led approach.

Issue	Labour	Liberal Democrat	Conservative
NHS	Greatly increased spending funded by National Insurance tax. Private sector services can be bought by NHS, but all care free at point of delivery	Greatly increased spending financed by extra income tax. Service free at point of delivery. Greater autonomy for hospital and primary care trusts	More market inputs both internally and by using the private sector for some care. Care should be free except for selective means-tested charges
Education	Increase quality and choice in all state schools. Encourage special subject schools. 50% of age group in higher education. Universities free to charge top-up fees	Increase spending through tax increases. Favours improved state sector through much greater local autonomy	More choice in state schools. Provide access for poorer children to expanded private sector. Emphasis on quality in higher education
Transport	Encourage investment in roads and rail to ease congestion. Private/public partnership OK. Part-privatise London tube	Reduce road expenditure. Greatly increase spending on public transport. More emphasis on local government control	Emphasis on road investment plus more use of the private sector in rail and city transport
Law enforcement	More community policing. Heavier sentences for serious offenders. More preventative approaches. Soften law on marijuana use	Devolve powers to run police authorities. More community policing and community participation in crime prevention	More police. Tougher sentencing. Little or no relaxation of drug laws

Table 27.2 *Party positions on the public services, 2003*

One thing is for sure: the Labour government firmly pinned its colours to the mast on these issues by promising very specific results. As we saw in earlier chapters, these included raising health expenditure to the EU average, increasing the number of 18–25-year-olds in higher education to 50 per cent, significantly reducing travel congestion within ten years and setting targets for a reduction in violent crime rates. Failure to meet these promises will almost certainly damage Labour's prospects at subsequent elections.

During 2002 and 2003 Labour was also haunted by an old spectre from the past: public sector trade union militancy. A number of groups ranging from firefighters to hospital consultants resisted attempts to link 'modernisation' (more flexible working practices) to pay increases. The simple truth is, of course, that the public services cannot be reformed without the co-operation of the people who run them. As a result the government was forced to choose between confrontation with the unions and compromising on its carefully worked out modernisation plans. It seems unlikely that this issue will go away. Labour remains firmly committed to modernising education, health and other public services. This has to mean taking on the public service professionals and persuading them to abandon across the board pay increases and uniform work practices in favour of pay rises related to the performance of individuals rather than of whole groups. But if health and education professionals refuse to accept dramatic changes in working practices, there is little the government can do about it without suffering politically damaging industrial action.

HOW HAVE BRITISH POLITICS CHANGED?

However the situation is evaluated it is clear that the entry of the European dimension into domestic affairs sharply distinguishes this period in British politics from anything that has gone before. The difference is enhanced by the coincidental shift in the political consensus from social democratic to neo-liberal. This holds in spite of Labour's search for a Third Way. For in a number of fundamental areas, and in particular the role of the market in economy and society New Labour is closer to the neo-liberal than to the social democratic position. True, Labour is more supportive of the Welfare State than the Conservative governments of 1979–97, more dedicated to combating 'exclusion', and generally more favourable to the EU. But in terms of its 'Third Way' flagship policies for the economy it has abandoned nationalisation for private ownership, it continues to support public–private partnerships, and courts business rather than trade union approval.

In terms of the machinery and organisation of government, there is some doubt whether the changes go far enough to mark out the last two decades as fundamentally different (see Table 27.3). The reason is that no government has been willing to give up its 'elective dictatorship' – the powers provided by party discipline, an unwritten constitution and a highly centralised form of government in which executive, legislative and judicial branches of government fuse and overlap. Reforms that have been carried out – select investigative committees,

Institution	Reformed after 1979	By whom	Characterisation
Cabinet and premiership	No	–	Continues to be 'elective dictatorship'
Parliament	Slightly	Cons	Investigative select committees
Political parties	Somewhat	Kinnock/Smith/ Blair/Hague/ Duncan-Smith	More disciplined and centralised: closer external regulation of practices and finance
General elections	No	–	Continue to give Parliamentary majority to plurality party
European and regional elections	Yes	Lab	Introduction of strong proportional element
Central administration	Yes	Cons/Lab	'Hiving off' and privatisation of subsidiary and administrative functions. Increasing use of political advisers
Local government	Yes	Cons/Lab	More central control over administrative functions, hiving off of some, territorial reorganisation, 'community politics', 'Cabinet' or 'executive' form of government
Devolution and regional assemblies	Yes	Lab/LibDem	Self-government for Scotland, Wales, Northern Ireland, London mayor; potential for conflict with centre
Quangos	Extended	Cons/Lab	Continue to be nominated by central government and to administer large areas of national life
Pressure groups (including unions and non-financial business)	Yes	Cons	Legal curbs, marginalised in policy making, change political to market relationships
City of London, finance, banks	Slightly	Cons/Lab	New self-regulatory measures: Bank of England freed to set interest rates
Police	Slightly	Cons	More centralised under government control
Security services	No	–	Slight moves to transparency; powers extended
Judges	No	–	Assert more autonomous powers of review
European Convention on Human Rights introduced	Yes	Lab	Increases in judges' powers of administrative review
Mass media (press and TV)	No	–	Shift to market model, investigative journalism

Table 27.3 *Institutional continuity and change, 1945–2003*

judicial review, incorporation of the Convention on Human Rights – do not fundamentally affect the powers of the central authorities. While devolution in Scotland, Wales and Northern Ireland transfers some powers from the centre to these areas, it does not affect in any way the way in which the centre continues to exercise its remaining and formidable powers over most of the United Kingdom.

Neither has local government reform or reorganisation altered the situation radically. The centre continues to depend on the administrative services of the local authorities, and indeed has strengthened its tight control of their policies and finances. However, it should be remembered that the councils themselves have found a new, more activist role in local representation and community politics.

Neither 'Next Steps' nor tight budgetary control have undermined the top civil servants' primary role as policy advisers to politicians and controllers of central administration. British ministers remain dependent on civil servants in the ministries, even under New Labour and its increasingly numerous and influential band of nominated advisers.

Alterations in the government and administration of the British State may have the potential to change the British system radically, but they have not yet fulfilled that potential. This is true, even though the administrative and local reorganisations of the Thatcher era, and the devolution carried through by Blair, are more far reaching than anything that happened in the 1950s and 1960s.

The radical policy reversal of the 1980s and 1990s and the impact of Europe certainly differentiate contemporary British politics fundamentally from the earlier post-war period. The stakes, the goals, the strategies have now radically altered. One significant indicator of a shift in thinking is the 'decline of decline'. In the 1980s political commentators were obsessed by the question of Britain's overall decline, especially what was termed 'relative economic decline', that is, slower economic growth than other countries. Both the left and right used this obsession to justify their preferred reforms and the sacrifices they entailed. In the early twenty-first century even with a not dissimilar long-term growth rate, the question of decline hardly enters into political debate. Britain has made the adjustment to the modern global economy and discussion is dominated, instead, by such questions as 'national sovereignty' versus 'Europe' and the quality of the public services.

We can thank Margaret Thatcher for that. Her 'radical right' policies changed the premises on which British politics were based and her energy and resolution ensured that changes were implemented. Her success in this respect may be gauged from the fact that Labour cannot turn the clock back in some respects (privatisation, for example), and has chosen not to do so in others (eg increasing direct taxation). Labour believes that the price of electoral success is acceptance of most elements of the new situation.

At the same time New Labour has found its own characteristic policies in what it claims to be a 'Third Way' – something between old Labour and neo-liberal Thatcherism. It has reversed Thatcherite centralisation with modest grants of devolution, it has tempered the market with a new stress on community, and it has returned to familiar ground with its pledges to improve the quality of life through improved public services.

ESSAYS

1. Why did 'Europe' decline in importance in British politics after the 2001 general election?

2. What evidence is there that the Liberal Democrats are now the true radical party in British politics?

3. Is the 'Third Way' simply neo-liberalism by another name?

4. Did New Labour's constitutional reforms transform British politics?

SUMMARY

This chapter has reviewed evidence that contemporary politics in Britain have been fundamentally transformed since 1979, and concludes that:

- Contemporary politics *are* very different, due partly to the neo-liberal Thatcherite policy revolution, which cannot be reversed, but also because of the strengthening of the European Union.

- This will be congenial to Labour's interventionist traditions, but there will be no going back to state socialism. Instead Labour governments have adapted neo-liberal approaches through their pursuit of a Third Way in politics.

- The major dimension to this is the emphasis on improving the quality of the public services and in particular health and education. Labour has forced a change in the political agenda in this area and obliged the Conservatives also to champion the public services.

- EU institutions and policies will probably become even more important in Britain, and will undermine the high degree of control exercised by British central governments.

PROJECTS

1. Outline the main differences between Labour and Conservatives on improving the public services. Who is more likely to succeed?

2. Write a brief on how the 'elective dictatorship' in Britain could be removed. What would be the advantages and disadvantages of the suggested changes?

FURTHER READING

For an assessment of the Thatcher and Major governments and their effects, see Dennis Kavanagh and Anthony Seldon (eds), *The Thatcher Effect: A Decade of Change* (Oxford: Clarendon Press, 1989) and *The Major Effect* (London: Macmillan, 1994). More specialised is Stephen P. Savage and Lynton Robins (eds), *Public Policy under Thatcher* (London: Macmillan, 1990). For a broad sweep across selected topics in British politics since 1945, see Lynton Robins and Bill Jones (eds), *Half a Century of British Politics* (Manchester: Manchester University Press, 1997).

Two excellent books written by journalists about British politics in the 1990s are Will Hutton, *The State We're In* (London: Vintage, rev. edn, 1996) and Simon Jenkins, *Accountable to None* (Harmondsworth: Penguin, 1997). Blair's 'Third Way' is assessed in Anthony Giddens, *The Third Way* (Oxford: Polity, 1998). Giddens answers critics in *The Third Way and its Critics* (Oxford: Polity, 2000). Assessments of the Blair governments include Peter Riddel, *The Blair Government* (London: Politico, 2002) and Anthony Seldon (ed.) *The Blair Effect* (London: Little, Brown, 2001).

USEFUL WEB SITES ON NEW LABOUR: NEW POLITICS FOR A NEW MILLENNIUM

Hotlinks to these sites can be found on the CWS website at http://www.booksites.net/budge.

The UK politics web site (www.ukpolitics.org.uk) is regularly updated and contains a variety of message boards and discussion lists related to the future of British politics in local, regional, national and international terms. Among a variety of topics you will find arguments concerned with the risks of an 'elective dictatorship' in Britain, the advantages and disadvantages of joining the European common currency and the like. A great deal of debate goes on in www.britpolitics.com, where the crucial questions on the development of British politics are addressed. Precious information on the direction that the main political parties might take in the following years can be gathered from the political speeches of their current leaders; for Tony Blair's speech at the 2002 Labour Party conference visit www.labour.org.uk/speeches; for Liberal Democrat leaders' speech to the party conference in 2002 visit www.libdems.org.uk/index.cfm/page.news/section.conference. Finally, Iain Duncan Smith's speech at the 2002 Conservative Party conference can be obtained from www.conservatives.com/conference/. It is worth regularly visiting the Trade Union Congress web site at www.tuc.org.uk.

The most important legislative matters under debate are available from www.parliament.uk, www.scotland.gov.uk, www.wales.gov.uk, and www.nics.gov.uk. For critical views on questions related to Britain and its integration to Europe visit the coalition known as Britain in Europe (www.britainineurope.org.uk). The Conservative Party (www.conservative-party.org.uk) somehow gathers most Eurosceptics. However, many related groups do as well: some of them are www.eusceptic.org, the Youth for a Free Europe (www.free-europe.org.uk), and the Bruges Group (www.brugesgroup.com).

For news and information on social and economic developments in Britain and the rest of the world visit the *Financial Times* www.ft.com, and the *Economist* www.economist.com.

New politics, new democracy?

The 'democratic deficit' of the European Union, that is the lack of accountability of its executive bodies (the Council of Ministers and the Commission) to an elected legislature such as the European Parliament or to national legislatures, is often criticised. The same criticism can be made of the UK government in relation to the House of Commons. The executive dominates Parliament, rather than the other way round. When select committees try to hold the government accountable for its actions as often as not they are fobbed off and their reports ignored. Whole areas of the executive, notably the security apparatus that most threatens civil liberties, are effectively screened from any scrutiny at all. In addition and notwithstanding recent trends towards devolution, Britain is an extraordinarily centralised country. Local governments have little power and almost no independent tax base, and in England a regional level of government simply does not exist.

None of this implies that Britain is not a democracy, even a liberal democracy. It does show, however, that even under an old-established, democratically advanced constitution there is room for improvement.

The last chapter focused on the transformation of British political life over the past 25 years. Here we examine the quality of democracy in Britain and ask whether the changes now working their way through politics will enhance or degrade this.

Liberal democracy has two aspects: popular control, and respect for individual and group rights. This chapter discusses how these stand now and how they might change. Accordingly it considers:

■ democratic control: what it is and where it operates
■ the electorate's choice between left and right
■ electoral control and reform
■ representation below the national level
■ pressure groups and policy
■ individual protection against administrative injustice
■ scrutiny of government and administration as a safeguard of individual rights
■ a written constitution.

LIBERAL DEMOCRACY: ELECTORAL CONTROL AND EFFECTIVE SCRUTINY

We are concerned with both control and scrutiny of the executive because of the dual nature of democracy as it now operates in most of the world, including Britain. Democracies tend not just to be democratic but also liberal. Their democratic character shows itself in rule by the majority, exercised by choosing between political parties on the basis of their record, candidates and programmes. The party or parties with the majority of votes should then form a government with a 'mandate' (authority) from the electorate to govern on the basis of their

28.1 **The electoral mandate**

This is the idea that the party (or parties) getting the most votes in an election will form a government that will carry through its electoral programme, as this has been supported by electors. The details of the argument are given below:

■ electors choose between parties at least in part on the basis of their programme

■ such programmes are distinguishable from each other so they offer electors a basis for choice

■ the party or parties that form the next government have a responsibility to carry out their programme in government, because this is a major basis on which they have been elected

■ they also have the authority to carry out their programme in government, as it has been selected by at least a sizeable number of electors as the best short-term programme for the country

■ parties do carry through their programmatic priorities in government.

Mandate
An instruction or command that carries legal or moral force. An electoral mandate is said to give the party winning an election the right to carry out its programme.

programme. In this way a rough correspondence between majority preferences and government policy is secured.

One obvious problem of British democracy is that no winning party since the Second World War has actually obtained a popular majority. Because of the workings of the electoral system, parties have obtained Parliamentary majorities with only a plurality (42–48 per cent) of the votes. One could say that the majority has, in fact, voted against the governing party, at least in a certain sense. This might be less true where the victor has occupied a centre position, thus making itself reasonably congenial to the majority if not actually representing them directly. But where the winning party has been at one of the ideological extremes, as in general elections from 1974–92, it has seemed like a minority government masquerading as a majority one. This is a real problem for democracy in Britain that we examine later in the chapter.

The liberal element in liberal democracy has some potential points of conflict with the democratic ideal that the majority should rule. Liberalism emphasises respect for individual and group rights, even when a majority might want to do away with them. Thus it sets bounds on what the majority can do.

Property rights are often involved in such a clash of principles, particularly in regard to progressive taxation where the property-less majority may wish to redistribute wealth through special taxes on the rich. Environmental concerns might also involve restrictions on the use of property that limit the owners' use of it.

Such difficult conflicts of principle often arise in day-to-day politics. In many other areas, however, liberalism and democracy are entirely compatible and even mutually reinforcing. This is because democratic principles themselves impose limits on what a current majority can do in the interests of future and possibly opposing majorities. Democratic procedures cannot, therefore, allow a current majority to punish or silence an opposing minority. Over time that minority may convince enough people of the rightness and justice of its claims to become a majority itself. In the interests of future majorities democratic procedures have to guarantee personal immunity to minority individuals and groups, and rights of debate, assembly, discussion and voting for all, even to persons holding unpopular or despised points of view.

This position brings democratic principles very close to liberal ones. Both are concerned with upholding rights even against a hostile (current) majority. Democratic procedures would, however, try to keep guaranteed rights to a minimum in order to leave a majority the maximum freedom of action. Liberalism would be more concerned with extending rights even at the cost of restricting majority rule.

In practice, civil rights are under so many threats that there is little real conflict between democratic and liberal principles. This is the case in Britain with regard to official secrecy, which drastically limits not only individuals' right to know enough even to claim their rights but (by the same token) also restricts full democratic debate and discussion.

In order to check on the extent to which popular majorities actually decide things in Britain we need to look at the way elections are conducted and how voting outcomes are reflected in the choice of governments and in the policies they pursue. We should also look to the future: will the conduct of elections change so as to reflect majority preferences better? There are two dimensions to this dynamic. What might be called national representation – the choice voters make between parties at the national level – and vertical representation, or the choice we are offered at the local, regional, and supranational (EU) levels.

On the side of rights – both liberal and democratic – we need to see how well these are protected and how efficiently infringements are investigated and corrected. Procedurally this involves appeals against injustice and powers of scrutiny, whether by courts, Parliament or media.

Electoral control and administrative scrutiny are thus the two major concerns of this chapter. At the end of the discussion we shall try to put together our conclusions about both of them, so as to form a rounded picture of the workings of liberal democracy in Britain and of its likely future development.

NATIONAL REPRESENTATION: ELECTORAL CHOICE BETWEEN LEFT AND RIGHT

In one sense elections are a defective democratic mechanism in Britain because a majority never elects a government. Instead, the single-member simple plurality constituency (or 'first past the post') system ensures that the party with the largest (but not a majority) vote gets a Parliamentary majority. Such a government has very wide powers even though it represents an electoral minority. There are very few restrictions within the unwritten constitution on what any government, even minority ones, can do (Chapter 4). Parliamentary sovereignty is all important, not the popular mandate, and in practice sovereignty is appropriated by the party with the majority of seats.

This situation may not be quite as undemocratic as it seems if the party which has that majority represents the 'centre' or the 'middle ground' of politics and thus comes closer to doing what most electors want anyway. To see what is involved here we need to examine the actual process of electoral campaigning and voting more closely, looking particularly at the way issues get narrowed down so as to simplify voting choices.

There are, of course, thousands of issues that could potentially enter into elections and provide a basis for choice between the political parties. It seems, however, from the evidence of the 'Essex Model' of voting that very few actually do. Basically, elections focus on the economy – particularly whether there should be more or less government intervention – on welfare, taxes and peaceful international co-operation versus aggressive assertion of national interests. These are the classic issues separating left and right in Britain, as in other countries (Chapter 17).

Why should all the complex debates and issues of British politics get crushed down to a simple one-dimensional choice between left and right? The reason is simple – this is the way both parties and media present party policy positions in election campaigns. There is an inevitable element of simplification in public presentation of the political choices involved that pushes political discussion and voting decisions into this one dimension.

Of course there is no *logical* reason why Labour, or the left in general, should combine internationalism with support for welfare and greater economic intervention. But it does. The Conservatives on their side combine support for (economic) freedom with hostility to a 'big' state and a nationalistic attitude abroad. Liberal Democrats support both freedom and welfare and thus tend to end up in the middle of the left–right spectrum, although in 1997 their environmentalism pushed them to the left of Labour.

We have already mapped out party positions along such a spectrum (in Figure 17.2) and traced the movement of the parties to left and right over the post-war period. Representing the important election issues in this direct way helps us see more clearly which party holds the 'centre' or 'middle ground' on the most important issues and whether this is the party that gets into government as a result of the election. This is summarised in Table 28.1, in which judgements as to which party was in the middle on the most important issues of the elections are made on the basis of Figure 17.2.

Over the range of 16 post-war elections from 1945 to 2001 inclusive, the middle party got into government eight times, or at half the elections. (This is on the generous view that the Conservative positions in 1951 and 1970 almost coincided with those of the Liberals, and so can be counted as 'middle' even though very slightly to the right of them, and that Labour in 1966 also practically coincided with the Liberals.)

What is more significant, however, is that six out of the eight occasions when the middle party, broadly defined, got into office occurred between 1951 and 1970! In 1974 a relatively extreme left-wing Labour Party won both elections, then an increasingly right-wing Conservative Party got into government from 1979–92. In other words, there was a tendency for parties taking an extreme ideological position rather than one based on the 'middle ground' to win office

Election year	45	50	51	55	59	64	66	70
Government party after election	Lab	Lab	Con	Con	Con	Lab	Lab	Con
Middle party on left–right issues	Lib	Con	Con (almost)	Con	Con	Lab	Lab (almost)	Con (almost)
Did middle party win?	No	No	Yes	Yes	Yes	Yes	Yes	Yes

Election year	74(i)	74(ii)	79	83	87	92	97	01
Government party after election	Lab	Lab	Con	Con	Con	Con	Lab	Lab
Middle party on left–right issues	Lib or Con	Lib	Lib	Lib–SD alliance	Lib–SD alliance	LD	Lab	Lab
Did middle party win?	No	No	No	No	No	No	Yes	Yes

Table 28.1 *The middle party in government, 1945–2001*

between 1971 and 1997. In that sense British governments moved further away from reflecting majority opinion in these years. Only New Labour, by shifting substantially rightwards, managed to reoccupy the centre in 1997 and make itself a more consensual government, a position it maintained in the election of 2001.

If Labour continues both to win elections and hold the middle ground we should see politics becoming less adversarial than they have been recently and more reflective of majority opinion, at least on the central issues where electoral choices are made. Close relationships with the Liberal Democrats should also strengthen these tendencies, as that party is quite likely to return to the centre position occupied during 1964–92. A coalition government of Labour and Liberal Democrats would even rest on a popular majority, producing a genuinely majoritarian government for the first time in the post-war period.

Such outcomes are very contingent ones, however, heavily dependent on the ebb and flow of electoral politics. The emergence of further non-majority-based governments from one or other ideological extreme remains a strong possibility. Indeed, they are quite likely under the workings of the present electoral system.

The rules of plurality voting, whereby the party with the single largest vote wins the seat, themselves encourage the emergence of governments with an electoral minority and Parliamentary majority. This is compounded by the fact that voting takes place within small, arbitrarily drawn constituencies that, in the current state of affairs, give Labour a large, inbuilt advantage over the Conservatives in the translation of votes into seats, making it again more likely that a Parliamentary majority will emerge from a voting plurality.

Only a change to some kind of PR (proportional representation) system that deliberately tried to match vote percentages to party seat percentages in reasonably large constituencies could guarantee that all electors received fair party representation in Parliament. Where this procedure has been applied, as in the elections to the Welsh Assembly and Scottish Parliament in 1999, it has produced

BRIEFINGS

28.2 The middle ground and the median voter

The view that the popular majority is better represented by a minority government if that is formed by the party holding the 'middle ground', that is, a centrist policy position, can be expressed more generally in terms of the median voter's choice and its relationship to other voters' choices. If electoral preferences can be arranged along a left–right policy spectrum corresponding to the party positions in Figure 17.2, then the median voter is the one who pushes the count over 50 per cent, going from either left or right. A simplified illustration of this is given as follows, for an electorate of five voters:

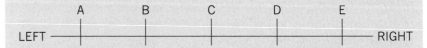

Middle ground
A political position roughly midway between the extremes of the political spectrum. The crucial point about the middle ground is not that it is in the middle but that it is assumed to be a position preferred by the majority of voters.

On this left–right dimension voters are placed in terms of their policy preferences from left to right. C is the middle (or 'median') voter. For a party to have a majority, it must get C to vote for it. In order to attract C the party has to come very near to C's position, otherwise the other party will come closer, get C's vote, obtain a majority and form the government. In this situation, whatever party forms the government will always adopt a policy position closer to C's preferences in order to win a majority. Even where there is a large electorate such as the British one, parties seeking extra votes will always have to move policy towards the median position (assuming they know where it is), as can be seen from the following diagram:

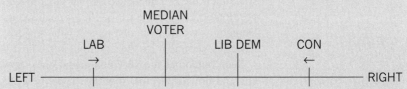

On this argument policy will always move towards C's (the median) position. This is very nice for C, of course, who will always get his or her way under ideal democratic conditions. But it is also a reasonable outcome for the other electors, indeed the best they can hope for. A and B would much prefer to have C's policies adopted than those of D and E. Similarly D and E prefer C to A and B. Thus the power of the median voter, and the adoption of that voter's preference by government, is the best way of meeting everybody's preferences under the existing distribution of opinion. The other voters do not get all they want but they get more than if the opposing wing could simply impose their own preferences.

In practice, of course, Britain has three large parties, so none can hope to get a majority on its own. However, if the party that the median voter supports gets into government, the policies pursued should approximate those which would have got a majority vote anyway, given the need to attract the median voter.

Instead, from 1974 to 1992, a party not responsive to the median voter got into government. This may account for the relatively extreme policies pursued by Conservative governments during this period. It may also explain why the politics of the period from 1950 to 1970 seem more consensual than those of later years. New Labour seems to have designed its policies to appeal to the median voter, perhaps ushering in a new era of (relatively) consensual politics.

either a coalition based on a majority of the vote (Scotland) or a minority executive forced to respond to majority opinion (Wales).

Unfortunately, as these examples show, PR could not guarantee any one party receiving an electoral majority; only that if it did not, it could not form a British government on its own. With three major parties in Britain and a number of minor ones the probability indeed is that none could gain either a majority of votes or a

Plate 28.1 *The late Donald Dewar, then the Scottish Labour Leader at the first Scottish Parliamentary election, May 1999. Under a semi-proportional voting system, Labour emerged as the largest, but not the majority, party in the new legislature*

majority of Parliamentary seats (unless two parties formed an electoral alliance with a common programme, pledged to form a government if it got a majority).

Otherwise, parties would have to negotiate coalition governments after the election, as in Scotland. These would certainly be based on a popular majority of votes. The problem is that electors would have voted for the different parties making up the government on the basis of their diverse policies and programmes. Even if the partners could compromise on these it would still not be quite what the electors had voted for. British commentators have traditionally been dismissive of coalition governments, seeing them as weak and unstable and not offering electors a clear-cut choice between alternative government programmes as the British system does. However, there is much to be said for coalition governments too.

CONTROVERSY

Coalition government versus single-party government

Arguments for single party government based on first past the post

1. The two major parties offer electors a clear-cut choice between alternative government programmes.

2. A cohesive Parliamentary majority ensures that the government programme gets through and the electoral mandate is fulfilled.

3. The largest single number of electors is represented by the party that gets into power (although this may not include the median voter).

4. The disadvantages of basing government on a popular minority are outweighed by the advantages of strong effective government.

5. Single-party government encourages adversarial politics, particularly between the two largest parties, as they are very much in a win or lose situation, and this clarifies the debate on the key political issues.

Arguments for coalition government based on PR

1. Some coalition governments are formed by parties that have fought the election with a common programme of government, as an electoral alliance (Germany, Scandinavia). If they get a majority they have a mandate just as much as a single-party government.

2. Many coalitions are strong and cohesive and have a clear programme of government (France, Germany, the Netherlands).

3. Coalitions are usually based on a popular majority that includes the median voter. Even though the supporting majority has not all voted for the same party, policy has a greater chance of representing majority rather than minority wishes.

4. Coalitions can be strong and effective too, as Germany and the Netherlands demonstrate. The Scottish Executive, formed by a coalition of Labour and Liberals, has been quite effective.

5. Coalitions generally encourage compromise and negotiation between the partner parties, and sometimes with the opposition too. No party and its supporters will lose out entirely under coalition government because all parties have to bear in mind that they might be partners with the others in a future coalition.

VERTICAL REPRESENTATION: LOCAL, REGIONAL, NATIONAL, AND SUPRANATIONAL ELECTIONS

A further criticism levelled at the British variety of democracy is that it is too centralised. Political scientists have distinguished between what they call 'first-order' and 'second-order' elections. First-order elections are those that elect the government that has the greatest impact in voters' lives. Usually this means national elections, while second-order elections are usually regional or local. In England, the first-order general elections dominate the democratic process to an extent that is unusual among developed democracies. In many systems, local, provincial and regional governments do much more than in England (although not now in the rest of the UK) and therefore they have a much higher status. This is true of most of the larger EU states, not to mention such countries as the United States and Australia. Turnout for these elections is closer to turnout levels for national elections, and the quality of the candidates running for office is often high. Usually they remain second-order elections, although in some highly decentralised systems such as the Swiss, regional elections can be first order, because the cantons (Swiss regional governments) have so many responsibilities.

Local government in England is unambiguously second order in status, with turnout in local elections often falling below 30 per cent. The same is true for elections to the European Parliament, where the British turnout is the lowest among all the EU states (Chapter 8). Perhaps this reflects just how irrelevant the European Parliament is for most voters compared to elections to the House of Commons. It is interesting, however, that when a sub-national government *is* seen as having important powers turnout shoots up. Just such a pattern has emerged with the Northern Irish Assembly and the Scottish Parliament – although much less so with the Welsh Assembly.

It follows, then, that further devolution to the English regions or to metropolitan areas could reinvigorate democracy in Britain. But as we saw in Chapter 10, Labour governments have been very slow to widen and deepen the devolution process. Perhaps this is unsurprising given that to do so would be to weaken central government power. Contrariwise, further devolution may help arrest the decline in interest in politics and the growing disillusionment with the system implied by the precipitous decline in turnout seen in the 2001 election.

Public interest in politics may also be given a boost should the European Parliament (or some other, new elected EU body) be given real powers and therefore have a discernible impact on people's day-to-day lives. However, there is little sign that the EU political process will be fundamentally reformed in the next few years.

Policy voting in referendums

It is clear that the 'big issues' such as the general left–right direction of the economy, public service priorities and foreign policy dominate political debate in Britain. Voting choices between the parties focus on these, since elections are at best a blunt instrument for exerting popular control. Popular decisions cannot

Referendum A vote in which only one issue or a small number of issues are put to the electorate, as against a general election in which the electorate chooses between parties on a broad range of political issues.

be fine-tuned in general elections, which take place only at four- or five-year intervals. They can only determine the overall direction of policy – the general priorities for governments to pursue – rather than how exactly they will be pursued. They also leave out all the other issues that do not fit on the left–right continuum – administrative reform, official secrecy, sleaze and corruption, environmental priorities, territorial management – many of which are important in their own right and have been the subject of preceding chapters.

In principle such issues could be decided separately by voting in popular 'initiatives' or referendums. Many European countries do have referendums on constitutional matters and the practice is spreading in Britain (for example, the Welsh and Scottish referendums on devolution in 1997, that on London government in 1998 and the promised all-British referendum on European Monetary Union).

Referendums, however, are called by governments at a time of their own choosing. Either the government senses it has an advantage and the vote will go the way it wants, or the parties are themselves internally divided and pass the hot potato on to the electorate so that they can avoid the decision themselves (as with the European Community referendum of 1975). Neither circumstance provides ideal conditions for unfettered popular choice.

In practice very few countries permit electors to have a vote on policy whenever a sizeable group of them wants one (a procedure known technically as a popular initiative, as opposed to a referendum, which is called by a government). This procedure is followed in about half the states of the USA, but not at federal level. In Europe it occurs in Italy and at a variety of levels – local, regional and federal – in Switzerland. The fact that Britain does not have popular initiatives does not make it notably less democratic than most other European countries.

Increased use of referendums from 1975 onwards does enhance the scope of popular control, but not very much, given the vast range of issues decided without reference to any kind of electoral process or popular vote. For evidence of popular influence over these we must look to other mechanisms, notably pressure group activity.

PRESSURE GROUP REPRESENTATION

As was pointed out in Chapter 11, there are tens of thousands of groups in Britain representing practically every activity and interest imaginable. On issues that affect them the relevant groups will become active, trying to influence the government through a variety of strategies. The theory of 'pluralist democracy' emphasises the extent to which every political decision will find an advocate or defender among groups and organisations, often not primarily political ones but with interests and members affected in this particular case.

Any specific issue decision will thus tend to be a compromise, attempting to reconcile the positions of the opposition groups. For example, on the right to open access to the countryside, the Ramblers' Association, which supports access, will confront the Country Landowners' Association and the National Farmers' Union, which oppose it. The final decision has been to allow restricted access with safeguards for crops, animals and game, giving all sides something of what they want but less than they would have preferred.

Pressure groups may thus focus popular preferences on detailed issues more precisely than political parties can. On many issues the majority of people may not be particularly involved and it is a question of two minorities confronting each other. Of course, one minority may be very much bigger than another. If the final decision favours the larger groups somewhat more, this would be in accordance with the democratic principle that the larger number should have more weight. In such cases, pressure group activity could supplement and complement the central democratic device of elections in a way that is perfectly compatible with their pre-eminence on the issues that do fall within their purview.

There are problems, however, with the idea that group representation can supplement party representation. These have already been spelled out in Chapter 12. Basically they relate to the fact that smaller groups often have more resources and influence than larger ones. Not only can they block proposals (even ones supported by a full popular majority) but they can also work to get their own privileges and monopolies covertly extended without the majority knowing. For example, the tobacco industry has been able to undermine administrative action to restrict smoking, and prevent legislation being proposed, by making large donations to political parties.

This may now be coming to light through the efforts of the Committee on Standards in Public Life. New legislation may force the parties to disclose the amount of donations and the identity of donors. However, this will not abolish the disparity of resources between the tobacco companies and their opponents. The former will still be able to influence decisions disproportionately by advertising, wining and dining supporters, employing consultants or threatening job losses. This often frustrates activists on the other side and causes demonstrations and street protests.

Disparities are even more pronounced where some pressure groups have privileged access to bureaucrats and politicians. It is an old tradition of British government to give some groups 'insider' status so that they are consulted before any action in their sphere is even formulated and are then allowed to intervene at every stage in the subsequent process. Traditional examples of insider groups have been the farmers' unions, hospital consultants, financiers and barristers; outsiders have been trade unions (except for brief periods), some manufacturers, environmentalists, consumers, and the larger and more popular groups.

Insider groups have been even more fortunate where they have had an institutional sponsor within the structure of government, as defence contractors have with the Ministry of Defence or the City of London with the Treasury and Bank of England. In both cases, government departments and agencies are almost obliged to defer to the organised interests because they can claim to operate in the national interest. In the case of defence, using foreign contractors could

Plate 28.2 *Changing the face of British democracy? Demonstrators take on Churchill*

jeopardise national security. With City interests, inflation and excessive government borrowing can damage not just the City, but the whole economy. The same argument is used by farmers who argued that only (subsidised) home-grown food can guarantee supply during wartime or an international emergency. In recent years, however, this argument has worn thin as the probability of a full-scale war has receded to almost zero. Farmers still receive subsidies, however, through the EU Common Agricultural Policy.

The important point here is that many groups do not *need* to organise and lobby the government because they are structurally advantaged. Big business and financial interests in particular dispose of such large resources, that any policy that threatens them can bring with it the prospect of job losses and disruption. Group representation thus seems more likely to magnify the imbalances of the electoral process in Britain rather than to compensate for them. Popular interests are able to make their voice heard and agitate on behalf of consumers, workers and environmentalists. Too often, however, their pleas take second place to those of wealthy entrenched interests that can operate both covertly and overtly through threats of economic disruption to advance their interests. Can scrutiny help? At least if it does not cancel out imbalances it can reveal what the richer pressure groups are up to under the cloak of official secrecy.

SCRUTINY AND RIGHTS

We associate scrutiny with defence of individual and group rights, because until decisions and their consequences are known rights can hardly be asserted against them. The defence of rights often involves publicity to get general support, lawsuits to have injustices overturned, media campaigns to alert Parliament and other bodies to a wrong. All these involve some scrutiny of public decisions by organisations or individuals, which is what we concentrate on here.

We need to make two preliminary points. As pointed out earlier, the defence of rights is a defining characteristic of the liberal side of liberal democracy. But it is also closely related to the democratic element as well, since one cannot have full debate or make informed popular decisions without maintaining procedural rights or knowing what is going on. The two sides of liberal democracy are thus mutually supportive, particularly on the matter of penetrating the cloak of official secrecy under which unjust and arbitrary decisions are often made.

It might well be asked, however, why the normal practices of Parliamentary democracy do not suffice for adequate scrutiny of decisions? This is the position taken by traditionalist MPs on both the Labour and Conservative sides, who claim that the winning party is elected to govern and should be allowed to get on with its mandate. The opposition should be left free to expose weaknesses in the government position or shortfalls in administration. If it does the job well, and the government makes too many mistakes, the opposition party will get public opinion on its side and win the next election, taking corrective action as the new government.

28.3 Scrutiny and the defence of rights: a case study

A recent case reveals just how much protection and scrutiny is needed against unjust administrative decisions. In 1985 most of the state-owned National Bus Company was sold off to private interests. It had run a pension scheme for its employees to which, as usual in an occupational scheme, both the employer and employees contributed. In 1985 this scheme had a surplus, over and above current obligations to members, of £114 million. Such a surplus seemed on the face of it to belong to the fund to distribute among members, particularly as they would be hit economically by the privatisation. Instead, it was appropriated by the company and ultimately went to the government's Department of Transport (DOT) as part of the profits of privatisation.

Attempts by a retired busman to query this decision were brushed off with threats of financial penalties for creating a nuisance, first by the DOT, then by the Public Accounts Committee of the Commons, and by the first pensions ombudsman. It was only the support of two investigative journalists that kept the matter going, until the second pensions ombudsman did take it on in 1994. In late 1997 the DOT were still resisting restitution of the money, and even investigation of the case. To keep the original complainants from suing the Department directly they had got the government official solicitor to instigate a lawsuit against the Department, using the Department's own lawyers! By this tactic they could keep the case going at least until the civil servants involved in the original appropriation of the surplus retired and most pensioners were dead or incapacitated. In 1999 the Department was finally ordered to distribute the surplus by the government – 14 years after it was expropriated. How quickly successor departments have complied remains unclear.

Unfortunately, what happened to the National Bus Company pension fund has been standard practice in the privatised utilities, where management has appropriated pension scheme surpluses wherever they could.

According to this view, the adversarial relationship of government and opposition guarantees effective scrutiny. To work, it demands that everyone be lined up in support of their own side. Any attempt to upstage this central confrontation by select committees, judicial review or media campaigns is at best irrelevant and at worst blunts the crucial central confrontation.

We have already exposed the shallowness of this point of view (Chapter 17). It is shown up even more by what has been said about the narrow, if highly important, range of issues on which party competition focuses. We can rely on party confrontations in the House of Commons to throw up differences on economic management, on the internal market in health, on welfare and work, and on Europe. When it comes to official secrecy, Civil Service incompetence and mismanagement, illicit payments to parties, and a range of other matters affecting individual and group rights, neither of the main parties is likely to institute major changes because they are both involved in the same abuses. Even if they are not, they are almost totally dependent on advice from civil servants, who are also involved. Leaving matters to ritual partisan debates in the Commons is a recipe for ignoring them altogether, which of course is just what many civil servants and party spin doctors want.

SCOPE OF SCRUTINY

We have looked at various forms of scrutiny in the preceding chapters, notably by the courts (including the European Court, Chapter 19), Parliamentary select committees (Chapter 18), and investigative journalism (Chapter 14). Encouragingly for the defence of rights, all these are on the increase.

Judicial review

The incorporation into British law of the European Convention on Human Rights in 1999 has extended the courts' powers of scrutiny and ability to reverse administrative decisions. Even before this important step was taken the courts were extending their own jurisdiction, taking their cue from the European Court of Justice and its very wide interpretation of its own powers.

Besides their explicit scrutiny of appeals against government administration, courts are often called on to make political decisions under the guise of legal judgments (Chapter 19). The problem here is that such decisions, based in the absence of other guidance on their own experience and prejudices, are very much affected by the closed and privileged background of the judiciary. Although the courts are necessary and powerful defenders of rights they often interpret them in a restrictive or even eccentric way.

There are two obvious remedies for this. One is to make the ruling norms, including constitutional ones, more explicit by writing them down, so judges are not forced to make decisions beyond their own competence. The other is to reform both the legal profession and the selection of judges so as to make them more open, accessible and representative of the general population.

Unfortunately, attempts to do both these things have been defeated. Lord Mckay, the Conservative Lord Chancellor at the end of the 1980s, tried to break down barriers between barristers and solicitors, and to get the latter appointed as judges. The barristers defeated him. Lord Irvine, the current Labour Lord Chancellor, backed off from making the appointment of judges less personal by putting it through a nomination committee.

Both Lord Chancellors have responded to calls for government economy by cutting legal aid, which enabled the poor and less well off to initiate and fight cases against employers and government. Both the law and legal profession are thus more accessible to the rich and powerful than the poor and downtrodden, although the latter need their help more. Overall, therefore, trends in judicial scrutiny have been mixed, giving it more scope in which to operate but restricting it to safe hands (elderly, conservative judges) and to insiders rather than outsiders.

Parliamentary select committees

It was one of the big surprises of the Thatcher period that a thoroughgoing reform and extension of the system of scrutiny was carried out in 1979, perhaps without proper appreciation of what the consequences might be. The predominant

Conservative philosophy of the period 1979–97 was certainly that 'government knows best' and that any scrutiny is best carried out through ritual confrontations in Parliament.

Despite this the select committees have functioned reasonably well and extended their scope. The corresponding committees of the House of Lords have also been very active, less prone to party interference than those of the Commons, and staffed by authoritative and able figures in the shape of the life peers who carry on the work.

The majority party for fear of embarrassing their leadership has watered down some reports of select committees. Such compromises are probably inevitable in politics, since one must always reckon with the pervasive presence of parties. The whips have also manipulated membership and the appointment of chairs. Enough searching investigative work has been done, however, even when embarrassing to the parties and government, to validate the work of select committees and to identify them as one of the most genuine and worthwhile constitutional innovations of the post-war period.

The trouble with select committees, Commons as well as Lords, is not with what they have been able to do but with what is not within their powers to do, that is, to have their criticisms and reports attended to. In the absence of any clearly defined constitutional role there is no obligation on the government as a whole, or on any individual minister, department or agency, to carry through their recommendations or even to respond to them. Indeed, as we have noted, the usual reaction of ministries to a critical report is to delay replying for two or three years in the justified hope that an election will intervene or the committee will be reformed, and the matter lost sight of.

Only by raising a political scandal through leakages to the press can a committee hope to get some response. Even then reactions are as likely to take the form of brazening the matter out as of redressing it. Again it appears that a remedy is to be sought in constitutional clarification. Until they are given coercive powers over civil servants the committees are likely to remain talking shops, unable to effect their recommendations no matter how many abuses they uncover.

Investigative journalism

We noted that, in spite of the growing concentration of ownership of the media, market forces have encouraged a tendency to muck raking and scandal mongering, which at the upper end has shaded over into investigative journalism. This mode of reporting has expanded steadily over the last three decades. Much of this book, in fact, could not have been written without it, as it would either have had to rely on what governments were willing to disclose (very little, and possibly untrue), or have been quite unable to sort out reality from legal fiction.

Investigative journalism has made British political life more transparent, and politicians more accountable, in the later post-war period than before. It is, however, a fragile plant. Severe libel laws, which put the onus of proof on the reporter and paper rather than the defendant, mean that the rich and powerful can always use legal threats to manipulate what is said about them. (Although their attempts can sometimes go seriously awry as the examples of Jonathan Aitken and Jeffrey

Archer, both of whom were imprisoned for perjury, show.) Official secrecy can be used to censor what is said and to smother investigations, even to justify the confiscation of embarrassing material just before transmission. Media proprietors can be induced to call the hounds off in return for favours or honours.

Again what is needed is the consolidation of rights to investigation, optimally as a constitutional right. Reforming the law of libel so as to allow a public interest defence for journalists – or even reversing the onus of proof in political cases, so that it is for the defendants to show that they are not doing what is alleged – would also free investigative journalism to be much more far reaching than it is at the moment. Doing the same with the Official Secrets Act (in its latest incarnation inappropriately termed the Freedom of Information Act) would be the greatest liberation of all. Forcing government, which is supposed to act on our behalf, to reveal whether it is actually doing so and how, would seem an obvious step along the road to the full, informed debate and discussion to which it must surely be subject in a democracy. Secrecy should be the exception, and should need to be justified, rather than being the rule, as it is now in British government.

Major obstacle to scrutiny: official secrecy

The blanket secrecy and obsessive defensiveness of administration and government in Britain are clearly the main obstacles to any kind of informed scrutiny. They are tempting for governments to maintain, as they act as defences against any kind of searching critique of what they are doing. New Labour seems to have modified its projected reforms on finding how useful secrecy can be in this regard.

Yet to a considerable extent this judgement may be mistaken. All sorts of conflicting political and social tendencies have combined to make secrecy into a weakness of governments rather than a defence. Leaks combined with investigative journalism tend, in the absence of balancing information, to turn small infractions of rules into major and destabilising scandals. Not knowing what their ramifications may be, owing to secrecy and attempted news management, much more may be suspected than what is actually there.

Secrecy centres on the security services and the ramifying arms industry, even though it spreads out to encompass vast administrative areas that have very little to do with either. The security services, indeed, often seem to form a state within a state, directed by a small Cabinet clique (if they are under control at all). The idea that two directors of MI6 might have been Soviet agents; that miners in 1984–5 were secretly harassed and spied on; that a campaign was carried out in the 1970s by the security services against the Prime Minister and the Labour government; that left-wing student leaders are routinely put under surveillance: all these surmises are surely more destabilising to British democracy than if they were openly discussed and checked. If found to be true, precautions could be taken against their recurrence. While official secrecy hides the truth no effective action can be taken to prevent a recurrence. In this, as in most other aspects, official secrecy is self-defeating. It is certainly inimical to British democracy.

The 2003 Hutton Inquiry into the death of the government arms expert Dr David Kelly, demonstrated many of the limitations of the existing system of accountability. Government officials, political advisers and political leaders were able to close ranks in such a way that protected the 'state' interest at the expense of those individuals and interests (including the BBC) that had publicised the claim that the government was exaggerating Iraq's potential to use weapons of mass destruction. Even so, the Hutton Inquiry represented an advance of sorts, if only because it involved direct testimony by all those involved in the affair, including security chiefs and the Prime Minister.

WRITING DOWN THE CONSTITUTION

Secrecy is a relic of the time when foreign policy was the major concern of British government and Britain was the major player abroad. It was also a time when government was the King's Government, and not responsible or accountable to Parliament except for taxation. Security is still part of the royal prerogative (exercised now by the Cabinet) and its managers are not accountable to anyone.

This is illogical and absurd in a modern democracy. Given the millions who died in the world wars, electors have as much right to know what is being done in their name in foreign policy as in welfare, the economy and other domestic matters.

There are those who laud the ambiguity and imprecision of the British constitution as a unique advantage, giving it a flexibility and adaptability that written constitutions do not have. As we have shown, however, its flexibility and adaptability are used mainly to get governments off the hook and to evade full scrutiny and democratic control.

Clearly, to extend democracy in Britain and to improve its functioning, the constitution needs to be codified and written down, so that everyone knows where he or she stands. Then and only then will it be possible to confront the other issues raised in this chapter: lack of clear guidelines for judicial action, absence of teeth for select committees, legal barriers to investigative journalism, reversal of official secrecy. A written constitution would also be able to tackle the issues of electoral representation and popular control, as well as relationships with European, regional and local governments.

Codification of the constitution
Producing a written constitution that makes it clearer, and more precise, explicit and systematic.

Writing down the British constitution would not be an enormous task, since it has already been done 40 or 50 times! Every time a British colony gained independence a constitution heavily modelled on (sometimes an exact copy of) the British was written for it. To find some of the main elements of the 'Westminster Model', with all its conventions and understandings, all one need do is read the Barbadian or Indian constitution and there it is.

Of course, such documents can be modified to serve the contemporary needs of Britain. Apart from anything else, ex-colonial constitutions contain many of the undesirable practices taken over from Britain, which we have listed earlier. However, these other documents give clear testimony of the practicability of writing down the British constitution. The only thing that prevents it in the British case is not practicability and workability but political will. It is easy and tempting for governments and bureaucracy to manipulate the unwritten constitution so as to make life easier for them. But making life easy for governments and civil servants should not be the prime concern for a self-respecting liberal democracy.

EVALUATING CURRENT DEVELOPMENTS

To some extent New Labour developed a 'constitutional project'. It wrote the European Convention on Human Rights into British law. It abolished the hereditary element in the House of Lords. It carried through its promise to give devolution to Scotland and Wales and a new local government to London. New electoral systems have been developed for each of these areas, while genuine proportional representation is now used for European elections in Britain and in Northern Ireland. All these developments may indicate a more open mind towards the central question (from a democratic point of view) of electoral reform.

However, it is difficult to see Labour agreeing, certainly in the near future, to a fully proportional electoral system for the British Parliament. The most one would expect would be an additional member system as for the Scottish Parliament, where a certain number of MPs are elected by PR additional to a majority who sit for constituencies. The final result is not exactly proportional but it would give Liberal Democrats more seats, while retaining the Labour lead over Conservatives in the constituencies.

If the Liberal Democrats win additional seats in forthcoming elections they could be attractive coalition partners for Labour. Government would finally be based on a popular majority to which it would be responsive on the central issues. This would enhance democratic control over the central policy process. Having two coalition partners privy to the secrets of government would also enhance scrutiny, as one party would keep an eye on the other and make sure that any administrative excesses were leaked.

Scrutiny should be helped in general by having more parliaments and assemblies. The debate inspired by the London Mayor Ken Livingstone into the private/public funding of the London Underground resulted in much closer scrutiny of the issue than would have been the case a few years earlier, even if he did lose the argument. Local and regional assemblies and parliaments might also help bring proliferating nominated quangos under control. They may also help to extend freedom of information in some areas, as has happened in Scotland where under pressure from the Liberal Democrats, the Parliament has eased official secrecy and in Wales where executive minutes are published on the World Wide Web!

However, New Labour has left the central processes of UK government, official secrecy and all, largely unreformed and unchecked. Parliament is still dominated on all matters by the leadership of the majority party. The security services have been given enhanced powers for the 'war on terrorism'. Unelected quangos have increased in number and been given new responsibilities. The elective dictatorship continues. In short, very little difference has been made to the Core Executive's place in the British constitution. Neither has the constitution been written down and codified.

New Labour's reforms, therefore, have advanced the country a little in democratic and liberal terms, but have not taken us very far. When all governments profit so much in the short term from existing arrangements, it is perhaps unrealistic to think they will ever reform them radically of their own free will.

ESSAYS

1. How can liberal democracy be reconciled with the existence of an 'elective dictatorship' in Britain?

2. Why has no recent British government won more than 50 per cent of the votes in general elections? What reforms might correct this situation?

3. Is Scotland now more democratic than England? Answer with respect to the functioning of the Scottish and the Westminster Parliaments.

4. Why do the security services have so much power in Britain? What reforms of the security services would you propose and why?

SUMMARY

This chapter has taken up the question raised at the beginning of this book: how healthy and extensive is British democracy? It has concluded that:

■ Britain is a liberal democracy.

■ The democratic element involves popular control.

■ The liberal element involves safeguards that are secured through scrutiny of the administration and other powerful bodies in Britain.

■ No post-war government, however, has been voted in by a popular majority even though the 'elective dictatorship' continues.

■ Some moves towards increased representation at the regional level involving Scotland, Wales and London have been taken, but moves towards further devolution have been halting.

■ Pressure groups can compensate for some of the defects of party representation but their role is limited because business and financial groups enjoy special influence over government policy.

■ Scrutiny by courts, select committees and investigative journalism is hampered by the lack of an adequate written constitution.

■ The constitution has been codified and spelled out many times in the form of ex-colonial constitutions. It would help British democracy if this could also be done in Britain.

■ New Labour's constitutional projects have usefully filled in gaps in the protection of rights and arrangements for scrutiny. But these changes are unlikely to raise the quality of British democracy substantially so long as the sometimes arbitrary powers of the government and central executive are left untouched.

MILESTONES

Milestones in British democracy, 1979–2003

	Scrutiny		Popular control
1979–97	– 'Stretching' of constitutional conventions to increase government power and ability to act, often secretly, without consultation		
1979	+ Parliamentary select committees reformed		
1979 onwards	+ Investigative journalism extends in depth and range, helped by increasing leaks from within the Civil Service and Cabinet	1979	+ Directly elected European Parliament
		1979–2003	– Nominated quangos and 'task forces' extend powers across a range of policy areas, often at expense of elected local government

	Scrutiny		Popular control
1984–5	– Ad hoc national police force created to break miners' strike. Illicit surveillance and harassment by security services	1980s	+ Local councils become increasingly politicised and discuss and criticise government policy
1989	– Official Secrets Act actually consolidates and strengthens official secrecy, with some minor liberalisation in unimportant areas		
1991	+ Consumers' and Citizen's Charters force publication of performance criteria by government departments and monopolies, thus giving a limited basis for redress of consumer rights		
1990s	+ Courts extend their powers of judicial review of administrative decisions		
1990s	– Security services' role expanded domestically by both Conservative and Labour governments		
1995–2002	+ Committees of investigation of corrupt links between political parties and business (Scott, Nolan etc)	1997	+ General election victory of Labour in part a reaction against arrogance and corruption of Conservative governments
		1997–2003	– Retention of existing quangos and creation of influential secret 'task forces' by Labour
1999	+ Incorporation of European Convention on Human Rights safeguards rights more and extends power of judicial scrutiny	1997–2003	+ Reintroduction of referendums on important constitutional issues
1998–2000	+ Abolition of the hereditary element in House of Lords	1998–?	– Only limited elected element proposed to replace hereditary and appointed peers
1997–2000	– Weakening of legislation to reform official secrecy	1998–9	+ Establishment of Welsh and Scottish Assemblies and all-London elected executive
			+ Local referenda to decide on design of local government including elected mayors
2000	– Executive system imposed on local government with secret 'Cabinet' meetings		
2003	+ Hutton Inquiry into the death of arms expert Dr David Kelly requires direct testimony by all those involved, including the Prime Minister		

Note: Positive developments for democracy are marked with +, negative ones with –. It can be seen from the chart that developments are mixed and degrade as well as enhance the quality of democracy.

PROJECTS

1. Prepare an audit of the constitutional reforms undertaken by Labour since 1997. Assess how these reforms have affected you and your friends and family personally, if at all.

2. Prepare an audit of the relative advantages and disadvantages of plurality versus proportional voting systems. Answer by comparing Britain with at least *two* other European countries.

FURTHER READING

R. Brazier, *Constitutional Reform* (Oxford: Clarendon Press, 1991) presents an account of the British constitution as it is and as it might be, while Stuart Weir and David Beetham assess democratic control in *Political Power and Democratic Control in Britain* (London: Routledge, 1999). On the new European order and the strategic choices it faces, see I. Budge et al, *The Politics of the New Europe* (Harlow: Addison Wesley Longman, 1997), Parts I and V. H. MacRae, *The World in 2020* (London: HarperCollins, 1995) presents an optimistic account of the future but Paul Kennedy, *Preparing for the Twenty-first Century* (London: Fontana, 1994) is more gloomy. On democracy in Britain see the special issue of *Political Quarterly* (1999). On New Labour's record on democracy, see Stuart Weir et al, *Democracy Under Blair: A Democratic Audit of the United Kingdom* (London: Politicos, 2002).

USEFUL WEB SITES ON NEW POLITICS, NEW DEMOCRACY

Hotlinks to these sites can be found on the CWS website at http://www.booksites.net/budge.

British democracy and politics are undoubtedly changing at a pace hardly ever seen before. A wide variety of issues that were regarded as secondary in the past have come to occupy the very centre of the political scene. Students of politics in Britain and around the world have the privileged opportunity to have access through the internet to the ideological debates, the decision-making processes and the legislative bodies where these changes occur. One of the leading arguments for changes in the UK system relates to the possibility of a widening of political participation. Most of the decisions taken in this respect are available from www.number-10.gov.uk. However, the government is not the only institution putting forward strategies for change; every political party has its own way of conceiving a 'wider democracy'. A full list of the main political parties in Britain is available from www.bubl.ac.uk/uk/parties.htm.

The main advocate of constitutional reform in the UK is Charter88, whose web site is available at www.charter88.org.uk. The Lord Chancellor's Department site (www.lcd.gov.uk) covers constitutional issues in England. The question of devolution is one of the epicentres of the debate on widening democracy; a recommendable starting point is the government's site at www.cabinet-office.gov.uk/constitution/devolution/devolution.htm.

Current issues and debates in British politics are the main concern of www.ukpolitics.org.uk and www.britpolitics.com. For the most relevant academic centres devoted to the analysis of politics in the UK, see the useful web sites section in Chapter 1 of this book. Finally, the role of the media in democratic change and the main web sites on this respect are analysed in Chapter 14.

Glossary

Accountability
To have to answer for one's conduct, or to be subject to review or evaluation by a higher body. The doctrine of ministerial accountability, for example, holds that government ministers are answerable to Parliament for their actions.

Administration
Either (1) the process of co-ordinating and implementing public policy through the machinery of public administration; or (2) another word for government – as in 'the Blair administration'.

Affirmative action
Policies designed to provide groups with redress for a past pattern of discrimination. Such policies often take the form of legal requirements that organisations, such as universities, businesses or state bureaucracies, should take positive steps to increase their numbers of minority groups that have suffered discrimination in the past. Known as affirmative action, or reverse discrimination in the USA, the term 'positive discrimination' is often used in the UK.

Agenda-setting theory
Argues that the media cannot determine what people think, but can have a strong influence over what people think about. By focusing on some issues but not others the media can highlight the importance of some issues in the public mind.

Balance of payments
(balance of trade)
A method of analysing the record of economic relations between a given country and the rest of the world, the balance of payments measures the surplus or deficit of exports over imports over a period of time. In practice, measuring the balance of payments is a complicated matter, but it is useful as a shorthand indicator of whether a country is 'paying its way' or spending more than it earns abroad.

Barristers and solicitors
Barristers are lawyers, mostly concentrated in London, who specialise in advocacy in court. They have more prestige than solicitors, who do the bulk of the legal work in preparation for court judgments but whose access to appear in the courts is restricted.

Beveridge Report
Resulted in the Welfare State, in which the government ensures the basic social and economic necessities of its citizens by financing and providing goods and services such as education, health care, housing and social security.

Bill of Rights
A formal statement of the rights and privileges that may be actually or theoretically claimed by citizens. Unlike a modern Bill of Rights, however, the one passed by Parliament in 1689 was more concerned to restrict the royal prerogative and assert the powers of Parliament. Britain's modern Bill of Rights dates not from 1689 but from the Human Rights Act of 1998.

Broadsheets
Serious national daily and Sunday papers, so called because of their size. Daily broadsheets are *The Times*, the *Daily Telegraph*, the *Guardian*, the *Independent*, and the *Financial Times*.

Cabinet	The committee of the leading members of the government who are empowered to make decisions on behalf of the government. The Cabinet is mainly, but not entirely, formed by heads of important departments of state and others who perform important functions of state.
Cabinet collegiality	The feeling among Cabinet members that they must act closely and co-operatively together, even when they conflict over policy issues and departmental interests.
Cabinet government	The theory that the Cabinet, not the Prime Minister, forms a collective political executive that, therefore, constrains the power of the Prime Minister. In Cabinet government the principle of collective responsibility ensures that the Cabinet either makes or is consulted about all important political decisions.
Cadre parties	Parties of like-minded and wealthy 'notables' who used their own money to fight political campaigns and relied upon their own personal supporters. Good examples are the Conservative and Liberal parties in Britain between about 1830 and the Reform Act of 1867.
Cartel	An arrangement between economic interests to limit competition by controlling their market in some way.
Cause groups (promotional groups)	Promote a general cause or idea. Unlike interest groups their members are not drawn from particular occupations but may come from a wide variety of social backgrounds.
Celtic fringe	Coined around 1900 to describe the northern and western peripheries of the British Isles (Scotland, Wales and Ireland) that voted Liberal, Labour or Nationalist rather than Conservative. The term is now used to refer to the Celtic periphery of the UK (Scotland, Ireland and Wales) whatever their voting patterns.
Civil liberties	The freedoms that should not normally be constrained by others, whether private individuals or the State. Civil liberties are often used as an argument against the extension of state power into areas of life regarded as private – for example, the enforced use of seat belts in cars or crash helmets for motorbike riders. Civil libertarians are those who use these arguments, or who are particularly conscious of the importance of civil liberties.
Civil servant	A servant of the Crown (ie the government) who is employed in a civilian capacity (not a member of the armed forces) and who is paid wholly and directly from central government funds (not local government, nationalised industries or quangos).
Civil Service anonymity	Civil servants are the confidential advisers of ministers and must not be asked questions about politically controversial matters or the policy advice they give.
Civil Service impartiality	The principle that civil servants should be politically neutral and serve their Cabinet ministers regardless of which party is in power and of what they may personally feel about their ministers' policies.
Civil society	The aspects of social and economic life (primarily voluntary associations and private organisations) that are outside the immediate control of the State. A strong civil society based on a large number and wide variety of private associations and organisations is thought to be the basis for democracy.

Class	Among the many and varied definitions of class, the most useful ranks the social and economic status of people according to their occupation, most notably into manual (working class) and non-manual (middle and upper class) groups, and then into subgroups or strata of these categories.
Coalition government	Where two or more parties combine to form the government, in contrast to single party government where all the offices of government are held by members of the same party. Britain has had single-party government for most (but not all) of the twentieth century.
Codification of the constitution	Producing a written constitution that makes it clearer, and more precise, explicit and systematic.
Cold War	The state of international relations between the West and the communist bloc that stopped short of outright war, but involved intense hostility and the stockpiling of arms and maintenance of large armies in case war should break out. The Cold War started in a serious manner in 1947, at the time of the Berlin blockade and airlift, but gradually died away in the 1970s as a result of international agreements and arms limitations.
Collective responsibility	The principle that decisions and policies of the Cabinet are binding on all members of the government, who must support them in public, to maintain a united front, or resign their government post.
Committee of Inquiry	A committee appointed by the government, but mainly composed of members outside Parliament, and charged with the job of inquiring into and reporting on a particular matter. Recent examples are the Nolan Committee on Standards in Public Life, the Scott Committee into 'arms to Iraq', and the (Lord Roy) Jenkins Committee on electoral systems.
Common law	Law that is overtly made by judges and which has become part of custom and precedent.
Community charge or **poll tax**	The local tax that replaced the rates (or property tax) in which every adult resident of a local authority paid the same amount. It came into operation in 1990 and was replaced by the council tax in 1993.
Community law	The treaties, legislation, and case law of the European Court of Justice, which are the legal basis of the European Union.
Constitution	A set of fundamental laws that determine what the central institutions and offices of the state are to be, their powers and duties, and how they relate to one another and to their citizens. Most constitutions are written and codified in a single document, but in Britain it is partly written but uncodified. Constitutional documents set the limits and powers of government and often state the rights and freedoms of citizens.
Constitutional convention	Unwritten understandings based on custom and practice that are held to be binding and are commonly observed even though they are not enforced by law or sanctions. An example in the British constitution is that of the Crown assenting to bills passed by Parliament.

Constitutional review The process by which laws and other acts of the legislature can be overruled by a court if the court holds them to conflict with constitutional rules, human rights, or other laws treated as superior to legislation. Prior to joining the European Economic Community no British court had this power.

Constructionism The practice by which the courts define and interpret the meaning of Acts of Parliament, especially where they are vague or general.

Content regulation Regulation of the content of the media by public bodies. Regulation of political content applies mainly to the electronic media (because of spectrum scarcity), and requires that news and current affairs programmes are accurate, balanced and impartial, but it also applies to the print media so far as pornography, violence and public decency are concerned.

Core Executive The network of institutions, people and practices that collect at the apex of power around the Prime Minister and the Cabinet, including the most powerful civil servants of Whitehall, the Cabinet Office, and the Prime Minister's Office. The core executive integrates policy in an otherwise rather fragmented decision-making structure.

Core party support The minimum voting support it is estimated a party can gain in a given election. The idea behind the concept is that core supporters are the diehard voters for a party in a given election.

Corporatism A system of policy making in which major economic interests work closely together within formal structures of government to formulate and implement public policies. Corporatism requires a formal government apparatus capable of concerting the main economic groups so that they can jointly formulate and implement binding policies. In this sense, Britain has never been a corporatist state, but had in the 1960s and 1970s a looser form of tripartite system.

Council tax The local tax that replaced the community charge in 1993, in which, like the rates, payment is related to property values and levied on all occupants of property. Business rates are set by central government and levied on non-domestic property.

Crossbench (non-aligned) groups Pressure groups that are not aligned with a party and try to maintain party political neutrality (such as crossbench groups in Parliament).

Cross-media ownership When the same person or company has financial interests in different forms of mass media – radio, TV and newspapers.

Cross-pressures Cross-pressures occur where political forces or influences push in different directions – for example, where someone with Labour sympathies reads a Conservative paper. Cross-pressures are likely to encourage moderate, centre-of the-road political attitudes and behaviour, or political inactivity in response to the difficulties they cause.

Decolonisation Colonies are foreign territories dominated by stronger states by means of military and economic power. Decolonisation, therefore, is the process of withdrawing from colonial relations with foreign countries so that they gain the autonomy of a sovereign state. In the case of the British Empire, colonial countries often became members of the Commonwealth.

Democratic deficit	A phrase usually applied to the EU to describe a lack of democratic accountability in its decision making. It is usually argued that the European Parliament is too weak in relation to the Commission, and especially the Council of Ministers.
Deregulation	The opposite of regulation, it involves the weakening or removal of state regulations in the interests of market competition. Deregulation was accompanied by privatisation in Britain in the 1980s and early 1990s.
Devolution	The delegation of specific powers by a higher level of government to a lower one. Unlike a federal system where the powers of the lower level are constitutionally guaranteed, devolved powers can always be taken back by the higher authority.
Discrimination	The practice of distinguishing (usually in order to disadvantage) between individuals or social groups on grounds or criteria (such as race, religion, gender or colour) that are not relevant to the circumstances under consideration.
Disposable income	More often known as 'take-home pay', disposable income refers to income after taxes have been paid.
Disproportionality (the opposite of proportionality)	Occurs when the seats in a representative body are not distributed in relationship to votes. Proportionality (proportional representation) occurs, therefore, when there is a closer relationship between the distribution of seats and votes. The British 'simple plurality' (first past the post) electoral system is often criticised for its disproportionality insofar as it advantages large parties and discriminates against small ones.
EC law	The treaties, legislation and case law of the European Court of Justice, which are the legal basis of the European Union.
Economic management	The process by which governments assume, to varying degrees, the task of managing the national economy by means of macro and/or micro economic policies. Government economic intervention may become so broad and pervasive that management turns into planning. Monetarism is associated with the idea that the government's role should be limited largely to management of the money supply, but Keynesian theory advocates more interventionist economic planning.
Egalitarian	Political views of policies based on a wish to achieve equality, or less inequality.
Elective dictatorship	The term used to describe the British political system as one in which, once elected, the leadership of the majority party in the House of Commons can do more or less what it wants without constitutional checks and balances, until it faces the electorate at the next general election.
Electoral volatility	Large changes in voting behaviour from one election to another.
Environmental impact assessment	A requirement of the European Union, which came into force in 1988, requiring all public and private projects above a given cost to be subject to environmental appraisal in which the advantages and disadvantages from the environmental point of view are laid out.
Environmentalism	A concern with the natural environment (including many things from the physical environment affecting 'the quality of life') and the belief that its protection should be given more importance, and economic growth less. Environmentalists

are sometimes referred to as 'ecologists' or 'conservationists'. In the 1970s and 1980s environmentalists began to form themselves into social movements and green parties.

Episodic groups   Groups that are not normally political, but become so when circumstances require. For example, football clubs are politically involved only when issues such as football ground safety or hooliganism become a political issue.

Equality of condition   The ideal objective of providing all citizens with equal access to income, wealth, education, employment, and other aspects of social life.

Equality of opportunity   The practice of ensuring that individuals compete on equal terms for goods, benefits and life chances, such as education, employment or housing, even though the outcome may be unequal. Equality of treatment does not involve treating all individuals as equals. For example, the mentally or physically handicapped should not be treated in the same way as those who are not so handicapped.

Equality of treatment   The application of the same rules and standards to all individuals and social groups.

Essex Model   A method of explaining past election results and predicting future ones based on a statistical analysis of the changing economic basis of previous election results.

Establishment   A vague term referring to the elite of public and private life that, some claim, run Britain irrespective of which party is in government. The Establishment consists of the small number of 'the great and the good' in the Civil Service, military, church, universities, political parties and business. Usually with public school and Oxford and Cambridge backgrounds, they are said to follow a consensus, middle-of-the-road and conservative approach to government and politics.

Ethnicity   A mixture or combination of different social characteristics (which may include race, culture, religion, or some other basis of common origin and social identity) that give different social groups a common consciousness, and which are thought to divide or separate them in some way from other social groups.

Euro   The name of the official common currency adopted by 11 members of the EU (Austria, Belgium, Finland, France, Germany, Ireland, Italy, Luxembourg, the Netherlands, Portugal, and Spain), with fixed conversion rates in their own currencies. Euro notes and coins were issued on 1 January 2002.

European Monetary System   The third and final stage of European financial integration, EMS provides for a single European currency (the euro), to replace existing national currencies, and a European central bank.

Europhiles   Those who are generally well disposed to the further integration of Europe within the framework of the European Union.

Europhobes   Those who are not generally well disposed to the further integration of Europe, at least within the framework of the European Union.

Exchange Rate Mechanism (ERM)   The ERM is the first stage of a European Union plan for financial integration. As part of the European Monetary System (EMS) introduced in 1979, the ERM was designed to minimise currency exchange fluctuation among members of the EU that belonged to the system. Each currency had an exchange rate against the European Currency Unit (ECU), and was supposed to fluctuate within a band either side of this exchange rate. Britain joined the ERM in October 1990, but international currency speculation against the pound drove it out again in September 1992 (Black Wednesday).

Executive

One of the three branches of government (with the legislative and judiciary). The executive is concerned with making government decisions and policies rather than with passing laws. In Britain the political executive is the Prime Minister and the Cabinet; in the EU the main executive is the Council of Ministers.

Executive agencies

Also known as 'Next Step agencies', these are the semi-autonomous agencies set up to carry out some of the administrative functions of government that were previously the responsibility of Civil Service departments.

False consciousness

The state of mind induced in the working class by the ruling class in order to conceal the real nature of capitalism.

Federal

A political structure that combines a central authority with a degree of constitutionally defined autonomy for sub-central units of government – usually territorial units of government such as states, regions or provinces. In discussions about the European Union in Britain, however, the term 'federal' is sometimes used as a code word by those critical of the idea of a 'European superstate', and sometimes as a word to describe a political structure, national or supranational, which is decentralised.

Fire brigade groups

Pressure groups formed to fight a specific issue and dissolved when it is over (eg the Anti-Poll Tax Federation).

Fiscal policy

A type of macro economic policy that uses taxation and public expenditure to manage the economy. Fiscal theories are particularly associated with the work of J. M. Keynes (*General Theory of Employment, Interest and Money*, 1936) who argued that fiscal tools should be used to promote economic development while avoiding the economic cycles of 'boom and bust'.

Framing effects
(of the media)

The argument that the media can exercise a subtle but strong effect on how public opinion thinks about politics in a general way, and how it reacts to particular events. For example, by focusing on bad news, the media can produce 'videomalaise'.

Franchise

In its political sense, the right to vote. In Britain the male franchise was extended in 1832, 1867, 1884 and 1918. The female franchise was partly introduced in 1918 and completed in 1928, by which time Britain had a universal franchise.

Free trade

The idea that international trade should not be restricted by protection in the form of tariffs, custom duties or import quotas that are designed to protect the domestic economy from foreign competition. Free trade policies are sometimes called 'laissez-faire' (allow to do) policies.

Freedom of information

Free public access to government information and records. Freedom of information is a necessary condition of open government. Under the public record acts of Britain some government records are open after 30 years.

Functional integration	A form of international integration based on pragmatic co-operation between states in specific areas of (usually) economic activity. The European Coal and Steel Community is an example. Functional integration is often contrasted with political integration that involves more ambitious blueprints for supranational government.
GATT	General Agreement on Tariffs and Trade – the series of agreements heavily promoted by the USA since the Second World War and designed to promote free trade in all products throughout the world.
Globalisation	The growing linkage of all countries of the world with each other through travel, tourism, trade and electronic communication. As anything done in one area now affects all the others, this means that countries like Britain can act less and less on their own and so creates a need for international political institutions such as the United Nations (UN) and the European Union (EU).
Glorious Revolution of 1688	Established the King's dependence on the support of Parliament and is thus a first step towards Parliamentary and constitutional government.
Government	A general term that refers either to the body which forms the political executive (as in 'the Labour government'), or the institutions which form the constitutional system (as in 'the British system of government'). In the second sense the government consists of those institutions that make the binding rules and decisions in a given territory.
Gross Domestic Product	The total value of all the goods and services bought and sold in the domestic economy.
Harmonisation	The attempt of the EU to create common product standards and specifications among its member states in the interests of a free and genuinely common market.
Hegemonic	In popular language, the term refers to an idea or practice that is widely accepted as correct, but the term originally meant a social class (the capitalists) or nation state that is so powerful that its view of the world is accepted even by those whose interests are not served by such a world view.
Human rights	Western ideas about 'rights' are traceable through the English Magna Carta, the United States Declaration of Independence and the French Declaration of the Rights of Man. The 1948 United Nations Universal Declaration of Human Rights proposed a number of fundamental rights, including those of 'life, liberty and security of the person', 'freedom of movement' and 'of thought, conscience and religion'.
Idealism	The view of politics, especially international relations, that emphasises the role of ideals and morality as a determinant of state policies, and hence the possibility of peaceful co-operation.
Ideology	A system of ideas, assumptions, values and beliefs that help us to explain the political world – what it is and why, and what it should be. Conservatism, liberalism, socialism, fascism and anarchism are main examples. Sometimes the word is used to describe a set of political ideas that are false or misleading. Marxists use the word in this way to describe the political ideas used by the ruling class to conceal the real nature of capitalism from the workers.

Imperialism	The practice of one nation controlling or dominating another state or territory, usually by military and economic means, and usually to the advantage of the imperial power. Imperialism (as in the British Empire) is often distinguished from colonialism in that it implies a greater degree of political integration of territories and their citizens, and in so far as imperialism is sometimes claimed to be a feature of advanced capitalism. The term 'imperialism' is now sometimes loosely applied to a strong international financial or cultural influence, as in 'US imperialism', which involves American films, clothes and speech.
Incomes policy	Government policy designed to secure economic growth and stability by regulating incomes and wages on the grounds that excess demand may be inflationary. Incomes policy was sometimes accompanied by a matching prices policy – hence prices and incomes policy.
Indicative planning	The practice of the state indicating targets or goals for such things as employment, inflation and output, without necessarily taking action of its own to achieve them.
Insider groups (established groups)	Pressure groups that are able to work closely with elected and appointed officials in central or local government.
Institutional racism	The collective failure of an organisation to provide an appropriate and professional service to people because of their colour, culture or ethnic origin. It can be seen or detected in processes, attitudes and behaviour which amount to discrimination through unwitting prejudice, ignorance, thoughtlessness and racist stereotyping which disadvantage minority ethnic people.
Interest groups (sectional groups)	Pressure groups that represent the interests of particular economic or occupational groups, especially business organisations, professional associations and trade unions.
Intergovernmental organisations	Allow national states to co-operate on specific matters while maintaining their national sovereignty. They contrast with supranational or federal organisations that wield some power over nation states.
International regimes	Are sets of international institutions and 'rules of the game' that are created and accepted by states in order to promote international co-operation and integration, as opposed to independent decision making and national competition. Major examples include the General Agreement on Tariffs and Trade (GATT), the Organisation for Security and Co-operation in Europe, and the Organization for Economic Co-operation and Development (OECD).
International Reserve Currency	A currency that many third world countries not directly linked with the sponsor country choose to make payments in, because it has a stable value.
Investigative journalism	In-depth and often critical journalism involving research that is usually time consuming and expensive. Examples include the *Washington Post*'s digging into the Watergate Affair in the United States of America, and the *Guardian*'s persistent inquiry into the cash for questions affair in Britain, 1995–7.
Iron law of oligarchy	The 'law' propounded by Robert Michels in 1911 whereby mass organisations cannot, by their very nature, be democratic and will always and of necessity be controlled by a small elite – the oligarchy.

Judicial review	The process whereby the courts supervise the way in which public officials and bodies carry out their duties. It includes the power to nullify actions that the courts believe to be illegal or unconstitutional.
Junior ministers	Ministers of state and parliamentary under-secretaries.
Keynesianism	Economic theory or policy derived from the writings of J. M. Keynes (1883–1946) that advocates some government economic intervention to achieve economic stability, growth and full employment. Keynesian policies were used widely in the western world, including Britain, in the 1945–80 period.
Kitchen Cabinet	The loose and informal policy advice group that Prime Ministers may collect around them, and which may include politicians, public officials and private citizens.
Knowledge gap	The result of the process whereby those with a good education and high status acquire knowledge faster than those with a poorer education and lower status.
Law	A body of rules enforced by the power of the state.
Left–right continuum	The continuum on which it is often convenient to locate parties, which stretches from the left-wing parties that believe in radical or revolutionary change, through the socialists and centre parties, to parties of the moderate right that oppose change, and to extremist parties of a Fascist or Nazi ideology. Although a simplification, the left–right continuum is often a convenient and accurate way of grouping and comparing parties.
Legislature	The law-making branch of government. In Britain it is the Queen in Parliament – the Queen, the House of Lords and the House of Commons.
Legitimation	The process of making something morally acceptable in the views of the population. A government, for example, is regarded as legitimate if it has gained power by winning a free and fair election.
Liberal democracy	The form of government practised in the West that tries to combine institutions of democratic government with liberal values about individual rights and responsibilities. Britain is democratic in the sense that it has the formal institutions of representative government such as free and regular elections, government under the law and formal political equality. It is a liberal democracy in the sense that it gives a certain independence and autonomy of government while trying to preserve the rights and freedoms of citizens.
Liberal individualism	Liberal ideology implies individualism (among other things), so in some senses adding the term individualism to liberalism is redundant. But the modern use of the term 'liberal individualism' suggests neo-liberal views that reject modern liberal ideology, which is fairly sympathetic to some forms of state intervention, and a return to classical nineteenth-century liberalism, which believes in a minimal, caretaker state.
Liberal internationalism	The view of international politics built on individualism that argues that individual rights are superior to nation state rights – for example, the idea that human rights are superior to state rights, or that the international community is entitled to impose human rights in countries whose governments do not recognise them.

Liberalism	Liberalism (with a capital 'L') refers to the beliefs and policies of the Liberal Party. In the nineteenth century Liberals were also liberals.
Liberalism	Liberalism (with a small 'l') is the political belief that individual rights should be protected by maximising freedom of choice by limiting the powers of government. It is therefore contrasted with socialism, which believes that state intervention can increase individual freedom. To confuse matters, the term 'liberal' is sometimes applied in the USA to opponents of the neo-liberal policies of the New Right.
Lobby system	The name given to specially selected correspondents of the main newspapers, TV and radio stations who are given confidential information by the government on a non-attributable basis. Not to be confused with 'the lobby', or pressure group system in Parliament. The lobby system for briefing journalists was widely criticised for giving the government too much influence over the news.
Macro economic policy	The branch of economic policy that deals with total or aggregate performance of the national economy, including monetary policy (money in circulation and interest rates), inflation, exchange rates, capital, employment and labour.
Magistrates' courts	Local courts, staffed by part-time and unpaid people (justices of the peace or JPs), that deal with minor crimes and decide which are more serious cases to be dealt with by Crown Courts.
Mandamus	The legal doctrine stating that local authorities must carry out the duties imposed on them by law. Authorities guilty of non-feasance (not doing their duty) can be issued with a writ of *mandamus*, ordering them to do their duty.
Mandarin power/ dictatorship of the official	The theory that, no matter which party forms the government, civil servants will exert a powerful influence over government, or even control the government, because of their ability, experience, expertise, training and special knowledge.
Mandarins	The comparatively small number (about 1,000) of very senior civil servants who have close and regular contact with ministers in their capacity as policy advisers.
Mandate	An instruction or command that carries legal or moral force. An electoral mandate is said to give the party winning an election the right to carry out its programme. In practice, party programmes are often so broad and vague, and people vote for them for so many different reasons, that it is difficult to claim that the winning party has a mandate for any given policy.
Market regulation	Regulation of the media market by public bodies.
Market testing	The process of deciding whether a public service should be produced at all, and, if so, whether it should be produced by the public sector, contracted out or privatised.
Mass parties	Are financed and organised with the help of a mass membership that both pays membership subscriptions and provides the human resources to conduct political campaigns.
Mass society	A society composed of isolated individuals who, because they have no deep roots in community and social life (civil society is weak), are liable to manipulation by political elites.

Micro economic policy	The branch of economic policy that deals not with the total performance of the economy but with the performance and behaviour of individual economic actors, including firms, trade unions, consumers and regional local governments.
Middle ground	A political position roughly midway between the extremes of the political spectrum. The crucial point about the middle ground is not that it is in the middle but that it is assumed to be a position occupied by the majority of voters.
Ministerial responsibility	The principle that ministers are responsible to Parliament for their own and all their department's actions. In theory, ministers are responsible for administrative failure in their department, and for any injustice it may cause, whether personally responsible or not.
Ministers	The 80 or 90 most senior government members consisting of the Prime Minister, Cabinet ministers (22–26 people), ministers of state (about 28), and parliamentary undersecretaries (about 33).
Monetarism	A revised version of neo-classical economics that, contrary to Keynesianism, argues that government should minimise its involvement in economic matters, except for controlling the money supply as a way of holding down inflation. In turn, the money supply consists mainly of the amount of cash and credit circulating in the economy. Monetarism is particularly associated with the work of Milton Friedman and the Chicago school and with the economic policies of the Thatcher government in the early 1980s.
Multimedia conglomeration	When the same company has financial interests in different media and (usually) in a range of other economic activities as well.
Nationalisation	The policy of taking firms, services or industries into public ownership, either because they are key parts of the economy, or because they form natural monopolies, or because they have failed in the open market.
Nationalism	Is more than patriotism, in that nationalists believe in sovereign state autonomy for the people they identify as belonging to a national community.
Natural law	The universal moral rules to which, it is claimed, human laws should conform.
Neo-liberal consensus	Agreement among different political groups and parties about neo-liberal politics, that is the political belief that individual rights should be protected by maximising freedom of choice, limiting the powers of government and promoting market economics. The consensus was at its strongest in Britain and the USA in the 1980s.
Neo-liberalism	The ideas associated with the New Right of the 1980s that market competition is the best means of guaranteeing political freedom and economic growth. In politics, neo-liberalism is particularly associated with the policies of Thatcher in Britain and President Reagan in the USA. However, to confuse matters, the term 'liberal' is often used in the United States of America to describe the moderate critics of neo-liberalism.
New Commonwealth	A coded term used to refer to non-white Commonwealth countries.
New Poor Law	Passed in 1834 to deal with the poor cheaply and efficiently. 'Workhouses' were set up everywhere into which those who needed relief had to go. Conditions

inside were tougher than those of the worst-paid employment outside to deter 'welfare dependence'.

New public management (NPM) The term applied to a mixed package of public sector reforms in many western states in the 1980s and 1990s, including the introduction of business management techniques and structures, the decentralisation and privatisation of public services, the use of performance targets, the introduction of internal markets, and greater use of private–public, semi-autonomous, and executive agencies. Also known as 'reinventing government', it is said to have had the effect of 'hollowing out the state', that is, reducing its operations and transferring some functions to the private sector or other bodies. NPM was introduced into Britain by the Thatcher governments and developed and modified by the Blair governments.

New Right The politicians and theorists of the 1980s who believed in the efficacy of market competition as the best means of guaranteeing political freedom and economic growth. The movement was 'new' in Britain in that it was opposed to the traditional 'one-nation' Tories (the 'wets'). It was particularly associated with the neo-liberal ideas and policies of Thatcher in Britain and Reagan in the USA.

New social movements Are organisations that emerged in the 1970s in order to influence public policy about such issues as the environment, nuclear energy and weapons, peace, women, and minorities. They have wider policy interests than most pressure groups, but are more loosely knit than political parties.

Next Steps The short title of the Ibbs Report (1988), which identified serious management failure in the Civil Service and recommended far-reaching reforms in the shape of executive agencies.

Nuclear deterrent The threatened use of nuclear weapons to prevent aggression on the part of foreign states, on the grounds that the aggressor nation will suffer too much damage to make the venture worthwhile. Nuclear deterrence, counter-strike and retaliation (all known sometimes as 'the balance of power' or 'the balance of terror') became a central feature of the Cold War.

Ombudsman A popular word of Swedish origin (meaning grievance officer) referring to the parliamentary commissioner for administration who investigates complaints of maladministration in public services.

Open government The relatively unconstrained flow of information about government to the general public, the media and representative bodies. Open government is relative, not absolute; all governments must keep some secrets, but critics of official secrecy in Britain claim that government is too secretive.

Orthodox economics The dominant economic theory of the first half of the twentieth century, which argued for minimal state intervention in the economy. Orthodox economics were widely practised in the western world until the advent of Keynesian economics.

Osmotherly Rules A set of rules, named after their author, Edward Osmotherly of the Civil Service Department, for the guidance of civil servants appearing before Commons Select Committees and designed to protect Civil Service impartiality, anonymity and secrecy.

Outsider groups	Do not have easy or official access to politicians and civil servants in Westminster and Whitehall, but are kept at arm's length because of who they are and what they represent.
Parliamentary sovereignty	The power of Parliament to make or repeal any law it wishes.
Party	An organisation of ideologically like-minded people who come together to seek power – often to fight elections with a view to gaining representation in decision-making bodies.
Party democracy	Either (1) the widespread distribution of power within a political party and/or (2) a system of national democracy resting on competitive parties.
Party factions	The sections or tendencies within parties that emphasise different features of party policy while subscribing to the overall aims of the party and its organisation. All parties contain such factions, but to varying degrees and strengths. Sometimes factions leave the main party to form their own (the Gang of Four and the SDP), and sometimes they are driven from it (Militant Tendency in the Labour Party).
Party families	Parties in different countries that share similar beliefs, principles, policies and, often, support groups. In Europe the three main party families are the Socialists (Labour and Social Democratic parties), Conservative (Conservative and Christian Democratic parties), and the Centre or Liberal parties.
Party manifesto	The document parties publish at the start of election campaigns outlining the programme of policies they intend to implement if elected to government.
Patronage	The giving of favours – office, contracts or honours – to supporters of the government.
Peak (umbrella) associations	Co-ordinate the activities of different organisations with the same general interests (eg the Trades Union Congress or the Council of Churches).
Pluralism	According to pluralist theory political decisions are the outcome of competition between many different groups representing many different interests. Power is fragmented and winners and losers in the pluralist battle change and vary according to the issue and its circumstances. Elites compete for the support of the non-elites and groups, which ensures democratic accountability.
Police	The civilian organisation established to maintain civil order. The creation of the Metropolitan Police in London in 1829 marks the beginning of the British police force.
Policing	The processes and arrangements, usually but not always involving the police, established to maintain civil order. All societies have to maintain order and so all engage in policing, although not all do so through a civilian police force.
Policy communities	Are small, stable, integrated and consensual groupings of government officials and pressure group leaders that form around particular issue areas.
Policy networks	Compared with policy communities, policy (or issue) networks are larger, looser, less integrated and more conflictual networks of political actors in a given policy area.

Political correctness A controversial term to describe the use of language about socially sensitive matters, such as race or gender, in a way that is designed not to give offence. Often the implication is that politically correct language is silly or absurd.

Positive planning Where the state takes direct action to achieve planning goals, as opposed to indicative planning where it sets out the goals but does not do anything itself to achieve them.

Poverty trap The idea that the Welfare State creates a vicious cycle of poverty for some social groups by imposing welfare systems that discourage people from taking responsibility for their own life or finding work. The cycle tends to continue, some claim, into the next generation of children who grow up in such a system.

Precedent A decision or practice of the past that is accepted as a guide for the present. In the law, precedents are past decisions of the courts that are thought to apply to similar legal problems or situations of the present.

Pressure groups Private, voluntary organisations that wish to influence or control particular public policies without actually becoming the government or controlling all public policy.

Prime Minister The head of the executive branch of government and chair of the Cabinet.

Prime ministerial government The theory that the office of the Prime Minister has become so powerful that he or she now forms a political executive similar to a president. In prime ministerial government the Prime Minister is 'the efficient secret of government', the Cabinet only a 'dignified part'.

Private members' bills Are introduced in Parliament by MPs or peers without government backing. Most (not all) fail, but in doing so they can influence future government legislation. Private members' bills may deal with any matter other than public expenditure.

Privatisation The opposite of nationalisation, privatisation is the returning of nationalised industries wholly or partly to the private sector. Privatisation was accompanied by deregulation in Britain in the 1980s and early 1990s.

Process-based approach The approach to judicial review which assumes that the principal task of the courts is to ensure that citizens can participate as fully and effectively as possible in the decision-making procedures of public bodies.

Progressive taxation Where higher income groups pay proportionately more in taxation than lower income groups.

Proportional representation (PR) A voting system which uses an allocation formula (there are many of them) that distributes seats among parties in proportion to their vote. PR tries to ensure that majorities and minorities are represented in proportion to their voting strength.

Public Sector Borrowing Requirement (PSBR) The amount borrowed by government to finance its annual expenditure. Keynesian theory argues that the PSBR should rise in times of economic depression in order to stimulate demand, and fall in times of rapid economic growth in order to prevent the economy from overheating. Monetarism argues that a large PSBR fuels inflation and crowds out capital for private investment.

Public service model	The idea that radio and TV should not be commercial but used in the public interest to educate, inform and entertain. The BBC under Lord Reith (its Director-General, 1927–38) is said by some to be the epitome of public service broadcasting.
Quangos	Quasi-autonomous non-governmental organisations financed by the government to perform public service functions but not under direct government control. Examples include the BBC and the Commission for Racial Equality (CRE). The advantage of quangos is that they can take sensitive political matters out of direct government control; the disadvantage is that they place public functions in the hands of unelected officials who are usually nominated by the government.
Racism	The practice of discriminating between individuals or groups on racial grounds.
Rate capping	The practice introduced in the 1980s whereby central government set a maximum rate level for local government in an attempt to control their expenditure.
Rational choice	An approach to political science that treats politics as the outcome of the interaction between rational individuals pursuing their own interests.
Realism	The view of politics, especially international relations, that emphasises the role of self-interest as a determinant of state policies, and hence the importance of power in these relations.
Referendum	A vote in which only one, or a small number of issues are put to the electorate, as against a general election in which the electorate chooses between parties on a broad range of political issues.
Regionalism	Regions are geographical areas within a state, and regionalism involves granting special forms of representation within national government to regions, or granting special powers and duties to regional forms of government. In Britain, the regions of Wales, Scotland, and Northern Ireland are examples.
Regressive taxation	Where lower income groups pay proportionately more in taxation than higher income groups.
Regulatory agencies	Offices of gas, water etc (Ofgas, Ofwat and so on) that enforce regulations and contracts binding public utility companies to provide a reasonable service for consumers and to protect the environment.
Reinforcement	Occurs where political forces push in the same direction – eg where someone with Labour sympathies reads a Labour paper. Reinforcing pressures are likely to confirm the individual's political attitudes and behaviour, and may encourage political activity.
Reinforcement theory (media effects)	Argues that the media do not create or mould public opinion so much as reinforce pre-existing opinion. This is because (1) the media adapt themselves to their consumers in their search for markets, and (2) consumers select the media and their messages to fit their own opinions, the result being that the media reflect consumer demand rather than creating it.
Representation	The process whereby one person acts on behalf, or in the interests, of another. Representative government entails the selection of representatives (usually by election) to make decisions, rather than direct participation of those represented.

Royal prerogative	Functions performed by ministers on behalf of the monarch. Before a constitutional monarchy was established the Crown had powers that were subject to no check or veto by Parliament, but now the royal prerogative is generally exercised by ministers.
Select committees	Committees of the House of Commons and the House of Lords which consider general political issues that are wider than a particular piece of legislation. The Public Accounts Committee of the House of Commons, which considers all accounts of money appropriated by Parliament, is a major example. Although membership is in proportion to party strength in the House, committees try to work in a non-party political manner, and chairs of committees are often members of opposition parties.
Selective benefits	Are state welfare benefits distributed according to individual circumstances such as income, age or disability.
'Short-termism'	A criticism often made by politicians of British managers and investors who are unwilling to pay for research and other developments that do not give an immediate profit.
Single-member simple plurality (SMSP)	The electoral system used in British general elections by which the country is divided into constituencies, each returning one member of Parliament who need only obtain more votes than any other candidate in that constituency to be elected.
Sleaze	A popular term, much used in the mid-1990s, referring to the corrupt or improper behaviour of public officials, initially mainly members of the Conservative government.
Social democratic	The ideology of that part of the political left which holds that political and social change can – and should – be achieved by means of peaceful reform rather than revolutionary violence. The British Labour Party is a social democratic party, as are the mainstream labour movements in Scandinavia and Germany.
Social democratic consensus	Agreement among different political groups and parties about the general principles of social democracy, that is, a generally moderate left or centre-left political programme. The consensus was strong in the 1950–79 period when all major parties accepted the broad principles of the Welfare State, the mixed economy, Keynesian economic policies and a NATO-based alliance against the USSR. The consensus was also known as 'Butskellism' after the left-wing Conservative leader R. A. B. Butler, and the right-wing Labour leader Hugh Gaitskell, who agreed on the broad issues of political policy, though not necessarily the details.
Sovereignty	The exclusive right to wield legitimate power within a territory. A sovereign state controls its own affairs, so far as any state can do so. Thus Parliamentary sovereignty means the power to make or repeal any law.
Spectrum scarcity	The shortage of broadcasting frequencies for radio and TV caused by the fact that the wavelengths available for public broadcasting on the spectrum are limited.
The Stability and Growth Pact	Was adopted at the Amsterdam meeting of the European Council in 1997 to ensure smooth progress towards fiscal convergence (Single Monetary Policy) and

price stability within the EU. The Pact committed EMU partners to aim for balanced or surplus budgets in the medium term.

Standing committees Committees of the House of Commons that examine bills after their second reading in order to make them more acceptable for their third reading. Committees are composed of party members in proportion to their numbers in the Commons.

State The set of public bodies and institutions that exercise sovereign power within a territory. The State makes binding laws and policies, and claims compliance with them by virtue of its monopoly of the legitimate use of physical force. In Britain it consists primarily of Parliament, the army, police, Civil Service and local government.

State law The sum total of laws passed by Parliament.

Statute law Law passed by Parliament (in contrast to European law or common law).

Stereotyping The practice of treating members of social groups as if they were all the same, often in a way that involves discrimination.

Stop–go cycle A pattern in which the economy swings between rapid growth that becomes inflationary, out of control, and 'overheated', followed by deflationary policies designed to slow growth and stabilise the economy.

Subsidiarity The principle whereby decisions should be taken at the lowest possible level of the political system – that is, at the level closest to the people affected by the decisions.

Sustainable development Development that meets the needs of the present without compromising the ability of future generations to meet their needs. The term was coined by the United Nations Commission on the Environment and Development, chaired by the Norwegian Prime Minister, Gro Harlem Brundtland, and spelled out in its report *Our Common Future* (1987).

Tabloids Less serious national and Sunday papers, so called because of their smaller format than broadsheets.

Tactical voting The practice of voting for a candidate who is not the first preference in order to keep out a less preferred candidate.

Targeted electioneering The practice whereby parties concentrate resources on those marginal seats that they think they have the best chance of gaining from another party, or the highest chance of losing to another party.

Task forces Are usually comparatively small, official groups specially created to do a particular and fairly limited job (write a report, investigate an issue or event, create a new government structure), and dissolved when they have completed the task. Task forces are normally under the direct control of those who create them, and they are often not constrained by the normal rules applying to public bodies. The Blair government is particularly associated with 'government by task force'.

Think tank An organisation set up to develop public policy proposals and to press for their adoption by government. Since think tanks are concerned with applied policy research and its implementation they are often connected with governments, parties or social movements. Major British examples include the government's own Central Policy Review Staff (1971–83), the Centre for Policy Studies (Conservative), and the Institute for Policy Research (Labour).

Tort: civil and criminal law

A tort is a civil wrong in English law. Civil law is the area of law dealing with business, property and 'normal' dealings between people. Criminal law is where violence, physical injury, theft and dangerous deception are involved.

Trade liberalisation

The process whereby international trade is increasingly opened up to market forces (free trade) by reducing trading tariffs, import and export controls, and other forms of protection.

Tripartism

Compared with corporatism, tripartism is a looser, less centralised and co-ordinated system that brings together three main interests (government, business, unions) in economic policy making. It is a consultative rather than a corporatist method of reaching and implementing decisions.

Tribunals

In Britain tribunals are quasi-judicial institutions set up to resolve conflicts between public or private individuals or bodies. They are a way of avoiding the expensive and time-consuming needs of the courts, and of settling a large number of fairly small and simple cases.

Two-tier local government

Where the functions of local government are divided between an upper level (counties, for example) and a lower level (boroughs or districts, for example).

Ultra vires

The doctrine whereby public bodies have only those powers granted explicitly or implicitly by Parliament, and no others.

Unilateralism

The belief that a country should voluntarily and independently renounce its (nuclear) weapons, either as a moral gesture that might be followed by others, and/or because unilateralists hold that nuclear weapons do not deter aggression and might even provoke it. The main unilateralist organisation in Britain is the Campaign for Nuclear Disarmament (CND).

Unilateralist

A person who holds that Britain should renounce nuclear weapons on its own (unilaterally) without waiting for multinational agreement to do so.

Unitary state

A state in which there is a single sovereign body, the central government. Unlike a federal state, the central government of a unitary state does not share power with smaller territorial areas within the state (states, regions or provinces) although it may devolve some powers to them. Britain, France, Sweden, Italy and Japan are unitary states; the USA, Germany, Austria and Switzerland are federal states.

Unitary system

Where local functions are controlled by only one layer of local government.

Universal benefits

Are state welfare benefits distributed to all groups and individuals who are eligible, irrespective of their particular circumstances.

Utopianism

A form of ideology which claims that it is possible to create a perfect or near-perfect society. However, some utopias are constructed by their creators not as feasible societies but as models against which to compare the real world. Plato's

Republic presents a utopia, as does Sir Thomas More's *Utopia* (1516), from which the modern word derives.

Videomalaise

The attitudes of political cynicism, despair, apathy and disillusionment (among others) that some social scientists claim are caused by the modern mass media, especially television.

Welfare State

A state in which the government ensures the basic social and economic necessities of its citizens by providing, through the revenues it raises from taxes and other sources, goods and services such as education, health, housing and social security. In Britain the Welfare State derives from the Beveridge Report of 1942.

Westminster Model

The form of liberal democracy that is modelled on the British system of government. It is best described and analysed by Walter Bagehot in *The English Constitution* (1867), and now involves: Parliamentary sovereignty and an unwritten constitution; representative democracy (rather than participatory or delegated democracy); an attempt to balance the need for strong government with the rights of citizens; an overlap between executive, legislative and judiciary; single ('winner takes all') party government; and the single-member simple plurality electoral system.

Whips

Officials appointed by Parliamentary parties in the Lords and the Commons to promote party discipline. A three-line whip is one requiring the voting support of all members of the party in Parliamentary divisions. The whips are also said to be the 'eyes and ears' of party leaders, who are too busy to maintain close and regular contact with backbench opinion.

White papers

Government documents outlining proposed legislation in order to permit discussion and consultation of the policy. White papers may be preceded by green papers, which are also consultative documents, but which outline various policy alternatives, rather than the firmer policy proposals that government sets out in its white papers.

World Trade Organisation

The international organisation set up in 1993 to police the GATT agreements.

Author index

Subject index

Page numbers in **bold** denote major discussion of topic
Page numbers in *italics* denote tables/illustrations